Impressionism

To my father Étienne and my children Barnabé and Valentine

French edition
Editorial Director: Julie Rouart
Administrative Manager: Delphine Montagne
Editor: Marion Doublet, assisted by Salomé Dolinski
Design: Audrey Sednaoui

English Edition
Editorial Director: Kate Mascaro
Editor: Helen Adedotun
Translated from the French by Elizabeth Heard
Copyediting: Penelope Isaac
Typesetting: Gravemaker+Scott
Proofreading: Lindsay Porter
Production: Barbara Jaegy and Julia Mirenda
Color Separation: Bussière, Paris
Printed in China by Toppan Leefung

Originally published in French as *Tout sur l'impressionnisme*

87, quai Panhard et Levassor
75647 Paris Cedex 13
editions.flammarion.com

17 18 19 3 2 1
ISBN: 978-2-08-020320-5
Legal Deposit: 09/2017

Impressionism

The Movement that Transformed Western Art

Véronique Bouruet Aubertot

Timeline and biographies by Sylvie Blin

Flammarion

Contents

Timeline 6

Impressionism and Its Era 16

Haussmann's Paris 18

A City of Pleasure and Spectacle 32

A World in Flux 44

The Photographic Revolution 62

The Art World 72

A New Vision of Landscape 94

Impressionism: A New Vision 104

Fresh Air 106

Favorite Haunts 120

The Non-Subject 136

Color First and Foremost 152

Capturing the Moment 168

Impressionism: A Dissident Movement 182

Fringe Exhibitions 184
–
Independent Trajectories 198
–
Art under Brutal Attack 214
–
A New Role for Dealers and Collectors 228
–
A Hard Life and Belated Recognition 246

Influence on a Grand Scale 258

A Generation of Post-"isms" 260
–
Plein Air Everywhere 272
–
A World of Infinite Possibilities 282

Biographies 292

Captions to the Virtual Galleries 358

Appendixes 362

Index 364
–
Selected Bibliography 367

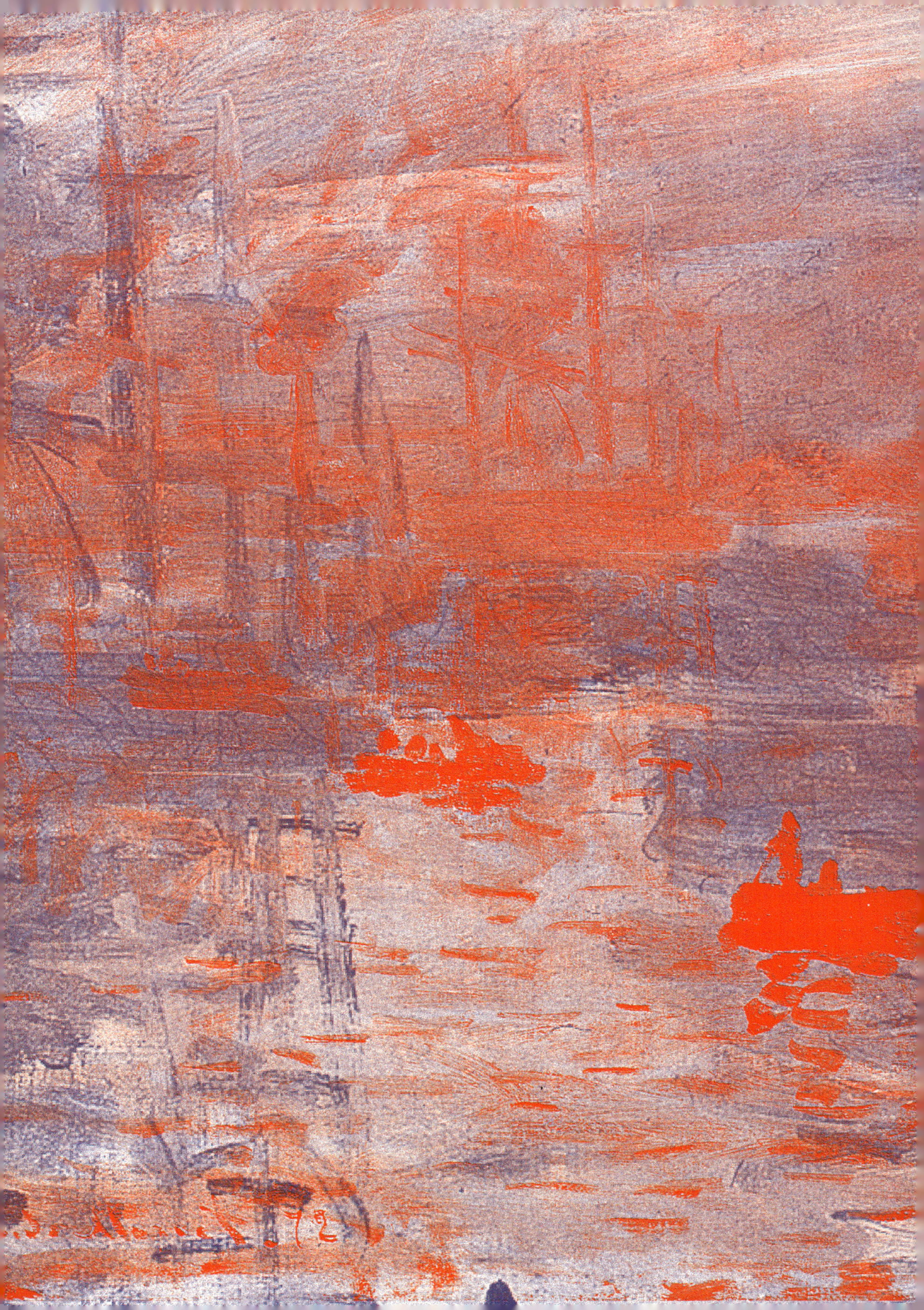

Timeline

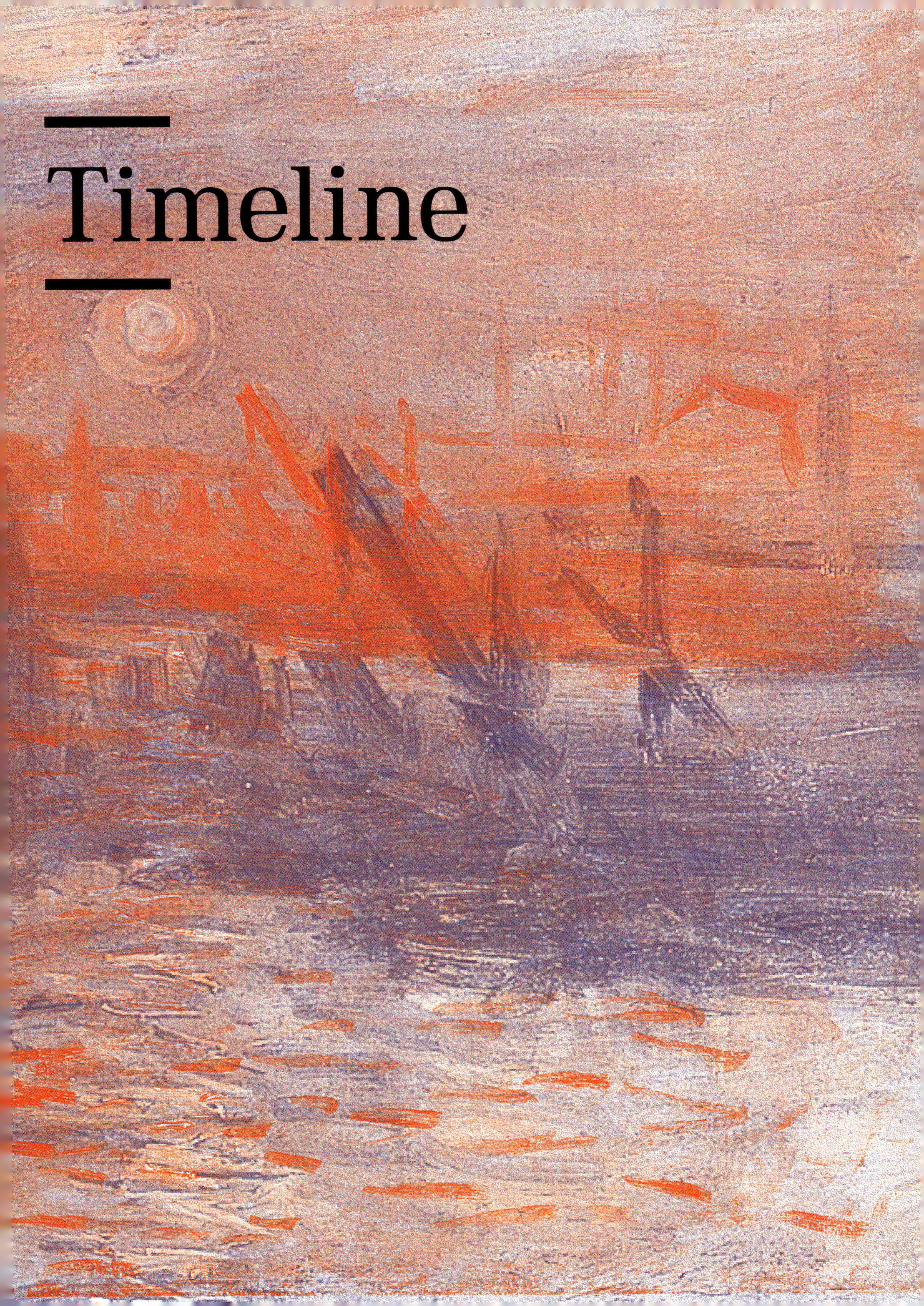

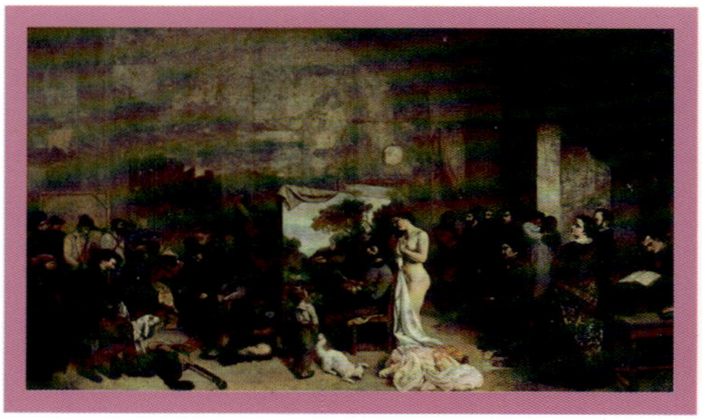

Jean-François Millet presents *The Sower* at the Salon.

–

Universal Exposition in London's Crystal Palace.

–

Louis-Napoleon Bonaparte's coup d'état is endorsed by plebiscite.

1851

▼ Presented at the 1850-51 Salon, *A Burial at Ornans* by Gustave Courbet creates a scandal.

Aristide Boucicaut opens Le Bon Marché, the first Parisian department store.

–

Alexandre Dumas fils publishes *The Lady of the Camellias.*

–

New constitution and restoration of the Empire: Louis-Napoléon Bonaparte becomes Napoléon III.

1852

Nadar opens a photography studio on Boulevard des Capucines in Paris.

–

Crimean War.

–

Nerval: *Daughters of Fire.*

1854

Universal Exposition in Paris.

–

▲ Gustave Courbet presents thirty-seven paintings, including *The Artist's Studio*, in his Pavilion of Realism.

–

The Paris urban renewal project is assigned to Haussmann.

1855

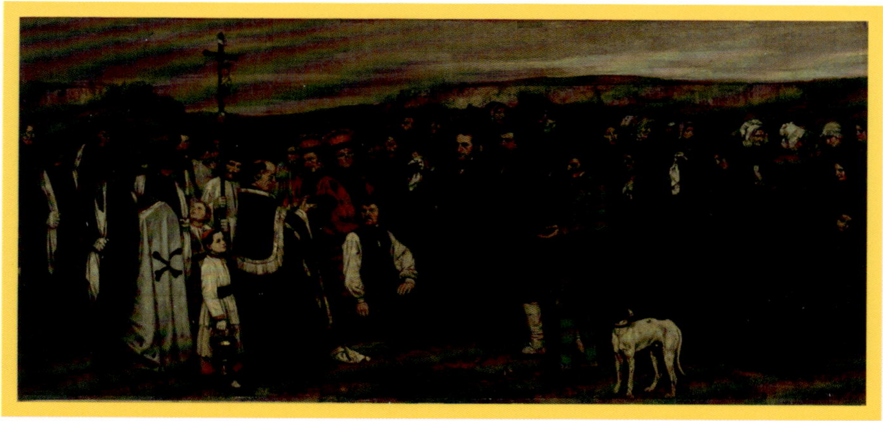

Daubigny fits out a barge as a floating studio called *Le Botin.*

–

The publication of *The Flowers of Evil* by Charles Baudelaire causes outrage: a trial ensues and six poems are censored.

–

1857

▼ Millet paints *The Angelus* and *Gleaners.*

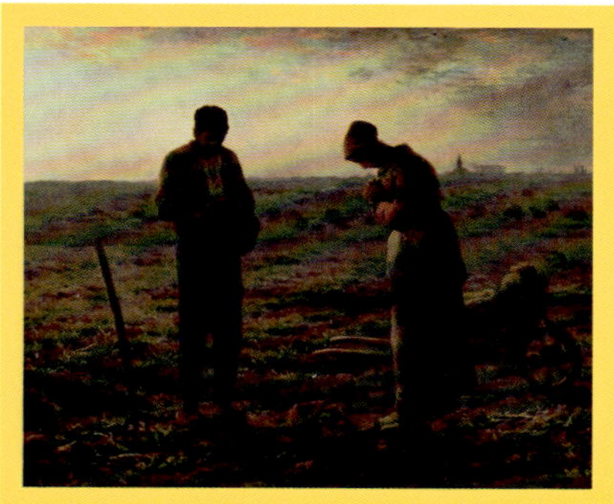

The painter François Bonvin opens his studio to display the pictures of painters refused by the Salon, including Fantin-Latour and Whistler.

–

Paint tubes with screw-on tops are marketed in France.

–

La Gazette des Beaux-arts is founded.

▲ Ingres: *The Turkish Bath.*

–

1859

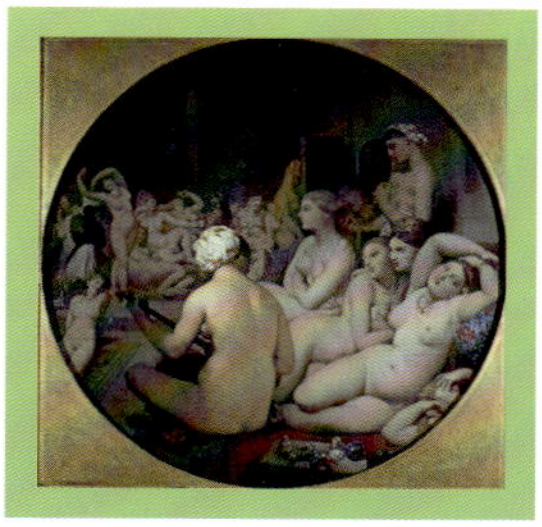

Death of Delacroix.

–

Reform of the administration of the École des Beaux-Arts: the Salon becomes an annual event.

–

1863

▼ The Salon des Refusés opens outside the official Salon, with the notable inclusion of Manet's *The Luncheon on the Grass.*

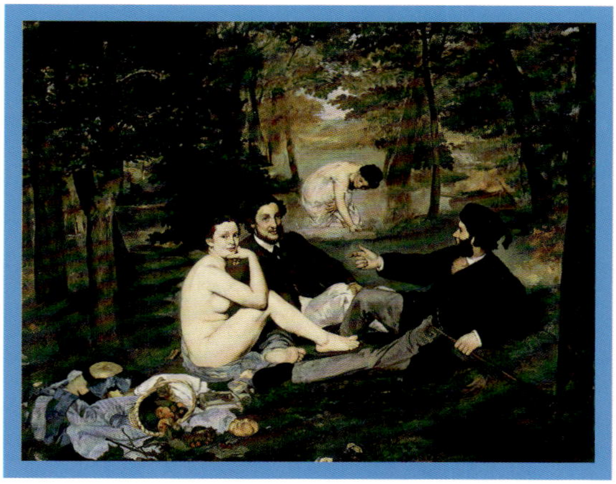

Publication of Chevreul's *On Colors and On Their Applications to Industrial Arts.*

–

Sale of Eugène Delacroix's studio; a retrospective exhibition was devoted to his work.

–

Cézanne and Rodin are rejected by the Salon.

–

1864

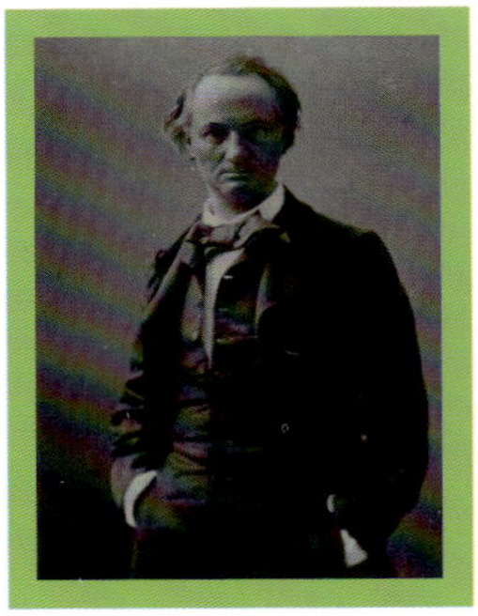

Monet paints *The Luncheon on the Grass.*

—

War and Peace by Tolstoy, *Alice's Adventures in Wonderland* by Lewis Carroll, *Tristan und Isolde* by Wagner.

1865

▼ Manet's *Olympia* is exhibited in the Salon, creating a scandal.

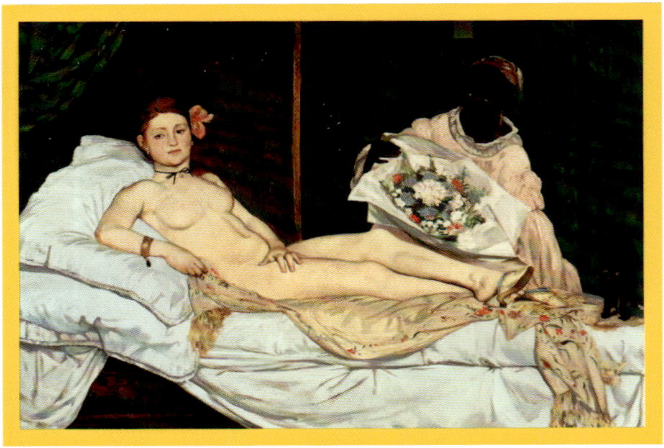

Universal Exposition in Paris.

—

Establishment of the Académie Julian, a private school accepting women.

—

▲ Death of Baudelaire.

—

Posthumous retrospective for Ingres.

1867

Daubigny and Millet resign from the Salon's jury, which has rejected submissions by Monet, Bazille, and Cézanne.

—

Franco-Prussian War.

—

▼ Death of Bazille.

1870

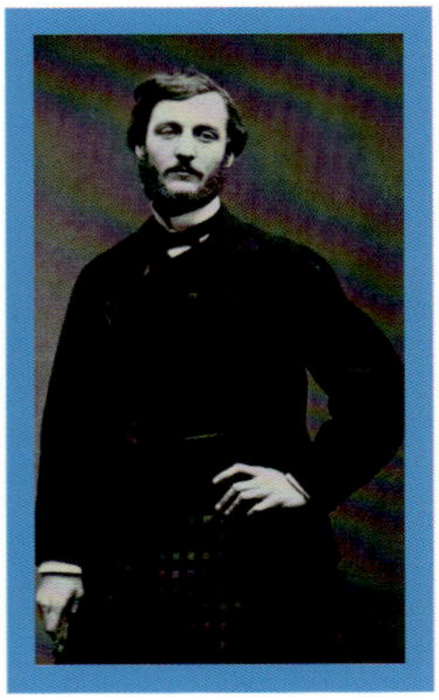

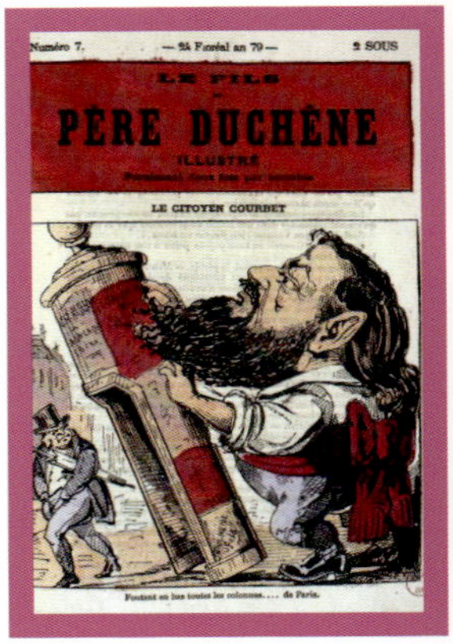

Inauguration of the Third Republic.

—

▲ The Paris Commune.

—

Courbet is imprisoned in the Sainte-Pélagie prison.

1871

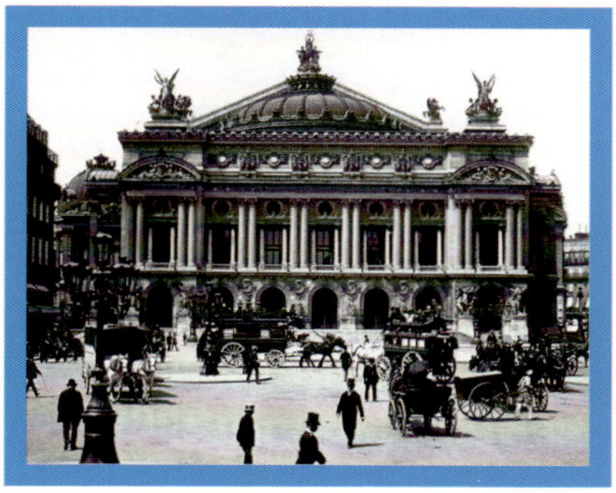

First exhibition by the Anonymous Cooperative Society of Artists (Painters, Sculptors, Engravers, etc.).

1874

▲ Inauguration of the new Opéra, built by Charles Garnier.

Bizet's *Carmen* is created for the Opéra-Comique.

1875

▼ Caillebotte: *The Floor Planers.*

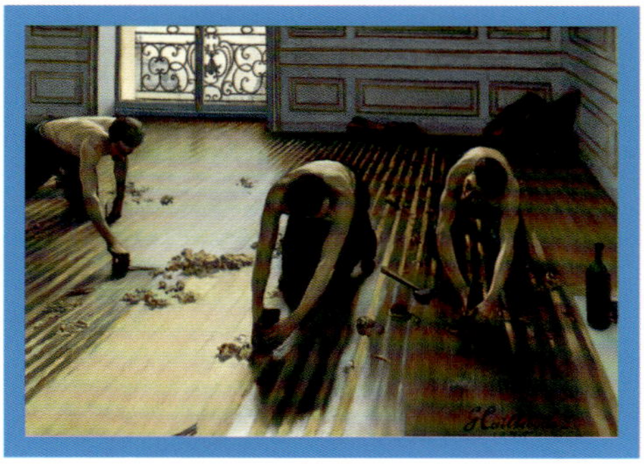

Edmond Duranty publishes *The New Painting*, a manifesto supporting impressionism and *plein air* painting.

"The Afternoon of a Faun" by Stéphane Mallarmé, illustrated by Manet, who presents his paintings to the public in his own studio.

1876

Second impressionist exhibition.

Rodin is accused of having made a cast of a living man for his sculpture *The Age of Bronze*, which is presented at the Salon.

Establishment of the Musée des Arts Décoratifs.

Third impressionist exhibition.

1877

▼ Monet paints a series on the Gare Saint-Lazare.

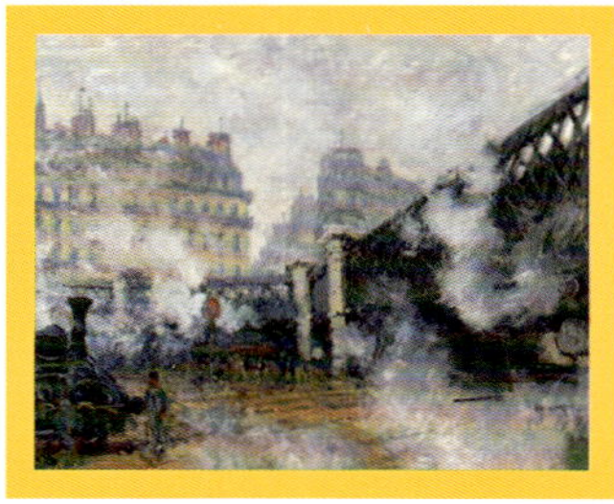

Universal Exposition in Paris.

—

Théodore Duret publishes *The History of the Impressionist Painters*, the first work devoted to the movement.

—

▼ **Eadweard Muybridge photographs a galloping horse,** confirming Étienne-Jules Marey's theory on animal locomotion.

1878

Fourth impressionist exhibition.

—

July 14 is proclaimed a national holiday and "La Marseillaise" becomes the national anthem.

1879

Fifth impressionist exhibition.

—

▼ **Rodin finishes *The Thinker*** and begins *The Gates of Hell*.

—

The tricolor is adopted as the national flag.

1880

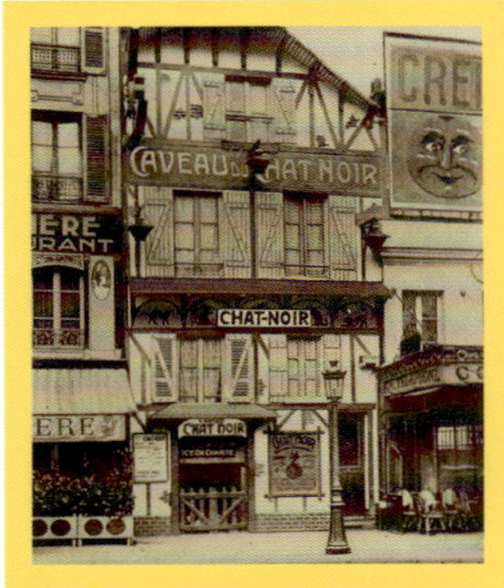

Sixth impressionist exhibition.

—

▲ **Le Chat Noir cabaret opens in Montmartre.**

—

Jules Vallès founds *Le Cri du peuple*, a socialist newspaper.

1881

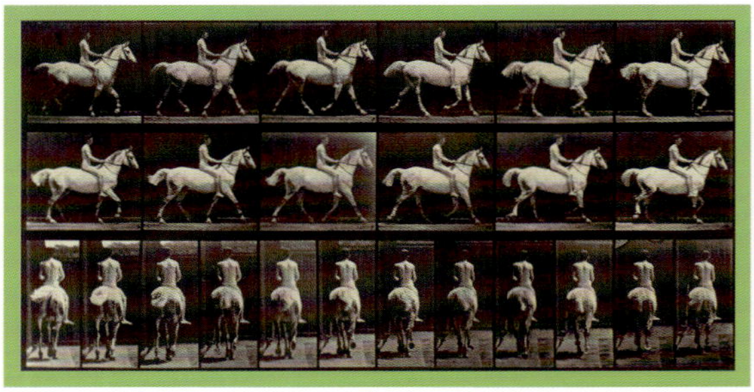

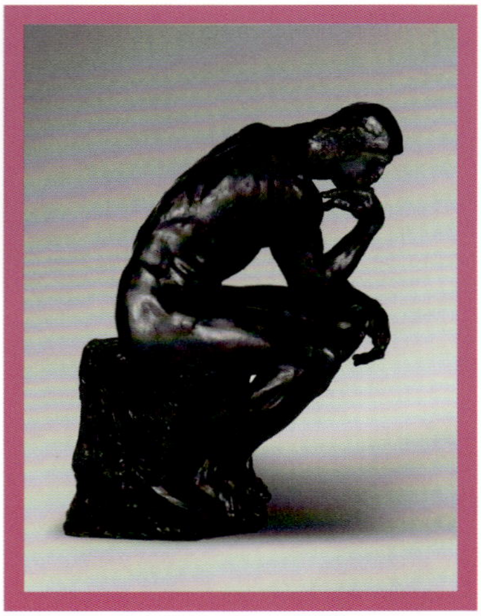

Courbet retrospective at the École des Beaux-Arts.

—

Seventh impressionist exhibition.

—

Nietzsche: *The Joyful Wisdom*, also known as *The Gay Science*.

1882

Monet moves to Giverny.

—

Death of Manet.

—

▼ **Retrospective of Japanese art in Paris.**

—

Foundation of Les XX group in Brussels.

1883

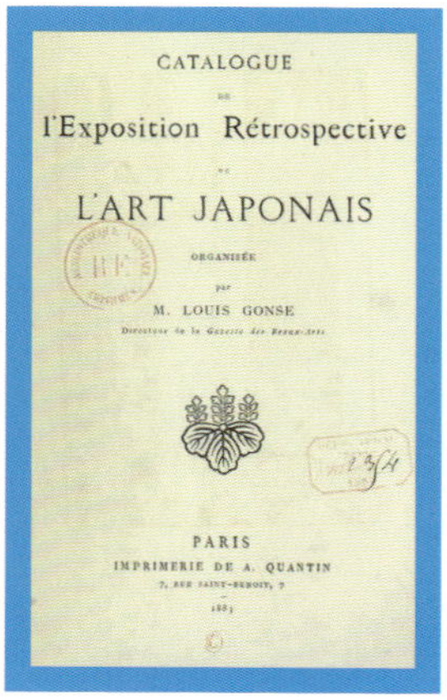

CATALOGUE

DE

l'Exposition Rétrospective

DE

L'ART JAPONAIS

ORGANISÉE

par

M. LOUIS GONSE

Directeur de la Gazette des Beaux-Arts

PARIS

IMPRIMERIE DE A. QUANTIN

7, RUE SAINT-BENOIT, 7

1883

Zola publishes his novel *His Masterpiece*, whose protagonist is based on Cézanne.

—

Symbolist manifesto.

1886

Eighth and last impressionist exhibition.

Van Gogh moves to Arles.

1888

▼ **In Pont-Aven, Paul Sérusier paints *The Talisman* under the direction of Paul Gauguin.**

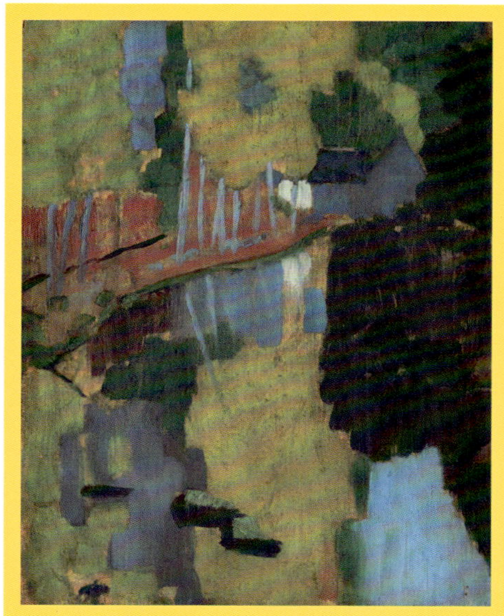

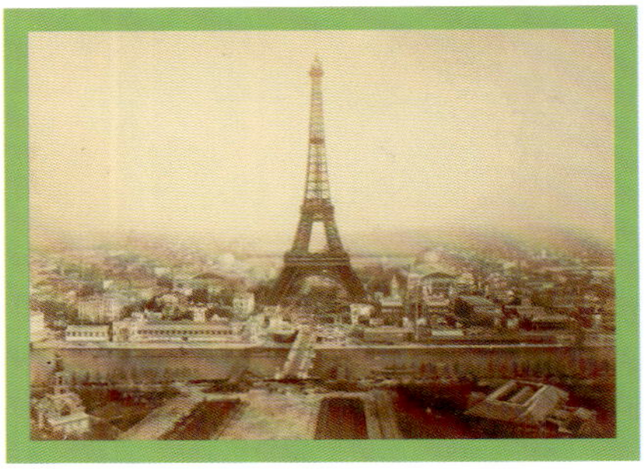

▲ Universal Exposition in Paris; inauguration of the Eiffel Tower.

–

Creation of the Nabi group.

–

Inauguration of the Musée Guimet in Paris.

1889

Manet's *Olympia* enters the Musée du Luxembourg, thanks to a public subscription.

–

1890

▼ Death of Vincent Van Gogh.

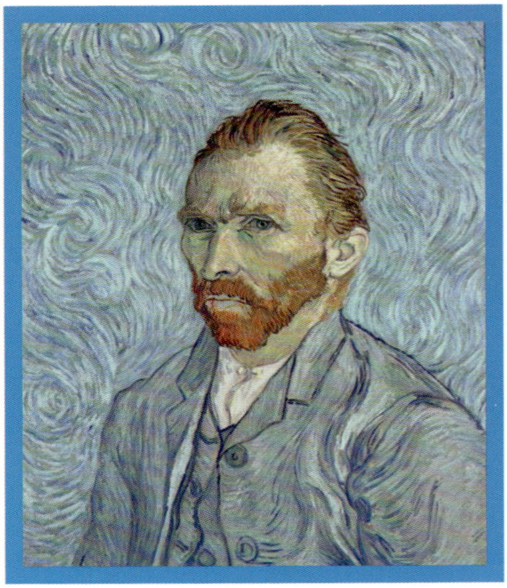

Gauguin leaves for Tahiti.

–

Death of Seurat and Rimbaud.

–

Oscar Wilde: *The Picture of Dorian Gray.*

–

▼ Consecration of the Sacré-Coeur basilica in Montmartre.

1891

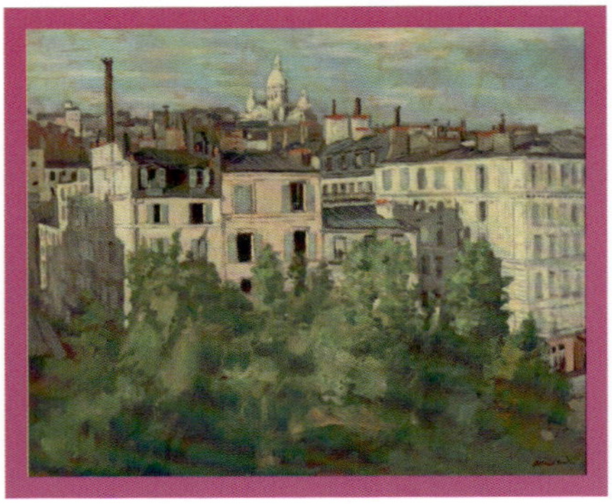

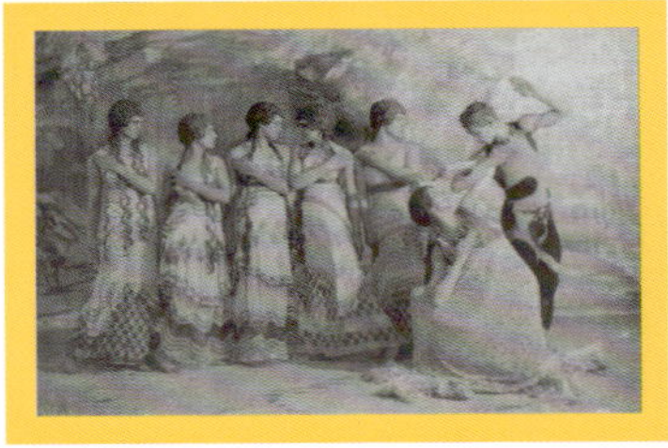

Signac's first visit to Saint-Tropez.

–

Maeterlinck: *Pelléas and Mélisande.*

–

Anarchist attacks: Ravachol is guillotined.

1892

▲ Debussy: *Prelude to the Afternoon of a Faun.*

1895

First international art exhibition in Venice.

—

▼ First public showing of a film in Paris.

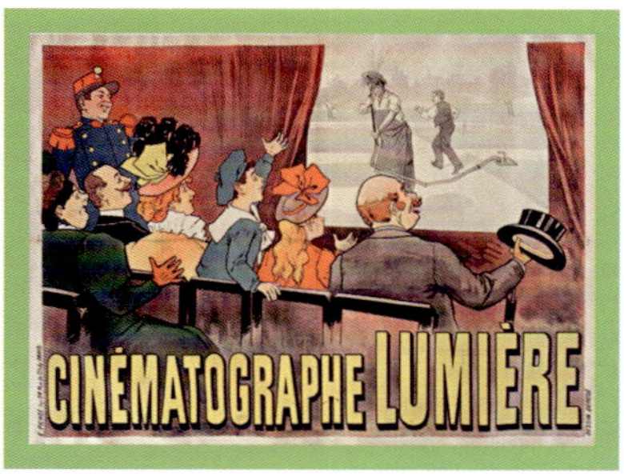

1897

A portion of Caillebotte's legacy is accepted by the State: the impressionists enter the Musée du Luxembourg.

—

Opening of the Castel Béranger, built by Hector Guimard in Paris.

1898

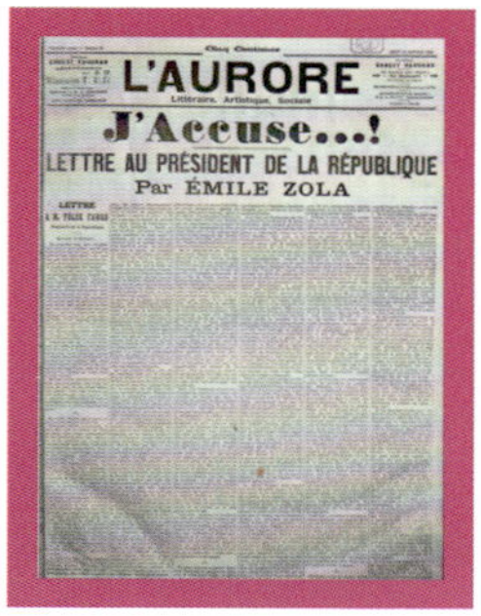
L'AURORE

J'Accuse...!

LETTRE AU PRÉSIDENT DE LA RÉPUBLIQUE

Par ÉMILE ZOLA

▲ Zola publishes his open letter "J'accuse."

—

Secession exhibitions in Berlin and Vienna.

—

Rodin's *Monument to Balzac* creates a scandal at the Salon des Indépendents: the commission is rejected.

1900

▼ Monet begins his *Water Lilies* series.

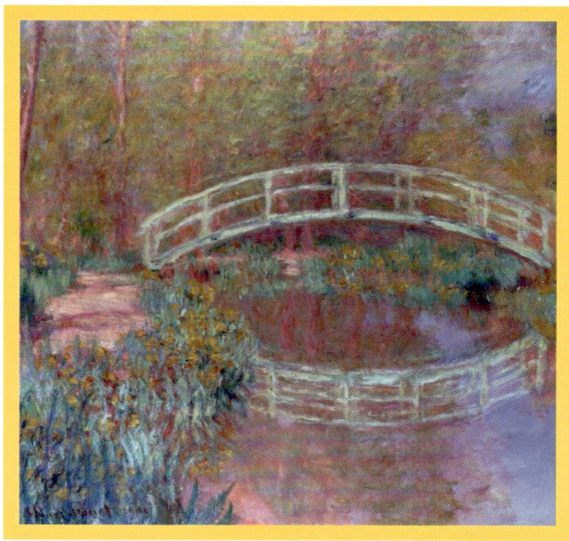

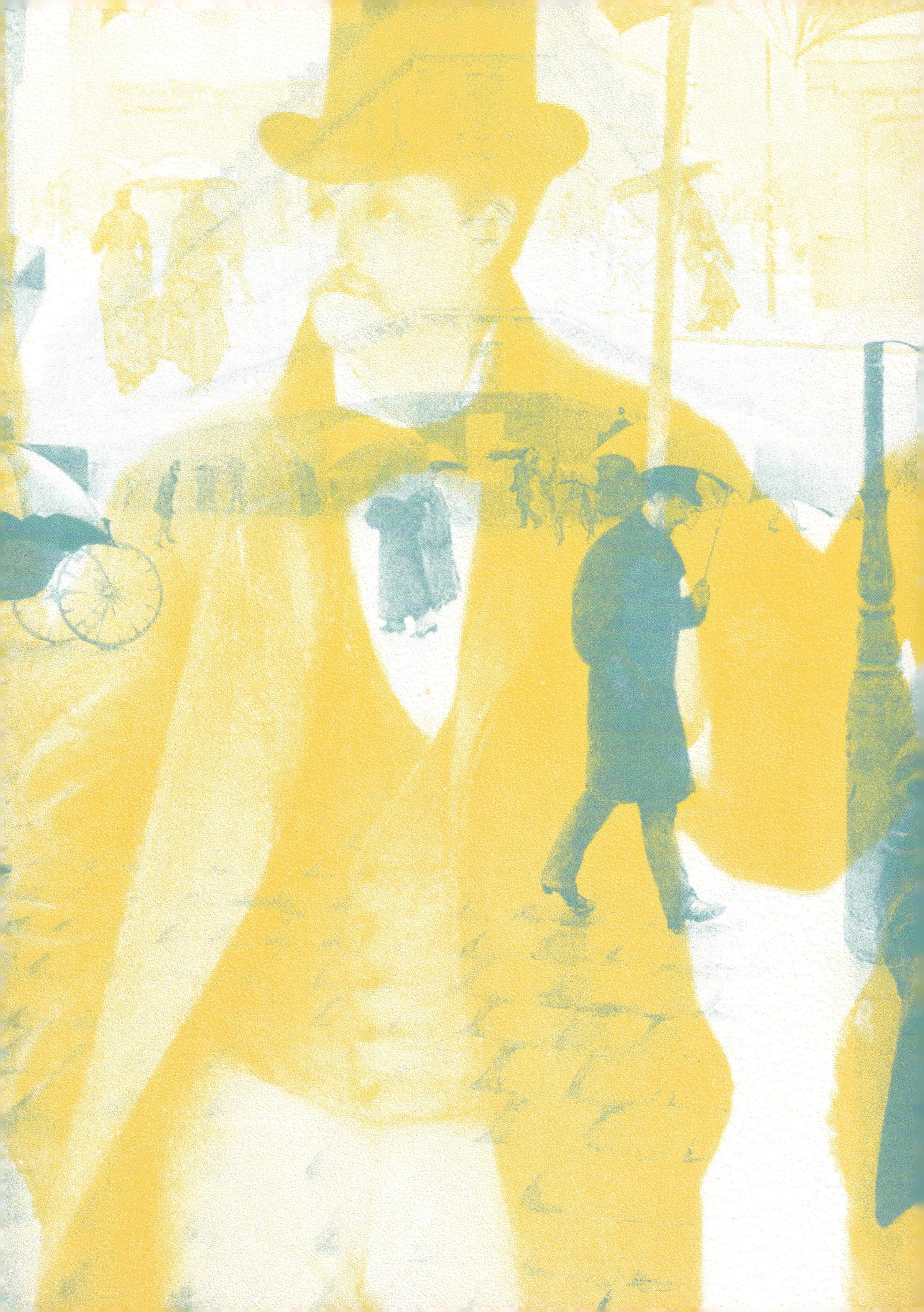

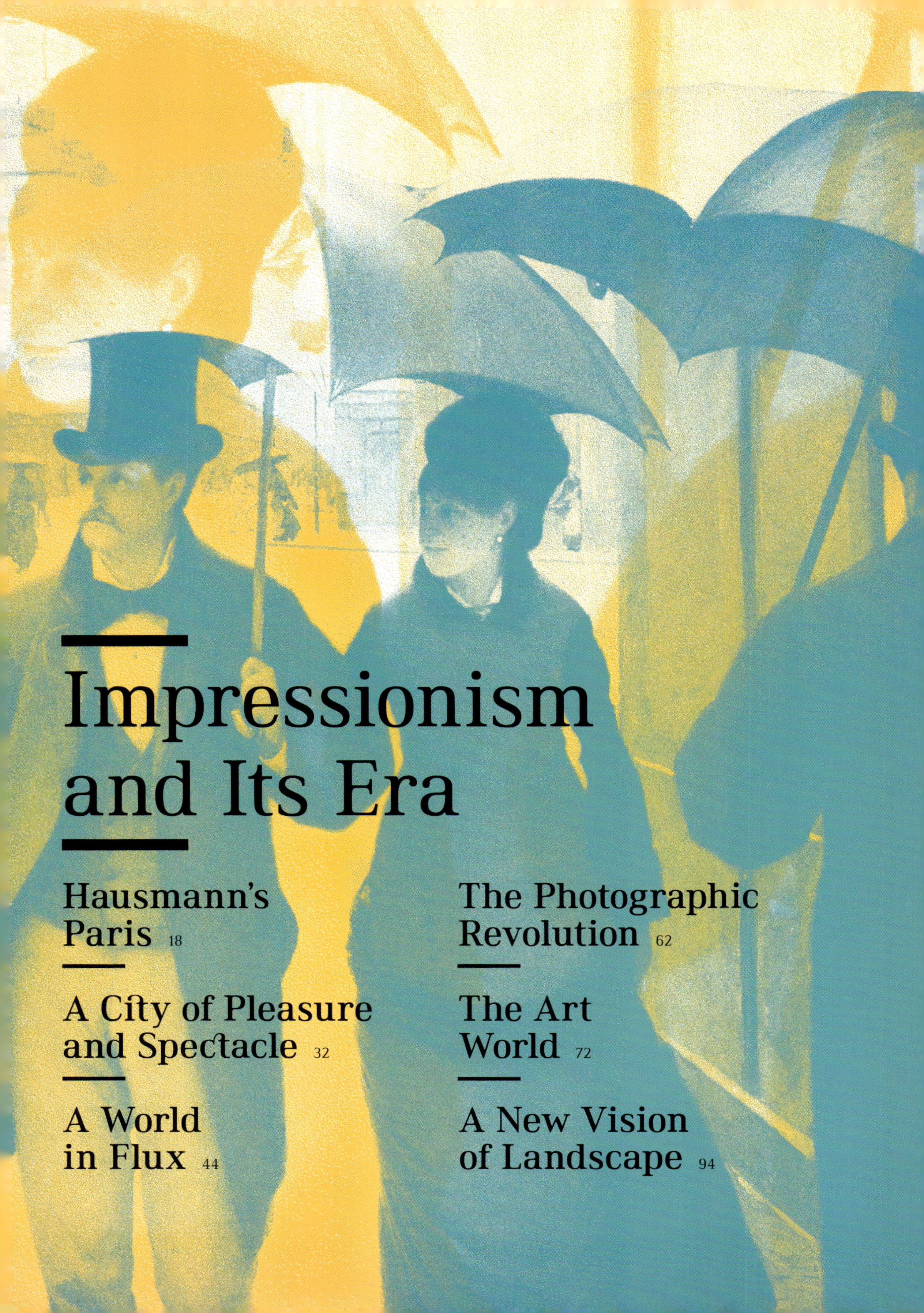

Impressionism and Its Era

Hausmann's Paris 18

A City of Pleasure and Spectacle 32

A World in Flux 44

The Photographic Revolution 62

The Art World 72

A New Vision of Landscape 94

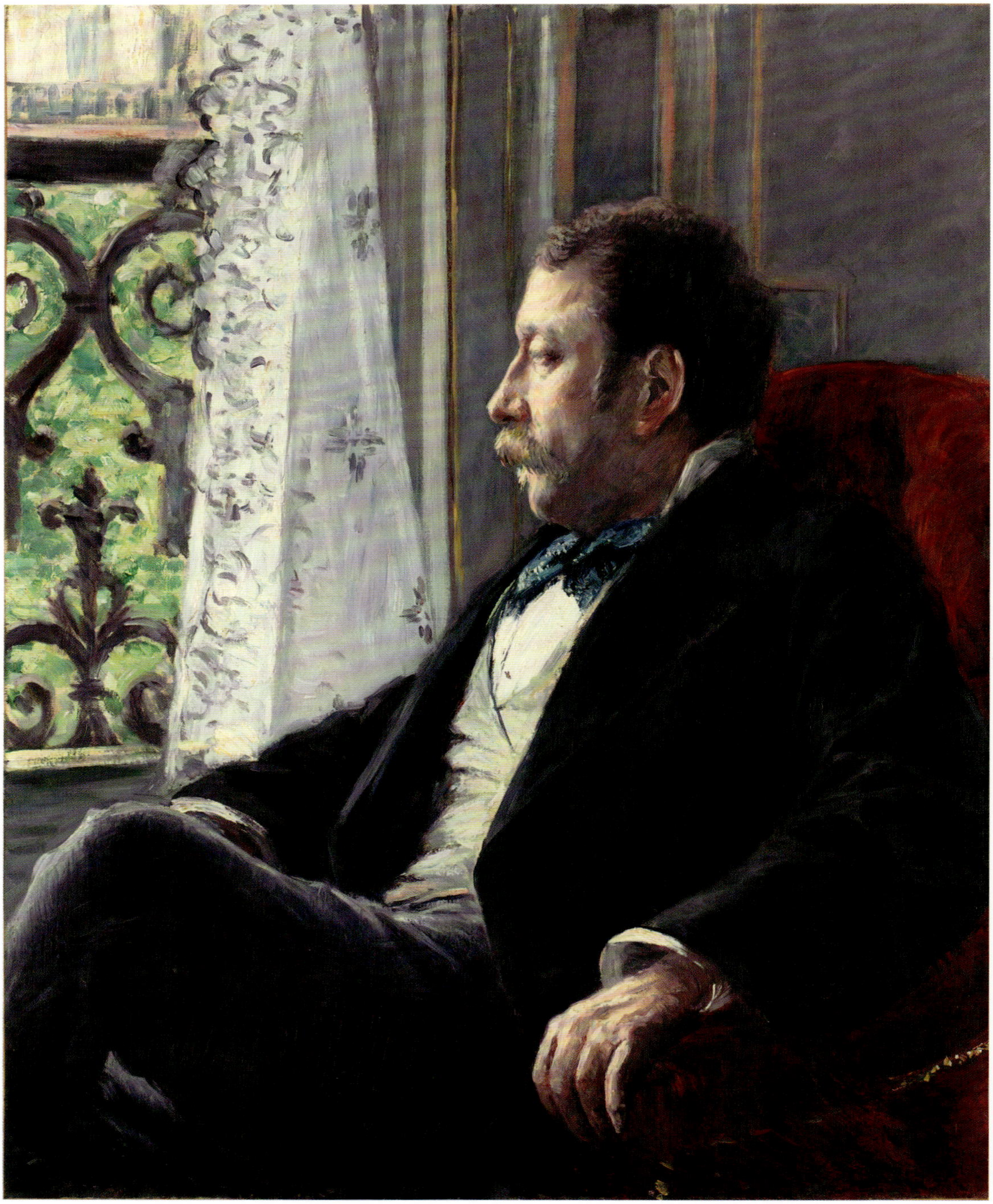

Gustave Caillebotte
Portrait of a Man
1880
Oil on canvas, 32 ¼ × 25 ½ in. (82 × 65 cm)
The Cleveland Museum of Art, Cleveland

Haussmann's Paris

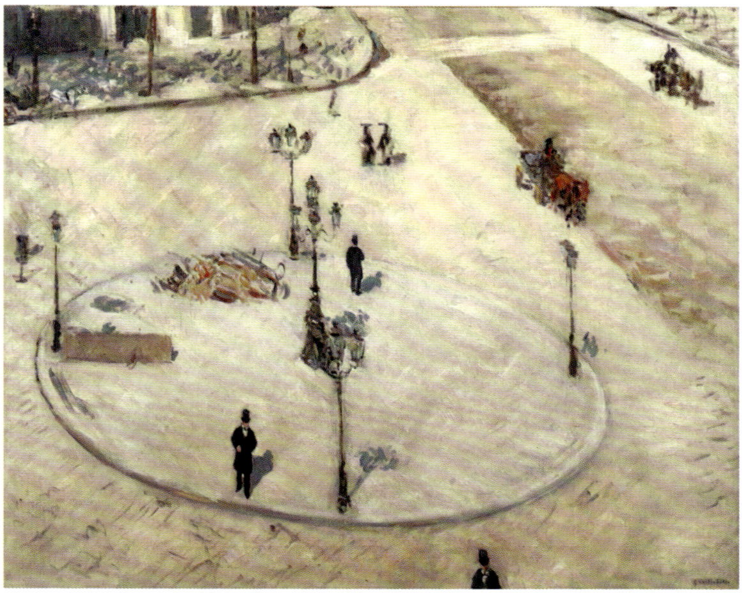

Gustave Caillebotte
The Refuge, Boulevard Haussmann
c. 1880
Oil on canvas, 2 ft. 8 in. × 3 ft. 3 ¾ in. (81 × 101 cm)
Private collection

It was a dilapidated, filthy city, crisscrossed with impenetrable alleyways. Typhus and cholera outbreaks were rampant, and cutpurses reigned unchallenged after nightfall. This was the face of early nineteenth-century Paris. Makeshift hovels festered like warts against monumental façades, and slums sprawled along the banks of the Seine. The impoverished masses lived in misery, while the more fortunate fled the city's center.

Napoleon III inaugurated the Second Empire following a coup d'état in 1851. He immediately initiated the project that would be remembered as his greatest achievement: the complete transformation of the city of Paris into "the capital of capitals."

The prevention of popular uprisings, which occurred frequently during that tumultuous period, was not the sole function of the broad thoroughfares planned for this reimagined vision of Paris. The wide new boulevards did indeed facilitate control and police counterattacks when

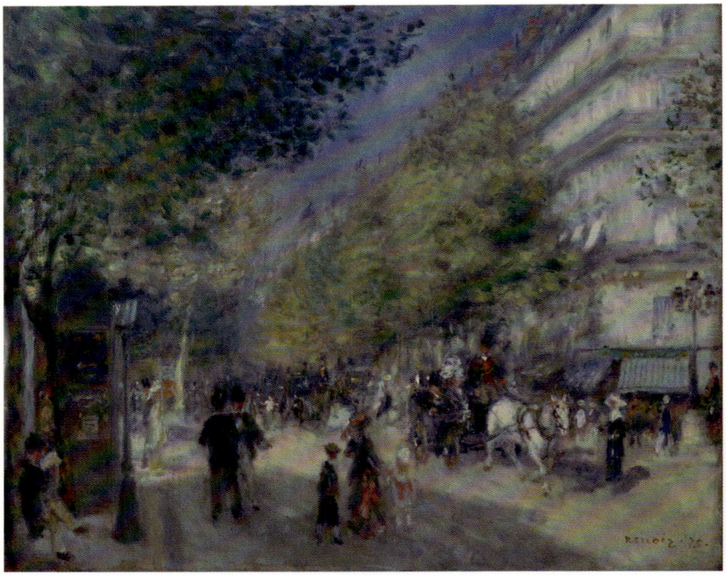

Auguste Renoir
The Grands Boulevards
1875
Oil on canvas, 20 ½ × 25 in. (52.1 × 63.5 cm)
Philadelphia Museum of Art, Philadelphia

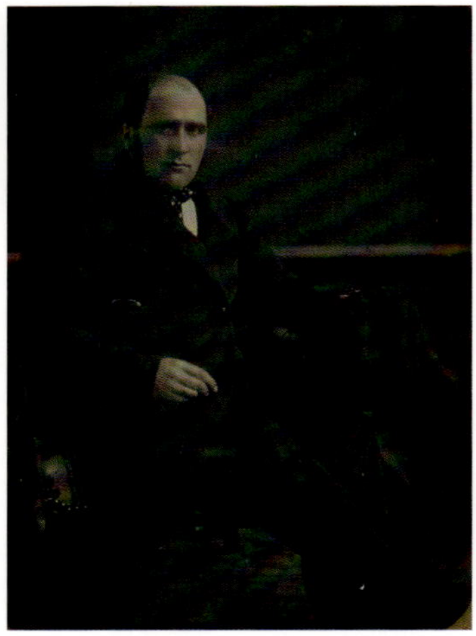

necessary, but they also addressed sanitation concerns, improving the lot of the most downtrodden inhabitants. Public health was a genuine concern for the emperor, as evidenced by his pamphlet on the eradication of poverty, published in 1844. Driven by exponential economic growth in a world experiencing rapid industrialization, Napoleon III's new plan for Paris drew inspiration from his formative experiences abroad. Exiled to the United States in 1837, he discovered a very different form of urban development, with broad avenues, fluid traffic circulation, running water, and gaslight illumination. Living in London between 1844 and 1848, he admired England's spacious landscaped parks.

It was a challenge to find the right man to bring about this metamorphosis, but the ideal candidate soon presented himself. In June 1853, Baron Haussmann, an ambitious senior civil servant, was appointed prefect of the Seine and charged with the mission of completely remodeling the capital city.

"Cuts everywhere. Paris slashed to pieces with a saber, its veins laid open to provide nourishment for a hundred thousand excavators and masons," as Zola wrote in *The Kill* (published in English in 1874), Paris was an immense, gaping construction site for almost twenty years. When Haussmann's work began it had been a medieval labyrinth, but he transformed the city into a modern capital.

Broad avenues were laid out geometrically, beginning with the "grand crossroads" formed by the Rue de Rivoli (the east-west axis) and the boulevards Sébastopol and Saint-Michel (north-south axis). The advent of railroads

"Monsieur Georges Eugène Haussmann, prefect of the Seine 1853–70, made the greatest impression on me. But, strangely, it wasn't so much his remarkable intelligence as the defects in his character that won me over. I encountered one of the most extraordinary figures of our time. Tall, strong, vigorous, and energetic, as well as polished and astute, this impressive man did not hesitate to show himself for what he was. He was visibly satisfied with his personal bearing." Minister of the Interior Persigny, 1853, quoted by André Morizet, *Du vieux Paris au Paris moderne : Haussmann et ses prédecesseurs*, 1932.

"I forgot to tell you that I found a room at the Grand Hôtel du Louvre, with a splendid view of the Avenue de l'Opéra.... I'm delighted to have the opportunity to paint these Parisian streets, which are habitually described as ugly, but which are actually so silvery, luminous, and animated."
Pissarro, letter to his son Lucien, 1897.

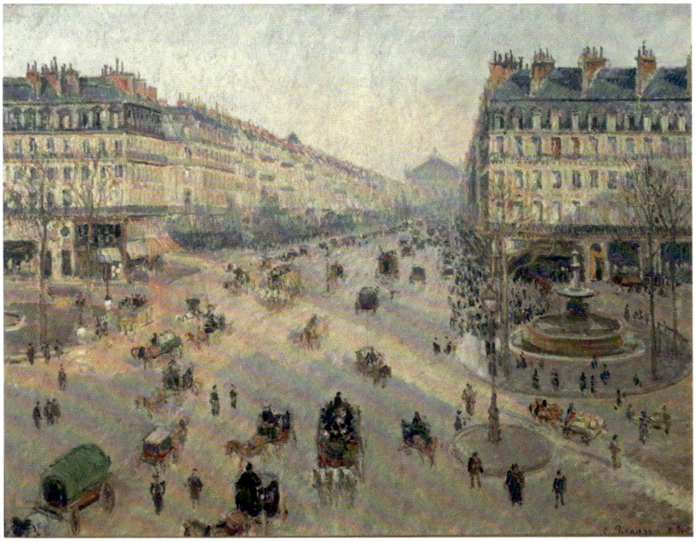

Camille Pissarro
The Avenue de l'Opéra: Sunlight, Winter Morning
1898
Oil on canvas, 2 ft. 4 ¾ in. × 3 ft. ¼ in. (73 × 91.8 cm)
Musée des Beaux-Arts, Reims

necessitated the construction of vast terminals. The Gare de Lyon was built in 1855 (by architect François-Alexis Cendrier) and the Gare du Nord in 1865 (by Jacques Hittorff). Iron and glass architecture triumphed with the new Halles (1853-56) by Victor Baltard and Félix Callet. Airy, clean, and well lit, the design won universal acclaim. A completely new type of housing was built at an astonishing rate in response to the needs of a population that almost doubled to two million within just fifty years.

The broad sidewalks of the Grands Boulevards attracted strolling pedestrians, café terraces were packed with customers, and theaters, restaurants, and department stores catered to a pleasure-seeking clientele. The sanitation and sewage systems were completely overhauled, putting an end to foul overflows and odors. Water and gas were available on every floor of the new buildings, and streetlights encouraged citizens to venture out at night, without worrying about their safety.

Paris annexed surrounding communities, extending its boundaries, and was organized into twenty arrondissements. Parks were designed by engineer Jean-Charles Adolphe Alphand for the city's cardinal points: the Bois de Boulogne to the west, the Bois de Vincennes to the east, the Parc des Buttes-Chaumont to the north, and the Parc Montsouris to the south. These green spaces provided picturesque vantage points and opportunities for pleasurable outings. Stately, clean, safe, and airy, the capital was transformed, perfectly attuned to the demands of both business and pleasure.

THE HAUSMANNIAN BUILDING

Today a symbol of Paris, the buildings referred to as "Haussmannian" were designed to offer visual uniformity and follow strictly defined building codes. Spare and almost austere, they strive for sobriety and clarity, with long balconies running along the third and sixth floors. Apartment buildings following this model sprouted like mushrooms; almost 1,240 of these structures were built between 1851 and 1900 within the Parisian city limits.

"The city still harbored a haphazard, picturesque jumble of dwellings dating from every era: houses with pointed gables, houses with little towers, hovels built of wood and brick, and stately private residences with pilasters and pediments. All around these palaces stretched a labyrinth of filthy, stinking alleys."

André Morizet, *Du vieux Paris au Paris moderne: Haussmann et ses prédecesseurs*, 1932.

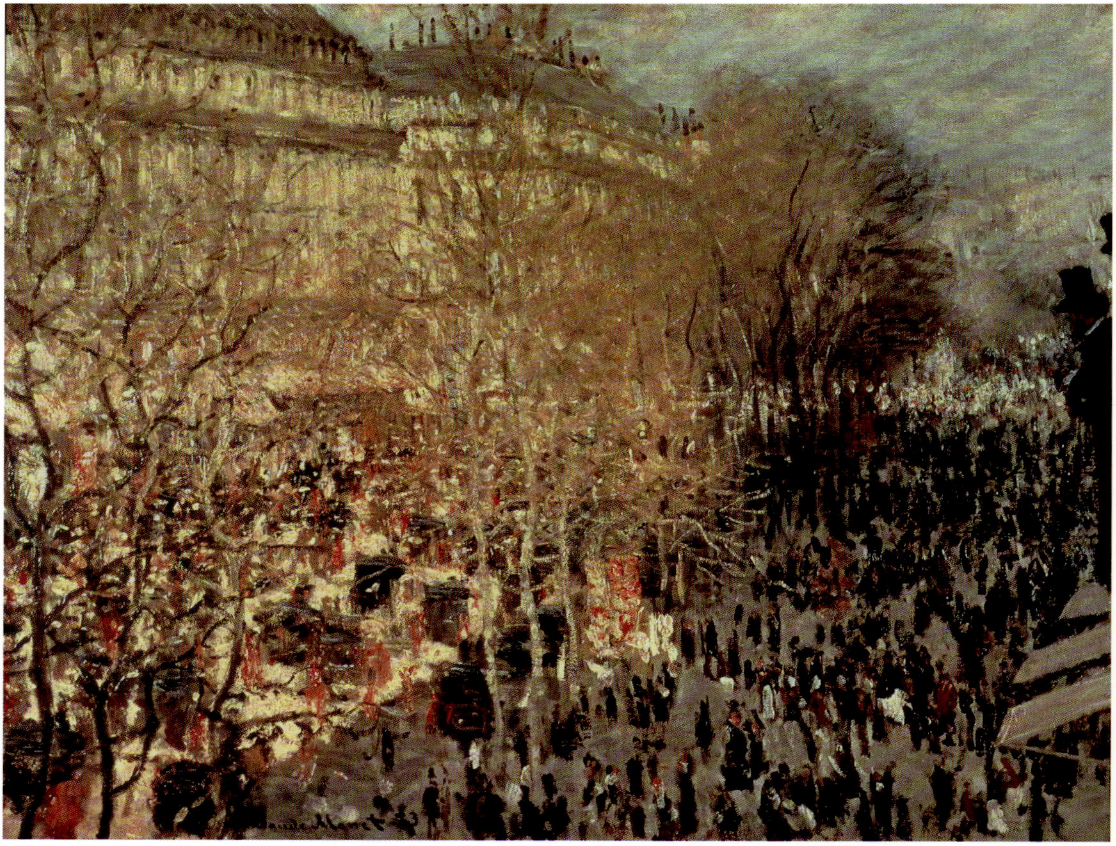

Claude Monet
Boulevard des Capucines
1873
Oil on canvas, 24 × 31 ½ in. (61 × 80 cm)
The Pushkin State Museum of Fine Arts, Moscow

The urban life so relished by the impressionists dismayed many observers, including the critic Louis Leroy. In *Le Charivari*, he wrote about this canvas, exhibited in 1874 at the first impressionist exhibition:
"Would you please explain what these innumerable tiny brushstrokes at the bottom of the canvas represent?"
"Why, of course," I replied. "They're pedestrians."
"What, are you telling me that I look like one of those when I'm walking down the Boulevard des Capucines? Hell and damnation! You're making fun of me!"

Auguste Renoir
The Pont Neuf
1872
Oil on canvas, 2 ft. 5 ½ in. × 3 ft. 1 in.
(75.3 × 93.7 cm)
National Gallery of Art, Washington, DC

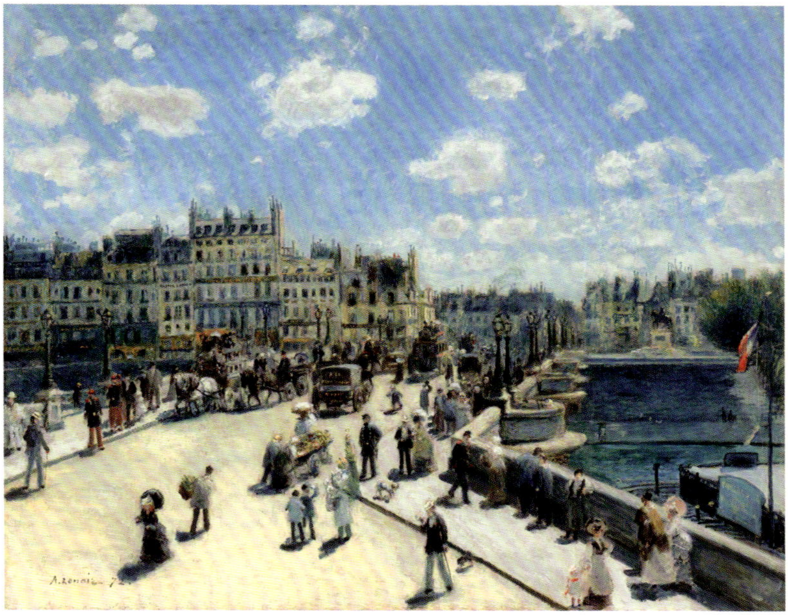

When Napoleon III declared himself emperor in 1851, Camille Pissarro was 21, Édouard Manet 19, and Edgard Degas 17. Alfred Sisley and Paul Cézanne were both 12, Claude Monet, 11, and Auguste Renoir, Berthe Morisot, Armand Guillaumin, and Frédéric Bazille were just 10.

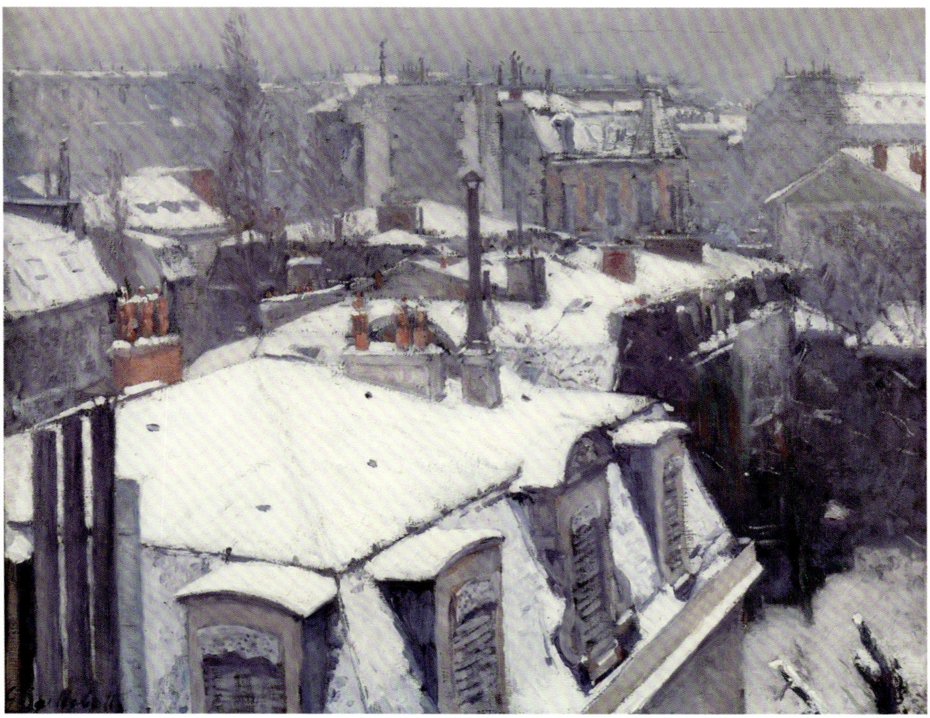

Gustave Caillebotte
View of Rooftops (Effect of Snow), also known as *Rooftops under Snow*
1878
Oil on canvas, 25 ¼ × 32 ¼ in.
(64 × 82 cm)
Musée d'Orsay, Paris

Windows over the city: this work introduced a novel subject to painting. It is perhaps the first view of the Parisian rooftops, which are so immediately recognizable to us today.

FOCUS

Japonisme

In 1853-54, the United States commissioned Commodore Perry to lead an expedition to Japan. His mission was to open trade routes, ending two centuries of isolationism, during which entering or leaving the Japanese archipelago without express authorization was punishable by immediate execution. This political turning point had instantaneous cultural repercussions. Westerners were fascinated by the artworks carried back by ship, rolled up in sheets of newspaper, or wedged between printed leaflets. Fascinated Europeans discovered striking illustrations in a completely unfamiliar style. Initially confined to a small elite audience, these *japoneries* or japonaiseries soon piqued the curiosity of many collectors, including Émile Guimet and Henri Cernuschi. They also captivated several writers, among them Baudelaire and the Goncourt brothers. It was in 1862, when Japan participated in London's Universal Exposition, that its distinctive art, with its porcelains, lacquers, bronzes, and prints, was revealed to a broad audience. Émile Guimet loaned many pieces from his collection to the Universal Exposition in 1878; they were an aesthetic revelation for many visitors.

Venturesome Collectors

Henri Cernuschi (1821-1896), a wealthy banker and ardent republican, horrified by the violence of the Commune, embarked on a voyage around the world that lasted from September 1871 until January 1873. He was accompanied by his close friend, the art critic Théodore Duret (1838-1927), a fervent advocate of the future impressionists. Cernuschi purchased almost five thousand works of art from Japan and China. Upon his return, he exhibited his collection at the Palais de l'Industrie for several months, spurring the emergence of *japonisme*. He bequeathed his collection and his town house overlooking the Parc Monceau to the city of Paris. The Musée Cernuschi opened to the public on October 26, 1898.

In 1876, Émile Guimet (1836-1918), the son of a wealthy Lyonnais industrialist, embarked on a lengthy tour of Japan, followed by visits to India and China. Three years later, he inaugurated a museum in Lyon that was dedicated to religious artifacts; it included countless treasures, which were transferred to Paris a decade later.

Shops Specializing in Japonaiseries

Located on Rue de Rivoli, La Porte Chinoise opened in 1862. It was the first shop to sell prints, ivories, and kakemonos. Baudelaire and the artists Bracquemond, Whistler, and Carolus-Duran enjoyed browsing there. In 1878, the shop's habitués included the Goncourt brothers, Zola, Manet, Degas, Monet, Cernuschi, and Duret.

The self-proclaimed "dealer in porcelains, and objets d'art of Japan and China," Siegfried Bing (1838–1905) opened L'Art Japonais in 1874. He offered all kinds of luxurious objects imported from the Far East. Bing contributed actively to the growth of *japonisme* with his publications and exhibitions.

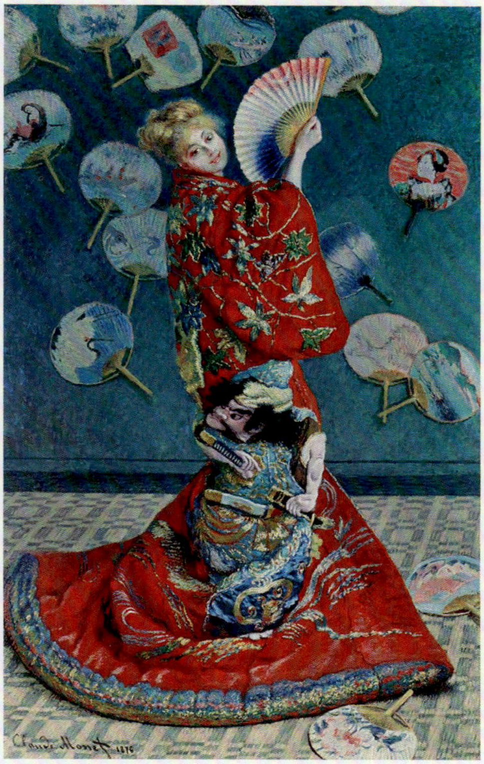

Claude Monet, *La Japonaise (Camille Monet in Japanese Costume)*, 1875
Oil on canvas, 7 ft. 7 in. × 4 ft. 8 in. (2.32× 1.42 m)
Museum of Fine Arts, Boston

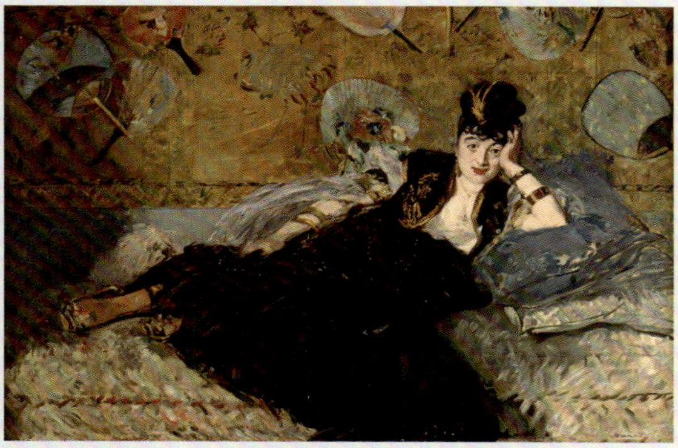

Édouard Manet, *Woman with Fans (Nina de Callias)*, 1873
Oil on canvas, 3 ft. 8 ½ in. × 5 ft. 5 ½ in. (1.13 × 1.67 m)
Musée d'Orsay, Paris

UKIYO-E

Ukiyo-e prints featured landscapes and everyday events as their favorite subjects. These "images of the floating world," by Japanese masters including Hokusai (1760–1849), Utamaro (1753–1806), and Hiroshige (1797–1858), had a profound influence on the future impressionists. In addition to this interest in subjects that seemed insignificant, or even banal, the Japanese approach to representation was entirely novel to western eyes, casting a fresh light on the world. The absence of perspective, the asymmetrical or off-center compositions, and the use of broad expanses of strong colors profoundly influenced Degas, Caillebotte, Monet, and Mary Cassatt, among others.

MARY CASSATT: ENGRAVING FIRST AND FOREMOST

A close friend of Degas and the impressionists, the American painter Mary Cassatt was particularly fascinated by the art of engraving. Her drypoints and colored lithographs demonstrate the influence of Japanese prints in their subject matter, their absence of perspective, the purity of their lines, and their use of broad areas of color.

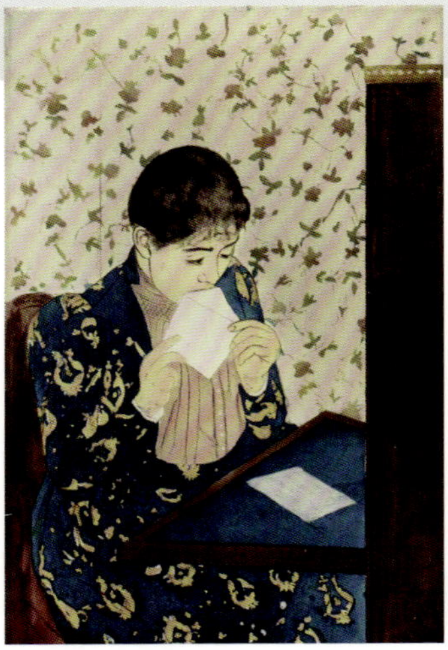

Mary Cassatt, *The Letter*, 1890–91
Colored etching, 13 ⅝ × 8 ⅞ in.
(34.6 × 22.7 cm)
Bibliothèque Nationale de France, Paris

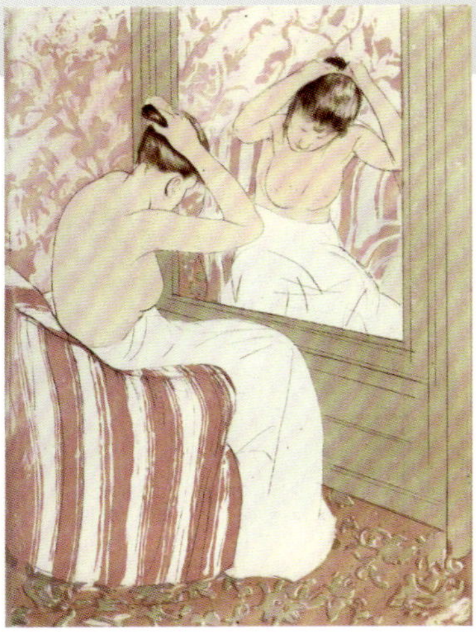

Mary Cassatt, *Woman Arranging Her Hair*, c. 1890–91
Aquatint, 14 ½ × 10 ½ in. (36.7 × 26.7 cm)
Bibliothèque Nationale de France, Paris

Monet called this his "Chinese painting." The view from above, the flattened composition without perspective, and the terrace in the foreground are all very reminiscent of Hokusai's work.

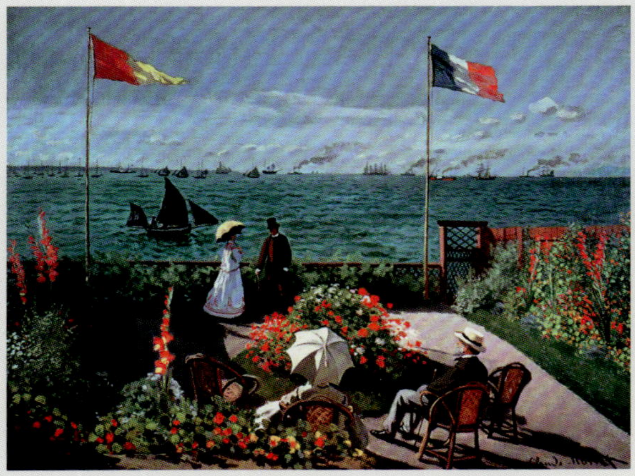

Claude Monet, *The Terrace at Sainte-Adresse*, 1867
Oil on canvas, 3 ft. 2 ½ in. × 4 ft. 3 ½ in. (98 × 130 cm)
The Metropolitan Museum of Art, New York

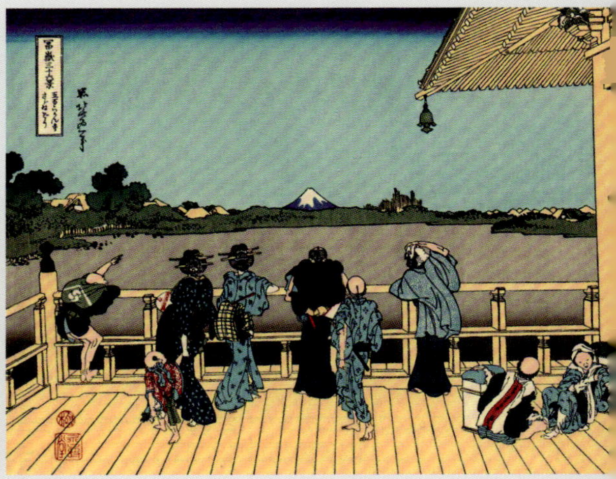

Hokusai, *Figures Looking at Mount Fuji from the Balcony of Sazaedō, One of the Buildings of the Temple of Gohyaku Rakanji at Edo*
Print from the series *Thirty-Six Views of Mount Fuji*, c. 1830
Woodblock print, ink, and color on paper, 10 ¼ × 15 ¼ in.
(26.2 × 38.6 cm)
Museum of Fine Arts, Boston

This Hiroshige landscape was one of the prints in Monet's collection. Its simplified rendition of space, eradicating any hint of perspective, is juxtaposed with a succession of colored picture planes. The landscape of Belle-Île, painted by Monet many years later, is strikingly similar.

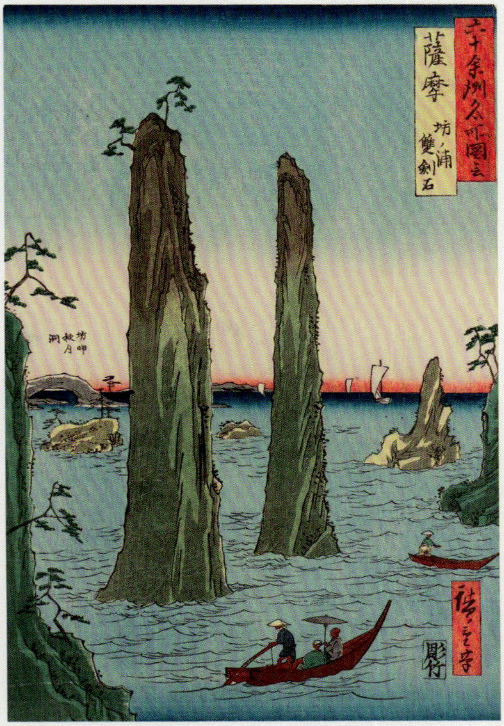

Hiroshige, *Rocks at Bo-No-Ura*, 1856
Woodblock print, ink, and color on paper, 13 ⅞ × 9 ⅝ in. (35.4 × 24.5 cm)
Museum of Fine Arts, Boston

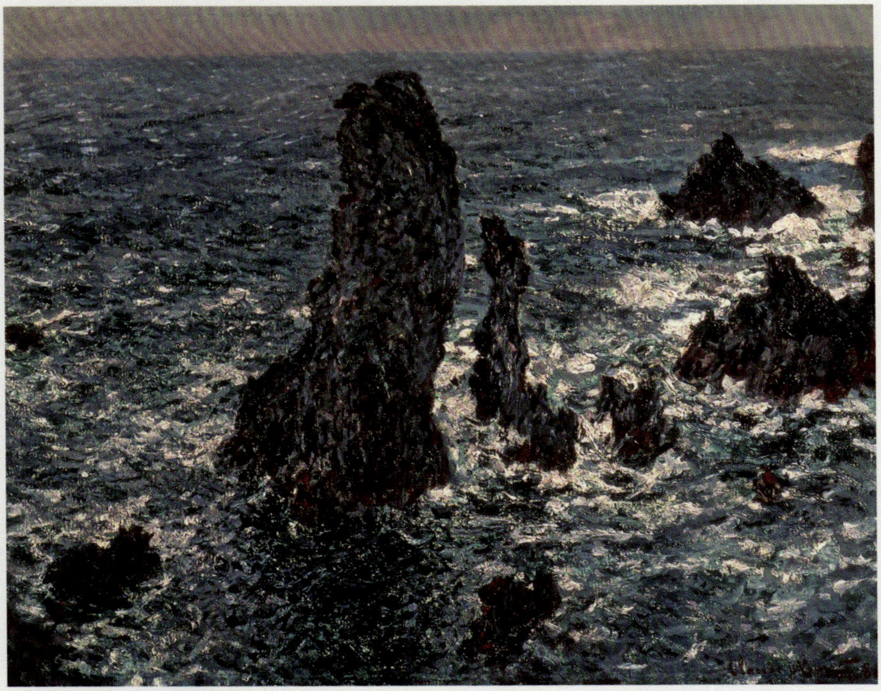

Claude Monet, *Rocks at Belle-Île*, 1886
Oil on canvas, 25 ⅝ × 31 ⅞ in. (65 × 81 cm)
The Pushkin State Museum of Fine Arts, Moscow

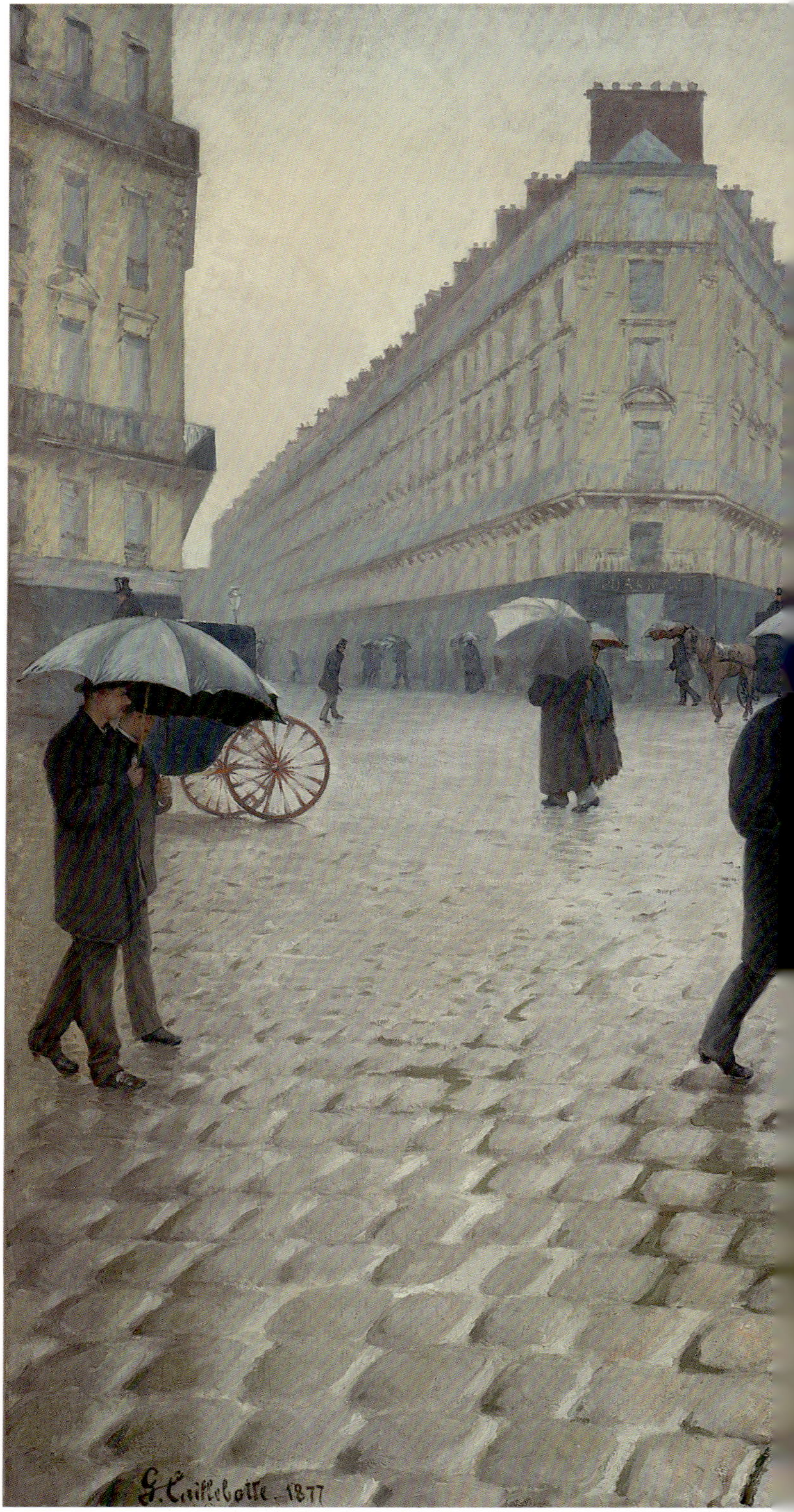

Gustave Caillebotte
Paris Street; Rainy Day
1877
Oil on canvas,
6 ft. 11 ½ in. × 9 ft. ¾ in.
(2.12 × 2.76 m)
The Art Institute
of Chicago, Chicago

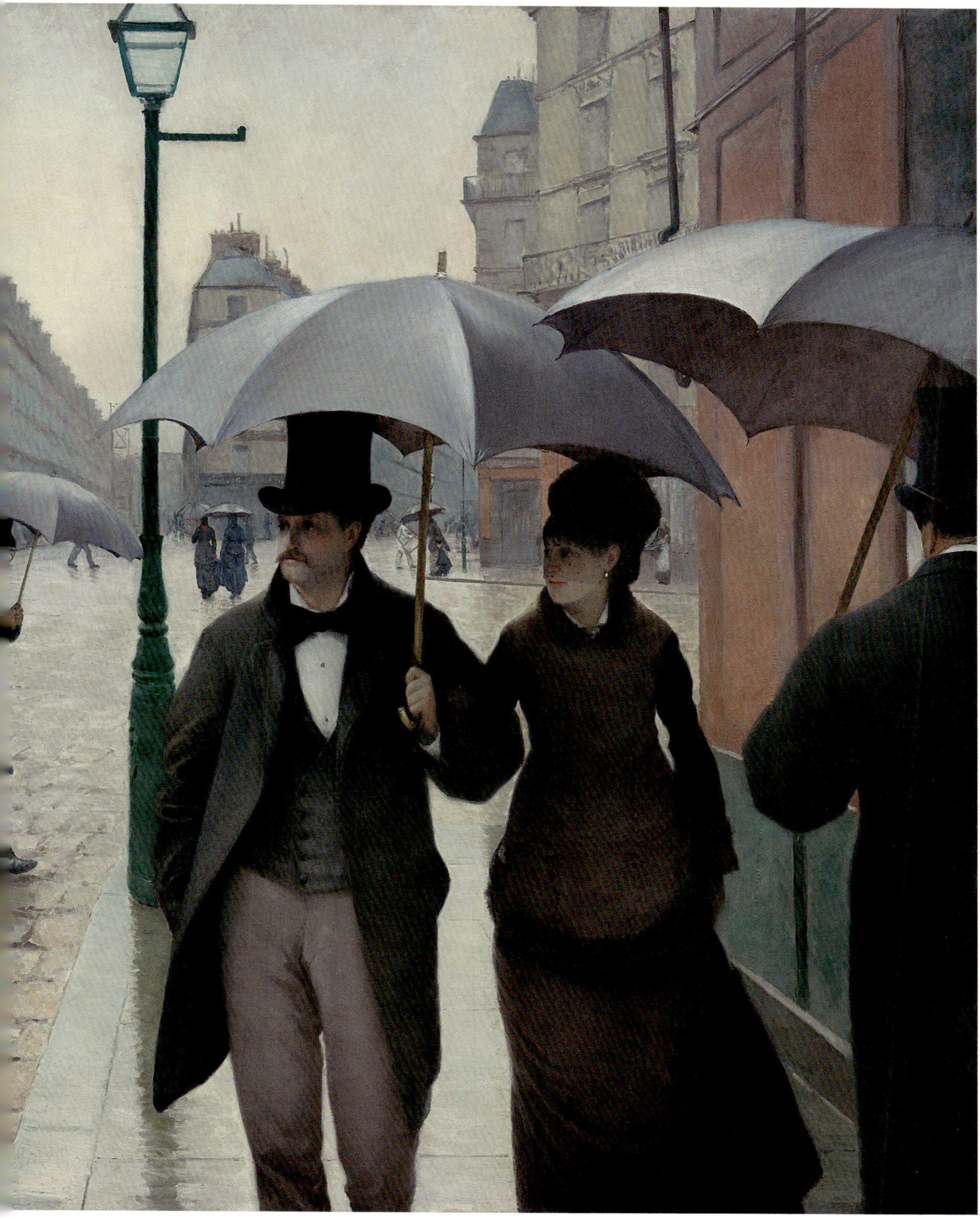

Paris Street; Rainy Day

Gustave Caillebotte, 1877

Displayed at the third impressionist exhibition in 1877, this Parisian scene demonstrates the distinctive qualities of the art of Gustave Caillebotte (1848–1894). While most impressionists tended toward *plein air* paintings of leisure activities, Caillebotte's passion was the new cityscape surrounding him. Capturing a fleeting moment, as in a photograph, his *Paris Street; Rainy Day* epitomizes the nineteenth-century world, in which Haussmann's Paris represented a newfound jewel.

MERCI, MONSIEUR CAILLEBOTTE!
A painter and artistic patron with a substantial private fortune, Gustave Caillebotte (1848–1894) was among the most active participants in the impressionist movement. Suffering from poor health, he was not yet thirty when he drafted a will leaving his large collection to the State. Following his death, only forty of the approximately sixty works he so generously offered were accepted, and then only after heated negotiations. The works by Degas, Monet, Pissarro, Renoir, Sisley, Cézanne, and Berthe Morisot are today among the treasures of the Musée d'Orsay's collection.

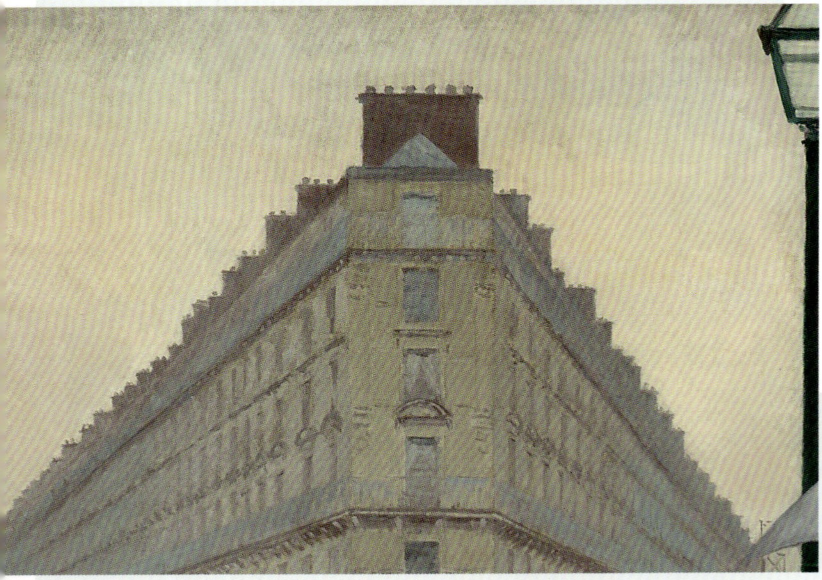

Solidly grounded by the lamppost as its central axis, the scene is set at a crossroads of Haussmann-style buildings. Caillebotte emphasizes the geometry and rigor of this new urban landscape. The viewer's eye is drawn to the line of receding rooftops, emphasized by the rows of long, narrow balconies.

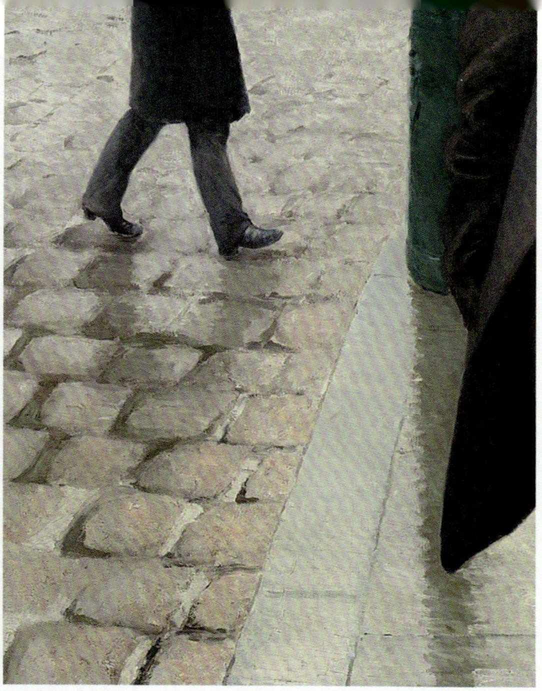

Like his impressionist friends, Caillebotte was attentive to the fleeting effects of weather. Bent beneath their umbrellas, somberly clad Parisians proceed along the sidewalk. Using the tip of his brush, the painter conveys the effect of the wet pavement and the shadow cast by the lamppost.

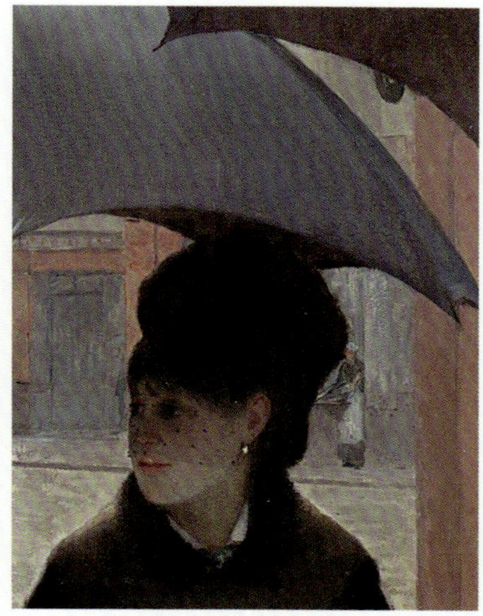

Like the gentleman accompanying her, the pretty young Parisienne's gaze is drawn to a scene set outside the picture's frame. A passing carriage, or an acquaintance? A shop window? It remains a mystery. Caillebotte composed a painting that captures the moment like a snapshot, hinting at events occurring outside the frame. A man seen from the back, about to cross their path, seems to be cut in half by the painting's frame.

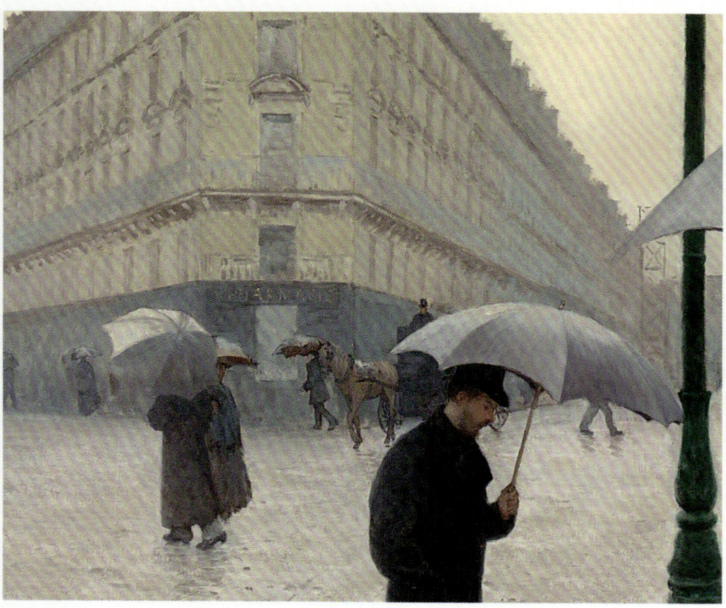

The curving umbrellas partly conceal a multitude of distant details that suggest the daily life of this new Paris. Anonymous passersby cross paths, absorbed in solitude or engaged in lively conversation; a laborer carrying his ladder avoids a woman who hoists up her skirt before crossing the street; two friends seen from the back walk together, and—a surrealist touch—two disembodied legs advance across the wet cobbles in the background.

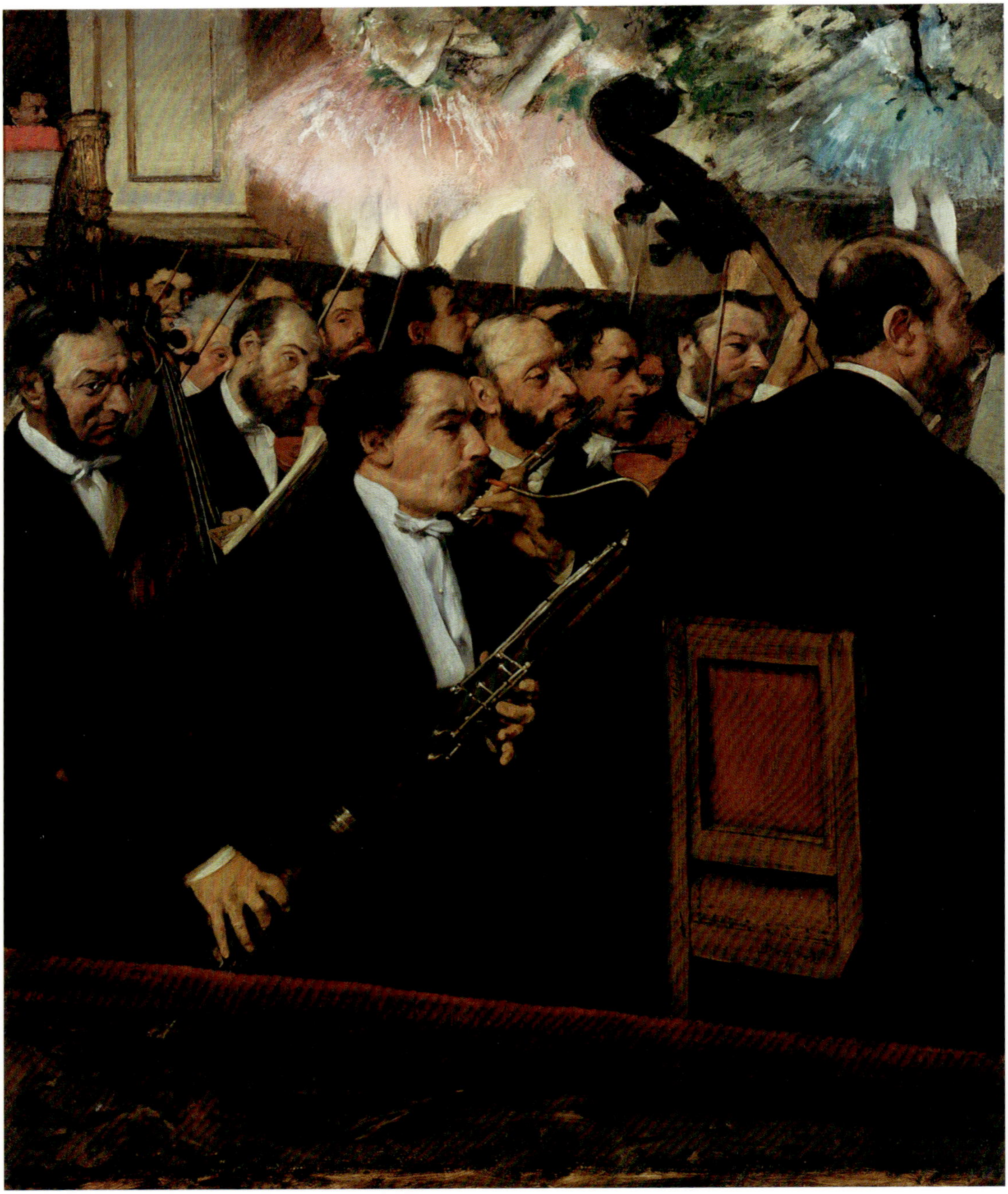

Edgar Degas
The Orchestra at the Opera
c. 1868–69
Oil on canvas, 22 ¼ × 18 ⅛ in.
(56.5 × 46.2 cm)
Musée d'Orsay, Paris

A City of Pleasure and Spectacle

"My dear Degas, surely you're not intending to revolutionize painting with double basses and dancers?"
"No, my dear fellow, no more than you are with your Christs suspended from lapel pins!"

Gustave Moreau and Edgard Degas, discussing their work in the Café La Rochefoucauld (at the corner of Rue La Rochefoucauld and Rue Notre-Dame-de-Lorette, not far from the symbolist master's residence-studio), quoted by Sophie Monneret in *L'Impressionnisme et son époque*, 1978.

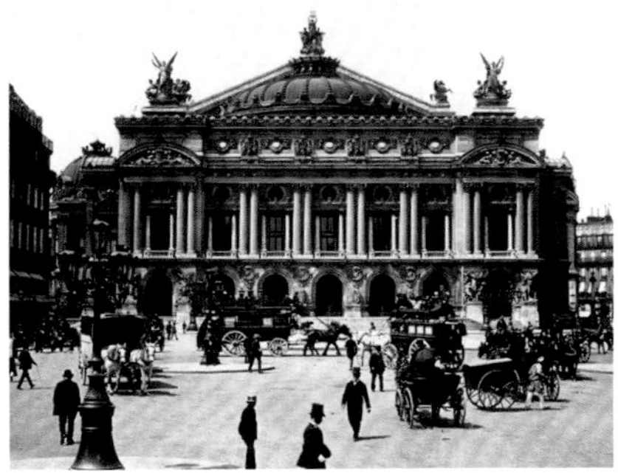

The Opéra Garnier
National Gallery, London

Building the Opéra was a long saga of unforeseen events and delays. The project was awarded to Charles Garnier in 1861, but work was halted by the Franco-Prussian War, and then restarted after a fire that devastated the temporary Opéra on Rue Le Pelletier in 1873. The monument was inaugurated in 1875, under the Third Republic. Napoleon III, who had commissioned the building, did not survive to see its completion. A focal point of the new Paris, the Opéra crowned the avenue of the same name, a spectacle and stage set in its own right, glittering with ornamentation. It became a model for opera houses worldwide.

Commissioned by Napoleon III, the new Paris seemed designed to be an ideal setting for the new governing class; aristocrats now mingled with the wealthy bourgeoisie. The Grands Boulevards, with their restaurants and spacious café terraces, welcomed passersby who sought recognition and access to Paris's social scene. The Bois de Boulogne was a popular destination; citizens went there to stroll, go boating, and skate, as well as seek new conquests. Scattered throughout the city, public gardens were places to gather and relax near ponds and bandstands.

Among the temples of sophisticated culture, the Comédie-Française, where "the Divine" Sarah Bernhardt held forth, the Opéra, the Odéon, and the Opéra-Comique all continued to attract the aristocracy, while also drawing members of the wealthy new bourgeoisie. Mingling parvenus with members of high society, these venues were indispensable markers of social status, and the aim of frequenting them was both to see and to be seen. Clothed in their finest attire and dripping with jewels, the great courtesans flaunted

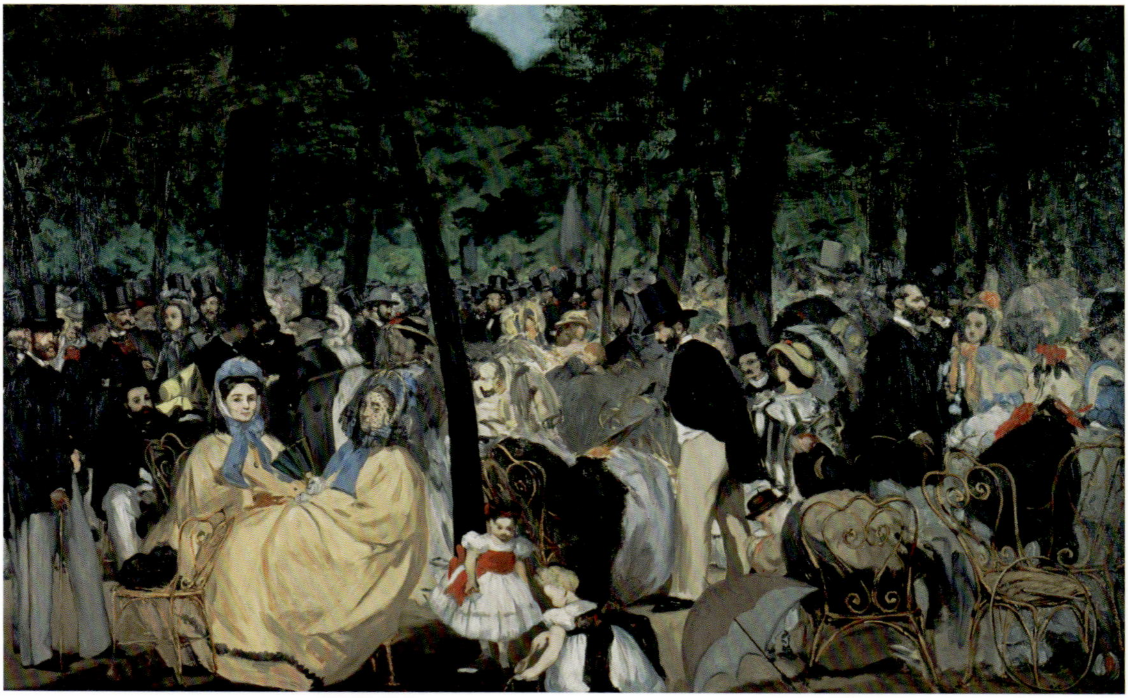

Édouard Manet
Music in the Tuileries
1862
Oil on canvas, 2 ft. 6 in. × 3 ft. 10 ½ in.
(76 × 118 cm)
National Gallery, London

Painting one of the places he frequented regularly, Manet depicts his own profile on the far left of the composition, and includes a number of his friends amid the crowd: Baudelaire, Offenbach, Fantin-Latour, and the art critic Champfleury.

their charms on balconies and in theater boxes, alongside duchesses and countesses.

Napoleon III's decree of January 6, 1864 (which granted theaters independence, gave them the freedom to set up without having to obtain state authorization first and to choose their own repertoires, and allowed the theater business to be determined by market forces) was revolutionary. Paris became the European capital of entertainment. Operetta was all the rage. The Théatre-des-Folies-Marigny, the Théâtre de la Renaissance, the Théâtre-Antoine, and the concert halls flourished, particularly along the Grands Boulevards. Their repertoire broadened, and vaudeville drew crowds, along with attractions including circuses and puppet shows. Les Ambassadeurs on the Champs-Élysées and the Ba-Ta-Clan on Boulevard Voltaire were popular venues for a new type of entertainment, where the bourgeois sat side by side with the lower classes. The café-concert offered a wide range of attractions, soon followed by music halls, which first appeared in 1869 with the Folies-Bergère and its more or less nude reviews. Cabarets, cafés, and dance halls were crowded side by side on the slopes of Montmartre. Paris had become a pleasure capital, and was also renowned for its houses of prostitution. These ran the gamut from simple brothels to palatial establishments that offered something for every proclivity and purse, from crowned heads of Europe to simple laborers.

"Parisian life is rich in poetic and wonderful subjects. The marvelous envelops us and saturates us like the atmosphere; but we fail to see it."

Charles Baudelaire, "The Salon of 1846."

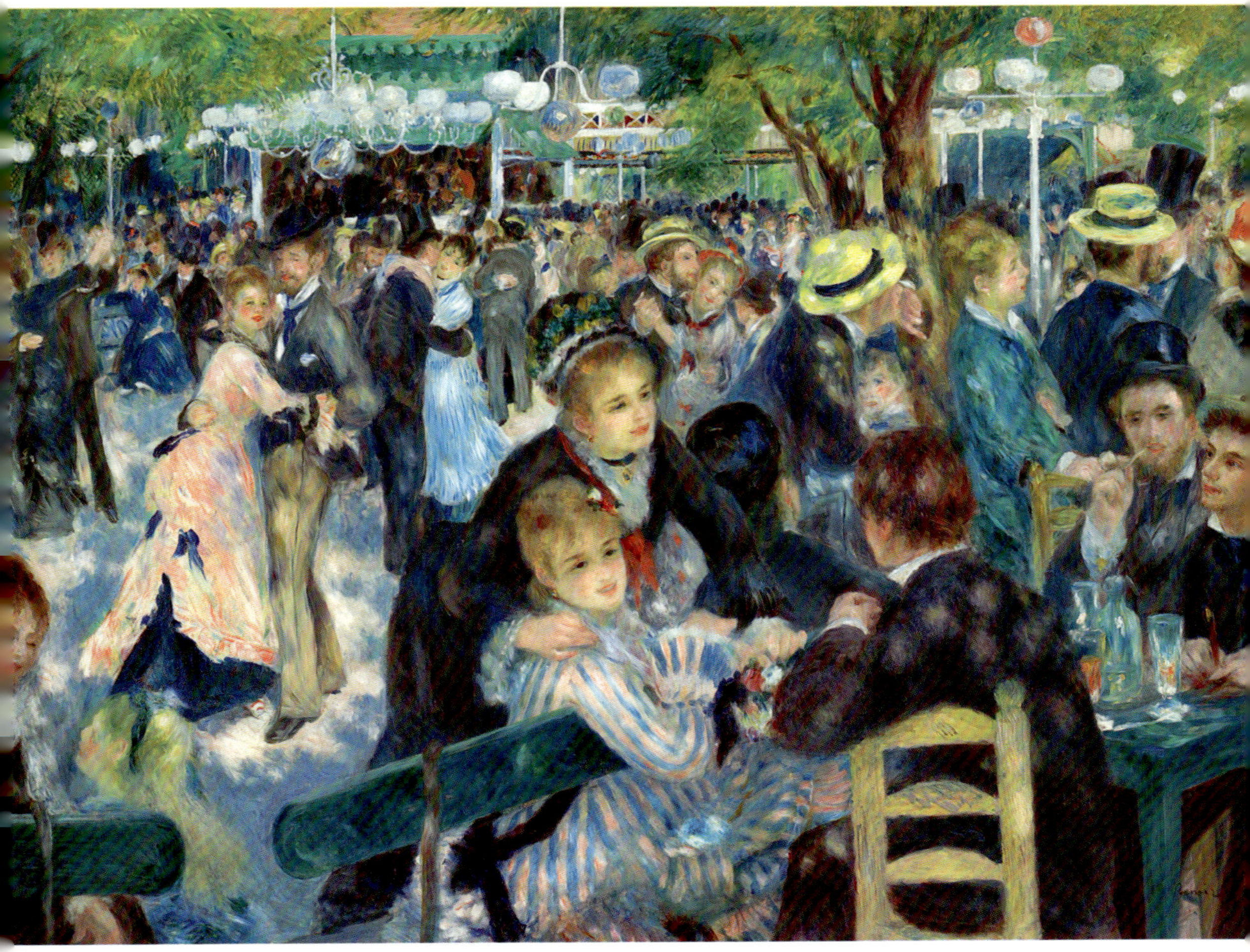

Presented at the third impressionist exhibition in 1877, this painting conveys the relaxed, exuberant atmosphere of a dance hall in Montmartre, located not far from Renoir's studio. Fit and fashionably turned out, bourgeois gentlemen in search of a good time mingle with seamstresses, laundresses, and laborers.

Auguste Renoir
Dance at Le Moulin de la Galette
1876
Oil on canvas, 4 ft. 3 ½ in. × 5 ft. 9 in. (1.31 × 1.75 m)
Musée d'Orsay, Paris

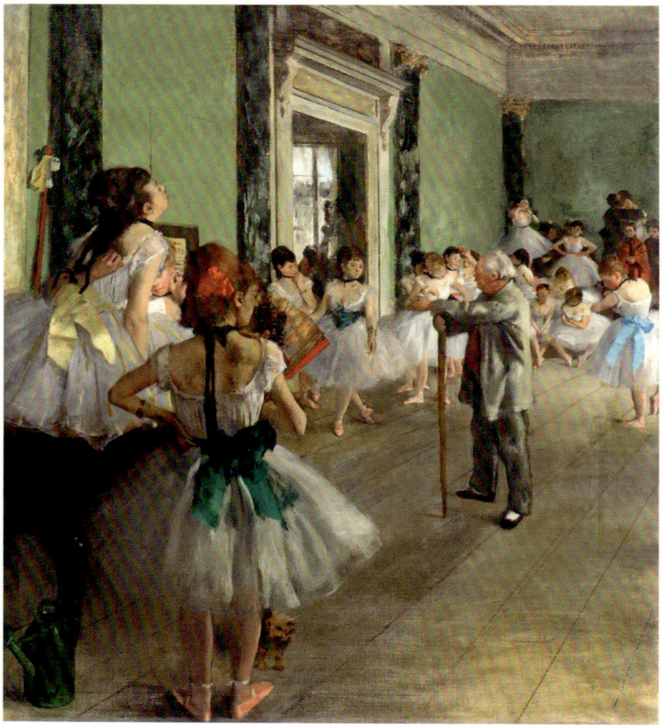

Edgar Degas
The Ballet Class
c. 1873–76
Oil on canvas, 33 ⅝ × 29 ½ in.
(85.5 × 75 cm)
Musée d'Orsay, Paris

IN THE WINGS

The stage wings and rehearsal rooms of the Opéra were an endless source of inspiration for Edgar Degas. Seemingly dashed off spontaneously, his works were actually carefully recomposed in his studio, and were based on sketches executed at the theater, studies of live models, and sometimes even photographs.

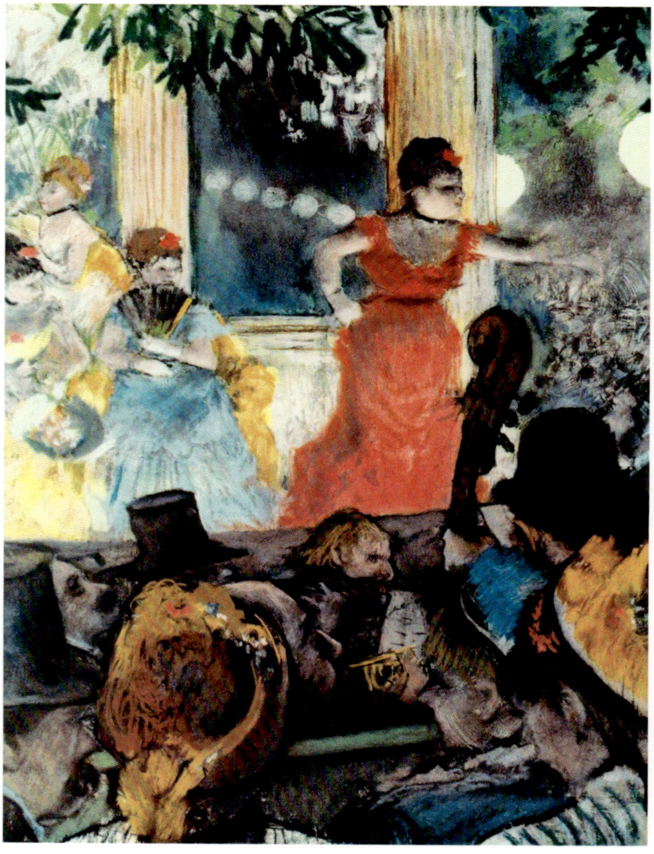

Edgar Degas
Café-Concert at Les Ambassadeurs
1876–77
Pastel on monotype, 14 ⅛ × 9 ⅞ in.
(36 × 25 cm)
Musée des Beaux-Arts, Lyon

IN THE LIMELIGHT

Gaslight lent its brilliance to nocturnal venues, including theaters, operas, cabarets, and concert halls. Acutely aware of lighting effects, Degas showed the dancers' and singers' ghostly, pallid faces, exposed to the harsh glare of the spotlights.

"The long working day was over, and the Paris of pleasure was illuminated, for a night of festivities. Cafés, wine merchants, and restaurants glowed.... Paris, just beginning to awaken to gaslight, was seized with an appetite for pleasure that soon became a hunger for anything that could be bought."

Émile Zola, *Paris*, 1898.

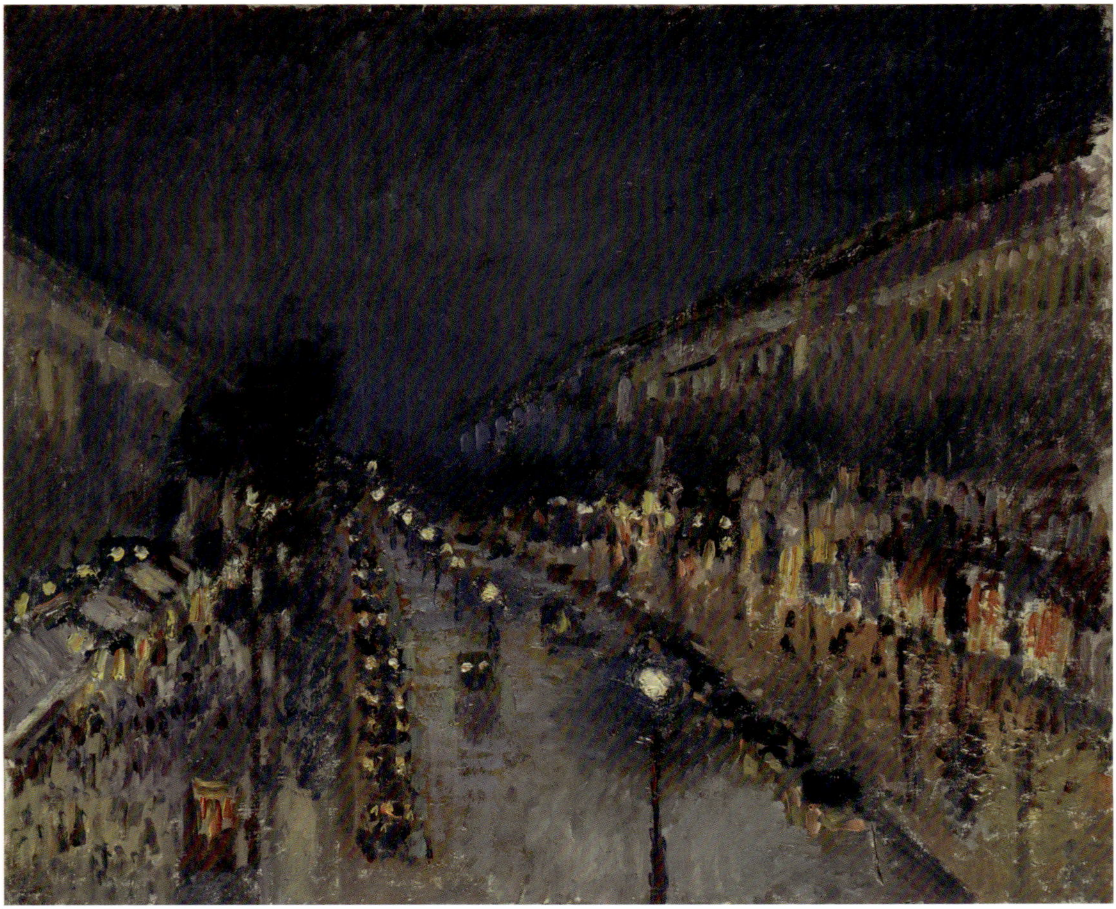

"The city had become an orgy of gold and women."

Emile Zola, *The Kill*, 1874.

Camille Pissarro
Le Boulevard Montmartre at Night
1897
Oil on canvas, 21 × 25 ½ in. (53.3 × 64.8 cm)
National Gallery, London

FOCUS

Cafés

In the nineteenth century, cafés, restaurants, and café-concerts played an essential role in artistic, intellectual, and political life. Friends would meet there informally, debate openly, and try to reshape the world.

The Café Guerbois

Located at 11 Avenue Grand-Rue-des-Batignolles (today Avenue de Clichy), the Café Guerbois became Manet's headquarters in the 1860s. A small band of regulars, calling themselves the "Groupe des Batignolles" after the newly developed neighborhood, gathered in this café close to Manet's studio. A fraternity formed around the man whom the future impressionists deemed their guardian spirit. In 1869-70, art critics Théodore Duret and Louis Edmond Duranty, the young writer Émile Zola, the artist and writer Zacharie Astruc, Antonin Proust (briefly the minister of arts: November 1881-January 1882), the painters Constantin Guys, Henri Fantin-Latour, Frédéric Bazille, Edgar Degas, Claude Monet, Pierre Auguste Renoir, Alfred Sisley, Paul Cézanne, and Camille Pissarro, and the photographer Nadar gathered in Manet's company for lively discussions; candor was the order of the day.

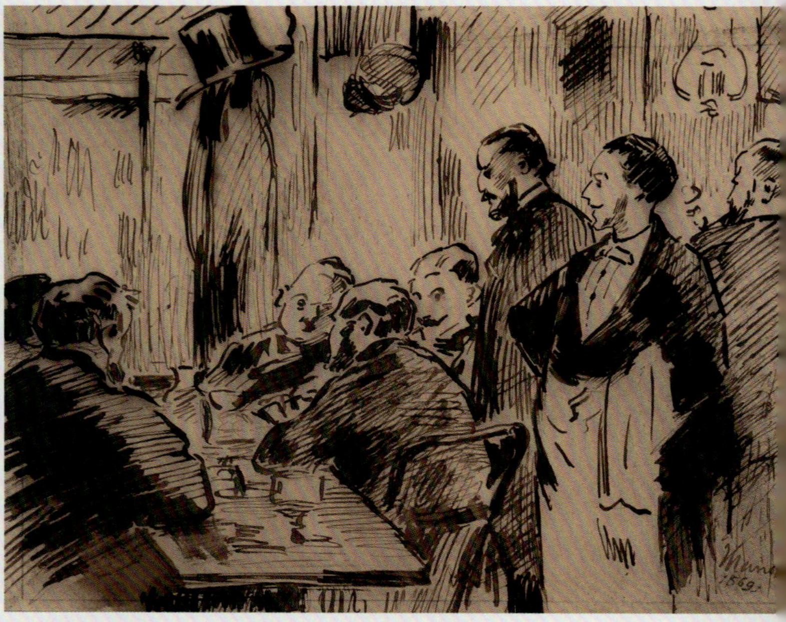

Édouard Manet, *Café Interior (Le Café Guerbois)*, c. 1869
Pen and India ink, 11 ⅝ × 15 ½ in. (29.5 × 39.5 cm)
Bibliothèque Nationale de France, Paris

"To their meetings in the Café Guerbois, Manet brought his paintings with their light tones and vivid colors, and Claude Monet, Pissarro, and Renoir brought the practices and techniques of plein air *painting. These encounters were bound to have fertile results. A powerful movement in art emerged that was soon to be identified as impressionism."*

Théodore Duret, *Les Peintres impressionnistes*, 1878.

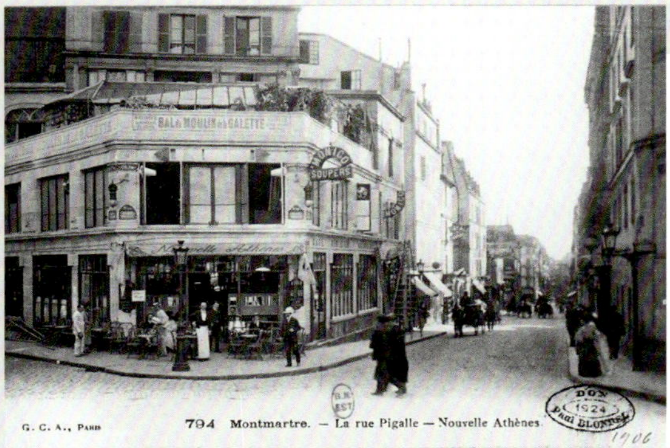

LA NOUVELLE ATHÈNES

In 1870, the Franco-Prussian War scattered the artistic community; Frédéric Bazille was among those who died at the front. The group's new rallying point was the Café de la Nouvelle Athènes at 9 Place Pigalle. The café quickly became the gathering place for contemporary artists, and an intellectual home for Bohemian society.

The Café de la Nouvelle Athènes in Montmartre, 1906
Postcard
Bibliothèque Nationale de France, Paris

COURBET AND THE BRASSERIES

At the center of the realist movement that revolved around Gustave Courbet were two venues: the Brasserie Andler-Keller on Rue Hautefeuille and, from 1863, the Brasserie des Martyrs, located on the same street. Thinkers, writers, painters, poets, and journalists gathered here. The social libertarian philosopher Proudhon, the journalist Castagnary, the writer Champfleury, and the poet Théodore de Banville all came, along with the art critic Louis Edmond Duranty, who founded the short-lived review Réalisme in 1856. Colorists, devoted followers of Ingres, and realists all thronged here to engage in verbal duels. Manet arrived with his friends Baudelaire. Monet and Pissarro, and the young medical student and future collector, Paul Gachet, stopped by to hear the debates as well.

"Nothing could be more interesting … than these causeries with their perpetual clash of opinions. They kept our wits sharpened, they encouraged us with stores of enthusiasm that for weeks and weeks kept us up, until the final shaping of the idea was accomplished. From them we emerged with a firmer will, with our thoughts clearer and more distinct."

Claude Monet, conversation in *Le Temps*, November 27, 1900 (quoted by John Rewald, *The History of Impressionism*, 1946).

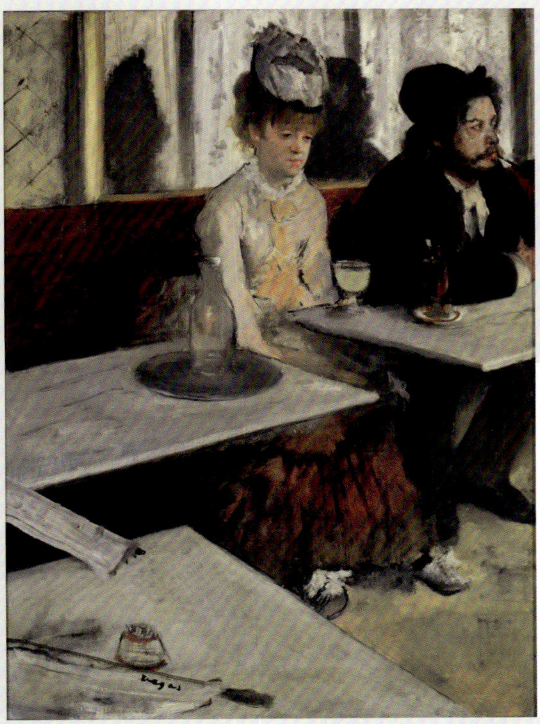

DEGAS, *THE ABSINTHE DRINKER*

It was Degas' friends—the painter and engraver Marcellin Desboutin and the actress Ellen Andrée, also an artist's model—who posed for his work titled *The Absinthe Drinker*. The scene is set in the Café de la Nouvelle Athènes; absinthe became emblematic of an era ravaged by widespread alcoholism.

Edgar Degas, *In a Café*, also known as *The Absinthe Drinker*, 1875–76
Oil on canvas, 3 ft. × 1 ¼ in. × 2 ft. 3 in. (92 × 68.5 cm)
Musée d'Orsay, Paris

Auguste Renoir
La Loge (The Theater Box)
1874
Oil on canvas, 31 ½ × 25 in. (80 × 63.5 cm)
The Samuel Courtauld Trust,
The Courtauld Gallery, London

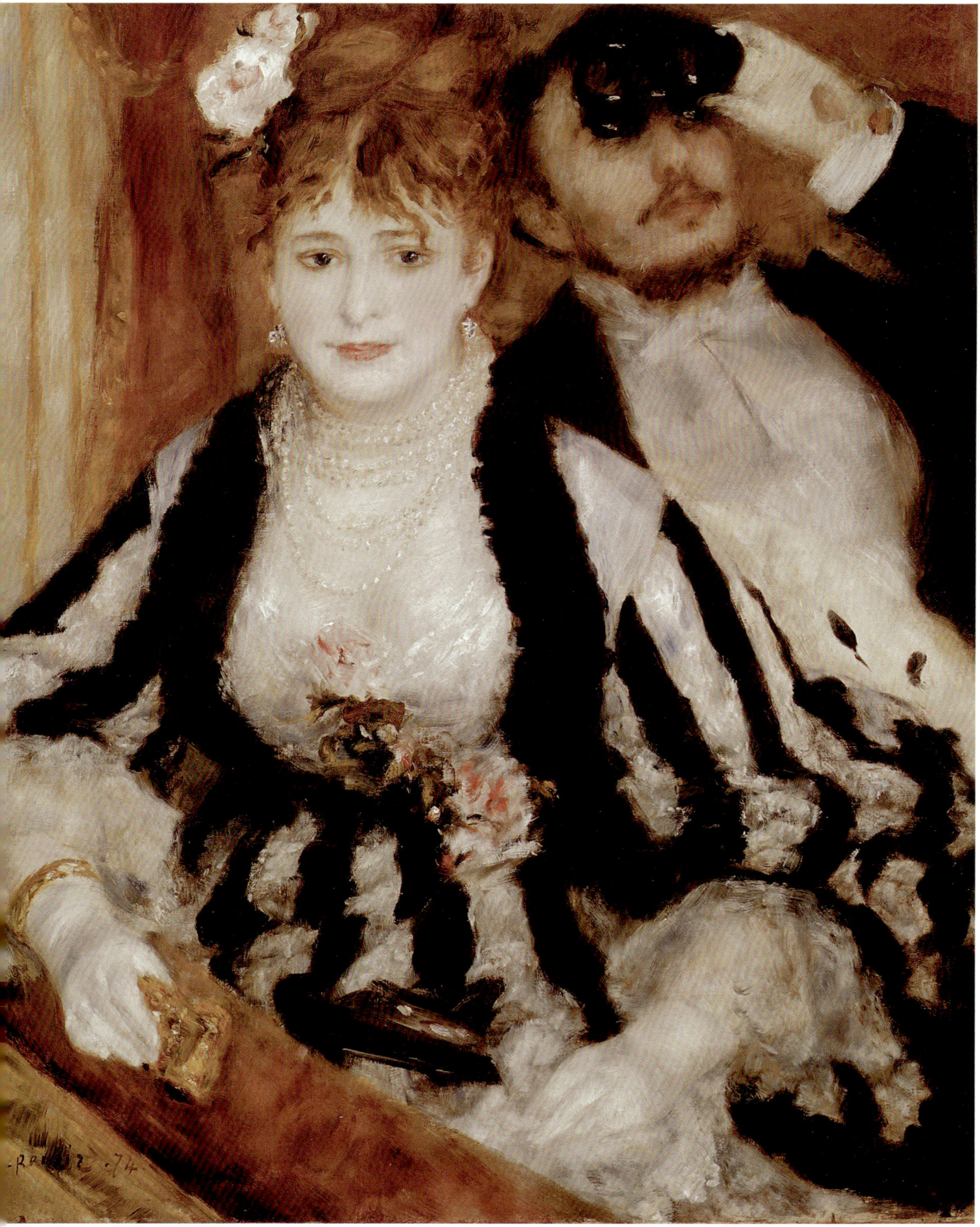

La Loge (The Theater Box)

Auguste Renoir, 1874

Paris was one long celebration during the Second Empire. Its concert halls flourished, and people flocked to theaters to see and be seen. Demimondaines mingled with society ladies, their every move observed and discussed in speculative murmurs; the performance occurred as much among the spectators as on the stage. The loges—theater boxes set above the stalls—formed balconies where audience members could rival one another for attention.

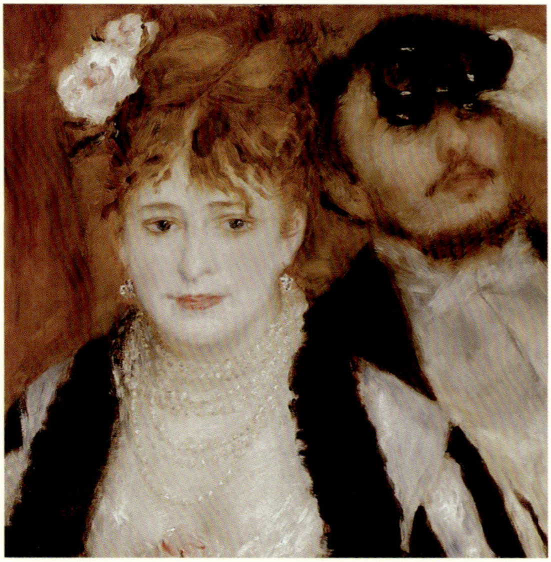

Rapid brushstrokes suggest the architecture of the loge. Renoir dwells in greater detail on the gown's lace trim, and loosely sketches the man's figure. In contrast, the artist lingers over the young woman's features meticulously and painstakingly, and carefully conveys the delicate hues of her porcelain complexion.

Roses are tucked in her hair and bodice; white-gloved hands grasp a black fan and a gold reticule. Nothing is left to chance in the young woman's toilette, which is as meticulous as it is elegant.

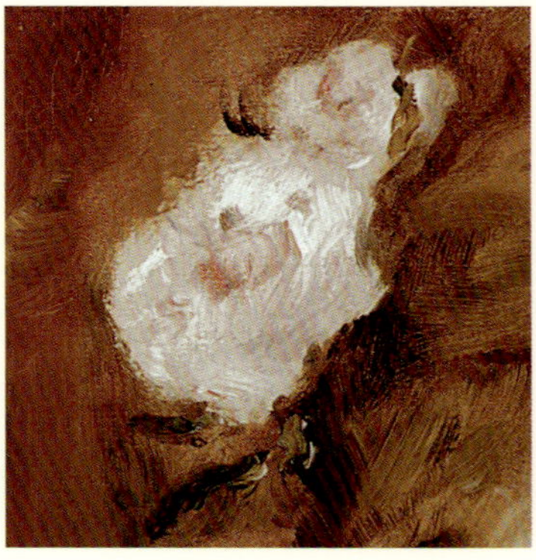

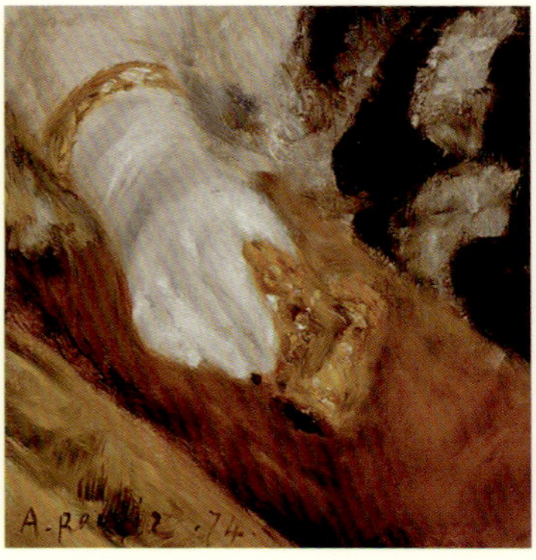

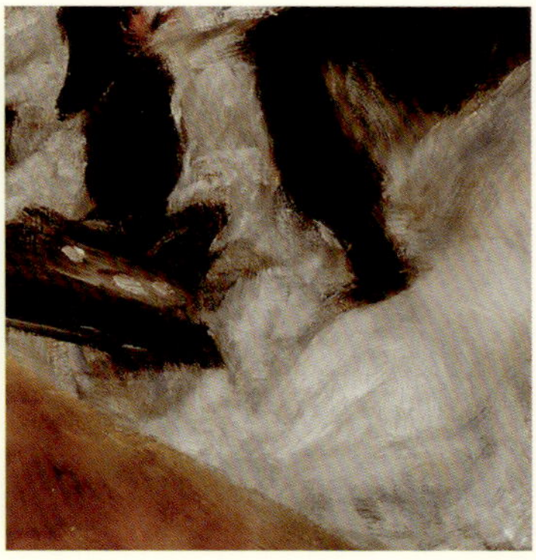

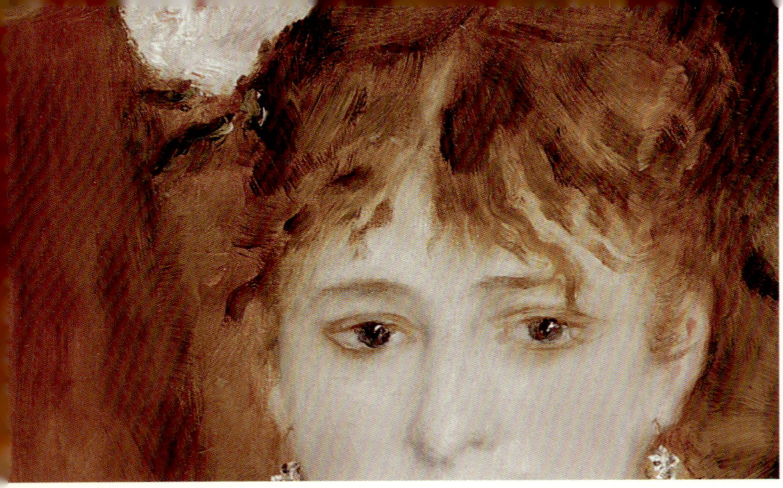

The only shadow in this painting is the suggestion of sadness in this lovely young woman's gaze.

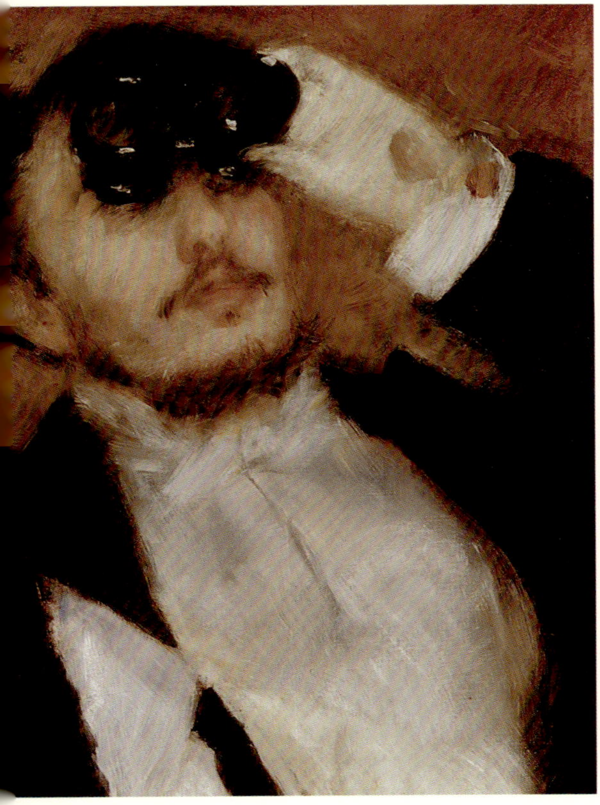

In the background, his body turned away from the woman, the man is absorbed by what he observes through his opera glasses. Instead of being directed toward the stage, he is pointing them at another loge, where perhaps a similar scene is being played out. Who is attending tonight's performance? And with whom? Such preoccupations were evidently the main incentive for this evening's outing, rather than the performance. Proust and Madame de Guermantes might be in the next loge.

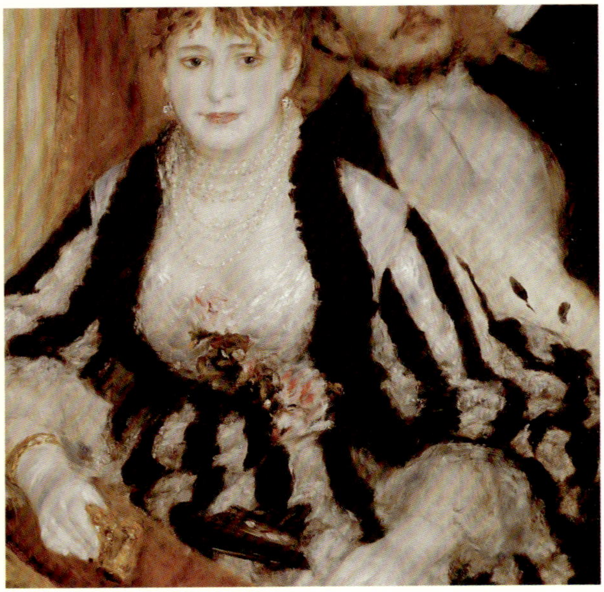

Leaning slightly toward the balcony's edge, this impeccably made-up woman, draped in pearls, resembles a jewel herself—perhaps a trophy for the man seated behind her.

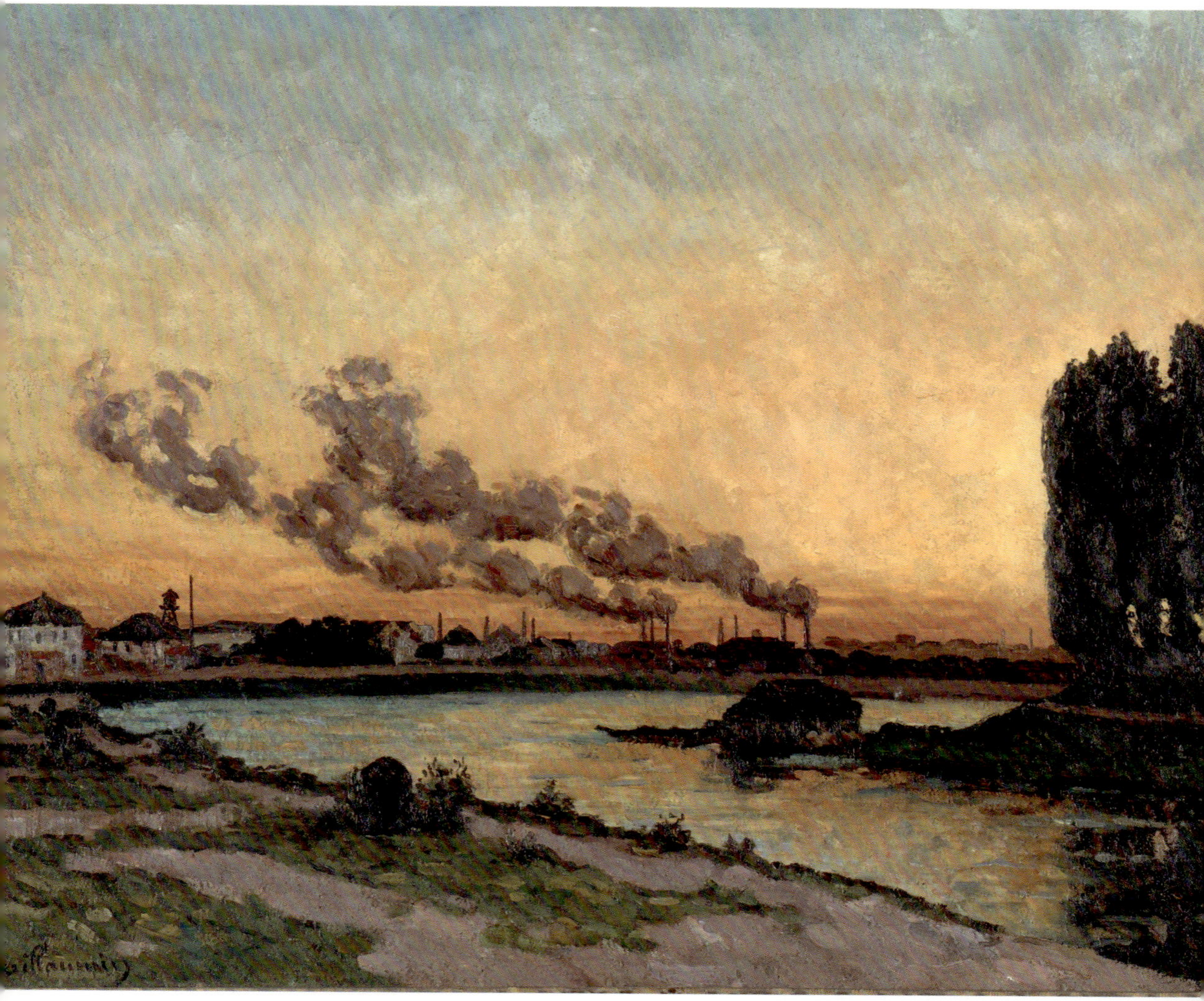

Armand Guillaumin
Sunset at Ivry
1878
Oil on canvas, 25 ⅝ × 31 ⅞ in.
(65 × 81 cm)
Musée d'Orsay, Paris

A World in Flux

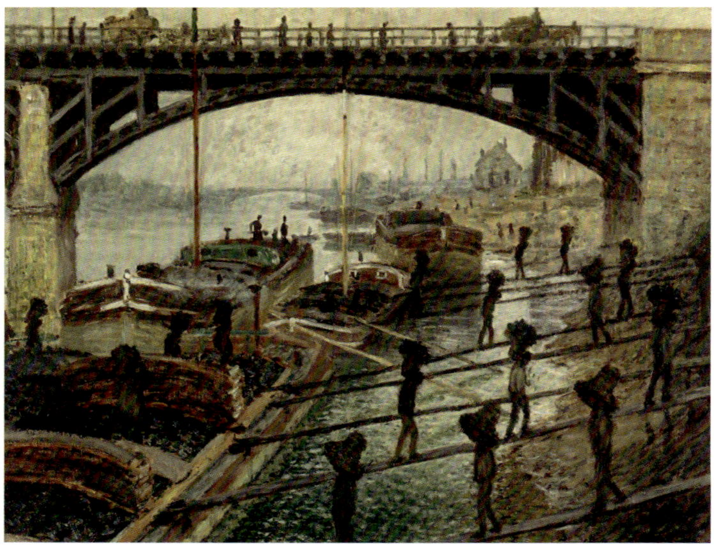

Claude Monet
The Coalmen, also known as
Men Unloading Coal
1875
Oil on canvas, 20 ⅞ × 26 in.
(55 × 66 cm)
Musée d'Orsay, Paris

The growth in trade and agriculture and the rapid industrialization of the country enriched the Second Empire, and Napoleon III celebrated his nation's triumph. He inaugurated the Universal Expositions to serve as showcases for this era of opulence. Empires were emerging in the fast-growing realms of finance and industry. Major banks were established (Crédit Lyonnais in 1863, Société Générale in 1864); metallurgy worked full tilt to support the frenetic growth of railroads and iron architecture; river traffic surged. Department stores were becoming the shrines of consumerism described by Zola in *Au bonheur des dames* (*The Ladies' Paradise*, 1883).

Entrepreneurial spirit, engineering and scientific progress, and exuberant innovation were the engines of an industrialized urban world undergoing explosive growth. This coincided with the emergence of a business bourgeoisie and the birth of an urban proletariat. Haussmann's building program pushed the working class out toward

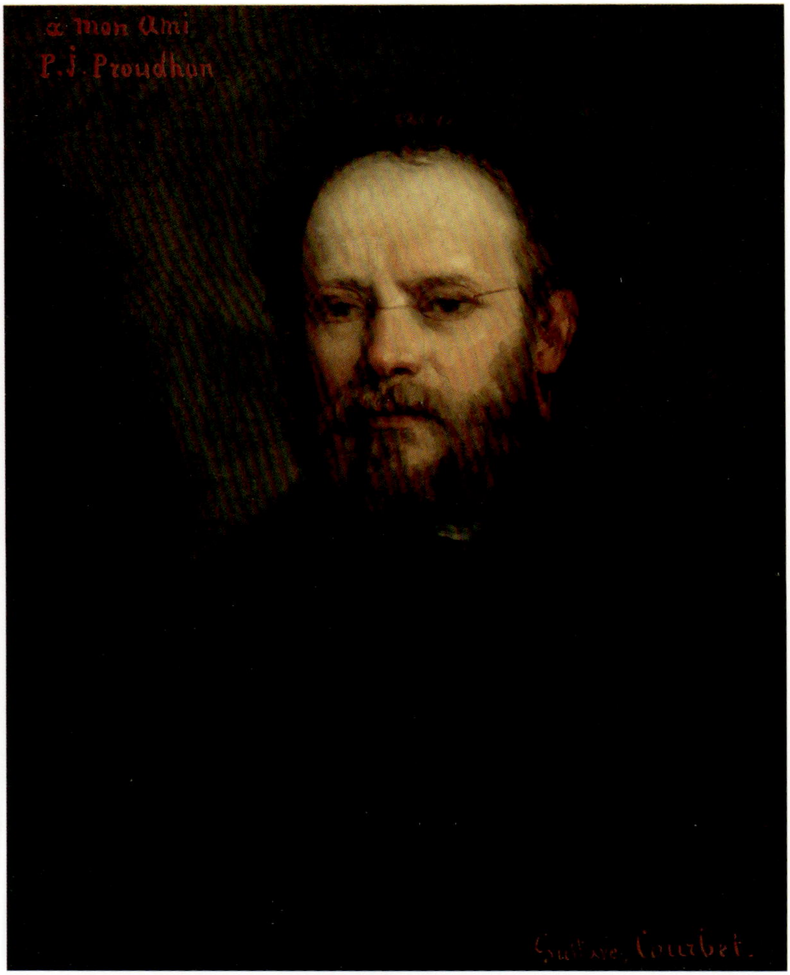

Gustave Courbet
Pierre Joseph Proudhon (1809-1865), Philosopher
1865
Oil on canvas, 28 ¾ × 21 ⅝ in.
(72 × 55 cm)
Musée d'Orsay, Paris

PIERRE JOSEPH PROUDHON

Pierre Joseph Proudhon was a socialist theorist and early advocate of anarchism, a fierce foe of private property and ardent defender of the common man. His activities as a journalist, polemicist, and politician took him from a seat in the National Assembly to a stint in prison, depending on the regime of the moment. He defended workers' rights in numerous publications. A close friend of Gustave Courbet, who was also born in the Franche-Comté, Proudhon was self-taught, working class, and a defender of realism in art.

the Belleville and Ménilmontant neighborhoods, and to the industrial basin of La Villette. The dispossessed sometimes made their voices heard, as in the Commune uprising that was bloodily suppressed in 1871; the oppressed masses had attempted to burn the Palais des Tuileries to the ground. Karl Marx in Germany and Pierre Joseph Proudhon in France revealed the workings of burgeoning capitalism and took up the cause of those left behind in its wake. The realist movement emerged in art, spearheaded by Gustave Courbet (1818-1877). He was determined to depict the contemporary world and social reality as they were.

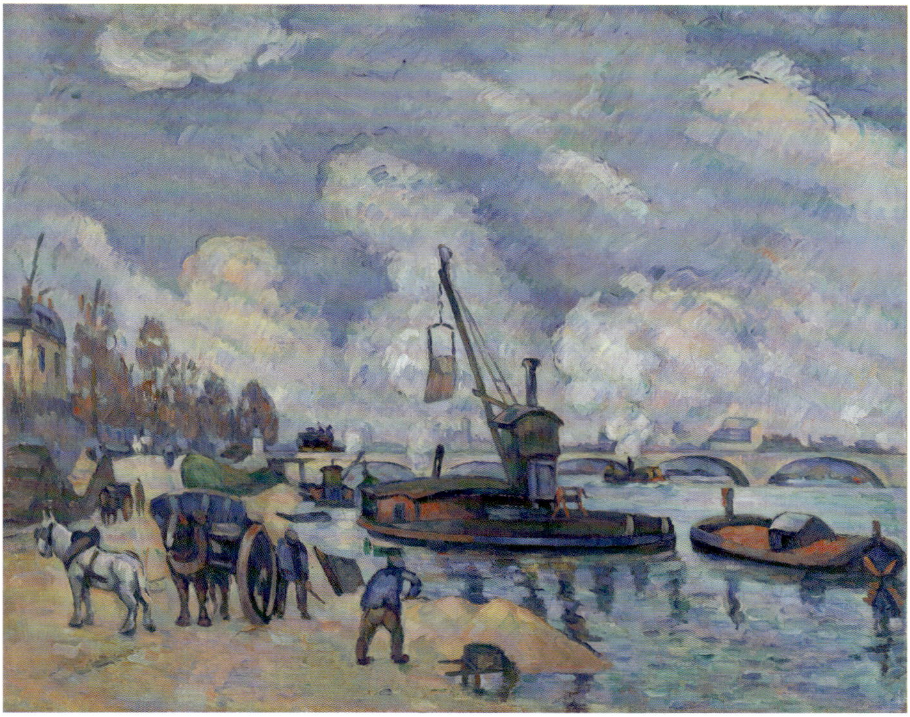

Paul Cézanne
On Bercy Quay in Paris
1867
Oil on canvas,
23 ⅜ × 28 ½ in.
(59.5 × 72.5 cm)
Kunsthalle, Hamburg

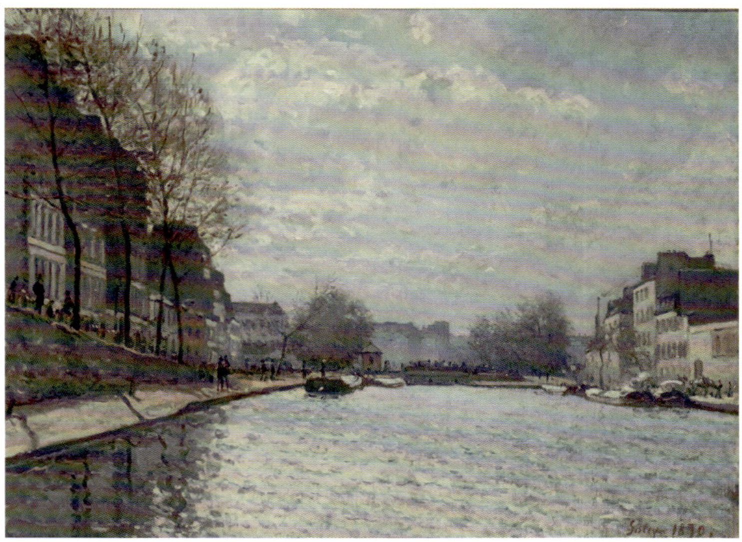

Alfred Sisley
View of the Canal Saint-Martin
1870
Oil on canvas, 19 ⅝ × 25 ⅝ in.
(50 × 65 cm)
Musée d'Orsay, Paris

"All the eastern portion of the city, the abodes of misery and toil, seemed submerged beneath ruddy steam, amid which the panting of workshops and factories could be divined; while westwards, towards the districts of wealth and enjoyment, the fog broke and lightened, becoming but a fine and motionless veil of vapour."

Émile Zola, *Paris*, 1898.

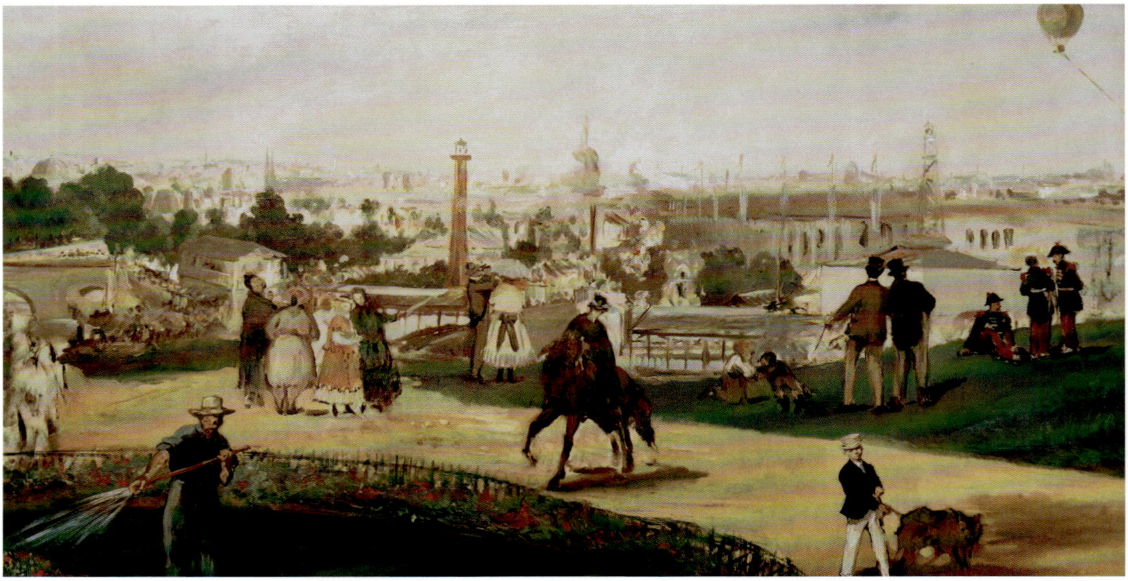

Édouard Manet
The 1867 Universal Exposition
1867
Oil on canvas, 3 ft. 6 ½ in. × 6 ft. 3 ½ in.
(1.08 × 1.97 m)
Nasjonalgalleriet, Oslo

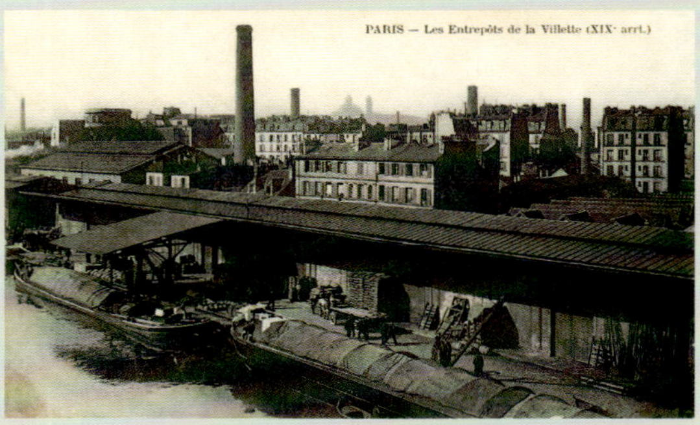

As is always the case with major urban renewal projects, Haussmann's work, which made the Paris we recognize today, also determined a new social hierarchy that is still perceptible now. High rents in the rebuilt center drove the disadvantaged away; they took refuge in the capital's peripheral working-class neighborhoods to the northeast, which were largely untouched by renovations. The typical Haussmann building was intended to accommodate every social stratum—bourgeois families on the second (main) floor, servants and employees on the third and forth, workers on the fifth, and domestic servants, students, and the impoverished beneath the eaves—but, in practice, this was not always the case. The fashionable residential areas lay to the west around the Champ-de-Mars and the Place de l'Étoile; theaters, offices, restaurants, and department stores were concentrated in the city center, while to the east, the impoverished masses teemed amid dense fumes emanating from the factories in the nineteenth and twentieth arrondissements.

By an imperial decree of March 8, 1853, Napoleon III ordered the first Universal Exposition to be held in Paris. The model had originated in England where, two years earlier, the world's first such exhibition had captivated visitors, who had marveled at the cast-iron and glass Crystal Palace built to house it. In Paris, five Universal Expositions, celebrating advances in French industry and engineering, followed: in 1855, 1867, 1878, 1889, and 1900.The 1855 exhibition was held on the Champs-Élysées. It was the first to boast a palatial structure, standing proudly beside the Palais de l'Industrie, that was wholly dedicated to the fine arts, displaying officially recognized works.

The Universal Exposition on the Champ-de-Mars in 1867 hosted forty-one countries and 52,000 exhibitors from all over the world. Drums and trumpets celebrated the triumph of the Second Empire in Haussmann's Paris, a city that was beautiful, new, and completely modernized.

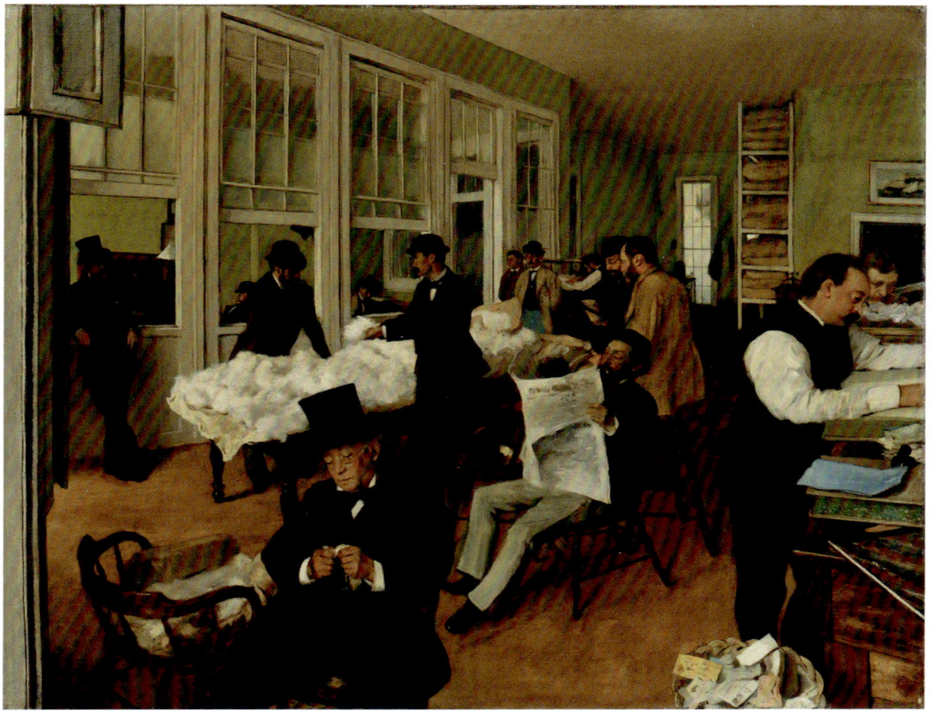

Edgar Degas
A Cotton Office in New Orleans
1873
Oil on canvas, 2ft. 4 ¾ in. × 3 ft. ¼ in. (73 × 92 cm)
Musée des Beaux-Arts, Pau

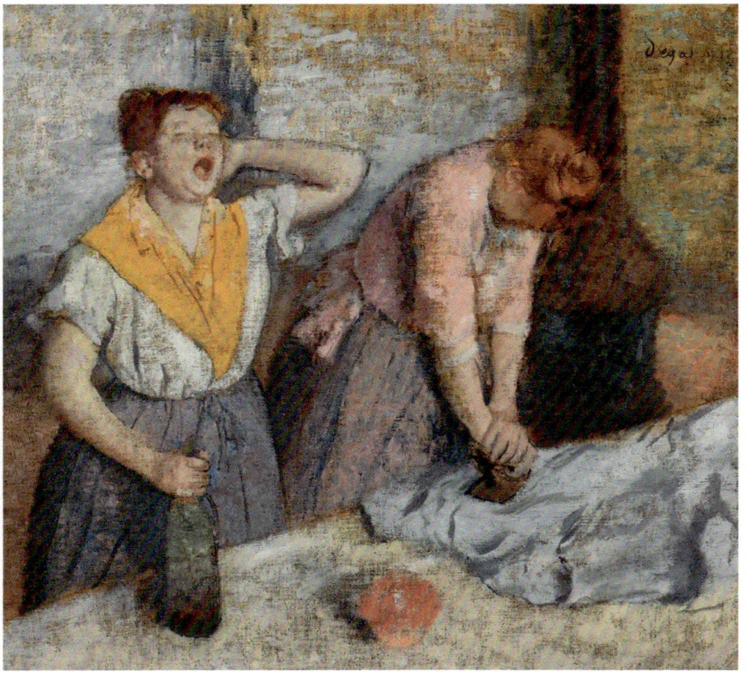

Edgar Degas
Women Ironing
c. 1884–86
Oil on canvas, 29 ⅞ × 32 in. (76 × 81.5 cm)
Musée d'Orsay, Paris

PEOPLE AT WORK

An aristocrat who condensed his last name for his artistic career (de Gas became Degas), Degas was an attentive observer of the worker's experience. In this painting, he depicts the exhaustion and nearly animalistic yawns of the laundresses, for whom the bottle of wine seems their only support. Unlike Pissarro and Courbet, Degas eschews militancy or social commentary. As if captured in a snapshot, the scene demonstrates his rigorous attention to the women's movements and gestures; there is no exaggerated sense of heroism or victimhood here.

FOCUS

The Tools of Painting

Technical developments and scientific discoveries, in a period when engineers and chemists were spurred on to ever greater ingenuity, provided advances that modern painters were quick to adopt.

The Invention of Paint Tubes

For centuries, artists prepared their own paints, grinding pigments and mixing them with a binder, like chefs creating a dish. The first industrially produced colors were sold "ready to use" in the nineteenth century. They were initially transported in pig bladders, which was not a very convenient method. Packaging was much improved by an English invention of 1841; this consisted of a flexible tube made from a thin sheet of tin, which could be tightly sealed with a clamp. The finishing touch came in 1859, when the firm Lefranc introduced an even better paint tube to the French market, which had a screw-on top, a design that endures to this day.

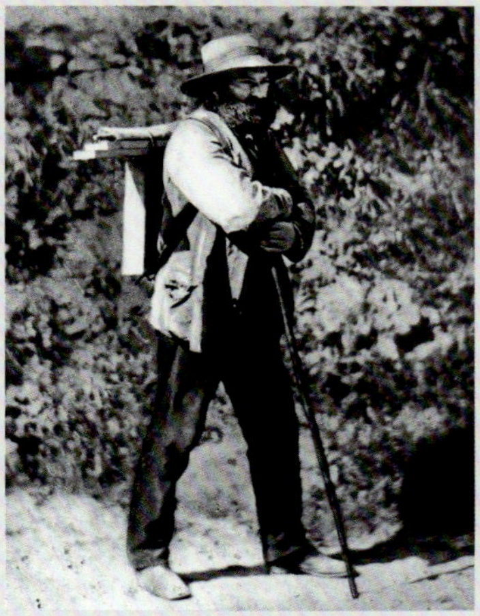

Paul Cézanne in Auvers-sur-Oise, c. 1874

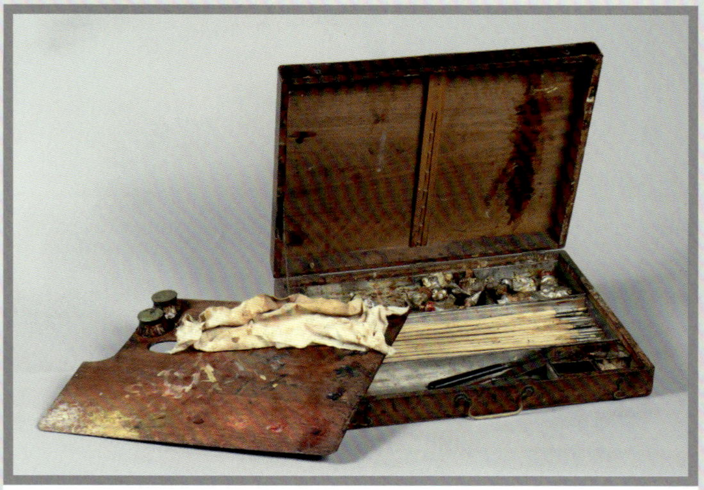

PORTABLE EQUIPMENT

In the eighteenth century, a few intrepid artists attempted to work *en plein air*. But painting outdoors required an expedition, complete with heavily laden donkey loaded with all the necessary equipment. With the invention of the paint tube, the process was simplified. Portable easels and paint boxes were displayed in the windows of art suppliers, and in the catalogs of specialized firms such as Lefranc. *Plein air* painting had become accessible to all.

Auguste Renoir's palette and paint box
Paris, Musée d'Orsay

The Science of Color

Michel Eugène Chevreul (1754–1845) was a chemist employed in the Gobelins manufactory, where he became director of the dye workshop in 1824. In 1839 he published an impressive volume on color theory, translated into English in 1854 as *The Principles of Harmony and Contrast of Colors.* Its significance was not immediately apparent. Chevreul demonstrated the role of colors, known as "complementary," on coloristic effects and luminosity. The concept is simple: viewed side by side, complementary colors enhance each other, while non-complementary colors seem dull and "dirty." For example, a shade of red may veer toward the scarlet beside a green, and, in turn, red juxtaposed with another color will seem less vivid. Lengthy and dense, Chevreul's treatise was over seven hundred pages long and had a very limited readership. However, his weekly lessons for professionals helped to disseminate his ideas. These were summarized in a simple, almost intuitive fashion, with the color wheel that he published to illustrate his theories. Showing the complete chromatic spectrum, each color appears opposite its complementary hue.

THE NEO-IMPRESSIONISTS

Led by Seurat, the neo-impressionists followed Chevreul's principles to the letter and adopted a pointillist approach to painting, juxtaposing brushstrokes of pure color. Abandoning the practice of blending colors on a palette, they let the viewer's eye produce the desired coloristic effect. Identified as a movement in 1886 by the critic Félix Fénéon, neo-impressionism recognized Pissarro as its mentor, and he was enthusiastic about the research carried out by the young pioneers, Seurat and Signac. They were advocates of "divisionism," and had an almost clinical approach to art. Both artists visited the Gobelins factory in 1884 to meet Chevreul; the elderly chemist was then ninety-eight years old. They regarded him as a mentor, and it was a revelatory meeting.

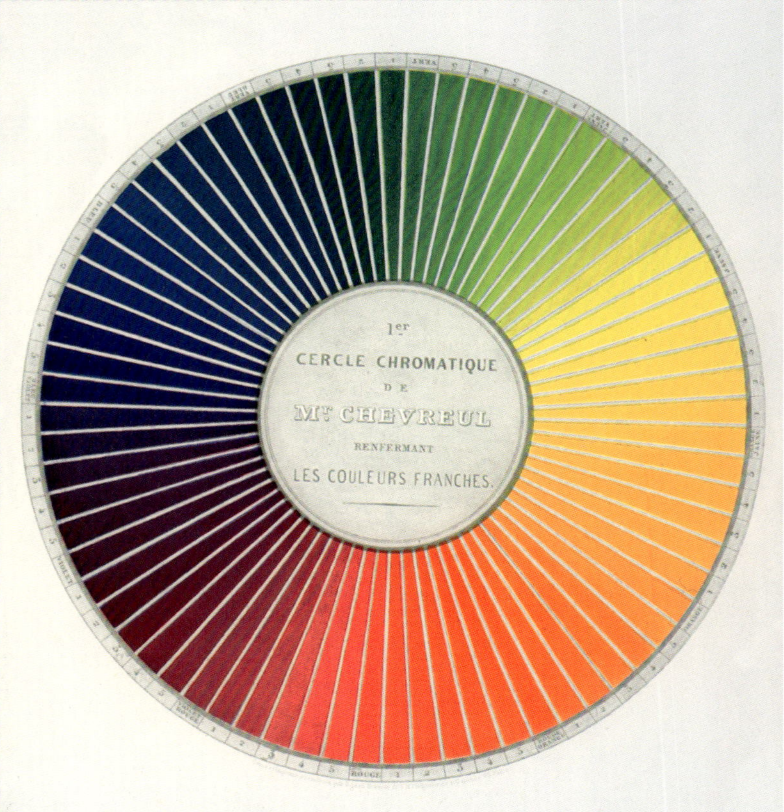

First chromatic wheel encompassing primary, secondary, and tertiary colors, 1861
Musée des Beaux-Arts, Rennes

The *Plein Air* Idyll

As the world industrialized, there was an obsessive longing to flee the urban inferno and its poisonous air, polluted by belching factory chimneys. People clamored to board the "pleasure trains" on Sundays, abandoning business attire to lounge on the banks of the Seine for the afternoon. The wealthier flocked to the early seaside resorts.

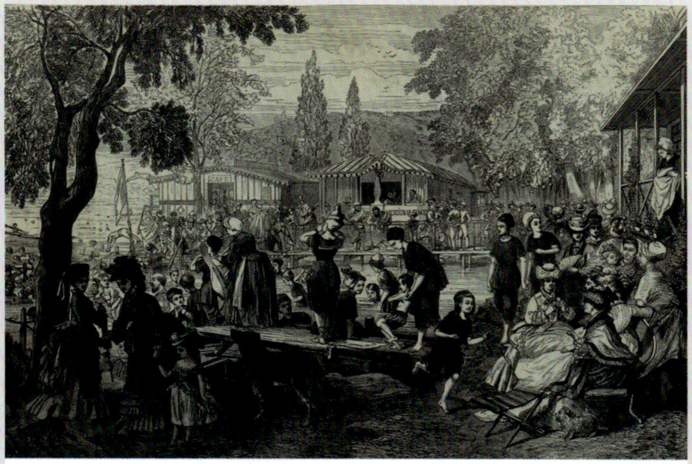

Paris in the Summer: Swimming at La Grenouillère
The Illustrated London News, September 25, 1875
Engraving, private collection

SUNDAY IN THE COUNTRY

Chatou, Croissy, Bougival, and Argenteuil became Sunday destinations. Visitors enjoyed boating and a picnic lunch on the grass, or a swim in the floating riverside establishments like La Grenouillère. One could also have a good meal and take a turn round the floor in one of the earliest dance halls.

"Imagine a huge boat transformed into a café, where boaters, male and female, attired in eccentric outfits, crowd together, laughing and cavorting to the music of a badly tuned piano. There's a place to swim, a real frog pond that's part of the establishment. And the frogs are generally quite attractive, shapely, and plump to everyone's satisfaction. La Grenouillère (but let's keep it between ourselves) is not exactly a spot I'd recommend to clergymen."

On La Grenouillère, *Guide Conty des environs de Paris*, 1888.

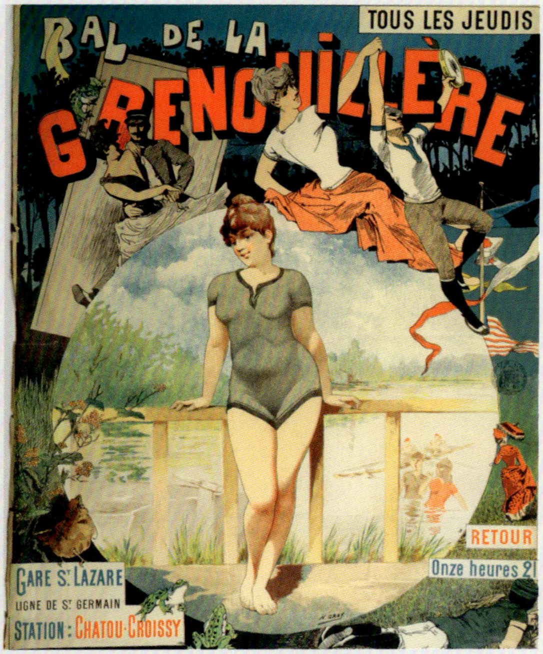

Henri Gray (?), advertising poster for a dance at La Grenouillère
Color lithograph, private collection

LA GRENOUILLÈRE

Located on the Seine, by the Ile de Croissy, between Chatou and Bougival, La Grenouillère—laughingly called "Trouville-sur-Seine" after the fashionable Normandy seaside resort—was one of the era's most popular venues. An enormous pontoon boat housed a ballroom and restaurant. There was a long barge with bathing cabins, and a beach. Canoes could be rented for the day. It was a recreational destination for ordinary people, but no one was immune to its charms: in 1869 it received a visit from Emperor Napoleon III and Empress Eugénie.

A SENSUAL SIESTA

Spare time, a country picnic, an afternoon of idling on the banks of the Seine—this subject was to be a favorite of the impressionists fifteen years later, but it appears here for the first time. The languor and sensuality of these women enjoying a Sunday afternoon siesta were considered intolerable. The scene, depicted on a monumental scale, created a scandal.

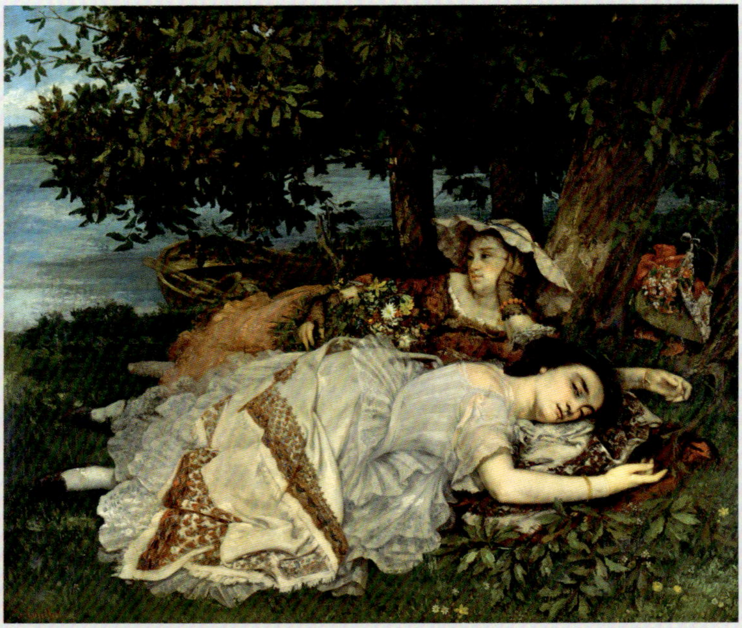
Gustave Courbet, *Young Women by the Seine (Summer)*, 1856–57
Oil on canvas, 5 ft. 8 ½ in. × 6 ft. 9 in. (1.74 × 2.06 m)
Petit-Palais, Musée des Beaux-Arts de la Ville de Paris, Paris

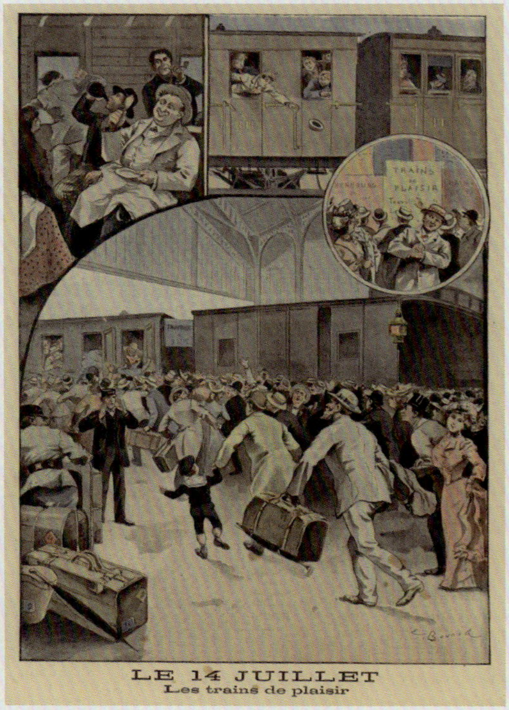

Ernest Auguste Bouard, *The Pleasure Trains, July 14*
Color lithograph
Private collection

"You'd taste the day's experiences, the fatigue, the haste, the exhilarating fresh air, the rippling water, the dappled sunlight, the shimmers that dazed and dazzled you during these outings. There was an almost animal hunger for life created by the surging river, the blinding light, and the beautiful weather."

Edmond and Jules de Goncourt, *Manette Salomon*, 1865.

THE *TRAINS DE PLAISIR*

The "pleasure trains" departed from the Gare Saint-Lazare on Sunday mornings, filled with excited Parisians, and carried them back in the evening, weary but content. They were depicted in humorous caricatures in illustrated publications of the day.

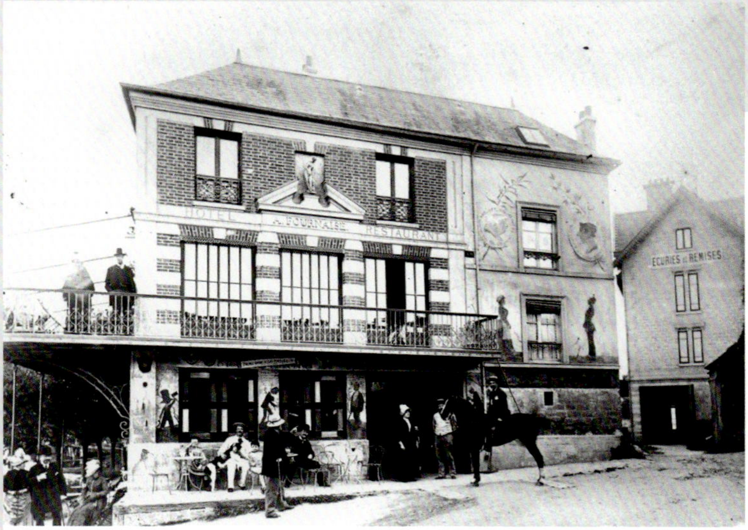

The Hotel Fournaise at Chatou, c. 1880
Private collection

THE HOTEL FOURNAISE

The Hotel Fournaise was a boaters' rendezvous on the banks of the Seine in Chatou. A boatbuilder himself, Monsieur Fournaise had his workshop here and organized regattas. His wife managed the restaurant. Both were assisted by their son and daughter Alphonse and Alphonsine. Renoir immortalized the spot in his famous *Luncheon of the Boating Party*, and also painted a portrait of the charming young Alphonsine.

THE FIRST SEASIDE RESORTS

The first seaside resorts were the exclusive retreats of high society in the nineteenth century. People traveled there to experience the newly discovered pleasures of sea bathing, and to enjoy amusements and entertainment of every kind, from casinos to racetracks and luxurious grand hotels. In the 1820s, the duchesse de Berry put Dieppe on the map. It was later succeeded by Trouville and then Deauville, which was constructed on former marshlands between 1860 and 1864. Readily accessible by railroad, the Normandy coast had the wind in its sails.

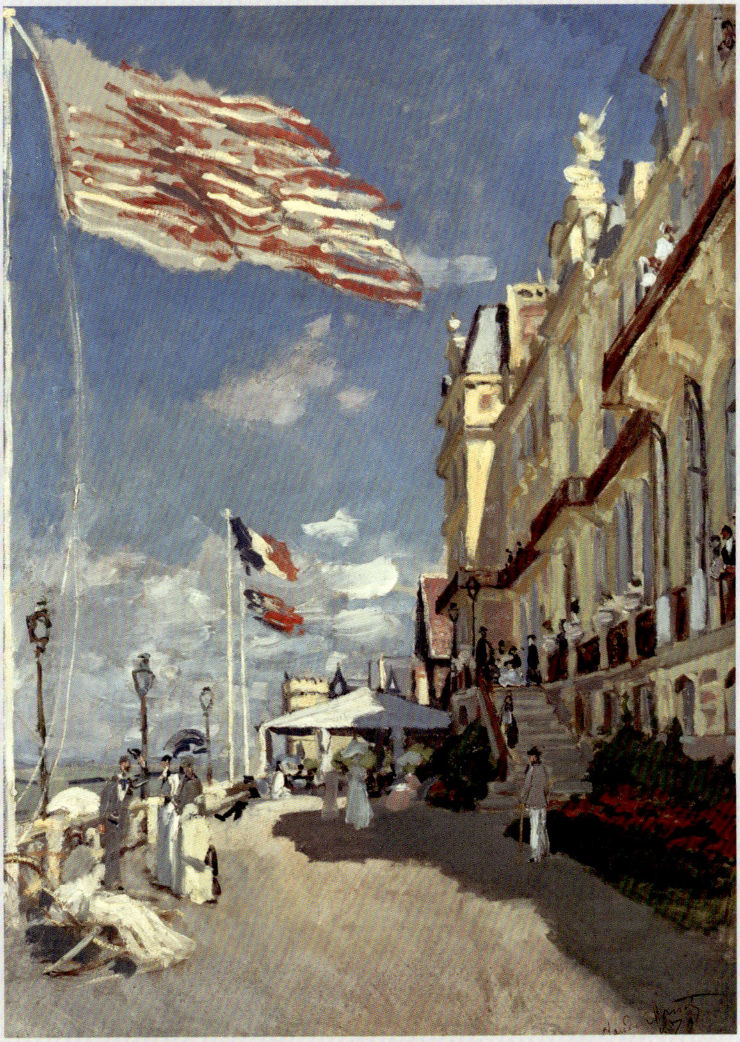

Claude Monet, *Hôtel des Roches Noires, Trouville*, 1870
Oil on canvas, 31 ⅞ × 23 in. (81 × 58.5 cm)
Musée d'Orsay, Paris

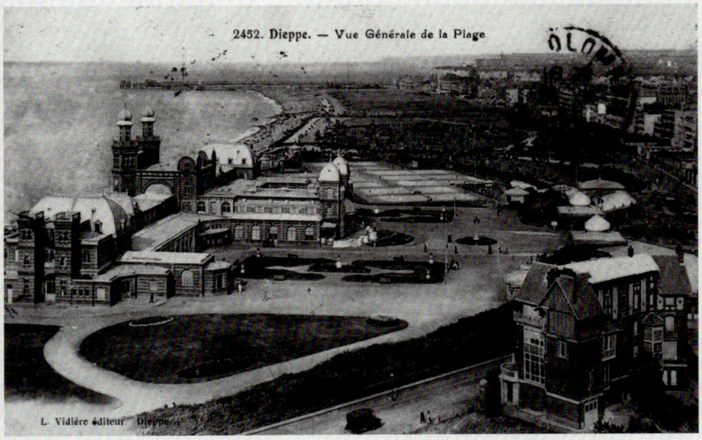

General view of the town and beach of Dieppe, early twentieth century

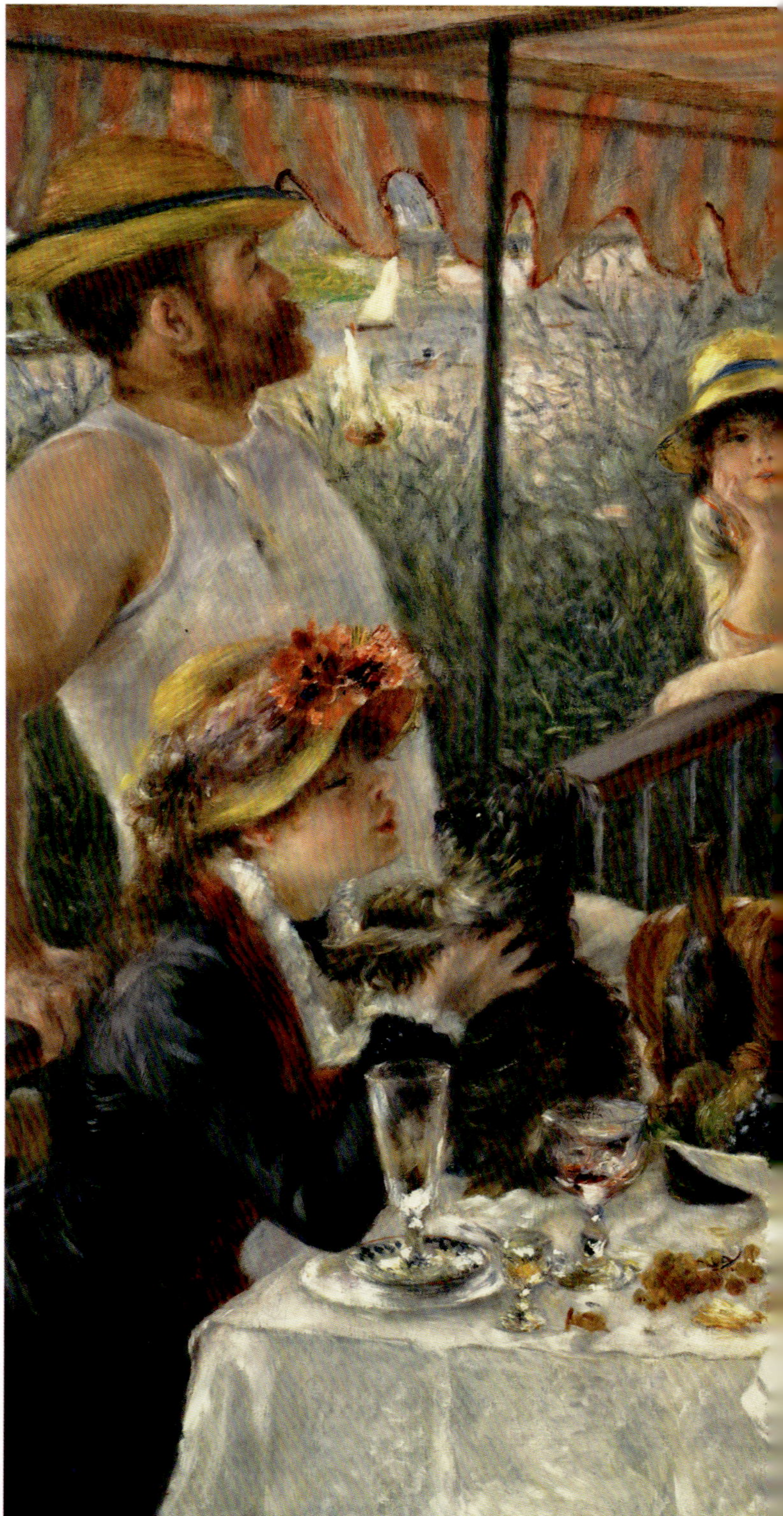

Auguste Renoir
The Luncheon of the Boating Party
1881
Oil on canvas, 4 ft. 3 in. × 5 ft. 7 ¾ in. (1.29 × 1.72 m)
Phillips Collection, Washington, DC

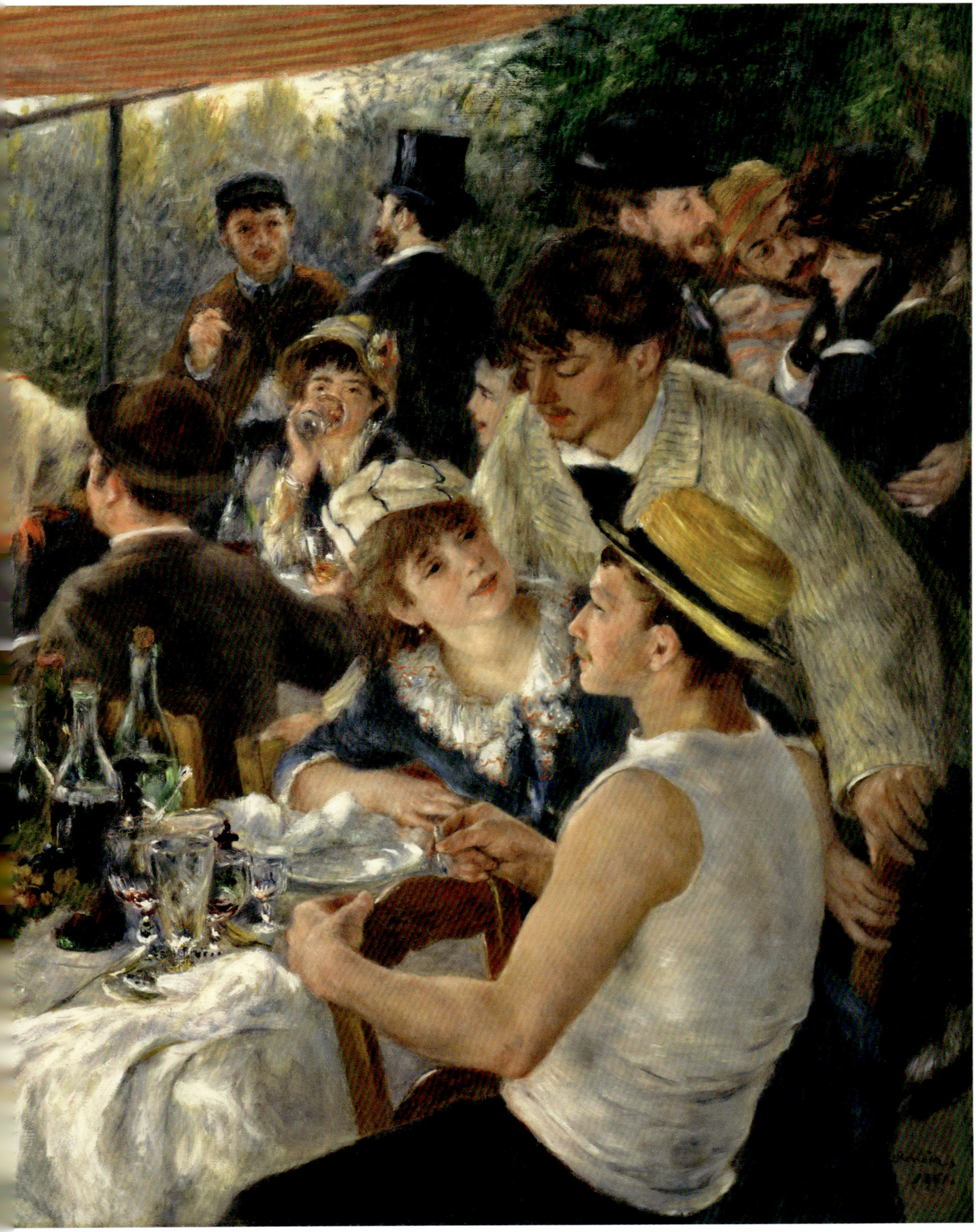

The Luncheon of the Boating Party

Auguste Renoir, 1881

Celebrating the pleasure felt by all enjoying a convivial meal, *The Luncheon of the Boating Party* was painted on the terrace of the Hotel Fournaise restaurant; it is like a manifesto for joie de vivre. Renoir's canvas fixes a fleeting moment in time, like a camera's snapshot.

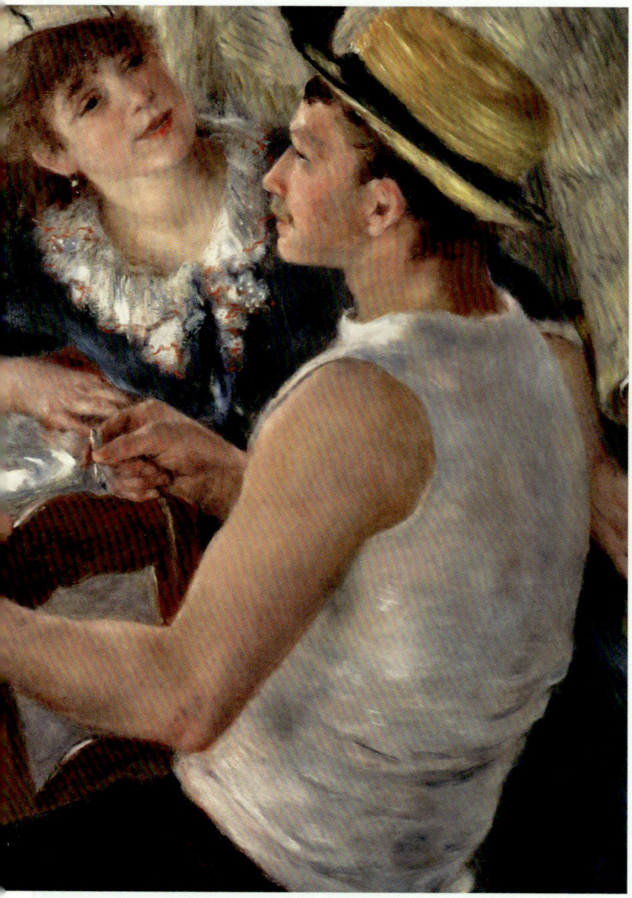

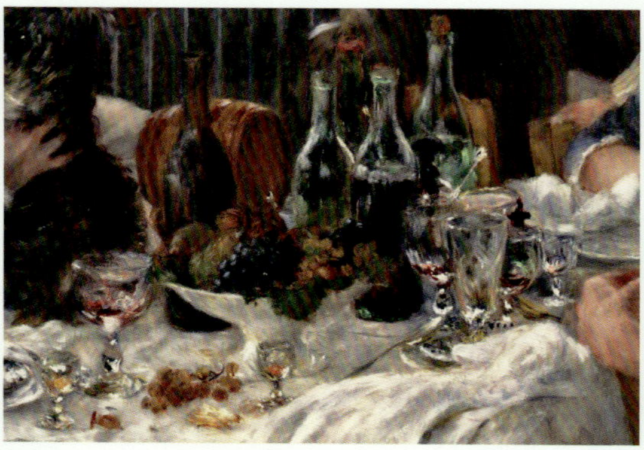

The closely observed leftovers, strewn on the table, demonstrate Renoir's epicurean side; he was always appreciative of sensory pleasures.

Athletic young boaters in their singlets and straw hats seem to be flaunting their muscly arms. Gustave Caillebotte is pictured straddling his chair.

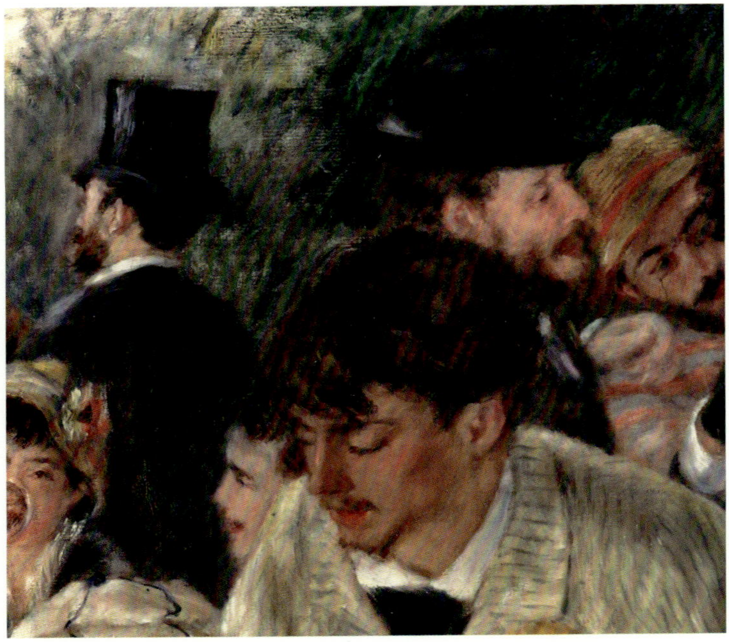

The elegant gentleman in the background, dressed in a top hat and suit, shows us the social mix at these leisure retreats, where seamstresses mingled with the bourgeoisie.

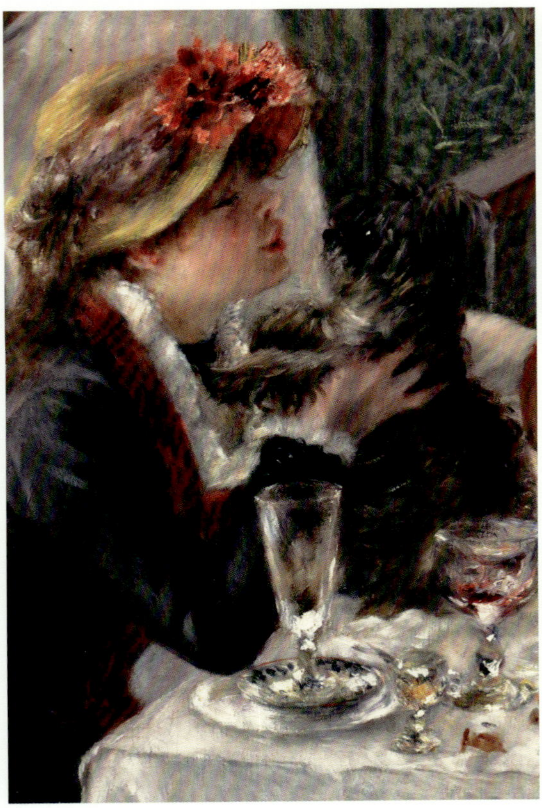

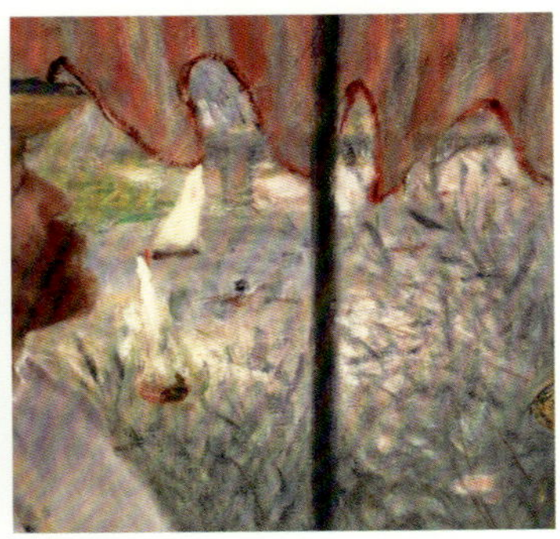

The sails of the boat in the background recall the fêtes, regattas, and nautical competitions organized on the Seine.

Shown playing with a little dog, the charming Aline Charigot wears a flower-trimmed hat. She was the companion and future wife of Auguste Renoir. Behind her is the journalist Paul Lhote and, leaning on the railing further back, Alphonsine Fournaise, the landlord's daughter.

Auguste Renoir
Père Fournaise
1875
Oil on canvas, 22 ⅛ × 18 ½ in. (56.2 × 47 cm)
Sterling and Francine Clark Art Institute, Williamstown

"I'm at Fournaise's place all the time. I find as many stunning girls to paint there as I could possibly wish for.... I've brought Fournaise plenty of customers, and he's thanked me by commissioning portraits of himself and his daughter."

Renoir, letter to Ambroise Vollard, quoted by Jean-Paul Crespelle in *La Vie quotidienne des impressionnistes*, 1981.

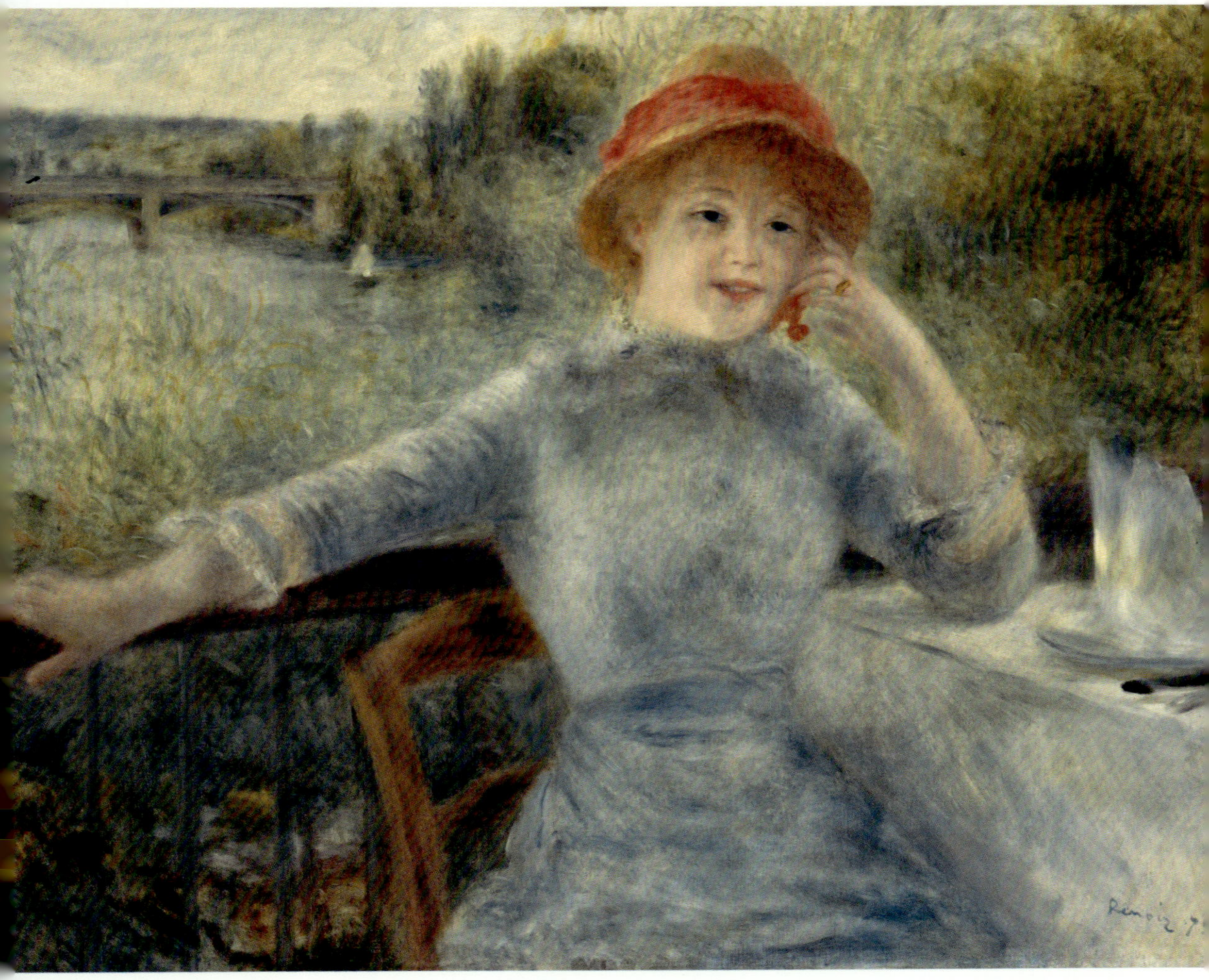

Auguste Renoir
Alphonsine Fournaise (1845–1937),
formerly known as
At La Grenouillère
1879
Oil on canvas, 2 ft. 5 in. × 3 ft. 1 in.
(73.5 × 93 cm)
Musée d'Orsay, Paris

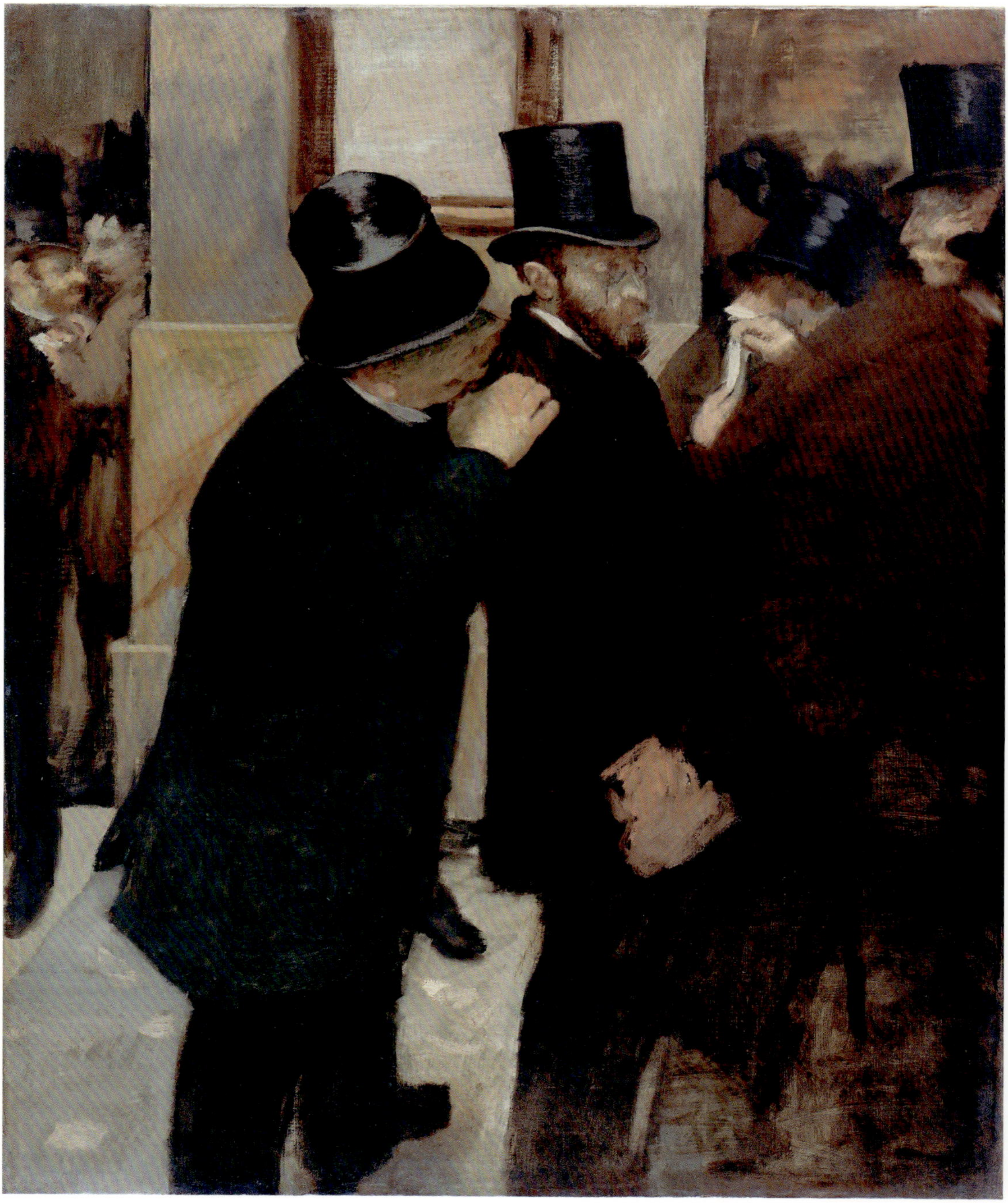

Edgar Degas
Portraits at the Stock Exchange
1878–79
Oil on canvas, 3 ft. 3 ½ ft. × 2 in. 8 ¼ in.
(100 × 82 cm)
Musée d'Orsay, Paris

The Photographic Revolution

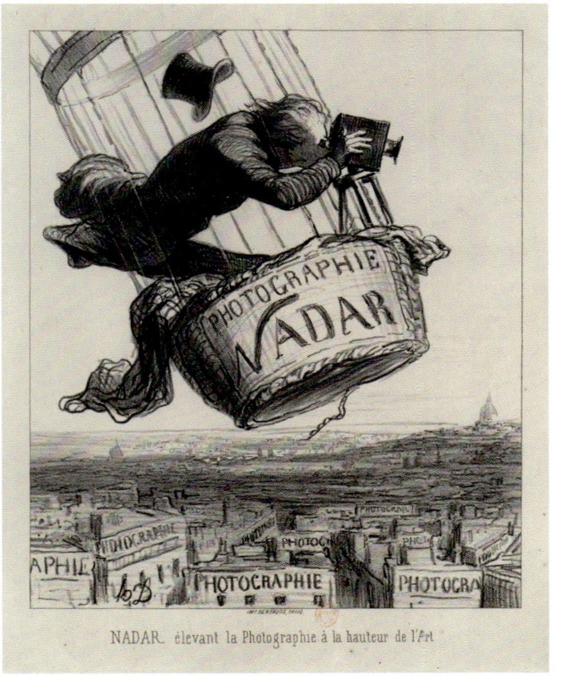

Honoré Daumier
Nadar Elevating Photography to the Level of Art
1862
Bibliothèque Nationale de France, Paris

Solemnly announced by Arago in his speech before the Académie des Sciences on January 6, 1839, photography was an invention that would forever revolutionize the world of images. Achieving a faithful likeness of reality through mechanical means was an earthshaking invention, attributed to Daguerre, among others. The technique would lead to a fundamental redefinition of art during the nineteenth century. The process took off immediately, but not without encountering some resistance. Defenders and detractors of photography confronted each other, debating the crucial question of whether the process was merely a vulgar technological device or an authentic art form. Perhaps the question was moot, because the production of images had been irrevocably altered. Nicknamed "the pencil of nature" by William Henry Fox Talbot (1800-1877), the English inventor who had been developing alternative photographic processes, photography liberated art forever from its function of accurately representing reality. Baudelaire saw photographic portraiture as an expression of vulgarity, but it created an immediate sensation, to the

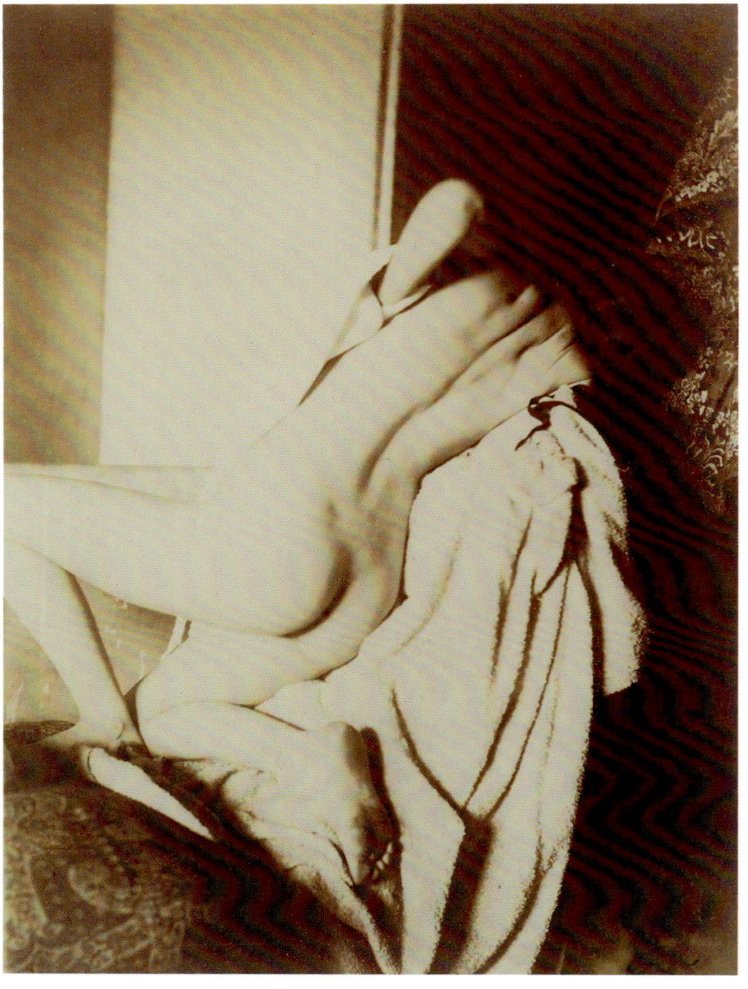

Edgar Degas
After the Bath, Woman Drying Her Back
1895
Gelatin silver print
The J. Paul Getty Museum, Los Angeles

profound dismay of many artists, who lamented the demise of "the painter's bread and butter."

Technical advances in photography came quickly, and led to the development of photographs using silver gelatin plates in 1871. The revolution entered a new phase: there were no more interminable posing sessions and equipment was much less cumbersome. Photographers could now freeze movement, capture the fleeting moment, and operate more easily outdoors.

Snapshots revealed a surprising, almost incredible, visual reality. Photography opened the eye to a broader vision. A new understanding of the world was evolving, changing forever the perception of the real. Painting as practiced by the impressionists gradually incorporated key aspects of photography: cropping, bird's-eye views, and low-angle perspectives; fluidity and spontaneity.

MOVEMENT DEMYSTIFIED

On both sides of the Atlantic, the French physiologist Étienne-Jules Marey, and the San Francisco-based English photographer Eadweard Muybridge, began to develop studies of movement and locomotion in 1872, using photography as a tool. These studies soon had a major impact on the art world. In its November 29 issue, the journal *Gil Blas* described an exhibition of Muybridge's photographs being held in the new studio of Meissonier, who was among the most academic of artists. It was attended by many painters and prominent artistic figures. Muybridge's studies of galloping horses (1878) would alter the way artists represented this gait, which had heretofore been left to the individual artists' interpretation. Muybridge's monumental work, *Animal Locomotion*, published in eleven volumes with 100,000 photographs, appeared in 1887.

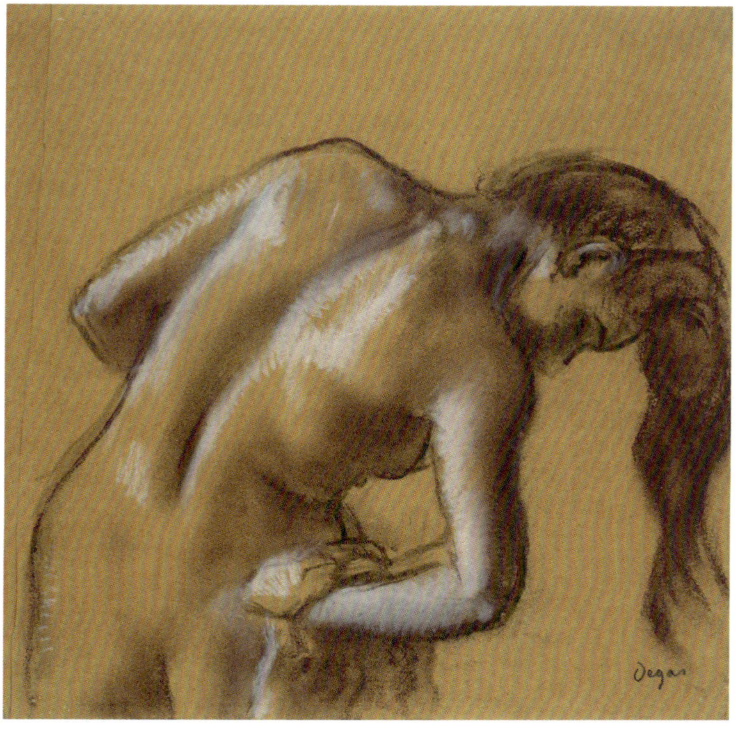

Edgar Degas
Woman Drying Herself
c. 1892
Charcoal and pastel with white highlights, 10 ⅜ × 10 ⅜ in. (26.4 × 26.4 cm)

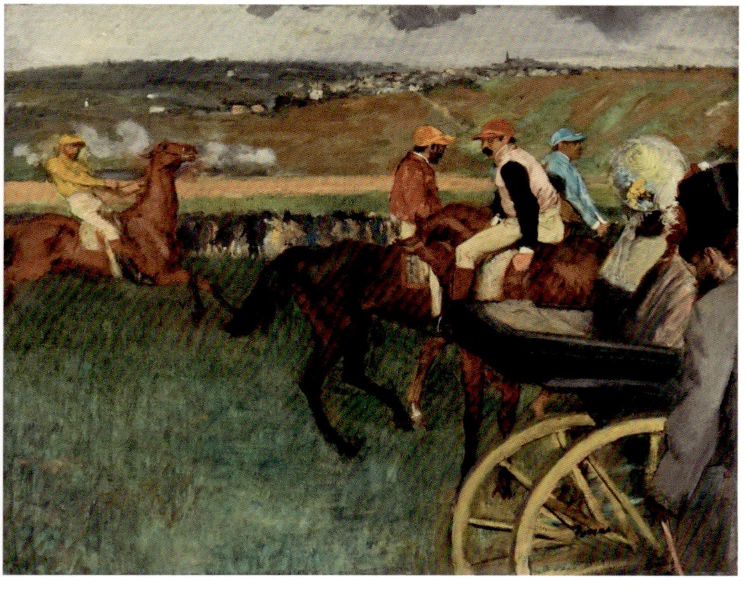

Edgar Degas
The Racecourse, Amateur Jockeys near a Carriage
1876–87
Oil on canvas, 26 × 31 ⅞ in. (66 × 81 cm)
Musée d'Orsay, Paris

Degas was a photographer himself and often composed his paintings like snapshots. Here, a figure seen from the back and cropped by the picture frame partially hides the vehicle driving away on the right. Jockeys cross paths, indifferent to one another, while in the background the breath of a whinnying horse creates a halo of vapor.

The fleeting passage of clouds and trees reflected in water was a favorite subject for pioneering photographers, as it also was for painters.

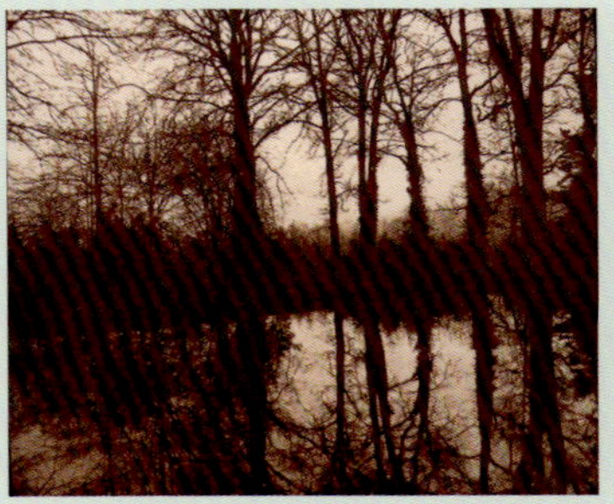

William Henry Fox Talbot
Trees Reflected in Water, Lacock Abbey
1843
Salted paper print, 6 ½ × 7 ½ in.
(16.4 × 19.1 cm)
Musée d'Orsay, Paris

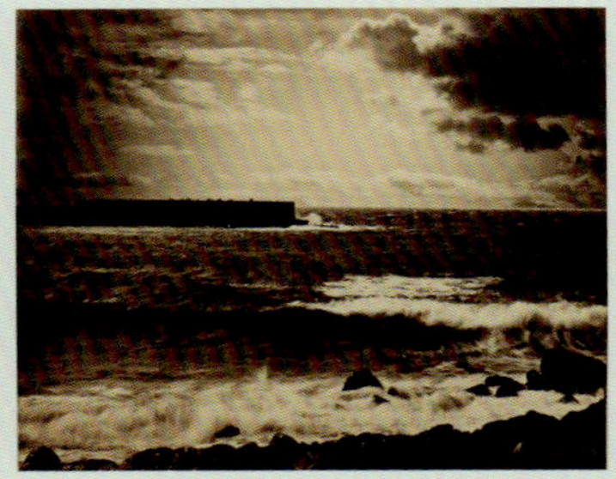

Gustave Le Gray
The Great Wave
1857
Albumin paper print from two negatives,
13 ½ × 16 ½ in. (34.3 × 41.9 cm)
Musée d'Orsay, Paris

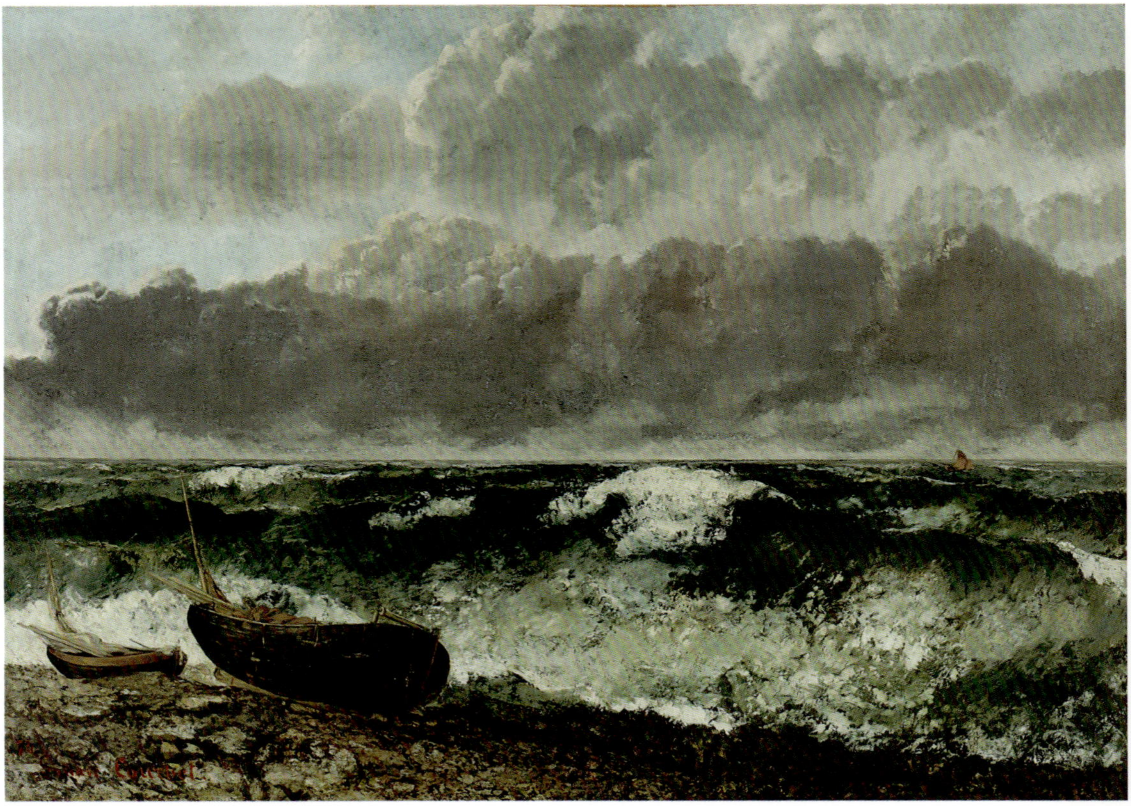

Gustave Courbet
The Wave, also known as *The Stormy Sea*
1870
Oil on canvas, 3 ft. 9 ½ in. × 5 ft. 3 in.
(1.16 × 1.60 m)
Nationalgalerie, Berlin

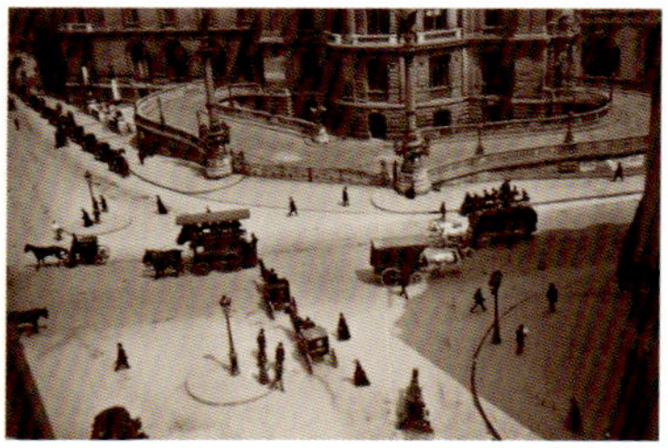

Martial Caillebotte
Rue Auber and Rue Scribe, 1892–95
Photographic print from a gelatin silver bromide negative, 4 ½ × 6 ⅛ in. (11.5 × 15.5 cm)
Private collection

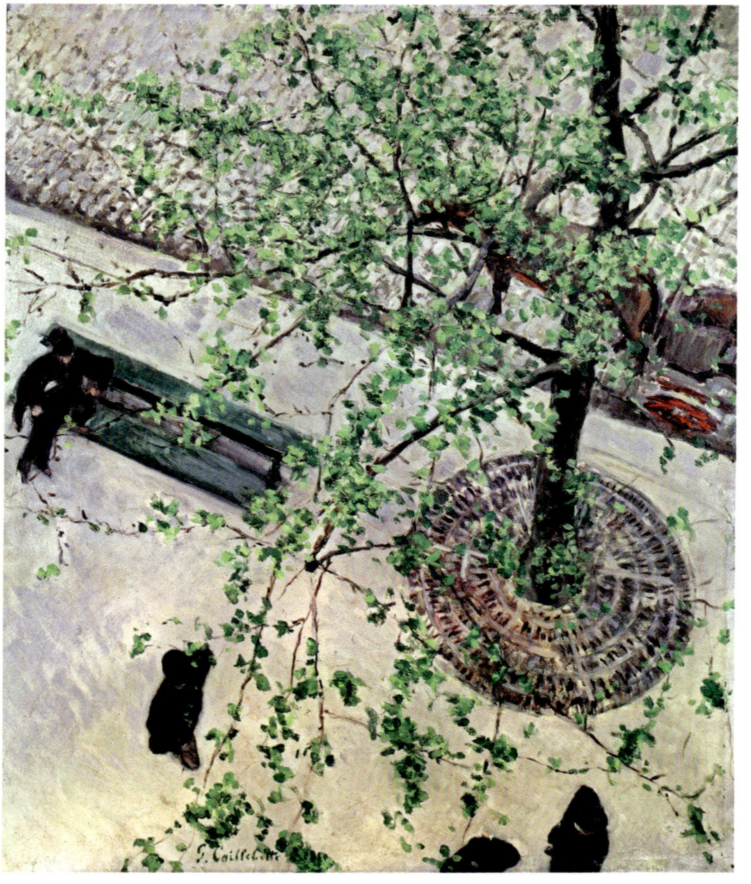

Gustave Caillebotte
The Boulevard Seen from Above
c. 1880
Oil on canvas, 25 ⅝ × 21 ¼ in. (65 × 54 cm)
Private collection

Striking in its modernity, this bird's-eye view of a street corner in Paris, captured from a balcony, is derived directly from the evolving vocabulary of photography.

NADAR AND THE FIRST IMPRESSIONIST EXHIBITION

A former habitué of the Café Guerbois, Félix Tournachon, known as Nadar, was a caricaturist, writer, aeronaut, and photographer. In 1874, he offered his studio at 35 Boulevard des Capucines for the first impressionist exhibition.

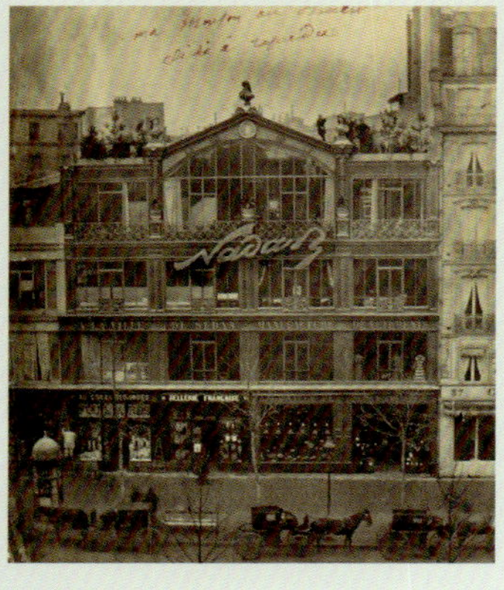

Nadar
Nadar's Studio at 35 Boulevard des Capucines
c. 1861
Albumin paper print from a collodion glass plate negative, 9 ⅞ × 7 ⅝ in. (25 × 19.4 cm)
Bibliothèque Nationale de France, Paris

IMAGES IN THE SPOTLIGHT

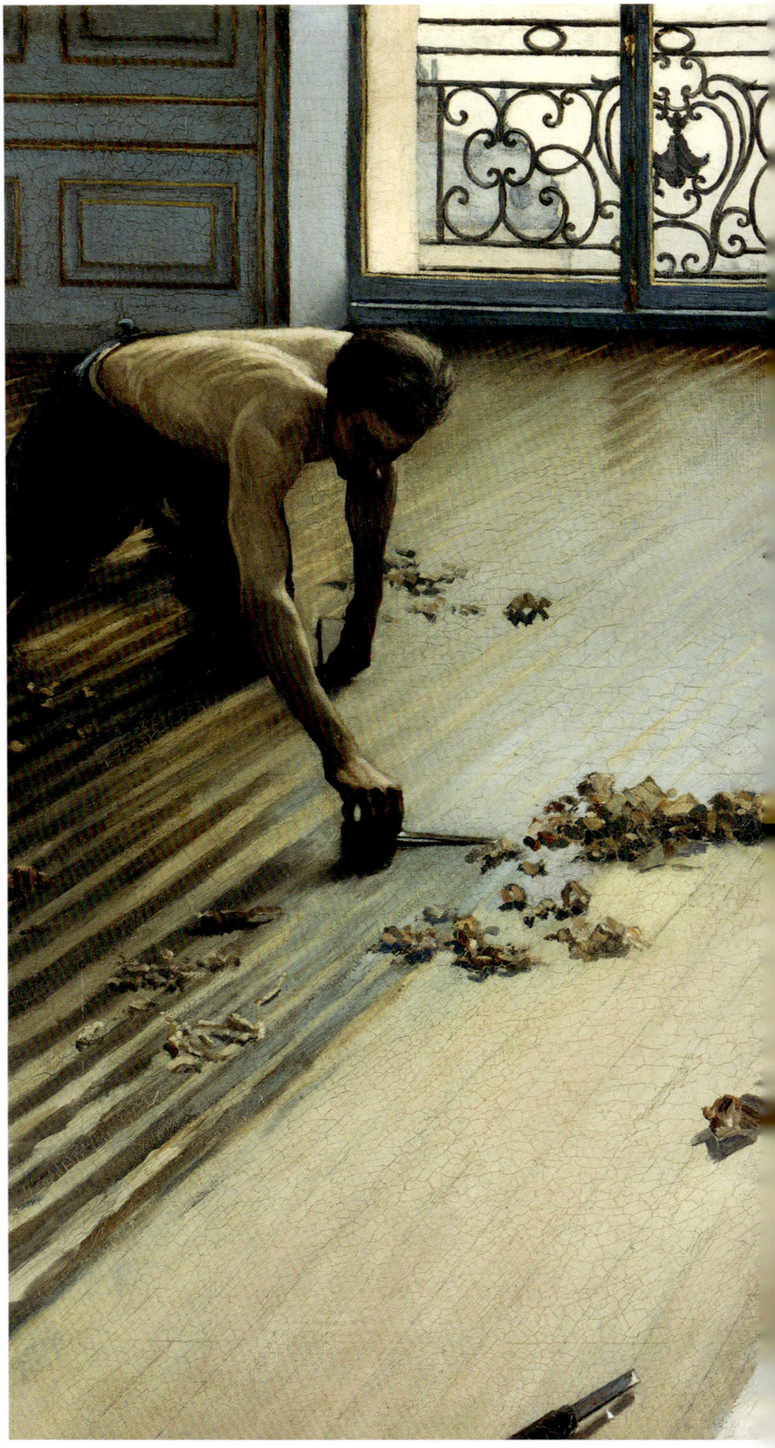

Gustave Caillebotte
The Floor Planers
1875
Oil on canvas,
3 ft. 4 ¼ in. × 4 ft. 9 ½ in.
(1.02 × 1.46 m)
Musée d'Orsay, Paris

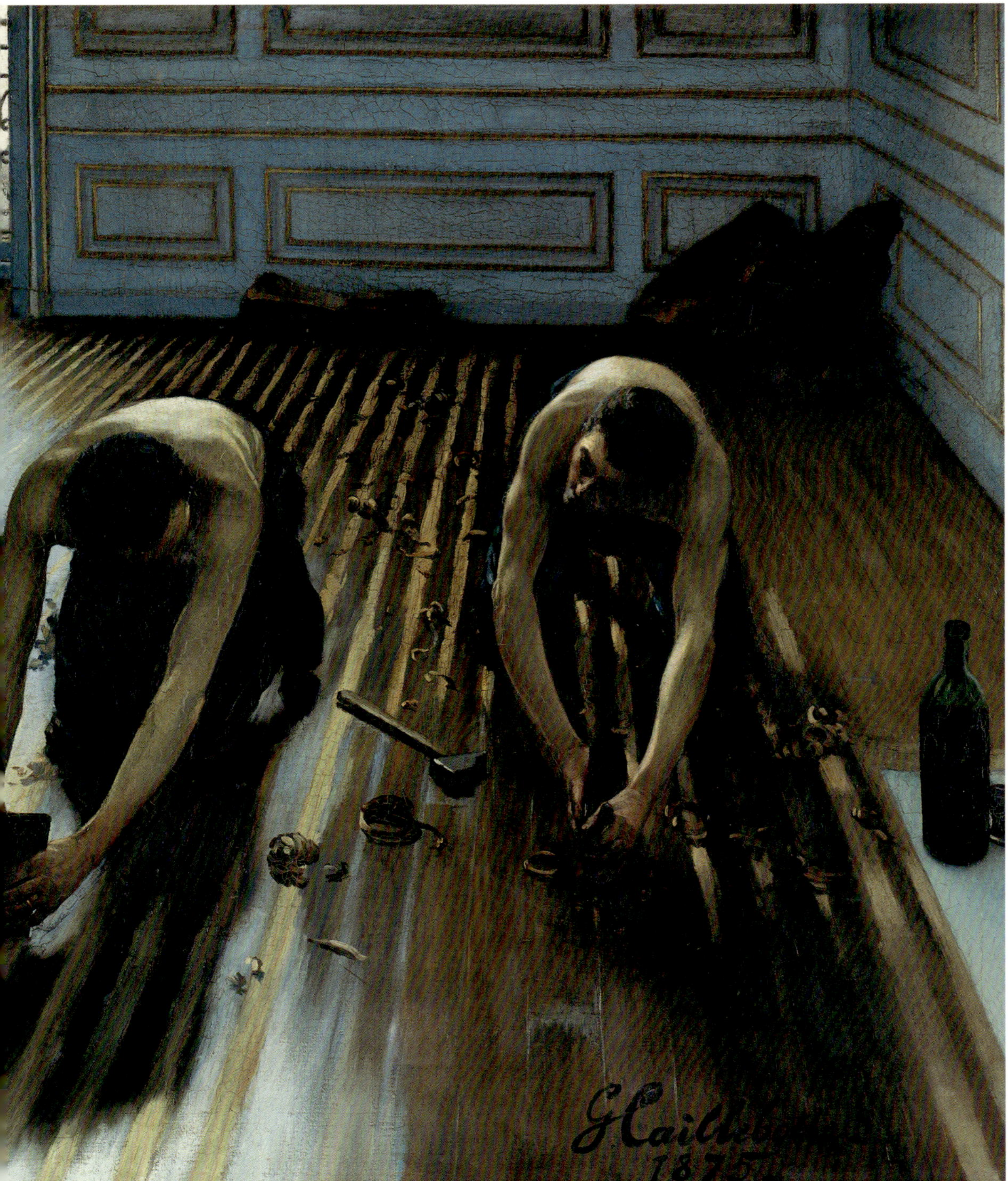
G. Caillebotte
1875

The Floor Planers

Gustave Caillebotte, 1875

Rejected by the 1875 Salon, this canvas was hung at the second impressionist exhibition in 1876. Gustave Caillebotte officially joined the group at that time. One of the first paintings to depict the urban working class, this canvas is notable both for its subject matter and its pictorial approach, which is clearly influenced by photography.

Directly inspired by a photographic perspective, the elevated point of view is accentuated by the receding lines of the wooden floorboards.

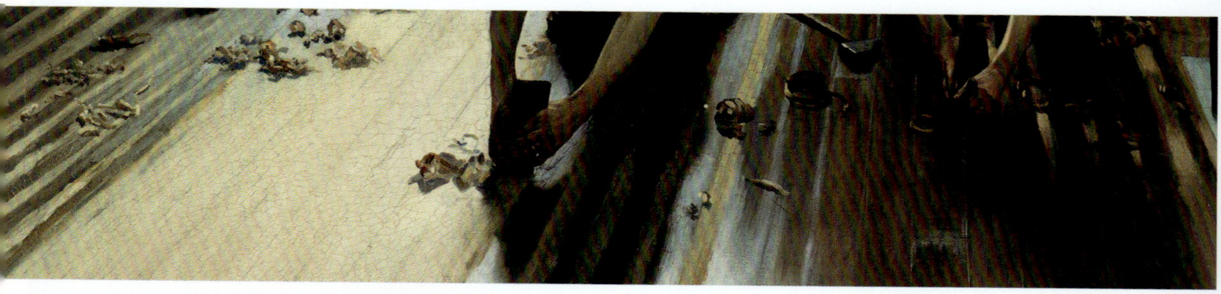

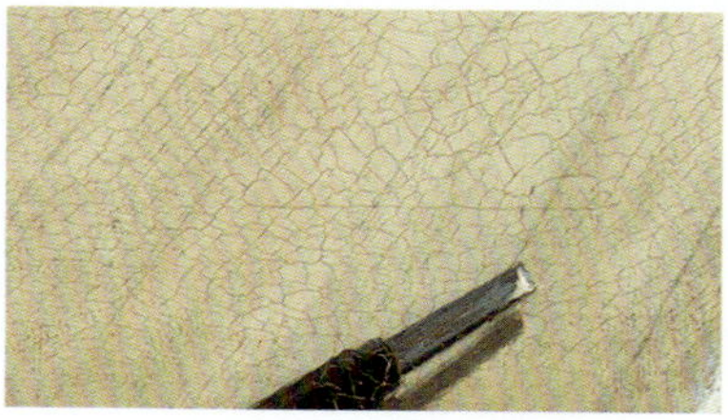

The chisel in the foreground is a nod to the tradition in eighteenth-century still lifes, where a knife often indicated the depth of a table while creating a transition between the pictorial space and the real world.

In the right foreground stands a bottle of cheap red wine, as also featured in Women Ironing by Degas, who—along with Caillebotte—was the only other impressionist artist to be drawn to the world of urban work. It was the only source of refreshment for these laborers, whose meager personal effects appear bundled at the back of the room.

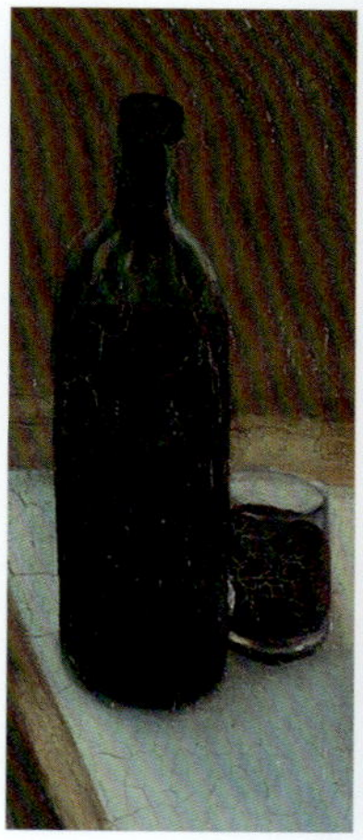

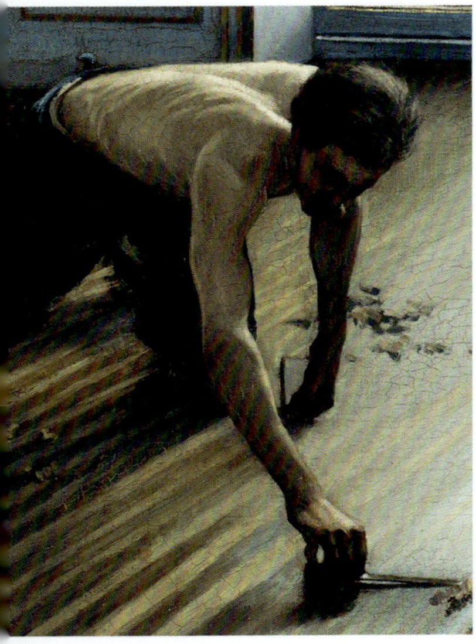

Photographs freeze movement, and this sensibility imbues the painting. Caillebotte does not compose his subjects within the constraints of the frame; he captures the reality of the scene like a camera's lens.

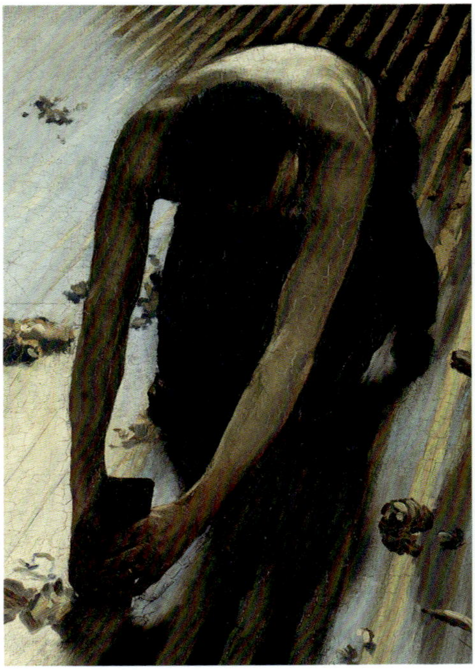

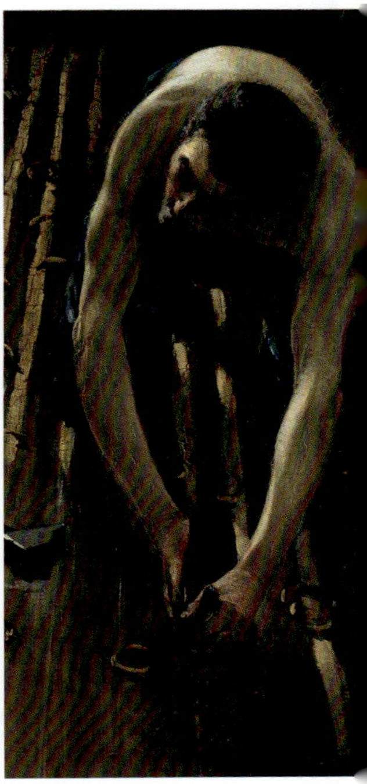

The men's bodies, stripped to the waist, catch light, which emphasizes their powerful musculature. Reminiscent of academic studies, these "nudes" are not Greek gods, but real men caught in the midst of their daily reality—hard manual labor.

Through the window, a luminous outside world can be glimpsed. Sunlit Haussmann buildings contrast with the dim lighting of the room where these men are engaged in backbreaking labor.

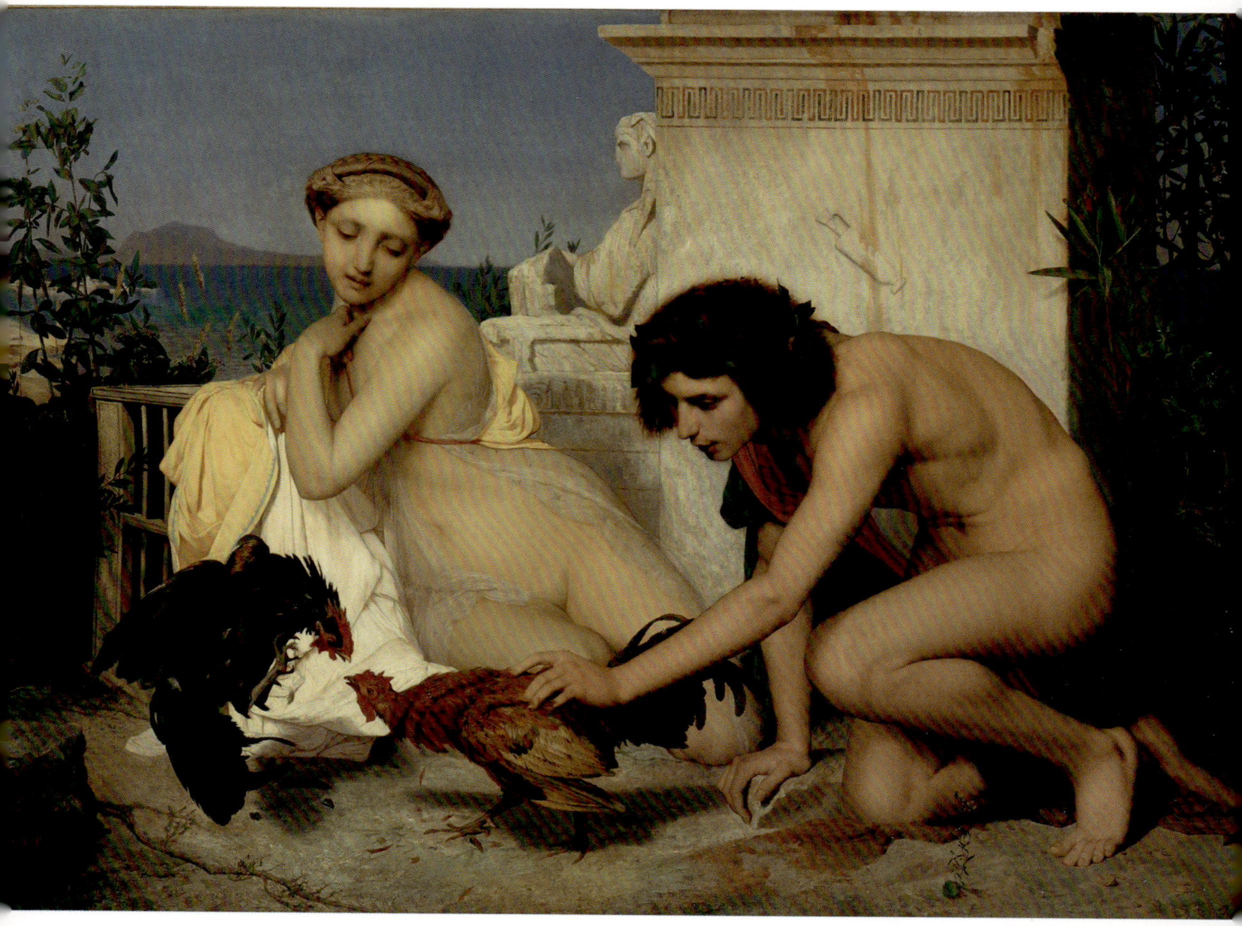

Jean Léon Gérôme
Young Greeks and a Cock Fight,
also known as *The Cock Fight*
1846
Oil on canvas, 4 ft. 8 ¼ in. × 6 ft. 8 ½ in. (1.43 × 2.04 m)
Musée d'Orsay, Paris

The Art World

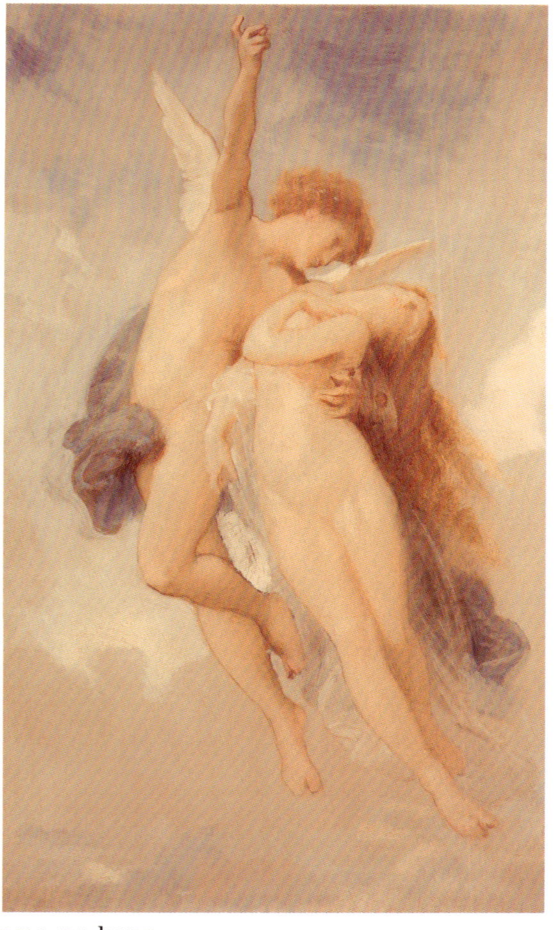

Still subject to the constraints of a system established during the reign of Louis XIV, the nineteenth-century art world was completely dominated by the Académie des Beaux-Arts and the annual exhibition known as the "Salon." Art was a career path like the army or government administration. Students followed an established series of obligatory steps, winning the recognition and awards that gradually earned them a reputation. The hurdles were laid out clearly: attending the École des Beaux-Arts; competing for the Prix de Rome, which offered the opportunity to study at the Villa Medici; admission to the annual Salon, the only exhibition where works were subject to jury vetting each year; winning medals; professorships at the École des Beaux-Arts; and finally the ultimate recognition, election to the Académie des Beaux-Arts. Without these credentials, there was no hope of professional success. Repeatedly copying the same hackneyed models, academic artists were mired in the classical tradition. They defended their hard-won privileges tooth and nail. They shared, often begrudgingly, the allocation of official commissions and monuments that proliferated under the Second Empire and the Third Republic. Any form

William Adolphe Bouguereau
Cupid and Psyche
1889
Oil on canvas
Private collection

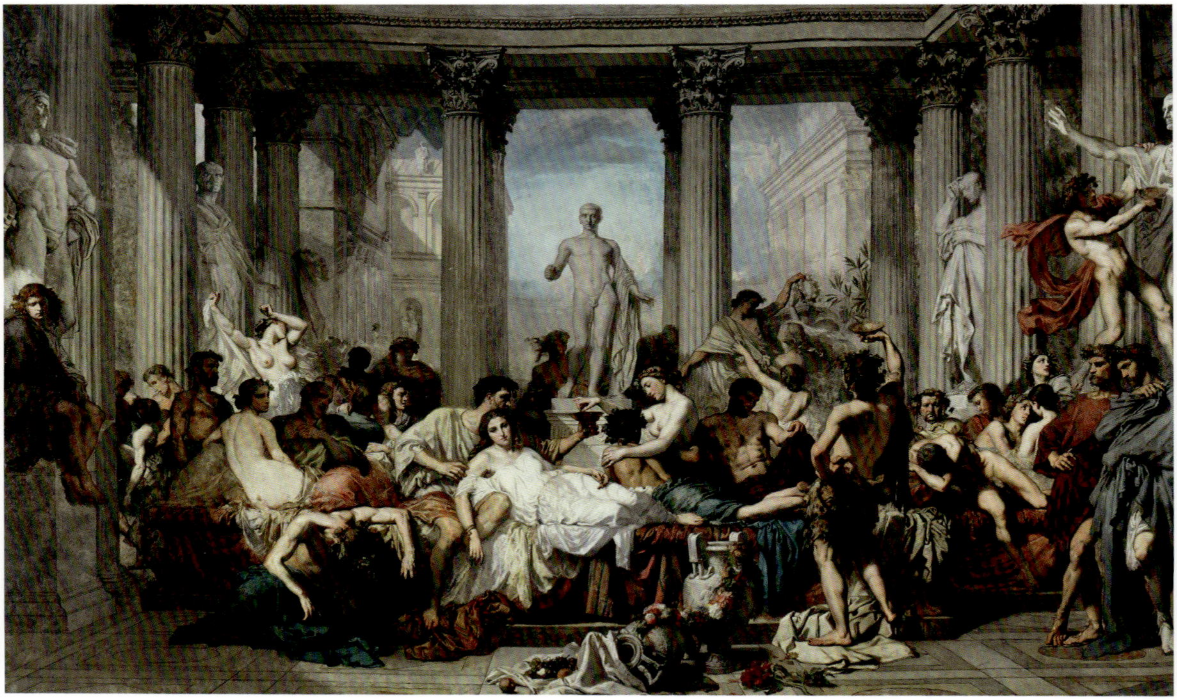

Thomas Couture
The Romans of the Decadence,
also known as *Roman Orgy*
1847
Oil on canvas, 15 ft. 5 ¾ in. × 25 ft. 4 in.
(4.72 × 7.72 m)
Musée d'Orsay, Paris

of artistic expression that diverged from the Academy's classical doctrines was harshly criticized. Delacroix's flamboyant palette and romantic élan were viciously attacked. Courbet's realism was deemed insufferable, and Millet and his peasants were regarded as heretical. "This is painting by democrats, men who don't change their linen; they wish to impose themselves on cultured people; their art displeases and disgusts me," declared the Count of Nieuwerkerke, the imperial director of the École des Beaux-Arts.

The Second Empire's governing class expected art to be a reassuring mirror, conventional and flattering. History painting was the ne plus ultra, a noble genre that duplicated classical models and the iconography of a distant past. The scale of these works, which sometimes assumed monumental proportions, was still considered a demonstration of artistic mastery. Lauded by art critics, Bouguereau, Couture, Meissonier, Gérôme, and Cabanel scooped up honors and medals for their porcelain-skinned Venuses, idealized nudes, grandiloquent compositions, anachronistic subjects, and sleight-of-hand effects.

Stifling and stale, it was a situation that was becoming unsustainable, as the photographer Maxime Du Camp observed in 1858. "Scientific progress is prodigious, industry is accomplishing miracles, and we remain impervious,

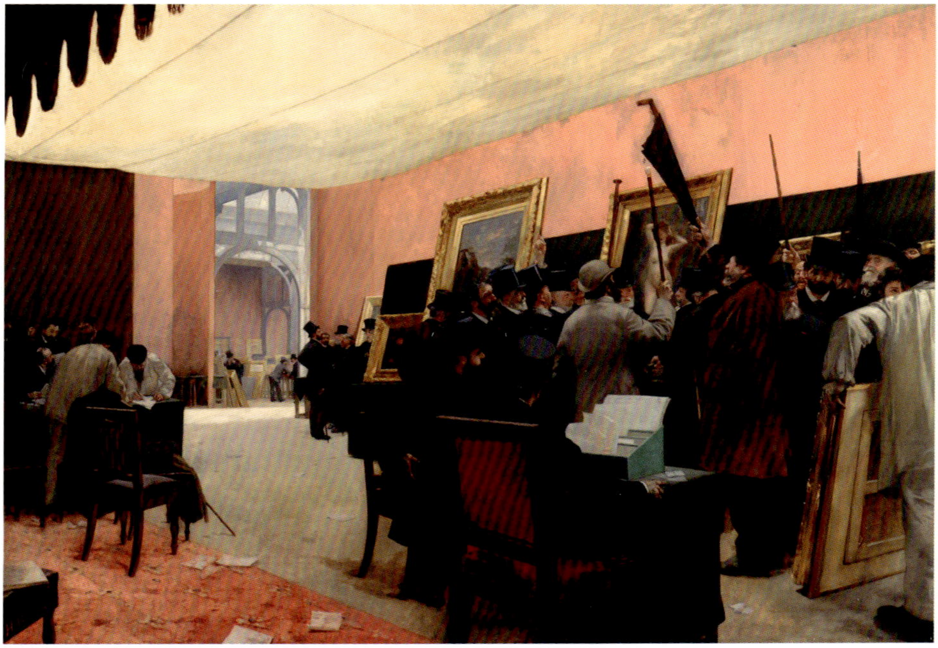

Henri Gervex
A Meeting of the Painting Jury of the Salon of French Artists
1885
Oil on canvas, 9 ft. 9 ¾ in. × 13 ft. 9 in. (2.99 × 4.19 m)
Musée d'Orsay, Paris

THE SALON
"The Salon stifles and corrupts the feeling for the grand, the beautiful; artists are driven to exhibit there by the attractions of profit, the desire to get themselves noticed at any price, by the supposed good fortune of an eccentric subject that is capable of producing an effect and leading to an advantageous sale. Thus the Salon is literally no more than a picture shop, a bazaar in which the tremendous number of objects is overwhelming, and business rules instead of art."
Ingres, member of the Académie des Beaux-Arts, professor and, in 1850, president at the École des Beaux-Arts (John Rewald, *The History of Impressionism*, 1946).

unaware, ridiculous, strumming the false chords on our lyres, closing our eyes so as not to see, stubbornly looking back to a past that offers us nothing. Steam power is discovered, while we sing of Venus, daughter of the salt sea; electricity is discovered, and we chant the praises of Bacchus, friend of the crimson grape. It's ludicrous."

It did indeed seem absurd that artwork should turn its back so resolutely on its own time. It was a system that shut the door on new generations of artists, and soon raised questions in the mind of Napoleon III himself. When the Salon's jury refused 2,783 of the 5,000 works submitted in 1863, the emperor sensed a potentially explosive situation and arrived in person to draw his own conclusions. He immediately decided to establish a Salon des Refusés as a counterpart to the official Salon, the annual showcase for art. It was to be a forum where those rejected from the Salon could display their work. Manet and his friends, Fantin-Latour, Whistler, Cézanne, Jongkind, Pissarro, and Guillaumin leapt at the opportunity. From its opening day, the Salon des Refusés attracted massive audiences, but the result was cruelly disappointing: people attended to jeer, criticize, and mock the works. The battle had just begun.

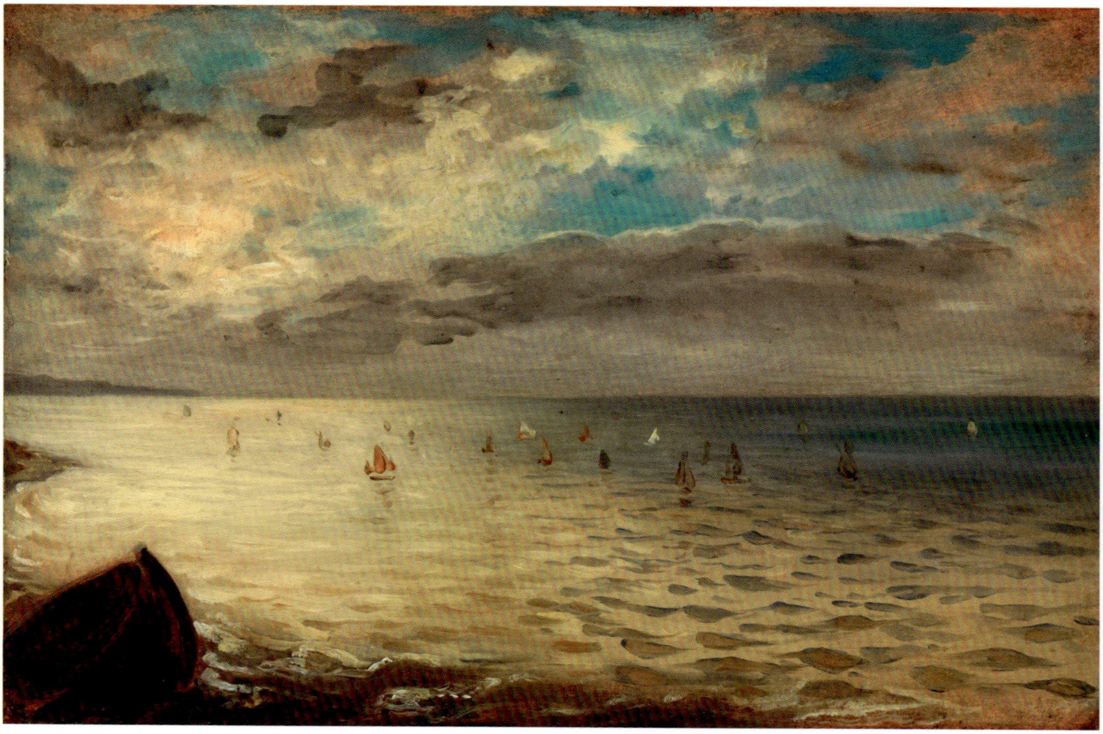

Eugène Delacroix
The Sea from the Heights of Dieppe
1852
Oil on wood, 14 ⅛ × 20 ½ in. (36 × 52 cm)
Paris, Musée du Louvre

DOWN WITH THE COLORISTS!

The standard-bearer of romanticism, Delacroix (1798–1863) followed Géricault and others, reviving the heated debate over the primacy of color versus drawing. In the tradition of Rubens, Veronese, and Titian, Delacroix made color the primary focus of his work, with expressive, loose, and lively brushstrokes. In 1832 he traveled to Morocco, where he was dazzled by the light of North Africa, an experience that pushed him further in the direction of the colorists. Ingres versus Delacroix, the purity of the line versus the expressiveness of color—the nineteenth century was riven by this ancient enmity between color and drawing, of which the latter, according to the Academy, was the one and only pillar of art.

INDEPENDENT PERSONALITIES

Refusing to be discouraged by the rejection of some of his canvases by the 1855 Universal Exposition, Courbet built his own pavilion. Located outside the official enclosure, at the foot of Avenue Montaigne, the Pavillon du Réalisme presented thirty-seven of the master's works, including *The Artist's Studio* (1854–55) and *A Burial at Ornans* (1849–50). Manet followed his example during the 1867 Universal Exposition—he and Courbet both built their own pavilions.

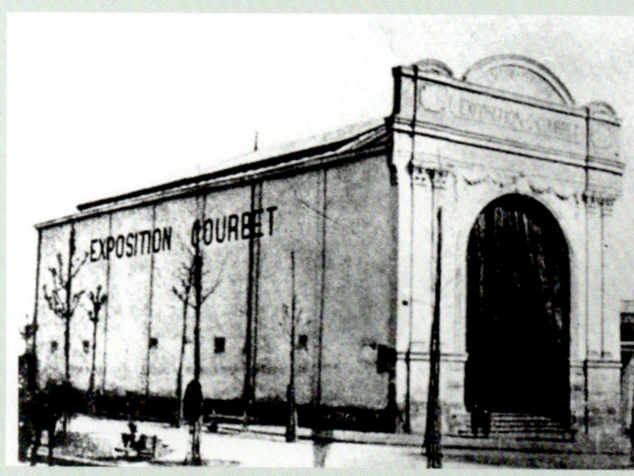

Gustave Courbet's private exhibition in 1867
Private collection

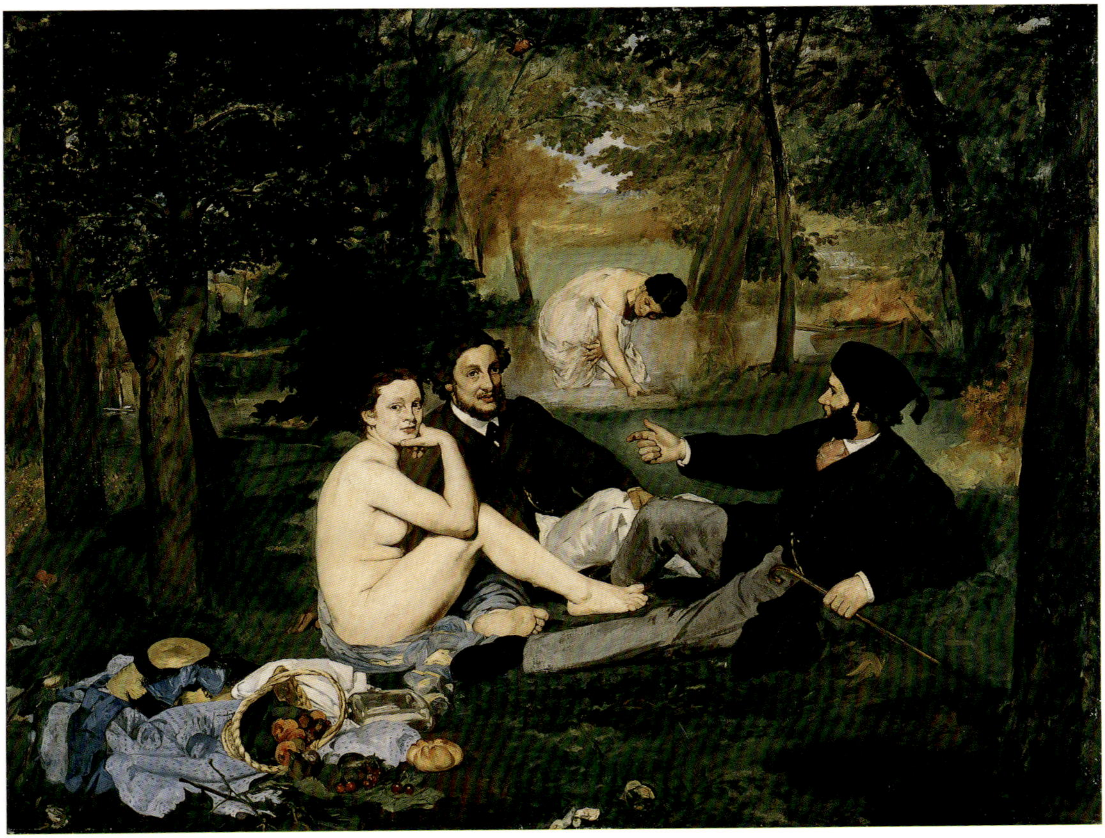

The Luncheon on the Grass
Exhibited at the Salon des Refusés in 1863, Manet's work alludes to the Renaissance iconography of *The Pastoral Concert*, now attributed to Titian, and also draws inspiration from the country fêtes so popular during his own day. But on closer inspection the viewer can see that the men are wearing contemporary clothing and the naked women look very realistic. Audiences and critics were as scandalized by the subject matter as by the style and treatment.

Édouard Manet
The Luncheon on the Grass
1863
Oil on canvas, 6 ft. 10 in. × 8 ft. 8 in.
(2.08 × 2.65 m)
Musée d'Orsay, Paris

CREATION OF THE SALON DES REFUSÉS

To the great chagrin of the Academy's official artists, Napoleon III established the Salon des Refusés in 1863, allowing painters who had been rejected by the official Salon's jury to display their work.

"Numerous petitions were submitted to the emperor concerning artworks that had been rejected by the Exposition's jury. His Majesty wished to allow the public to judge the legitimacy of these claims and decided that works of art that had been refused would be exhibited in another part of the Palais de l'Industrie. This exhibition was to be optional, and artists who did not wish to participate could simply inform the administration, which would immediately return their works to them."

Le Moniteur universel, April 24, 1863.

FOCUS

Training

"They're taught beauty the same way they're taught algebra," declared Delacroix on the topic of the courses offered by the École des Beaux-Arts. The study of antiquity and the copying of plaster casts were the pillars of an artistic training whose overriding objective was to mold students to conform to an inflexible set of standards.

DRAWING REIGNS SUPREME

It seems incredible, but until 1863, drawing was the only subject taught in the studios of the École des Beaux-Arts. Students who wished to learn painting and sculpture had to attend independent or "free" ateliers outside the Academy. Initiated by Viollet-le-Duc and Prosper Mérimée and approved reluctantly by the Count of Nieuwerkerke, superintendent of the École des Beaux-Arts, the teaching reform was made official on November 15, 1863. The elderly Ingres opposed the move with all his remaining energy, but new courses were gradually offered: anatomical drawing, history, and archeology—and even, at last, painting. Among the members of the impressionist group, only Degas and Renoir briefly studied there.

THE MUSÉE DU LOUVRE:
A BREATH OF FRESH AIR

A few painters, like Pissarro, declared that the Louvre should be burned to the ground. But for other artists, the museum was a source of inspiration and even subversiveness. Weary of dry instruction that revolved around copying the art of antiquity, artists came to the Louvre to search for new visions and admire and copy the great colorists, from Titian to Tintoretto and Rubens. They were also intrigued by Spanish artists such as Velázquez. Manet and Berthe Morisot met at the museum in 1868, and Manet encountered Degas in 1862. Degas met Mary Cassatt there some years later.

Edgar Degas, *Mary Cassatt at the Louvre: The Paintings Gallery,* 1885
Etching, aquatint, and drypoint highlighted with pastel on tan wove paper, 12 × 5 in. (30.5 × 12.7 cm) without the margins; 12 3/8 × 5 in. (31.3 × 12.7 cm) overall
The Art Institute of Chicago, Chicago

THE ASPIRING ARTIST: A WARRIOR'S TALE

"A young man demonstrates an inclination toward painting or sculpture.... More often than not, this young man must overcome the resistance of his parents, who would prefer to see him enter the École Centrale where he'd be trained for a business career. His resources are doubted, his aptitude must be demonstrated. If his initial efforts do not meet with success, he is viewed as misguided or lazy—no more allowance. So he has to run after conventional success. The young artist enters the École, wins an award... but at what price? He operates under the condition that he must adhere exactly, unswervingly, to the limits imposed by the faculty. He must tamely follow the beaten path, entertaining no ideas save those disseminated by his professors, and above all avoid any claim to having any original ideas of his own.... And let's remember that the bulk of the student body naturally includes more mediocrities than genuine talents, and that the majority will always take the side of the established routine. There is no end to the mockery for anyone who manifests any inclination toward originality. How is it possible for a poor fellow, scorned by his teachers, mocked by his comrades, and threatened by his parents, to avoid the road more traveled? How could he have enough strength, enough self-confidence, enough courage to shake off this yoke that goes by the name of classical education and chart his own course instead?"

Viollet-le-Duc, architect and member of the Commission des Monuments Historiques, "The Teaching of the Arts," *Gazette des Beaux-Arts*, June 1862.

FREE ACADEMIES: PLAN B

Within this highly restrictive framework, some artists offered lessons in their studios to respond to the desire for greater freedom of expression. Opened by Charles Suisse (1846–1906) in his studio on the Île de la Cité, the Académie Suisse offered freedom in the choice of subject matter and technique. Manet, Monet, Pissarro, Guillaumin, and Cézanne all worked there between 1856 and 1862. There were no professors or students; the artists acted according to their inclinations. In 1862, Charles Gleyre (1804–1874), an academic luminary but a liberal professor, welcomed Renoir, Monet, Bazille, and Sisley into his studio. The initial core of what was to become the future impressionist group formed there.

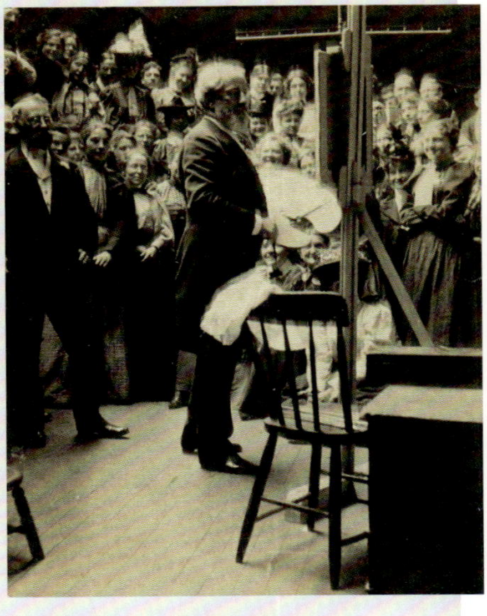

Portrait of Carolus-Duran in His Studio
April 12, 1898
Silver print, 4 ¾ × 3 ⅝ in. (12 × 9.3 cm)
Musée d'Orsay, Paris

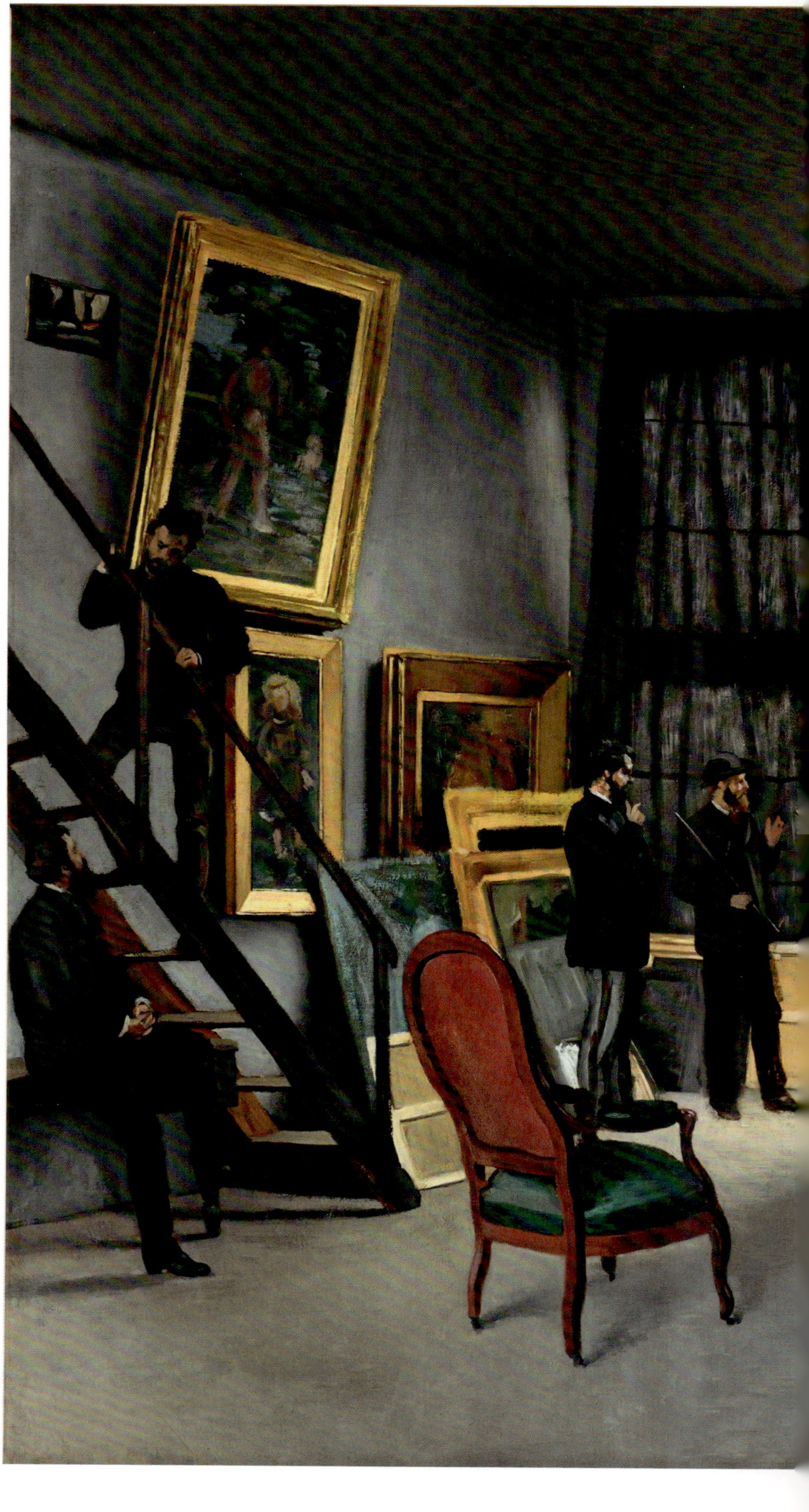

Frédéric Bazille
Bazille's Studio
1870
Oil on canvas,
3 ft. 2 ½ in. × 4 ft. 2 ½ in.
(98 × 128.5 cm)
Musée d'Orsay, Paris

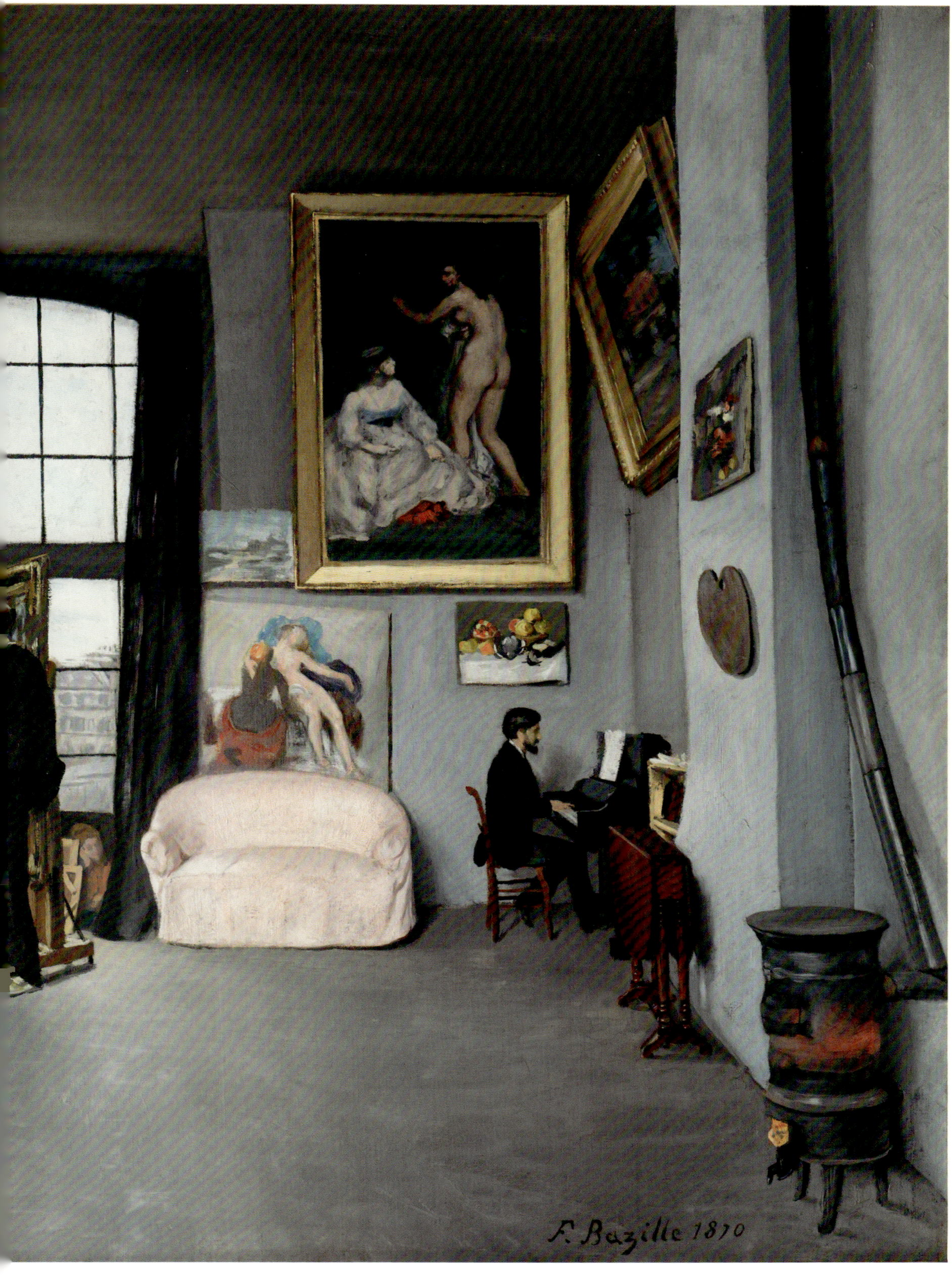
F. Bazille 1870

Bazille's Studio

Frédéric Bazille, 1870

As the impressionists abandoned schools and the academic system, the studio became an intellectual forum. Ateliers were no longer the lairs of artists guarding their secrets, where models posed and subjects were contrived. The impressionists found their subjects outdoors, and the studio became a gathering place where painters could meet for discussion and artistic debate.

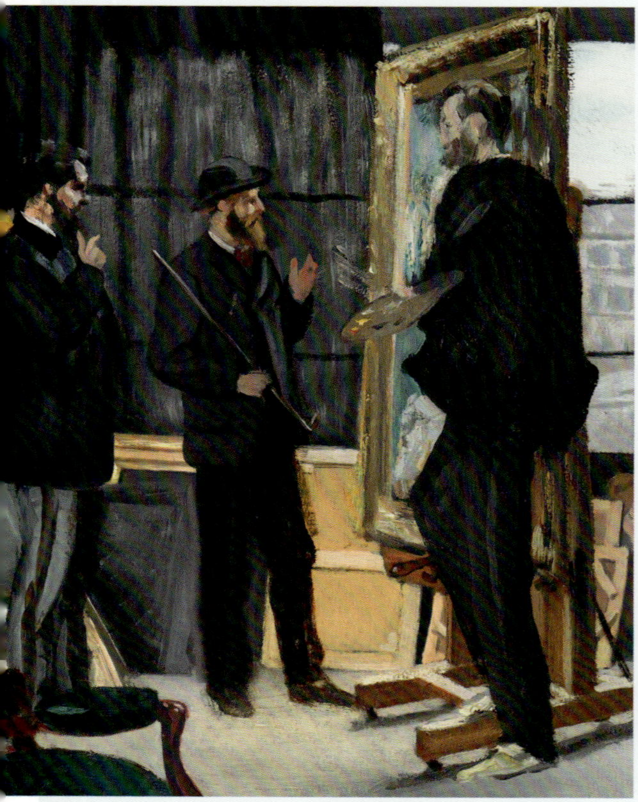

Manet, standing in front of the easel, brush in hand, seems to be giving a lesson to Monet, who is just behind him, and to Bazille, who is holding a palette. The painting is a subtle homage to the man the impressionists had chosen as their leader.

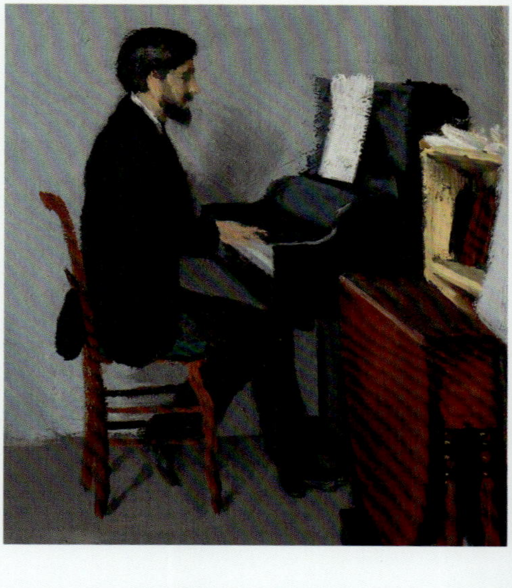

Seated at the piano, musician Edmond Maître demonstrates how the studio had become a kind of open house where visitors were free to express themselves. Bazille, a music lover, organized musical soirées in his studio; Gabriel Fauré sometimes joined in.

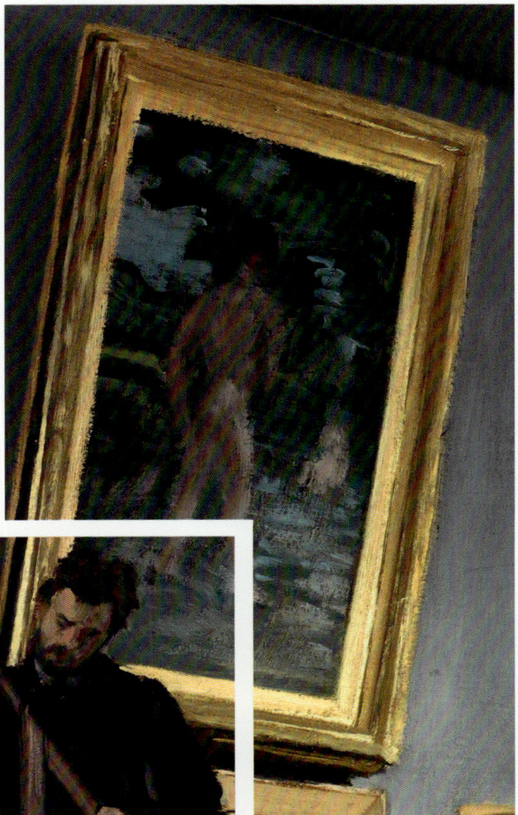

The Fisherman with a Net *can be seen hanging on the left. The artist took advantage of his wall space to display his works as if in a museum gallery.*

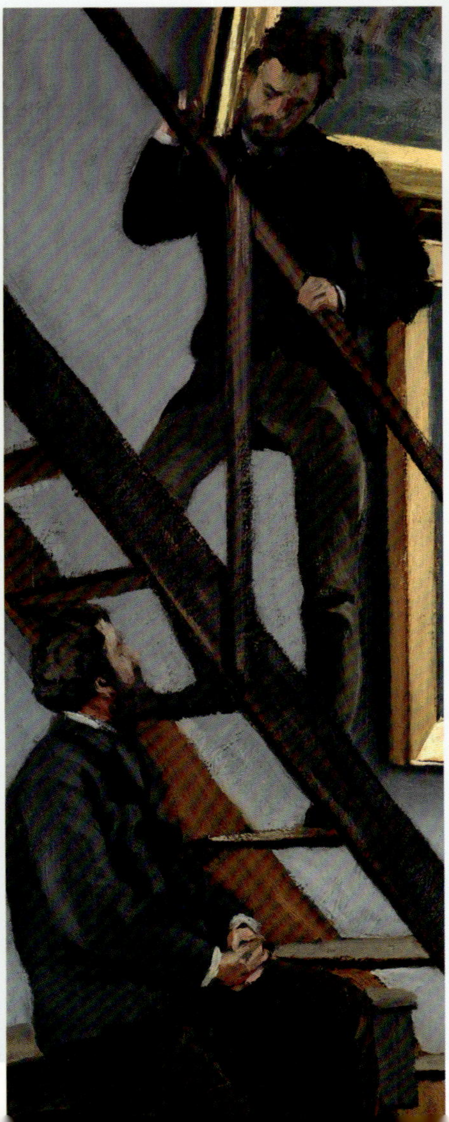

Pausing on the staircase, Zola converses with Renoir, who is seated nonchalantly on a table. Bazille received his comrades in his studio in the Batignolles district, not far from the Café Guerbois, where these young painters would gather around Manet in the evening.

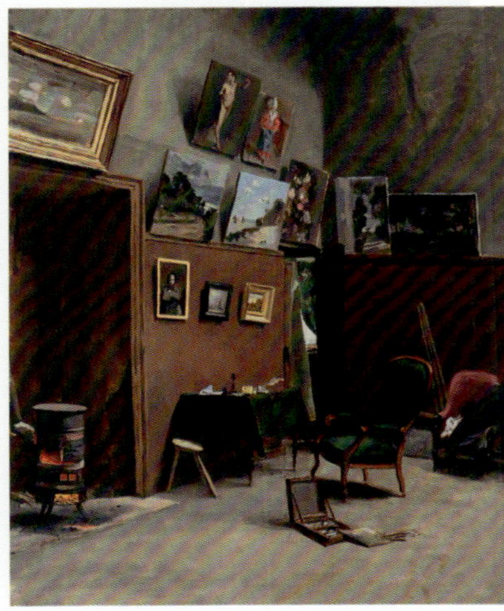

Frédéric Bazille
Corner of the Studio on Rue de Furstenberg
1881
Oil on canvas, 31 ½ in. × 25 ⅝ in.
(80 × 65 cm)
Musée Fabre, Montpellier

Frédéric Bazille arrived in Paris in 1862. He generously shared his various studios with his friends Gleyre, Monet, and Renoir, beginning with this space on Rue de Furstenberg. Empty of people, the studio became a subject in its own right for the painter.

FOCUS

Manet: A Spiritual Father

Édouard Manet (1832–1883) was chosen very early on as a spiritual father by the younger generation of painters who were hungry for something new. As their elder, Manet willingly assumed the role of mentor without indulging in any theorizing. He was an artistic dissident, and although he searched for honor and recognition his entire life, he stood out for his independence and distinctiveness. In an artistic world that endlessly revisited tired, anachronistic themes, Manet was revolutionary in painting scenes of the daily life surrounding him. He depicted identifiable individuals dressed in contemporary clothing, or unclothed, unashamedly revealing their bodies. He pursued topics that the Academy and the École des Beaux-Arts discouraged. He haunted the Louvre and was fascinated by Spanish painting. The artist scorned rules and conventions, and his technique was judged "flat," with the absence of modeling considered jarring. It was seen as outrageous that Manet employed patches of color, with brushstrokes left visible. The sometimes harsh light in his canvases struck some as offensive. Moreover, he drew his inspiration from contemporary life: men and women relaxing on the beach, or frequenting bars and café-théâtres; the expansion of the railroads. His work embraced so many pre-impressionist themes.

PROFESSION: ARTIST

Édouard Manet was born into a prominent family. Learning of his son's plan to become an artist, Édouard's father initially tried to discourage him, shipping him off to Rio de Janeiro. But it was no use—on his return in 1850, Édouard entered the studio of the academic painter Thomas Couture. "On my first day, I was given a classical piece to copy," he remembered. "I turned it over and over in every direction. It seemed more interesting upside down." His personal fortune allowed him to devote himself to his art, unhampered by the need to earn a living.

"Manet was as important to us as Cimabue or Giotto were to the Italians of the Quattrocento."

Auguste Renoir, quoted by Jean Renoir in *Renoir, My Father*, 1962 (2001).

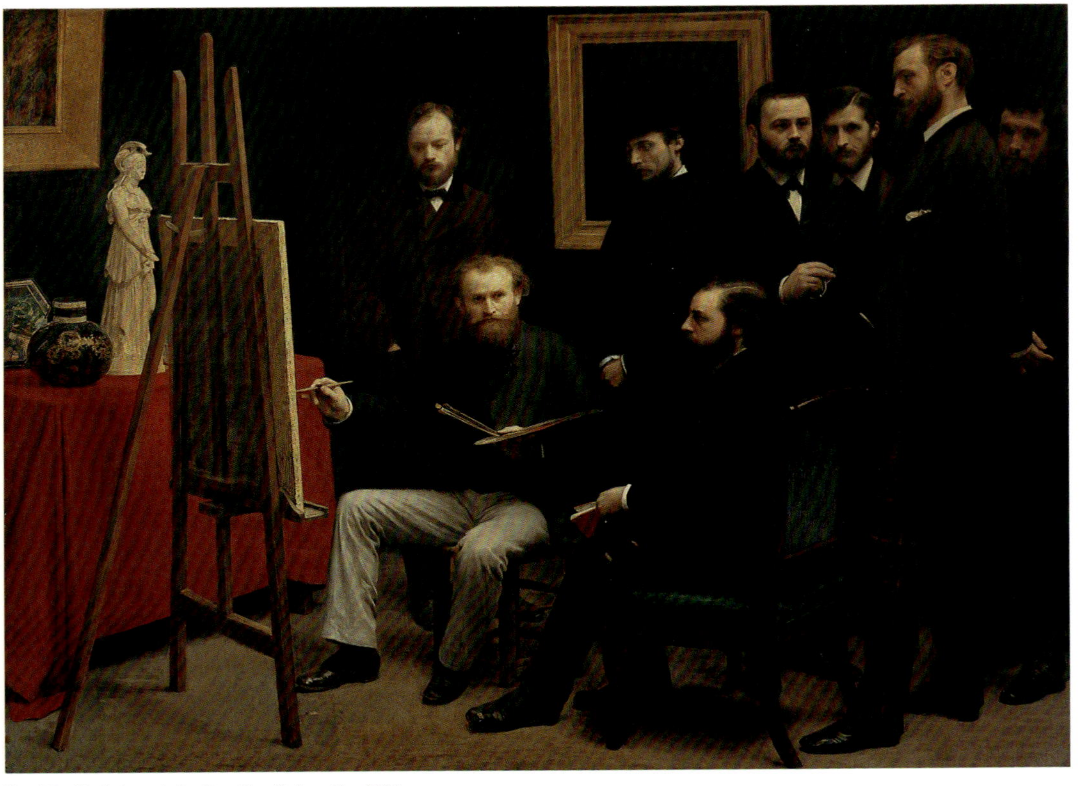

Henri Fantin-Latour, *A Studio at Les Batignolles*, 1870
Oil on canvas, 6 ft. 8 ¼ in. × 8 ft. 11 ¾ in. (2.04 × 2.74 m)
Musée d'Orsay, Paris

THE ÉCOLE DES BATIGNOLLES

Manet is seated at his easel, brush in hand. Surrounding him, from left to right, Fantin-Latour depicts the German painter Otto Scholderer, Auguste Renoir (wearing a hat), Zacharie Astruc, an artist and journalist (sitting), Émile Zola, a leading spokesman for the new approach to painting, Edmond Maître, an official in the Hôtel de Ville at the time, Frédéric Bazille, who was to perish in the war just a few months later at the age of twenty-eight, and finally, Claude Monet in the shadowy background. Exhibited in that year's Salon, the work was a manifesto for this group that coalesced spontaneously around Manet. The École des Batignolles was named after the new neighborhood where Manet had his studio. They all gathered at the Café Guerbois, their favorite haunt not far from the Place Clichy. Painted the same year as Bazille's *The Artist's Studio*, this work gives a completely different view of this community of artists. The clothing is somber, the poses rigid, the likenesses seem contrived, and the figures seem posed. It is a far cry from Bazille's painting, where the figures, atmosphere, light, and ideas seem to circulate freely.

"The true painter will be the person who knows how to seize the epic side of contemporary life. Through color and drawing he will show us how to see and understand that we possess grandeur and poetry, even in our cravats and polished boots."

Charles Baudelaire, "The Salon of 1845."

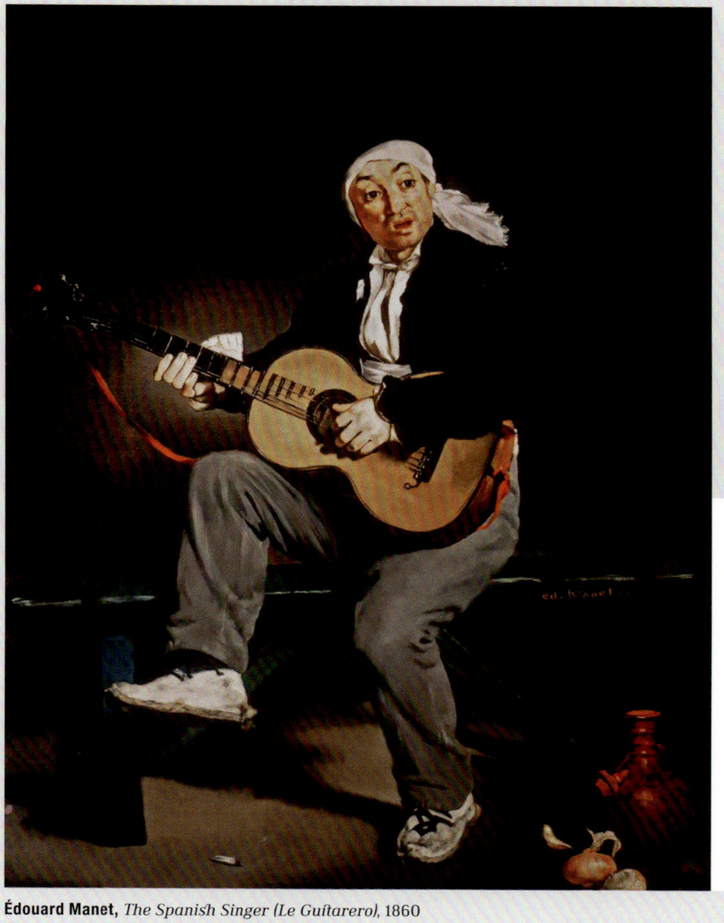

Édouard Manet, *The Spanish Singer (Le Guitarero)*, 1860
Oil on canvas, 4 ft. 10 in. × 3 ft 9 in. (1.47 × 1.14 m)
The Metropolitan Museum of Art, New York

"Caramba! Here's a guitar player who's not just a character from the Opéra-Comique.... There's tremendous talent in this life-sized figure, painted in heavy impasto, with bold brushstrokes and true-to-life colors."

Théophile Gautier.

"You sensed his good breeding. Under his broad brow and a distinctively straight nose, his lips, curving upward, seemed mocking. His gaze was clear. His eyes were small but very lively.... Few men could match his charm."

Antonin Proust, *Édouard Manet: Souvenirs*, 1897.

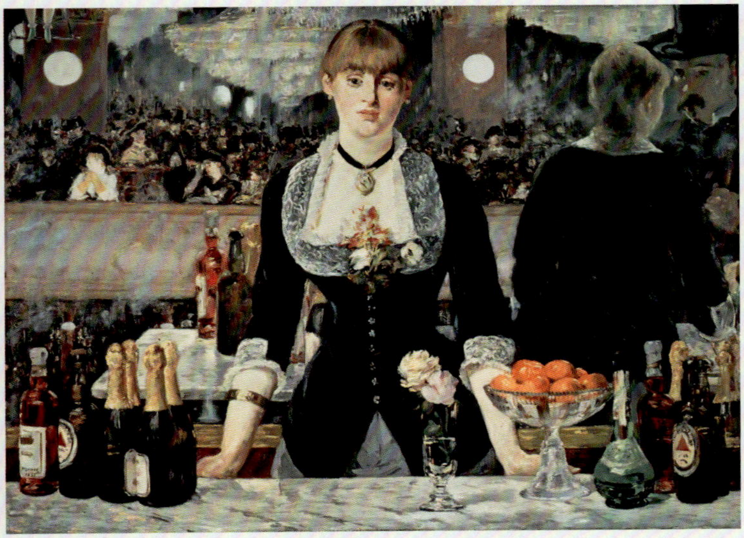

"No one heeds the wind that will blow tomorrow, but nevertheless the heroism of modern life surrounds us and urges us on."

Charles Baudelaire, "The Salon of 1845."

Édouard Manet, *A Bar at the Folies-Bergère*, 1882
Oil on canvas, 3 ft. 1 ¾ in. × 4 ft. 3 ¼ in. (96 × 130 cm)
Courtauld Institute Galleries, London

"Reconstituting historic figures—what a joke! There's just one truth: paint what you see with the first brushstroke."

Édouard Manet, quoted in Antonin Proust, *Édouard Manet: Souvenirs*, 1897.

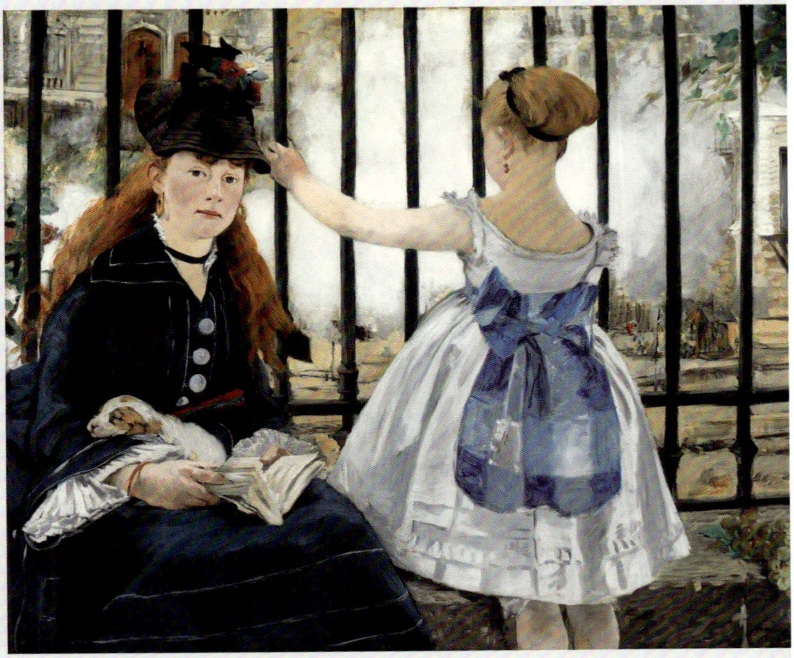

Édouard Manet, *The Railway*, 1873
Oil on canvas, 3 ft. ¾ in. × 3 ft. 8 in. (93.3 × 111.5 cm)
National Gallery of Art Washington, DC

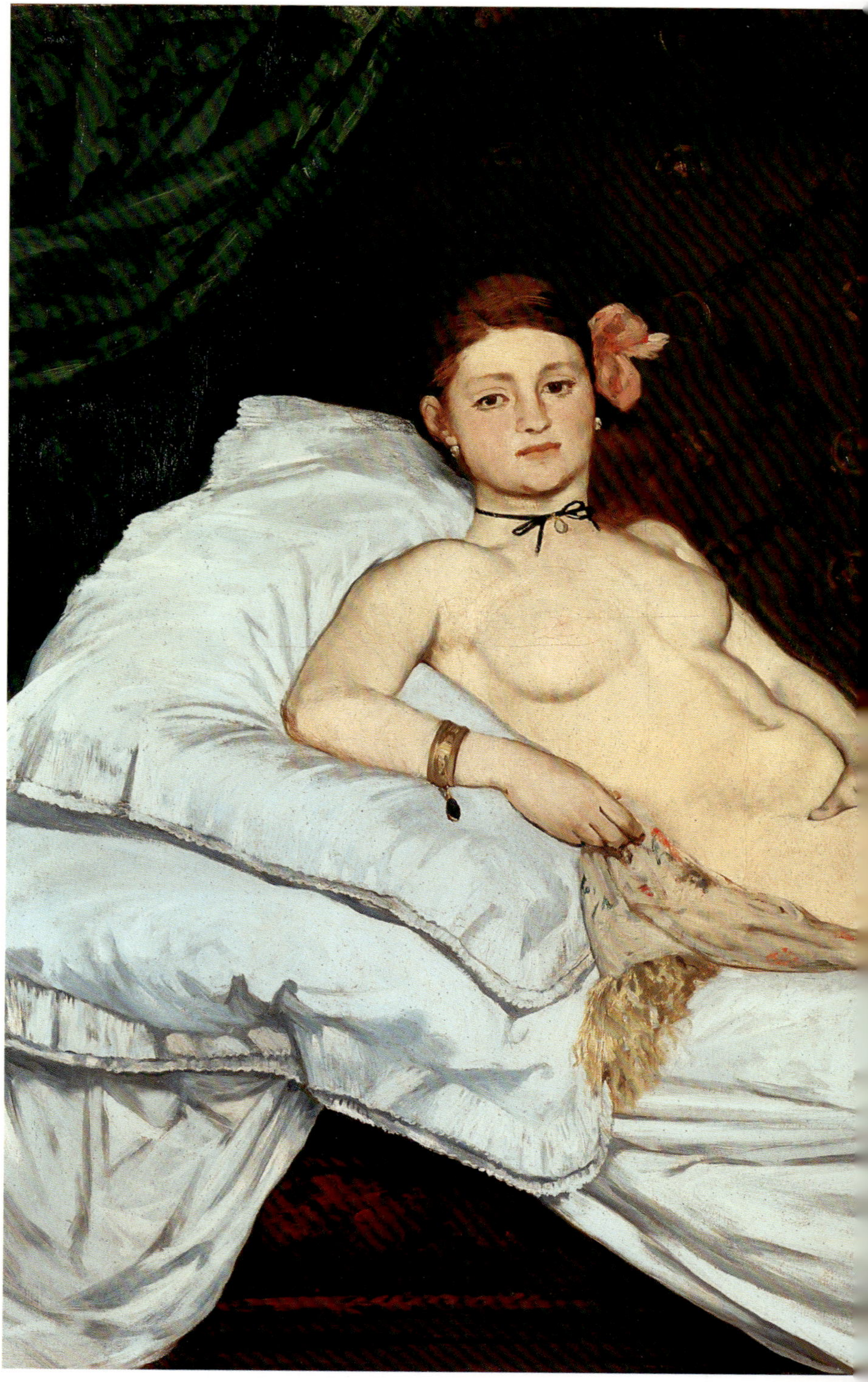

Édouard Manet
Olympia
1863
Oil on canvas,
4 ft. 3 ¼ in. × 6 ft. 2 ¾ in.
(1.30 × 1.90 m)
Musée d'Orsay, Paris

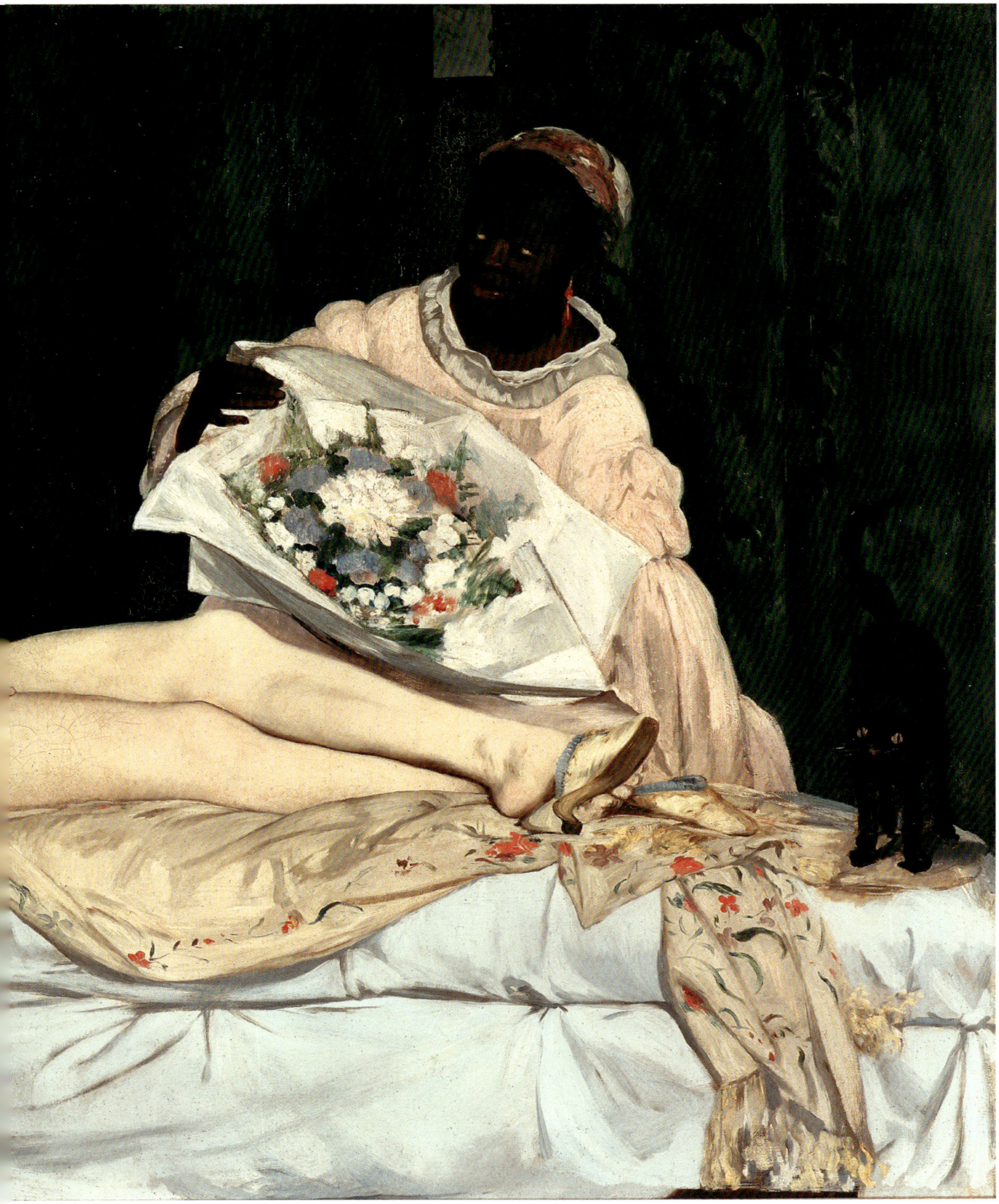

Olympia
Édouard Manet, 1863

Édouard Manet's *Olympia* was accepted by the Salon of 1865, even though *The Luncheon on the Grass* had been refused two years earlier. Nevertheless, the nude unleashed harsh criticism and created a tremendous scandal.

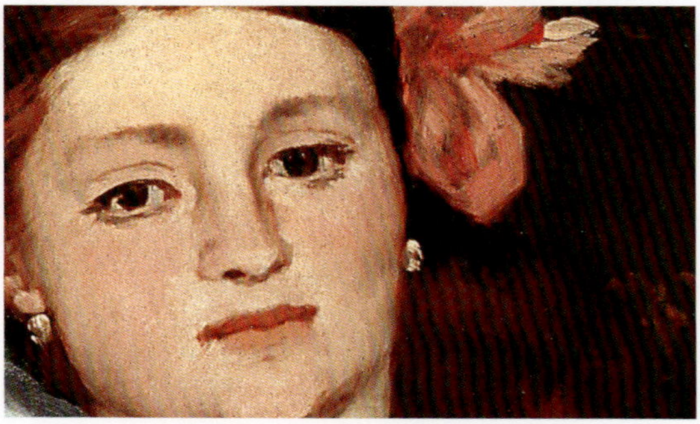

With an expression that is both absent and arrogant, she stares the viewer down.

The model's cupped hand both conceals and draws attention to her sex. She lies displayed on her bed like a coveted object in a shop window.

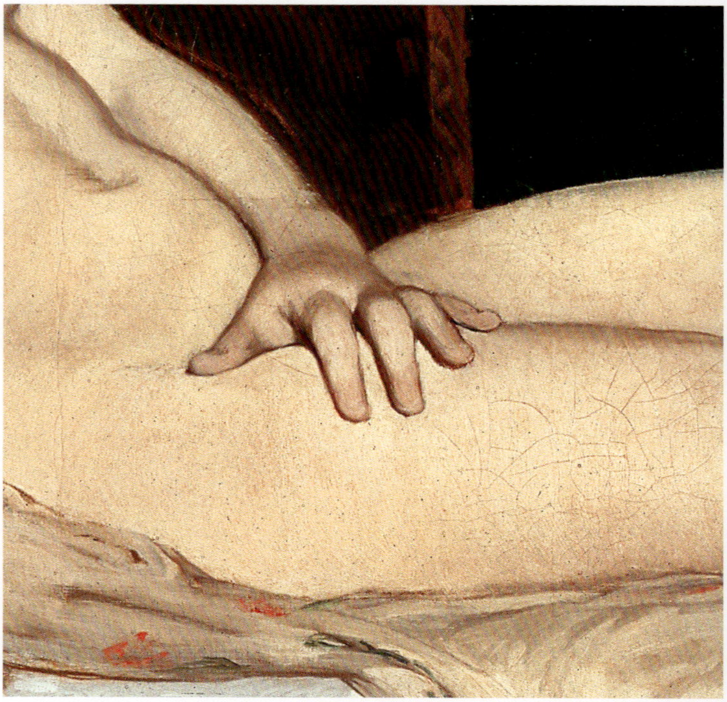

VICTORINE MEURENT
Victorine Meurent's blond Venetian beauty and dark brown eyes haunted Manet. He first met his favorite model in 1862, and she appeared in his work over the years, posing in a toreador costume (*Mlle V. in the Costume of an Espada*, 1862), as a street singer in a painting of the same name (1862), eating lunch in the company of two gentlemen (*The Luncheon on the Grass*, 1863), sniffing a bunch of violets (*Woman with a Parrot*, 1866), and totally naked, as we see her here.

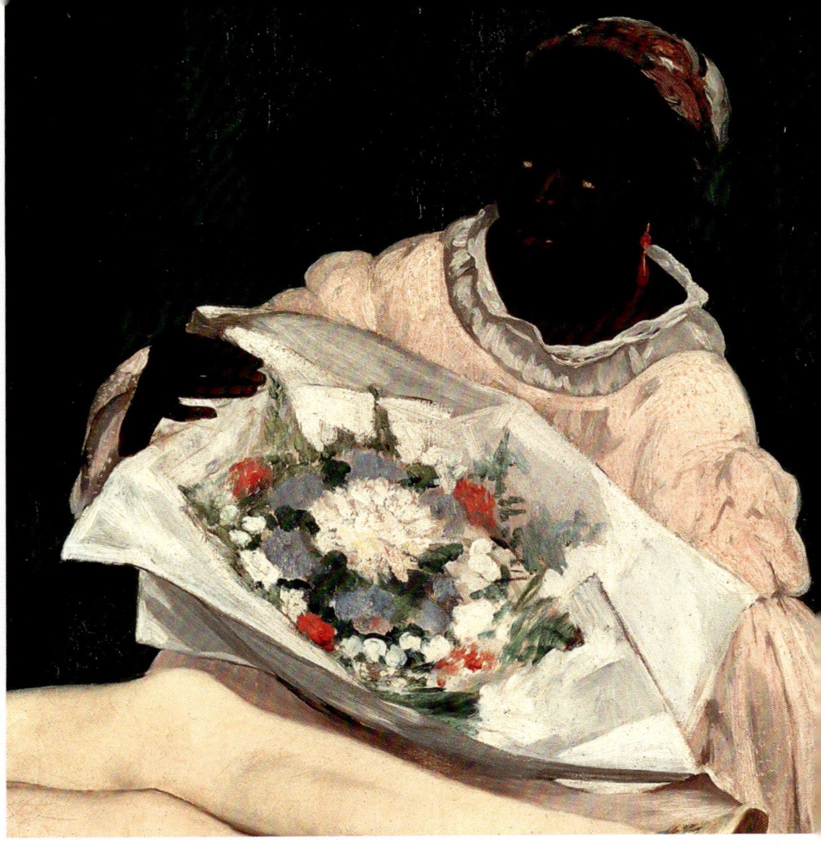

Proffered by a black maidservant, the bouquet of flowers is superciliously ignored by its intended recipient, but it dominates the center of the composition.

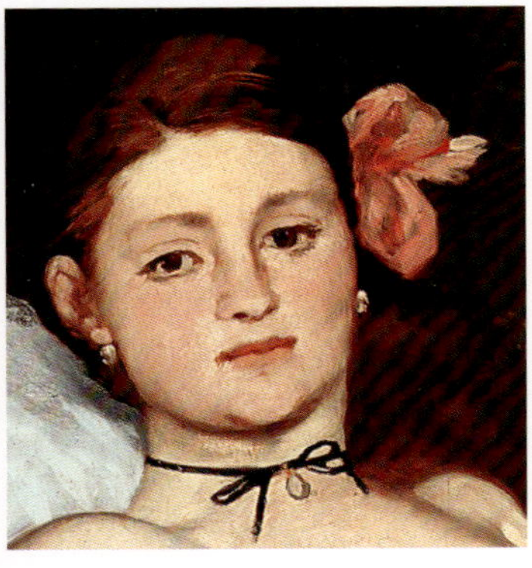

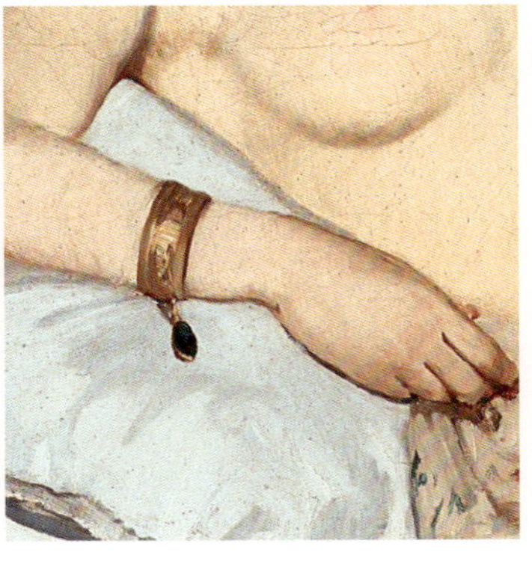

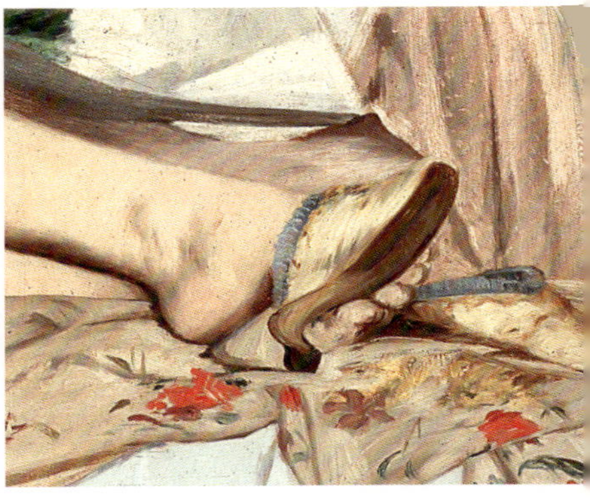

The accessories—her jewels, the flowers behind her ear, her slippers—make it clear that this nude is neither a goddess nor a woman in the privacy of her dressing room. She is adorned to seduce, a sexual temptation put on display. It's unclear who possesses whom. Courtesans of the era devoured their protectors' fortunes voraciously.

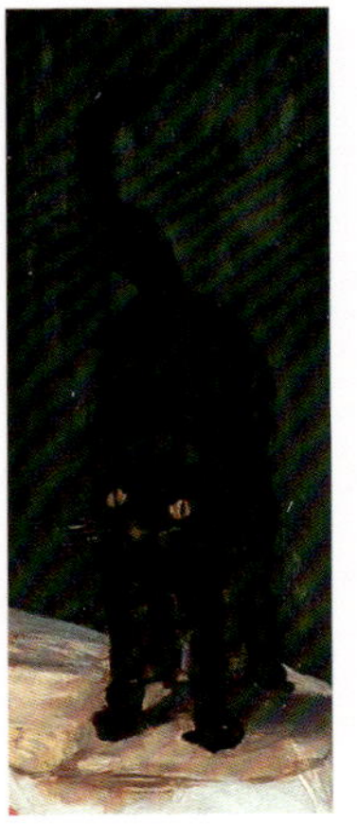

The black cat creates a note of unease; its arched back closes the composition with a question mark.

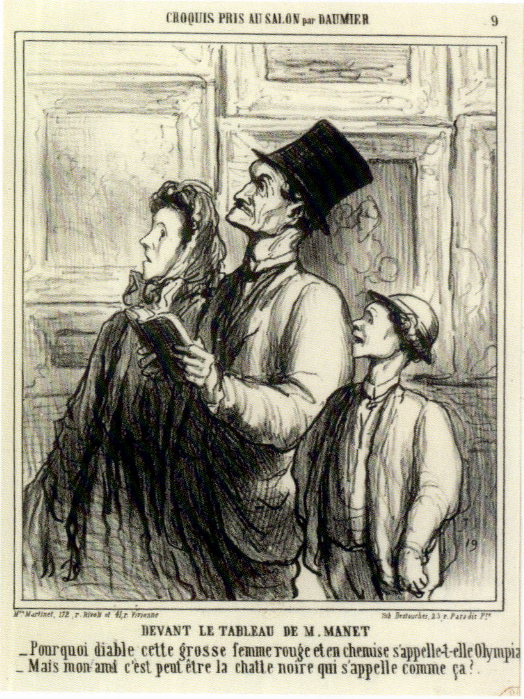

Honoré Daumier
In Front of Monsieur Manet's Painting
Le Charivari, May 14, 1865
Bibliothèque Nationale de France, Paris

"THE ROYAL ROAD"

For many years, the French public considered *Olympia* to be offensive and unacceptable. Claude Monet fervently championed the painting, urging its admission to the Louvre following Manet's death. It took a year of concerted effort. In 1890, Monet launched a subscription to underwrite the painting's purchase. But, having collected the necessary sum, the problems continued, because the museum had to be persuaded to accept *Olympia* into its collections. After tricky negotiations, the gift of the work was finally accepted, but the painting was exhibited in the Musée du Luxembourg, which was then devoted to the work of contemporary artists.

SCANDAL AT THE 1865 SALON

"Who is this odalisque with her yellowish belly, an ignoble model from who knows where, with the temerity to represent Olympia?"

Jules Claretie, *Le Figaro*, 1865.

"Olympia is inexplicable from any point of view, even if accepted for what she is, a scrawny creature stretched out on a sheet. Her flesh tones are murky, the model is a nobody."

Théophile Gautier, *Le Moniteur universel*, 1865.

"The crowd throngs close, as if visiting a morgue, when confronted with Monsieur Manet's overripe Olympia. Art that has sunk so low does not even deserve our scorn."

Paul de Saint-Victor, "Le Salon de 1865," *La Presse*, May 28, 1865.

"Insults rain down on me like hailstones. I've never had such a reception.... I should so much like to have your sound opinion of my work, for all this outcry is disturbing, and clearly somebody is wrong."

Édouard Manet, letter to Baudelaire, May 4, 1865
(quoted in the catalog of the Manet exhibition at the Grand Palais, 1983).

If the Olympia canvas was not ripped to pieces and destroyed, it was thanks to the precautions taken by the exhibition's administration.... I've rarely seen Manet more despondent."

Antonin Proust, in *Édouard Manet: Souvenirs*, 1897.

Alexandre Cabanel
The Birth of Venus
1863
Oil on canvas, 4 ft. 3 ¼ in. × 7 ft. 4 ¼ in. (1.30 × 2.25 m)
Musée d'Orsay, Paris

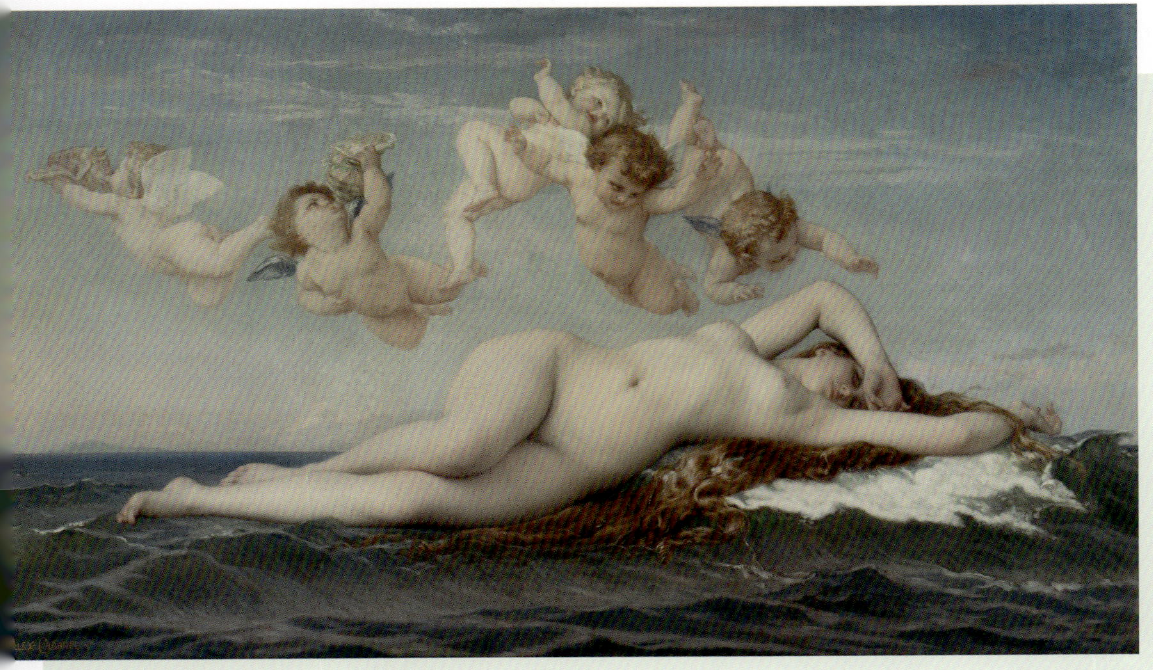

WHY SUCH OUTRAGE?

While difficult to comprehend today, the uproar generated by *Olympia* was due to the fact that it was a painting of an actual nude woman, rather than an assemblage of idealized body parts as advocated by Beaux-Arts teaching. Viewers could actually identify the model. There is no mythological excuse for her nudity, and she is far from being a fetching odalisque. Furthermore, the subject is clearly a prostitute. Alexandre Cabanel's *The Birth of Venus* (1863), well received in the Salon two years earlier, demonstrates what was acceptable and admired in depictions of the female nude at the time.

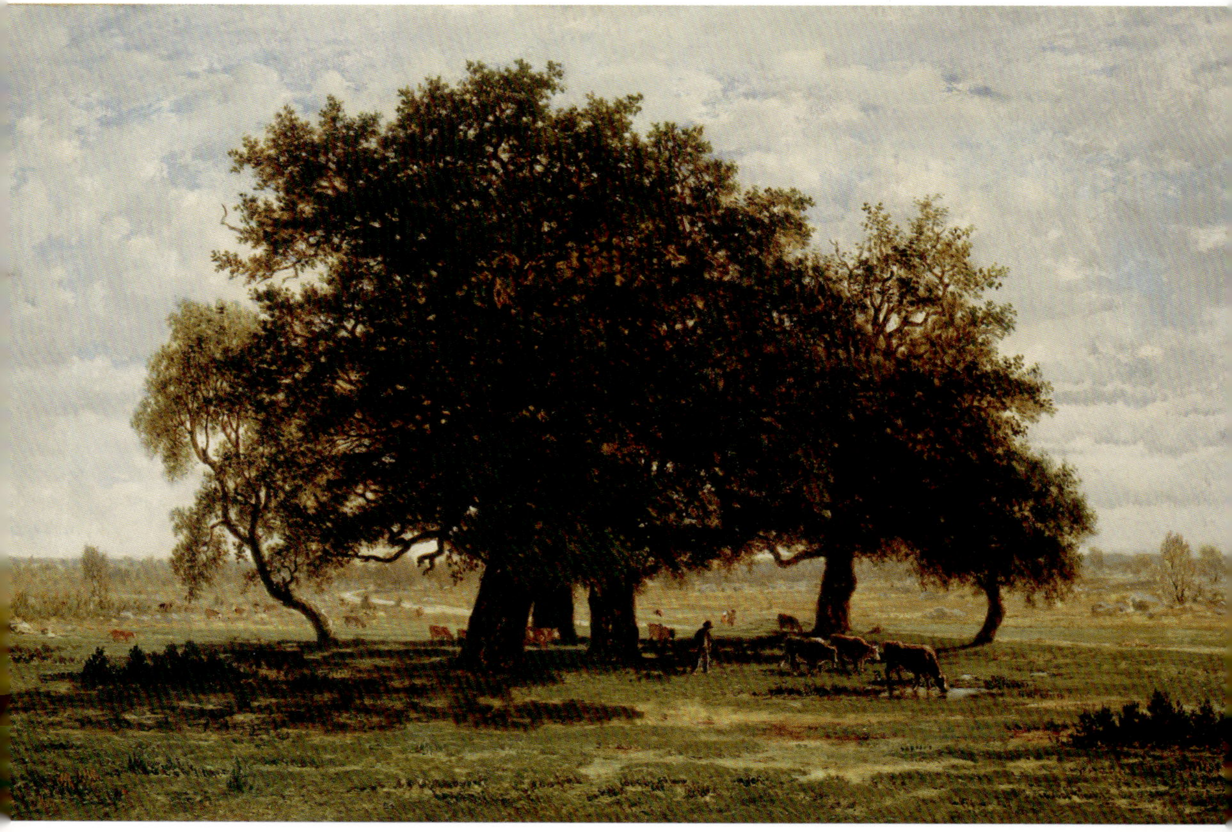

Théodore Rousseau
Oaks at Apremont
1855
Oil on canvas, 2 ft. 1 in. × 3 ft. 3 in. (63 × 99 cm)
Musée du Louvre, Paris

A New Vision of Landscape

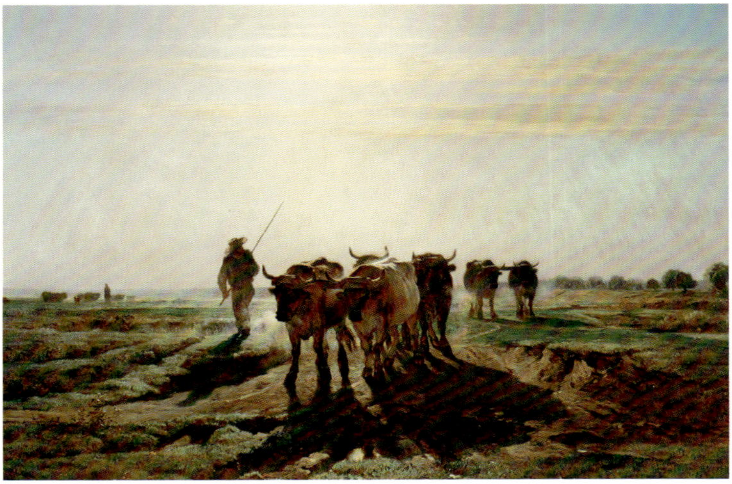

Constant Troyon
Oxen Going to Labor in the Fields: Morning
1855
Oil on canvas, 8 ft. 10 in. × 13 ft. 1 ½ in.
(2.60 × 4.00 m)
Musée d'Orsay, Paris

For centuries, landscape was considered a minor genre in the hierarchy established by the Académie des Beaux-Art. Landscapes had long been consigned to the role of mere background for elaborate compositions and history subjects. Rocks that looked as if they were made of cardboard and unrealistic trees were scattered implausibly across an artificial countryside that was rightly referred to as "recomposed." Landscape served as a stage set, where all that really mattered was the moral of the story and the lofty deeds depicted in the foreground. Nineteenth-century academic painters did not acknowledge landscape as a worthy subject in its own right, and they remained faithful to this guiding principle, which was in the traditional mainstream. Nymphs scampered across meadows that suggested theater curtains, and heroes flexed their muscles against a backdrop that resembled wallpaper. The gulf between art and contemporary reality was the widest it had ever been.

Several dissident movements emerged during the nineteenth century, demonstrating a lively interest in landscape

A CONTROVERSIAL VISION
A celebrated author of the time, Paul de Saint-Victor summed up the aversion to this new approach to landscape painting in 1855: "We prefer the *lucus*, the sacred grove, where fauns traverse the woodlands and woodcutters ply their trade; the Greek spring, where nymphs bathe in a Flemish pool and ducks paddle by, where the half-nude shepherd drives his rams and goats with his Virgilian staff along Poussin's bucolic pathways, rather than a pipe-smoking peasant who treads a country path in one of Ruysdael's works."

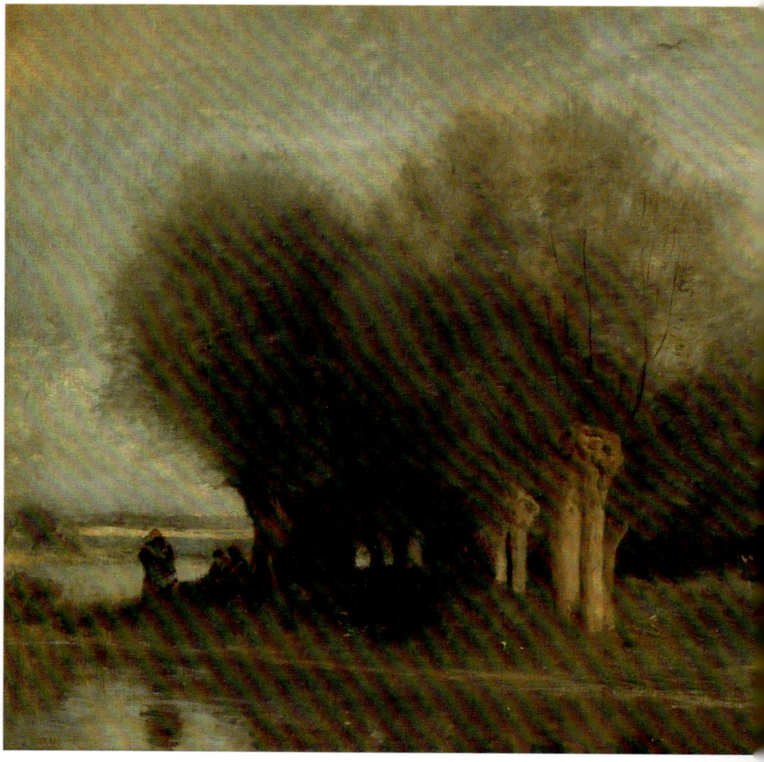

Jean-Baptiste-Camille Corot
Willows Beside the Water
c. 1855
Oil on canvas, 18 ⅛ × 24 ⅜ in. (46 × 62 cm)
Musée d'Orsay, Paris

as a subject in its own right. A shift began toward a new vision of the countryside, which reached its climax in the 1870s with the advent of impressionism. Gustave Courbet (1819–1877), the standard-bearer of realism, followed the motto, "Paint what you see, what you wish, what you feel." He daringly painted prosaic subjects and landscapes that showed the countryside of his native Franche-Comté. A rebel, he adopted the large-scale format traditionally reserved for history paintings. In *The Angelus* (1857–59) and *Gleaners* (1857), Jean-François Millet (1814–1875) also rendered scenes of humble rural life, the reality closest to his own experience. There was a fresh sensitivity to nature, even among the established bemedaled and recognized artists of the Academy. Classical equilibrium predominated in the work of Jean-Baptiste-Camille Corot (1796–1875). A few mythological figures still appear, but he painted trees that were very close to realistic renderings, where air seems to rustle through the leaves. The light in these paintings is no longer that of the studio, even though the final versions of his works were executed based on *plein air* sketches and drawings. There was a longing to quit Paris, the hotbed of urban corruption, and seek out close contact with nature.

"Never lose the first impression that moves you."
Jean-Baptiste-Camille Corot.

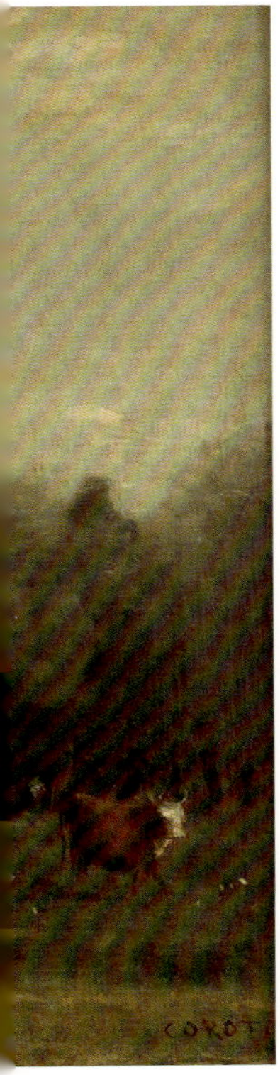

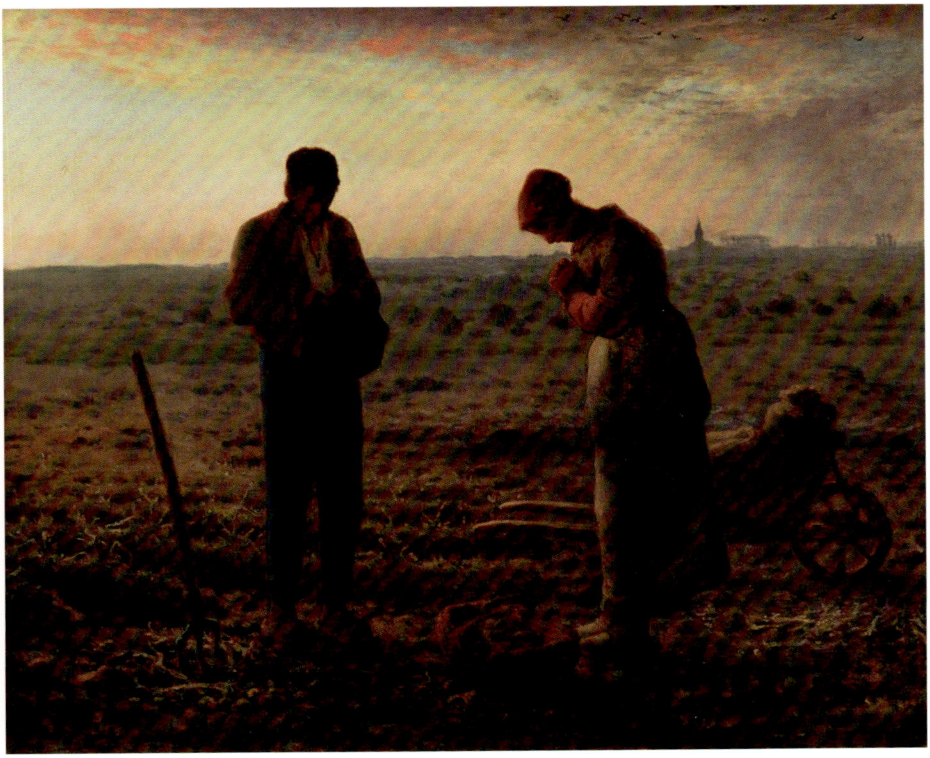

"Make the trivial serve as an expression of the sublime."

Jean-François Millet.

Jean-François Millet
The Angelus
1857–59
Oil on canvas,
21 ⅞ × 26 in.
(55.5 × 66 cm)
Musée d'Orsay, Paris

By mid-century the forest of Fontainebleau was accessible by carriage or train. It offered clean air and a fresh vision of the world. Artists flocked there to paint studies of rocks, foliage, trees, and picturesque details. A small coterie of devotees, known as the Fontainebleau or Barbizon school, gathered in the village. Sometimes taking up full-time residence, or boarding at the Auberge Ganne, Jean-François Millet, Théodore Rousseau (1812-1867), Constant Troyon (1810-1865), and Narcisse Díaz de la Peña (1807-1876) relished the simple life and closeness to nature. They felt no need of any narrative pretext for their paintings. A forest clearing or border (de la Peña), racing dogs or laboring oxen (Troyon), a pond surrounded by lofty oaks in Apremont (Rousseau) were fully satisfying subjects for these painters. Charles François Daubigny (1817-1878) initially moved to Barbizon in 1860, and subsequently to Auvers-sur-Oise. He was the first artist to execute an entirely *plein air* painting with no finishing in his studio. The future impressionists followed in the footsteps of these pioneering painters who had a fresh perspective on the French landscape. With the end of the upheavals of the Franco-Prussian war in 1870, these artists took the first steps in a new direction.

LE BOTIN

It is said that Daubigny stretched his canvas between posts on the beach at Villerville to better capture the passage of the clouds above. He was the first to execute paintings entirely outdoors. Fascinated by aquatic scenes, he built *Le Botin*, a studio boat, in 1857, so he could meander and paint at his leisure along the river banks. It was a brilliant notion that inspired Claude Monet.

EXILE TO LONDON

During the Franco-Prussian War in 1870, Monet and Pissarro decided to take their chances in London. Scornful of the Pre-Raphaelitism that dominated the art scene, they spent their days at the National Gallery, discovering the atmospheric landscapes of Turner, Constable, and Bonington. Just as the British school of landscape painting, which tended toward sensitive realism, had captivated Géricault and Delacroix, it proved a revelation to Monet and Pissarro.

They encountered Daubigny, who was also in exile there. He introduced them to the art dealer Paul Durand-Ruel (1831–1922), also fleeing war-torn France. Durand-Ruel organized painting exhibitions in a gallery he leased on New Bond Street. He soon took an interest in the two young painters and decided to support them. As Monet recollected forty years later: "Thanks to Daubigny and Durand-Ruel, my few friends and I didn't starve to death on the sidewalks of London in 1870: these are things you don't forget" (Claude Monet, letter to Moreau-Nélaton, 1924).

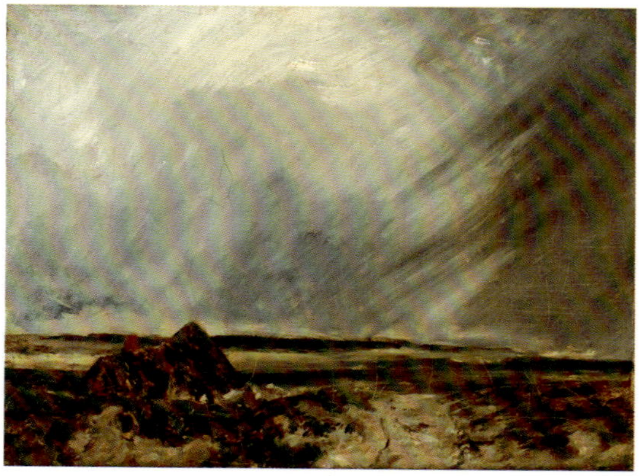

Richard Parkes Bonington
A Heathland
1825–26
Oil on canvas, 21 ⅞ × 14 ⅜ in. (29 × 36.5 cm)
Musée Fabre, Montpellier

John Constable
Study of the Sky
1806
Gray paper, pastel, 7 × 4 ⅝ in. (18 × 11.8 cm)
Musée du Louvre, Paris

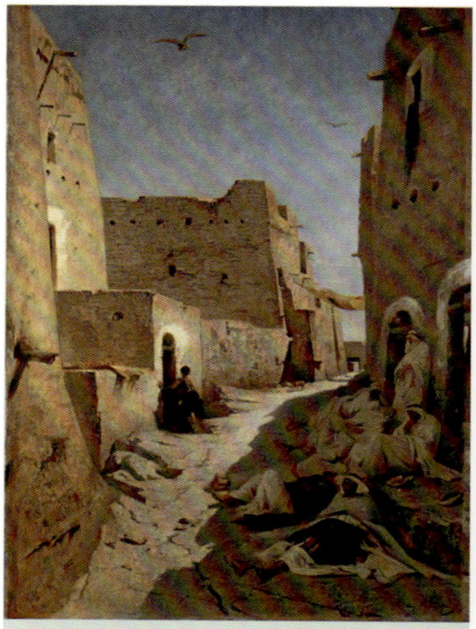

Eugène Fromentin
The Bab-El-Gharbi Road, Laghouat
1859
Oil on canvas, 4 ft. 8 in. × 3 ft. 4 ¼ in. (1.42 × 1.02 m)
Musée de la Chartreuse, Douai

LIGHT FROM DISTANT LANDS

During the Second Empire, the French colonial domain came to encompass large parts of North and sub-Saharan Africa and Asia. A group of adventurous artists, known as "Orientalists," left France to explore these new worlds, searching for picturesque subjects and passionate emotions. Although their smooth, highly finished works were academic in style, they brought back a new sense of warm, saturated light, a far cry from the dim studios in Paris. Back home, they set to work, sketchbooks in hand. As horizons broadened, this fantasized foreign world became a specialty for some of these artists, such as Eugène Fromentin.

"You have to know countryside to paint it. I know my own countryside, so that's what I paint. This forest floor is my home, that river is the Loue. Visit the place, and you'll see my painting."

Gustave Courbet.

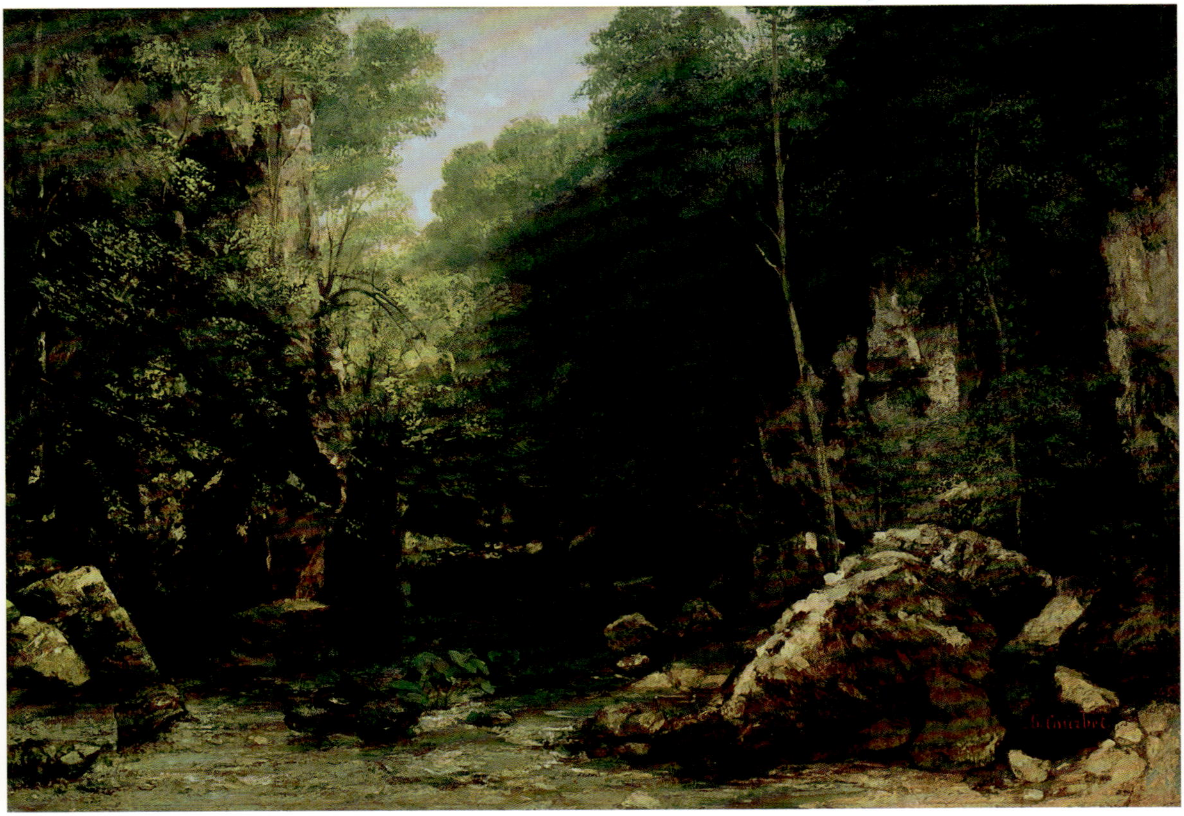

Gustave Courbet
The Black Stream, also known as
The Stream of the Puits Noir
1865
Oil on canvas, 3 ft. 1 in. × 4 ft. 5 ¼ in. (94 × 135 cm)
Musée d'Orsay, Paris

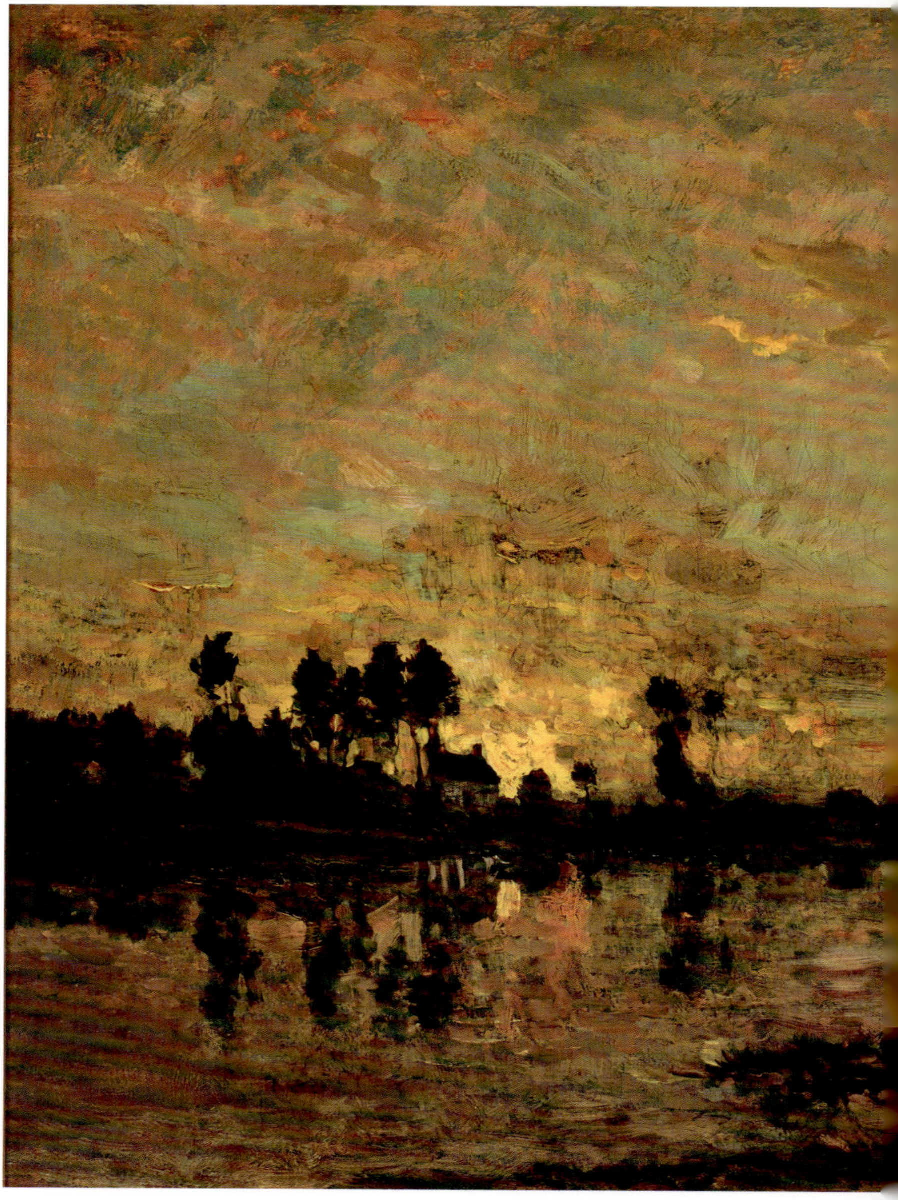

Charles François Daubigny
Sunset on the Oise
1865
Oil on wood (mahogany),
15 ⅜ × 26 ⅜ in. (39 × 67 cm)
Musée des Beaux-Arts, Angers

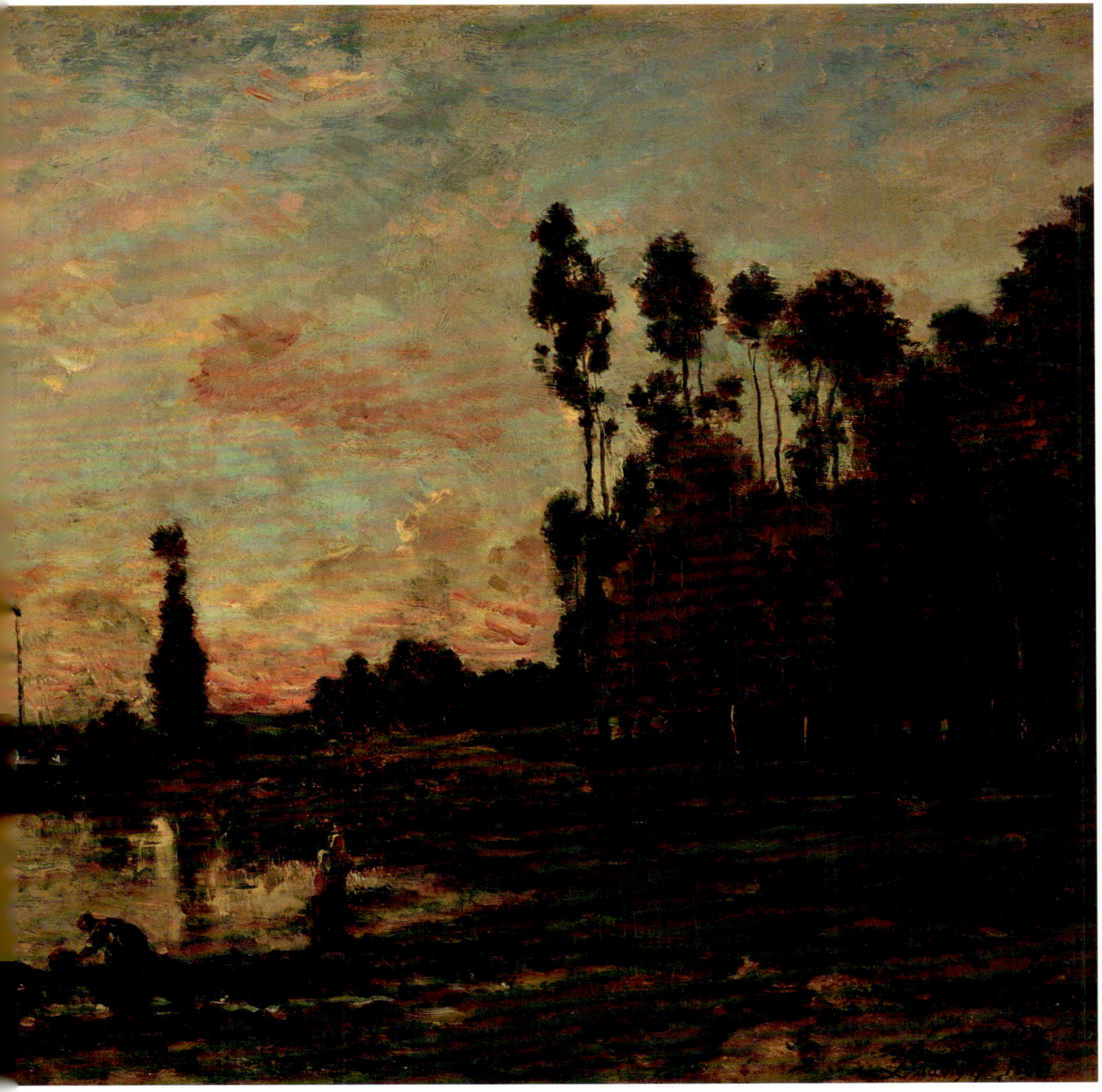

Sunset on the Oise

Charles François Daubigny, 1865

Recognized by the establishment, Charles François Daubigny (1817–1878) was close to the Barbizon painters for a while. He later distanced himself from them and laid claim to a new vision of landscape that heralded impressionism.

The water's edge and the sea were already among Daubigny's favorite subjects. He was the first to consider a painting executed entirely outdoors as a finished work.

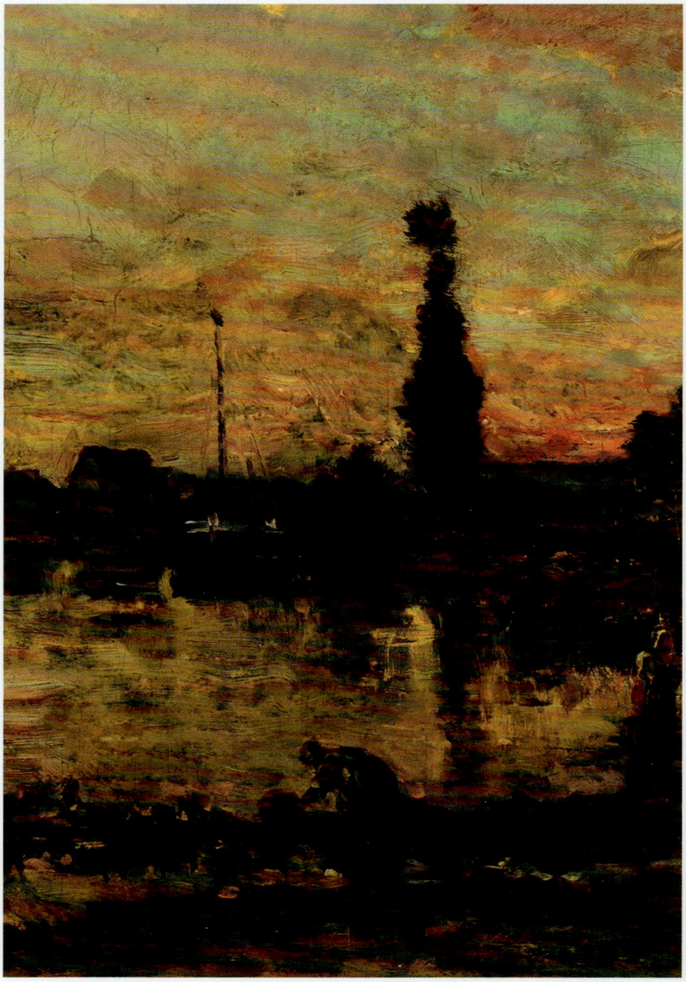

DAUBIGNY, FRIEND OF THE FUTURE IMPRESSIONISTS

A member of the Salon's jury, Charles François Daubigny took an interest in the next generation of artists and successfully got Bazille, Monet, Pissarro, Renoir, Degas, Sisley, and Morisot accepted to the 1868 Salon. Even though the superintendent of the École des Beaux-Arts, the Count of Nieuwerkerke, expressed his outrage, Émile Zola—a supporter of Daubigny's—declared: "Traditional landscape is dead, slain by life and reality" (minutes of the Salon, 1868). When Monet and Sisley were rejected by later Salons, Daubigny resigned, soon followed by his highly respected friend, Corot. Exiled to London during the war of 1870, Daubigny encountered Pissarro and Monet, whom he supported and introduced to the art dealer Durand-Ruel. Returning to France after the conflict, he welcomed them with open arms to his house in Auvers-sur-Oise, as he did Cézanne the following year.

"It is impossible to mistake the time of day when Monsieur Daubigny paints; he is a painter of the moment, of a fleeting impression."

Odilon Redon, *La Gironde*, 1868.

Clearly visible, free, and fluid, his brushstrokes convey the movements and vividly colorful effects of the sky. The act of creation is clearly affirmed, and proclaimed with a freedom that is striking when compared with the smooth, polished finish of the academic painters. Impressionism is imminent.

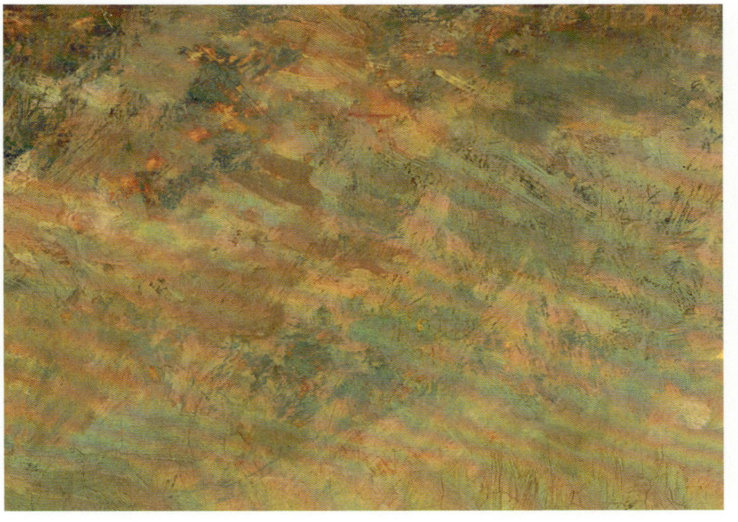

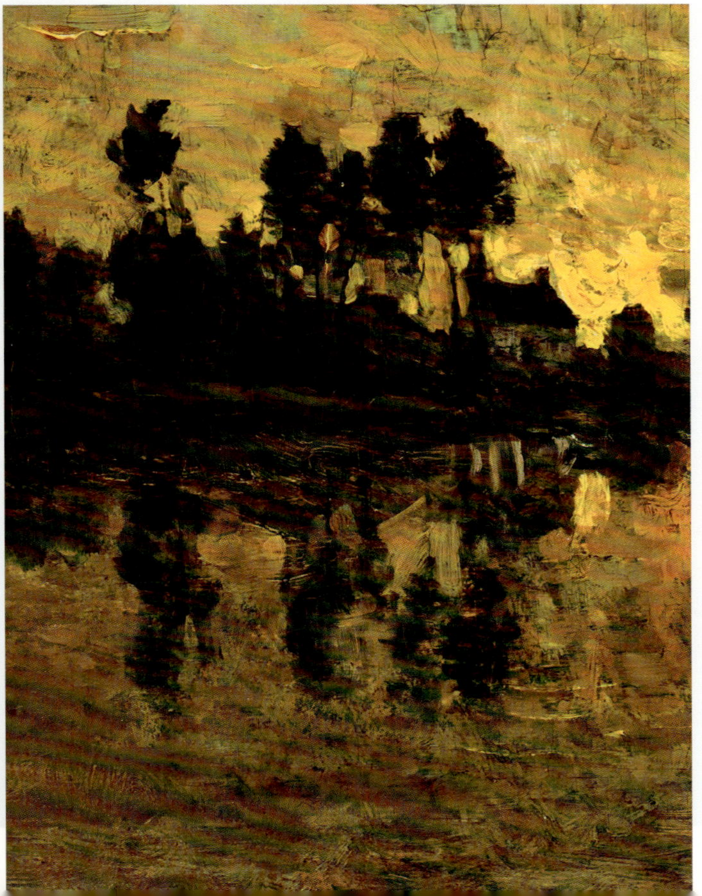

The essence of this painting is the artist's close attention to the reflections of trees mirrored in water. These effects later became a central theme of impressionism.

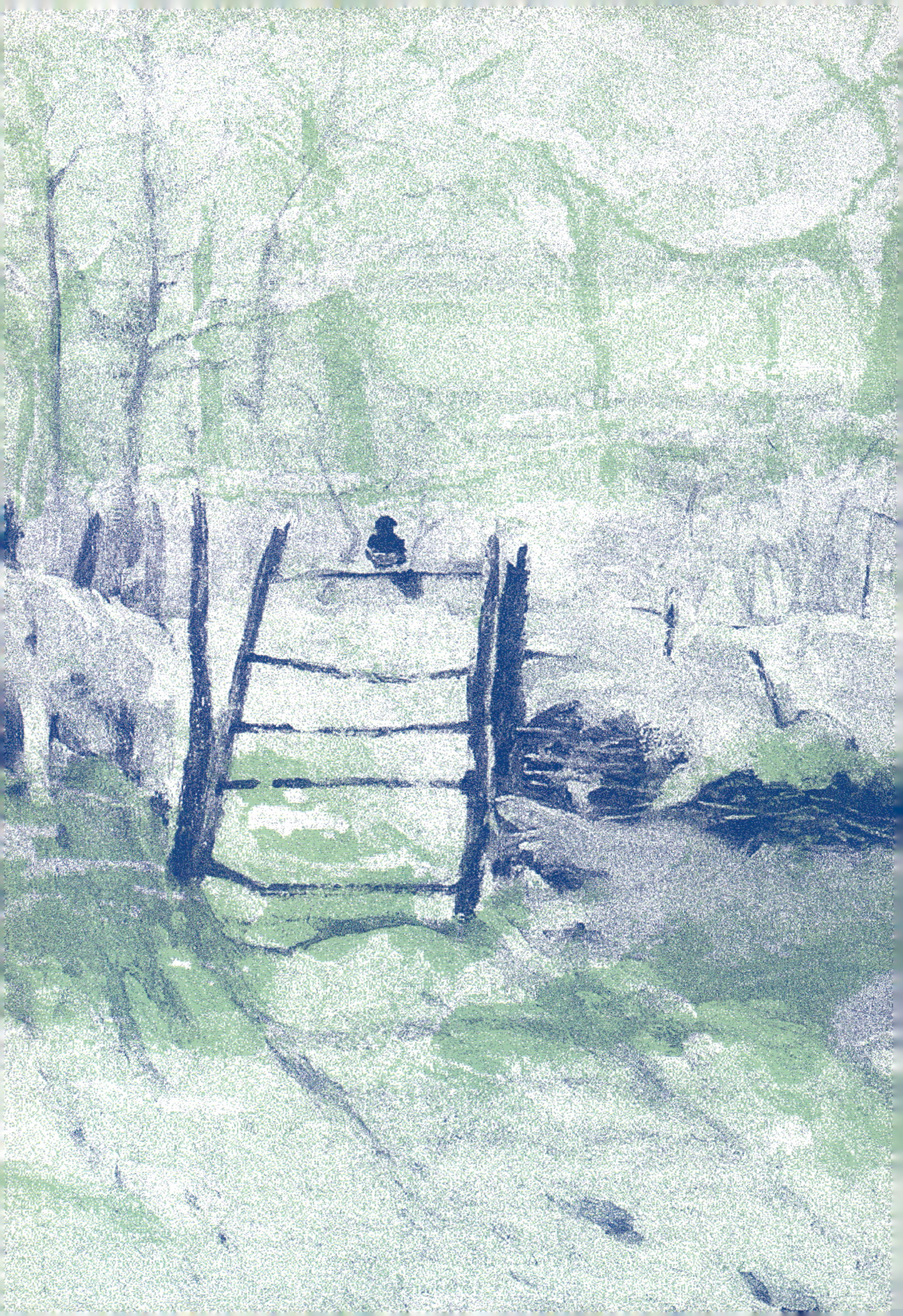

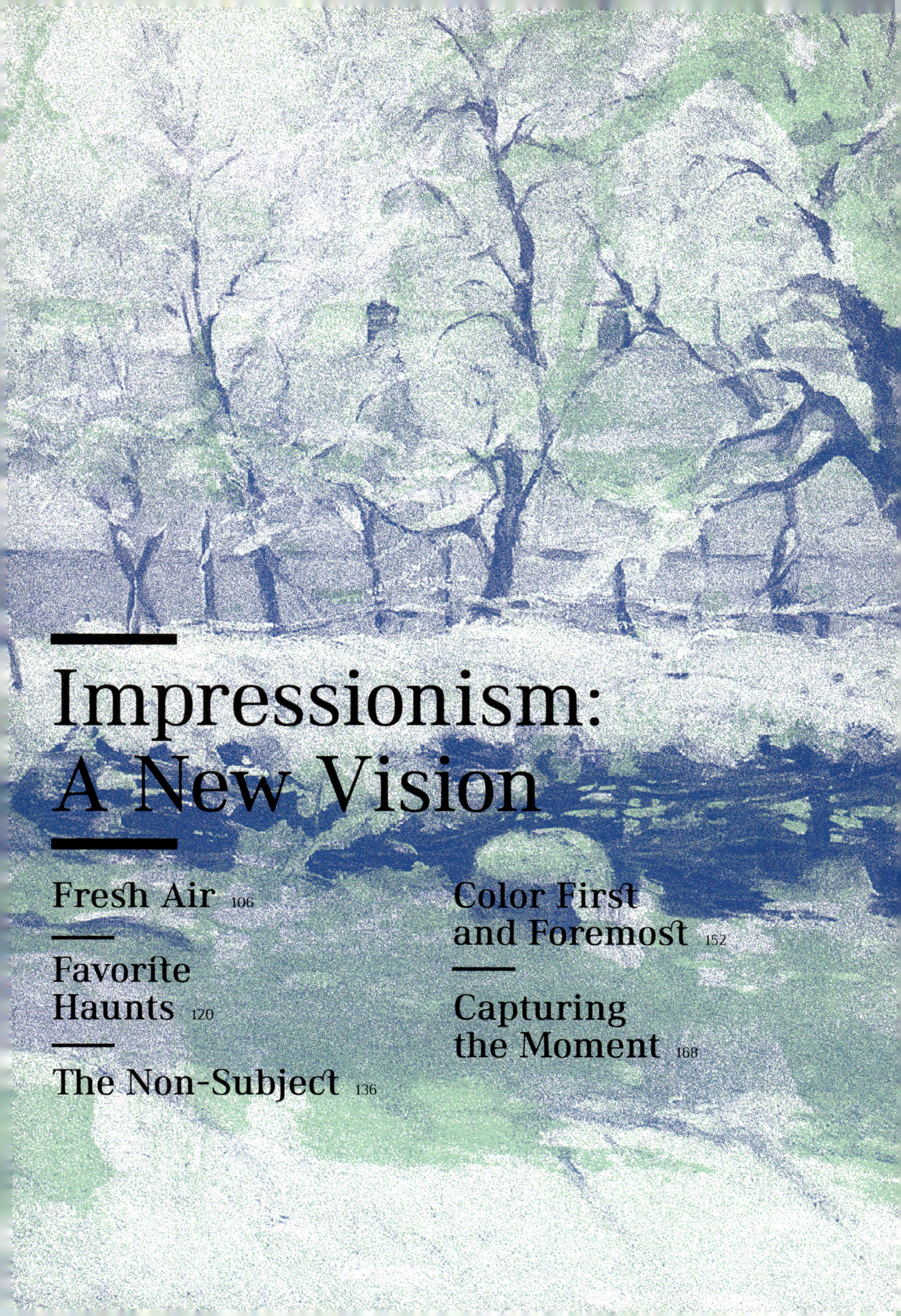

Impressionism: A New Vision

Fresh Air 106

Favorite Haunts 120

The Non-Subject 136

Color First and Foremost 152

Capturing the Moment 168

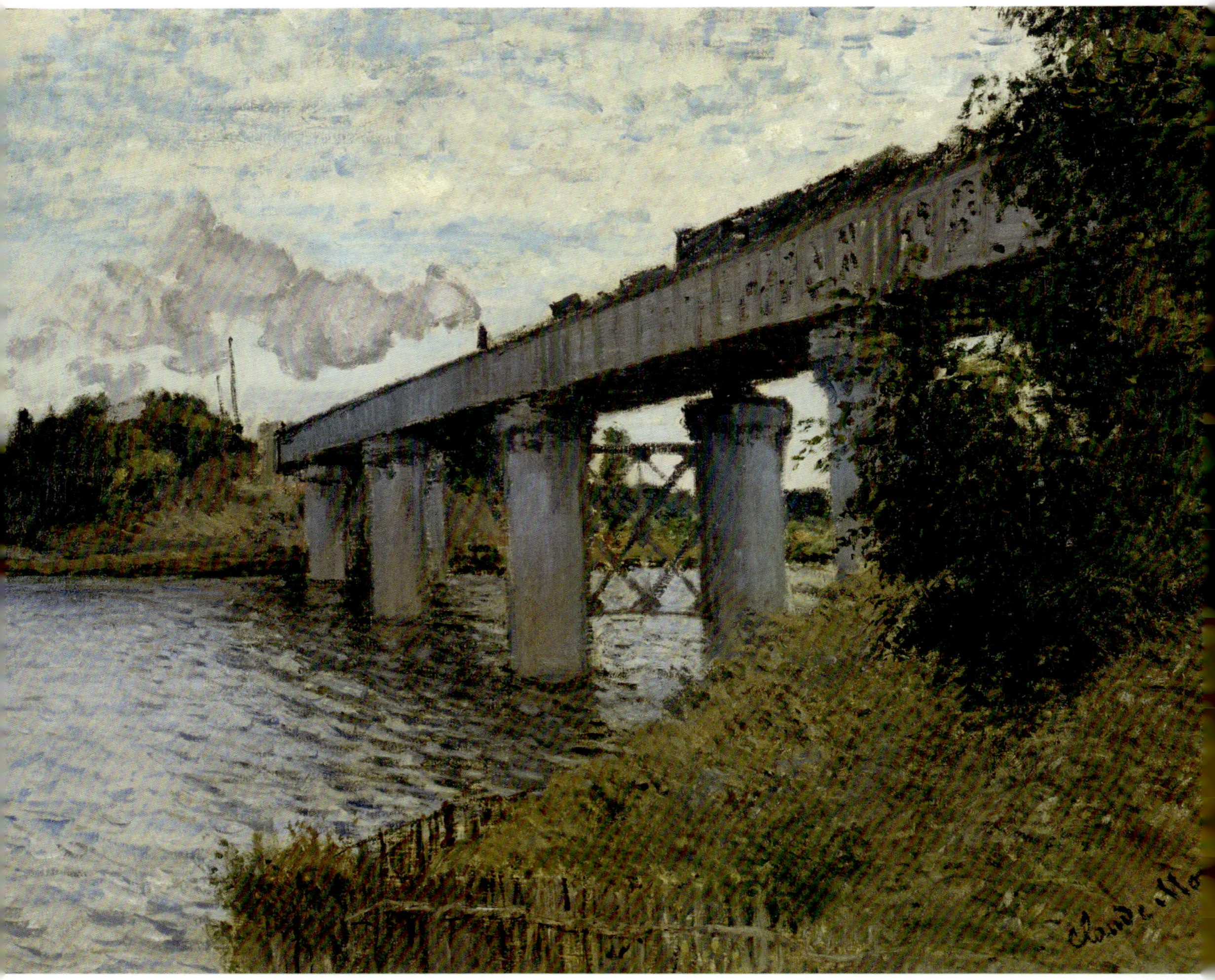

Claude Monet
The Railway Bridge at Argenteuil (Val-d'Oise)
1873–74
Oil on canvas, 21 ⅝ × 28 ⅜ in. (55 × 72 cm)
Musée d'Orsay, Paris

Fresh Air

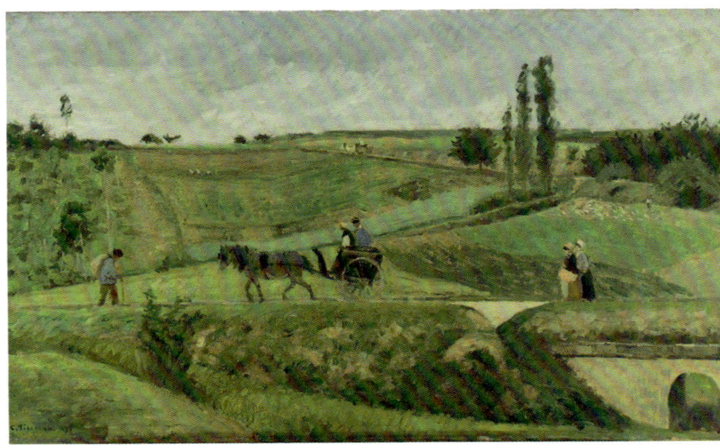

Camille Pissarro
The Road to Ennery
1874
Oil on canvas, 1 ft. 9 ½ in. × 3 ft.
(55 × 92 cm)
Musée d'Orsay, Paris

"Let's get away from here! This place is bad for us–there's no authenticity." This was how the young Claude Monet, newly arrived in Paris, viewed his surroundings. He was trying to lure Sisley, Renoir, and Bazille, his fellow students in Gleyre's studio, to join him in *plein air* painting. It was a radical notion to set up easels outside to study the movements of the clouds and variations in light. Providence had provided Monet with visionary mentors early in his career. He had already ventured into *plein air* painting on the beaches of Normandy with Boudin (1824-1898) and Jongkind (1819-1891). Weary of studying plaster casts and academic subjects, the four friends decided to pursue their explorations in the leafy outdoors. In March 1863, they set their sights on Fontainebleau, a near-wilderness that lay close to Paris. The Barbizon school had already earned the forest a reputation in the art world, but these four young men had revolutionary ambitions. They worked with a daringly different palette, devoid of the brownish "chicory juice" that dimmed the canvases of their

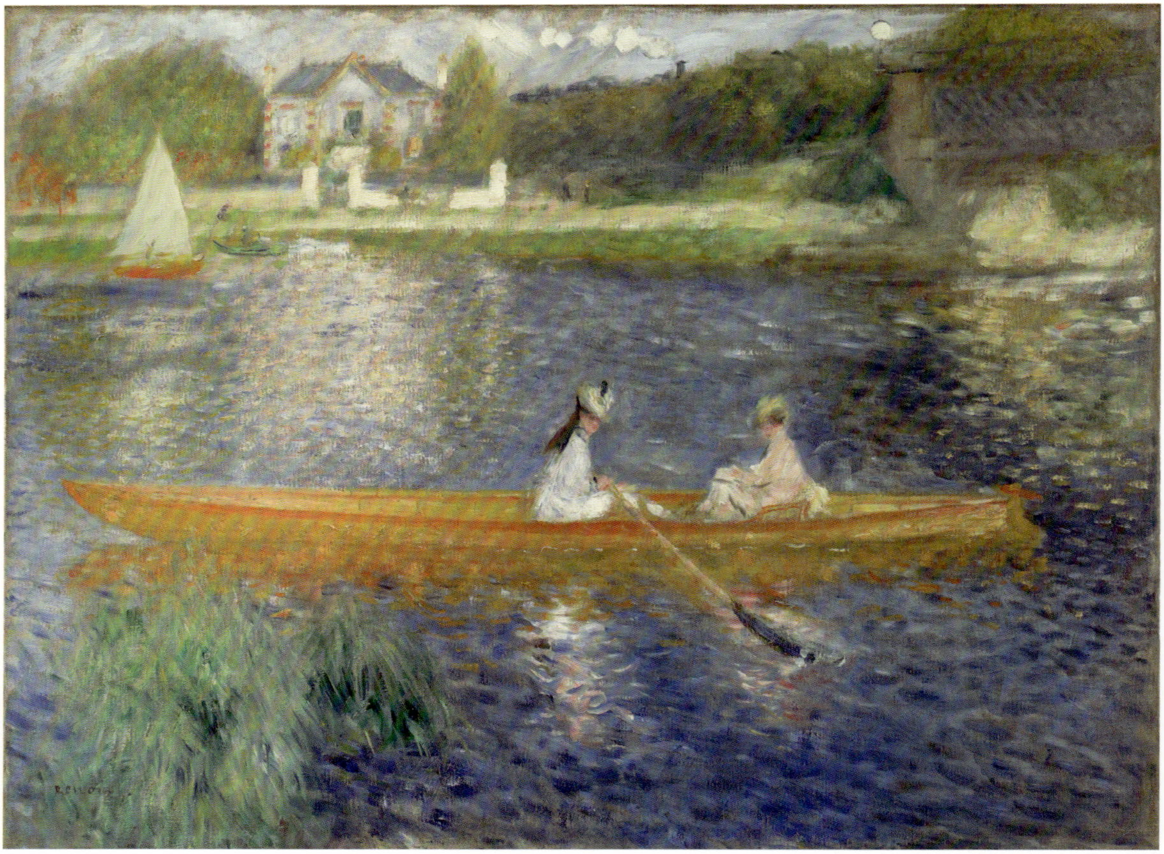

Auguste Renoir
The Skiff
1875
Oil on canvas, 2 ft. 4 in. × 3 ft. (71 × 92 cm)
National Gallery, London

elders. Renoir and Sisley visited the villages of Chailly and Marlotte, and Monet, Bazille, and Pissarro eagerly joined them. These became favorite spots, but the painters also enlarged the scope of their travels. Despite family disputes, Monet returned to paint on the Normandy coast, inviting his friend Bazille to join him in the spring of 1864; Courbet also came in 1865. Eventually, most of the future impressionists found themselves on the banks of the Seine, where river regattas and Sunday outings provided inexhaustible sources of inspiration. Lifelong friends, united in their artistic experimentation, the young painters gathered around Manet for conversations in the Café Guerbois. They encouraged each other, taking the train out from Paris to paint in Argenteuil or Chatou, enthusiastically lining up their easels side by side, immersed in nature. Following the Franco-Prussian War in 1870, which claimed Bazille's life, most members of the group chose to live outside Paris for financial as well as artistic reasons; they longed to be close to the natural world. Monet chose Argenteuil; Pissarro went to Pontoise, and Sisley to Louveciennes. Renoir alone remained steadfastly in Paris, loyal to Montmartre.

Édouard Manet
Monet Painting in His Studio-Boat
1874
Oil on canvas, 2 ft. 8 ¼ in. × 3 ft. 3 ½ in.
(82 × 100 cm)
Neue Pinakothek, Munich

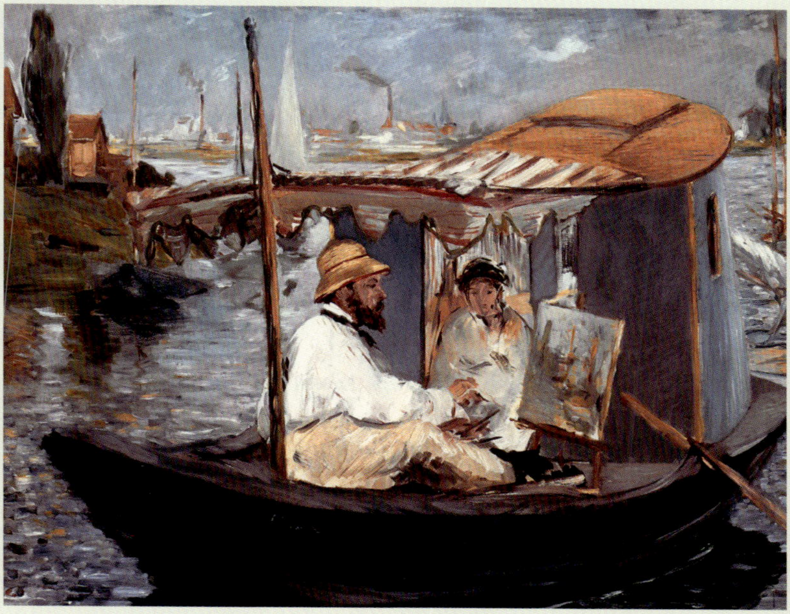

MONET AND HIS STUDIO-BOAT

Utterly devoted to painting, and longing to be at one with nature, Claude Monet lived in Argenteuil from 1871 until 1878. He purchased an old barge and converted it into a waterborne studio, following the example of his predecessor Daubigny and his *Botin*. Manet depicted his friend painting on the river. Camille, Monet's first wife, appears in the background. She died prematurely in 1879, aged just thirty-two.

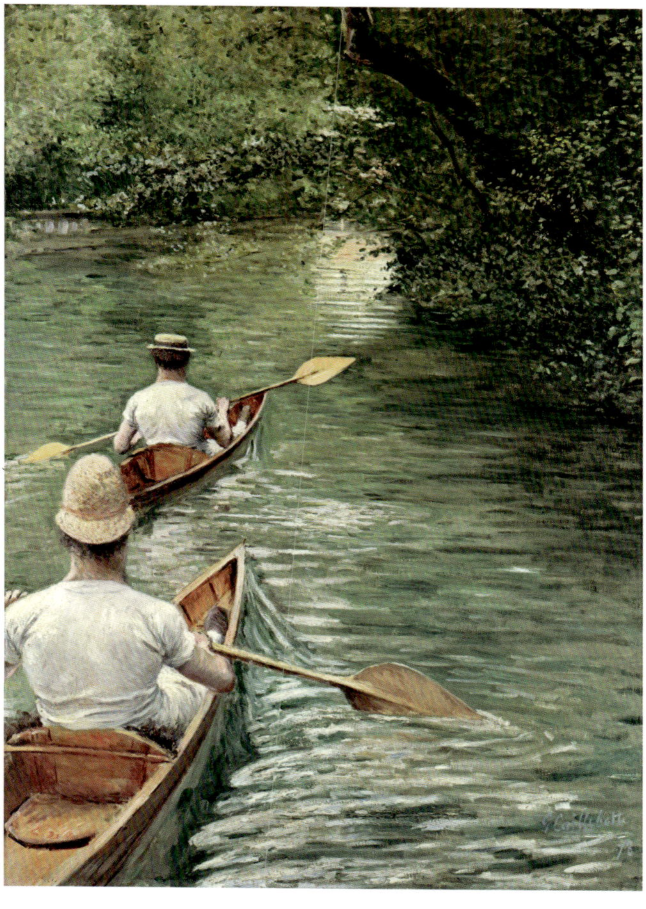

Gustave Caillebotte
The Canoe Paddlers
1878
Oil on canvas, 5 ft. 1 ¼ in. × 3 ft. 6 ¾ in.
(1.56 × 1.09 m)
Musée des Beaux-Arts, Rennes

An accomplished athlete, Gustave Caillebotte was more than a spectator at the regattas and boating trips that were so popular along the Seine. The almost photographic framing of this painting suggests the movement of the canoes as they glide through the water. The effort of the paddlers is skillfully emphasized by the dynamic diagonals of the composition.

FOUR YOUNG MEN OF THEIR TIME

Passionately devoted to studying painting, Claude Monet (1840–1926) was the son of a prosperous Le Havre merchant. In exchange for his father's financial support, he promised to enter the atelier of a prominent painter. Shortly after arriving in Paris, Monet started attending the unconventional Académie Suisse, as well as Gleyre's studio, but soon turned his back on these as well. Predictably, Monet's father cut off his allowance, condemning his son to poverty. Frédéric Bazille (1841–1870), the son of a prominent Montpellier family, came to Paris to study medicine as well as art. He intended to divide his time equally between the two fields, but he soon chose painting. He generously shared his parents' allowance to help support his friends. Alfred Sisley (1839–1899) was the son of a wealthy British merchant family residing in Paris, but he preferred art to business. He fell into financial difficulties, as did his father, who was bankrupted during the Franco-Prussian War. Auguste Renoir (1841–1919) was from a different social background, the son of a tailor and a dressmaker. He was just thirteen years old when he began his apprenticeship as a porcelain artisan, but he soon began to pursue his ambition to be a painter, despite the financial insecurity.

"Renoir brought bread from his house so we wouldn't starve. For a week we'd had no bread, no fire to cook with, no light—it was dreadful."
Monet, letter to Bazille, August 9, 1869.

"We don't eat every day, but I am happy anyway, because—when we are painting—Monet is good company.… I do almost nothing because I don't have many paints."
Renoir, letter to Bazille, autumn 1869.

LA FERME SAINT-SIMÉON

In 1854, Boudin adopted the habit of crossing the Seine estuary to settle in at the Auberge La Ferme Saint-Siméon on the road from Honfleur to Villerville. It was a tranquil, bucolic retreat—"Forty francs a month for room and board"—and it attracted a coterie of painters, including Corot, Jongking, Courbet, and Monet, who in turn encouraged Bazille to join them.

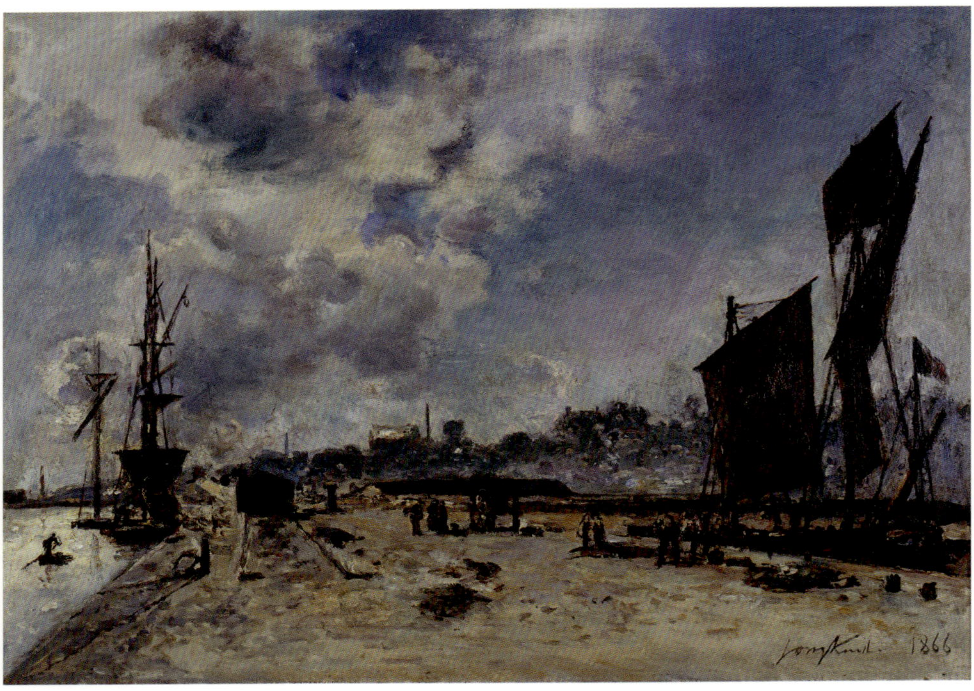

Johan Barthold Jongkind
Quai at Honfleur
1866
Oil on canvas,
12 ¾ × 18 ⅛ in.
(32.5 × 46 cm)
Musée d'Art Moderne André-Malraux, Le Havre
Olivier Senn Collection

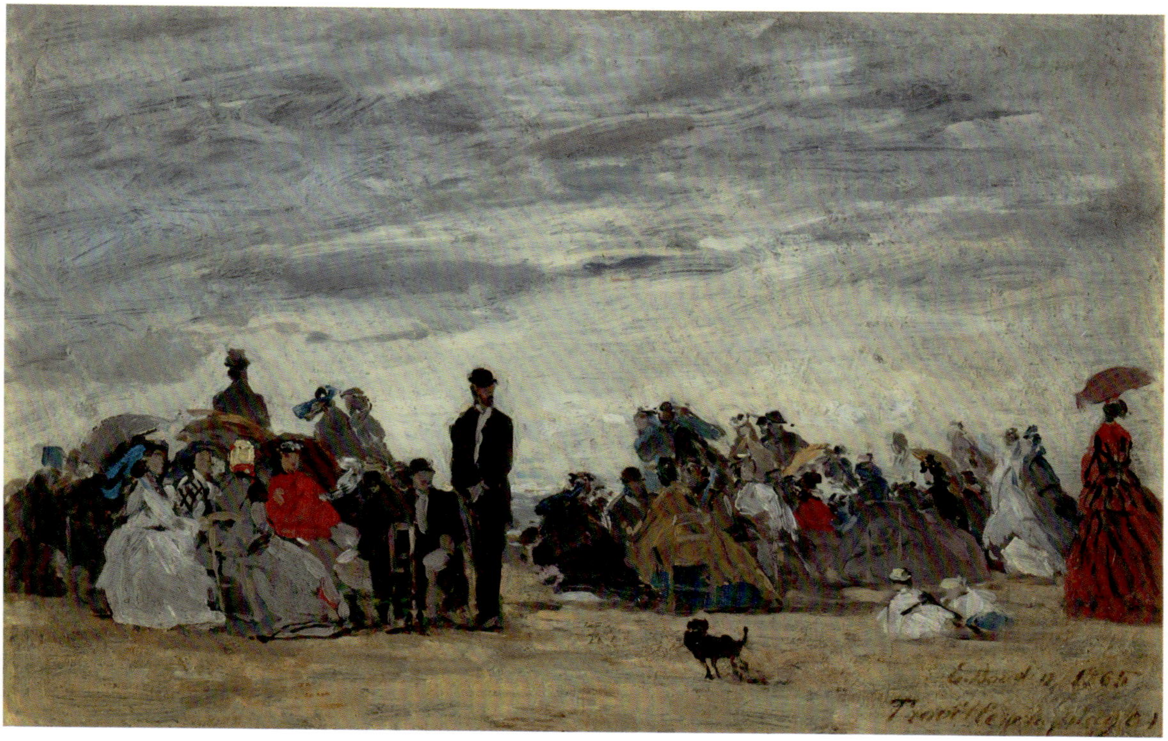

Eugène Boudin
The Beach at Trouville
1865
Oil on cardboard, 10 ⅜ × 16 in.
(26.5 × 40.5 cm)
Musée d'Orsay, Paris

AT SCHOOL ON THE BEACH

Initially a cabin boy on his father's boat, and later a stationer and framer in Le Havre, Eugène Boudin (1824–1898) used his spare time to paint the lively and fashionable crowds on the beach of Trouville. His shop displayed the works of artists passing through the area, including Jean-Baptiste Isabey, Troyon, and Millet. With Millet's encouragement, Boudin decided to devote himself exclusively to painting in 1854. His submissions to the Salon were eventually accepted, and he earned a degree of recognition. It was Boudin who, in 1862, introduced Trouville beach scenes, illustrating the newly discovered charms of seaside resorts. One day, Boudin came across caricatures by a seventeen year old by the name of Monet, and he encouraged the young man to set up his easel outdoors. Monet kept three of Boudin's drawings in his bedroom in Giverny, and he always expressed his unswerving gratitude for the guidance he had received in the early days of his career.

"At his insistence, I agreed to work with him en plein air. *I bought a box of paints and we left for Rouelles, without much confidence on my part. Boudin set up his easel and started to work. I studied him with a certain degree of apprehension. Then I looked more closely, and all of a sudden it was like a veil had been torn away. Now I understood; now I grasped what painting could be."*

Claude Monet, on Eugène Boudin (quoted by Jean Clay, in *Impressionism*, 1971).

FOCUS

Painting Side by Side

Lifelong friends who shared a commitment to artistic experimentation, the impressionists engaged in debate, visited each other, and traveled together to paint from nature.

Fontainebleau

Weary of academic studies, Monet, Renoir, Sisley, and Bazille followed in their elders' footsteps to Barbizon. They then turned their attention to the forest of Fontainebleau, where they painted their first *plein air* canvases together.

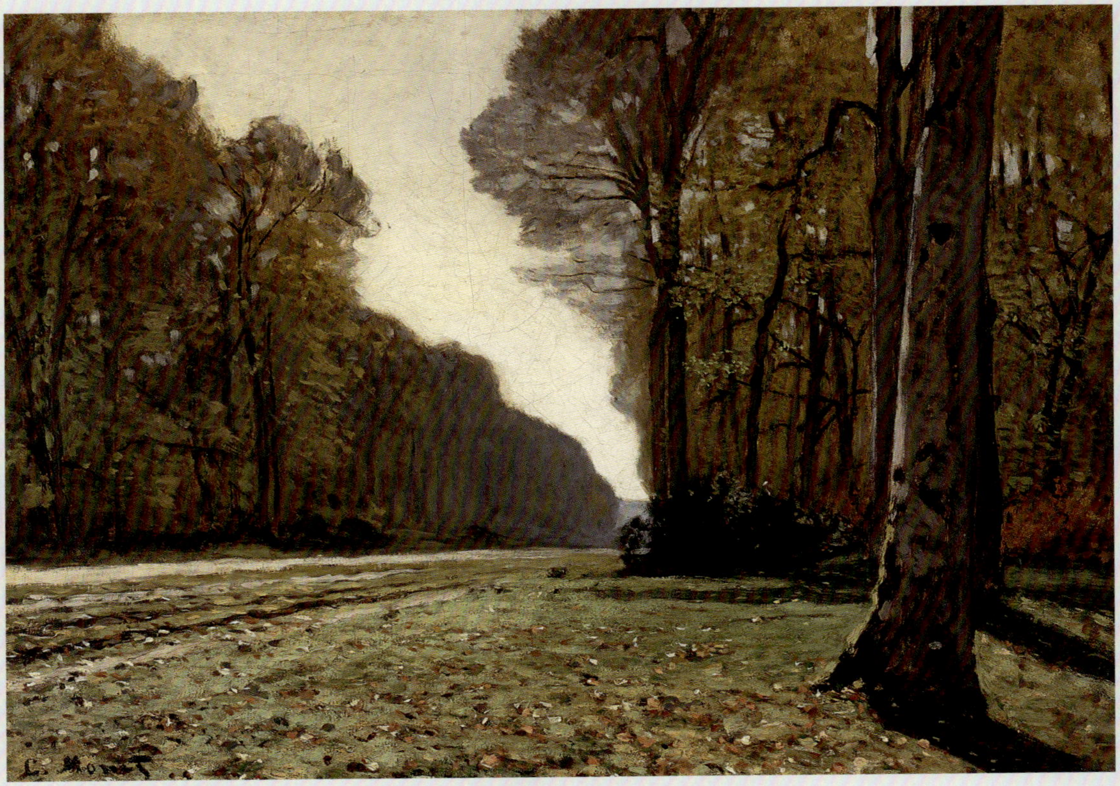

Claude Monet, *The Road from Chailly (Forest of Fontainebleau)*, c. 1865
Oil on canvas, 17 ⅛ × 23 ¼ in. (43.5 × 59 cm), Musée d'Orsay, Paris

Monet uses the vanishing point of this broad avenue to build his diagonal composition. Sensitive to the effects of light, he renders the halo of mist on the treetops, the shadows cast by the tree trunks, and the splashes of light on the ground.

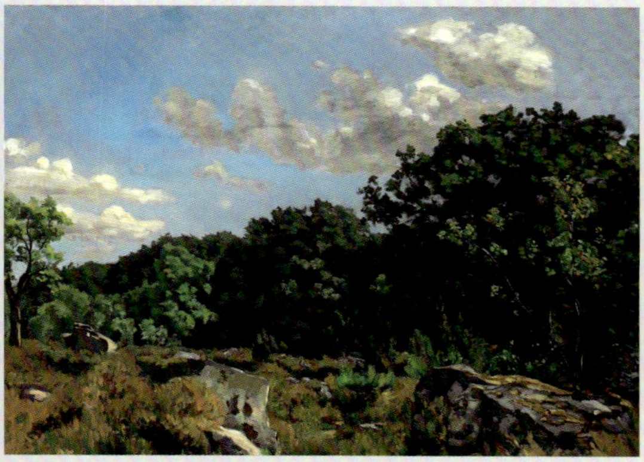

Frédéric Bazille, *Landscape in Chailly*, 1865
Oil on canvas, 2 ft. 8 in. × 3 ft. 3 ½ in. (81 × 100.3 cm)
The Art Institute of Chicago, Chicago

Bazille prefers a different point of view, ignoring perspective and focusing on the picturesque, wild aspect of the rocks in the foreground. The bright sunshine evokes the light of the south of France where he grew up.

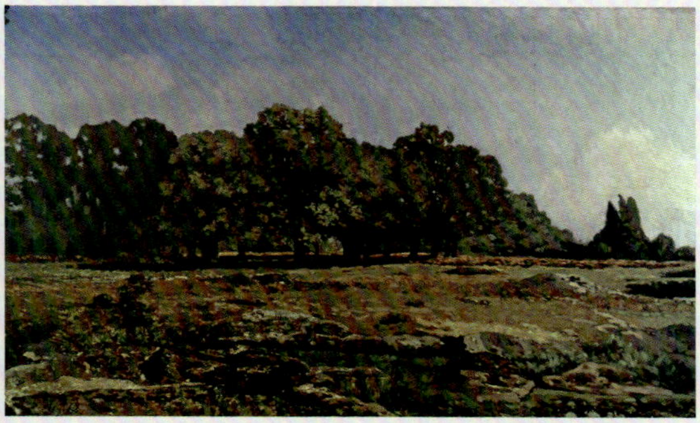

Alfred Sisley, *Grove of Chestnut Trees at La Celle-Saint-Cloud*, 1865
Oil on canvas, 4 ft. 2 ¾ in. × 6 ft. 10 in. (1.29 × 2.08 m)
Petit Palais, Musée des Beaux-Arts de la Ville de Paris, Paris

More likely painted at Fontainebleau than at La Celle-Saint-Cloud, this Sisley canvas seems less daring, more in the tradition of predecessors such as Théodore Rousseau and Corot.

La Grenouillère

Nicknamed "Trouville-sur-Seine," La Grenouillère was a popular bathing establishment beside the Seine, near Bougival. Accessible by train, it attracted enormous crowds on Sundays. Monet and Renoir came here to paint together, setting up their easels side by side. In these two paintings, the artists have chosen exactly the same point of view; only a few details indicate a different time of day.

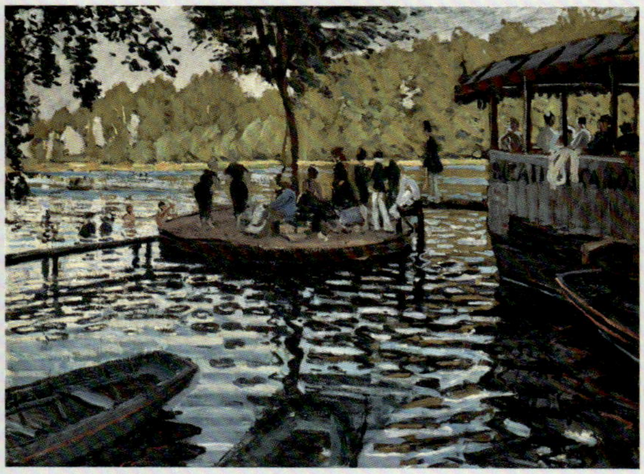

Claude Monet, *La Grenouillère*, 1869
Oil on canvas, 2 ft. 5 ½ in. × 3 ft. 3 ¼ in. (74.6 × 99.7 cm)
The Metropolitan Museum of Art, New York

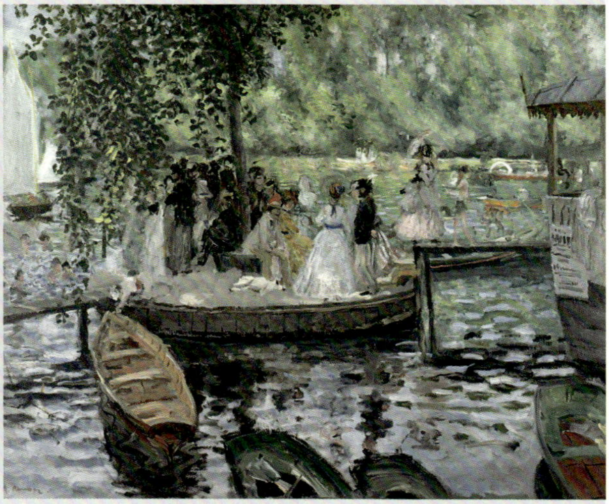

Auguste Renoir, *La Grenouillère*, 1869
Oil on canvas, 26 ⅛ × 31 ⅞ in. (66.5 × 81 cm)
National Museum, Stockholm

Monet at Home in Argenteuil

Between 1871 and 1878, Monet lived in Argenteuil, where he welcomed Manet one sunny day. Renoir turned up as well, and the guests spontaneously picked up their brushes. Renoir chose a small format, while Manet opted for a larger composition. The approach is slightly different, but both versions of the scene are tender and full of charm.

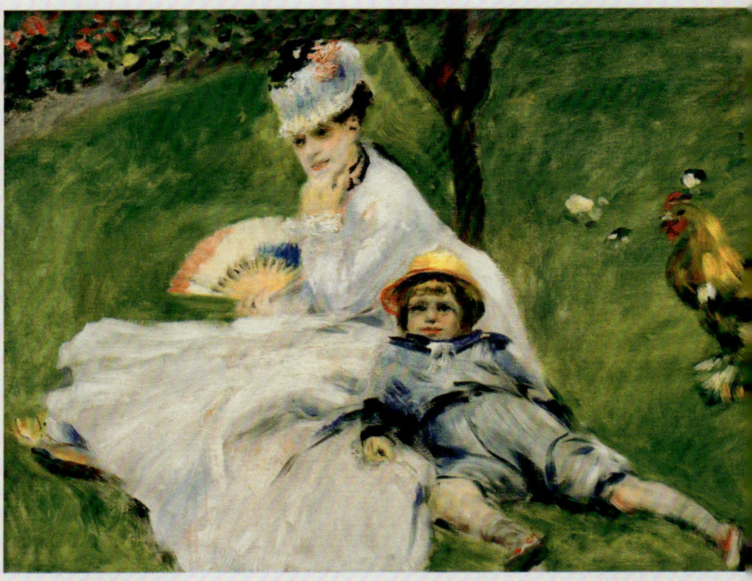

Auguste Renoir, *Camille Monet and Her Son Jean in the Garden in Argenteuil*, 1874
Oil on canvas, 19 ⅞ × 26 ¾ in. (50.4 × 68 cm)
National Gallery of Art, Washington, DC

The Promenade

In this case, Monet and Renoir did not work side by side, nor did they choose the same subject. But the similarities between these two works, which were painted several years apart, are striking. We see a grassy meadow scattered with poppies. A path winds its way downward, and two groups of figures are visible at different levels. In both paintings we see a return from a country outing in the heat of a summer afternoon.

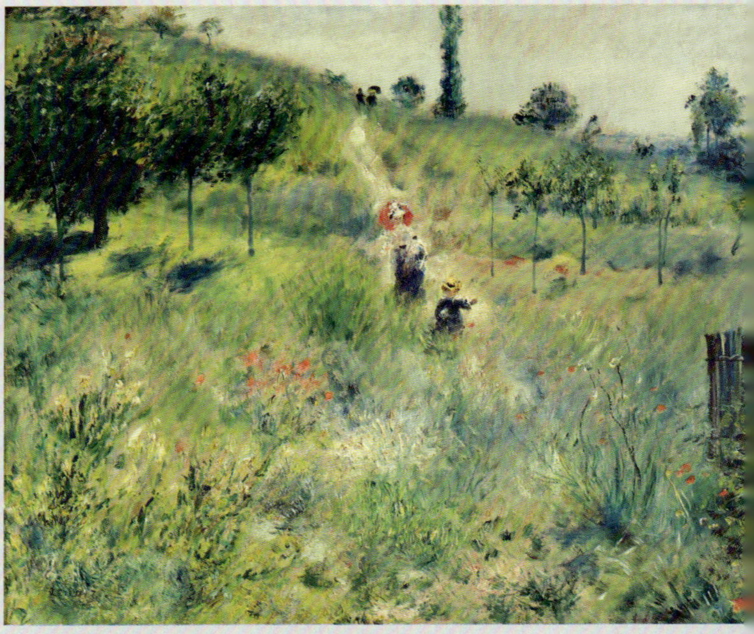

Auguste Renoir, *Path Leading through Tall Grass*, c. 1876–77
Oil on canvas, 23 ⅝ × 29 ⅛ in. (60 × 74 cm)
Musée d'Orsay, Paris

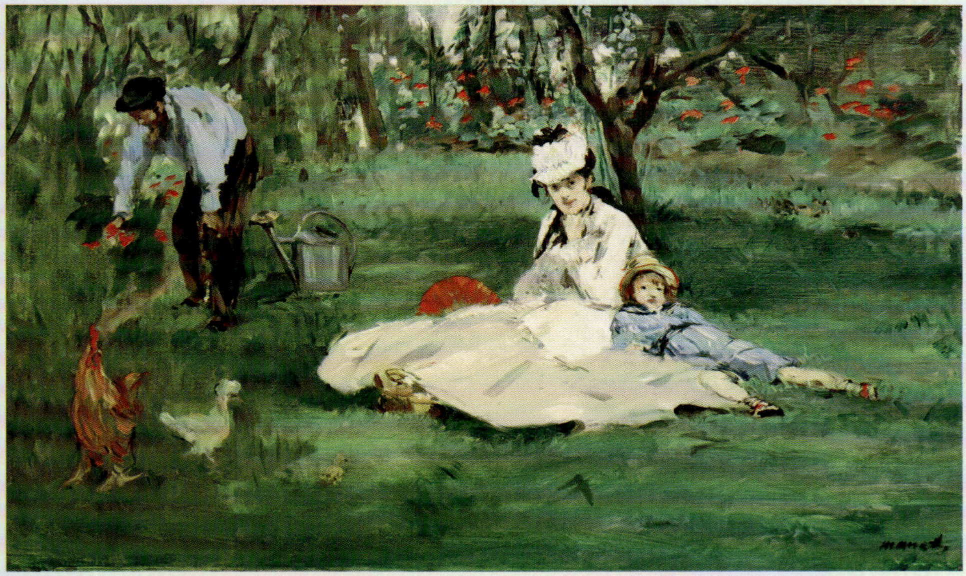

Édouard Manet, *The Monet Family in the Garden,* 1874
Oil on canvas, 2 ft. × 3 ft. 3 in. (61 × 99.7 cm)
The Metropolitan Museum of Art, New York

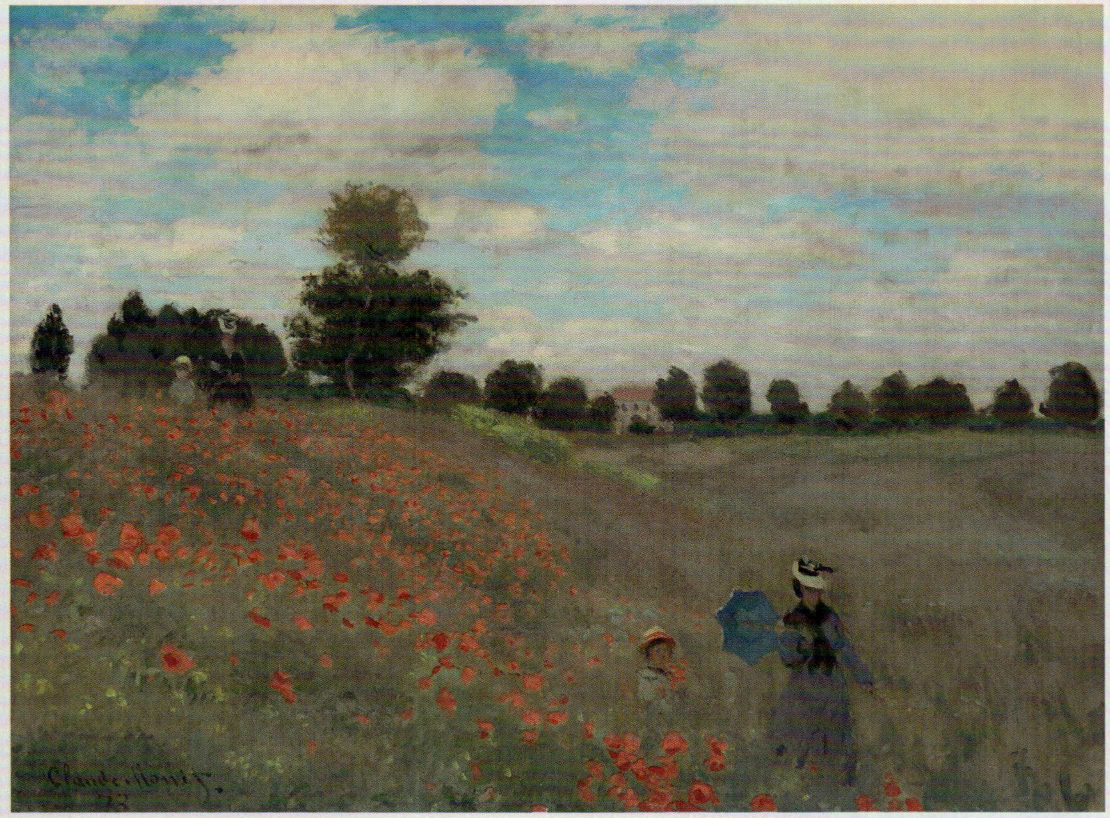

Claude Monet, *Poppies, near Argenteuil,* 1873
Oil on canvas, 19 ⅝ × 25 ⅝ in. (50 × 65 cm), Musée d'Orsay, Paris

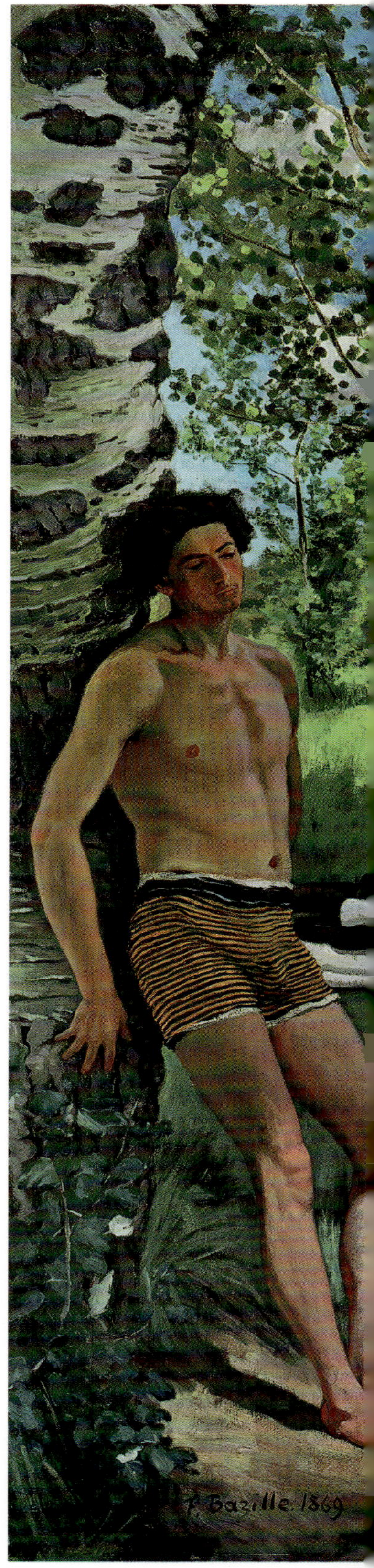

Frédéric Bazille
Summer Scene
1869
Oil on canvas, 5 ft. 1 ½ in. × 5 ft. 2 ¼ in.
(1.56 × 1.58 m)
Fogg Art Museum, Harvard University
Art Museums, Cambridge

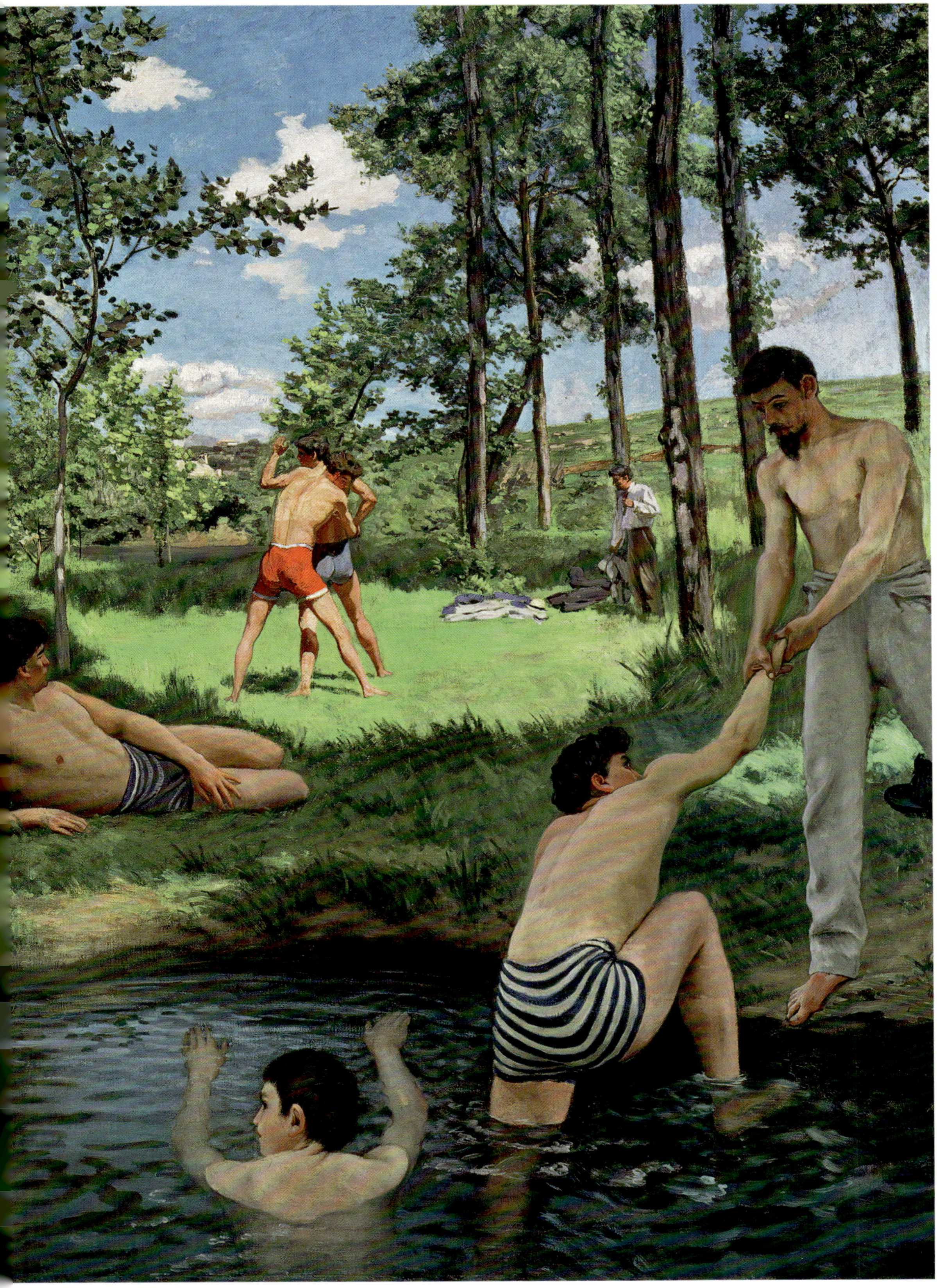

Summer Scene

Frédéric Bazille, 1869

Frédéric Bazille, a native of Montpellier, celebrates the joys of summer in this sensuous scene that evokes the delights of bathing and outdoor recreation.

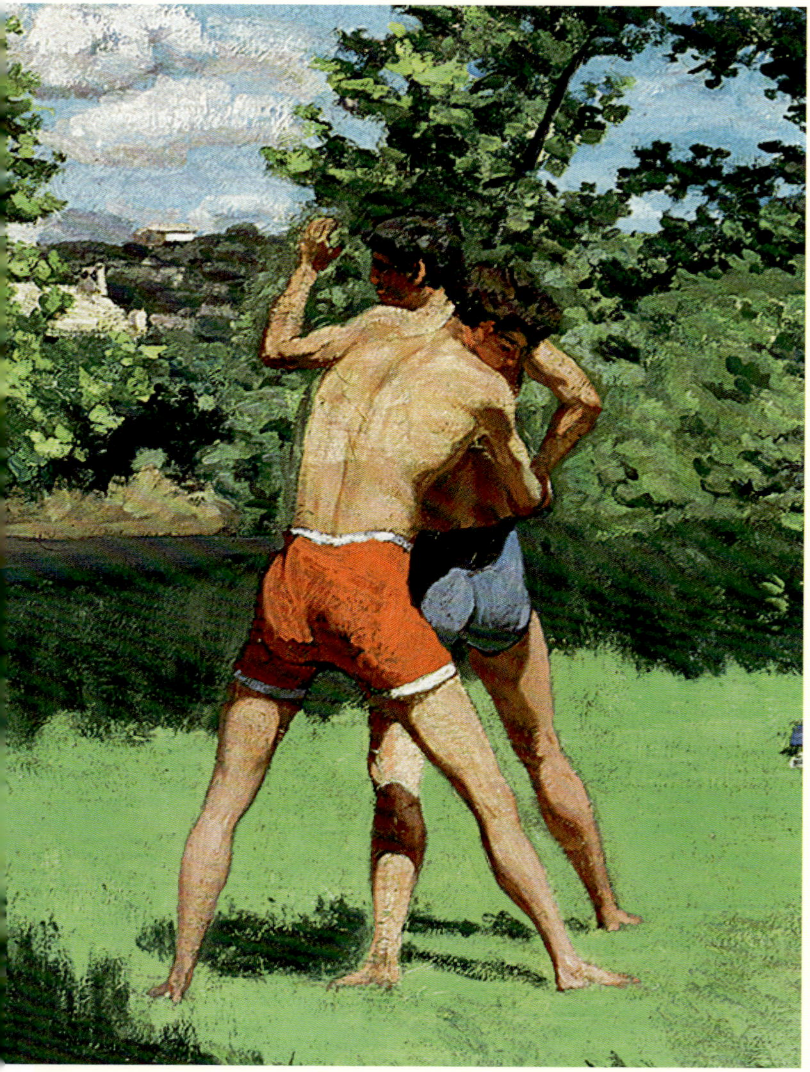

In the background, two friends practicing wrestling are rendered in patches of light and shadow under the powerful Mediterranean sun.

A DIP IN FRESH WATER

In the nineteenth century, people began to realize that they could enjoy the water outdoors as well as inside. Suddenly, sea bathing became widely popular, and Norman fishing villages and ports were transformed into chic seaside resorts. The fashion for recreational swimming also took hold on the banks of the Seine and other rivers. Attracted by the sense of freedom and communion with nature, the impressionists immediately embraced this *plein air* theme, which they adopted and explored exhaustively in their work.

"How long must we wait until eyes that have been clouded by tradition can bear to see light that is natural, clear, and true?"

Pierre Puvis de Chavannes, letter to Berthe Morisot, 1872.

With visible effort, this swimmer is hoisted out of the water. The artist shows the striped fabric of his bathing costume stretching across his body.

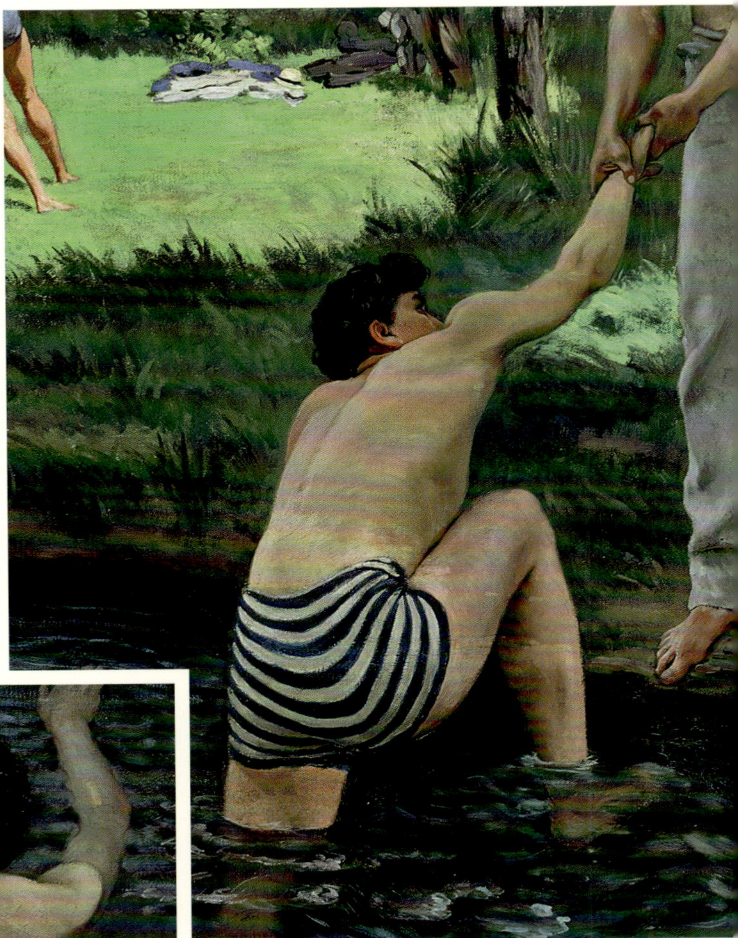

The artist captures the reflections in the pond. The water is not opaque; the swimmer's body can be glimpsed beneath its surface.

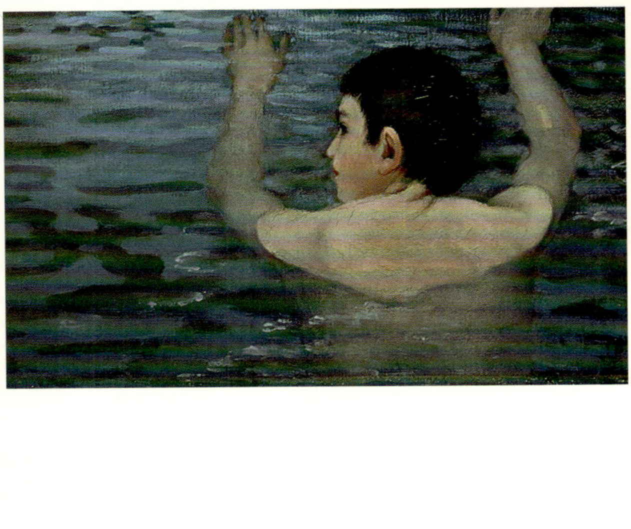

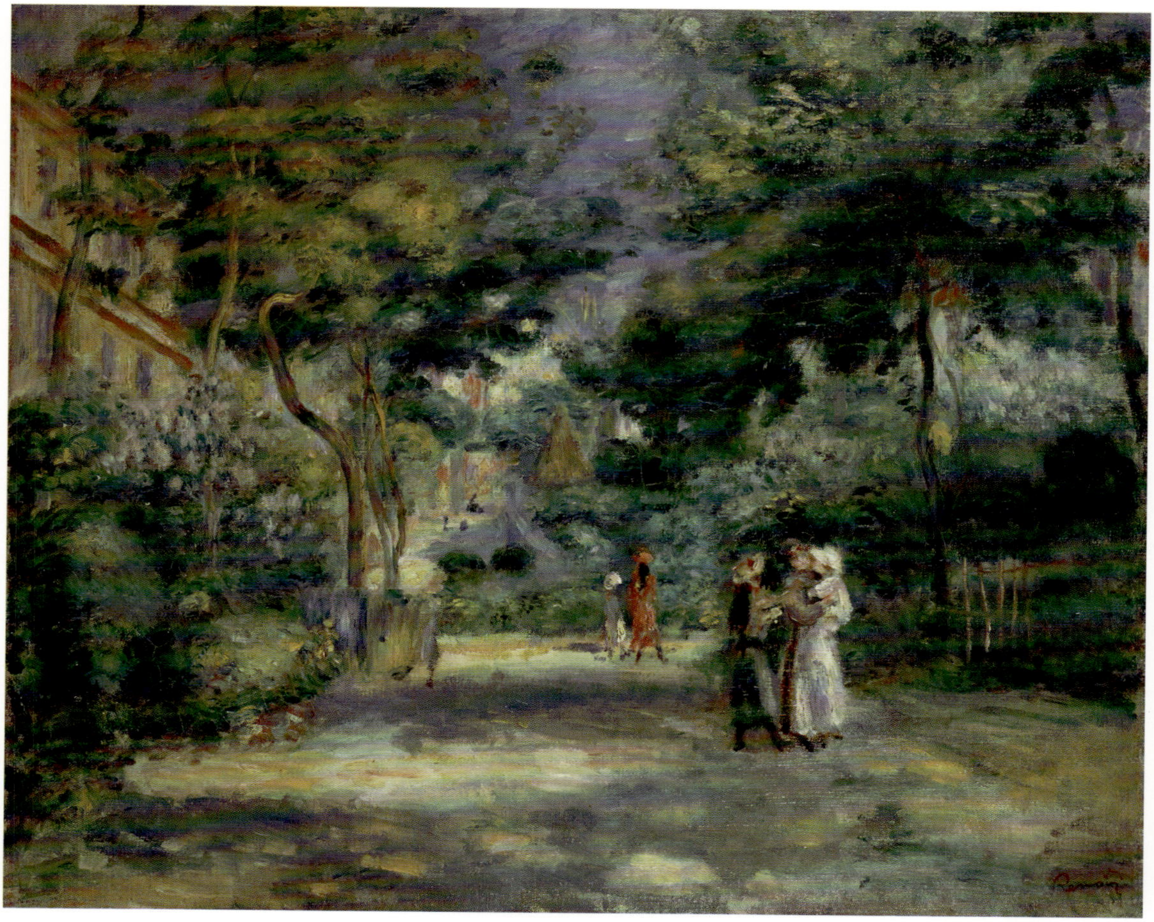

Auguste Renoir
The Gardens of Montmartre
c. 1890
Oil on canvas, 18 ⅛ × 21 ⅝ in.
(46 × 55 cm)
Ashmolean Museum, Oxford

Favorite Haunts

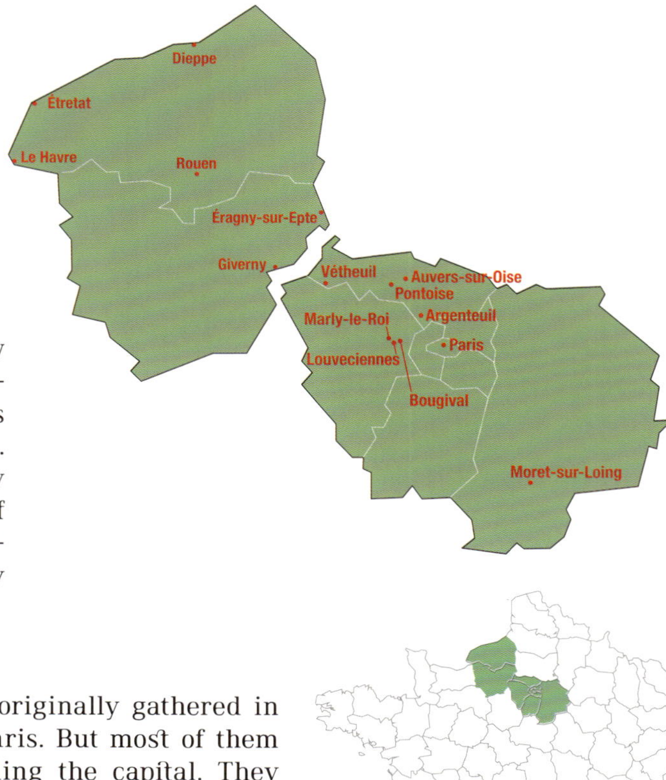

Always on the lookout for new perspectives, the impressionists selected favorite locations to serve as their open-air studios. Most chose to live on the Normandy coast or along the looping course of the Seine. Their landscapes proliferated, painted at every time of day and in every season.

Paris

The brotherhood of impressionists originally gathered in the cafés and open academies of Paris. But most of them soon moved out to areas surrounding the capital. They wanted to be close to their favorite subjects (landscapes, leisure activities, and the open air) and escape the high cost of urban living. Renoir was the exception: he remained in the vicinity of Montmartre before eventually moving to Collettes in Cagnes-sur-Mer in 1903.

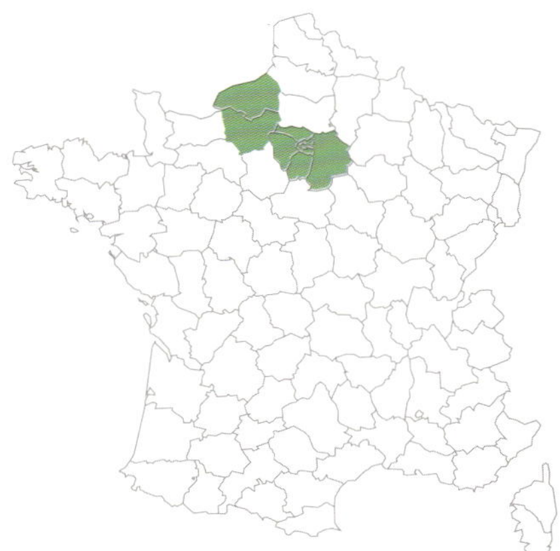

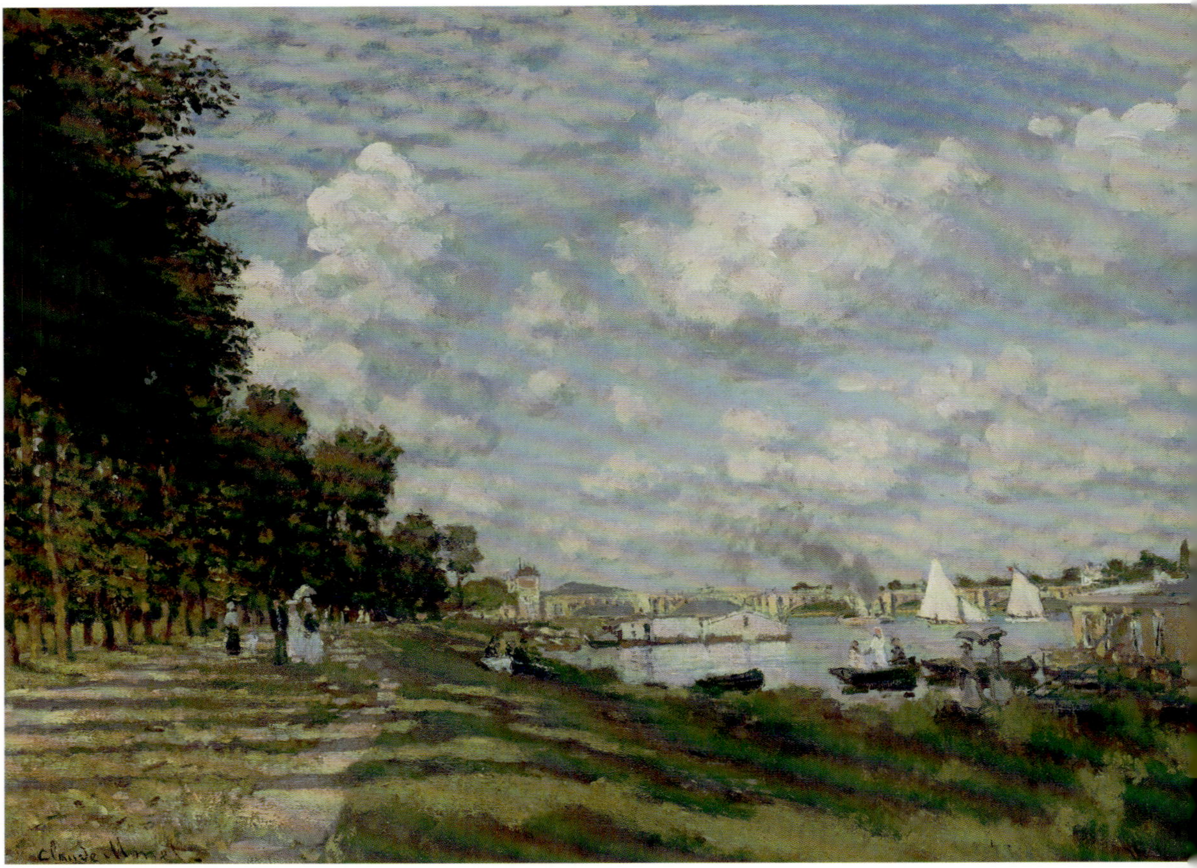

Claude Monet
The Basin at Argenteuil
c. 1872
Oil on canvas, 23 ⅝ × 31 ⅝ in.
(60 × 80.5 cm)
Musée d'Orsay, Paris

Argenteuil

This was the destination for all (or most of) the impressionists in the early 1870s. They could travel there–on a day's outing–by train from the Gare Saint-Lazare. Monet moved to Argenteuil in 1871; Renoir and Sisley often visited. Manet spent the summer with Monet in 1874, and they enjoyed practicing *plein air* painting together.

Louveciennes

Pissarro settled here in 1869. Exiled during the Franco-Prussian War in 1870, he found his studio pillaged, with over a thousand canvases destroyed upon his return. He painted numerous views of Louveciennes in the months following.

Éragny-sur-Epte

Pissarro settled here in 1884 and lived in the village until his death in 1903. He often invited his friends Monet, Paul Cézanne, Vincent Van Gogh, and Paul Gauguin to his garden, which became one of his favorite subjects.

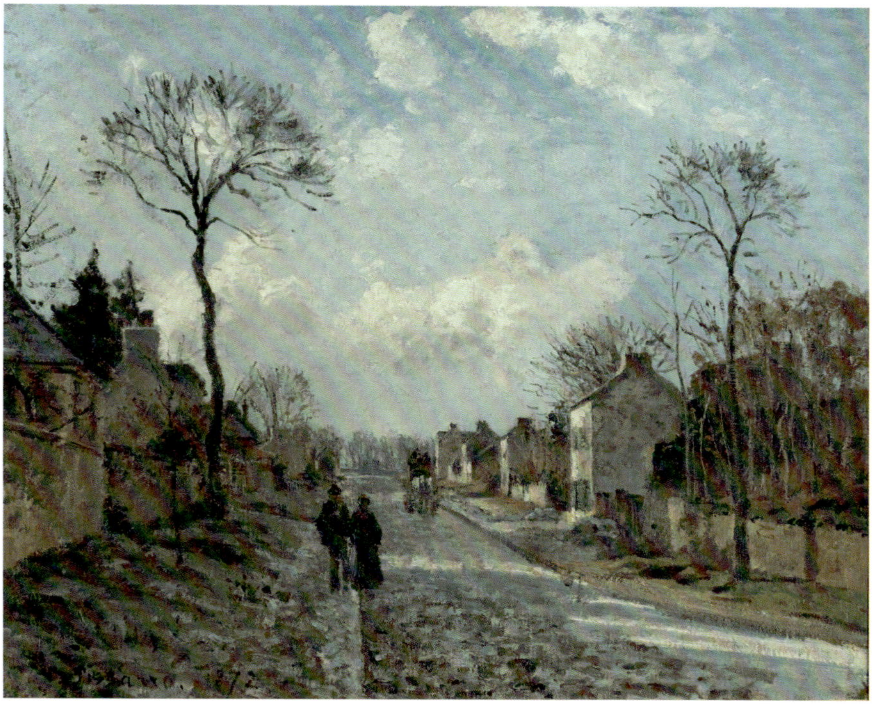

Camille Pissarro
The Road from Louveciennes
1872
Oil on canvas,
23 ⅝ × 30 ⅞ in.
(60 × 73.5 cm)
Musée d'Orsay, Paris

Camille Pissarro
Landscape in Éragny: Church and Farm in Éragny
1895
Oil on canvas,
23 ⅝ × 28 ⅞ in.
(60 × 73.4 cm)
Musée d'Orsay, Paris

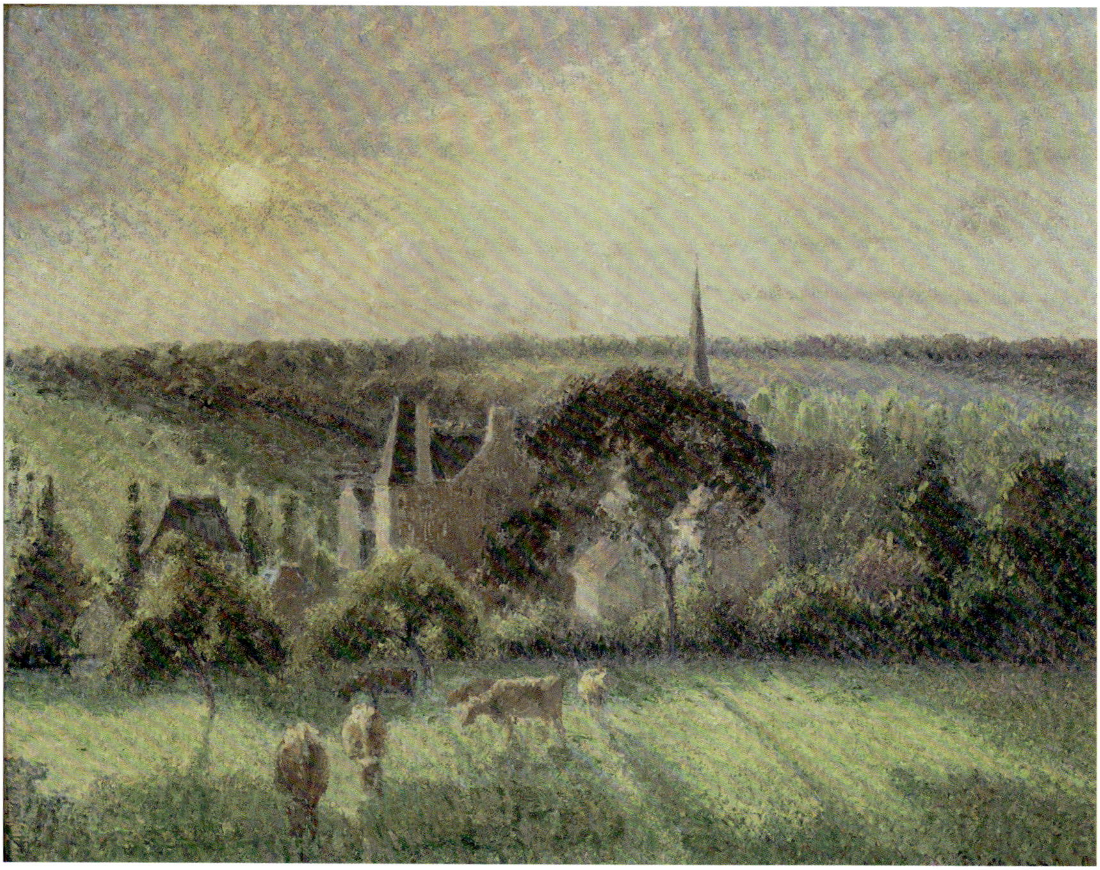

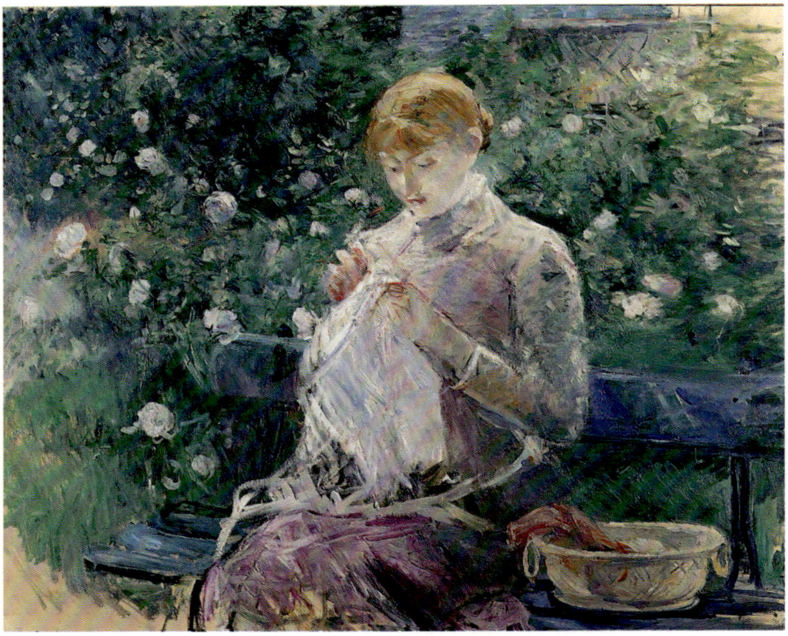

Berthe Morisot
Pasie Sewing in the Garden in Bougival
1881
Oil on board,
2 ft. 8 ¼ in. × 3 ft. 3 ¾ in.
(81.7 × 101 cm)
Musée des Beaux-Arts, Pau

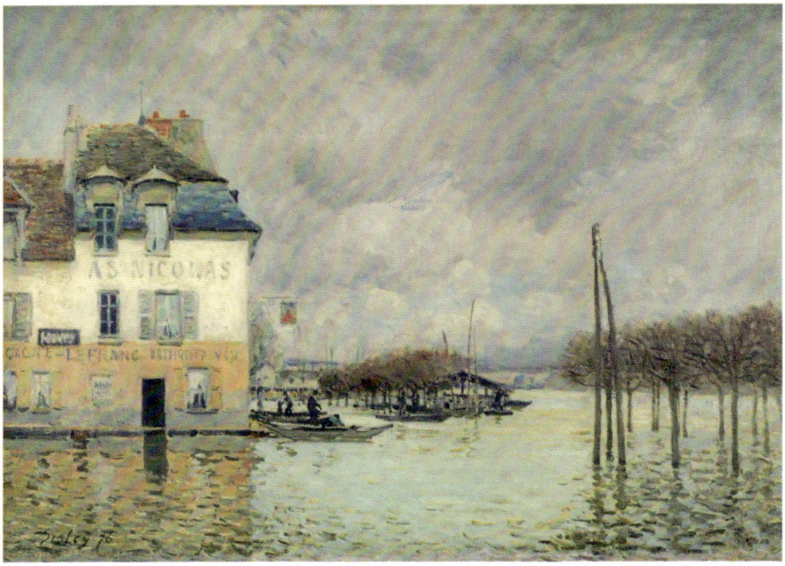

Alfred Sisley
The Flood at Port-Marly
1876
Oil on canvas, 23 ⅝ × 31 ⅞ in.
(60 × 81 cm)
Musée d'Orsay, Paris

Bougival

From 1881 until 1884, Berthe Morisot and her husband Eugène Manet rented a house in Bougival, where they spent beautiful summer days with their daughter Julie. The garden, where the little girl played while her nursemaid sewed, became an inexhaustible source of inspiration for Berthe's paintings.

Marly-le-Roi

Sisley moved to Marly-le-Roi in 1875. He was living there during the great flood of 1876, and he painted a series of six

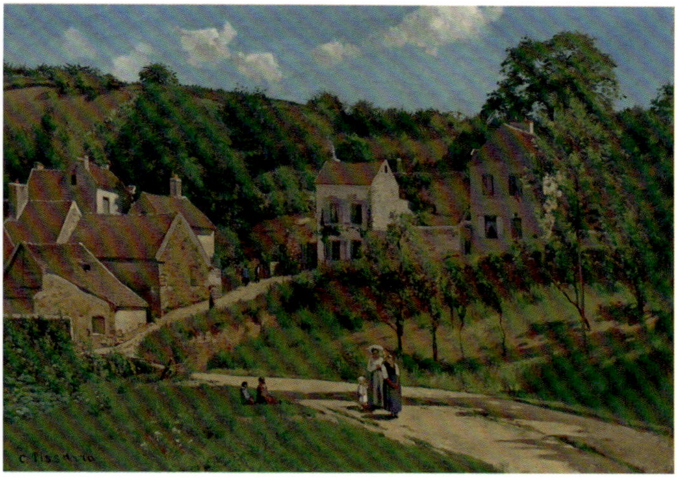

Camille Pissarro
The Hermitage at Pontoise
1867
Oil on canvas,
4 ft. 11 ½ in. × 6 ft. 7 in.
(1.51 × 2.01 m)
The Solomon R. Guggenheim Museum, New York

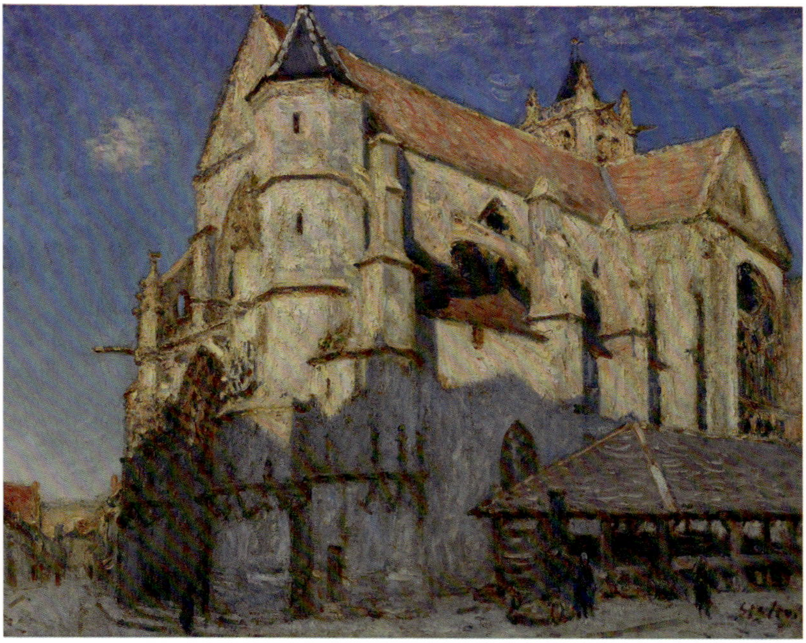

Alfred Sisley
The Church at Moret, Full Sunlight
1893
Oil on canvas,
26 ⅜ × 32 ⅛ in.
(67 × 81.5 cm)
Musée des Beaux-Arts, Rouen

views of the local wine merchant's house. With the building's foundations below water, its owner improvised a little launching stage beside his door.

Pontoise

Pissarro lived here from 1866 until 1869 and returned in 1872. He generously invited his friends Cézanne, Gauguin, and Armand Guillaumin to work there by his side.

Moret-sur-Loing

Sisley made his final move to Moret-sur-Loing in 1882 and lived there until his death in 1899. This view of the church was one of a series of twelve canvases that the artist painted between 1893 and 1894.

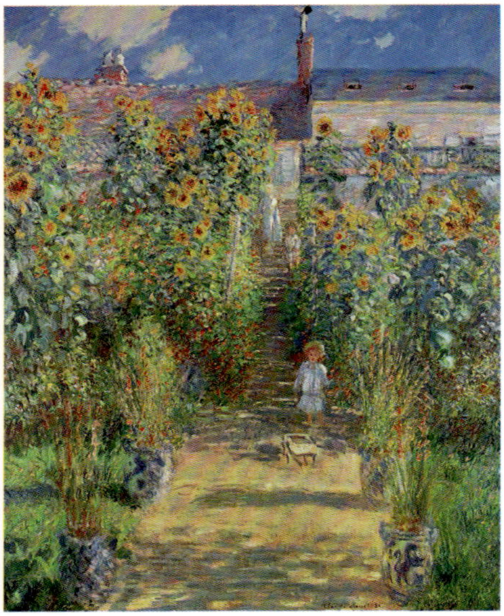

Claude Monet
The Artist's Garden at Vétheuil
1880
Oil on canvas,
4 ft. 11 ¾ in. × 3 ft. 11 ½ in.
(1.52 × 1.21 m)
National Gallery of Art, Washington, DC

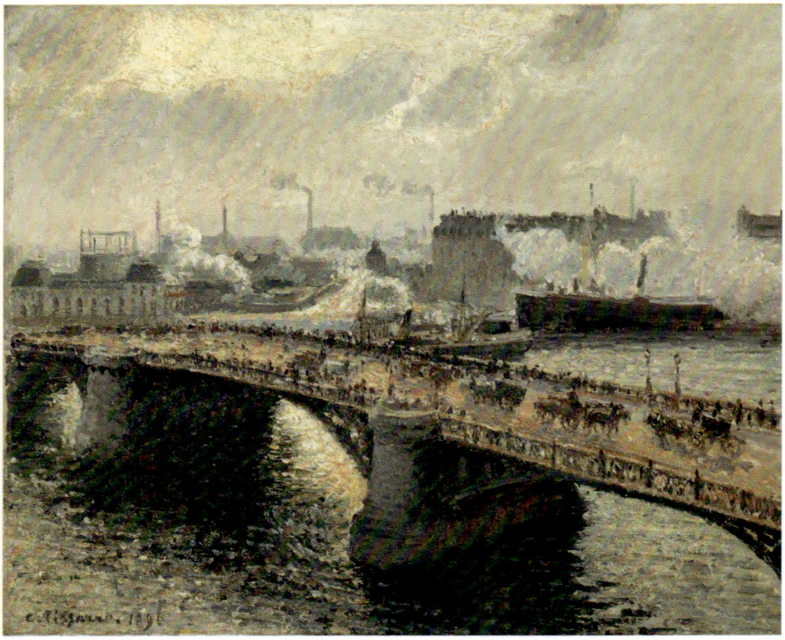

Camille Pissarro
Pont Boieldieu, Rouen: Sunset, Misty Weather
1896
Oil on canvas, 21 ¼ × 25 ⅝ in. (54 × 65 cm)
Musée des Beaux-Arts, Rouen

Vétheuil

Monet moved to Vétheuil with his family in 1878. They were soon joined by Alice Hoschedé and her six children. Camille, Monet's first wife, died here of cancer the following year.

Rouen

Located between Paris and the Normandy coast, Rouen was an obligatory stop along the way. Pissarro, Gauguin, and Monet (painting his legendary cathedral scenes) enjoyed stays of various lengths.

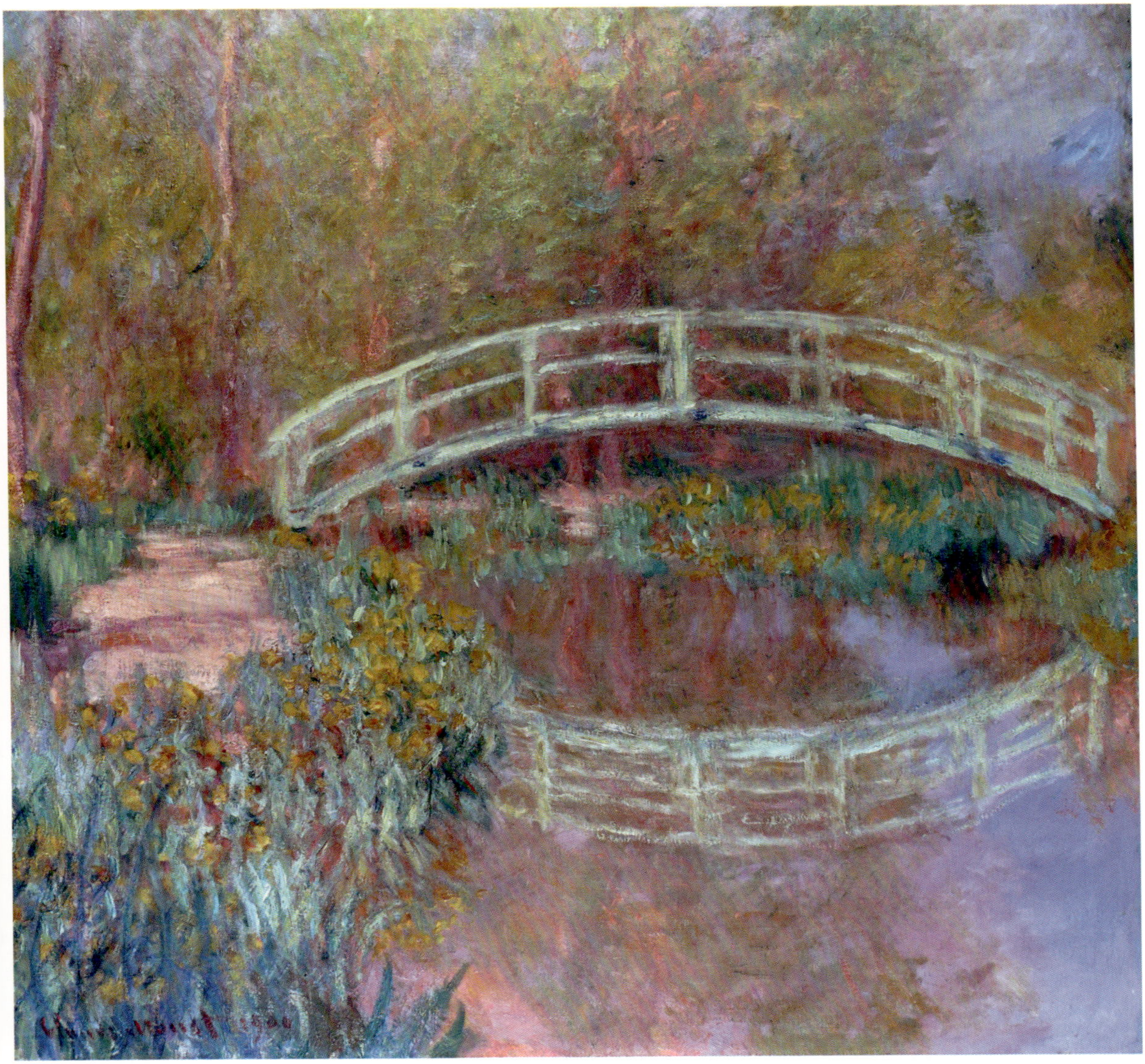

Claude Monet
The Water Lily Pond: Water Irises
1900
Oil on canvas, 2 ft. 11 in. × 3 ft.
(89 × 92 cm)
Private collection

Giverny

Monet settled in Giverny in 1883 and lived there until his death in 1926. His garden became his great obsession in the final years of his life.

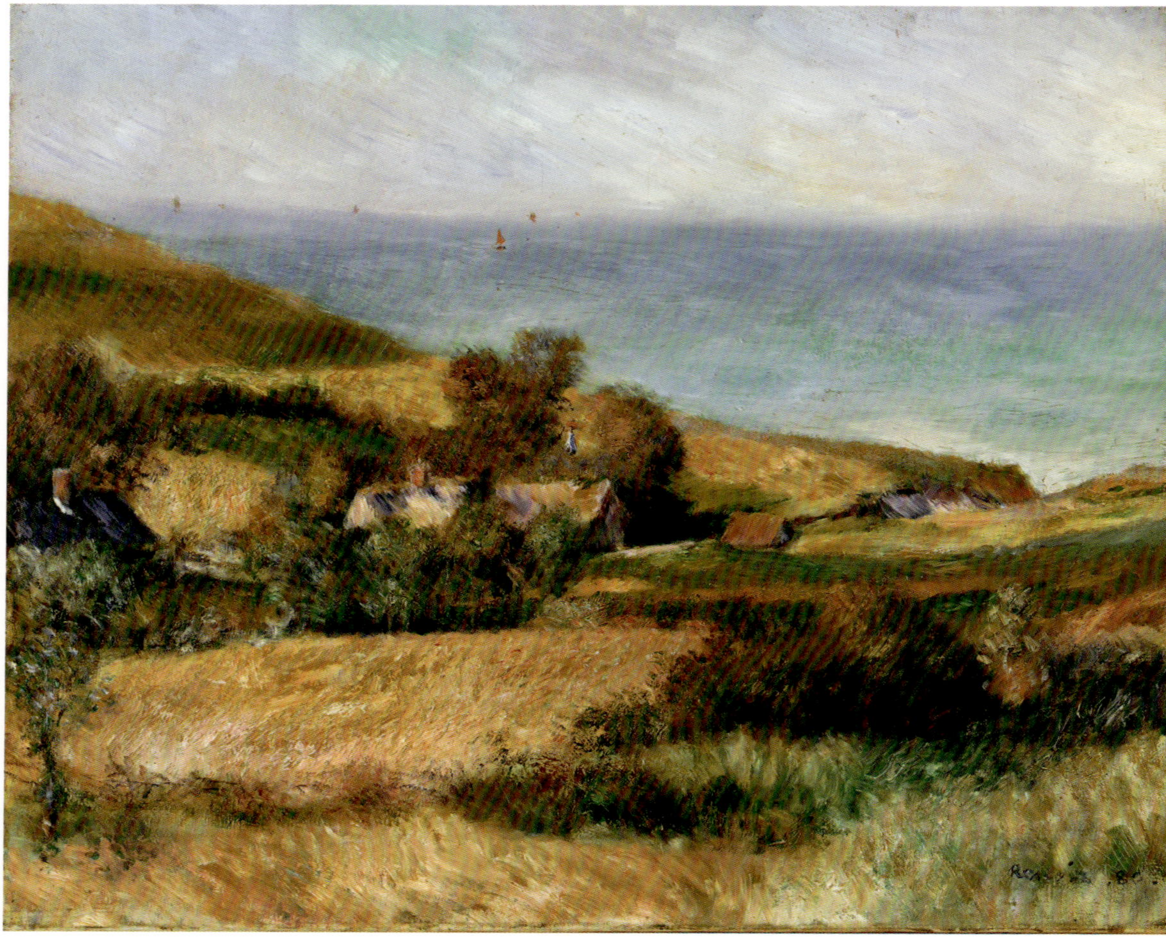

Auguste Renoir
View of the Seacoast near Wargemont in Normandy
1880
Oil on canvas, 19 ⅞ × 24 ½ in. (50.5 × 62.2 cm)
The Metropolitan Museum of Art, New York

Dieppe

Sophisticated and cosmopolitan, the seaside resort of Dieppe was attractive to artists. Monet visited in 1882 but he soon came to prefer Pourville, which was very close by and much less crowded. He carefully planned his visits, which were dedicated exclusively to painting, sometimes traveling to the coast at Varengeville. In 1879, Renoir visited the nearby Château de Wargemont at the invitation of his patron Bérard, the owner of this family property. Pissarro came later, in 1901 and 1902, to paint numerous views of the town and its port.

Étretat

Monet set up his easel by the famous cliffs of Étretat in the winters of 1868 and 1869. He returned every year between 1883 and 1886. It was here that he met Guy de Maupassant, who had come to garner inspiration for his writing in 1885.

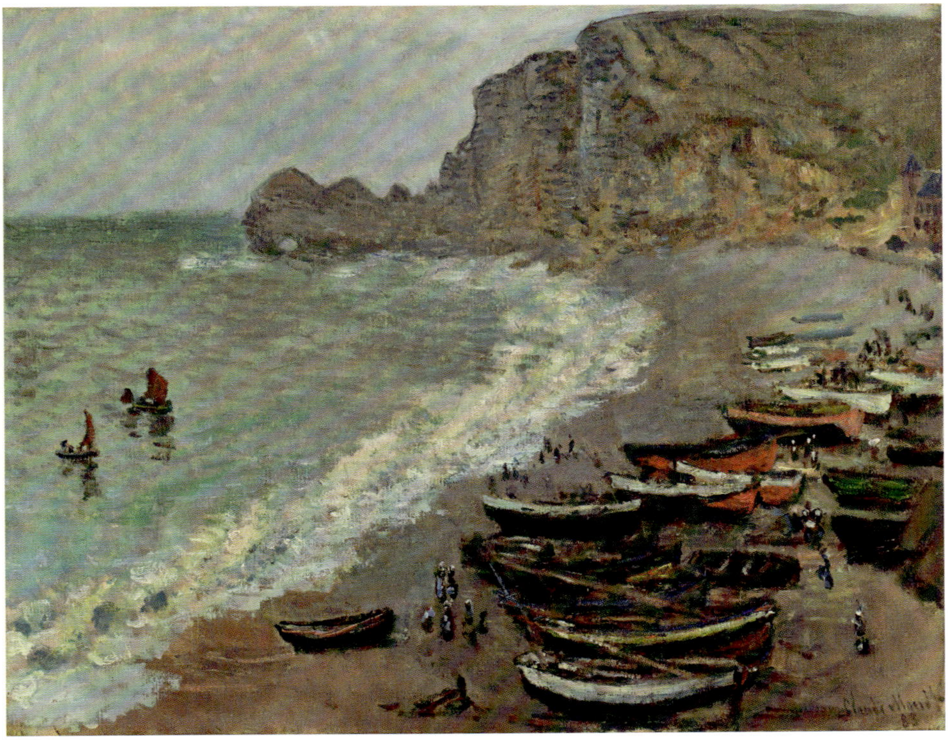

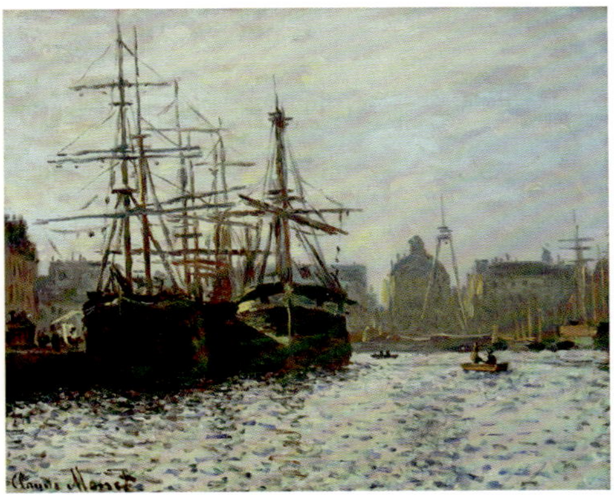

Claude Monet
Étretat: the Beach and Port of Amont
1883
Oil on canvas, 26 × 31 ⅞ in. (66 × 81 cm)
Musée d'Orsay, Paris

Claude Monet
The Bassin du Commerce, Le Havre
1874
Oil on canvas, 15 × 18 ⅛ in. (38 × 46 cm)
Musée d'Art Moderne et d'Art Contemporain, Liège

Le Havre

A native of Le Havre, Monet returned to the town frequently during the 1860s and 1870s, despite conflicts with his father. It was here, as a young boy, that he had the meeting with Boudin that proved a turning point, and where he acquired the desire to capture the ceaselessly changing scenery of the seaside.

FOCUS

Gardens

Alongside massive industrialization and urban development, the nineteenth century witnessed the ascendency of green spaces, both public and private. The era embraced gardens in all their forms: pleasure gardens, kitchen gardens, which enhanced the quality of daily life, and the parks that served as the green lungs of Haussmann's newly salubrious Paris. As domesticated enclaves of nature, private gardens were frequently used as settings by the impressionists. They painted figures *en plein air*, capturing the play of light and shadow and the fleeting moments of everyday life.

Monet, the Passionate Gardener

In Paris, Monet painted the Parc Monceau and the Tuileries and Luxembourg gardens. He cultivated a garden in every place he lived thereafter–Argenteuil, Vétheuil, and Giverny. He always took great care of these oases. They were places of privacy to be shared with family and friends, or for solitary contemplation, or–above all–for painting. The importance of these spaces to the artist reached its apogee in Giverny.

When Monet composed this large canvas in 1866, he was striving to incorporate figures into a *plein air* setting. This painting, which was rejected by the 1867 Salon, inaugurated the theme of women in a garden, which became a recurrent one in his work.

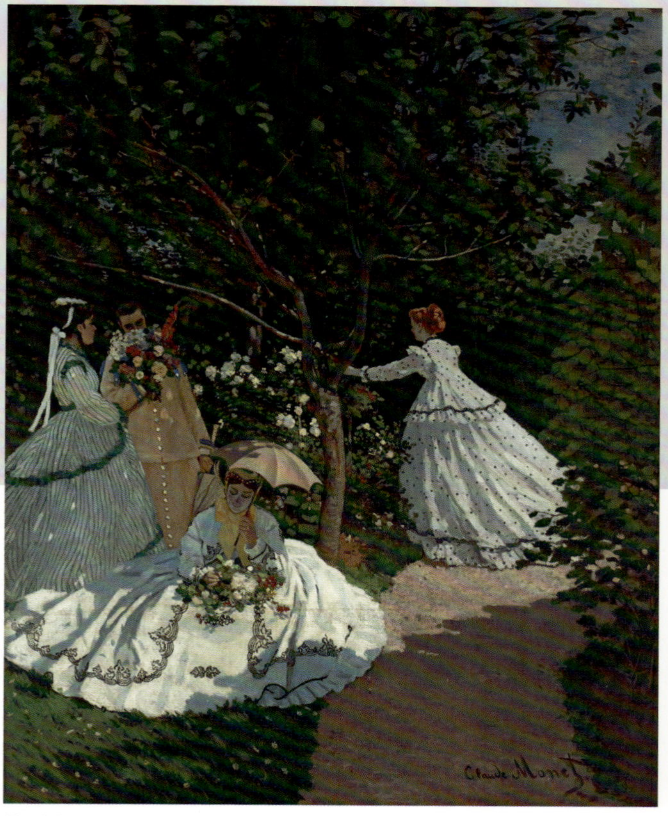

Claude Monet, *Women in the Garden*, c. 1866
Oil on canvas, 8 ft. 4 ½ in. × 6 ft. 8 ¾ in. (2.55 × 2.05 m), Musée d'Orsay, Paris

Monet and his visiting friends used the garden in Argenteuil as the subject for many compositions. Here we see his son Jean in the center, while his first wife Camille stands at the top of the steps. We recognize the blue faïence planters lined up along the façade, which were to follow Monet from house to house, all the way to his final residence in Giverny.

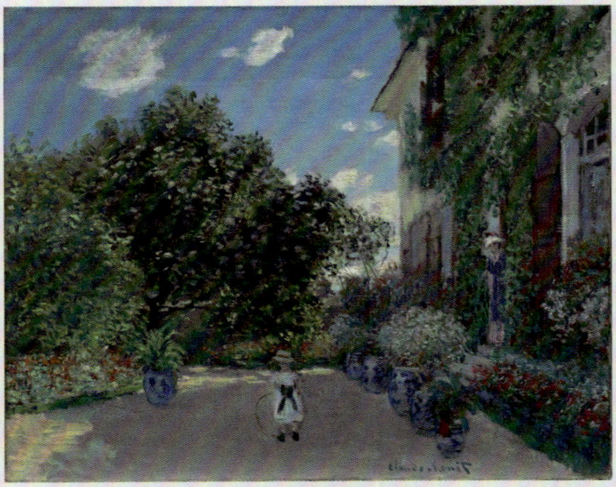

Claude Monet, *The Artist's House at Argenteuil*, 1873
Oil on canvas, 23 ¾ × 28 ⅞ in. (60.2 × 73.3 cm)
The Art Institute of Chicago, Chicago

Monet's house in Argenteuil was a gathering place for the impressionists, who were initiated into *plein air* painting in an atmosphere of joyous camaraderie.

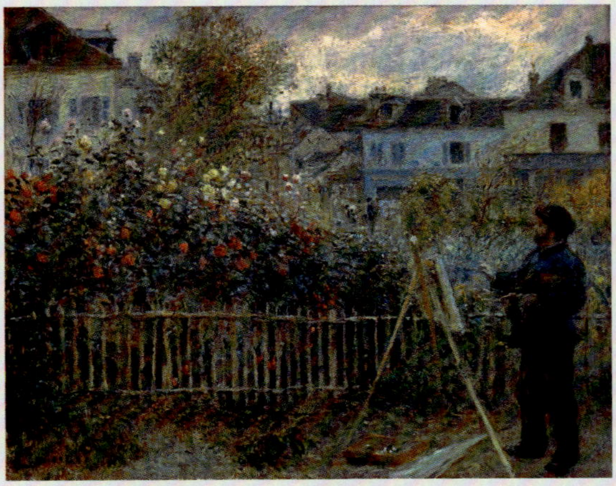

Auguste Renoir, *Monet Painting in His Garden at Argenteuil*, 1873
Oil on canvas, 18 ⅛ × 23 ⅝ in. (46 × 60 cm)
Wadsworth Atheneum, Hartford

Transformed by the painter, the garden in Giverny became a lavish extravaganza, an explosion of color that represented the climax of Monet's passion for nature and *plein air* painting.

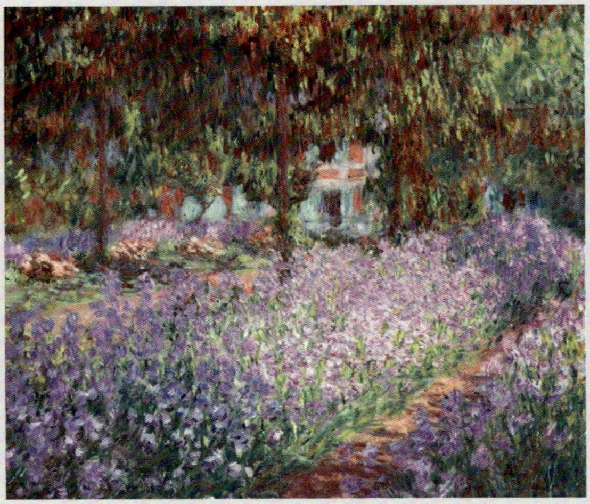

Claude Monet, *The Artist's Garden at Giverny*, 1900
Oil on canvas, 31 ⅞ × 23 ⅝ in. (81 × 92 cm)
Musée d'Orsay, Paris

Renoir in Collettes

Renoir spent the last twelve years of his life at Collettes, his property in Cagnes-sur-Mer. Gravely affected by arthritis, and physically exhausted, he used his garden as a place where he could experiment with an approach to painting that was utterly free of constraints.

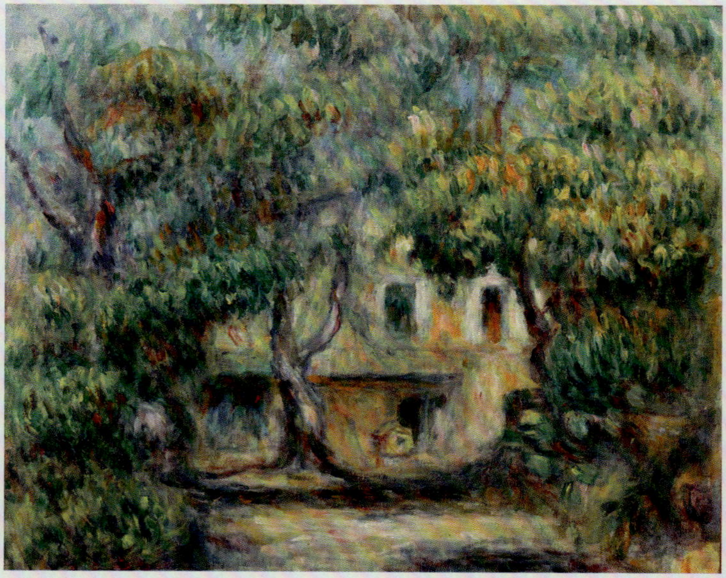

Auguste Renoir, *The Farm in Collettes*, 1915
Oil on canvas, 18 ⅛ × 20 ⅛ in. (46 × 51 cm)
Musée Renoir, Cagnes-sur-Mer

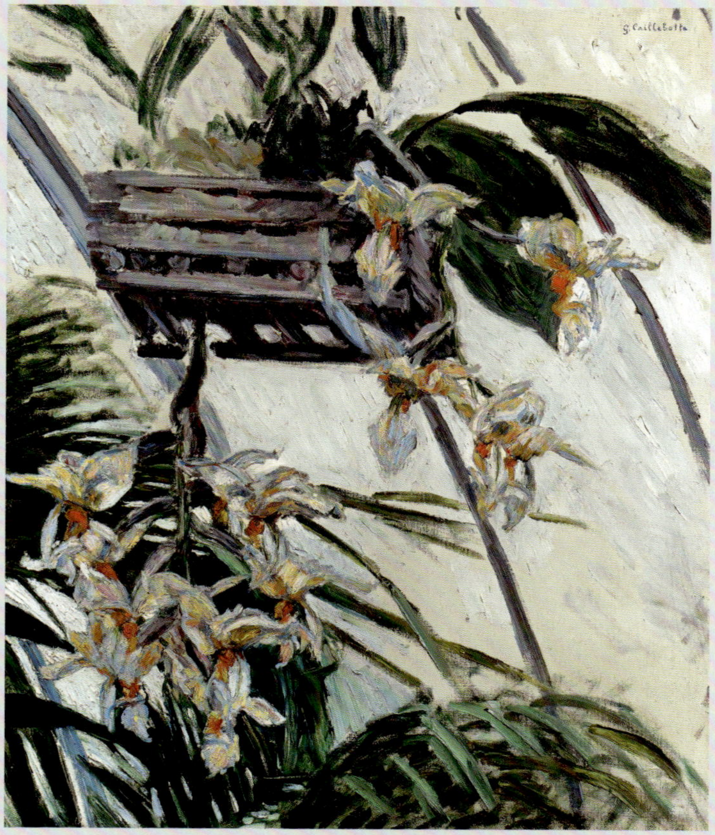

Gustave Caillebotte, *Orchids*, 1893
Oil on canvas, 25 ⅝ × 21 ¼ in. (65 × 54 cm), private collection

Caillebotte, the Horticulturist

Caillebotte painted around a hundred views of the park surrounding his family's property in Yerres before acquiring his own home in Petit Gennevilliers in 1881. It was on the banks of the Seine, across from Argenteuil. Increasingly absent from his Parisian residence, Caillebotte devoted himself to painting, as well as to his passions for sailing and gardening. He propagated plants, built a greenhouse, and exchanged cuttings with his friend Claude Monet, also a keen horticulturist.

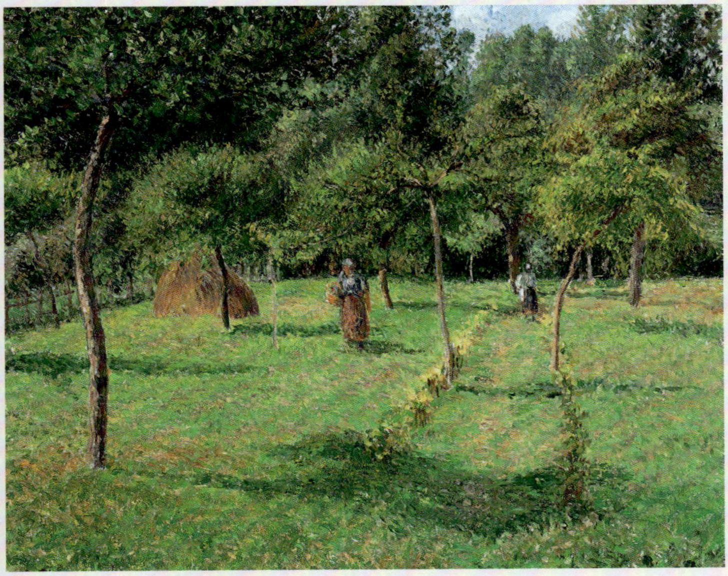

Camille Pissarro, *The Garden at Éragny*, 1896
Oil on canvas, 21 ½ × 25 ¾ in. (54.6 × 65.4 cm)
Thyssen-Bornemisza, Madrid

Pissarro in Éragny

Pissarro settled in Éragny in 1884 and focused his attention on the garden surrounding his new home. Apple trees in flower, summer heat, and sunsets proved an inexhaustible source of inspiration for him.

Berthe Morisot in Her Garden

Berthe Morisot's work frequently shows the garden of the house in Bougival that she rented between 1881 and 1884. Somewhat less frequently, she also painted the Bois de Boulogne, which was close to where she lived from 1883. As a woman, she was more restricted in painting outdoors, so the garden became her favorite setting. She loved to surprise her daughter Julie when she was absorbed in her games. Morisot and her husband Eugène Manet bought a property in Mesnil in 1891, which appears in the works she painted toward the end of her life.

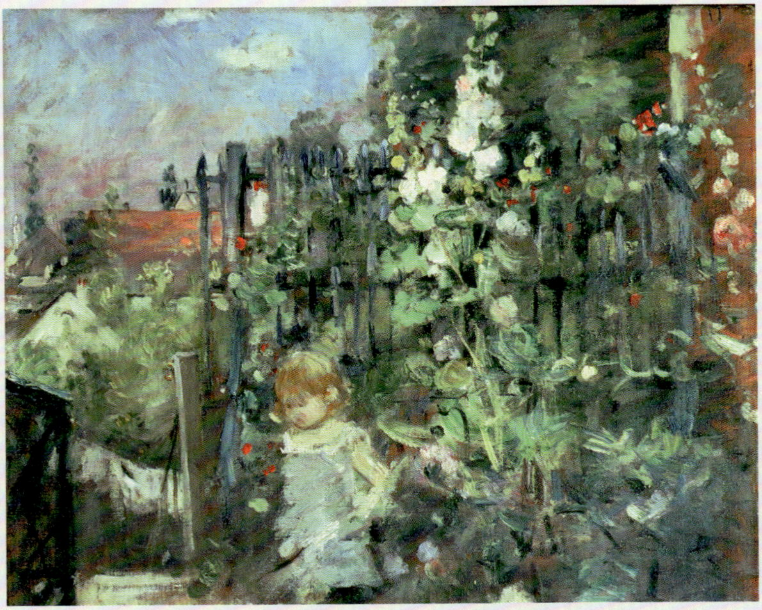

Berthe Morisot, *Child with Hollyhocks*, 1881
Oil on canvas, 19 ⅞ × 16 ⅝ in. (50.6 × 42.2 cm), private collection

FOCUS

Giverny

Monet had no sooner arrived in Giverny than he embarked on the installation of irrigation and terracing systems to create the garden of his dreams. He redirected a little tributary of the Epte and built a Japanese bridge over the stream. Having painted *en plein air* for his entire life, the master impressionist fashioned his own outdoor world in Giverny, which became the inexhaustible inspiration for his painting for the remaining years of his life.

This painting is modest in scale compared to most of the innumerable compositions that Monet devoted to his pools of water lilies. It was a subject he revisited endlessly in his spectacular compositions.

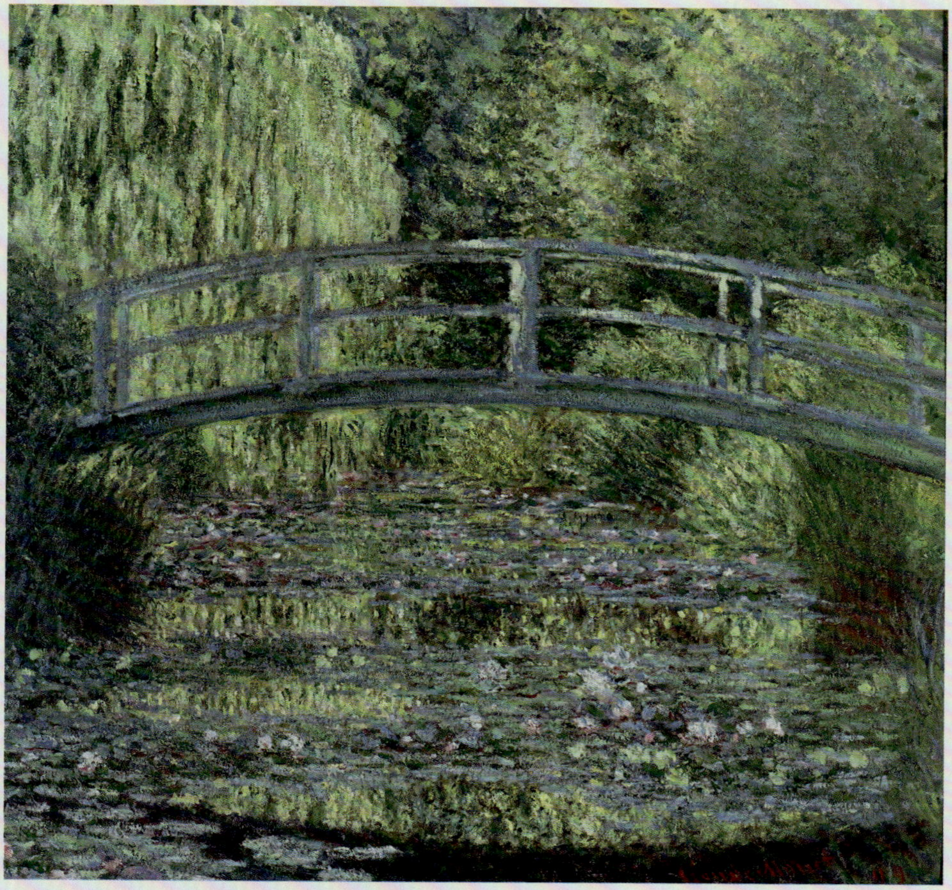

Claude Monet, *The Water Lily Pond: Harmony in Green*, 1899
Oil on canvas, 2 ft. 11 in. × 3 ft. 1 in. (89 × 93 cm)
Musée d'Orsay, Paris

The walls of Monet's house were covered with impressionist paintings and Japanese prints from his collection. His library included numerous tomes on horticulture. In his bedroom, three sketches by Boudin were always at his side.

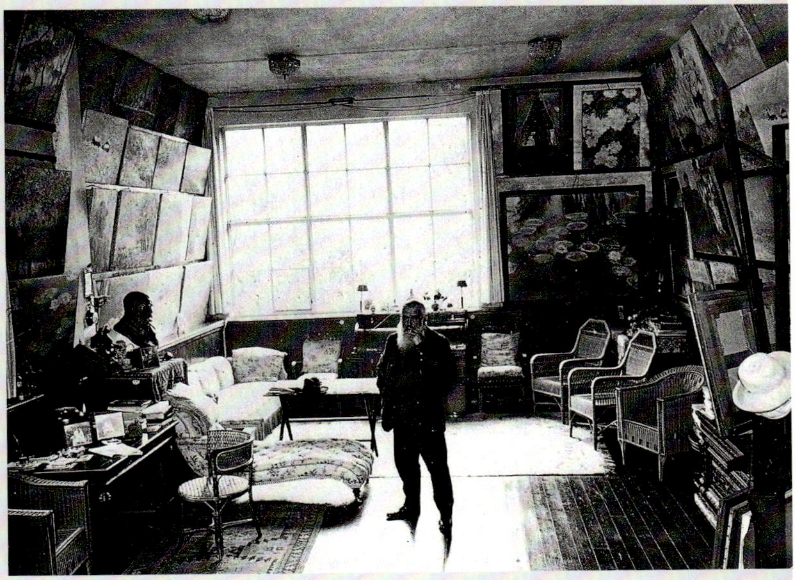

CULTIVATING HIS GARDEN

Monet once stated that his garden was his greatest work of art. He took great care over every detail at Giverny, deciding on all the installations and plantings. Still fascinated by Oriental art, Monet built the Japanese-style bridge that frequently appears in his paintings.

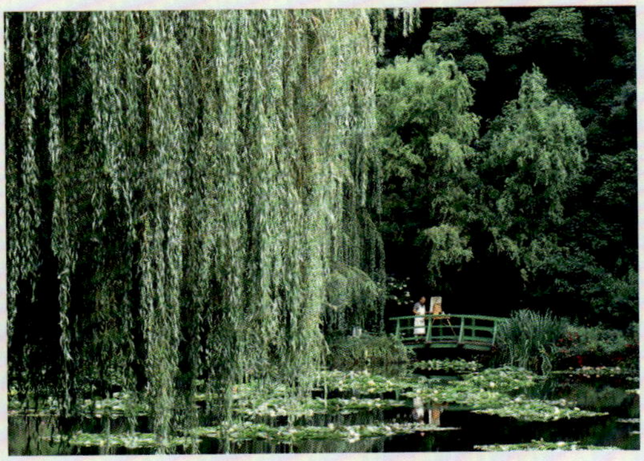

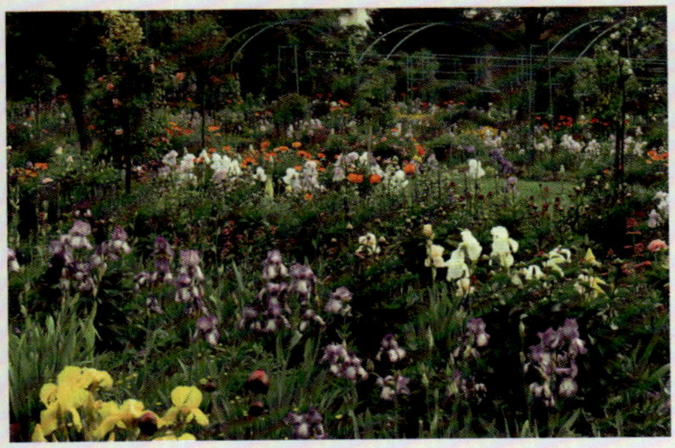

Monet designed his flowerbeds meticulously, mixing combinations like colors on a canvas.

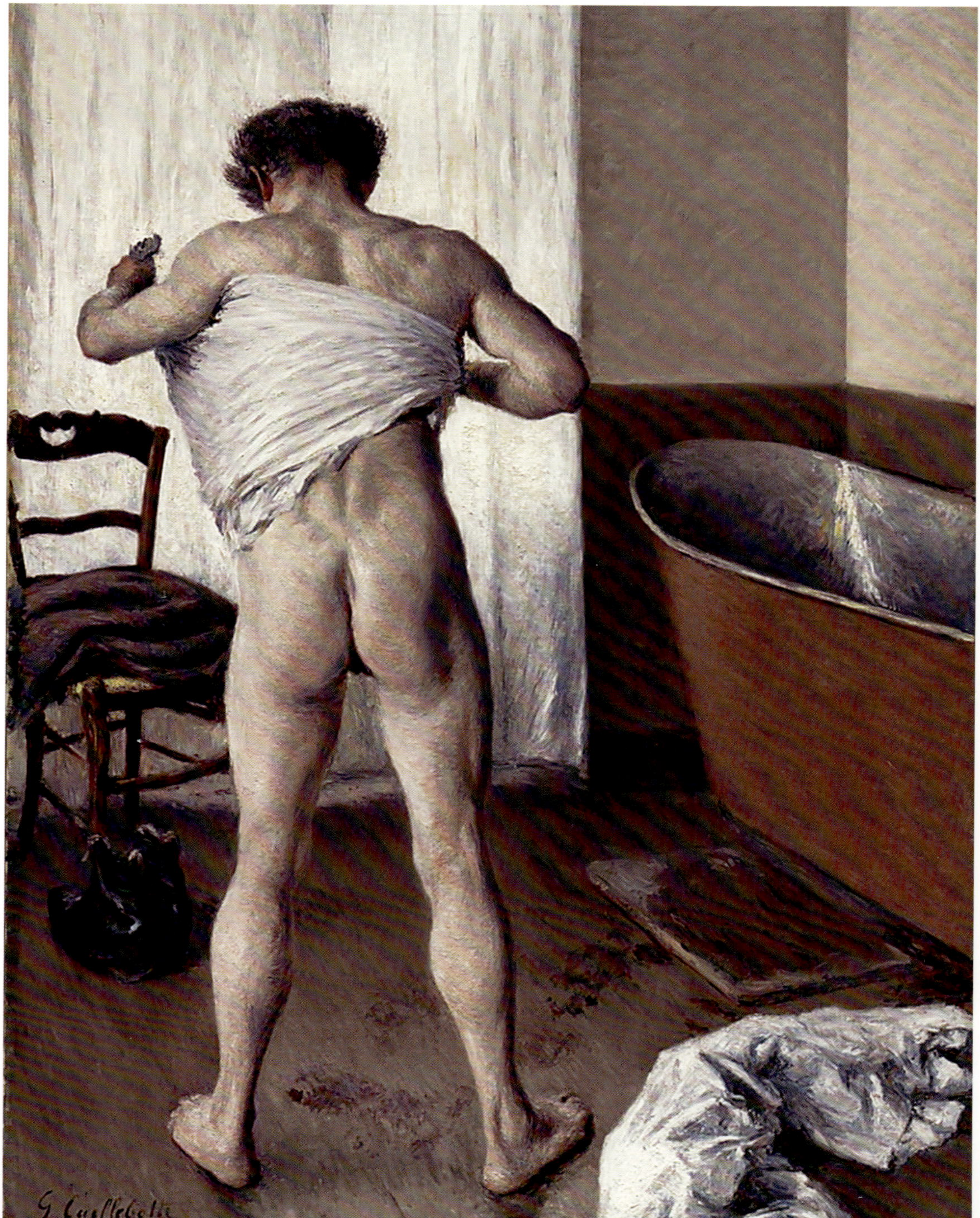

Gustave Caillebotte
Man at His Bath
1884
Oil on canvas, 4 ft. 9 in. × 3 ft. 9 in.
(1.45 × 1.14 m)
Museum of Fine Arts, Boston

The Non-Subject

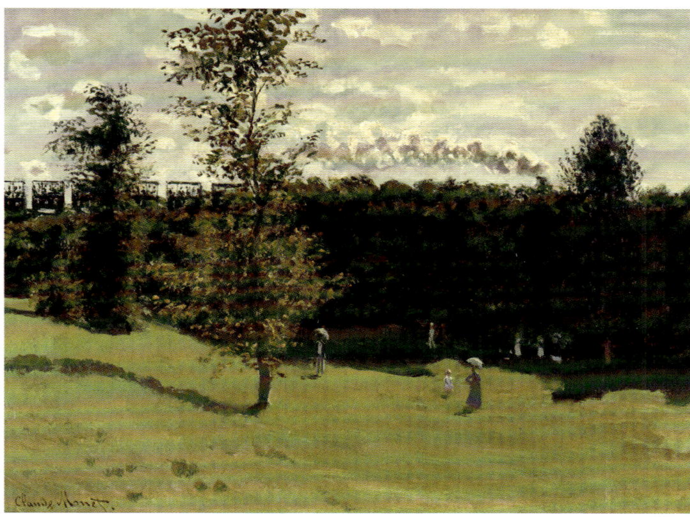

Claude Monet
Train in the Countryside
c. 1870–71
Oil on canvas, 19 ⅝ × 25 ⅝ in.
(50 × 65 cm)
Musée d'Orsay, Paris

While gods continued their reign on Olympus, and heroes still dueled on the walls of the Salon, the impressionists resolutely rejected these lofty subjects and ambitious compositions, turning their attention to more mundane topics: everyday occurrences, idle moments, free time. Alert to their surroundings, they loved such brief interludes, seeking to convey their poetry and emotion. A road stretching into the distance, a playful child, a ray of sunlight, a woman sewing, a train traveling across the countryside, a gust of wind: all these "non-events" were worthy of their attention. Their favorite subjects included scenes as delightful and negligible as chasing butterflies or enjoying a boat outing. The shimmering reality of life entered into their paintings, which embraced these ephemeral moments in an ode to life's simple pleasures. These works eschewed lofty deeds and actions, eliminating narrative and anecdote. Even when the impressionists took on a more public scene, such as a racetrack or the Paris Opéra, they painted

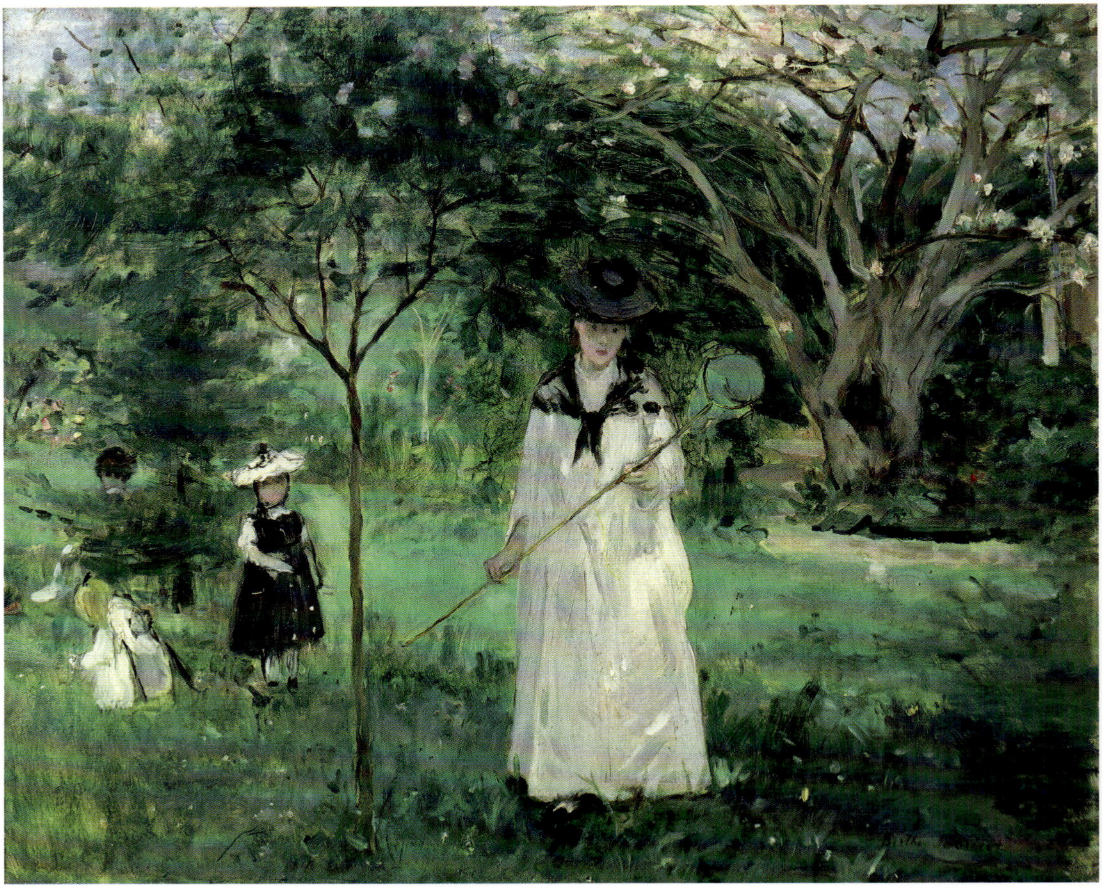

Berthe Morisot
Chasing Butterflies
1874
Oil on canvas, 18 ⅛ × 22 in. (46 × 56 cm)
Musée d'Orsay, Paris

events on the sidelines. They never showed the victory in a race or any details of an opera performance. If there is such an event, it is not the featured subject. The paintings always show the moments before or after–the intermission, the rehearsal, or the downtime. The authenticity of the poses and the moment in time absorbed all their attention. The impressionists focused on their own era; they did not seek subjects other than those that surrounded them in the real world. It was no concern of theirs if the subject matter might seem trivial or uninteresting to some viewers. That was not the issue. Anything might catch their eye–even an exhausted little girl sprawled in a chair, or raindrops making circles in a pond during a downpour. Captured in

LIFE ON A SMALL SCALE
It was a return to reality. With the impressionists, paintings assumed more modest proportions. No more of the vast scenes and monumental canvases that official art imposed on viewers. These were paintings that could be carried under the arm and propped on an outdoor easel or hung on the walls of a collector's apartment.

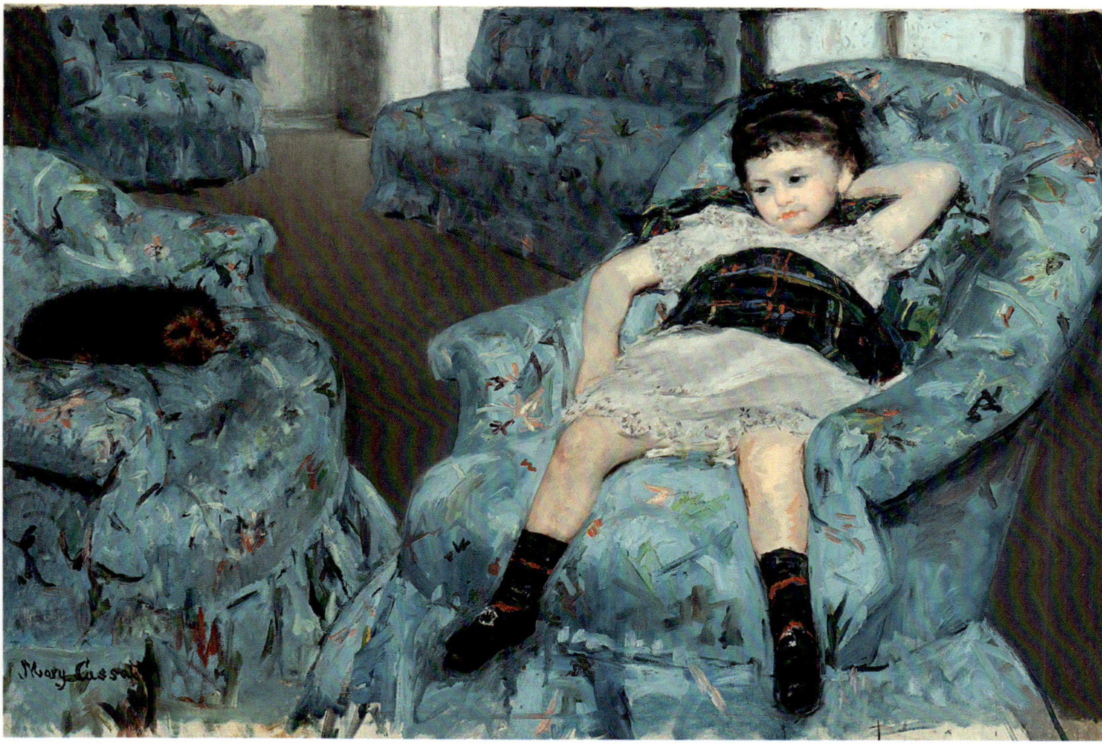

Mary Cassatt
Little Girl in a Blue Armchair
1878
Oil on canvas, 2 ft. 11 ¼ in. × 4 ft. 3 in.
(89.5 × 129.8 cm)
National Gallery of Art, Washington, DC

swift brushstrokes, every moment of life could be rich and full in the eyes of someone who could see and feel. It was a philosophy of life, but more importantly, it was a turning point in the history of art. The impressionists were no longer painting a subject–they were painting a picture. Painting itself was now the sole and true topic of impressionist art.

"Until now, art was concerned with nothing but gods, heroes, and saints. It's time for it to occupy itself with mere mortals."

Pierre Joseph Proudhon, 1865.

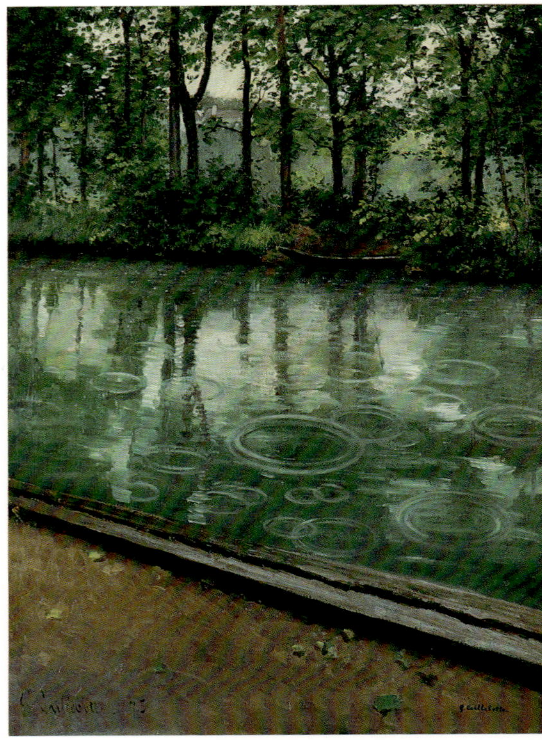

Depicting a non-event that is both daringly novel and inconsequential, this incredibly modern composition is remarkable for its non-subject and its cropped picture space. The circles created by the impact of raindrops falling on a pool have fully absorbed Caillebotte's attention.

Gustave Caillebotte
The Yerres: Effect of Rain
1875
Oil on canvas, 31 ⅞ × 23 ¼ in. (81 × 59 cm)
Indiana University Art Museum, Bloomington

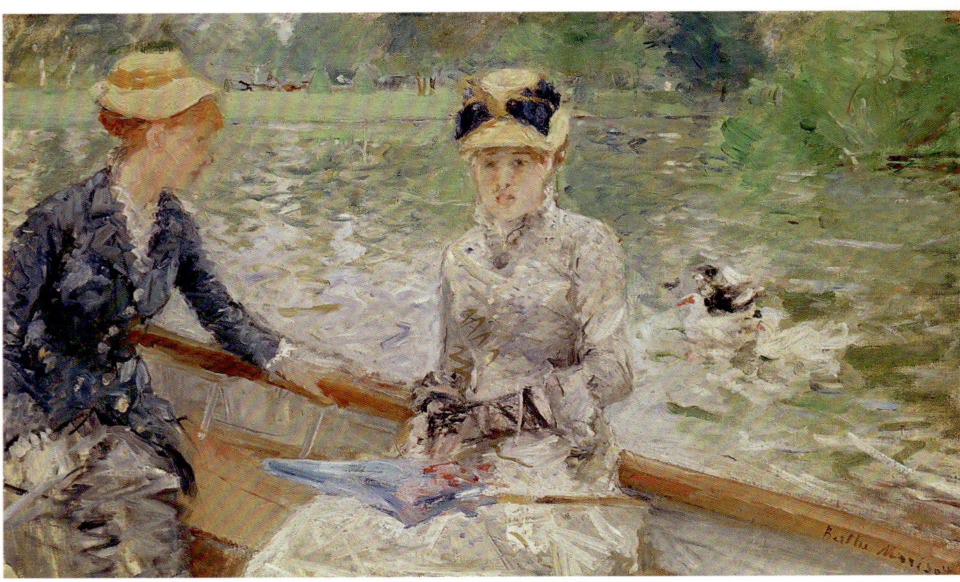

Berthe Morisot
Summer Day
1879
Oil on canvas, 18 × 29 ⅝ in. (45.7 × 75.3 cm)
National Gallery, London

This scene captures a moment, probably in the Bois de Boulogne, a favorite spot for Berthe Morisot. Two stylish young ladies are posed in a boat. As if captured in a snapshot, one turns away, her face in profile, apparently distracted by a passing flock of ducks.

Like any good bourgeois Parisian, Degas frequented the races, which were considered very fashionable. The public thoroughly enjoyed this form of entertainment, imported from Great Britain. But Degas did not take as his subject the finishing line or the excited spectators in the stands. He was much more interested in the intermission time between races, and the interplay of light and shadow.

Edgar Degas
The Parade, also known as
Racehorses in Front of the Tribunes
c. 1866–68
Oil on paper mounted on canvas,
18 ⅛ × 24 in. (46 × 61 cm)
Musée d'Orsay, Paris

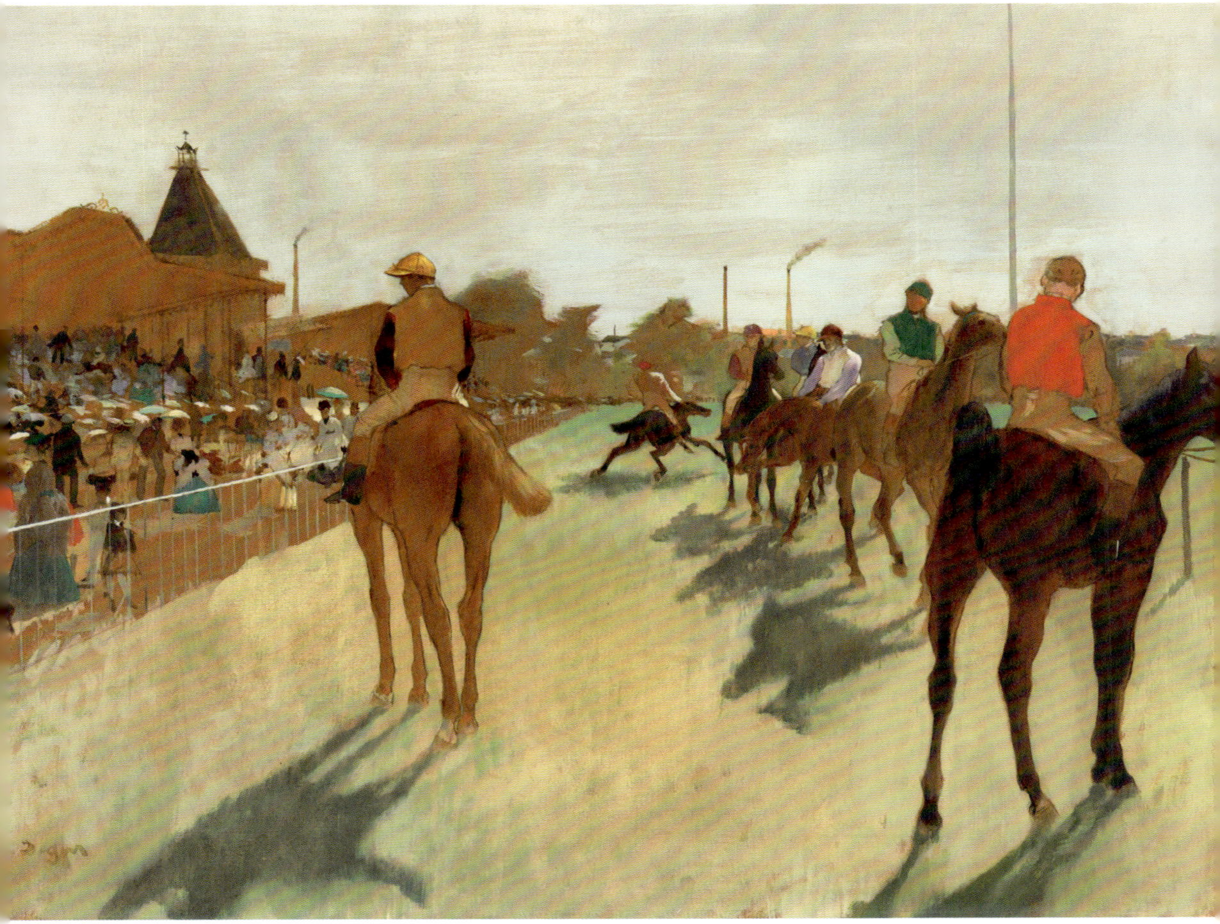

"Treating a subject for its tonalities rather than the subject itself is what distinguishes the impressionists from other painters."

Georges Rivière, 1877.

Family Life

Highly conscious of their surroundings, the impressionists introduced a theme that had hitherto been absent from French art. Family life, which had been hidden and private, was suddenly displayed on walls. Little or nothing is actually occurring in these pictures. We see a woman sewing, someone reading, someone else rather bored, others sitting in the parlor or dining in the garden. These people are no more heroic or attractive than nature intended. They are just normal people living their daily lives—observed by a painter who regards them with affection.

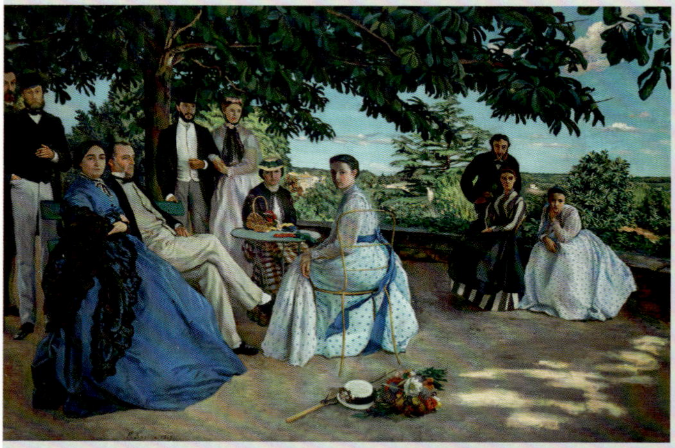

Frédéric Bazille, *Family Reunion,* also known as *Family Portraits,* 1867
Oil on canvas, 4 ft. 11 ¾ in. × 7 ft. 7 ¼ in. (1.52 × 2.30 m)
Musée d'Orsay, Paris

When visiting his family home in Méric, near Montpellier, Bazille executed a huge group portrait, showing his close relatives on the terrace. Turned toward the painter's easel, as if toward a camera, the figures seem to engage with us, giving the picture a powerful impact. The men's self-assurance and the women's mild reserve combine to evoke the conventions of bourgeois existence. It was an authentic view of contemporary life that was completely novel at the time. Painted *en plein air* beneath the Mediterranean sun, and later retouched in Bazille's studio, the work demonstrates the painter's mastery of light. He is shown standing at the far left of the composition.

Berthe Morisot became a mother late in life, and her daughter Julie was one of her favorite subjects. We see the child grow from one painting to the next as the artist captures the poetic world of childhood with a heightened maternal sensibility.

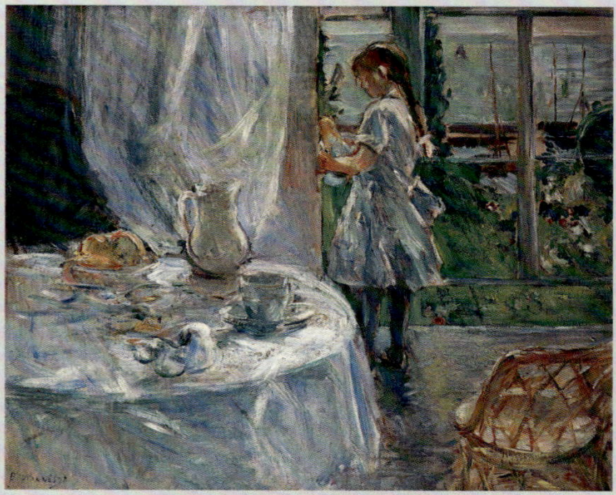

Berthe Morisot, *Cottage Interior,* also known as *Child with a Doll,* 1886
Oil on canvas, 19 ⅝ × 23 ⅝ in. (50 × 60 cm)
Musée d'Ixelles, Brussels

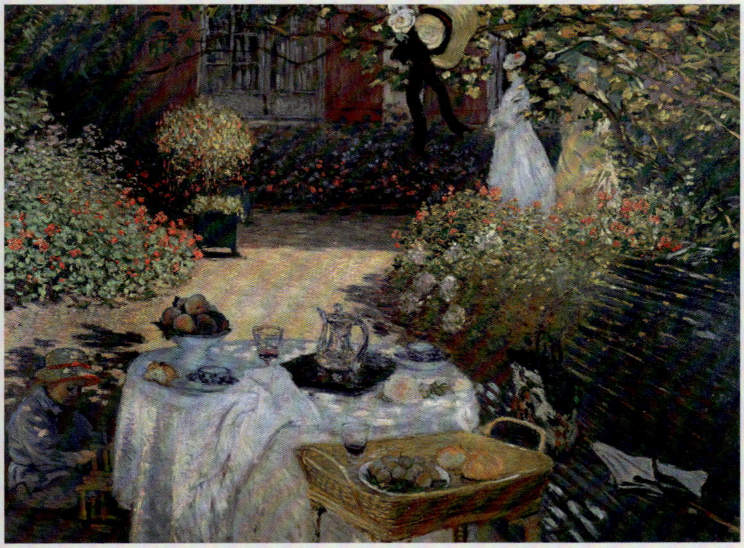

Claude Monet, *Luncheon: Monet's Garden in Argenteuil*, c. 1873
Oil on canvas, 5 ft. 3 in. × 6 ft. 7 ¼ in. (1.60 × 2.01 m)
Musée d'Orsay, Paris

During his years in Argenteuil, Monet tirelessly painted Camille and their young son busy in the garden. Despite the family's money worries, a peaceful joy and a leisurely air pervade these compositions. Monet takes obvious pleasure in painting spontaneously, creating the effect of a snapshot and showing his little family in their daily occupations. It's a beautiful day; the table has not yet been cleared; a hat dangles from a tree branch; a bag and parasol lie forgotten on a bench. Little Jean plays quietly in the shade. Dressed in white, Camille appears in the background, heightening the delightful impression of spontaneity. This intimate, unscripted approach would later inspire the Nabis.

Caillebotte decided to depict his relatives in the family property in Yerres, where he painted numerous canvases in the 1870s. He shows his cousin, aunt, and a family friend, with his mother in the background. The composition is aligned along a powerful diagonal. Bent intently over their work, to the point that their features are hard to see, these women seem to be cloistered within their domestic life, in keeping with the rules of bourgeois convention.

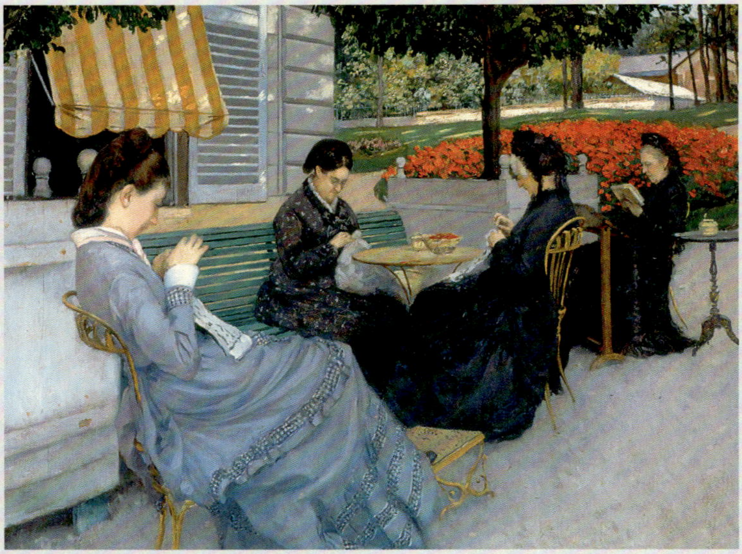

Gustave Caillebotte, *Portraits in the Country*, 1876
Oil on canvas, 3 ft. 2 ¾ in. × 3 ft. 7 ¾ in. (98.5 × 111 cm)
Musée Baron-Gérard, Bayeux

FOCUS

Nature in Its Own Right

As *plein air* painters, the impressionists made nature itself one of the great motifs of their art. The colors of autumn, the reflections of sunlight on water, a storm, or simply a gust of wind sufficed as subject matter. The genre's limitations had been codified by the Academy. Landscape, which had been constrained by rigid rules relegating it to a backdrop for history scenes, was freed from these limitations. No more papier-mâché cliffs, or trees in leaf no matter the season, or horizons fading into the distance. For the impressionists, nature and the elements required no pretext to appear in their canvases.

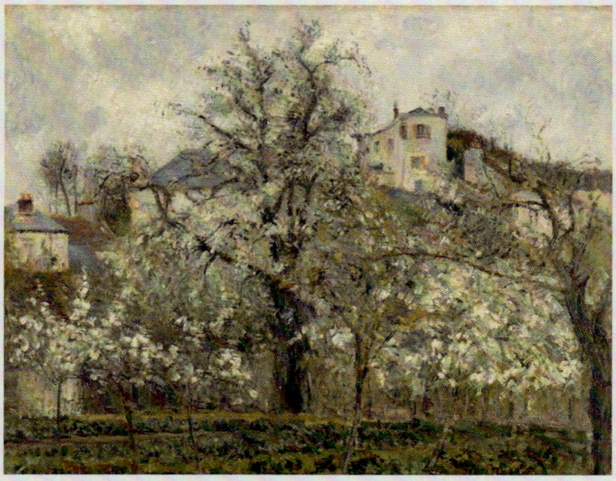

Camille Pissarro, *Spring Plum Trees in Flower,* also known as *Kitchen Garden, Trees in Flower: Spring, Pontoise,* 1877
Oil on canvas, 25 ⅞ × 31 ⅞ in. (65.5 × 81 cm), Musée d'Orsay, Paris

The Seasons

Corot still allowed the occasional nymph to stroll through his woodlands, and the Barbizon painters welcomed humble peasants or placid cows to their compositions. But now a revolution was under way, with the impressionists completely disassociating landscape from all the clichés expected by the Academy. Nature was a worthy subject in its own right. It was inexhaustible, in fact. Captivated by its magic, the impressionists were dedicated to capturing the many faces of the natural world through the transitory passage of the seasons.

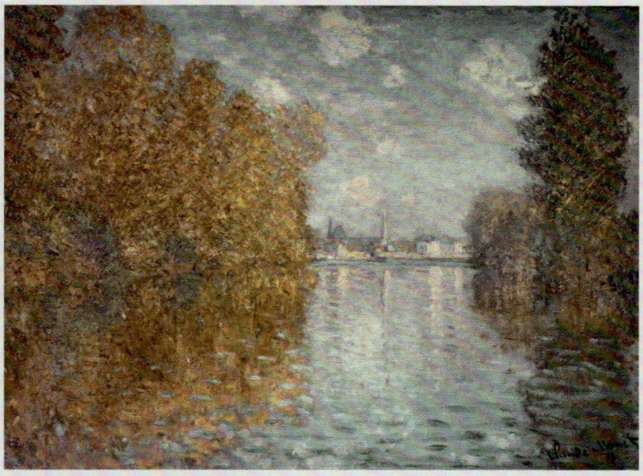

Claude Monet, *Autumn Effect at Argenteuil,* 1873
Oil on canvas, 21 ⅝ × 29 ⅜ in. (55 × 74.5 cm)
The Courtauld Gallery, London

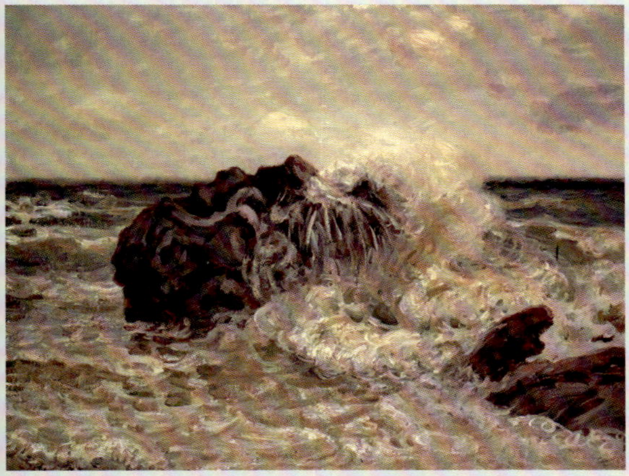

Alfred Sisley, *The Wave, Lady's Cove, Langland Bay*, 1897
Oil on canvas, 25 ⅝ × 31 ½ in. (65 × 81.5 cm)
Private collection

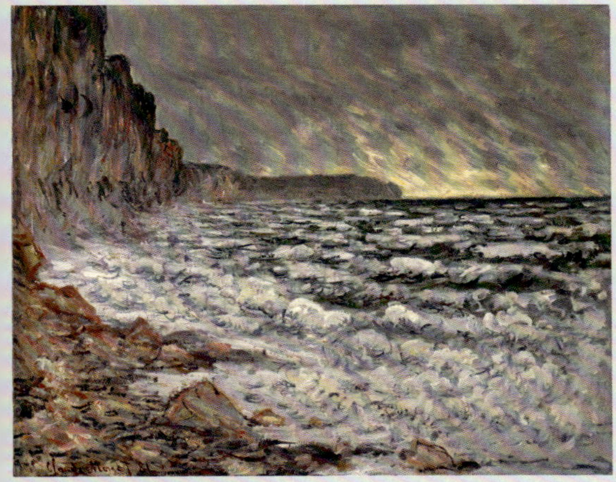

Claude Monet, *Fécamp, Seashore*, 1881
Oil on canvas, 25 ⅝ × 31 ½ in. (65 × 80 cm)
Musée des Beaux-Arts André-Malraux, Le Havre

The Sea

Fierce gunfire from fleets of battleships, or humble fishermen wresting a meager living from the ocean–the sea was no stranger to art, whether featured in heroic war spectacles or heartrending genre scenes. But the impressionists treated the subject entirely freshly. They did not need any excuse to produce a seascape. The sea appeared in its own right, in its full spectrum of colors, tempestuous or peaceful, thundering or majestically calm. The viewer could almost smell the sea spray.

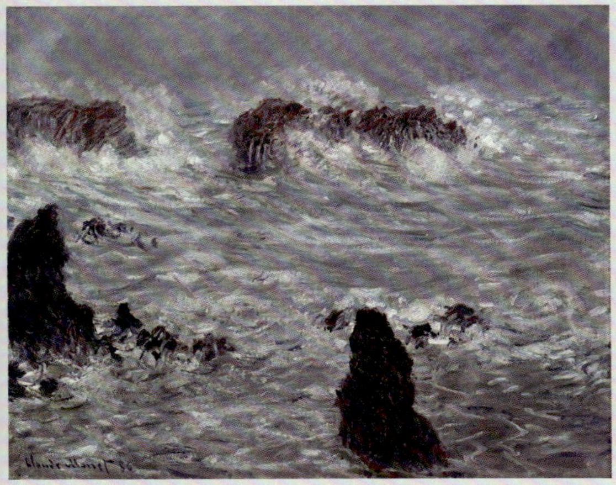

Claude Monet, *Storm on the Côte Belle-Île*, 1886
Oil on canvas, 25 ⅝ × 32 in. (65 × 81.5 cm)
Musée d'Orsay, Paris

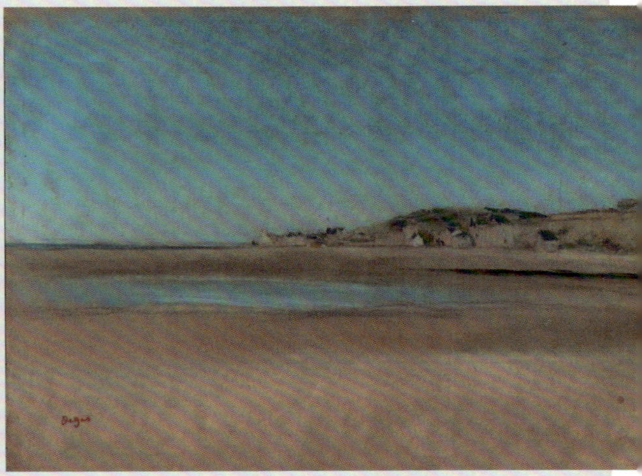

Edgar Degas, *Houses beside the Sea*, c. 1869
Pastel, 12 ⅜ × 18 ¼ in. (31.4 × 46.5 cm)
Musée d'Orsay, conserved at the Musée du Louvre, Paris

The Water's Edge

Painting their beloved banks of the Seine, the impressionists made water and the play of reflections one of their great themes. Constantly in motion, and sparkling with changing reflections, water was a subject that fascinated the impressionists above all others. When evoked by their brushstrokes, water was no longer a uniform, opaque mass, immobile like a sheet of metal. It revealed its transparency and its infinite range of tones, reflecting clouds, riverbanks, boats, and the sunlight, all perpetually changing.

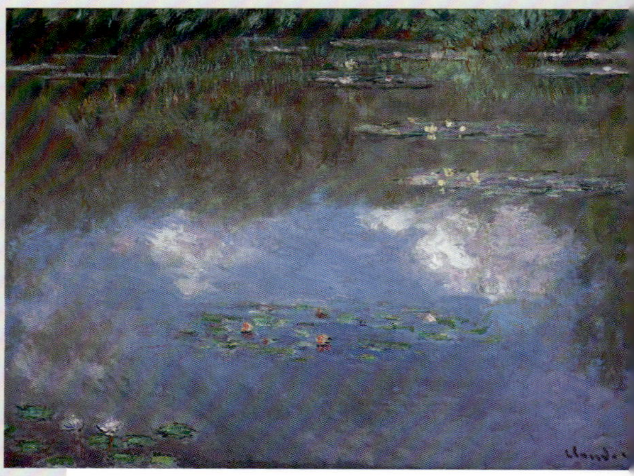

Claude Monet, *Water Lilies, Water Landscape, Clouds*, 1903
Oil on canvas, 2 ft. 4 ¾ in. × 3 ft. 3 ½ in. (73 × 100 cm)
Private collection

"Yet again I've taken on the impossible: Depicting water with grasses undulating beneath.... It's wonderful to behold, but it's madness to try to do this. But then I always take on such things."
Monet, letter to Gustave Geoffroy, June 22, 1890.

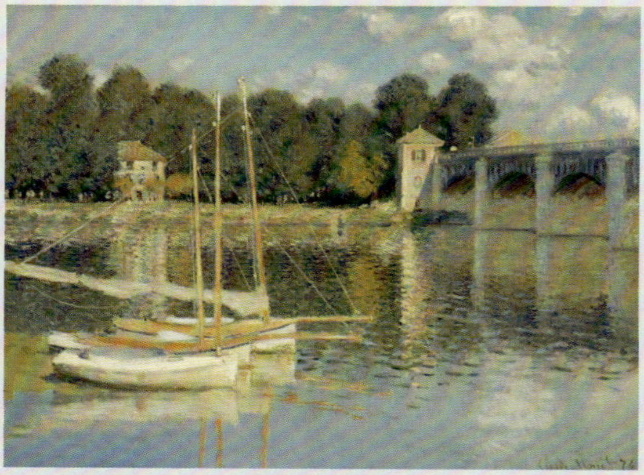

Claude Monet, *The Argenteuil Bridge*, 1874
Oil on canvas, 23 ⅞ × 31 ½ in. (60.5 × 80 cm), Musée d'Orsay, Paris

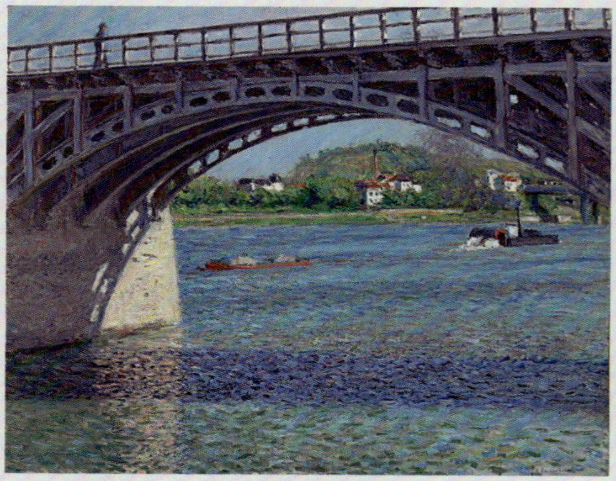

Gustave Caillebotte, *The Bridge at Argenteuil and the Seine*, c. 1883
Oil on canvas, 25 ¾ × 32 ⅛ in. (65.5 × 81.6 cm)
Private collection

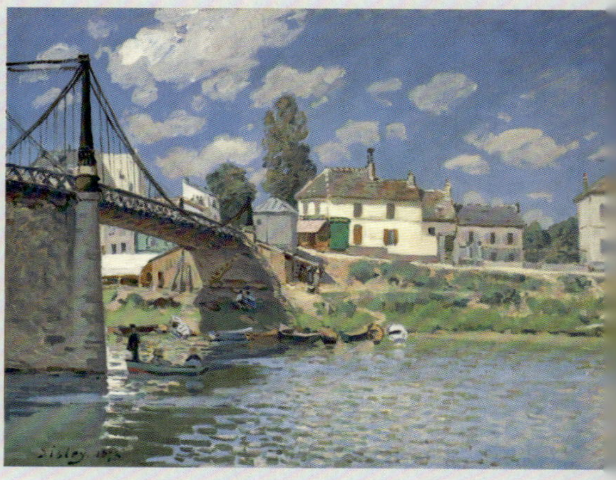

Alfred Sisley, *The Bridge at Villeneuve-la-Garenne*, 1872
Oil on canvas, 19 ⅛ × 25 ¾ in. (49.5 × 65.4 cm)
The Metropolitan Museum of Art, New York

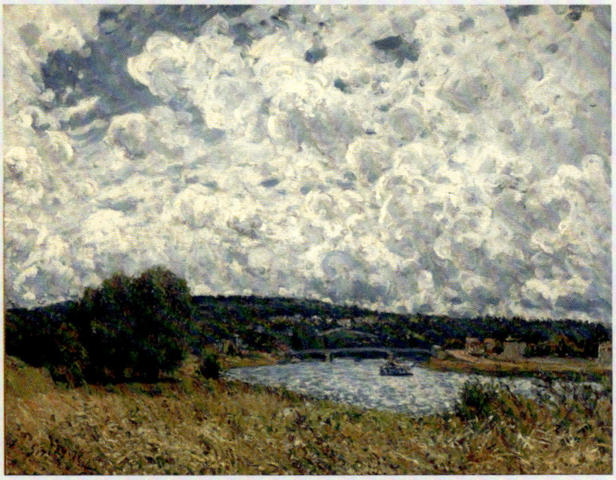

Alfred Sisley, *The Seine at Suresnes*, 1877
Oil on canvas, 23 ⅞ × 20 ⅞ in. (60.5 × 73.5 cm), Musée d'Orsay, Paris

The Sky

Passing clouds, bursts of sunlight, storms, the splendor of a sunset—for the impressionists, the constant mutability of the sky was a subject in its own right. When they left their studios to paint *en plein air*, their main goal was to find and render the shimmer of natural light. They never tired of the infinite variations of the sky, toward which the artist's eye always turned when painting outside; it was no longer restricted to a narrow band of blue or gray at the top of the canvas. Mighty events transpired there that deserved the artist's attention. The horizon line lowered and a vast new space was opened up to the painter's brush.

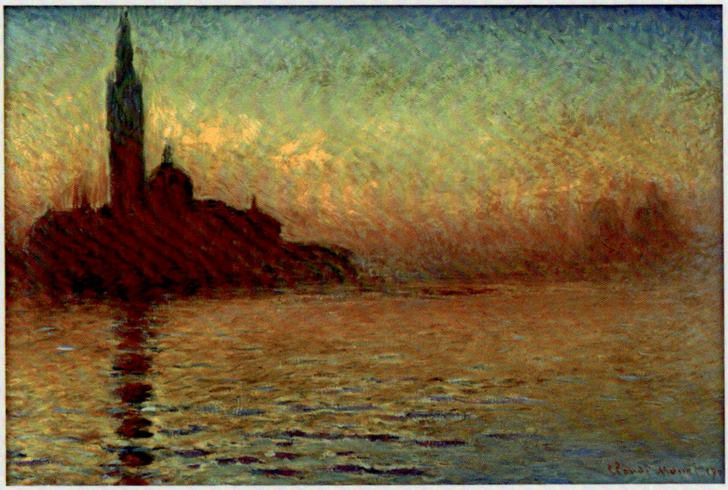

Claude Monet, *San Giorgio Maggiore by Twilight*, 1908
Oil on canvas, 2 ft. 1 ¾ in. × 3 ft. ½ in. (65.2 × 92.4 cm), National Museum of Wales, Cardiff

Strong Wind, Storm, Snow Effect, Frost Effect, Sun Setting or *Impression, Sunrise:* the impressionists employed a novel vocabulary for their picture titles, which spoke volumes about their innovative intentions. Capturing a fleeting light effect or atmospheric shift was a seemingly impossible challenge.

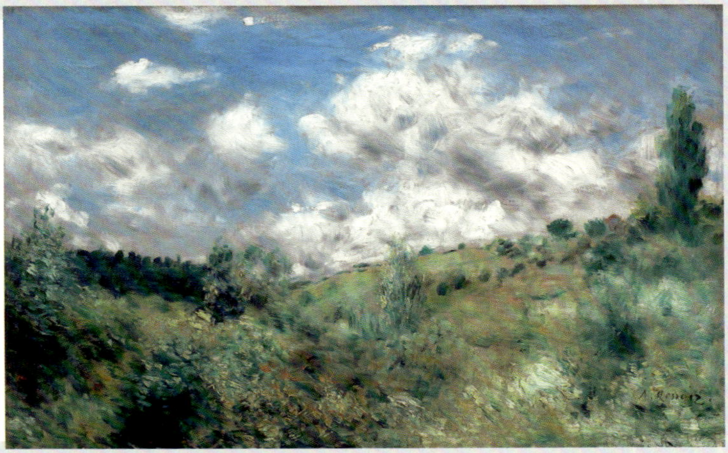

Auguste Renoir, *The Gust of Wind*, c. 1872
Oil on canvas, 20 ½ × 32 ½ in. (52 × 82.5 cm), Fitzwilliam Museum, Cambridge

Auguste Renoir
The Swing
1876
Oil on canvas,
3 ft. ¼ in. × 2 ft. 4 ¾ in.
(92 × 73 cm)
Musée d'Orsay, Paris

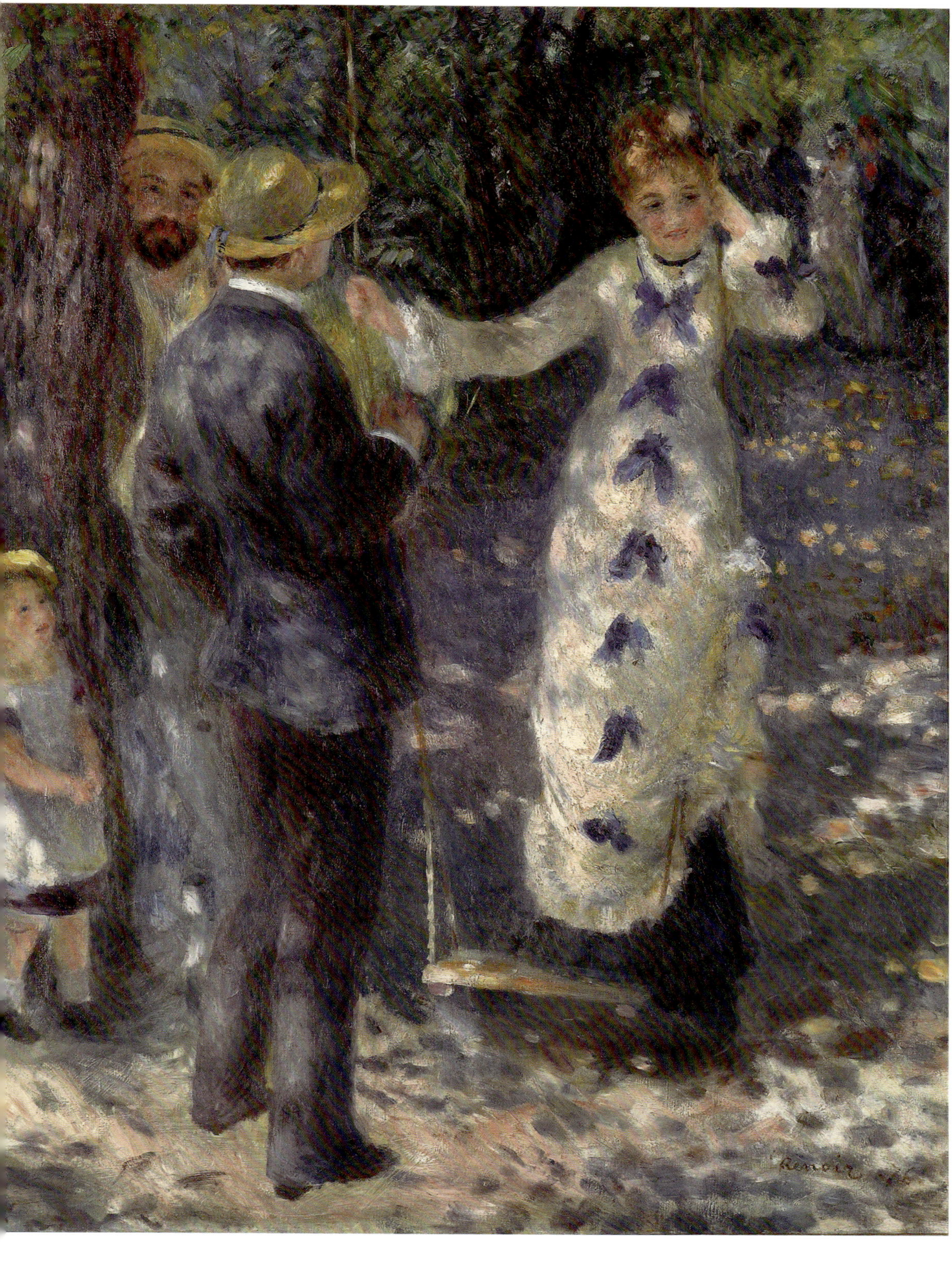

The Swing

Auguste Renoir, 1876

There is not really much going on near this swing, and yet.... A man seen from the back, a woman averting her gaze, a face emerging from the background, a little girl observing the scene from one side: the impressionists abandoned grandiose scenes in favor of everyday events captured as if in photographs.

Jeanne, a young resident of Montmartre, appears here between Edmond, Auguste Renoir's brother, and the painter Norbert Goeneutte. All three models also appear among the dancers in Dance at Le Moulin de la Galette.

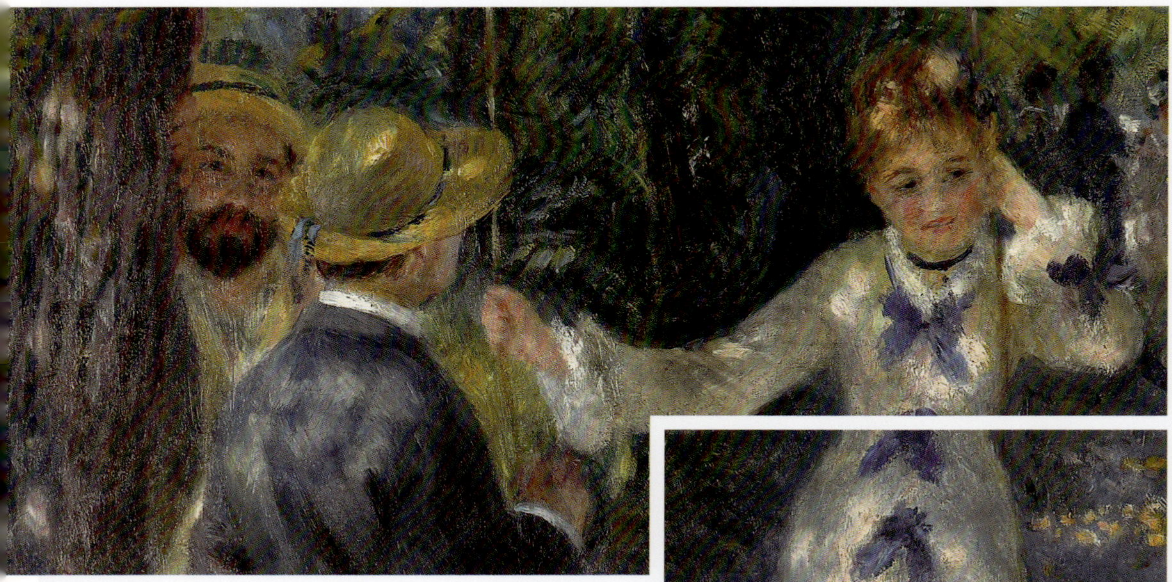

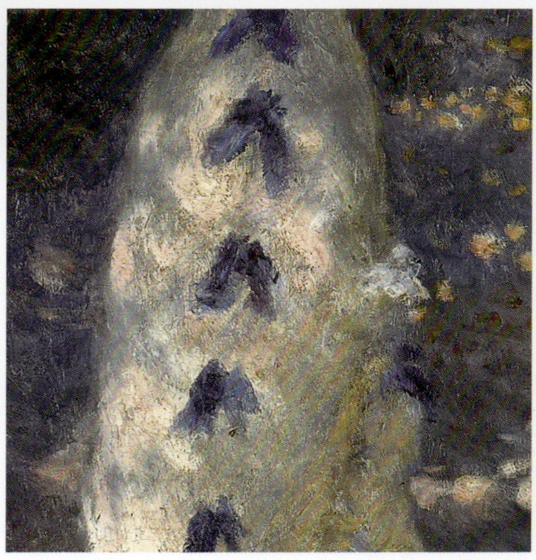

Renoir conveys the sparkling sunlight filtered through the leaves using splashes of light and shadow. This rendering was roundly condemned by critics.

Created in the summer of 1876, at the same time as *Dance at Le Moulin de la Galette*, this painting captures the carefree atmosphere of a Sunday afternoon in a place where working-class people gathered for relaxation. It was one of Renoir's favorite themes.

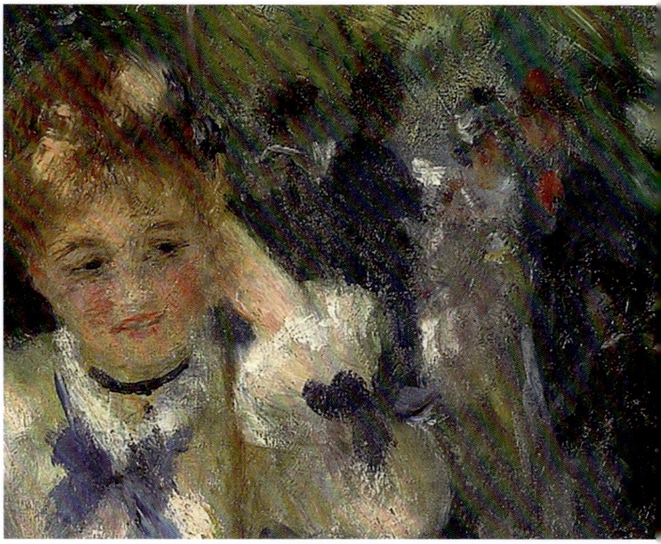

As if hastily sketched into the background, the group of figures in the distance sets the foreground scene within a larger context.

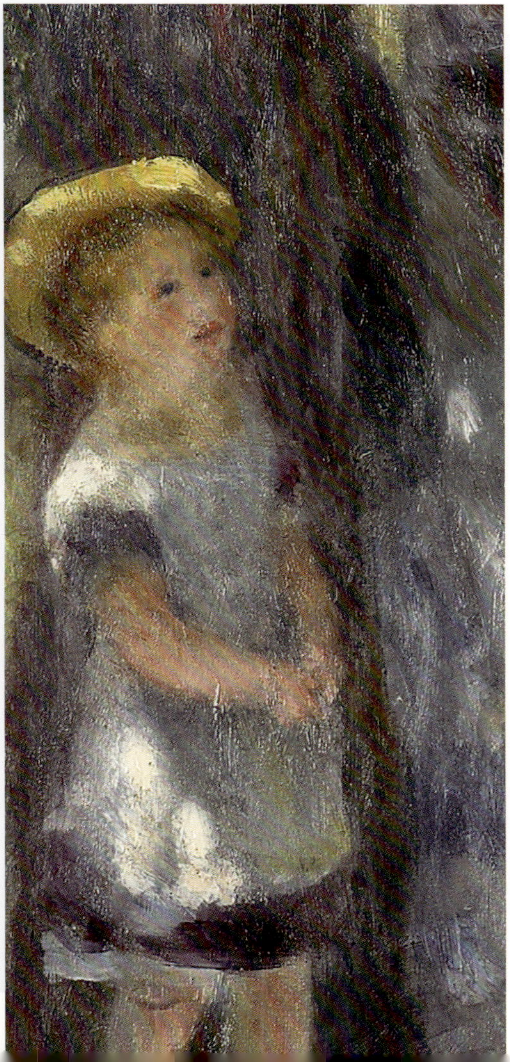

"I think a picture should be a delightful thing, happy and pretty–yes, pretty! There are enough troubles in the world, without spending our time making more of them."

Auguste Renoir.

The little girl's wondering gaze contrasts with the young woman's modest sideways glance. A skilled painter of children, Renoir marvelously captures the girl's charm and innocence.

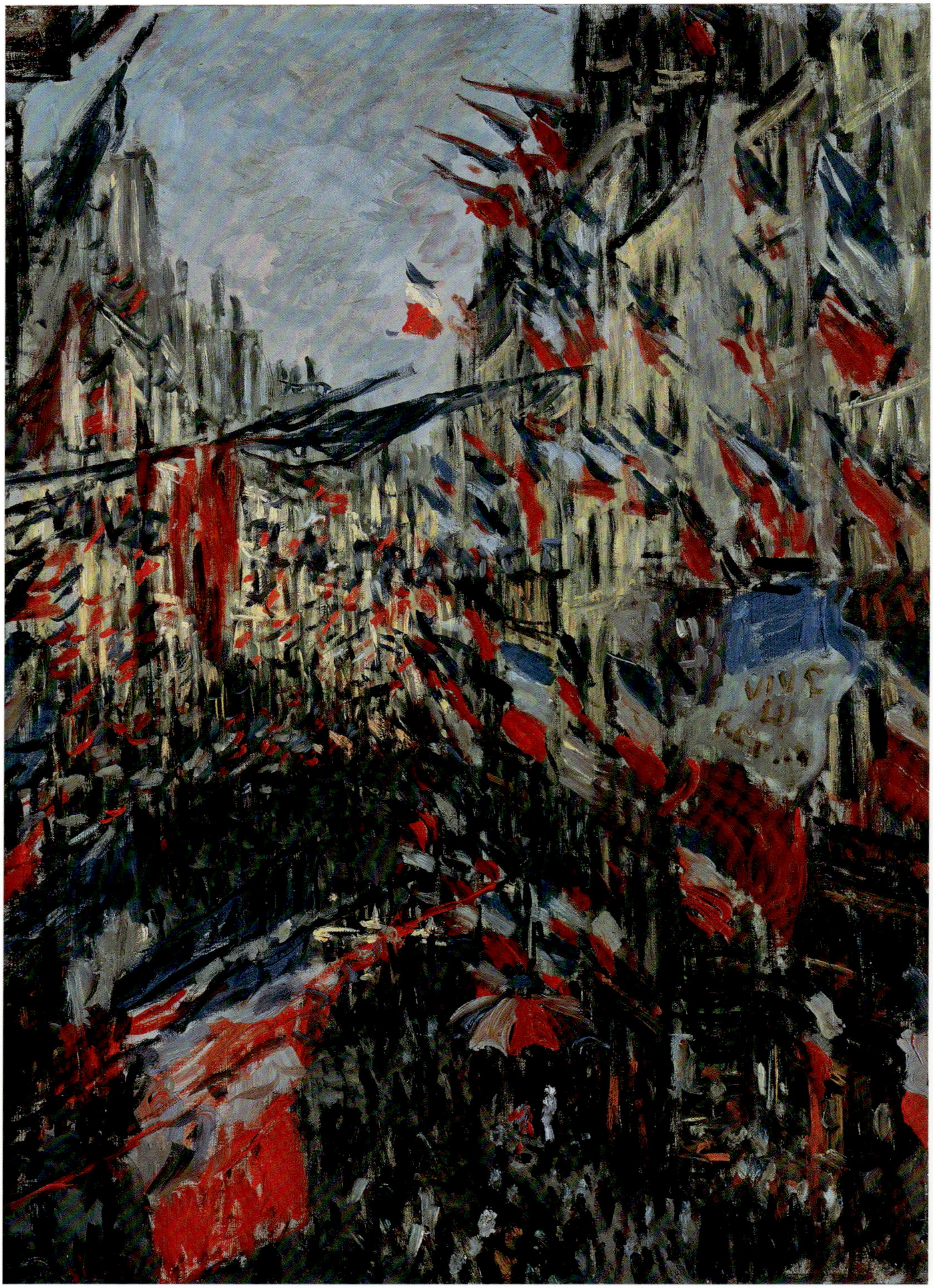

Claude Monet
The Rue Saint-Denis: Celebration of June 30, 1878
1878
Oil on canvas, 29 ⅞ × 20 ½ in. (76 × 52 cm)
Musée des Beaux-Arts, Rouen

Color First and Foremost

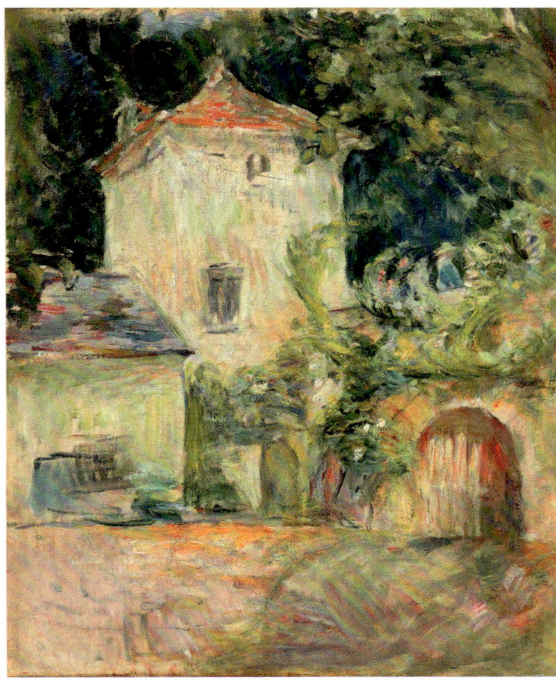

Berthe Morisot
Pigeon Loft at the Château du Mesnil, Juziers
1892
Oil on canvas, 16 ⅛ × 13 in. (41 × 33 cm)
Private collection

Radical from many points of view, the impressionists' innovative decision to set up their easels outdoors revolutionized painting by ignoring the norms of representational art. Embracing the direct and sensory experience of the outdoors, rather than recomposing the subject according to the rules and presuppositions of the studio, the impressionists quickly developed a new style of painting that addressed the challenge they had taken on. No more studies, no more preparatory drawings, no more professional models, no more local color. All the rules inculcated by the École des Beaux-Arts, the schools, and the academies were abruptly abandoned. Color reigned, applied in light, rapid brushstrokes. It assumed complete dominance over forms, tonalities, and impressions. Drawing, a purely intellectual construct, which outlined forms that were colored in later, was all but eliminated. There was nothing but vibrations of color, light, and movement. As Camille Mauclair so accurately observed: "While the academic painter sees only the exterior drawing enclosing the model's form, the impressionist sees the actual living lines that are without

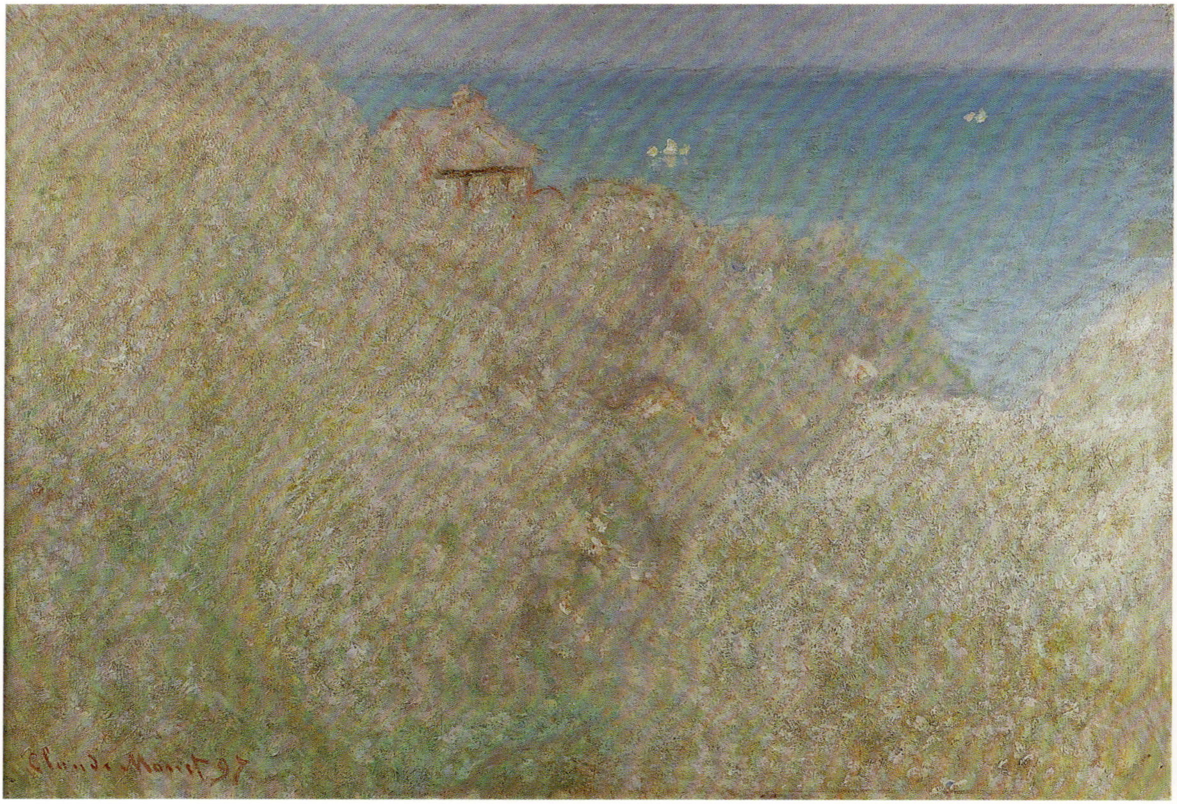

Claude Monet
Cliff at Varengeville (Gorge du Petit Ailly)
Oil on canvas, 2 ft. 1 ½ in. × 3 ft. ¼ in. (65 × 92 cm)
Musée des Beaux-Arts André-Malraux, Le Havre

geometric form but built up through thousands of irregular brushstrokes. Seen from a distance, they create life. While the academic painter depicts things by arranging them in their respective planes, following a system that can be reduced to a purely theoretical design, the impressionist's perspective is created by thousands of tiny tones and stipples, and by the variety of atmospheric conditions. It is not immobilized but rather constantly in motion." (*L'Impressionnisme: Son histoire, son esthétique, ses maîtres*, 1903). This exhilarating and extreme approach very often led to the elimination of conventional perspective; instead the space was constructed using a succession of colored picture planes. There were no more vanishing points or outlines. Drawing, once the unassailable pillar of academic art, had run its course. Color had once been applied meticulously

NO MORE "LOCAL COLOR"

The impressionists put an end to "local color," the academic principle that dictated that objects and surfaces be rendered without taking into account the way they are modified by light, atmospheric conditions, and neighboring hues. This fundamental change in the point of view was supported by Chevreul's scientific research on color, by *plein air* painting directly from nature, and by the study of master colorists of the past. The lesson learned was that color was everything.

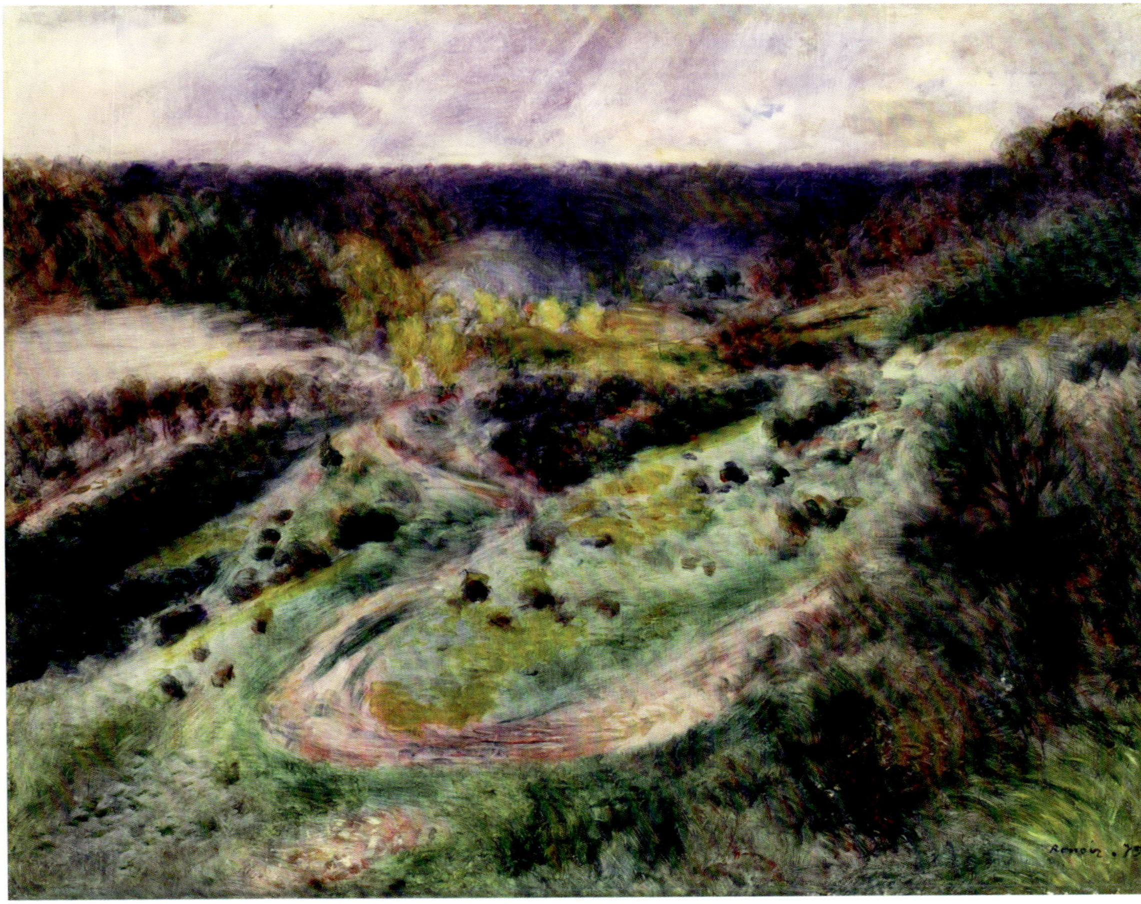

Auguste Renoir
Road at Wargemont
1879
Oil on canvas
Toledo Museum of Art, Toledo

so as to eradicate any trace of brushstrokes, but now the transition from one tone to another was obvious, with no attempt at concealment. The impressionists' ideal subjects were streets decked out for national celebrations, or landscapes in which light brought out colors and heat waves dissolved the contours of forms. The resulting work was akin to a sketch, very different from what viewers had come to expect. Audiences were shocked. But the revolution had begun, and it was unstoppable. The liberation of color continued, pushed to the limit by Monet and Renoir in the later years of their careers. In their wake came the fauvists in the early years of the twentieth century.

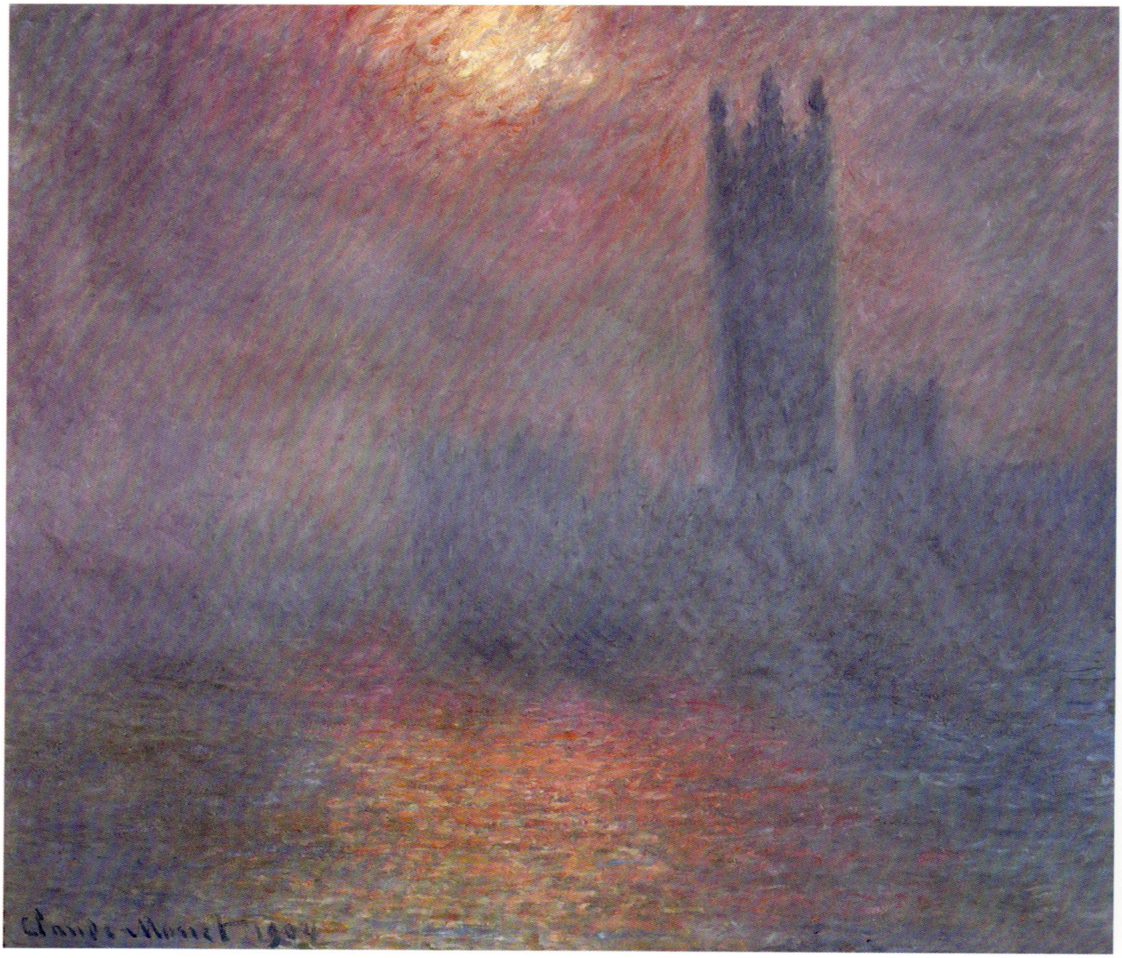

Fragmented into a multitude of colored dashes, Monet's brushstrokes render the diffraction of sunlight in London fog. Every form seems evanescent and insubstantial, even the majestic architecture of the Houses of Parliament.

Claude Monet
Houses of Parliament: The Sun Shining through the Fog
1904
Oil on canvas, 2 ft. 8 in. × 3 ft. ¼ in. (81 × 92 cm)
Musée d'Orsay, Paris

"Look at Titian, look at Rubens, and you'll realize that their shadows are a glaze, so thin that you can see through it. The shadows aren't black; no shadow is actually black. It always has color. Nature knows nothing but color, and black and white are not colors."

Auguste Renoir.

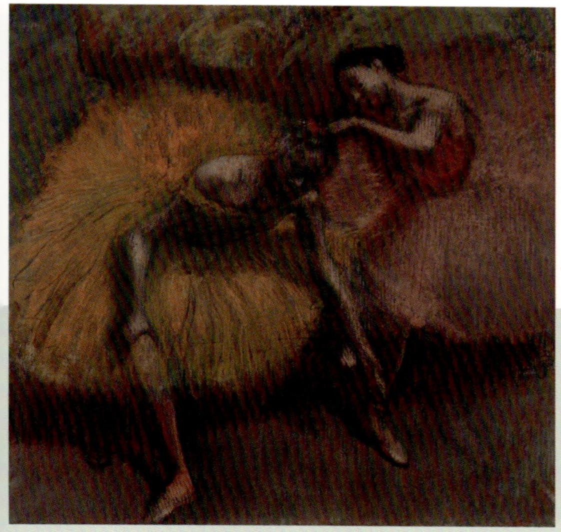

Edgar Degas
Two Dancers, Yellow and Pink
1898
Pastel, 3 ft. 5 ¾ in. × 3 ft. 6 ½ in. (1.06 × 1.08 m)
Museo de Bellas Artes, Buenos Aires

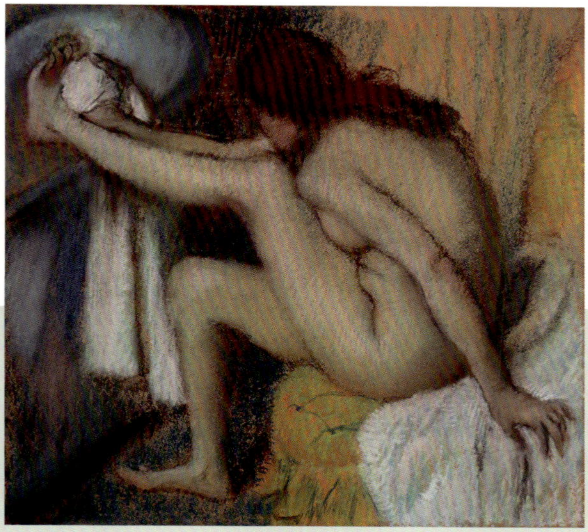

Edgar Degas
After the Bath, Woman Drying Her Left Foot
1886
Pastel on board, 19 ¾ × 21 ¼ in. (50.2 × 54 cm)
The Metropolitan Museum of Art, New York

DEGAS AND THE ART OF PASTEL

Degas was conscientious in his drawing and restrained in his palette when painting, but he allowed vibrant hues when working in pastels, which show the swift movement of his hand. He reserved the medium for intimate private scenes, capturing fleeting moments, and preserving them forever. In this scene of a woman bathing, the space defies conventional perspective and is conveyed entirely by the structure of colored picture planes. In the sketch of the two dancers, the brightly colored tutus are the focal point of the composition.

"Some imagined this juxtaposing of brushstrokes to be easy, because it seemed imprecise compared to good rigorous drawing as it's taught at school. In reality, the impressionist technique is incredibly difficult.... The eye recomposes what the brush has dissociated, and one finds oneself perplexed at all the science, all the secret order which has presided over this accumulation of spots which seem projected in a furious shower. It is a veritable orchestral piece, where every colour is an instrument with a distinct part, and where the hours with their different tints represent the successive themes."

Camille Mauclair, *L'Impressionnisme: Son histoire, son esthétique, ses maîtres*, 1903.

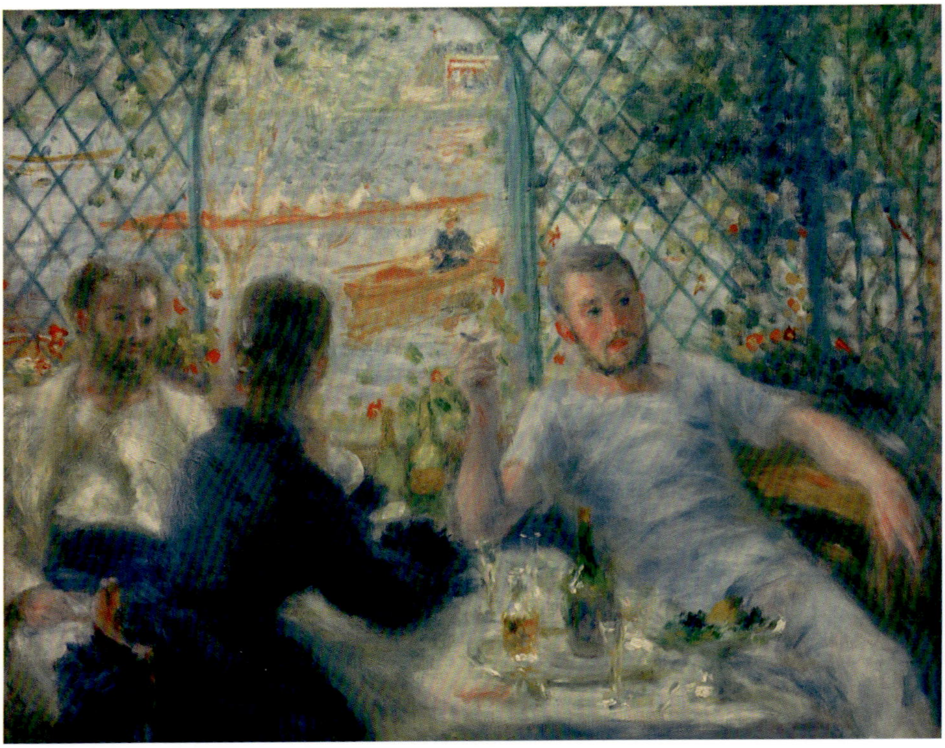

Auguste Renoir
Lunch at the Restaurant Fournaise,
also known as *The Rowers' Lunch*
1875
Oil on canvas, 21 ⅝ × 26 in.
(55.1 × 65.9 cm)
Art Institute of Chicago, Chicago

Constructed through a series of colored plains, the picture renders space as a multicolored powdering of brushstrokes, whose acid tonalities convey the intense light of a summer day. The effect is dazzling.

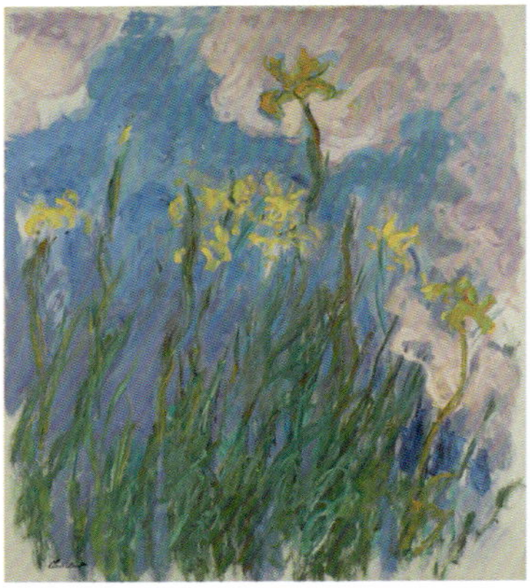

Claude Monet
Yellow Irises
1924–25
Oil on canvas, 4 ft. 11 in. × 4 ft. 3 ¼ in.
(1.50 × 1.30 m)
Michel Monet Collection, Giverny
Alice Tériade Collection, Paris

"The impressionist sees and represents nature just as it is, that is, solely in colored vibrations. Not design, nor light, nor relief, nor perspective, nor chiaroscuro–such childish classifications: in reality all of that is resolved in colored vibrations."

Jules Laforgue, "Critique d'art," *Mélanges posthumes*, 1903.

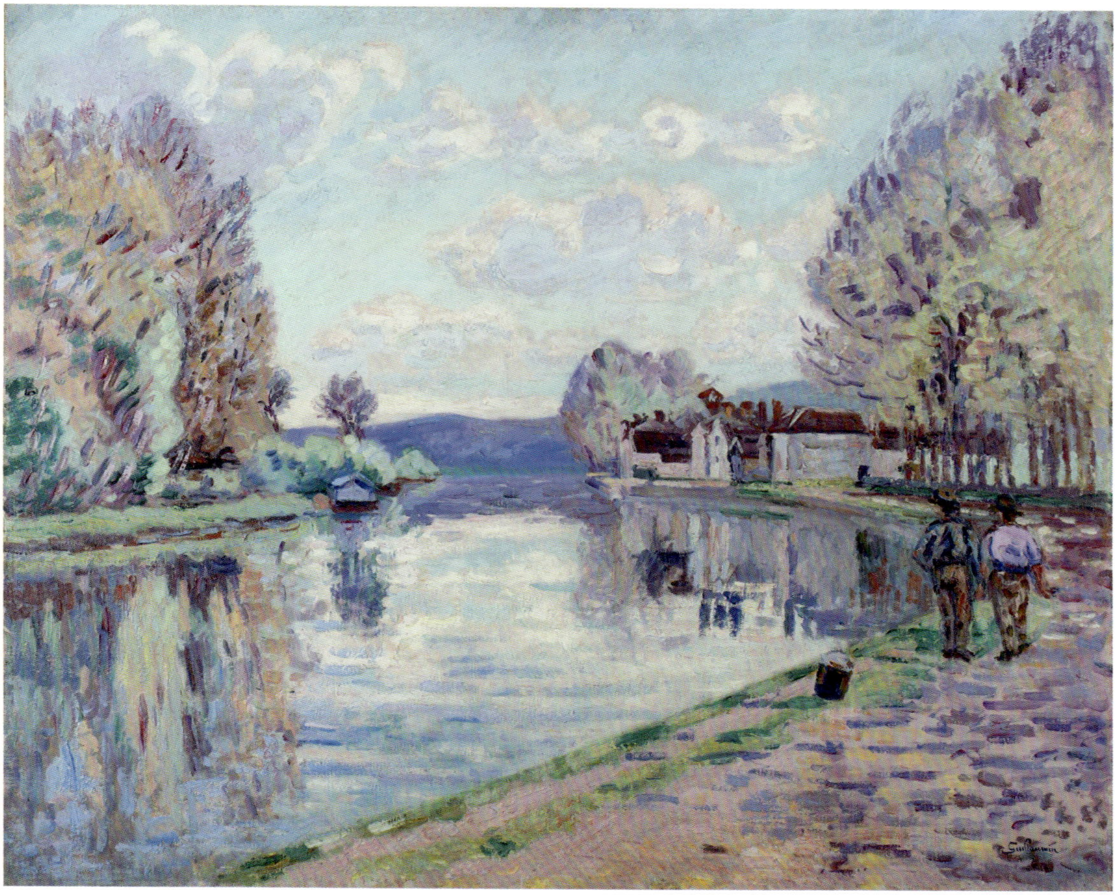

Armand Guillaumin
The Seine at Samois
c. 1898
Oil on canvas, 23 ⅝ × 28 ¾ in.
(60 × 73 cm)
Musée d'Art Moderne André-Malraux,
Le Havre

PISSARRO'S PAINTING LESSON

"Precise drawing is dry and hampers the impression of the whole, it destroys all sensations. Do not define too closely the outlines of things; it is the brush stroke of the right value and color which should produce the drawing.... Paint the essential character of things, try to convey it by any means whatsoever, without bothering about technique.... Don't work bit by bit, but paint everything at once by placing tones everywhere, with brush strokes and try to put down your perception immediately.... Don't be afraid of putting on color, refine the work little by little. Don't proceed according to rules and principles, but paint what you observe and feel.... Don't be timid in front of nature: one must be bold, at the risk of being deceived and making mistakes. One must have only one master—nature; she is the one always to be consulted."

Pissarro's advice to the young painter Le Bail, quoted by John Rewald, *The History of Impressionism*, 1946.

FOCUS

Snow

Attuned to shifting atmospheric phenomena, the impressionists found that their intuitions were confirmed when they studied snow. Shadows were not black, but colored, because they were subject to the principle of reflection. It was a challenge to sell this observation, but it was the source of infinite pictorial experiments for these painters.

The impressionists chose unassuming landscapes for their snow scenes. The subjects were the pretext for testing the subtlety of their palettes and their skill at conveying all the variations of the colored reflections. The clear colors of the impressionist style were expressed in all their beauty, opening the eyes of an audience habituated to the dark palette of the many nineteenth-century artists who used murkier hues. This powerful luminosity was shocking, as was the color treatment of the shadows and the reflections on the snow. Until this time, the vision created in the studio rendered snow as a uniformly white expanse. A dazzling exercise in virtuosity, the subject was one that Monet, Pissarro, and Sisley explored throughout their careers.

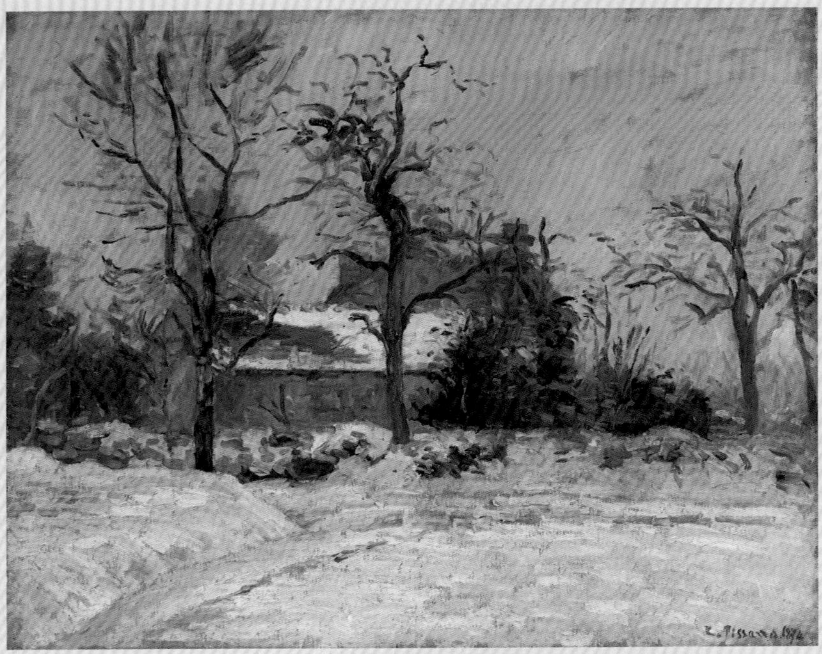

Camille Pissarro, *Piette's House at Montfoucault: Snow Effect*, 1874
Oil on canvas, 23 ⅝ × 28 ¼ in. (60 × 73.5 cm), Fitzwilliam Museum, Cambridge

"With the advent of winter, impressionists paint snow. If they see that the shadows cast by the sun are blue, they unhesitatingly paint blue shadows. And the public laughs."

Théodore Duret, *Les Peintres impressionnistes*, 1878.

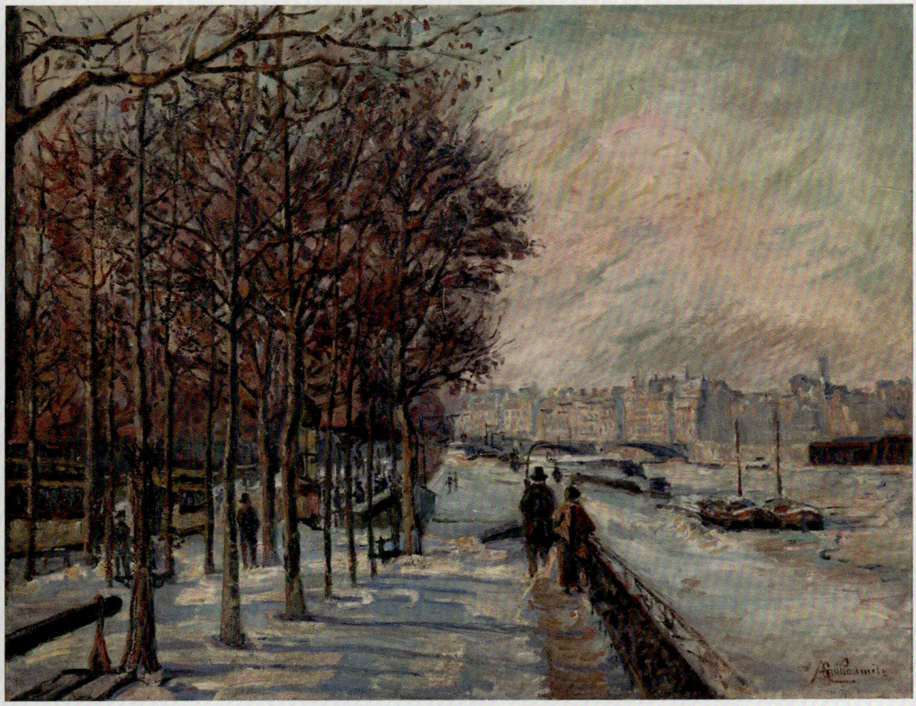

Armand Guillaumin, *Place Valhubert, Paris*, 1875
Oil on canvas, 25 ⅜ × 31 ⅞ in. (64.5 × 81 cm)
Musée d'Orsay, Paris

Painted outdoors near Étretat five years before the first impressionist exhibition, this snowy landscape has no hint of narrative, save for a magpie perched on a stile. The painting demonstrates Monet's early fascination with the ephemeral, fleeting effects offered by the close observation of nature. A slash of sunlight cuts across the planes of shadow, and light gives this painting its structure, while the range of pastel colors in the whites is a pictorial tour de force. When submitted to the 1869 Salon, the work was refused because the jury was not accustomed to such a bright, luminous palette.

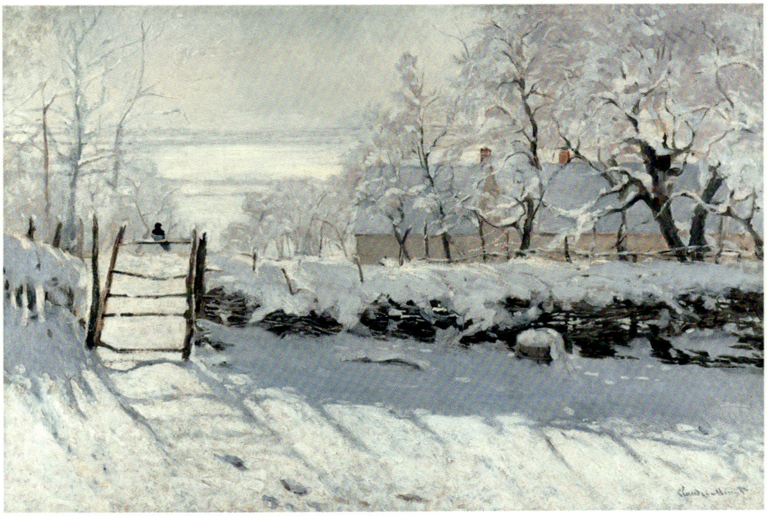

Claude Monet, *The Magpie*, 1868–69
Oil on canvas, 2 ft. 11 in. × 4 ft. 3 ¼ in. (89 × 130 cm), Musée d'Orsay, Paris

A recurrent topic in Pissarro's work, snow scenes always—as in paintings by the other impressionists—show nature slumbering beneath a thick white cloak. An exception that proves the rule, this city view shows pedestrians on a Parisian boulevard overtaken by a storm, in a subtle harmony of black and white.

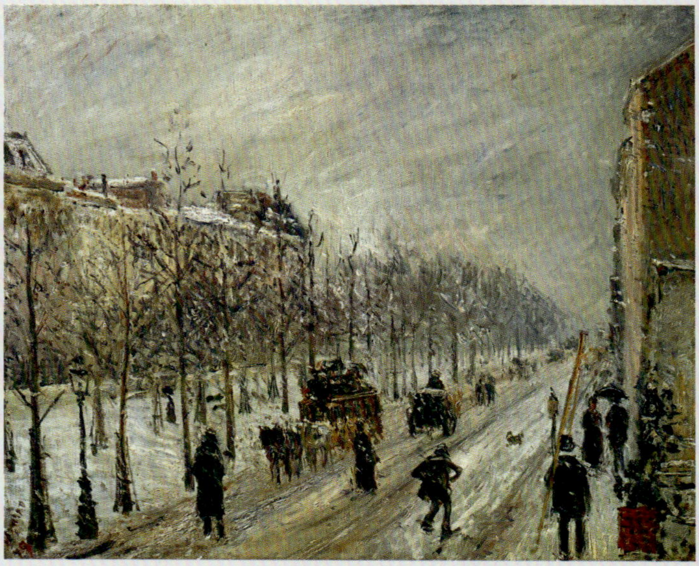

Camille Pissarro, *The Outer Boulevards: Snow Effect*, 1879
Oil on canvas, 21 ¼ × 25 ⅝ in. (54 × 65 cm)
Musée Marmottan Monet, Paris

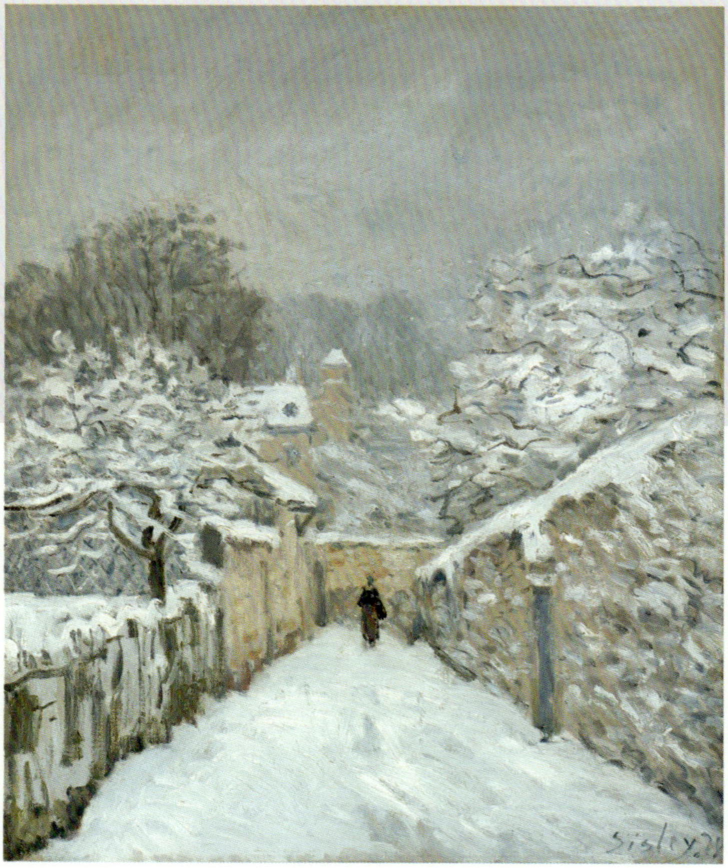

Alfred Sisley, *Snow at Louveciennes*, 1878
Oil on canvas, 24 × 19 ⅝ in. (61 × 50 cm), Musée d'Orsay, Paris

Sisley was a private, solitary man. He painted many snowscapes, whose soft, melancholy effects seem to echo his own retiring disposition. As is often the case in his landscapes, the path extends towards the horizon. Here it is punctuated by a dark silhouette, seen from the back, in the precise center of the composition. A profound sense of stillness emanates from the scene; it may superficially seem uneventful, but the swift brushstrokes enliven the surface.

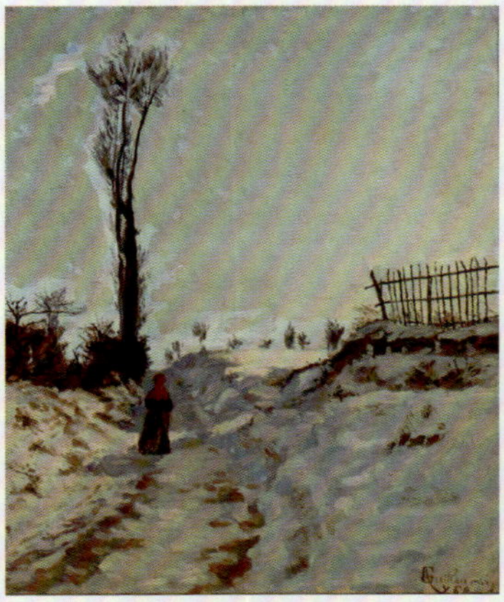

Armand Guillaumin, *Rutted Path, Effect of Snow,* 1869
Oil on canvas, 26 × 21 ⅝ in. (66 × 55 cm)
Musée d'Orsay, Paris

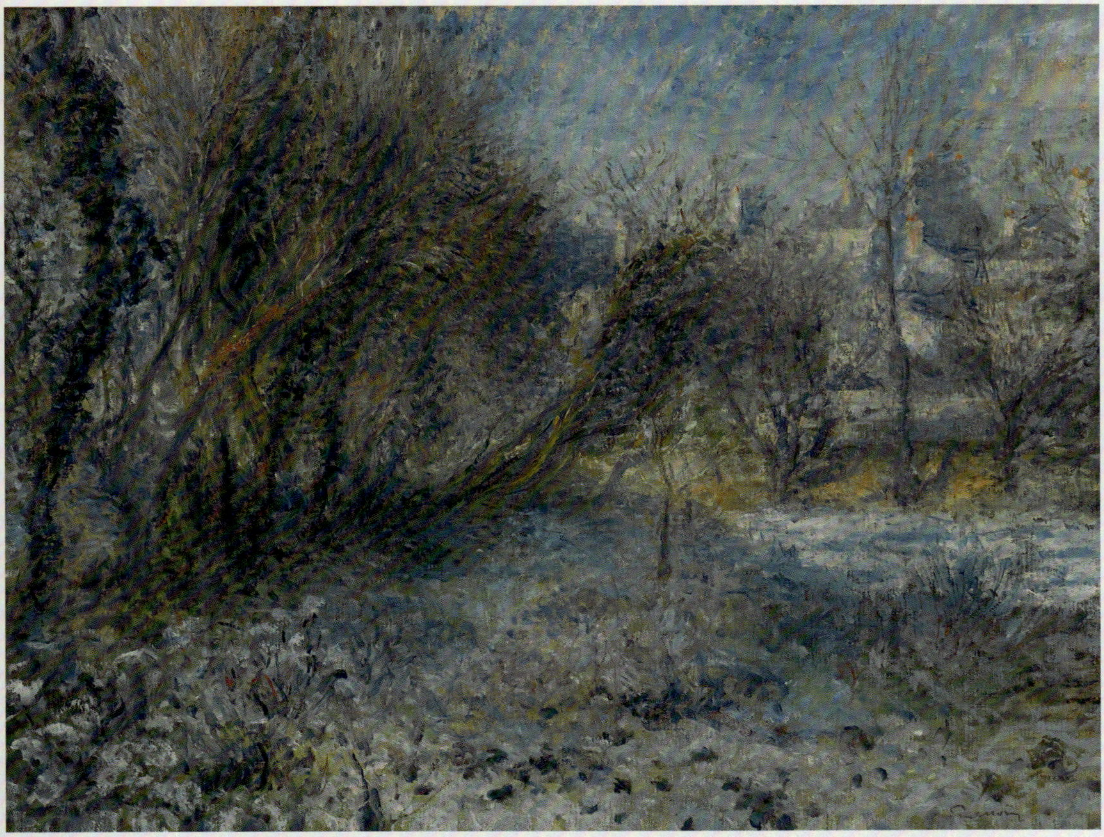

Auguste Renoir, *Snow-Covered Landscape,* c. 1875
Oil on canvas, 20 × 26 in. (51 × 66 cm), Musée de l'Orangerie, Paris

"White does not exist in nature.... You admit that you have a sky above that snow. Your sky is blue. That blue must show up in the snow. In the morning there is green and yellow in the sky. These colors also have to appear in the sky if you paint your picture in the morning. If you paint it in the evening, you'd have to use red and yellow."

Auguste Renoir.

IMAGES IN THE SPOTLIGHT

Claude Monet
Turkeys
1876–77
Oil on canvas,
4 ft. 10 in. × 5 ft. 7 ¾ in.
(1.47 × 1.72 m)
Musée d'Orsay, Paris

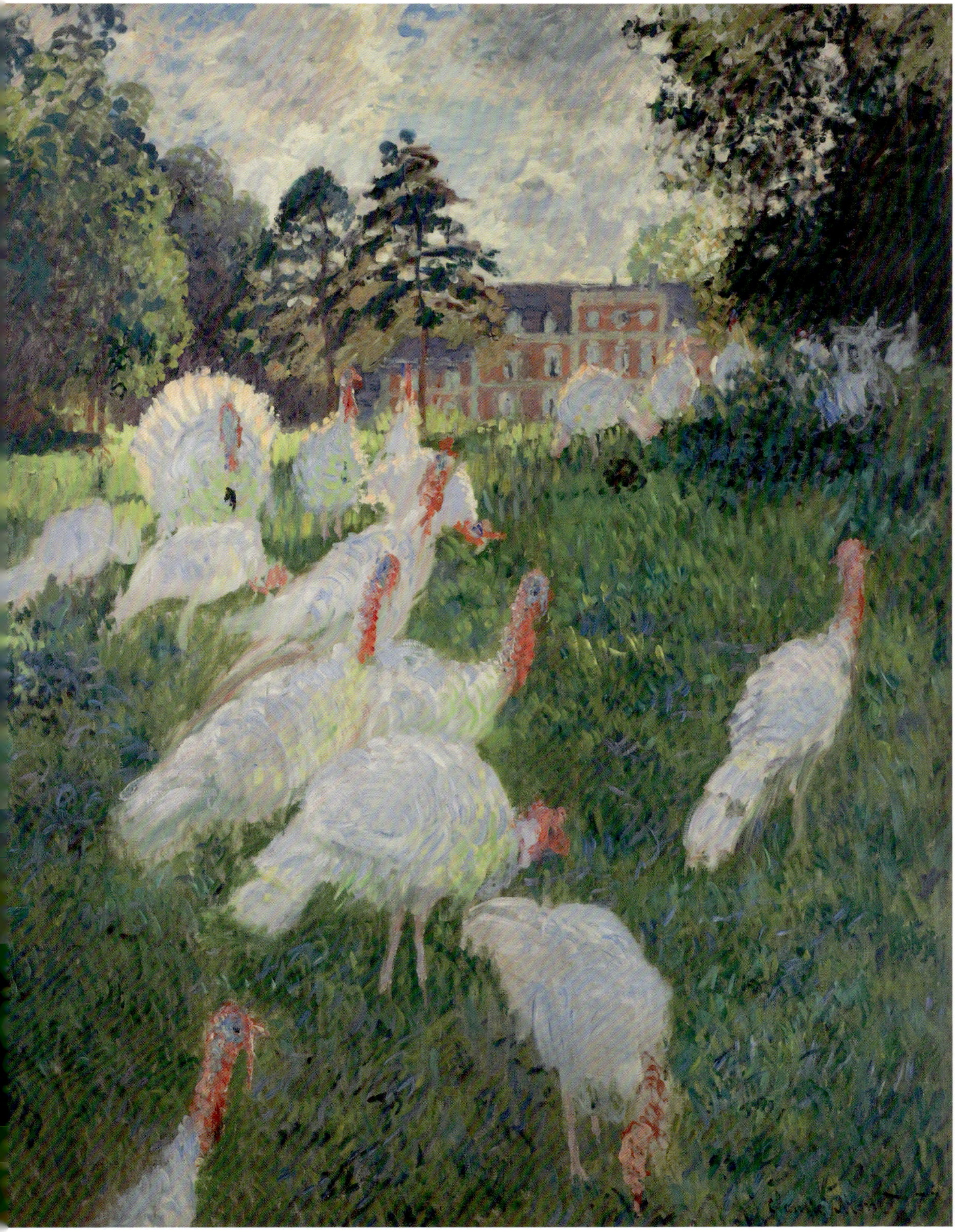

Turkeys

Claude Monet, 1876–77

Commissioned from Monet by Ernest Hoschedé for the large drawing room in his château in Montgeron, this audacious composition was originally one of four decorative panels. The patron's château is relegated to a minuscule presence in the background, yielding pride of place to a flock of turkeys. The subject matter may seem incongruous, but color is the real topic of this painting.

The turkeys' white plumage has tints of blue to convey the volume and the shadows that, for the impressionists, were never black.

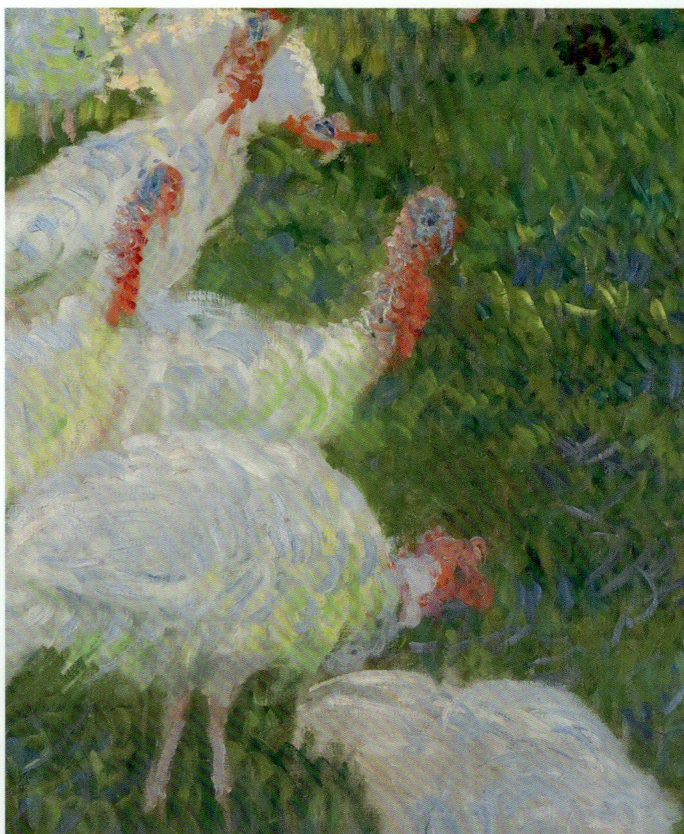

The turkey, stretching its neck and turning its head toward the foreground, tells us that the picture is merely a fragment of a much larger world. Monet introduces the entirely novel notion of an "off-camera" view. The pictorial composition is not a world unto itself.

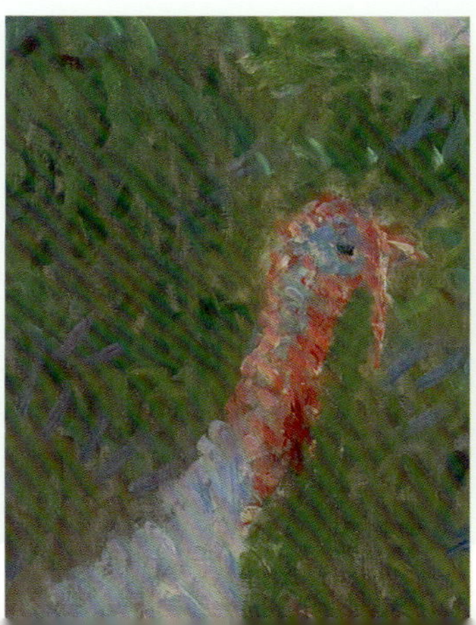

"This clever panel is delightfully executed, as delightfully as the most remarkable Japanese drawings. It evoked... hysterical laughter. They swooned, they writhed, and they held their bellies... and I'm referring to some very respectable bellies!"

Octave Mirbeau, "Notes on Art: Claude Monet," *La France*, November 21, 1884.

A VERY SPECIAL PAINTING

Daring in its subject matter, as well as the way of life and sense of the natural world it depicts, this work was displayed in the third impressionist exhibition in 1877. It did not win unanimous approbation, to put it mildly. Monet was particularly fond of this painting and kept track of the work as it passed among collectors. In 1903, he told Durand-Ruel that he wanted to reacquire it, but his wish was never fulfilled.

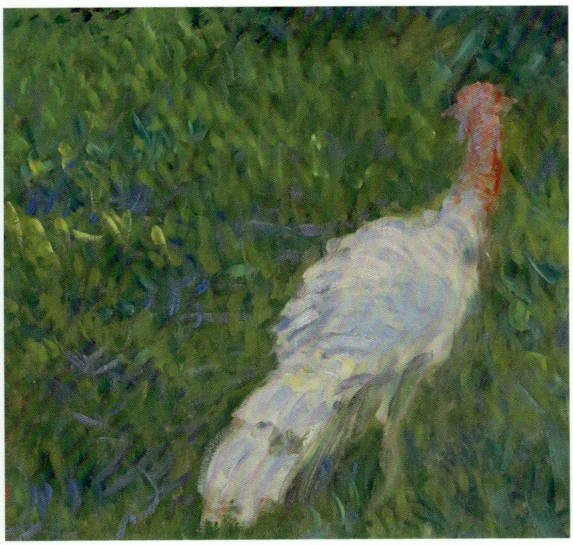

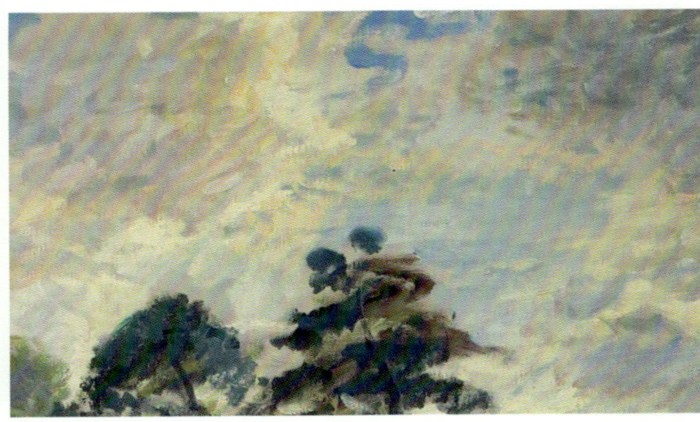

Monet's deft, rapid brushstrokes adapt flexibly and capably to his subject, whether he is depicting grasses or clouds in the sky.

The ray of sunlight shining through the turkey's tail feathers creates a halo. The effect demonstrates Monet's interest in light effects, which were among his favorite subjects.

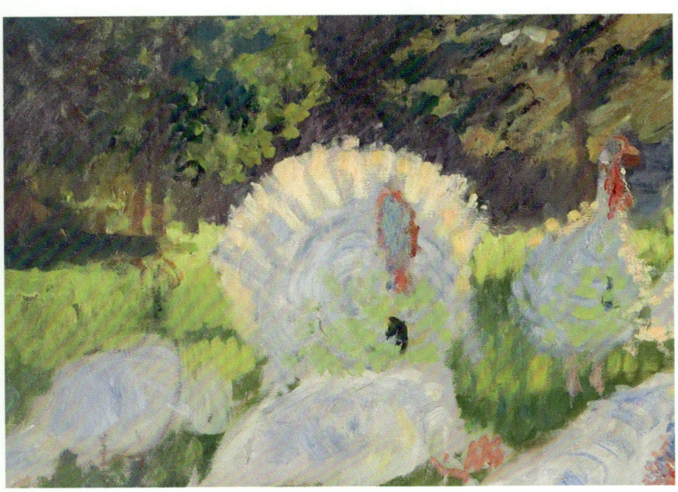

"'Just look at the house! Why, the turkeys couldn't walk in at the door. The perspective is all wrong....' For art was not for us then as it is now—a mere emotion, right or wrong only in proportion to its intensity; we believed then in the grammar of art, perspective, anatomy."

George Moore, *Confessions of a Young Man*, 1917.

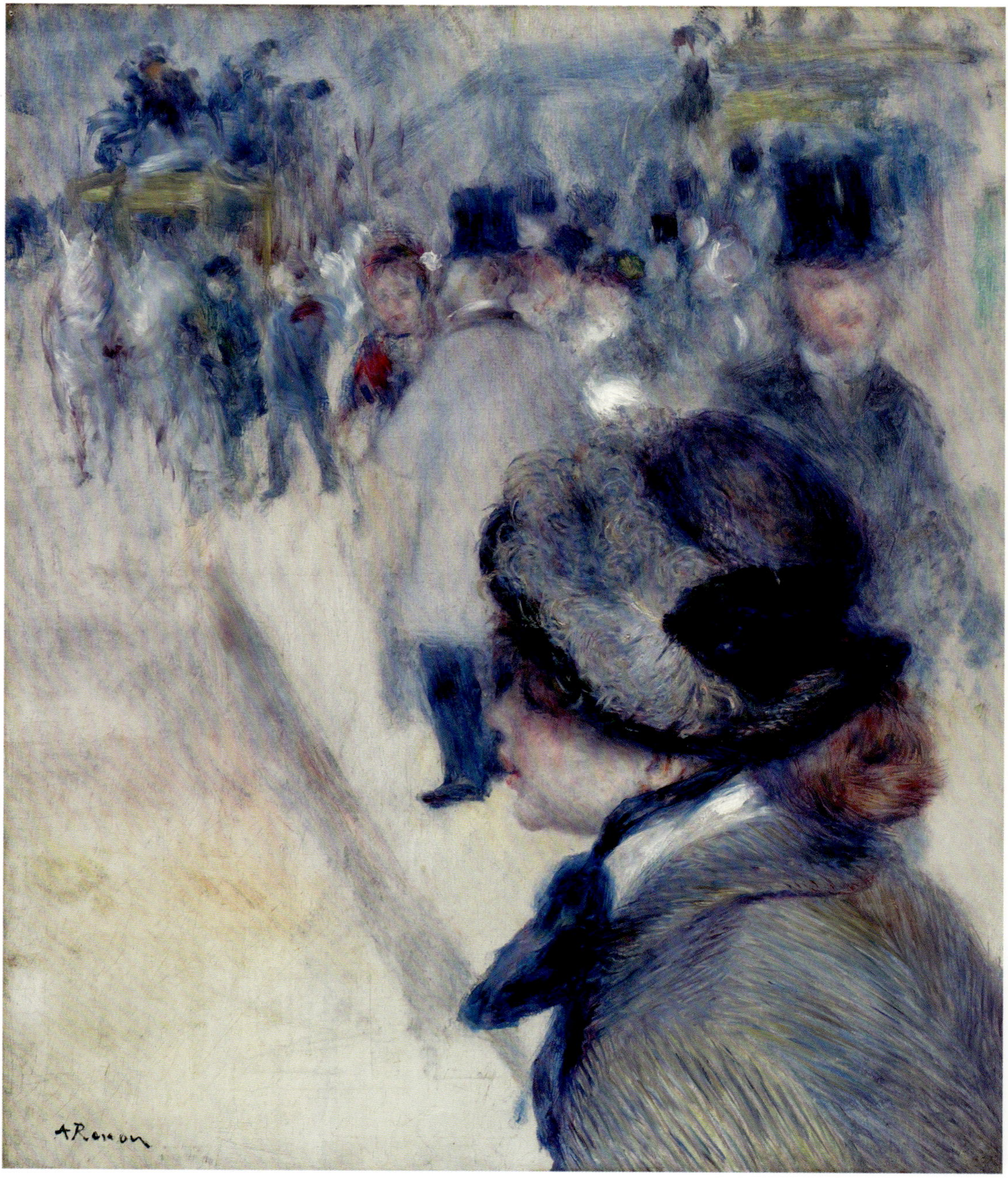

Auguste Renoir
Place Clichy
c. 1880
Oil on canvas, 25 ¼ × 21 in. (64 × 53.5 cm)
Fitzwilliam Museum, Cambridge

Capturing the Moment

"The juxtaposition of such strokes and washes carried out in the open air on any given subject matter were realised so quickly that they came faster than the thought that accompanied them."

Alain Tapié, "Physics of Nature, Physics of Painting," 2010.

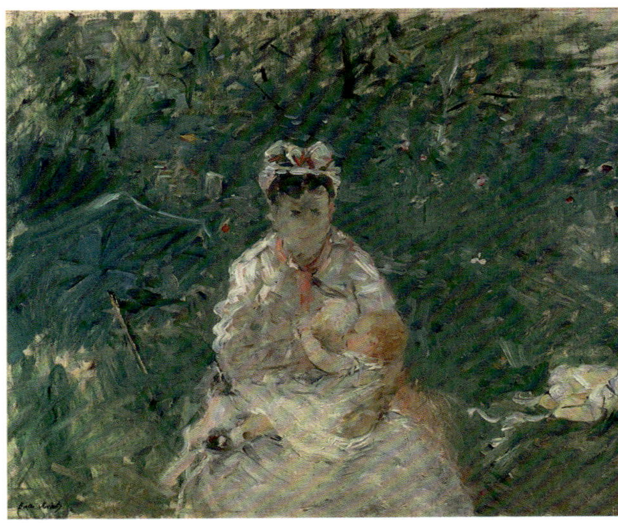

Berthe Morisot
The Nurse
1879
Oil on canvas, 19 ⅝ × 24 in. (50 × 61 cm)
Private collection, Washington, DC

Inquisitive about the contemporary world, and following their own subjectivity as artists, the impressionists broke with tradition in stepping out into the real world. Ridding their pictures of all academic affectations, they looked at their surroundings with a fresh, unaffected gaze. For them, the world was a blank page where everything could be reinvented. Novel subjects presented themselves, fresh sensations were awoken, and experimentation became part of the creative act. Suddenly, painting was no longer a question of applying rules or reproducing the commonplace, but actually entailed an act of creation.

Setting up an easel outdoors was a natural response to the desire to be closer to the realities of the world and their own feelings. This decisive initiative had powerful implications. First of all, it required the painter to capture the moment by working swiftly. By refusing to revisit their paintings back in the studio, the impressionists chose to retain intact the first impression, the painter's equivalent of the writer's first draft. They imposed speed upon themselves; there was no opportunity for retouching or second thoughts.

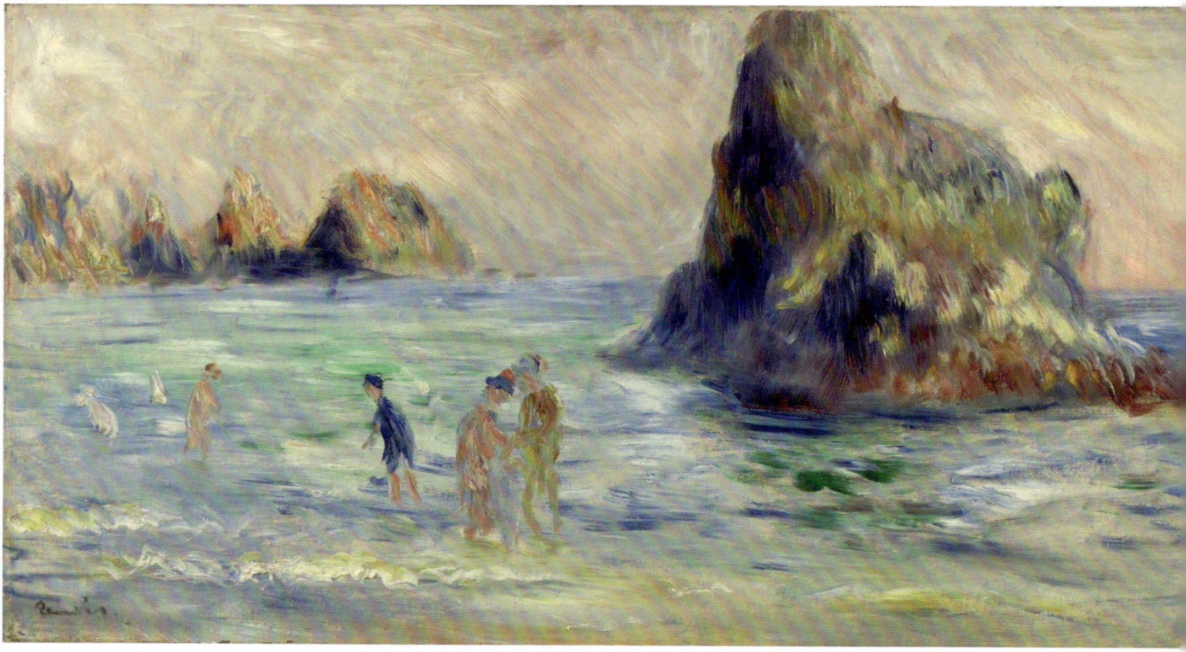

Auguste Renoir
Moulin Huet Bay, Guernsey
c. 1883
Oil on canvas, 11 ½ × 21 ¼ in. (29.2 × 54 cm)
National Gallery, London

Capturing the transience of the moment, following the first impulse of artistic creation, before the child turns her head or a cloud obscures the sun, the artist must paint quickly, almost at one with the subject. This revolutionary approach broke away from all the methodical steps taught in the academies. It liberated the brushstroke, which became both color and drawing, capturing the ephemeral with the tip of a paintbrush, a moment in time. Painting became a physical act, spontaneous and emotional rather than deliberate and cerebral. These works were executed directly on to the canvas without preparatory drawings. Paintings retained an unfinished quality, reminiscent of a sketch–a criticism often levied by the impressionists' critics. Some, like Monet and Berthe Morisot, remained faithful to this practice throughout their careers, although it was both demanding and intuitive. Others, such as Renoir, abandoned the approach for a while, or never embraced it, like Degas. But whatever their personal choices, whether or not they permanently embraced *plein air* painting, or whether they preferred the water's edge or the city's

"They tried to convey the motion, the movement, the vibration, and the interplay of passersby as if they were trembling leaves, or glinting water, or the vibration of sun-drenched air, like the sheen of the sun's rays; they knew how to capture the soft embrace of a gray sky."

Edmond Duranty,
"The New Painting," 1876.

Degas excelled at framing his subjects like photographs, inventing a new approach to the depiction of space. Always interested in conveying the reality that lay before him, he brought a fresh vision to well-worn subjects as conventional as a woman at her toilette. The Degas model was a far cry from the traditional bathing Venus. Manet's approach was raw in comparison, and was seen as banal—even indecent—by his audience.

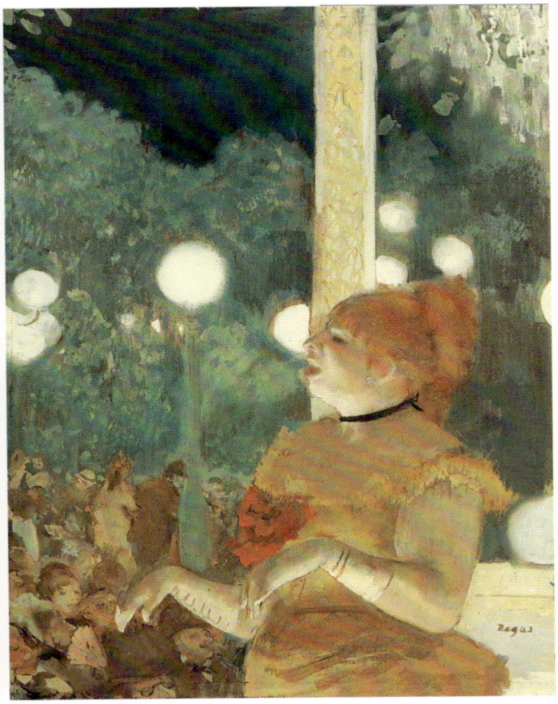

Edgar Degas
The Café Concert, also known as
The Song of the Dog
c. 1876–77
Gouache and pastel on monotype,
22 ¼ × 17 ⅞ in. (57.5 × 45.5 cm)
Henry Havemeyer Jr. Collection, New York

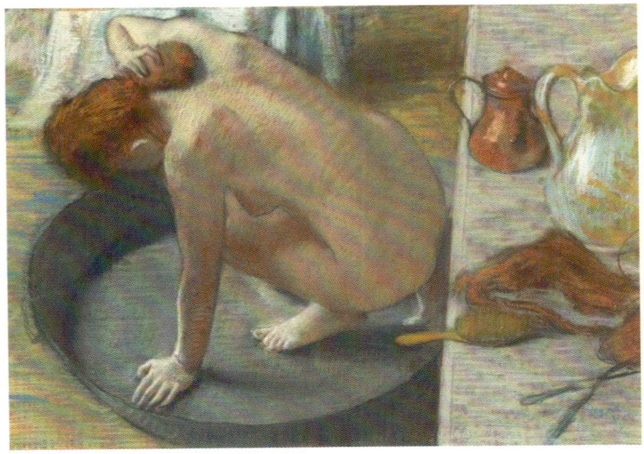

Edgar Degas
The Tub
1886
Pastel on board, 23 ⅝ × 32 ⅝ in. (60 × 83 cm)
Musée d'Orsay, Paris

streets as their subjects, all of these artists shared the challenge of capturing life on the fly. The photographic snapshot haunted their awareness. Figures are cropped exiting or entering the frame; forms appear in a blurred movement, as they do in the reality we experience. The impermanence of modern life and the ephemeral mood of our time attracted them, in contrast to the permanence and immobility of tradition. Always devoted to landscape, and painting from life, Monet made the transitory fluctuations of the atmosphere the focus of his entire career. Flags fluttering in the wind and the splendor of a sunset called to him earlier in life; in his later years he was obsessed by the endless reflections in the water-lily pond in Giverny. Berthe Morisot also pursued this ambition, coupled with humility, to remain committed to painting her first impressions of a subject. Even artists like Degas and Caillebotte, who painted partially or entirely in their studios, were united in their quest for reality and spontaneity. The photographic aesthetic inhabited these artists, and is evident in every one of their canvases. Life is there, vibrating in

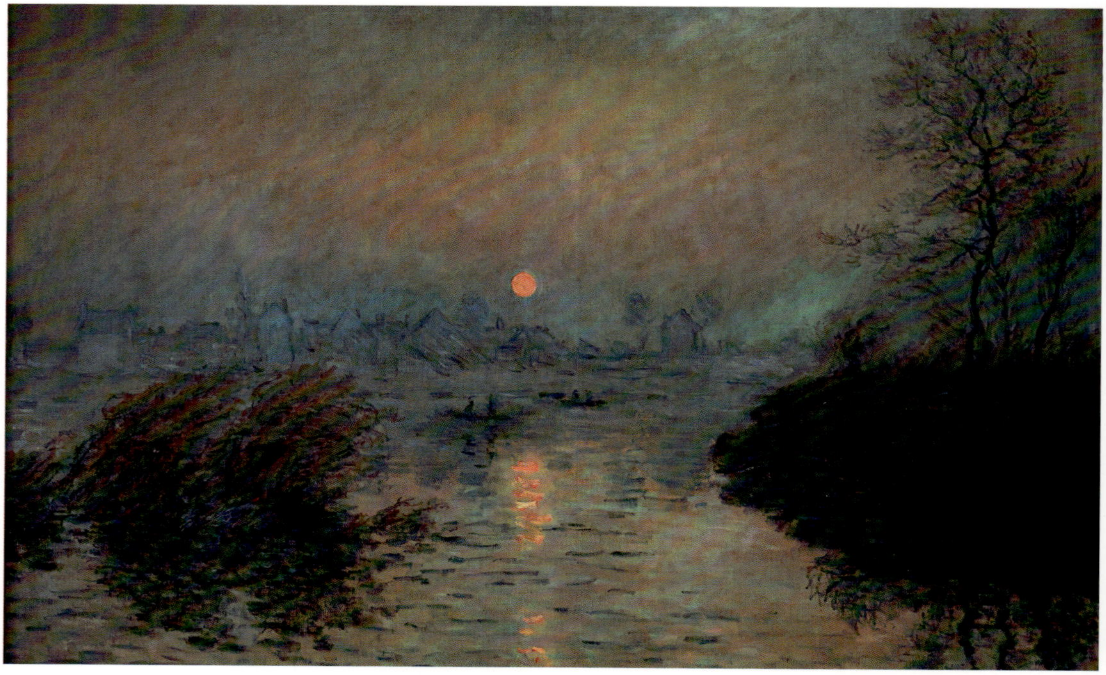

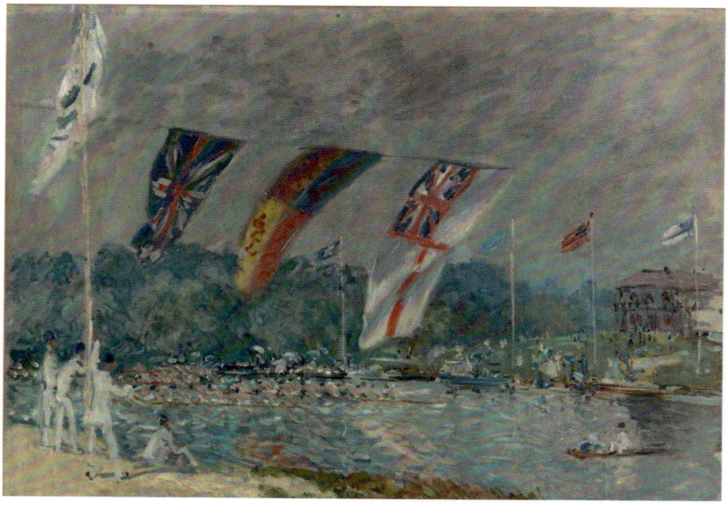

Claude Monet
Sunset on the Seine at Lavacourt: Winter Effect
1880
Oil on canvas, 3 ft. 4 in. × 4 ft. 11 in. (1.02 × 1.50 m)
Petit Palais, Musée des Beaux-Arts de la Ville de Paris, Paris

Alfred Sisley
Regatta at Molesey
1874
Oil on canvas, 2 ft. 2 in. × 3 ft. (66 × 91.5 cm)
Musée d'Orsay, Paris

Sisley was a painter of subtle landscapes devoid of human figures, but he was also skilled at conveying the bustling atmosphere at sporting events, or flags snapping in the breeze.

these figures, captured in the midst of their daily activities. They're sometimes glimpsed in the process of entering into the picture plane or escaping its frame. The cabaret singers hold forth; the Opéra's child dancers rehearse or stand yawning in the wings; pedestrians stride along the streets of Paris with hurried steps; oarsmen flex their muscles in the summer sunlight—all fixed in the moment.

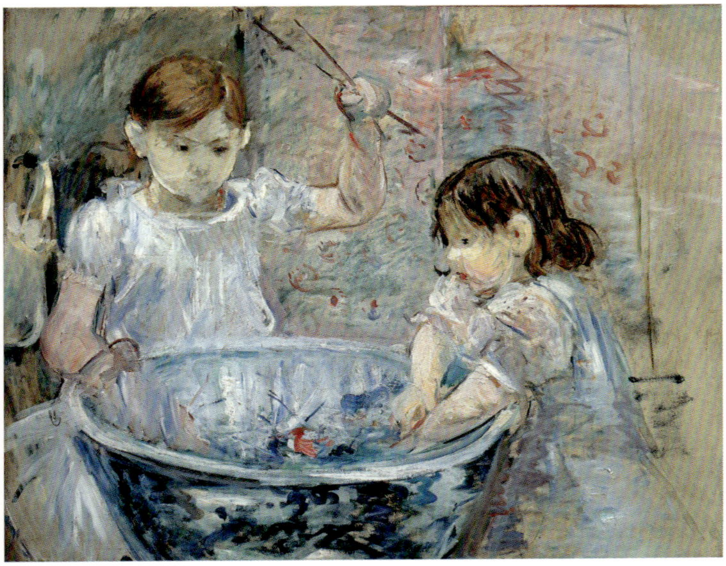

Berthe Morisot
Children with a Bowl
1886
Oil on canvas, 2 ft. 4 ¾ in. × 3 ft. ¼ in.
(73 × 92 cm)
Musée Marmottan-Monet, Paris

Conveying childhood with sensitivity, Berthe Morisot captured this playful moment in her apartment on the Rue de Villejust in Paris. She used her brush deftly, to draw as well as to paint. Critics often reproached her for the unfinished quality that went hand in hand with her spontaneity.

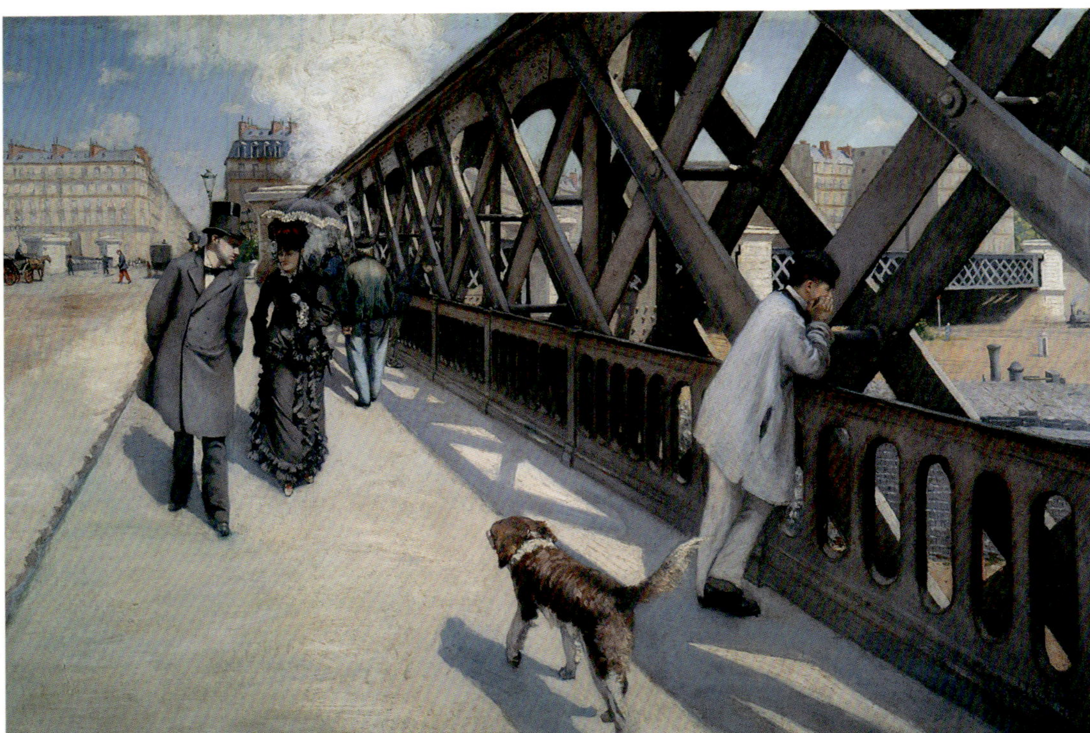

Gustave Caillebotte
The Pont de l'Europe
1876
Oil on canvas, 4 ft. 1 in. × 5 ft. 11 in.
(1.25 × 1.82 m)
Musée du Petit Palais, Geneva

This composition is a snapshot of urban life, firmly anchored by the receding diagonal of the sidewalk and the metal latticework of the recently constructed Pont de l'Europe. A couple passes by, engrossed in conversation; smoke billows from a train; and a dog trots purposefully into the foreground of the pictorial space.

FOCUS

The Series

The almost insurmountable challenge of capturing ephemeral moments led the impressionists to return tirelessly to the same subjects–landscape for Monet, her daughter Julie for Berthe Morisot, and dancers in rehearsal for Degas. This obsessive preoccupation led some of the artists to undertake series of paintings. This practice might be considered the fulfillment of a quest–or acknowledgement of defeat.

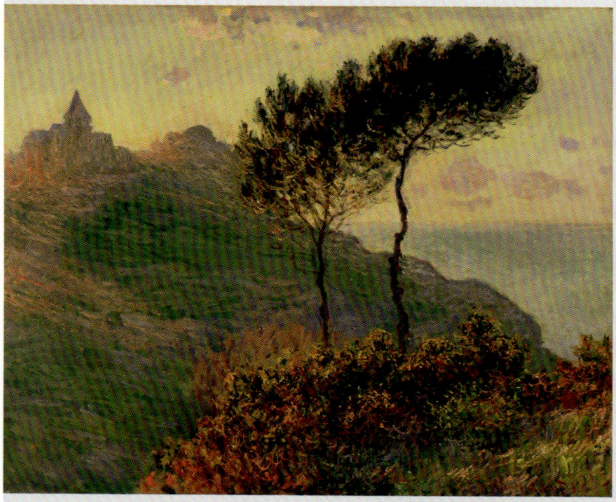

Claude Monet, *The Church at Varengeville, Backlit*, 1882
Oil on canvas, 25 ⅝ × 31 ⅞ in. (65 × 81 cm)
University of Birmingham, The Barber Institute of Fine Arts, Birmingham

"I often followed Claude Monet in his search for impressions. He actually wasn't a painter, he was a hunter. He was often trailed by children carrying his canvases; there might be five or six of them representing the same subject, at various times of day, with different effects. He picked them up then put them aside, one after another, depending on the changing light and atmosphere. And the painter, contemplating his subject, bided his time, alert to shifting sunlight and shadows, capturing a ray of sunlight or a passing cloud with a few brushstrokes.... I've seen him seize a dazzling flash of light from a white cliff and affix it to the canvas with a flood of yellow tones that conveyed the effect of this elusive, blinding light in a strangely startling and fleeting fashion. On another occasion, he seemed to actually grab a downpour over the sea.... It was actual rain that he had painted."
Guy de Maupassant, "La Vie d'un paysagiste," *Gil Blas*, September 28, 1886.

Monet

An early adopter of painting from nature, Monet soon dedicated himself almost exclusively to landscape, a genre he was determined to make his own. The studio-boat that he had created in 1876 allowed him to immerse himself as deeply as possible in the natural world. When living in Pourville and Étretat in the early 1880s, he went through periods when he painted as if possessed. He would bring along an entire series of paintings that he perched on his easel, one after another, depending on the light or time of day. Some of these subjects, like the customs house in Varengeville or the Manneporte at Étretat were repeated again and again, obsessively. When he settled in Giverny, Monet developed a succession of projects for painting in series. He would select a specific subject, always painting it from the same point of view at different times of day, from dawn till twilight. The views of London's Houses of Parliament in 1900 reflected the same preoccupation, although slightly less systematically. For the last twenty years of his life, the water lilies in his garden at Giverny were virtually his sole subject, a testimony to the intensity of his desire to paint a single scene in its infinite variations, and to become as one with it.

"Every day I add something and discover something I hadn't yet noticed. It's so difficult, but I'm making progress.... I'm shattered, I can't stand any more of this.... I had a night filled with nightmares; the cathedral was collapsing on top of me, and I couldn't tell whether it was blue, pink, or yellow."

Monet, letter to his wife Alice Hoschedé, Rouen, April 3, 1892.

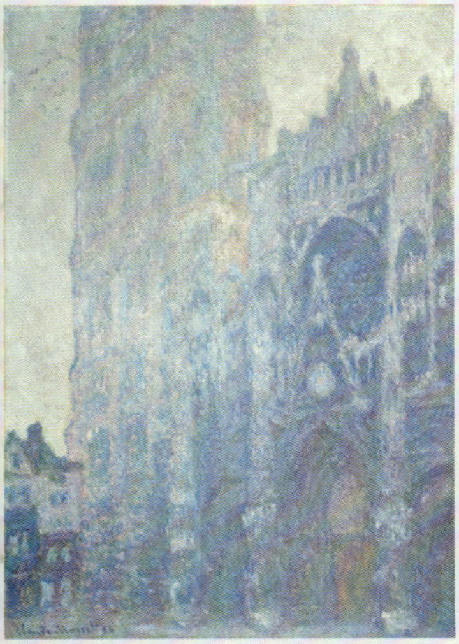

Claude Monet, *Rouen Cathedral, the Portal and the Tour Saint-Romain (Morning Effect),* also known as *Harmony in White*, 1893–94
Oil on canvas, 3 ft. 6 in. × 2 ft. 4 ¾ in. (106.5 × 73.2 cm)
Musée d'Orsay, Paris

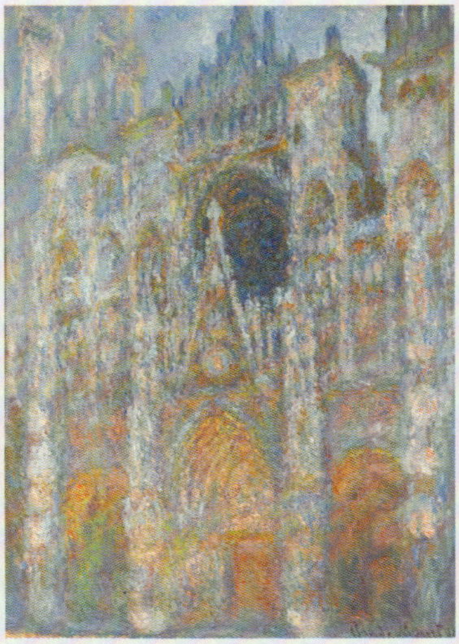

Claude Monet, *Rouen Cathedral, the Portal (Morning Sun),* also known as *Harmony in Blue*, 1893–94
Oil on canvas, 3 ft. ¼ in. × 2 ft. ¾ in. (92.2 × 63 cm)
Musée d'Orsay, Paris

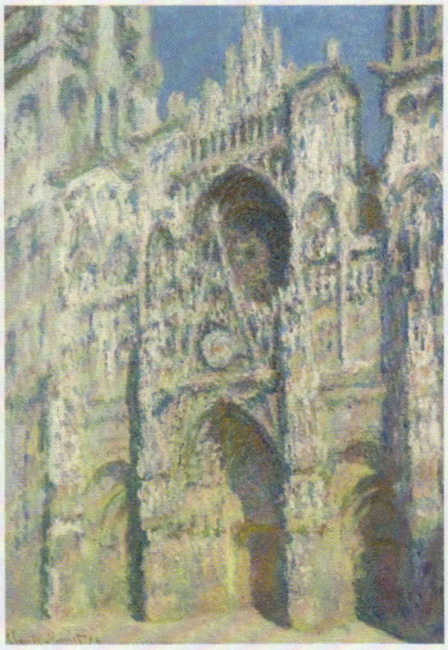

Claude Monet, *Rouen Cathedral, the Portal and the Tour Saint-Romain (Bright Sun),* also known as *Harmony in Blue and Gold*, 1893–94
Oil on canvas, 3 ft. 6 ¼ in. × 2 ft. 5 in. (107 × 73.5 cm)
Musée d'Orsay, Paris

THE CATHEDRAL OF ROUEN

Created during two visits to Rouen in 1892 and 1893, between February and mid-April, his paintings of Rouen Cathedral were later revisited by Monet in his studio. These works pushed to the extreme the systematic approach to painting in series; it was an approach with which the artist had already experimented. The building's western façade appears repeatedly, generally from an identical point of view. Light is the true and only subject here—not the monument. The architecture's substance dissolves amid the shimmering brushstrokes.

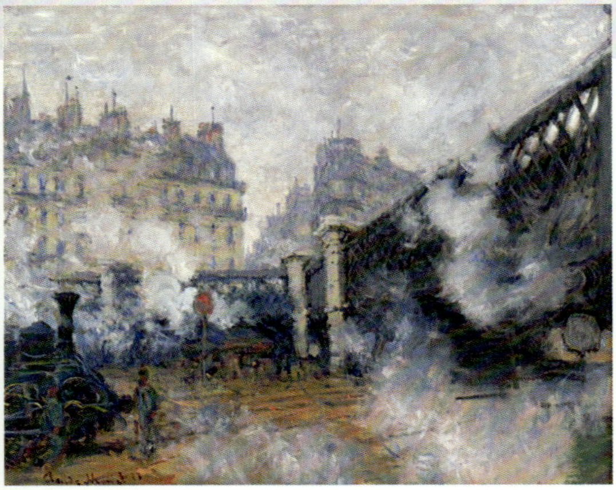

Claude Monet, *The Pont de l'Europe, Gare Saint-Lazare*, 1877
Oil on canvas, 25 ¼ × 31 ⅞ in. (64 × 81 cm), Musée Marmottan-Monet, Paris

Fascinated by scenes of contemporary life and the visual effect of smoke billowing from steam engines, in January 1877 Monet obtained permission to set up his easel in the middle of the Gare Saint-Lazare. He painted twelve canvases, some of which were shown at the third impressionist exhibition that spring. The points of view vary from painting to painting, but we already see the painter's fascination with exploring the same subject in multiple compositions.

THE HAYSTACKS

Whether heaped with snow or submerged in the golden light of summer, at dusk or at dawn, haystacks fascinated Monet. Newly settled in Giverny, he was enamored of this subject, which he explored in over twenty canvases. The haystacks were ideal for studying the light at various times of day and in different seasons.

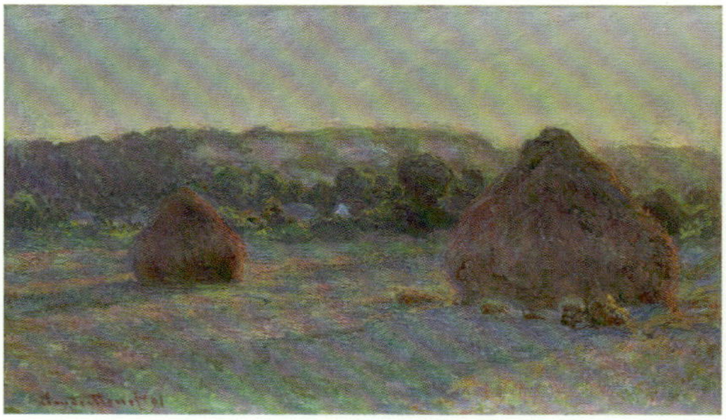

Claude Monet, *Stacks of Wheat (End of Summer)*, 1890–91, oil on canvas, 1 ft. 11 ½ in. × 3 ft. 3 ½ in. (60 × 100.5 cm), The Art Institute of Chicago, Chicago

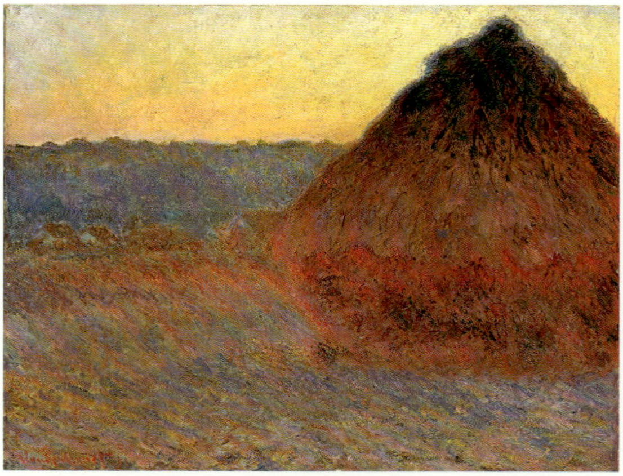

Claude Monet, *Haystack*, 1891
Oil on canvas, 2 ft. 4 ¾ in. × 3 ft. ¼ in. (73 × 92 cm), private collection

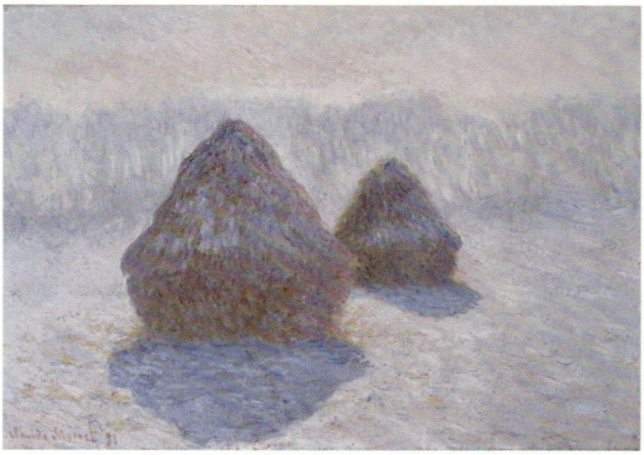

Claude Monet, *Haystacks (Effect of Snow and Sun)*, 1891
Oil on canvas, 2 ft. 1 ¾ in. × 3 ft. ¼ in. (65.4 × 92.1 cm)
The Metropolitan Museum of Art, New York

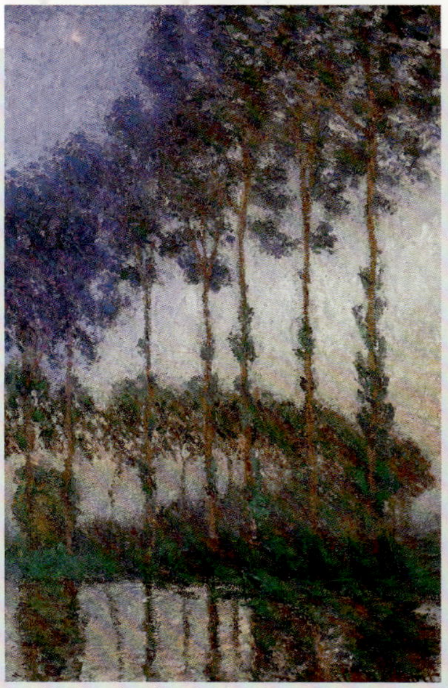

Claude Monet, *Poplars on the Banks of the Epte, Twilight*, 1891
Oil on canvas, 3 ft. 3 ½ in. × 2 ft. 1 ½ in.
(100 × 65 cm)
Museum of Fine Art, Boston

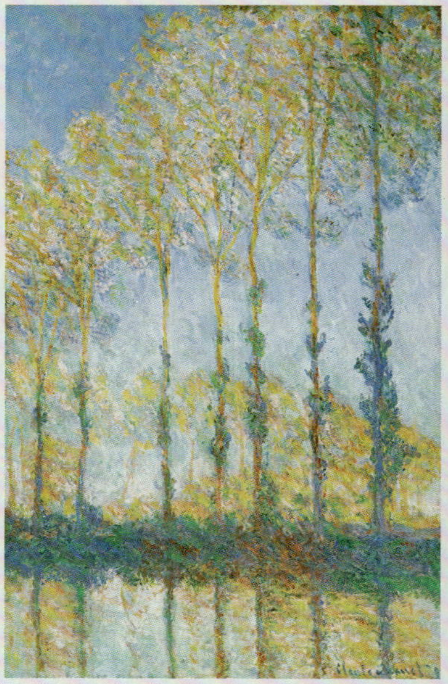

Claude Monet, *Poplars, White and Yellow Effect*, 1891
Oil on canvas, 3 ft. 3 ½ in. × 2 ft. 1 ½ in.
(100 × 65 cm)
Philadelphia Museum of Art, Philadelphia

The same year, Monet executed a series depicting the lofty poplars that lined the banks of the Epte, across from the Île aux Orties near Giverny. Durand-Ruel exhibited fifteen of these pictures in March, the first time that the dealer had presented works in a series.

Sisley

Sisley devoted himself entirely to landscapes, and willingly painted the same subjects again and again. He sometimes created actual series, although in a more haphazard, less systematic manner than Monet.

He witnessed the flood in Port-Marly in 1876. The event awoke a fascination that spurred him to paint six views at various times of day and at differing flood stages, almost from the same point of view. Certain subjects reappear again and again like leitmotifs in his paintings: the banks of the Loing, its bridges, and views of Moret. In 1893 and 1894, he embarked on a new series of fourteen canvases depicting the church in Moret, just across the street from his lodgings. Once again, light, whether evening, morning, or midday, is the real subject here.

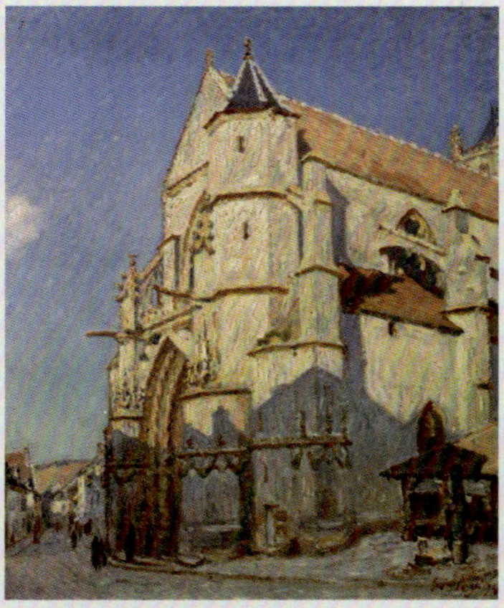

Alfred Sisley, *The Church at Moret, Evening*, 1894
Oil on canvas, 3 ft. 3 ¾ in. × 2 ft. 8 ½ in. (101 × 82 cm)
Petit Palais, Musée des Beaux-Arts de la Ville de Paris, Paris

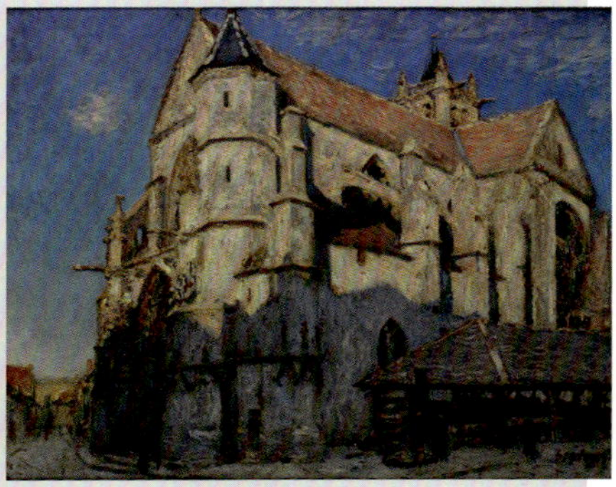

Alfred Sisley, *The Church at Moret, Full Sunlight*, 1893
Oil on canvas, 26 ⅜ × 32 in. (67 × 81.5 cm)
Musée des Beaux-Arts, Rouen

Pissarro

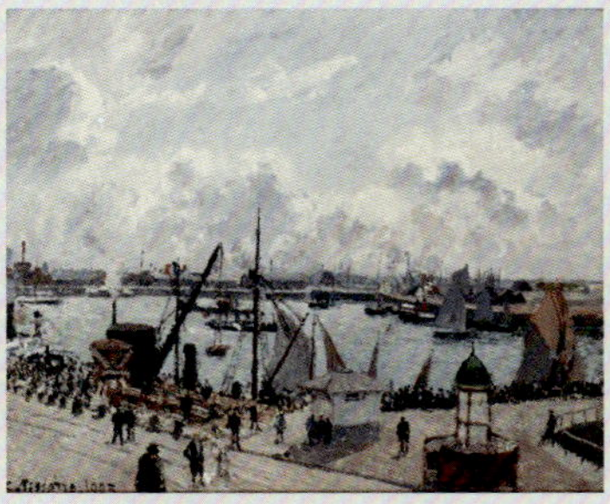

Camille Pissarro, *The Pilots' Jetty at Le Havre*, 1903
Oil on canvas, 25 ⅝ × 21 ½ in. (54.5 × 65 cm)
Musée d'Art Moderne André-Malraux, Le Havre

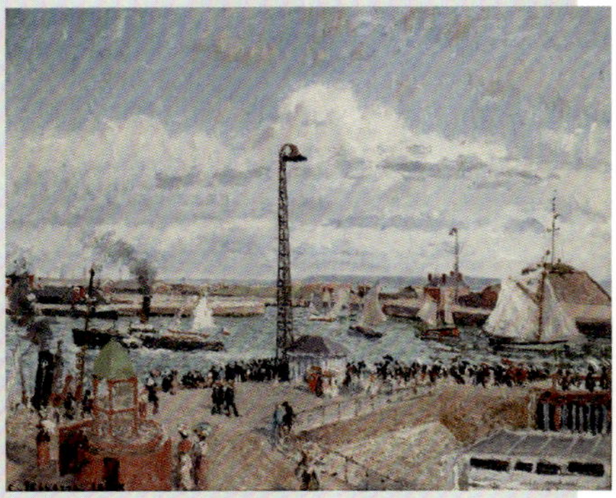

Camille Pissarro, *The Outer Harbour of Le Havre, Morning, Sun, Tide*, 1903
Oil on canvas, 21 ½ × 25 ¾ in. (54.5 × 65.3 cm)
Musée d'Art Moderne André-Malraux, Le Havre

Toward the end of his life, Pissarro embarked on studies of the same subject, some over a sustained period and some more randomly. Between 1883 and 1903, he developed a significant series of paintings based on the three Norman ports of Rouen, Dieppe, and Le Havre. In the course of seven separate stays, Pissarro adopted the same point of view to paint landscapes that were sometimes sunlit, and sometimes rainy or foggy. In 1898, he rented a room at the Hôtel du Louvre in Paris, overlooking the Place du Théâtre-Français and the Avenue de l'Opéra, so he could paint this view at his leisure. Working from an apartment on the Rue de Rivoli during the following two years, he created a series of views of the Carrousel and the Tuileries. He then devoted himself to painting the Pont-Neuf and the Pont Royal between 1901 and 1903, while continuing to paint other subjects as well.

IMAGES IN THE SPOTLIGHT

Claude Monet
Study of a Figure Outdoors: Woman with a Parasol, Facing Left
1886
Oil on canvas, 4 ft. 3 ½ in. × 2 ft. 10 ½ in. (131 × 88 cm)
Musée d'Orsay, Paris

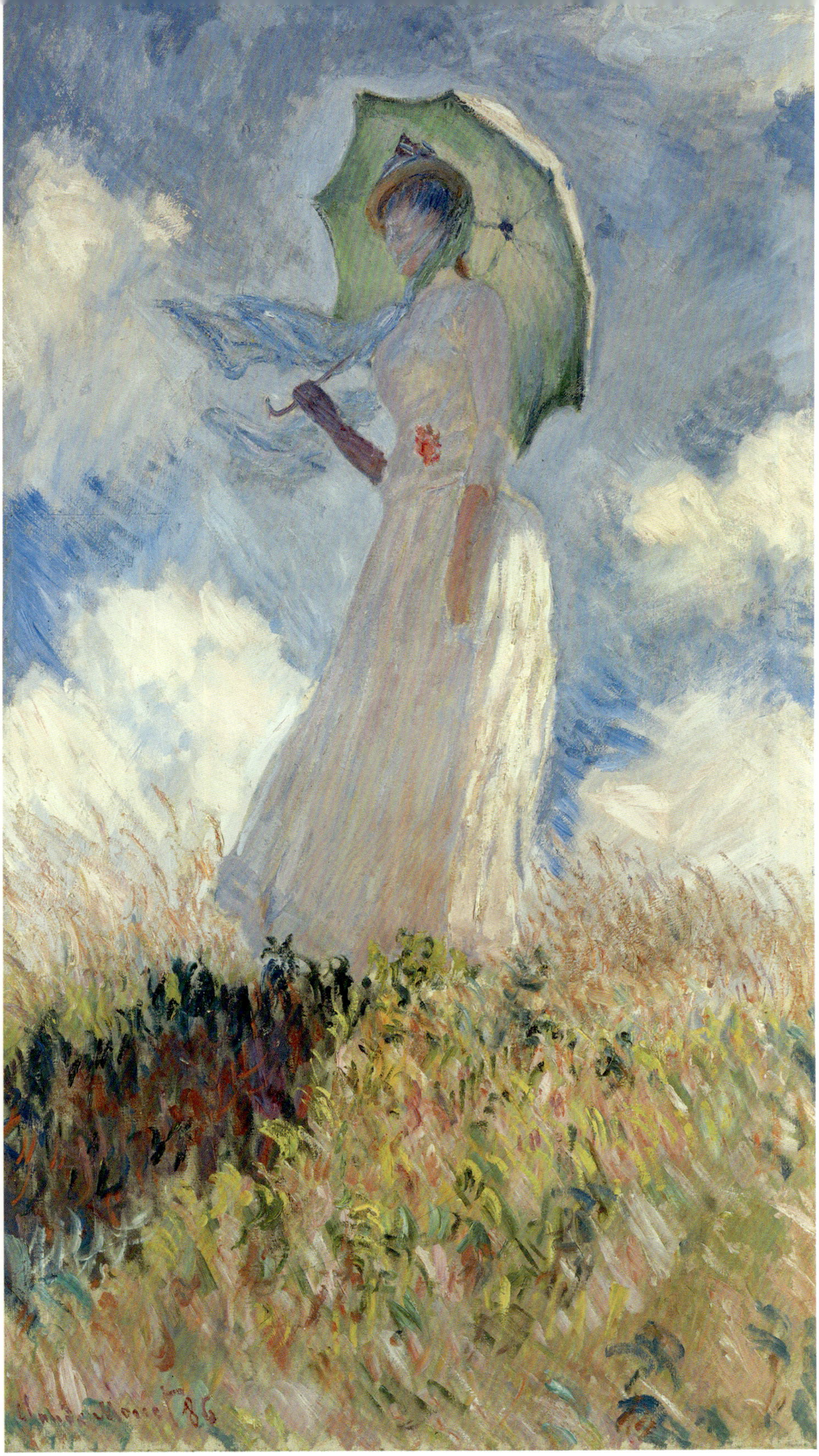

Study of a Figure Outdoors: Woman with a Parasol, Facing Left

Claude Monet, 1886

In this work dated 1886, Monet strove to capture Suzanne Hoschedé in a fleeting moment. His stepdaughter and one of his favorite models, she is shown returning from a walk. He painted two compositions in which a young woman appears silhouetted against the sky. In one case she is turned to the right and in the other to the left, as shown here.

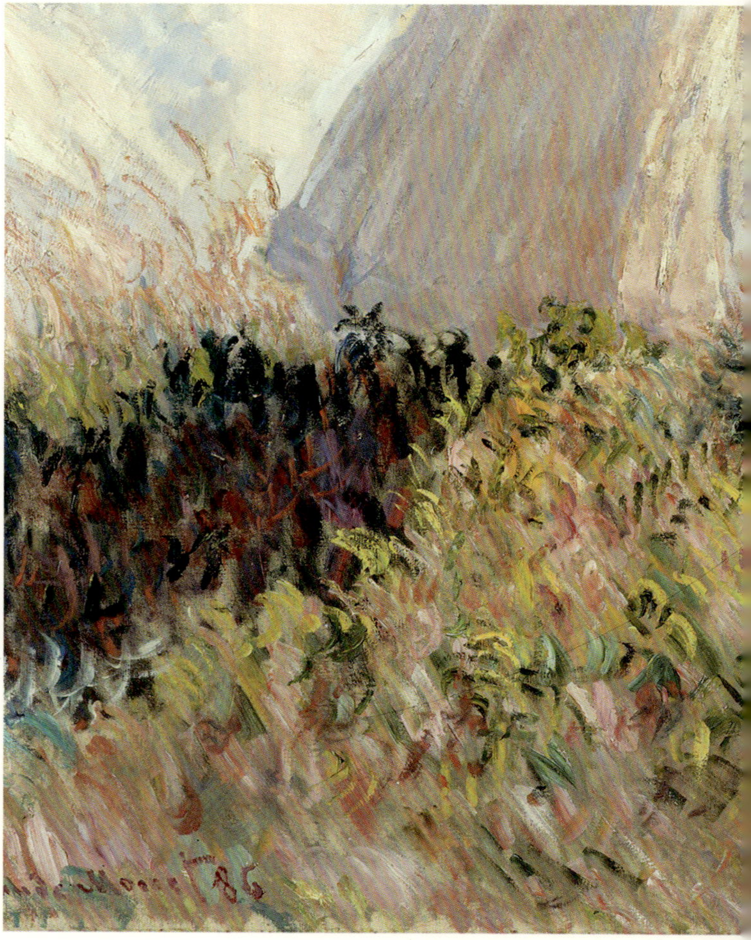

The overlapping small, quick brushstrokes are enough to convey the grasses bending in the wind—green, yellow, blue, brown, and mauve. Monet depicts a colorful vision of nature just as he sees it, without presuppositions.

Movements of the sky and water are among Claude Monet's great subjects. His rapid brushstrokes rendered atmospheric changes in a style that was close to a masterly sketch.

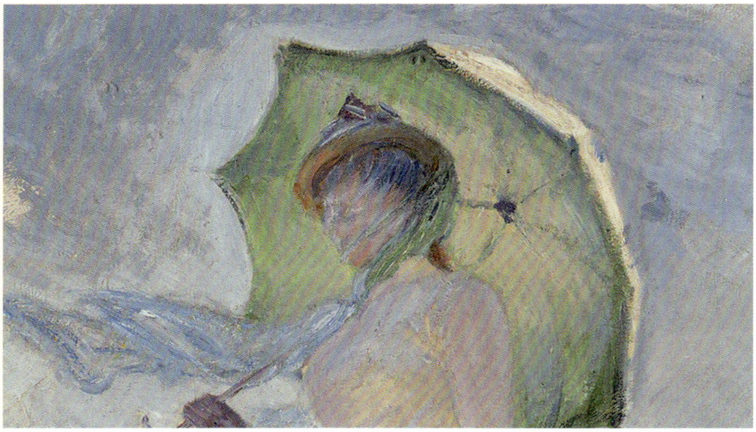

Some observers believe that the vision of Suzanne Hoschedé poised on the hilltop would have reminded Monet of his first wife Camille, who died young. He had often painted her with their son Jean. This hypothesis is supported by the young woman's indistinct features, which are obscured by her light veil.

Painted eleven years earlier, this picture showing the artist's wife Camille and their son is strikingly similar, whether the resemblance is deliberate or not. The composition is virtually identical, with the woman's figure, shaded by a parasol, seen from below and silhouetted against the blue summer sky. Only the child in the background is missing from the later work.

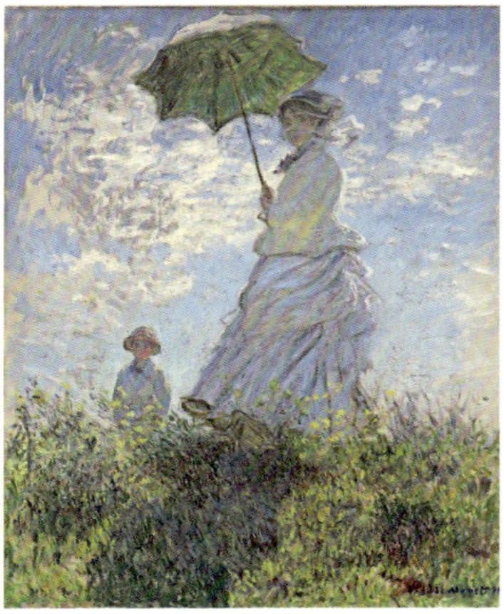

Claude Monet
Woman with a Parasol–Madame Monet and Her Son
1875
Oil on canvas, 3 ft. 3 ½ in. × 2 ft. 8 in. (100 × 81 cm)
National Gallery of Art, Washington, DC

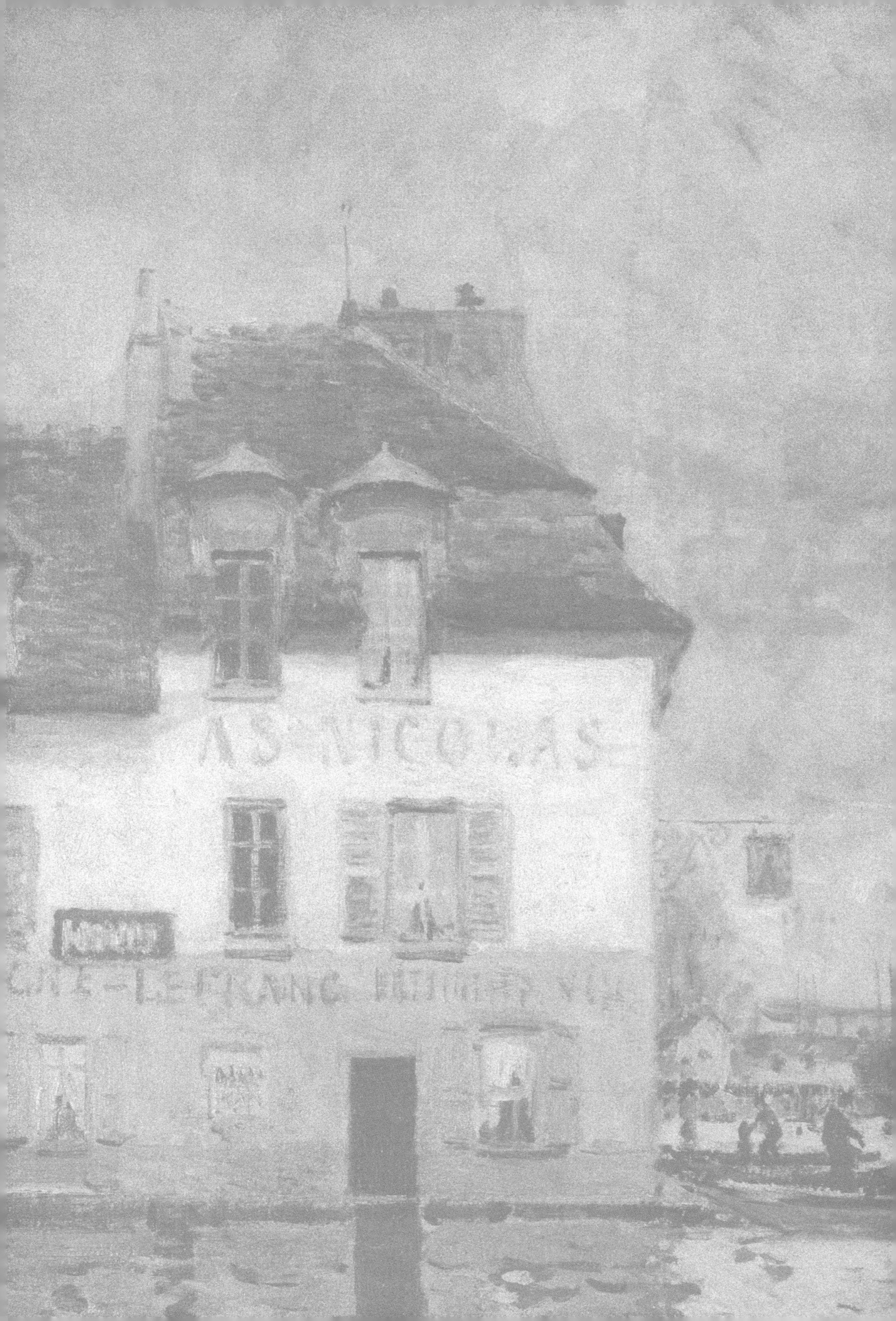

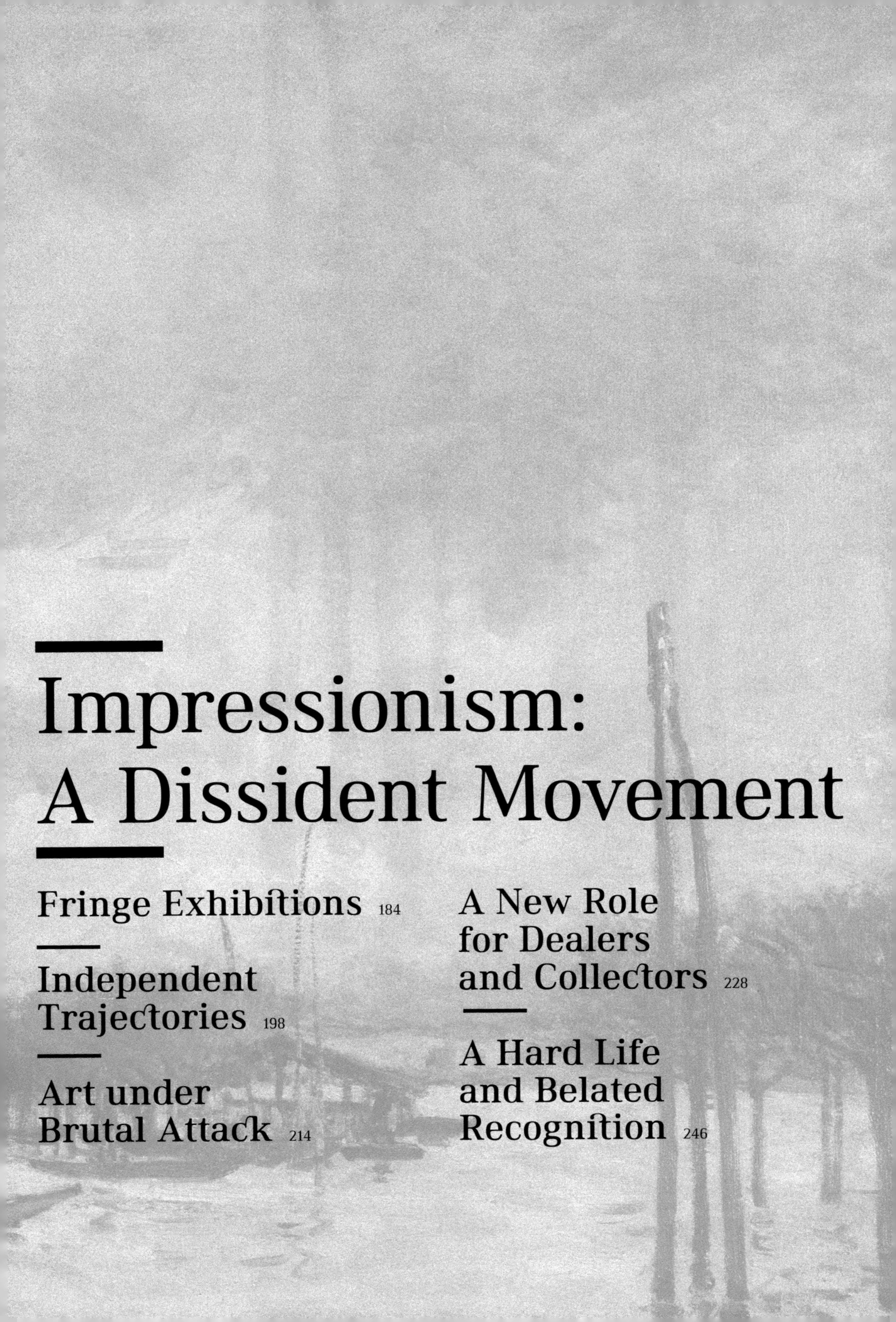

Impressionism: A Dissident Movement

Fringe Exhibitions 184

Independent Trajectories 198

Art under Brutal Attack 214

A New Role for Dealers and Collectors 228

A Hard Life and Belated Recognition 246

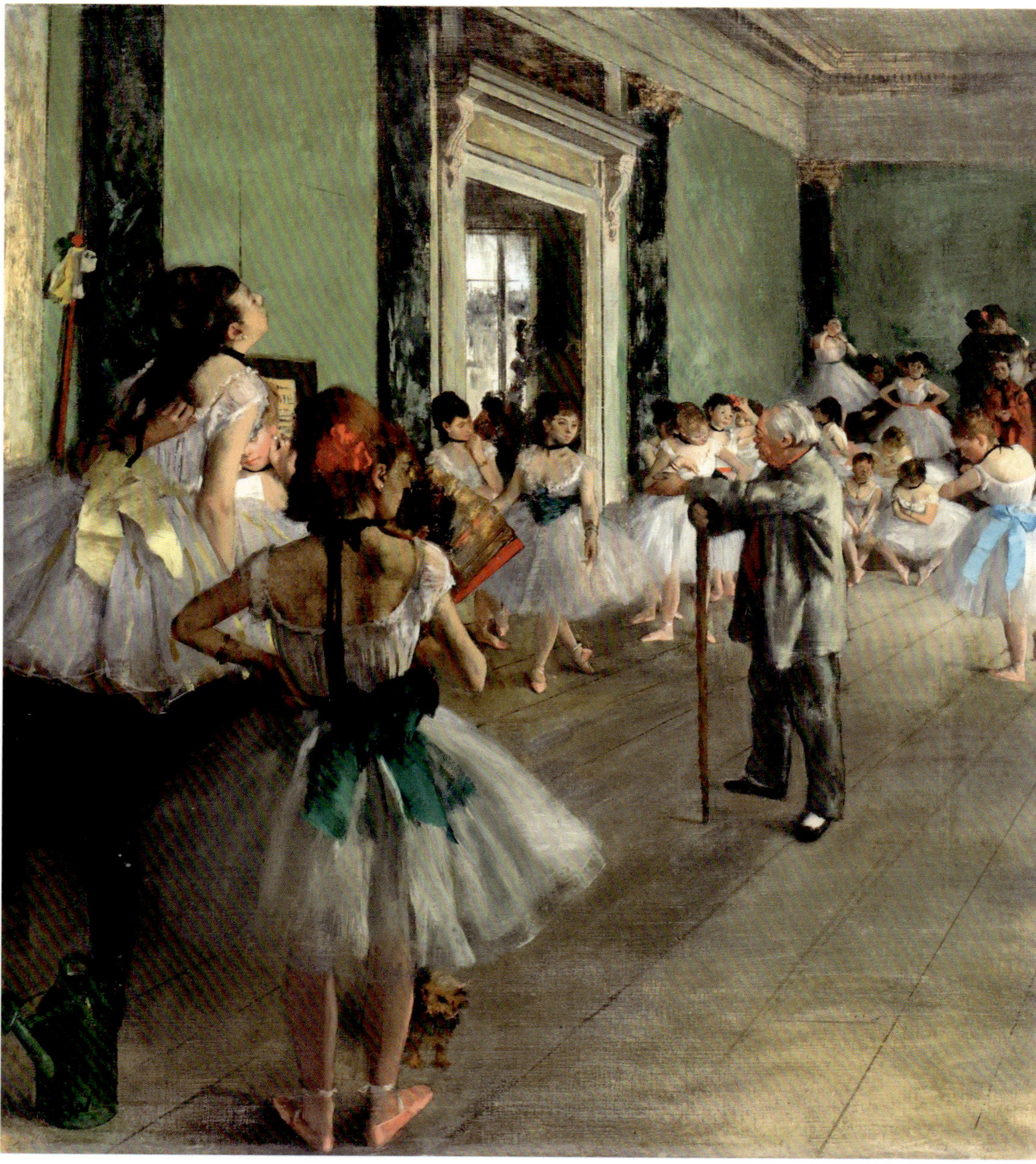

Edgar Degas
The Ballet Class
c. 1873–76
Oil on canvas, 33 ⅜ × 29 ½ in. (85.5 × 75 cm)
Musée d'Orsay, Paris

Fringe Exhibitions

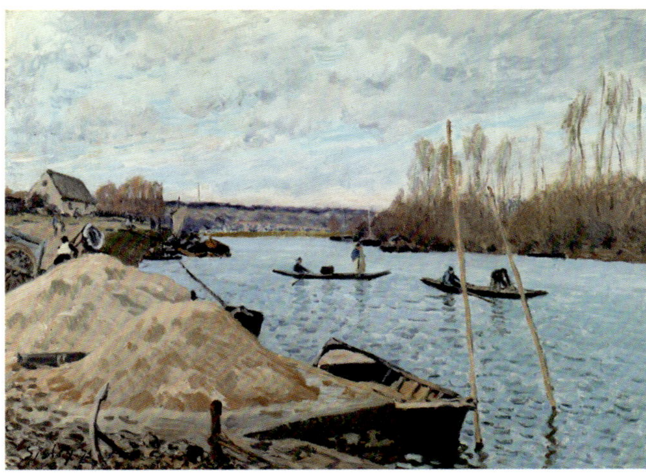

Alfred Sisley
The Seine at Port-Marly, Piles of Sand
1875
Oil on canvas, 21 ⅝ × 29 ⅛ in.
(55 × 74 cm)
Art Institute of Chicago, Chicago

Even outside the Salon, where rejection was almost a foregone conclusion, French landscape painting offered little opportunity to independent artists. Refusing to conform to a model that did not suit them, the future impressionists themselves had to find an audience for their paintings. Various ideas circulated during their gatherings at the Café Guerbois, and later at the Nouvelle Athènes. The fact that they were forbidden to exhibit their work was intolerable, and the best response was to organize an exhibition of their own. They took inspiration from the example of their revered elders. Courbet had built his own pavilion on the outskirts of the 1855 Universal Exposition, and Courbet, followed by Manet, revived the experiment twelve years later during the Universal Exposition of 1867.

An initial attempt by a small group was unsuccessful, lacking the necessary resources; the Franco-Prussian War of 1870-1 and the Commune of March-May 1871 then followed. After this period of chaos passed, the project was revived, encouraged by Monet, who raised the idea again in 1873. Everyone endorsed the concept. There was

AT THE TIME OF THE FIRST EXHIBITION: Monet was 34, Renoir 33, Sisley 35, Degas 40, Cézanne 35, and Pissarro 44.

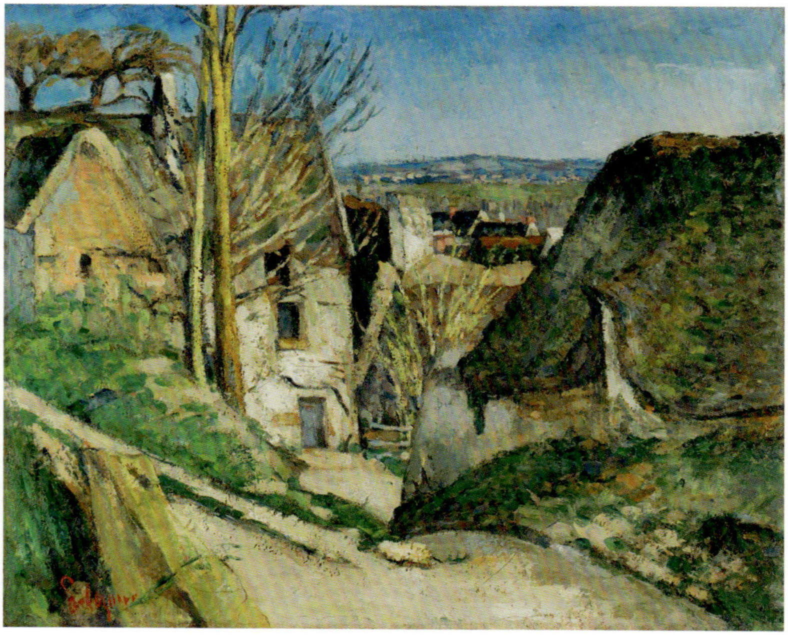

Paul Cézanne
The Hanged Man's House, Auvers-sur-Oise
1873
Oil on canvas, 21 ⅝ × 26 in. (55 × 66 cm)
Musée d'Orsay, Paris

a development phase during which they envisioned a new format. Everyone had their own point of view, and they had to find common ground. The initial idea of inviting eminent predecessors like Courbet and Corot was ultimately abandoned. Manet declined to participate, although he was very close to the group and followed their progress at every exhibition; he preferred, despite the affronts, to court official recognition and the honors conferred by the Salon.

The challenge of the Salon was inescapable: it was the sole point of reference for French art, and from the outset it was at the heart of the debate, constantly rearing its head like a primordial sea serpent. Could an artist exhibit with the impressionists as well as at the Salon? Did there have to be a choice, or could one participate in both? After all, an artist had to make a living. Or, conversely, would they have to formally secede from the Salon and noisily declare their individualism in order to attract attention? Their positions fluctuated over time, and the format changed over the course of the eight impressionist exhibitions held between 1874 and 1886.

In the end, administrative issues had to be worked out, because this, too, was uncharted territory. Almost anarchic in his thinking, Pissarro suggested that his friends should draw inspiration from the system adopted by guilds and other corporate bodies. The charter of the Anonymous Cooperative Society of Artists (Painters, Sculptors, Engravers, etc.) was finalized on December 27, 1873. It was agreed

THE GERM OF AN IDEA

In 1867, Bazille wrote in a letter to his family: "I won't submit another thing to the jury. It is too absurd ... to be exposed to the caprices of the administration.... What I want to tell you is this: a dozen talented young artists here think like me. We've decided to rent a big studio every year where we'll exhibit our own works, as many as we wish to. We'll also invite other artists we admire to send their pictures. Courbet, Corot, Díaz, Daubigny, and many others you may not be familiar with, have promised to send their pictures, and strongly support our idea." But it was impossible to raise the necessary funds, and the project stagnated. The enthusiastic Bazille, who perished in the war of 1870, did not live to see the achievement of this goal seven years later.

Camille Pissarro
Red Roofs: Corner of a Village, Winter
1877
Oil on canvas, 21 ¼ × 25 ⅝ in. (54 × 65 cm)
Musée d'Orsay, Paris

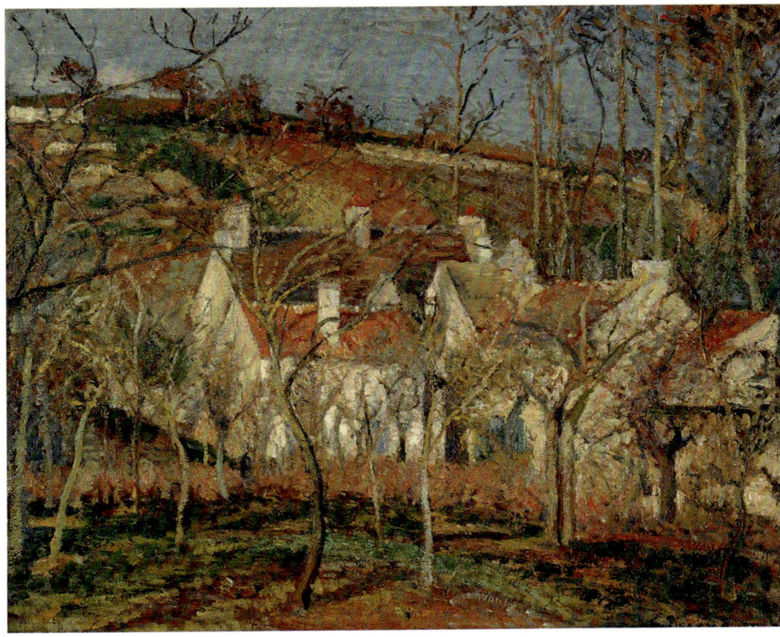

"Our exhibition is going well. It's a success. The critics are eating us alive and accusing us of not working. I'm getting back to my work—it's better than reading. You learn nothing whatsoever from these people."
Pissarro, letter to Duret, May 5, 1874.

"The public doesn't appreciate, or understand, good painting. They award a medal to Gérôme and leave Corot aside. The people who do grasp it and brave the scorn and contempt are few in number and very rarely millionaires. That doesn't mean we should be discouraged. Everything will come along in time, even wealth and fame; while we're waiting, the judgment of true connoisseurs and friends makes up for the oblivion of idiots."
Duret, letter to Pissarro, June 2, 1874.

that each participant would pay an annual contribution and remit ten percent of their profits from sales. Then there was the delicate question of how to hang and value each artist's work. Eventually, they decided on a system combining a lottery with the practical consideration of the paintings' measurements. Despite the complexities of implementing and accommodating various points of view, the collective will was strong. Fortune seemed to favor them, at least on this occasion. A former habitué of the Café Guerbois, the photographer Nadar was just moving out of his quarters on Boulevard des Capucines. The rooms were empty and he generously offered to make them available. It was a blessing, and the exhibition opened on April 15, 1874. It was a debacle, however: the criticism of this new kind of painting was ferocious. Endless taunts, each more scathing than the last, rained down from all quarters.

ATTENDANCE
With four thousand works on display, the Salon received between eight and ten thousand visitors a day, but the first impressionist exhibition saw its audience decline from 175 visitors on its opening day to fifty-four when it closed. In the evening, only a handful of idle passersby came to stroll through the galleries. Even harder to bear, their reaction was to scoff.

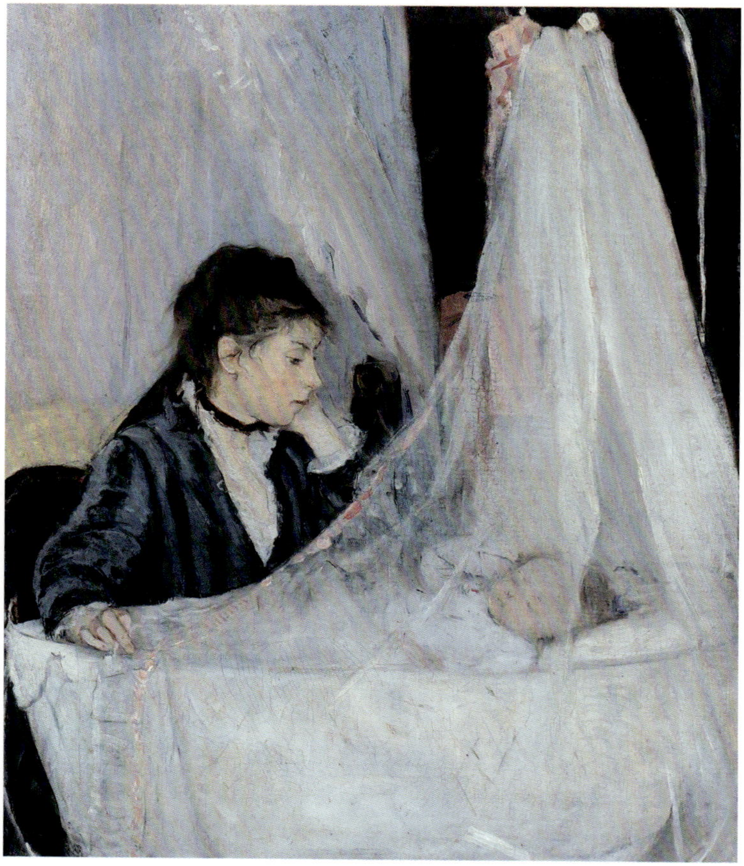

Disturbed by the criticism she read in the papers, Madame Morisot, Berthe's mother, dispatched Guichard—her daughter's former painting instructor—to the exhibition so he could give his opinion: *"I've seen Nadar's galleries," he wrote, "and I want to give you my genuine impression immediately. As I entered, dear lady, my heart fell when I saw your daughter's works hanging in this noxious setting. I told myself, 'You can't surround yourself with such fools and escape with impunity.' Manet was right to raise objections to the exhibition."*

Berthe Morisot
The Cradle
1872
Oil on canvas, 22 × 18 ⅛ in. (56 × 46 cm)
Musée d'Orsay, Paris

"It was the hilarity of a crowd of people who'd come for the amusement, getting increasingly excited, bursting out in laughter for no reason, entertained as much by pretty things as by the gambling tables.... They elbowed each other, twisted about... and every canvas had its moment, with people calling each other over to point out a good one to ridicule, with quips circulating from mouth to mouth... expressing all their idiocies, the nasty, stupid sneers that the sight of an original work of art evokes from bourgeois imbeciles."

Émile Zola, *His Masterpiece*, 1902.

THE FIRST IMPRESSIONIST EXHIBITION

Opening: April 5, 1874.
Entry price: 1 franc.
Catalog price: 20 centimes.
Opening hours: 10:00 a.m.–6:00 p.m. and 8:00–10:00 p.m. (the evening hours were a first).
Number of works: 175.
Participants: Cézanne (three canvases including *Modern Olympia*); Degas (ten paintings, pastels, and drawings); Guillaumin (three landscapes); Monet (five paintings and seven sketches); Berthe Morisot (nine paintings, watercolors, and drawings); Pissarro (five landscapes); Renoir (six canvases including *La Loge* [*The Theater Box*] and *The Dancer* as well as one pastel); and Sisley (five landscapes). Other participants (with 111 works) were Astruc, Attendu, Béliard, Boudin, Bracquemond, Brandon, Bureau, Cals, Colin, Debras, Latouche, Lepic, Lépine, Levert, Meyer, De Molins, Mulot-Durivage, De Nittis, Auguste Ottin, Léon Ottin, Robert, and Rouart.
Financial proceeds: very meager, not even allowing all participants to cover their annual dues of 61.25 francs.

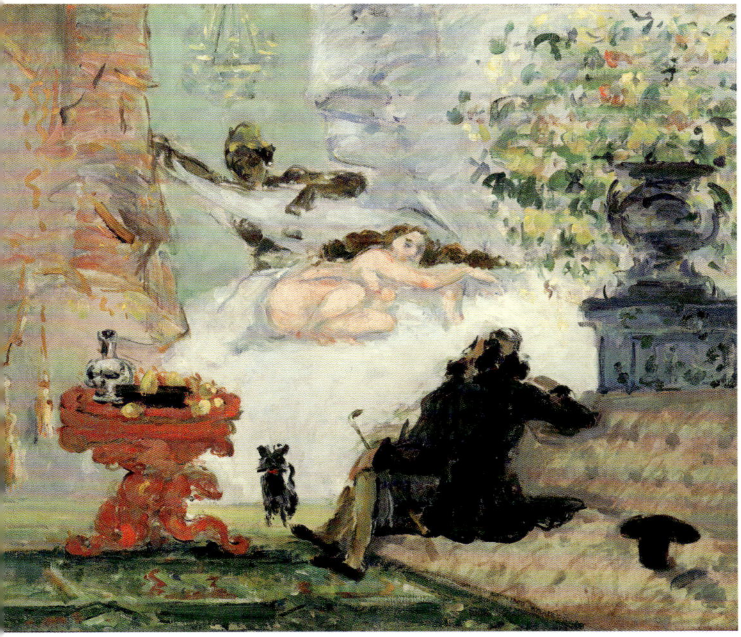

Paul Cézanne
A Modern Olympia
1873
Oil on canvas, 18 ⅛ × 21 ⅝ in. (46 × 55 cm)
Musée d'Orsay, Paris

On duty at the exhibition on the morning after Louis Leroy's article appeared, the painter Latouche wrote to Dr. Gachet, who had lent the impressionists a painting by Cézanne: "I'm standing guard over your Cézanne, but I can't guarantee anything; I'm afraid it will be returned to you in shreds."

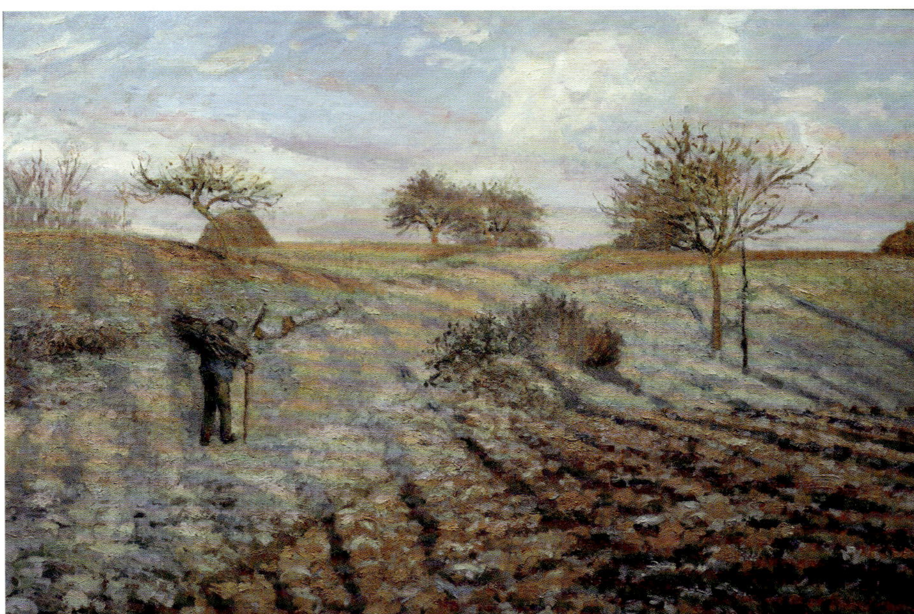

Camille Pissarro
White Frost
1873
Oil on canvas,
2 ft. 1 ½ in. × 3 ft. ½ in.
(65 × 93 cm)
Musée d'Orsay, Paris

"For the love of Michelangelo," he cried, "what is that?"
"You can see… some kind of white ice in very deep ruts."
"Those are ruts, that's ice? But these are paint scrapings from a palette spread evenly over a dirty canvas. There's neither head nor tail, top nor bottom, back nor front."

Extract from Louis Leroy's withering criticism published on April 25, 1874, in *Le Charivari*, where Leroy imagined a dialogue with an academic artist attending the exhibition with him.

The Impressionist Exhibition

Eight independent exhibitions were staged by the Anonymous Cooperative Society of Artists (Painters, Sculptors, Engravers, etc.) in the course of twelve years. After the initial launch in Nadar's studios in 1874, the shows were mounted almost yearly. Financial problems, diverging points of view, and conflicting personalities made each exhibition a new battleground, although the determination to exhibit, be seen, and gain recognition always rallied the group.

Second Exhibition, 1876

It was two years before the second exhibition opened its doors in the Galerie Durand-Ruel. Thirteen of the earlier participants were absent, including Cézanne, but Caillebotte was a notable addition to their ranks. The show was a near debacle. Despite the publication of Duranty's brochure "The New Painting: Concerning the Group of Artists Exhibiting at the Durand-Ruel Galleries," and a few other isolated positive articles, including that of Jules Antoine Castagnary in *L'Opinion*, incomprehension was almost universal. The press continued its attacks, particularly under the byline of *Le Figaro*'s critic Albert Wolff.

Location: Galerie Durand-Ruel,
11 Rue Le Pelletier.
Participants: Béliard, Bureau, Caillebotte, Cals, Degas, Desboutin, François, Legros, Lepic, Levert, Millet, Monet, Morisot, Ottin, Jr., Pissarro, Renoir, Rouart, Sisley, Tillot.

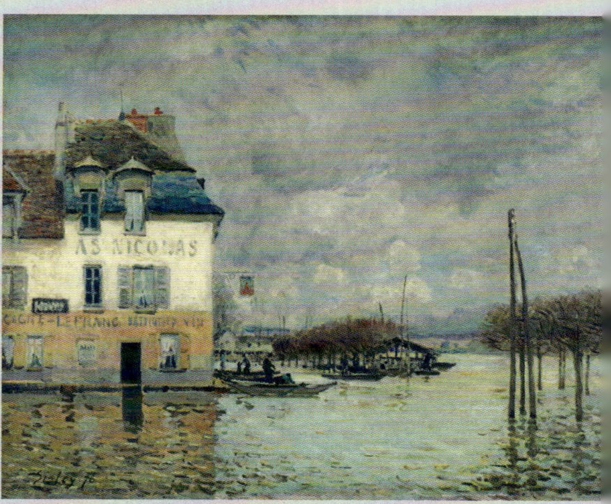

Alfred Sisley, *The Flood at Port-Marly*, 1876
Oil on canvas, 23 ⅝ × 31 ⅞ in. (60 × 81 cm)
Musée d'Orsay, Paris

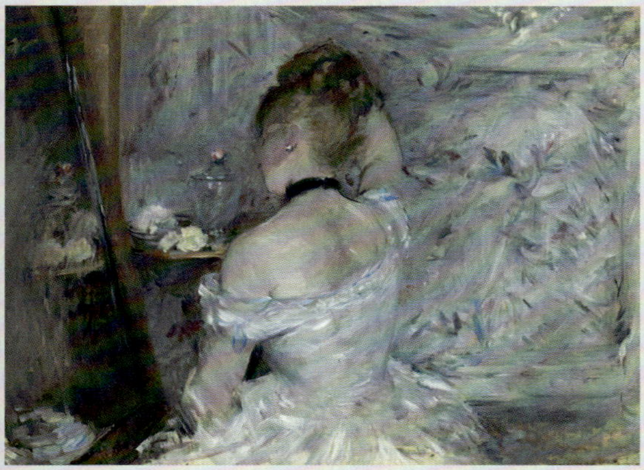

Berthe Morisot, *Young Woman at Her Toilette*, 1875, oil on canvas, 23 ¾ × 31 ⅝ in. (60.3 × 80.4 cm), The Art Institute of Chicago, Chicago

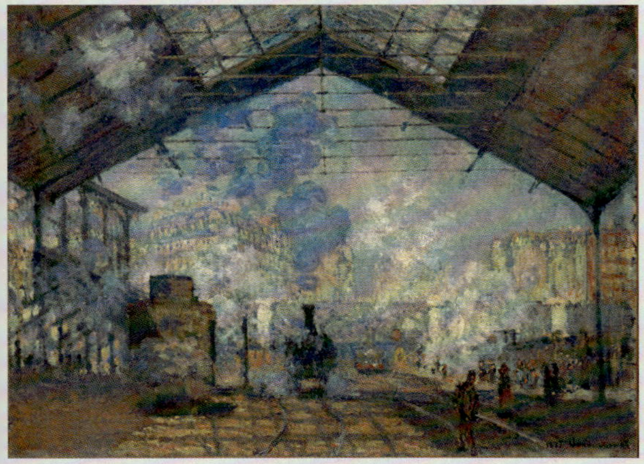

Claude Monet, *The Gare Saint-Lazare*, 1877
Oil on canvas, 2 ft. 5 ¾ in. × 3 ft. 5 in. (75.5 × 104 cm)
Musée d'Orsay, Paris

Third Exhibition, 1877

It was thanks to the energy and financial support of Caillebotte that the third exhibition was able to take place, in an apartment on Rue Le Pelletier, rented for the occasion. Critics continued to rail against these artists, although some observers were beginning to notice certain redeeming qualities in some painters, like Renoir, who exhibited his *Dance at Le Moulin de La Galette*. Cézanne, who was participating for the last time, had a prominent spot. Degas imposed the rule that artists could not exhibit at both the Salon and the impressionists' show.

Location: 6 Rue Le Pelletier.
Participants: Caillebotte, Cals, Cézanne, Cordey, Degas, Guillaumin, François, Franc-Lamy, Levert, Maureau, Monet, Morisot, Piette, Pissarro, Renoir, Rouart, Sisley, Tillot.

Fourth Exhibition, 1879

For the first time, the exhibition was not a financial disaster. The public continued to scoff, but the critics were less uniformly negative. Mary Cassatt and Paul Gauguin joined the venture. Weary of disputes within the group, Renoir, Sisley, Guillaumin, and Cézanne did not make an appearance, nor did Berthe Morisot, who had recently given birth. The situation with the critics and Renoir's success at the Salon the same year led Monet to abandon the fifth exhibition.

Location: 28 Avenue de l'Opéra.
Participants: Félix Bracquemond, Marie Bracquemond, Caillebotte, Cals, Cassatt, Degas, Forain, Gauguin, Lebourg, Monet, Pissarro, Rouart, Somm, Tillot, Zandomeneghi.

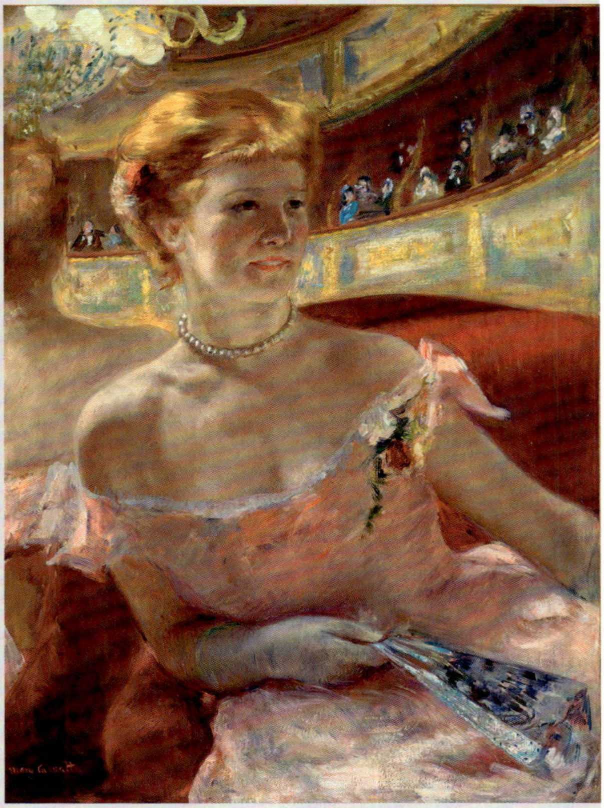

Mary Cassatt, *Woman with a Pearl Necklace in a Loge*, 1879
Oil on canvas, 32 × 23 ½ in. (81.3 × 59.7 cm)
Philadelphia Museum of Art, Philadelphia

Sixth Exhibition, 1881

When it returned to its original location seven years later, the impressionist group no longer resembled its earlier self. Monet, Renoir, and Sisley still stayed away, along with Caillebotte, who was dismayed by Degas's conduct. They negotiated a concession from Degas, persuading him to engineer the departure of Raffaëlli for the next exhibition and the re-inclusion of artists who had exhibited in the Salon.

Location: 35 Boulevard des Capucines.
Participants: Cassatt, Degas, Forain, Gauguin, Guillaumin, Morisot, Pissarro, Raffaëlli, Rouart, Tillot, Vidal, Vignon, Zandomeneghi.

Fifth Exhibition, 1880

Three great figures of the impressionist movement, Monet, Renoir, and Sisley, had lost faith in the event and did not participate. Degas, criticized for his authoritarianism, and no champion of unity, tried to force the inclusion of his friends, including Raffaëlli. Although the critical animosity diminished, the seeds of the group's dissolution had already been sown.

Location: 10 Rue des Pyramides.
Participants: Félix Bracquemond, Marie Bracquemond Caillebotte, Cassatt, Degas, Forain, Gauguin, Guillaumin, Lebourg, Levert, Berthe Morisot, Pissarro, Raffaëlli, Rouart, Tillot, Vidal, Vignon, Zandomeneghi.

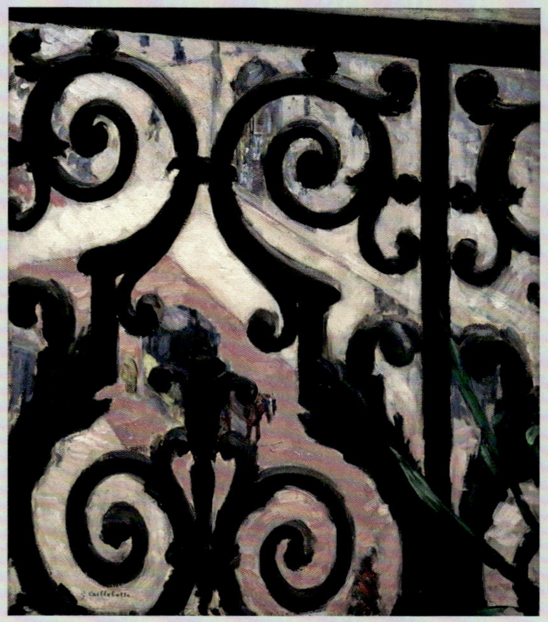

Gustave Caillebotte, *View Seen through a Balcony*, 1880
Oil on canvas, 25 ⅝ × 25 ⅜ in. (65 × 64 cm)
Musée Van Gogh, Amsterdam

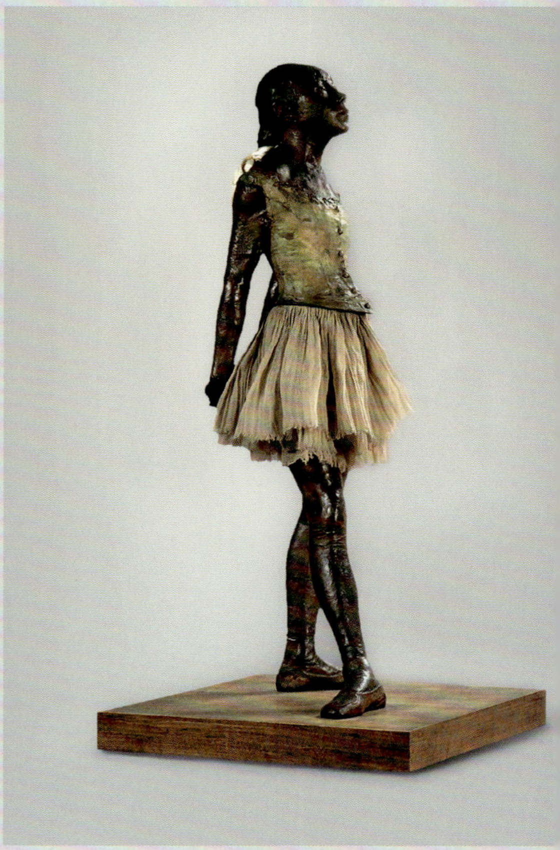

Edgar Degas, *Small Dancer Aged Fourteen*, also known as *Large Clothed Dancer*, 1881
Bronze patinated in various colors, tulle tutu, pink satin ribbon in the hair, wooden base, 3 ft. 2 ½ in. × 1 ft. 1 ¾ × 9 ¾ in. (98 × 35.2 × 24.5 cm)
Musée d'Orsay, Paris

Seventh Exhibition, 1882

With the removal of second-rate talents and the return of Renoir, Monet, and Sisley, this was certainly the most homogeneous of the impressionist exhibitions. Degas refused to participate, demonstrating his opposition. Durand-Ruel, who had rented the space where the exhibition was held, actively promoted the show to a press that was now less hostile. Henri Rouart offered to lease the premises for the next three years, but Durand-Ruel's financial difficulties prevented a repeat of the experiment, while dissensions among the group's members intensified.

Location: 251 Rue Saint-Honoré.
Participants: Caillebotte, Gauguin, Guillaumin, Monet, Morisot, Pissarro, Renoir, Sisley, Vignon.

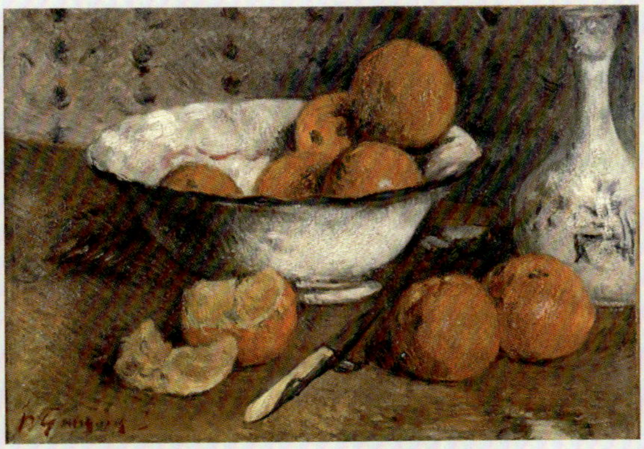

Paul Gauguin, *Still Life with Oranges*, c. 1880
Oil on canvas, 13 × 18 ⅛ in. (33 × 46 cm)
Musée des Beaux-Arts, Rennes

Eighth Exhibition, 1886

Organized by Berthe Morisot and her husband Eugène Manet, this final exhibition marked the last chapter of the collective venture. Monet, Renoir, Caillebotte, and Sisley broke away again, while Degas returned, satisfied that participating artists were once more forbidden to exhibit simultaneously at the Salon. The end of an adventure, the exhibition saw the emergence of new trends, with the inclusion of Seurat and Signac at the behest of their supporter Pissarro. Now it was neo-impressionism's turn to be ridiculed.

Location: at the corner of Rue Laffitte and the Grands Boulevards, above the restaurant La Maison Dorée.
Participants: Marie Bracquemond, Cassatt, Degas, Forain, Gauguin, Guillaumin, Morisot, Camille Pissarro, Lucien Pissarro, Redon, Rouart, Schuffenecker, Seurat, Signac, Tillot, Vignon, Zandomeneghi.

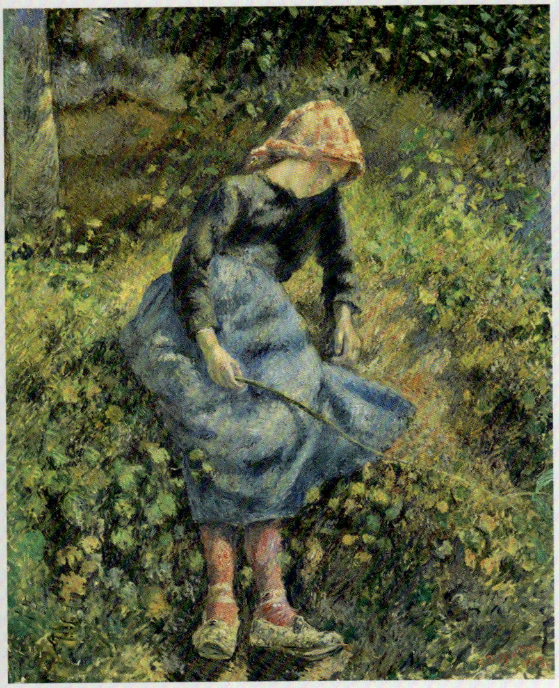

Camille Pissarro, *The Shepherdess*, 1881
Oil on canvas, 31 ⅞ × 25 ½ in. (81 × 64.8 cm)
Musée d'Orsay, Paris

A MODEL THAT INSPIRED OTHERS

On May 15, 1884, another independent exhibition born of a group initiative opened in an outbuilding by the Tuileries. The Society of Independent Artists had about a hundred members, whose only unifying principle was to put the Salon's rejection behind them. Needless to say, in the absence of any common style or ideology, the result was an exuberant free-for-all. There were a few valuable nuggets, though, with the inclusion of Odilon Redon, Georges Seurat, and Paul Signac.

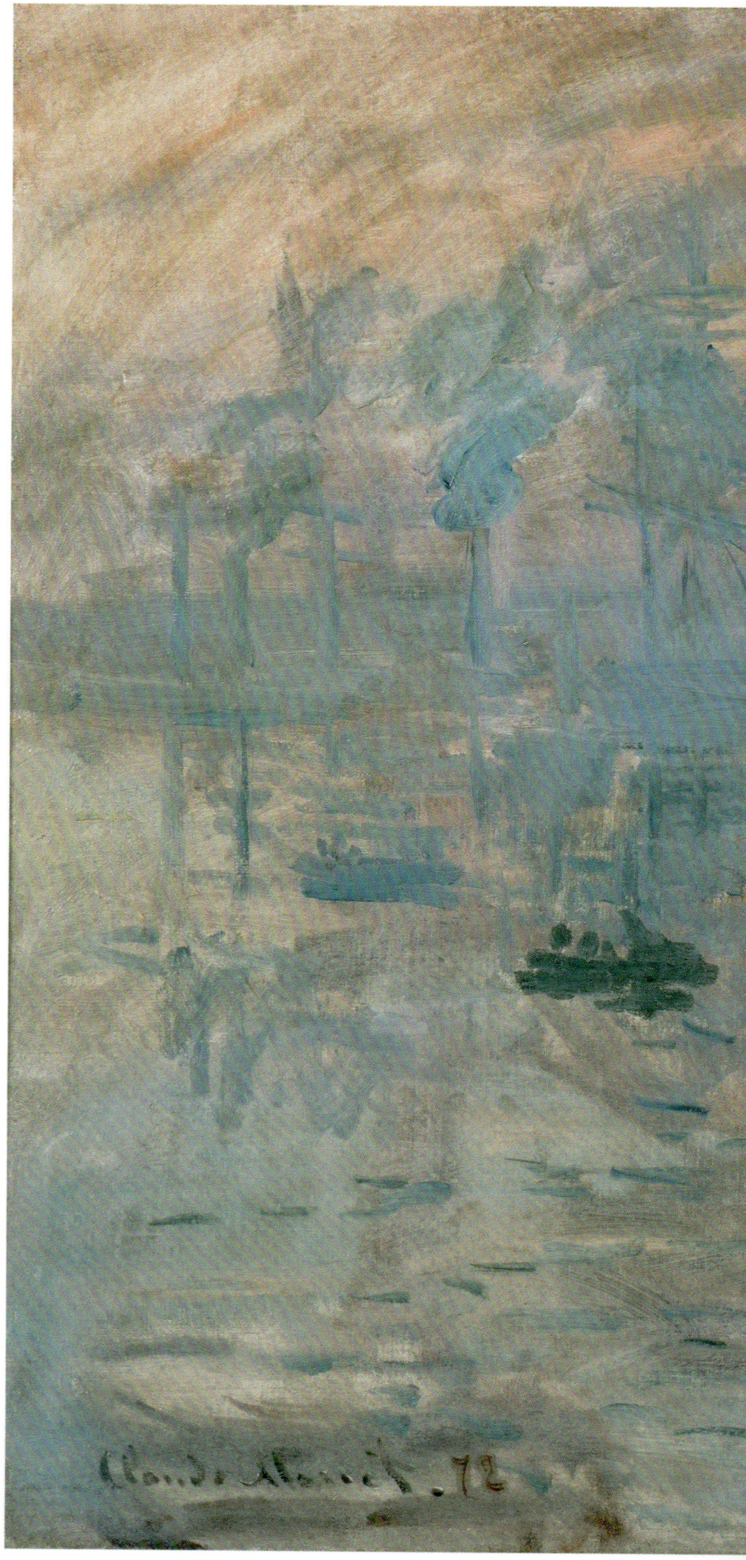

Claude Monet
Impression, Sunrise
1872
Oil on canvas, 18 ⅞ × 24 ⅞ in.
(48 × 63 cm)
Musée Marmottan, Paris

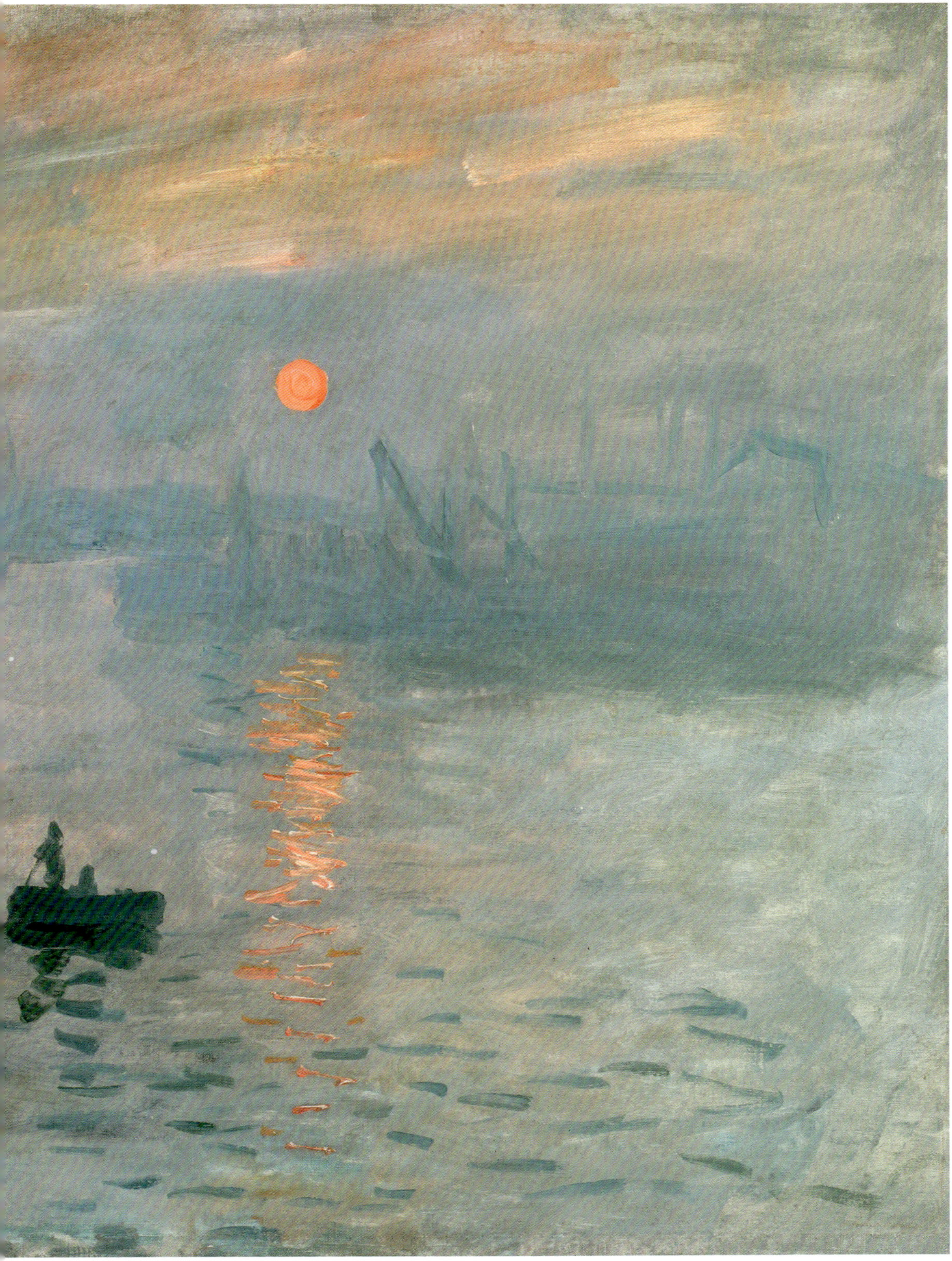

Impression, Sunrise

Claude Monet, 1872

Presented at the first impressionist exhibition in 1874, this canvas is considered to be the origin of the term "impressionism," which henceforth described works by this group of artists.

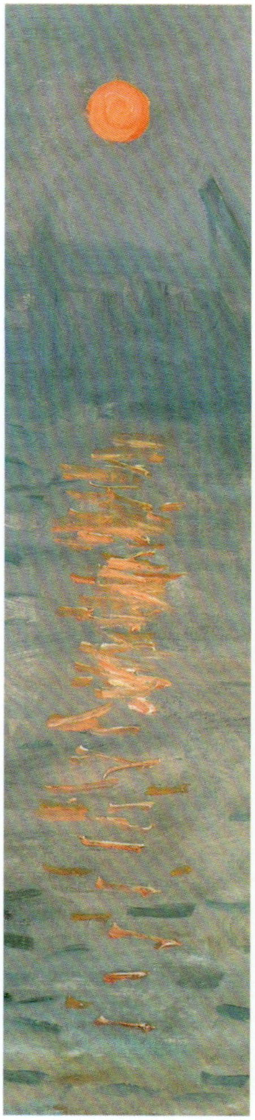

The reflections of the setting sun in the water are rapidly conveyed with simple orange hatchings.

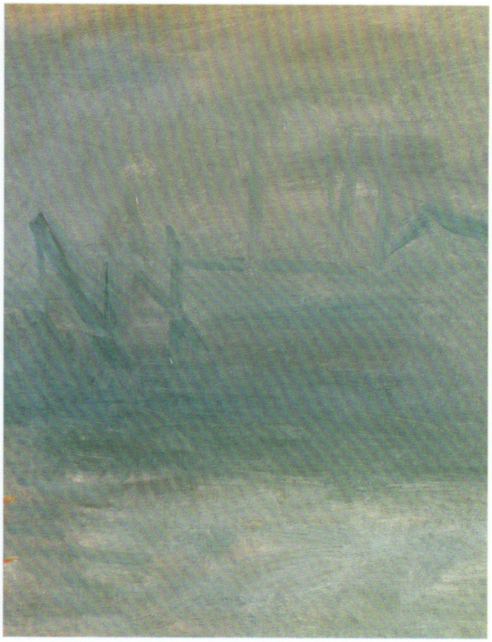

The cranes in the background are barely suggested; they are the only elements that allow us to identify this vast port as Le Havre.

"They asked me for a title for the catalog; the scene couldn't really pass for a view of Le Havre, so I replied, 'Put down Impression!'"

Claude Monet, quoted by M. Guillemot in *La Revue illustrée*, March 15, 1898.

"What does this picture represent? See the brochure." "Impression, Sunrise." "Impression, that's clear enough. I was just telling myself the same thing—I am impressed. So there must be an impression in there someplace.... And what a free hand, what assurance in the technique! Wallpaper in its early phases of production is more finished."

Louis Leroy, "Exhibition of the Impressionists," *Le Charivari*, April 25, 1874.

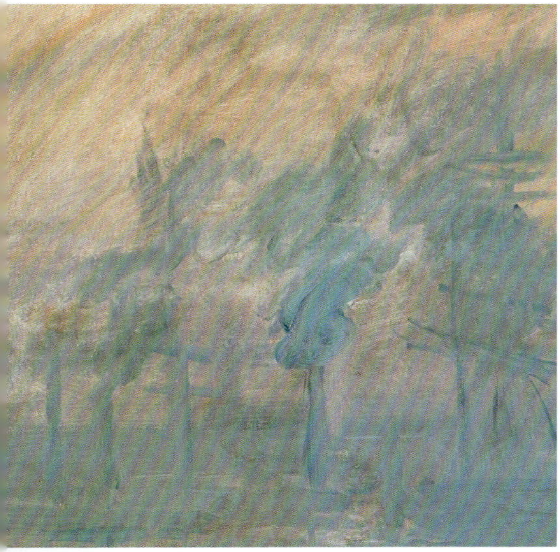

Flecked with brushstrokes, the sky reveals veils of mist, a subject dear to the artist, like water and reflections.

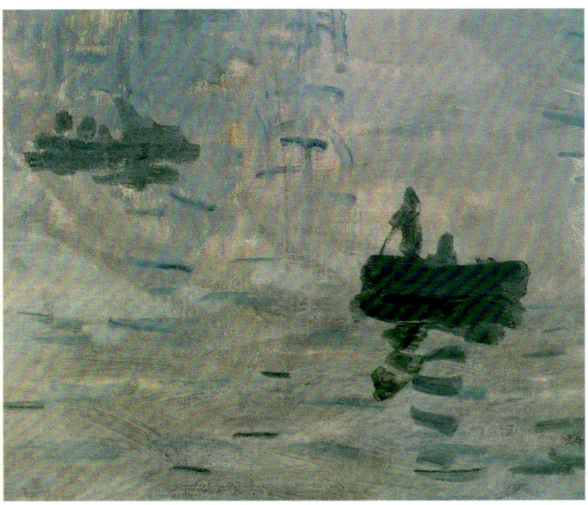

A rapidly sketched background punctuated by quick brushstrokes suffices to represent the sea.

IMPRESSIONISM IN THE AIR

"It seems certain that the word *impression* was frequently heard in the discussions of the painters [in the Café Guerbois]. Critics had used it for some time to characterize the efforts of such landscapists as Corot, Daubigny, and Jongkind. Rousseau himself had spoken of his attempts to remain faithful to the 'virgin impression of nature,' and even Manet, though not primarily interested in landscapes, had insisted on the occasion of his large show in 1867 that his intention was 'to convey his impression.'"
John Rewald, *The History of Impressionism*, 1946.

The word "impressionism," used derisively at the time of the first exhibition in 1874, would forever allude to the new group, although some of its members were hesitant to embrace the term, including Renoir, who was resistant to assimilation in any "school." Degas rejected the term, preferring "independent painters." Some advocates of the movement also rejected it, including Zola, who stubbornly referred to these painters as "naturalists." The critic Louis Edmond Duranty preferred the term "new painting," the title of the pamphlet published in 1876 for visitors to the second impressionist exhibition.

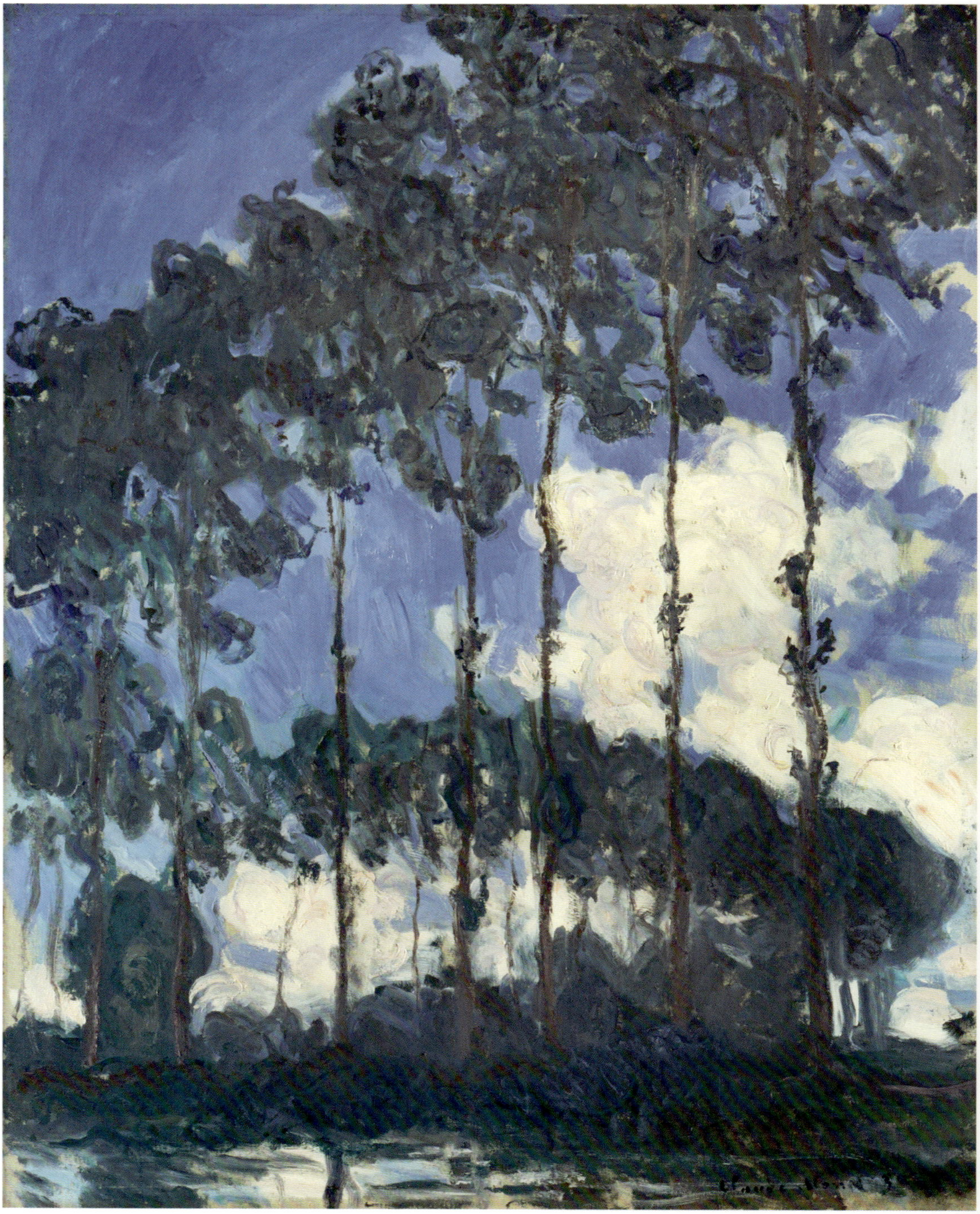

Claude Monet
Poplars on the Epte
1891
Oil on canvas, 35 ⅜ × 29 in.
(92.4 × 73.7 cm)
Tate Collection, London

Independent Trajectories

Far from designating a cohesive group, impressionism was more of a trend, liberally interpreted by individuals whose distinctive personalities led them to follow diverging paths—when they were not engaged in open conflict, that is. From the beginning of their association, every group decision was prefaced by animated, sometimes furious, discussion. Just six years after the first exhibition, it had to be acknowledged that consensus was not necessarily a realistic expectation. "I am still and always wish to be an impressionist," declared Monet in 1880, "but I now only rarely see my comrades, both men and women. The little sanctuary has turned into a commonplace school that opens its doors to any untalented hack who comes along." Was this an attack on Degas, who was constantly trying to attract additional artists to the group, or perhaps a way of justifying his desertion to participate in the Salon? Monet's revealing statement was made at a time when the great protagonists—Monet, Sisley, and Renoir—had abandoned the fifth exhibition. The inclusion of other artists diluted the original impressionist initiative, and the right to choose whether to exhibit at the Salon had always been a bone of contention. The painters' strong personalities and their increasingly divergent artistic paths further heightened the already acute existing tensions. The peremptory

IMPRESSIONIST DINNERS

Now scattered round and about Paris, the impressionist painters gathered for a monthly dinner at the Café Riche, near the Opéra. For Monet, Pissarro, Sisley, and Caillebotte, it was an opportunity to leave the country for an outing to Paris. Their friends, including the critic Duret and the writers Mallarmé and Huysmans, joined the group. These meetings admittedly lacked the spontaneous, ebullient sprit of the gatherings in the Café Guerbois and the Nouvelle Athènes, but they allowed the participants to remain in contact, despite some absentees like Pissarro, who couldn't always pay his share of the bill.

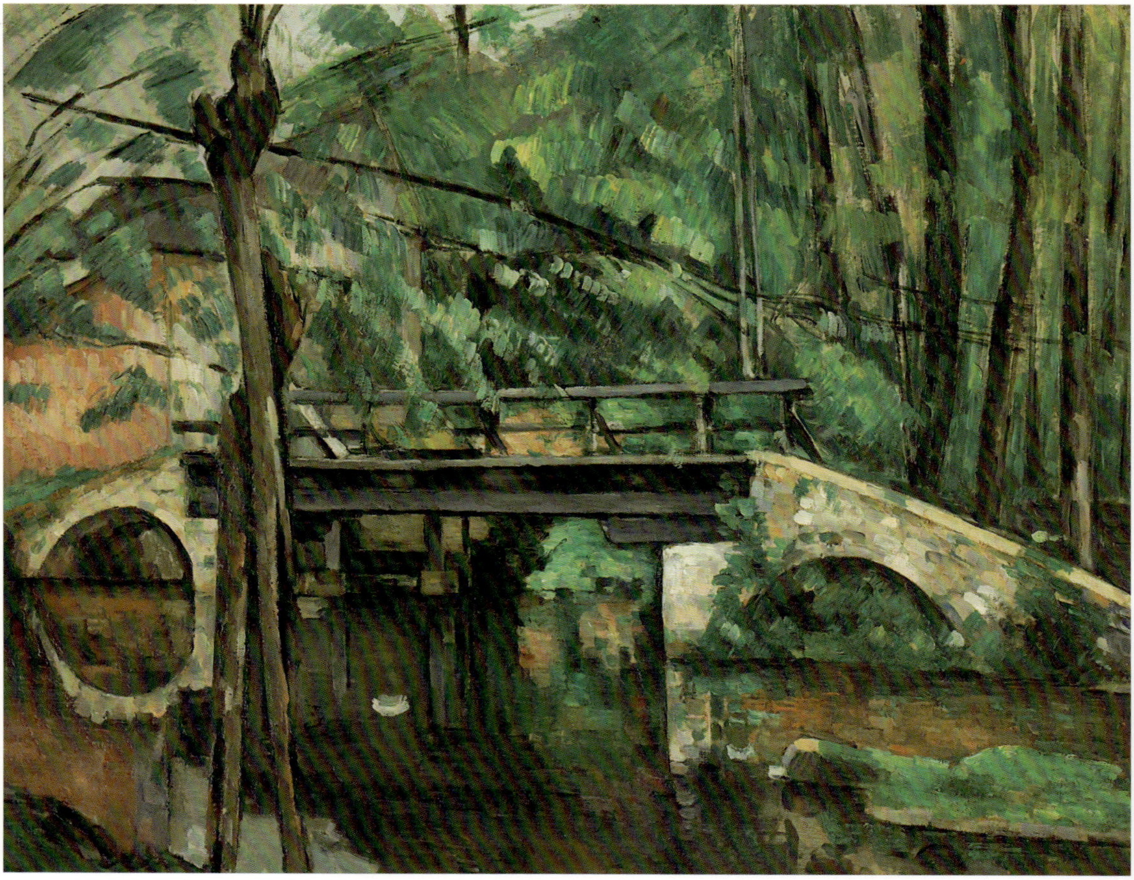

Paul Cézanne
The Bridge at Maincy
c. 1879
Oil on canvas, 23 × 28 ½ in. (58.5 × 72.5 cm)
Musée d'Orsay, Paris

"I wanted to make impressionism something strong and enduring, like the art in museums."

Paul Cézanne.

Degas took it upon himself to impose artists from outside the group. From 1879, Renoir pursued a different tangent, as did Cézanne, definitively. Monet bowed out of the fifth exhibition, followed by Sisley, both tired of the sense of stagnation. Caillebotte withdrew on the eve of the sixth exhibition, justly accusing Degas of sowing discord. Despite the return of Renoir, Monet, Sisley, and Caillebotte in 1882 for the seventh exhibition, the truce was short-lived. Long-standing conflicts ended with the dissolution of a group that had never been clearly defined but had cohabited thanks to artistic and social affinities. Over time, their individual trajectories diverged as the artists matured. Obsessed with landscape and painting from nature, Monet pushed even

DIFFERENT WORLDS

Manet and Berthe Morisot were both products of the wealthy, cultivated Parisian bourgeoisie, and they acted in keeping with their social status. Degas—with his shamelessly moody character—dispensed with such niceties. The group included its share of generous comrades, including Bazille, who came from a prosperous family in Montpellier, and Caillebotte, the heir to a substantial fortune. Sisley was the son of a wealthy merchant, but his situation changed following the events of 1870, which destroyed the family fortune. A retiring personality, he shared periods of poverty with the chronically struggling Monet, who had broken with his well-off family and remained bitter. Pissarro, originally from the Antilles, was always affable and generous despite his financial concerns.

Cézanne, the son of a milliner from Aix, enjoyed flaunting his strong local accent, outspokenness, and even his questionable character to his bourgeois Parisian audience. Renoir came from a working-class background and started as an apprentice porcelain painter. His impoverished origins became a thing of the past with his successes at the Salon, and he always had an air of irrepressibly good cheer about him. Apprenticed at the age of sixteen, Guillaumin worked for the Paris-Orléans railroad company. The job allowed him to escape poverty, but he was only able to paint during his brief hours of leisure—until 1892 when, in a true reversal of fortune, he won the jackpot in a state lottery and was finally able to devote himself to painting full time.

Claude Monet
Rough Sea at Étretat
1883
Oil on canvas,
2 ft. 8 in. × 3 ft. 3 ½ in.
(81 × 100 cm)
Musée des Beaux-Arts, Lyon

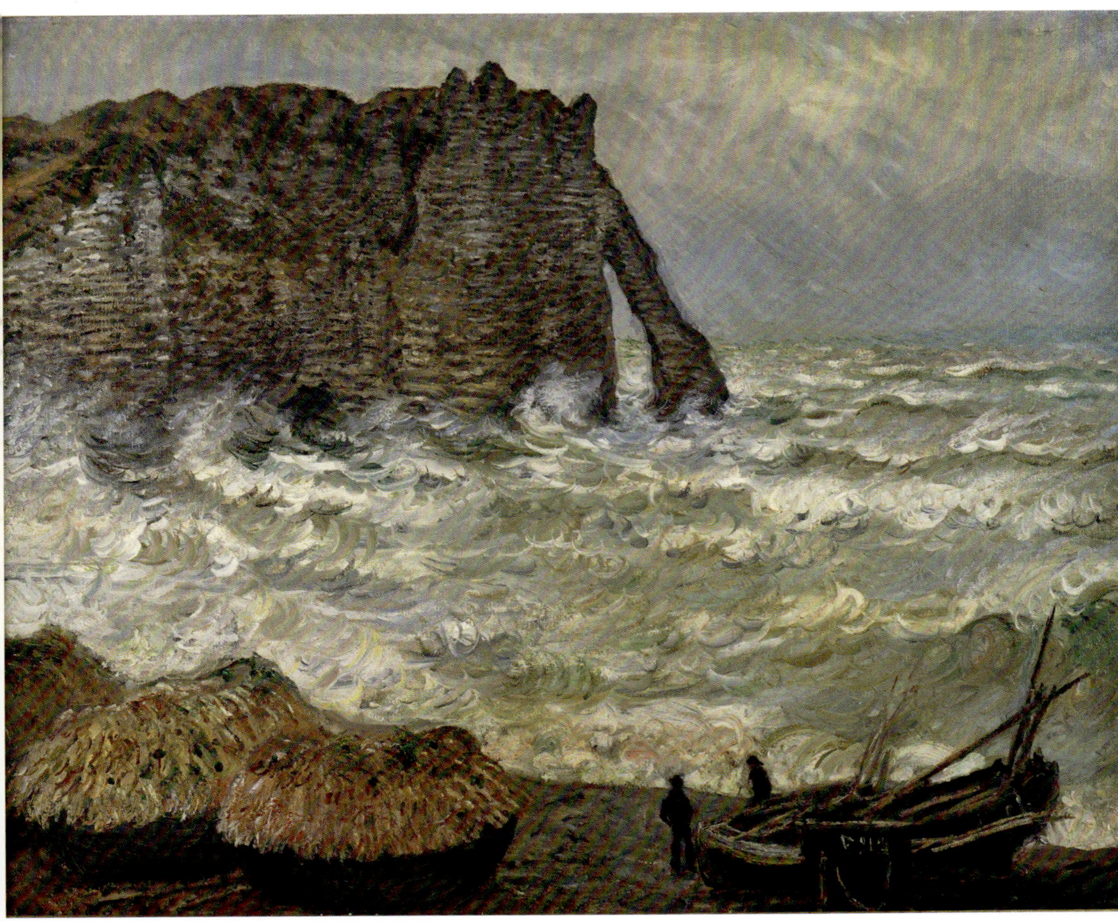

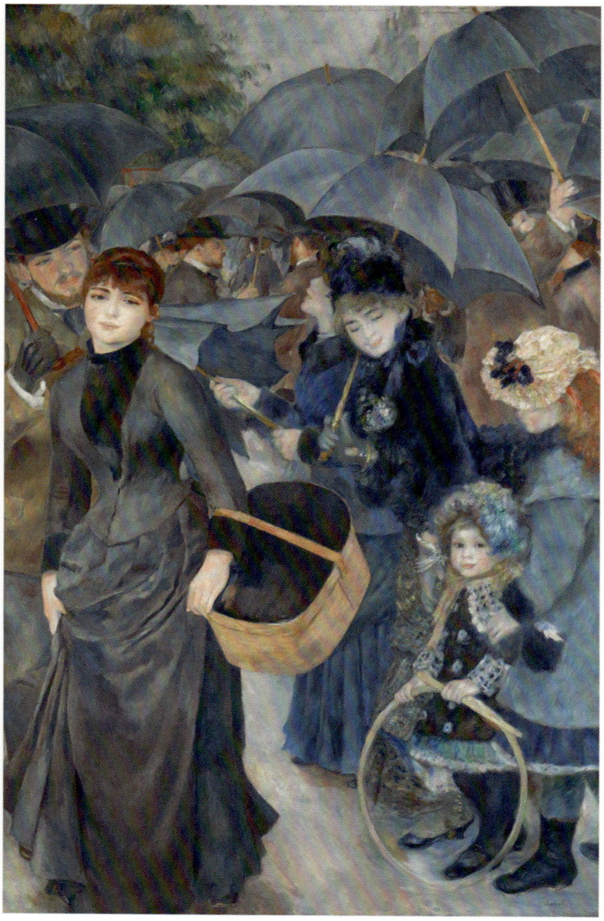

Auguste Renoir
The Umbrellas
c. 1880–86
Oil on canvas,
5 ft. 11 in. × 3 ft. 9 ¼ in.
(1.80 × 1.15 m)
National Gallery, London

"In 1883, a sort of break occurred in my work. I had got to the end of impressionism and had reached the conclusion that I could neither paint nor draw. In short, I had reached an impasse."

Auguste Renoir.

further with the dissolution of form. In contrast, Renoir gradually abandoned fragmented brushstrokes to adopt a degree of solidity in his work. Degas never painted directly from nature and was a fierce advocate of line and drawing as well as a certain degree of naturalism.

In addition to these fundamental disagreements, the artists had to face the fact that the impressionists' exhibitions, which were excoriated by critics, were for the most part a financial disaster. Even the unfailingly faithful Pissarro, the only one to participate in all eight impressionist exhibitions, considered withdrawing after the seventh exhibition. He reiterated the same idea a year later, lucidly observing: "The difficulty seems to be arriving at an understanding."

AN ACCCURATE PREMONITION

"In just a few short years, the painters who had gathered on Boulevard des Capucines were divided. The strongest among them understood that there were subjects that lent themselves to a rapid 'impression' in the form of a sketch, but other topics, which were far more numerous, demanded a more precise rendering."

Jules Antoine Castagnary, *Le Siècle*, April 29, 1874, writing about the first impressionist exhibition.

DEGAS: THE LEAST IMPRESSIONISTIC OF THE IMPRESSIONISTS

Opposed to this designation, Degas, who continued to argue for the expression "independent artists," condemned certain basic precepts of impressionism by his own approach to art. He was committed to line and drawing, and fiercely opposed the fragmentation of brushstrokes and forms. He never painted *en plein air*. Landscapes and atmospheric subtleties did not interest this urbane, acerbic figure. He expressed his version of modernity through choosing subjects that were grounded in the reality of his time, using his extraordinary photographic eye. Nevertheless, the impressionists unanimously recognized him as a great artist and considered him one of their own. They were not mistaken about this, although they were critical of his authoritarian demeanor and his wish to impose on the group minor painters such as Forain, Raffaëlli, and Zandomeneghi. Degas liked to emphasize their differences: "No art was ever less spontaneous than mine. What I do is the result of reflection and study of the great masters; of inspiration, spontaneity, temperament—temperament is the word—I know nothing."
Degas, quoted in George Heard Hamilton, *Painting and Sculpture in Europe: 1880–1940*, 1967.

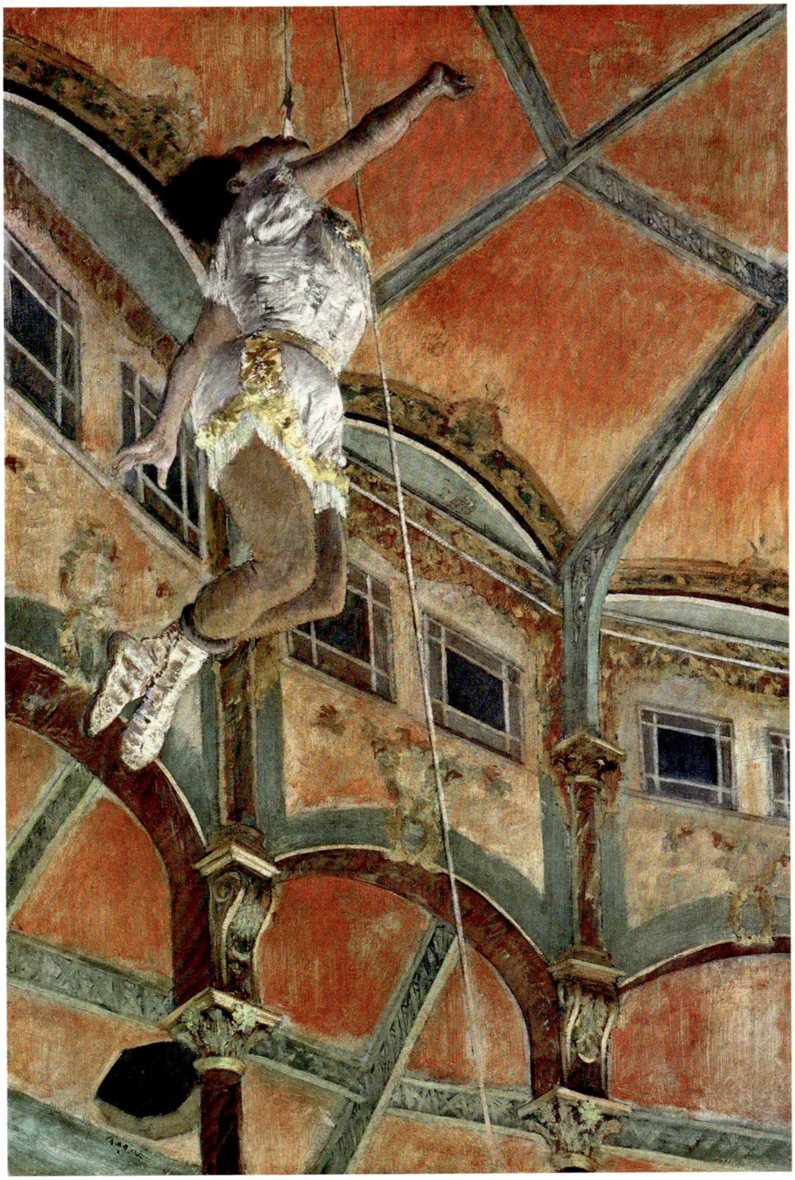

Edgar Degas
Miss Lala at the Cirque Fernando
1879
Oil on canvas,
3 ft. 10 in. × 2 ft. 6 ½ in.
(116.8 × 77.5 cm)
National Gallery, London

Distinctive Brushstrokes

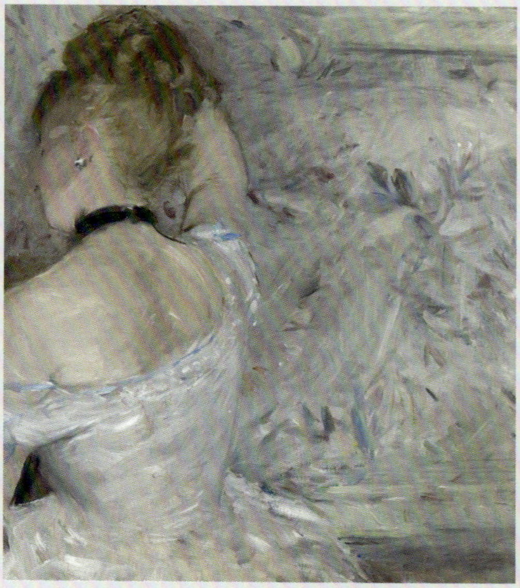

Berthe Morisot, *Young Woman at Her Toilette* (detail), 1875
Oil on canvas, 23 ¾ × 31 ⅝ in. (60.3 × 80.4 cm)
The Art Institute of Chicago, Chicago

BERTHE MORISOT
Her long, rapid brushstrokes produced works that were almost sketch-like.

EDGAR DEGAS
Faithful to drawing and painting in his studio, Degas developed a more carefully worked approach.

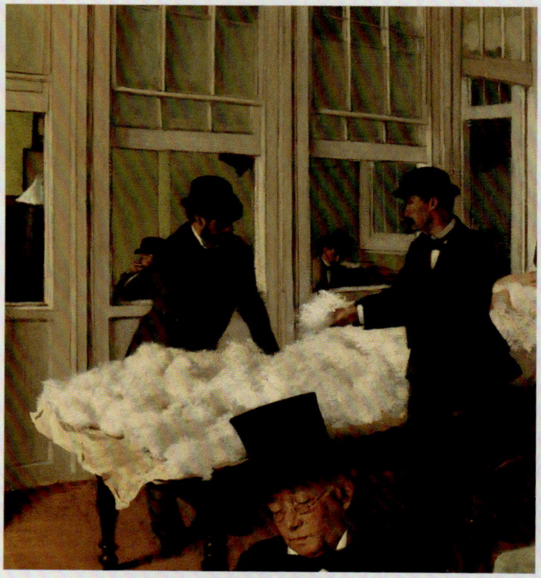

Edgar Degas, *A Cotton Office in New Orleans* (detail), 1873
Oil on canvas, 2 ft. 4 ¾ in. 3 ft ¼ in. (73 × 92 cm)
Musée des Beaux-Arts, Pau

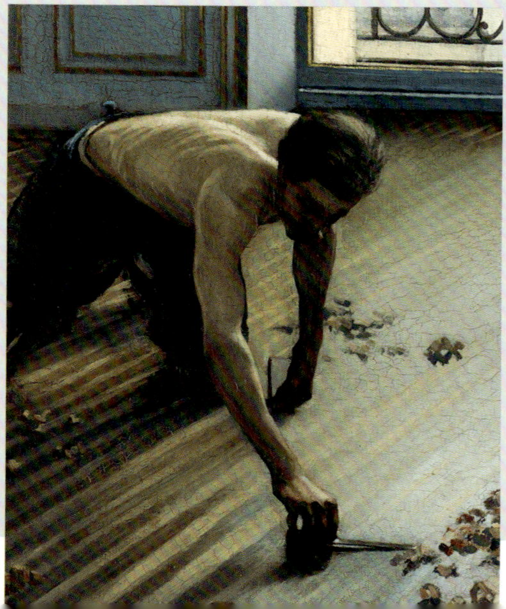

GUSTAVE CAILLEBOTTE
Like Degas, Caillebotte did not use fragmented brushstrokes.

Gustave Caillebotte, *The Floor Planers* (detail), 1875
Oil on canvas, 3 ft. 4 ¼ in. × 4 ft. 9 ½ in. (1.02 × 1.46 m)
Musée d'Orsay, Paris

FRÉDÉRIC BAZILLE

Bazille died young, before he could fully participate in the impressionist adventure, and he retained a fairly traditional approach.

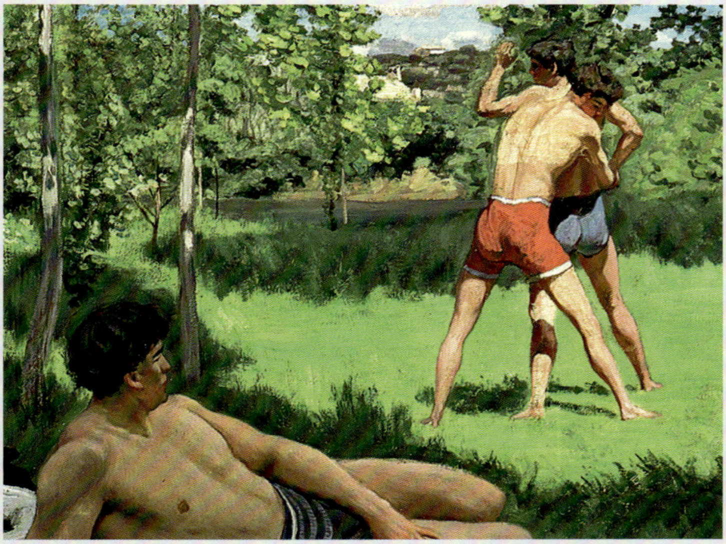

Frédéric Bazille, *Summer Scene* (detail), 1869
Oil on canvas, 5 ft. 1 ½ in. 5 ft. 2 ¼ in. (1.56 × 1.58 m)
Fogg Art Museum, Harvard University Art Museums, Cambridge

AUGUSTE RENOIR

Renoir used fragmented brushstrokes at the beginning of his career, but he adopted a more defined style, before embracing complete freedom toward the end of his life.

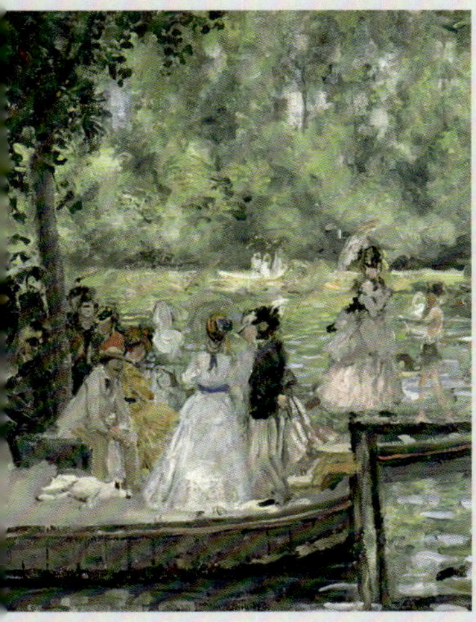

Auguste Renoir, *La Grenouillère* (detail), 1869
Oil on canvas, 26 ⅛ × 31 ⅞ in. (66.5 × 81 cm)
National Museum, Stockholm

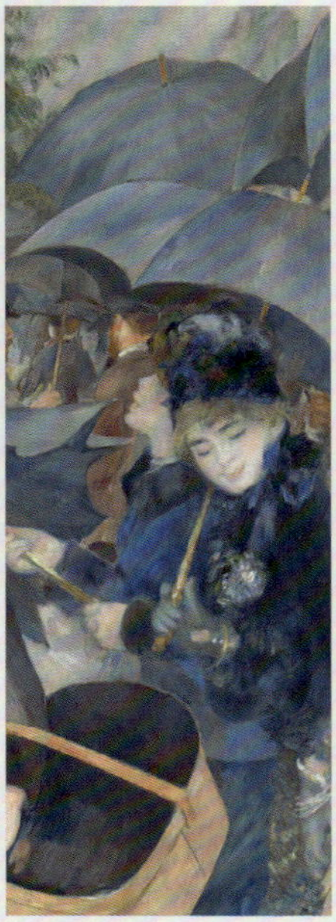

Auguste Renoir,
The Umbrellas (detail),
c. 1880–86
Oil on canvas,
5 ft. 11 in. × 3 ft. 9 ¼ in.
(1.80 × 1.15 m)
National Gallery, London

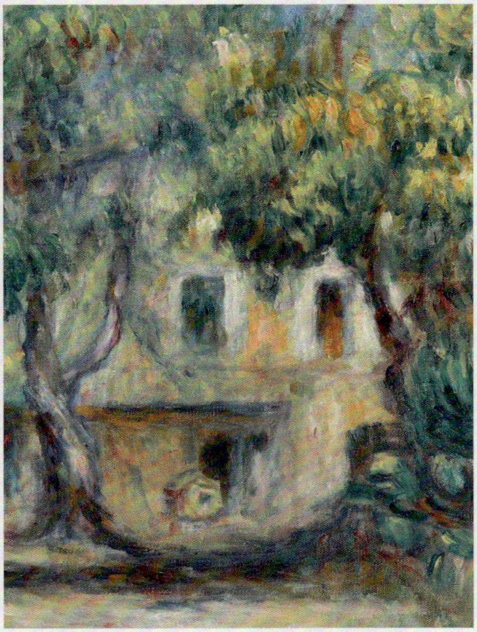

Auguste Renoir, *The Farm at Les Colettes* (detail), 1915
Oil on canvas, 18 ⅛ × 20 in. (46 × 51 cm)
Musée Renoir, Cagnes-sur-Mer

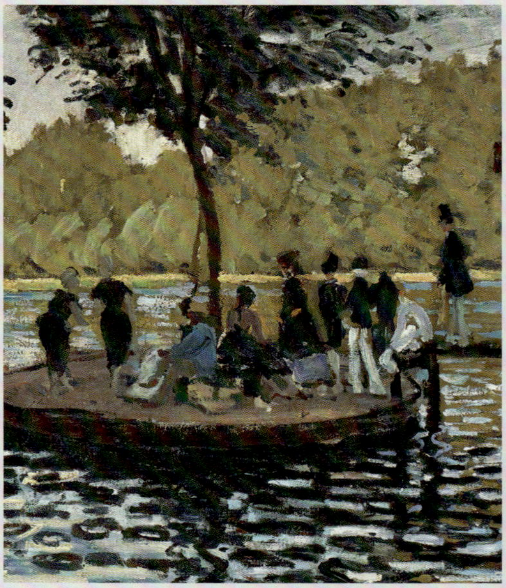

Claude Monet, *La Grenouillère* (detail), 1869
Oil on canvas, 2 ft. 5 ½ in. × 3 ft. 3 ¼ in. (74.6 × 99.7 cm)
The Metropolitan Museum of Art, New York

CLAUDE MONET
Originally his brushstrokes were like little commas, but they became increasingly free, approaching the point of complete disintegration and an almost reflexive form of expression at the end of his life.

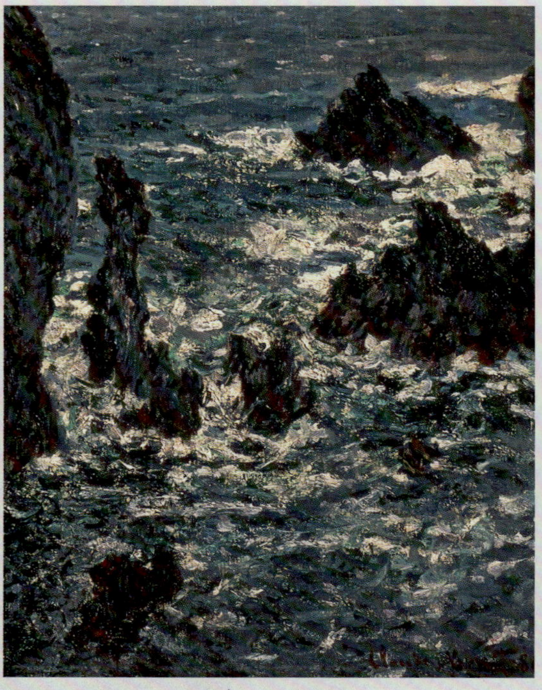

Claude Monet, *Rocks at Belle-Île* (detail), 1886
Oil on canvas, 25 ⅝ × 31 ⅞ in. (65 × 81 cm)
The Pushkin State Museum of Fine Arts, Moscow

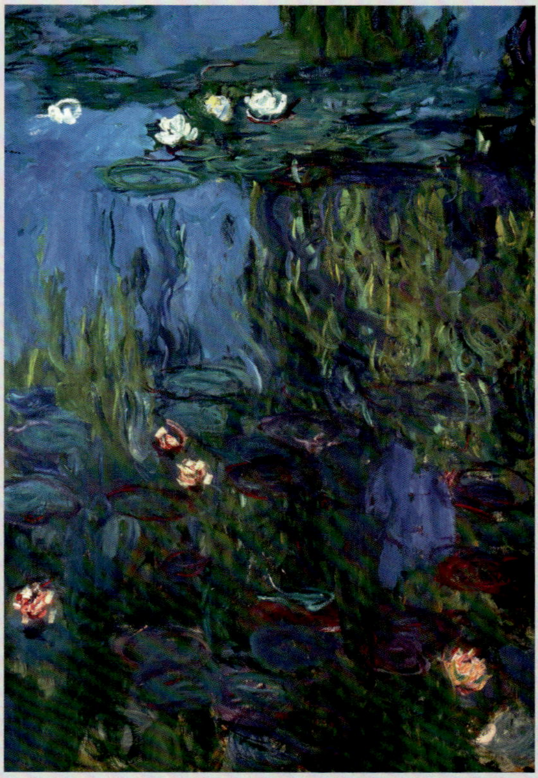

Claude Monet, *Water Lilies*, 1914–17
Oil on canvas, 6 ft. 6 ¾ in. × 4 ft. 11 in. (2.00 × 1.50 m),
now 5 ft. 7 in. × 4 ft. (1.70 × 1.22 m)
Private collection

ALFRED SISLEY

Usually lively but controlled, Sisley's brushstrokes occasionally showed freer movement.

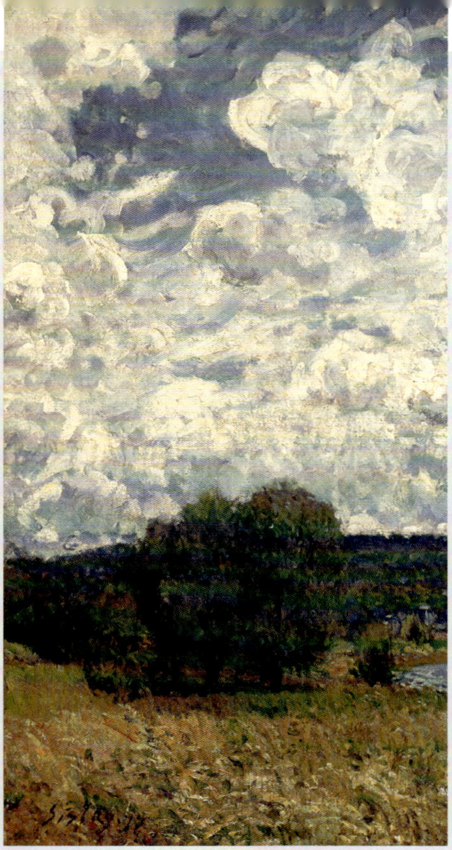

Alfred Sisley, *The Seine at Suresnes* (detail), 1877
Oil on canvas, 23 ⅞ × 28 ⅞ in. (60.5 × 73.5 cm)
Musée d'Orsay, Paris

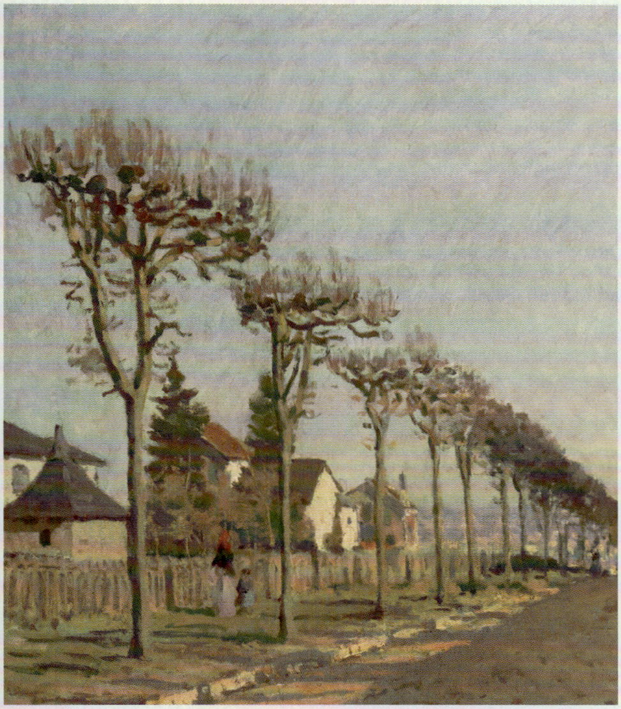

Alfred Sisley, *The Chemin de la Machine, Louveciennes* (detail), 1873
Oil on canvas, 21 ½ × 28 ¾ in. (54.5 × 73 cm)
Musée d'Orsay, Paris

CAMILLE PISSARRO

Pissarro's more structured brushstrokes suddenly fragmented when he adopted pointillism in 1886.

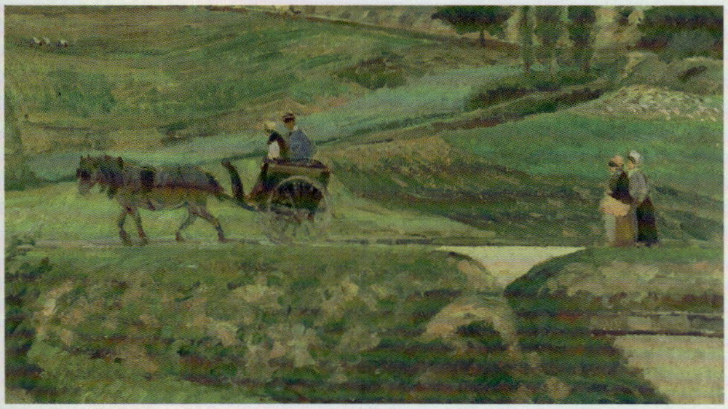

Camille Pissarro, *The Road to Ennery* (detail), 1874
Oil on canvas, 1 ft. 9 ¾ in. × 3 ft. ¼ in. (55 × 92 cm)
Musée d'Orsay, Paris

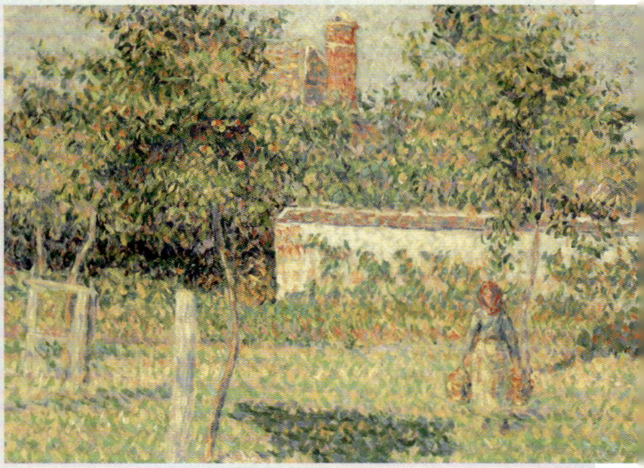

Camille Pissarro, *Woman in an Orchard,* also known as *Spring Sunshine in the Meadow at Éragny* (detail), 1887
Oil on canvas, 17 ⅞ × 25 ⅝ in. (45.4 × 65 cm)
Musée d'Orsay, Paris

FOCUS

A Woman's Place

For the first time in history, impressionism put male and female artists on an equal footing. Although it would not have been deemed appropriate at the time for women to participate in the discussions that took place in the cafés, Berthe Morisot and Mary Cassatt exhibited their work alongside their male counterparts, and their output was genuinely respected. These two women, one from the Parisian bourgeoisie and the other from the American upper-middle class, each had a distinguished artistic career. The quality of their painting was fully acknowledged, although they were somewhat restricted in their choice of subject matter by the conventions of the day. It was natural for them to paint scenes from their domestic lives. Berthe Morisot's daughter Julie was her primary model, and scenes of reading, bathing, and family life are recurrent in her work. After traveling through Europe, Mary Cassatt moved permanently to France in 1874. She had been friends with Degas since their meeting in 1877, and she exhibited with the impressionists, providing them with active support. Her paintings depict real women taking tea, reading, and on outings to the Opéra or to museums. Her engravings demonstrate her assimilation of Japanese art, which remained a powerful influence in her work. Manet's only student, Eva Gonzalès, here shown painting, was another example of a successful woman artist, although she died young in 1883.

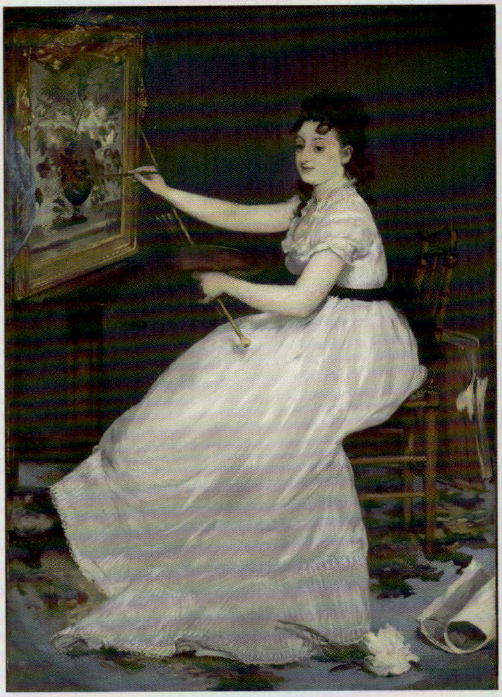

Édouard Manet, *Eva Gonzalès,* 1870
Oil on canvas, 6 ft. 3 ¼ in. × 4 ft. 4 ¼ in. (1.91 × 1.33 m)
National Gallery, London

"These women will become painters. Do you actually realize what this will mean?"

Joseph Guichard, the Morisot sisters' first art teacher, to their mother, Madame Morisot.

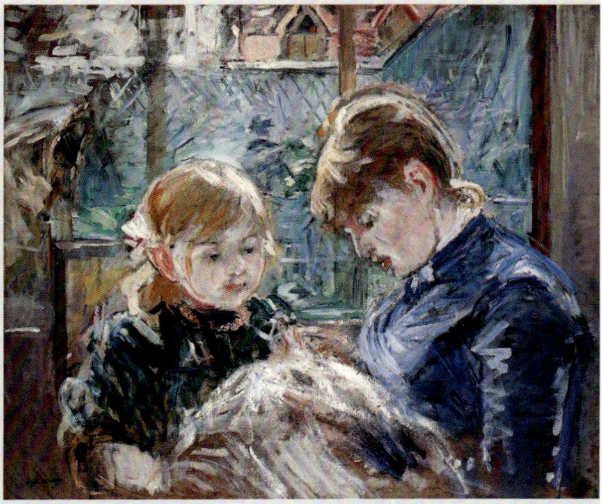

Berthe Morisot, *The Sewing Lesson (Julie and Her Nurse)*, 1884
Oil on canvas, 23 ¼ × 28 in. (59 × 71 cm)
Minneapolis Institute of Arts, Minneapolis

PROFESSION: NONE
Such was the entry recorded on Berthe Morisot's death certificate. The artistic revolution had its limits, even for a woman who had received unwavering support in her career from her husband Eugène Manet, the brother of Édouard Manet, who had been the first of them to meet her.

WOMEN, REAL WOMEN

For the impressionists, the female figure was no longer the statuesque body of a remote goddess. Suddenly wives, mothers, and children appeared, along with coquettish young women visiting their milliners and ladies attending performances, taking tea, or reading together. Real women leading real lives created an entirely unfamiliar iconography. Degas had no qualms about showing a woman just out of the tub, toweling herself vigorously, not concealing her vaguely animalistic quality.

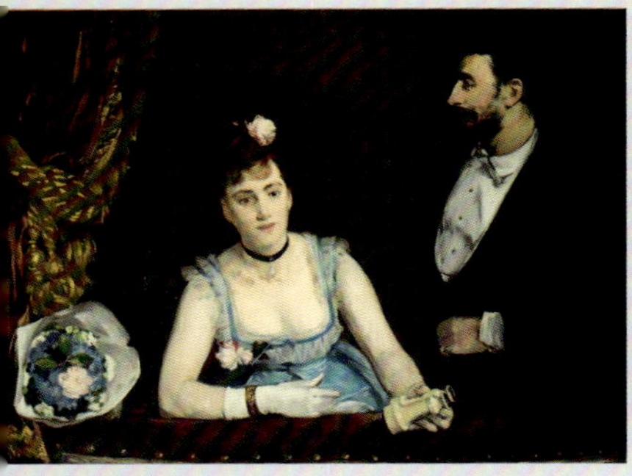

Eva Gonzalès, *A Box at the Théâtre des Italiens*, c. 1874
Oil on canvas, 3 ft. 2 ½ in. × 4 ft. ¾ in. (98 × 130 cm)
Musée d'Orsay, Paris

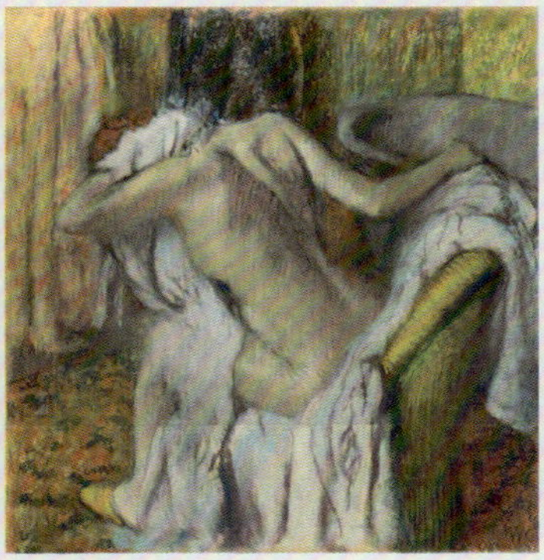

Edgar Degas, *After the Bath, Woman Drying Herself*, c. 1890–95
Pastel on board, 3 ft. 4 ¾ in. × 3 ft. 2 ¾ in. (103.5 × 98.5 cm)
National Gallery, London

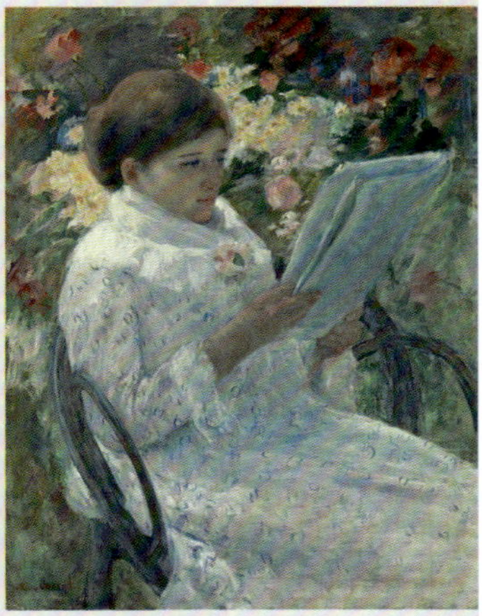

Mary Cassatt, *Woman Reading in the Garden*, 1878–79
Oil on canvas, 35 ⅜ × 25 ⅝ in. (89.9 × 65.2 cm)
The Art Institute of Chicago, Chicago

IMAGES IN THE SPOTLIGHT

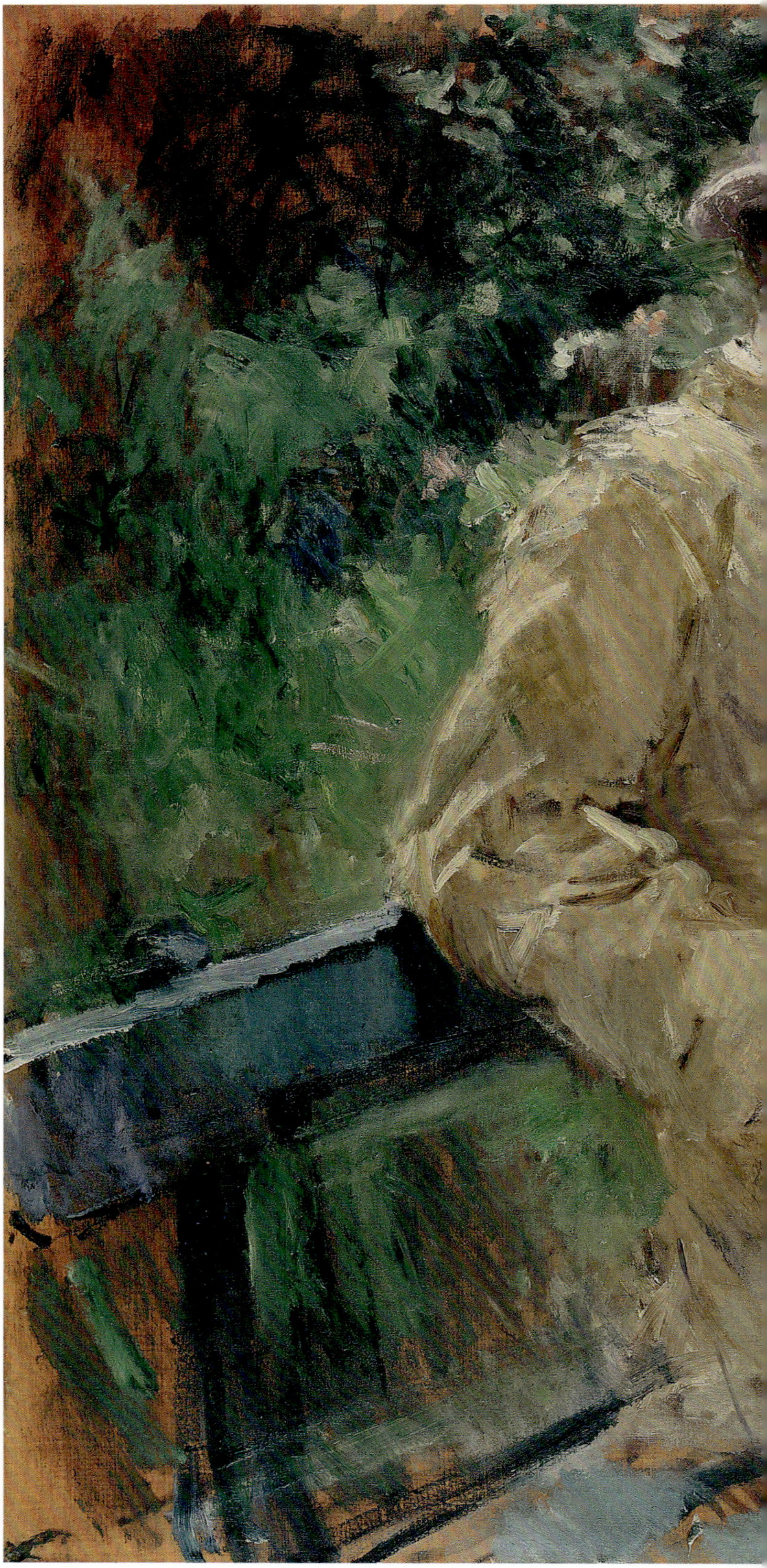

Berthe Morisot
Eugène Manet and His Daughter in the Garden at Bougival
1881
Oil on canvas,
2 ft. 4 ¾ in. × 3 ft. ¼ in.
(73 × 92 cm)
Musée Marmottan, Paris

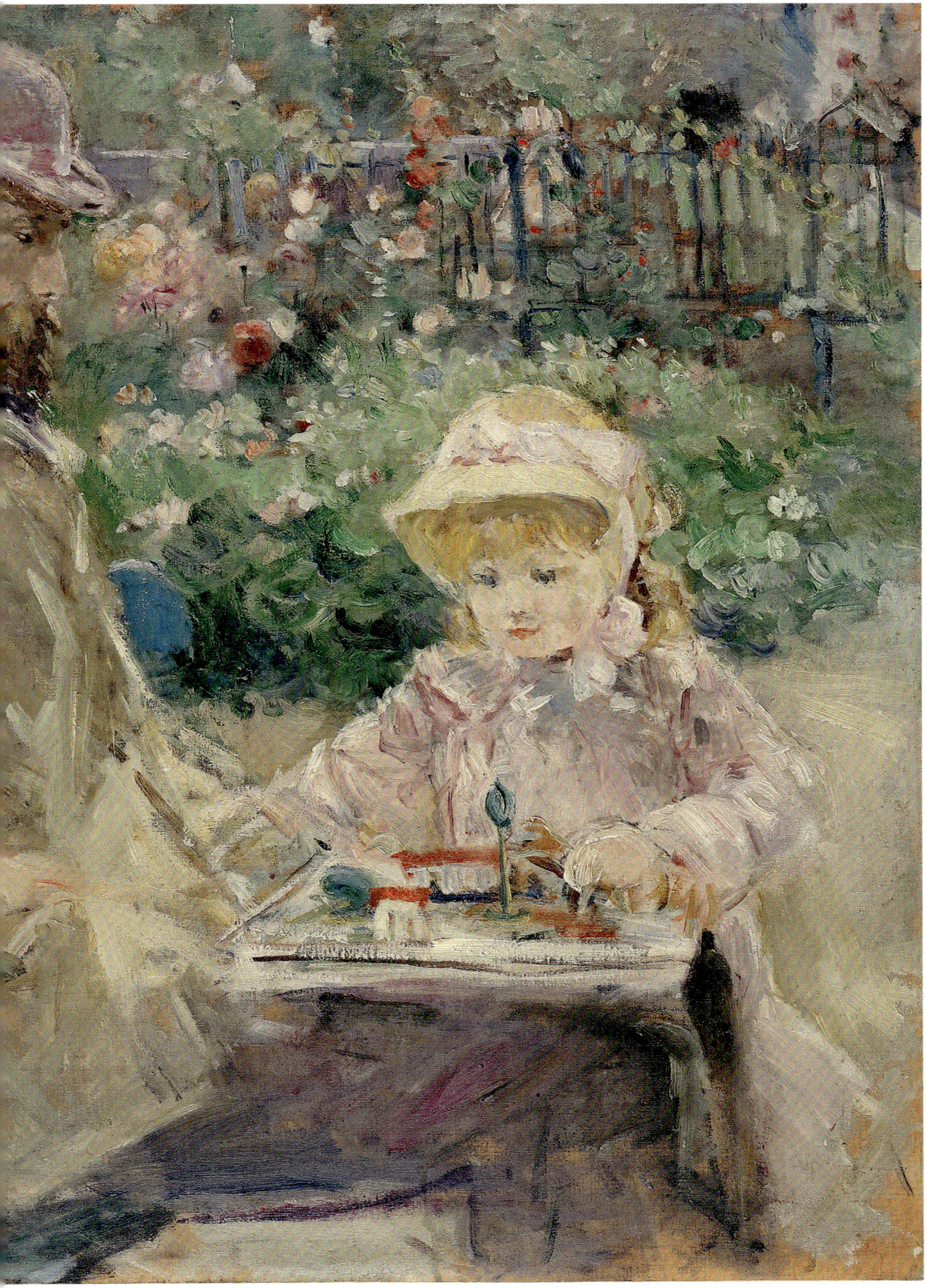

Eugène Manet and His Daughter in the Garden at Bougival

Berthe Morisot, 1881

Changing roles, changing points of view. Women artists created a new iconography. Berthe Morisot became a mother late in life with the birth of her daughter Julie. As an artist, she had a fresh perspective on this moment of family life, showing her husband Eugène Manet playing with their daughter.

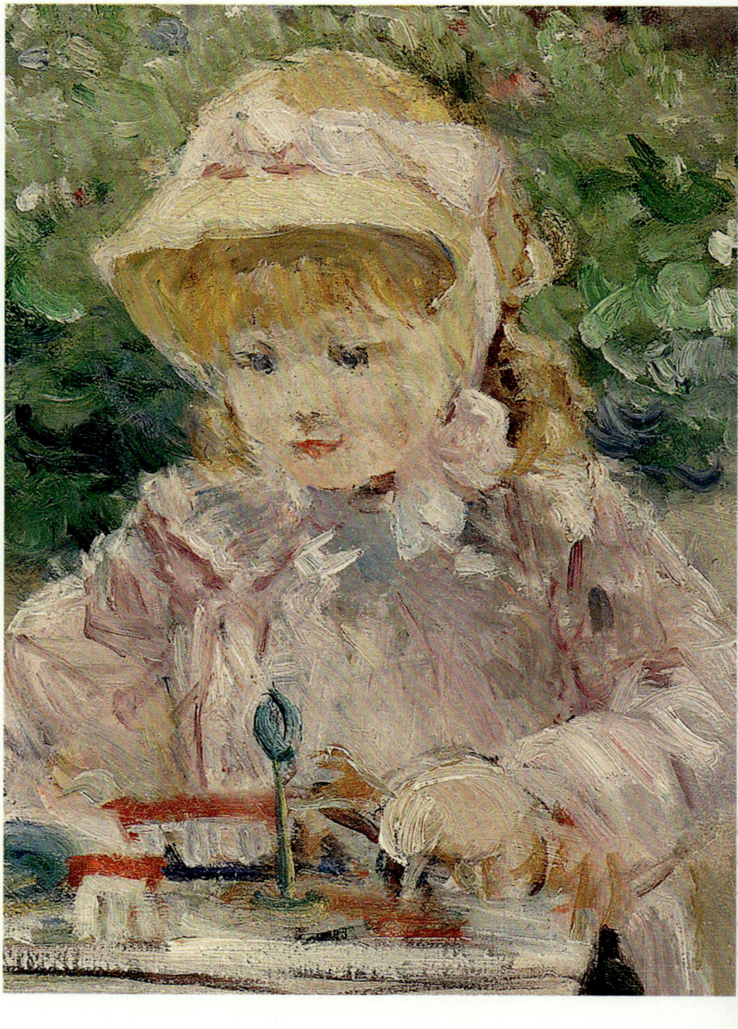

Full of freshness and life, Berthe Morisot's sketch depicts—with rapid brushstrokes—the features of her daughter Julie, who is an omnipresent model in her work.

"Duret, who knows what he's talking about, thinks that this year's exhibition is the best your group has had. I think so, too."

Eugène Manet, letter to Berthe Morisot, March 1882.

A loyal supporter of her artistic career, Eugène Manet stood by her during her adventure in the impressionist world, supervising the hanging of her pictures and even writing art reviews in the detailed reports that he sent to her when she was away from Paris.

A new vision of fatherhood emerges. He is no longer the family patriarch, but an affectionate man able to understand the child's perspective on life.

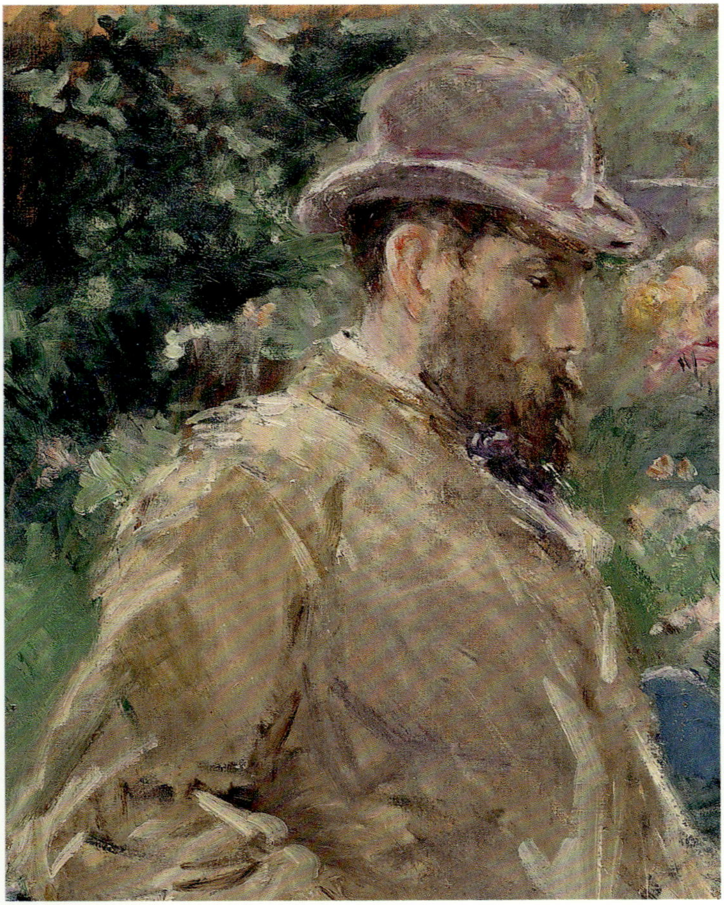

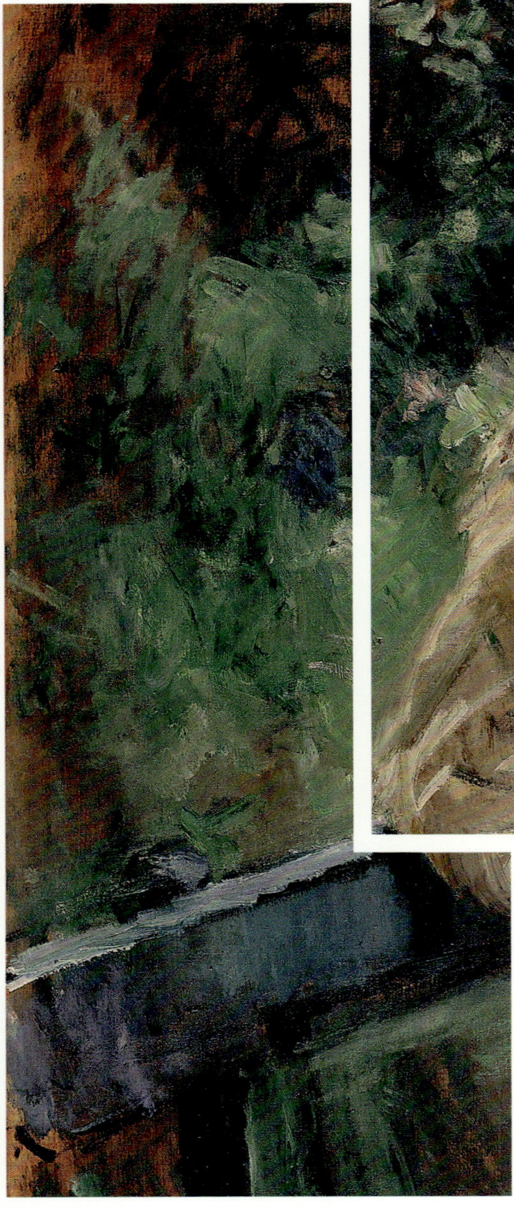

The artist's freedom of expression is revealed in her vigorous brushstrokes, which are content to merely suggest the foliage with broad movements of the brush: saying less to communicate more.

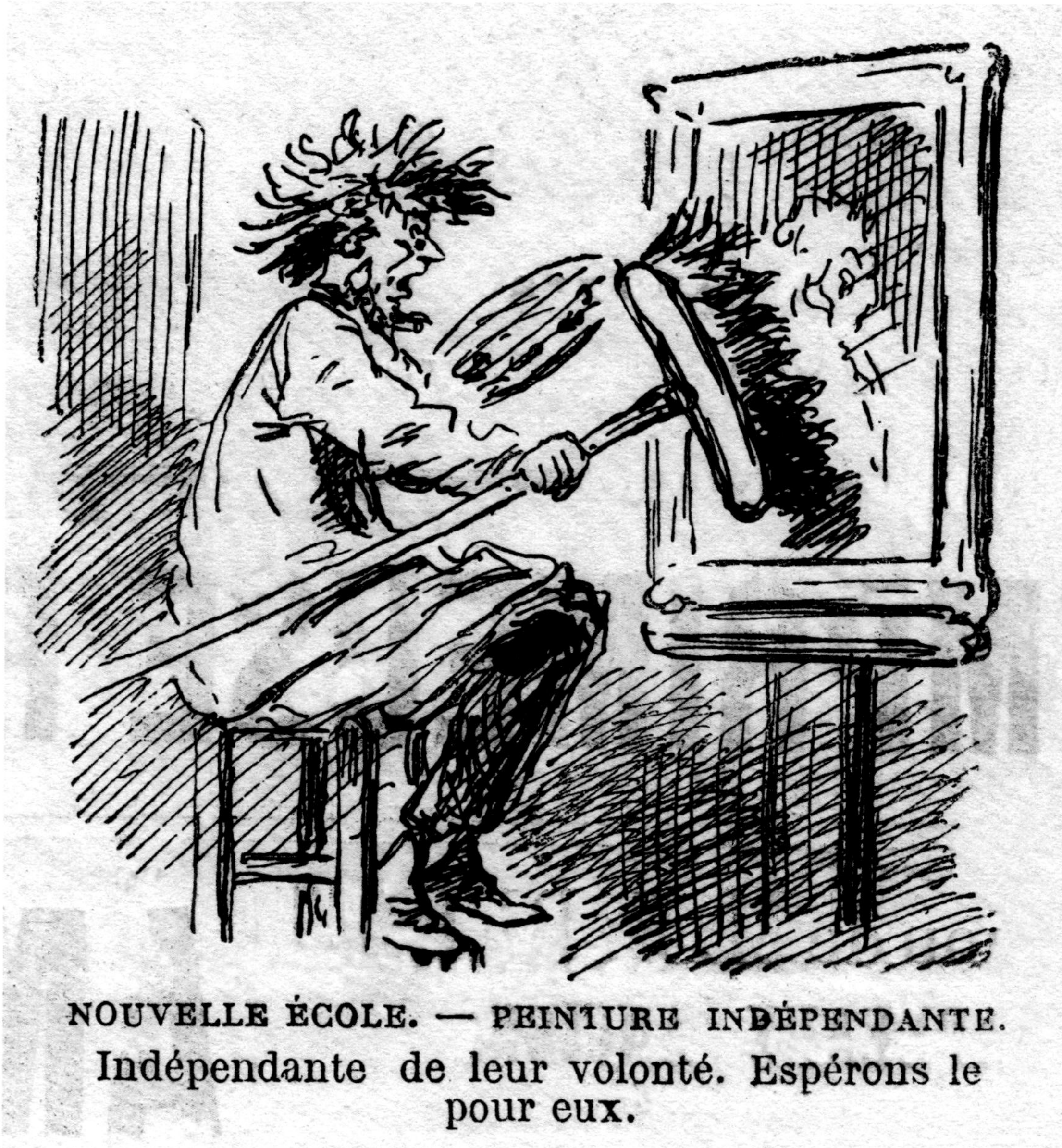

Cham
New School, Independent Painting
Le Charivari, April 1879
Wood engraving,
approximately 3 ⅛ × 3 ⅛ in. (8 × 8 cm)
Kharbine Tapabor Archives

Art under Brutal Attack

Published in *Le Charivari* on April 25, 1874, ten days after the opening of the first impressionist exhibition, the resounding criticism by Louis Leroy set the tone for the attacks that assailed the group for close to twenty years. Savaging the painters one by one, Leroy staged a fictional dialogue with an award-winning artist from the Salon, whom he guides from canvas to canvas through the entire exhibition. Although it is difficult to understand today, this new way of painting outraged viewers, who were used to seeing academic art. Their horror is reflected in the virulence of the attacks that rained down from all quarters. Viewers perceived the lack of respect for academic principles as a direct insult. The rapidity of impressionist work was interpreted as talentless daubing; it was "poorly drawn" and "badly painted." To cap it all, it was hard to discern any subject matter at all, and, if any existed, it was considered to be of no interest, or trivial at best. Writing in *La Presse* on April 29, 1874, E. Cardon provided a mock recipe for cooking up one of these new paintings. "Smear three quarters of the canvas with black and white, scrub the rest with yellow,

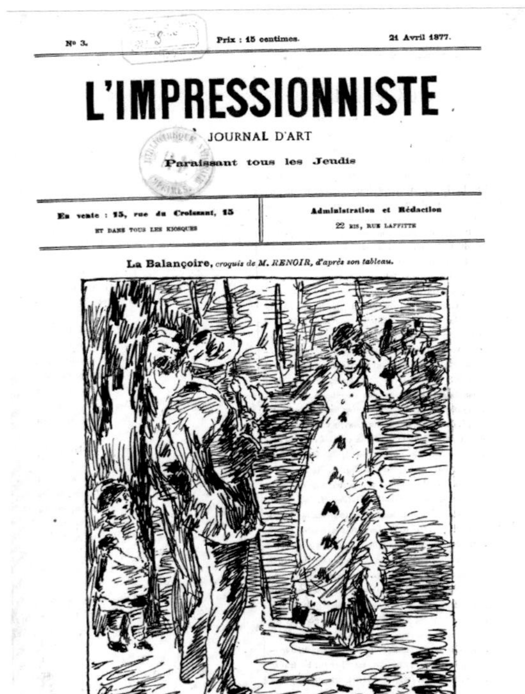
N° 3. Prix : 15 centimes. 21 Avril 1877.

L'IMPRESSIONNISTE

JOURNAL D'ART

Paraissant tous les Jeudis

En vente : 15, rue du Croissant, 15
ET DANS TOUS LES KIOSQUES

Administration et Rédaction
22 BIS, RUE LAFFITTE

La Balançoire, *croquis de M. RENOIR, d'après son tableau.*

Cover of *L'Impressionniste*
April 21, 1877
Bibliothèque Nationale de France, Paris

From the founding of the Anonymous Cooperative Society of Artists (Painters, Sculptors, Engravers, etc.), in 1873, their statutes had envisioned the publication of a review covering their activities and their art. The journal became a reality with the third exhibition in 1877. Georges Rivière (1855–1943), Renoir's friend, was a journalist who undertook to publish five issues that year. But the venture was short-lived, due to lack of adequate funding.

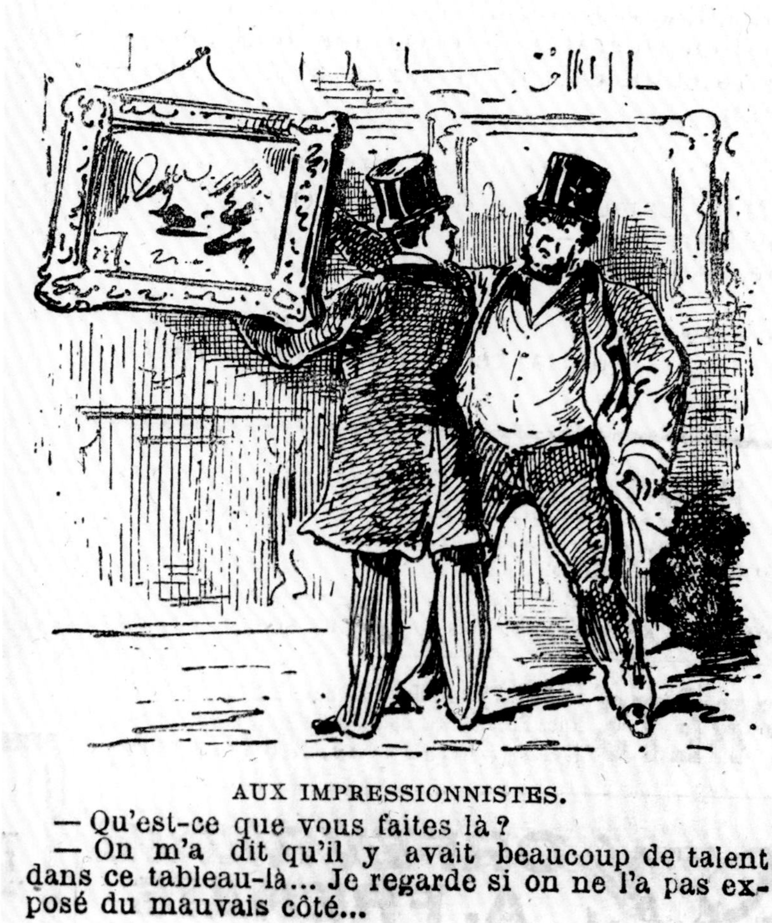

Pif
Aux impressionnistes
Le Charivari, April 10, 1881
Wood engraving,
approximately 3 ⅛ × 3 ⅛ in. (8 × 8 cm)
Kharbine Tapabor Archives

randomly scatter red and blue spots here and there, and you'll get an impression.... The famous Salon des Refusés cannot be mentioned without bursting into laughter, and that was the Louvre compared to the exhibition on Boulevard des Capucines." The well-known critic Jules Claretie was more measured in his wording, but equally decisive: the impressionists seemed to have simply "declared war on beauty," as he wrote in his book *L'Art et les artistes français*, 1876. He elaborated on this, five years later, writing in *Le Temps* about the sixth impressionist exhibition (1881). "What would we say if writers took a notion to publish their handwritten notes, observations, and off-the-cuff remarks jotted down on the fly? We'd tell them to edit them and finish their work properly. It would be a simple matter of respect for the audience if the 'independent' painters would

WHY SUCH HATRED?

"Nineteenth-century bourgeois society was positivist and pragmatic; for them the rejection of traditional modeling techniques was a dangerous symptom. A social order that considered itself to be universal and definitive realized that—in every area—history was moving on.... Every impressionist painting tells a tale of liberation: life had escaped the stifling system of symbols that strove to constrain it. The raw reality of the impressionist vision defied the traditional order that some thought convention could contain.

Jean Clay, *Histoire de l'impressionnisme*, 1971.

"Try to make Monsieur Pissarro understand that trees are not purple, that the sky is not the color of fresh butter, and that in no country on earth will you find the things he paints, and that no thinking person can tolerate such absurdities. Try to make Monsieur Degas see reason. Tell him that art does in fact have some qualities that you can put a name to: drawing, color, execution, control. He'd laugh in your face and call you a reactionary. Try to explain to Monsieur Renoir that a woman's torso is not a heap of decomposing flesh with green patches, laced with purple blotches that indicate complete putrefaction in a cadaver!"
Albert Wolff, *Le Figaro*, April 3, 1876.

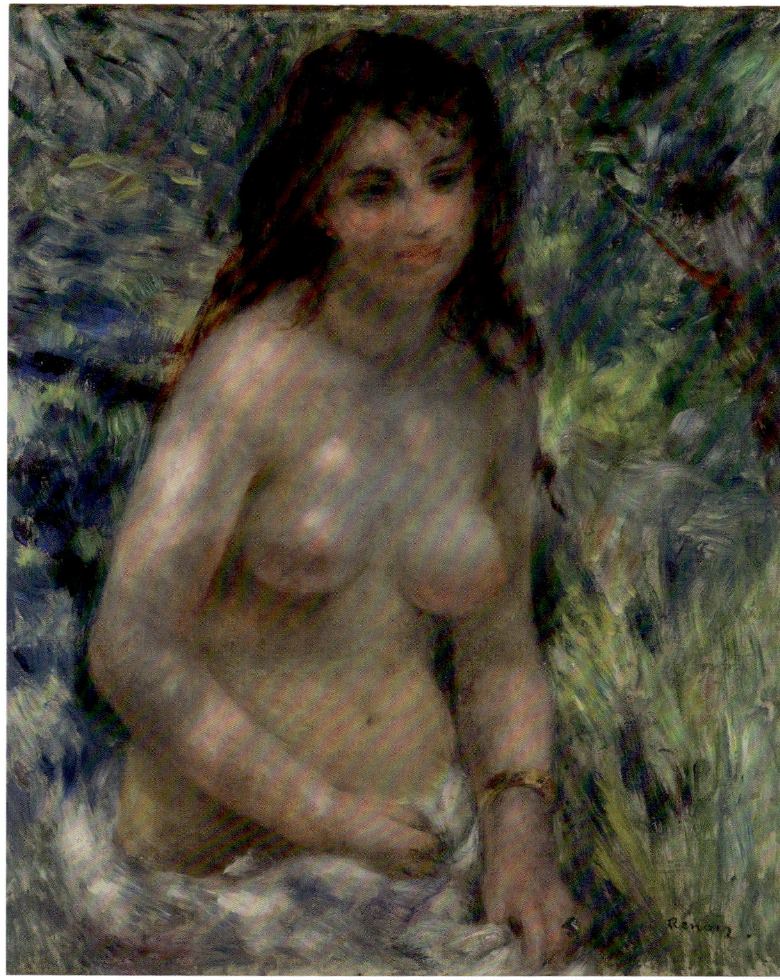

Auguste Renoir
Study of Torso, Effect of Sun
1875
Oil on canvas, 31 ⅞ × 25 ⅝ in. (81 × 65 cm)
Musée d'Orsay, Paris

consent to pursue their works beyond a mere sketch." In the *Courrier de France*, April 6, 1877, F. O. S'quare reminisced three years after the first impressionist exhibition, proof of the event's lasting impact: "The public mind was indignant. It was horrible, stupid, and messy; these paintings made no sense." The shockwaves were genuine and they left an enduring mark.

There was a near-unanimous opinion that the liberties taken by the impressionists–the unfinished aspect of their canvases that contrasted so sharply with the polished perfection of academic pointing–were genuine outrages. The public's incomprehension was total. The only plausible explanation for such disruptiveness must be that they were insane. This argument was advanced from the outset, even at the time of the first exhibition. It was expressed by Leroy

STEADFAST
CHAMPIONS

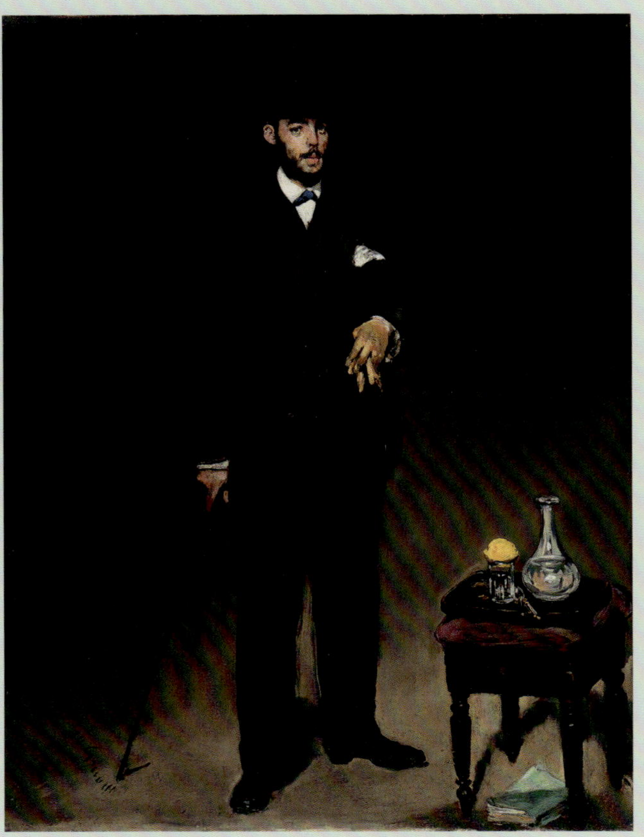

THÉODORE DURET
(1838–1927)
Present at the first gatherings in the Café Guerbois, the art critic Théodore Duret was also a collector and admirer of Far Eastern art. He attentively followed the careers of Manet, Pissarro, Monet, Renoir, and Sisley. He gave moral—and sometimes financial—support to his friends. His work *Histoire des peintres impressionnistes*, published in 1906, was the first thorough analysis of the movement. Short-term financial problems forced him to sell his impressionist collection to art dealer Georges Petit in 1894. Duret remained an invaluable observer of the emergence of this decisive artistic movement.

in his article in *Le Charivari.* Observing the recognized academic painter Joseph Vincent, who accompanied him on his visit to the show, he saw the man practically lose his reason. "It was the last straw. The venerable Vincent's brain came under attack from too many sides at once and spun completely off course. He stopped by a city security officer who was guarding these treasures and, mistaking him for a portrait, began to offer me very emphatic critical observations." The hypothesis of mental illness, all the more dangerous due to its potential contagion, was revived by Albert Wolff in *Le Figaro* (April 3, 1876) at the time of the second impressionist exhibition. "They've just opened an exhibition said to be of paintings. The innocent passerby who is lured in by the flags that decorate the façade enters and is confronted with a hideous spectacle: works by five or six maniacs, one of them a woman, are displayed here, a collection of unfortunate attempts fueled by mad ambition. Some viewers dissolve in laughter, but my heart sank."

PERSISTENT ANIMOSITY
Although its extreme virulence moderated over time, criticism continued in the same vein, accusing the artists of visual aberration, deliberate affront, an absence of professionalism, and, as always, insanity. Albert Wolff, the influential critic at *Le Figaro*, continued to pursue the theme of madness in 1880:
"Seeing these things did not give much pleasure. Aside from some interesting drawings, I saw nothing but canvases with no redeeming features, the works of madmen who mistake pebbles for pearls."

LOUIS EDMOND DURANTY
(1833–1880)
A keen observer of innovative developments in painting, the art critic Louis Edmond Duranty published a review, *Le Réalisme*, in 1856–57, designed to defend Courbet and his followers. He was a close friend of Degas, and attended the first gatherings in the Café Guerbois, where the animated discussions led him to the point of a duel with Manet. It turned out to be just a brief difference of opinion that demonstrated the intensity of the debates. He wrote the pamphlet *La Nouvelle Peinture* for the second impressionist exhibition in 1876, and published it as a catalog for the show. In 1879, his glowing review of the fourth impressionist exhibition was published in the influential supplement to the *La Gazette des Beaux-arts*. Always close to these artists, he tirelessly championed his comrades and supported their bold experiments.

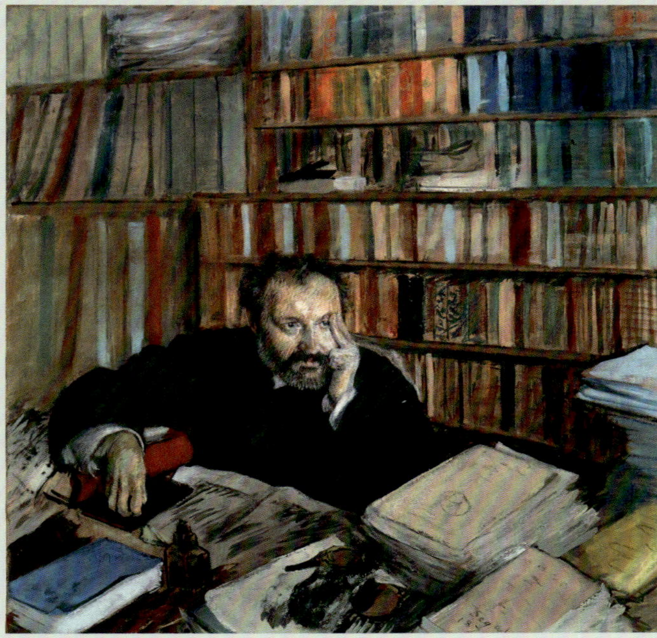

Facing page: Édouard Manet
Portrait of Théodore Duret
1868
Oil on canvas, 18 ½ × 17 in. (46.5 × 35.5 cm)
Petit Palais, Musée des Beaux-Arts de la Ville de Paris, Paris

Edgar Degas
Portrait of Edmond Duranty
1879
Pastel and tempera on wood,
3 ft. 3 ¾ in. × 3 ft. 3 ½ in. (1.01 × 1.00 m)
Burrel Collection, Glasgow Museums and Art Gallery, Glasgow

A FEW DISSENTING VOICES

In the face of these onslaughts, each more virulent than the last, Jules Antoine Castagnary published a rare positive review in *Le Siècle* on April 29, 1874. "There is talent here, lots of talent. These young painters have a way of understanding nature that is neither tedious nor banal. It's animated, precise, luminous—it's delightful. What quick minds and lively brushstrokes. Yes, it's sketchy, but how eloquent these suggestions are!" Two years later he published another article in *Le Siècle*, defending the second impressionist exhibition. Armand Silvestre, writing in *La Presse*, was one of the few other voices to champion the impressionists. In the daily paper *Le Voltaire*, the writer Huysmans mentions the fourth impressionist exhibition in 1879. He judged the work of "these rabble-rousers, who are so disparaged and scorned" to be considerably more interesting than the paintings in the Salon. It was a homage of sorts.

FOCUS

In the Words of Writers

While art critics brutally attacked the representatives of the new painting, writers raised their voices in the movement's defense. Some authors saw echoes of their own literary explorations in these works. Others, weary of sterile academicism, recognized the audacity of genuine artistic expression. Ties of friendship and support created a bond between these painters and writers. Like Zola, Mallarmé was among the earliest to write in favor of Manet and take an interest in Monet, Renoir, Degas, and Berthe Morisot. More sporadically, Guy de Maupassant, Paul Valéry (who was very close to the Morisot family), and Joris-Karl Huysmans, who later turned to symbolism, all demonstrated their interest in the newly emerging approach to painting. The poets Jules Laforgue and Octave Mirbeau were even more militant advocates, who also wrote perceptively on behalf of impressionism.

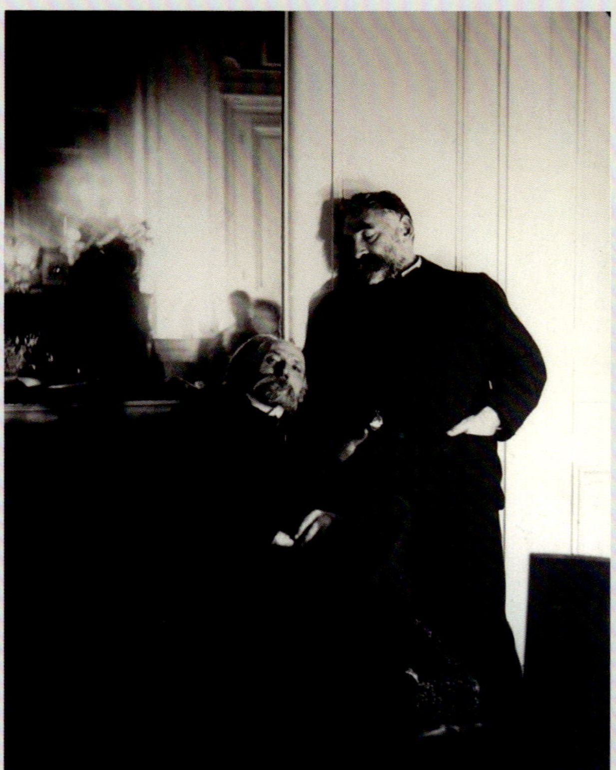

This photograph was taken by Degas on December 16, 1895, in the apartment of Julie Manet and her cousins Paule and Jeannie Gobillard, at 40 Rue de Villejust in Paris (today Rue Paul-Valéry). This portrait demonstrates the close ties uniting the three men with the Manet and Morisot families.

Edgar Degas, *Portrait of Stéphane Mallarmé and Auguste Renoir,* 1895
Photographic print
Paris, Bibliothèque Jacques Doucet

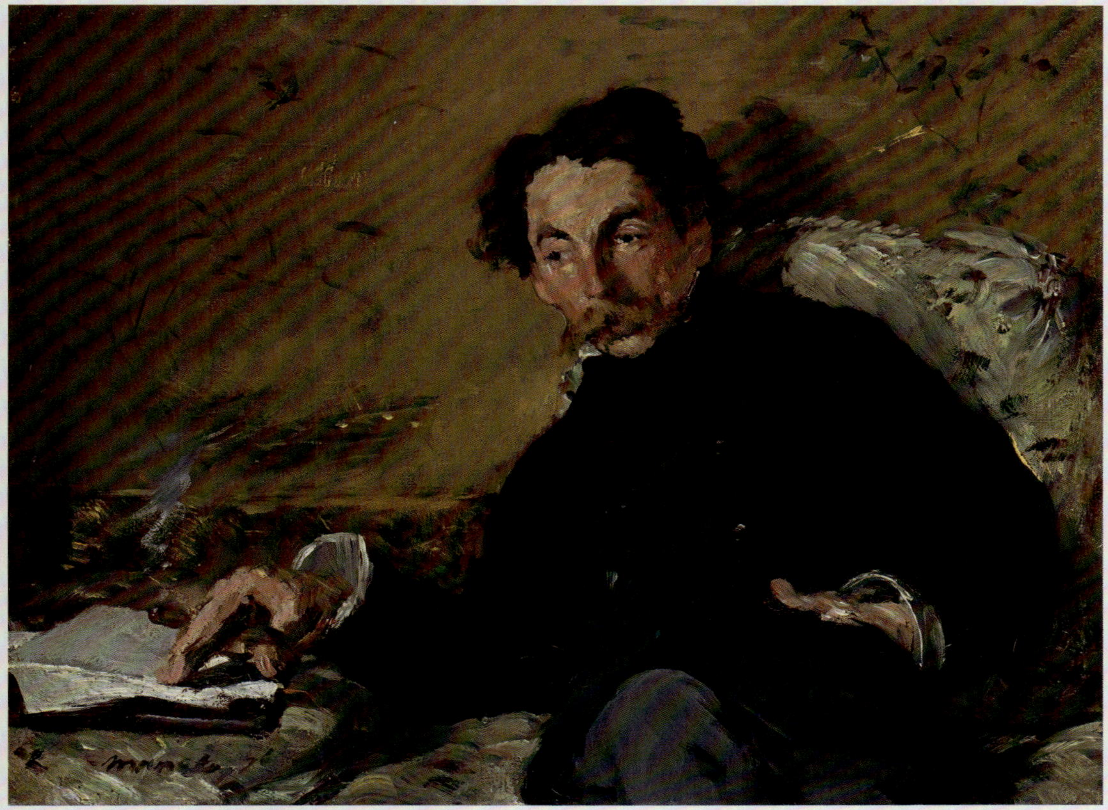

Édouard Manet, *Portrait of Stéphane Mallarmé*, 1876
Oil on canvas, 10 ⅝ × 14 ⅛ in. (27 × 36 cm)
Musée d'Orsay, Paris

Nonchalantly slouched on a sofa, Mallarmé poses in his friend's studio on Rue Saint-Pétersbourg. It was his habit to stop by for a visit after teaching English courses at the Lycée Condorcet. This picture was owned by the poet's family until 1928, when it was acquired by the French State.

STÉPHANE MALLARMÉ (1842–1898)

Close to the painters Manet, Renoir, Degas, and Berthe Morisot (who chose him to tutor her only child Julie), Mallarmé took up his pen in 1874 to sharply criticize the dictates of the Salon. "The jury has nothing to say but 'This is a picture' and 'This is not a picture.' It does not have the right to hide them," he thundered in *La Renaissance artistique et littéraire* (April 12, 1874). He turned to Manet, who was still widely ridiculed, to illustrate his poem "L'Après-midi d'un faune" (1876). A year earlier, he had solicited Manet's help for his French translation of "The Raven" by Edgar Allan Poe. "I saw my beloved friend Manet every day for ten years, and I miss him dreadfully today," he wrote in a letter to Verlaine in 1885, two years after the painter's death. Mallarmé wrote several prefaces for the painters who were his friends, including one for the retrospective exhibition of Berthe Morisot's work in Durand-Ruel's gallery in 1896, the year after her death. He offered this definition of impressionism, which remains wonderfully precise and comprehensive: "Don't paint the thing—paint the effect it produces."

"Monet, along with Whistler, is the artist who captivates me the most.… You might even say that he actually invented the sea."

Octave Mirbeau, *Gil Blas*, April 13, 1887.

OCTAVE MIRBEAU (1850–1917)

A passionate observer of the art of his time, Octave Mirbeau wrote about art and published articles with "the enthusiasm of a poet," in the words of the critic Geffroy. He supported Monet, Renoir, and Berthe Morisot, and unhesitatingly condemned the Salon's official artists. He was one of the habitués of the Charpentiers' salon for collectors, and attended dinners with the impressionists at Café Riche. He visited Caillebotte and Monet, whom he particularly admired, sharing his passion for gardening. Mirbeau wrote for the popular press (*Gil Blas, L'Écho de Paris, Le Journal*). He also wrote the preface of the catalog for the joint Rodin/Monet exhibition at Georges Petit's gallery in 1889. He took an interest in the work of Gauguin and Van Gogh, and maintained an extensive correspondence with Pissarro. Mirbeau amassed a significant impressionist collection that was sold by his widow after his death.

"I am so very glad to have found in you a warm, sensitive, conscientious, and sympathetic advocate. Thank you, Monsieur, you have bound up my many wounds and relieved many torments."

Pissarro, letter to Octave Mirbeau, May 1887, following the publication of one of his articles.

JULES LAFORGUE (1860–1887)

Jules Laforgue published his first writings on art at the age of twenty-one. An admirer of Pissarro, Sisley, Monet, Morisot, Renoir, Degas, and Mary Cassatt, he devoted himself in 1882 and 1883 to writing a well-reasoned study of the impressionist movement. His remarkably astute work was not published during his lifetime. It appeared in *Mélanges posthumes* in 1903. The poet advocated the abolition of the Salon, judging, in a very avant-garde manner "that artists should display their works with sellers, as writers publish their books with publishing houses." Following Laforgue's early death, his friend, the critic Félix Fénéon, committed himself to publishing some of Laforgue's writings and drawings.

"The impressionist is a modernist painter who is gifted with an exceptionally sensitive eye. He forgets the images that have accumulated through the centuries in museums, forgets the academic education of the eye (drawing and perspective, coloring), so as to live and observe clearly and simply in the luminous spectacle of the open air—outside the studio, whether it's a city street, the countryside, or an interior. He manages to recreate the vision of a natural eye that sees naturally, and he paints as naively as he sees."

Jules Laforgue, *Mélanges posthumes*, 1903.

ÉMILE ZOLA (1840–1902)

The standard-bearer for naturalism in literature, Zola championed the paintings of Manet and the circle of artists who rejected the Academy to take a fresh look at the modern world. A childhood friend of Cézanne's, and close to the impressionists, he frequently appeared at their gatherings and is often shown in their paintings. He insisted on referring to them as "naturalists" rather than "impressionists." Ultimately, though, Zola disavowed the movement, concluding that impressionism had not given rise to any genuine talents. As he wrote in 1880 in the daily paper *Le Voltaire*: "They're all precursors; the man of true genius has not yet been born. They see what they wish and we think they're right, but we look in vain for a masterpiece that exemplifies this approach.... They remain inadequate to the demands of what they are attempting to do; they stutter, unable to find the proper word." This total change of mind was unequivocally expressed when he visited his last Salon in 1896: "Good heavens! Was it this that I fought for so hard? For this garish painting.... Good lord! Was I mad? It's really terribly ugly—it revolts me!"

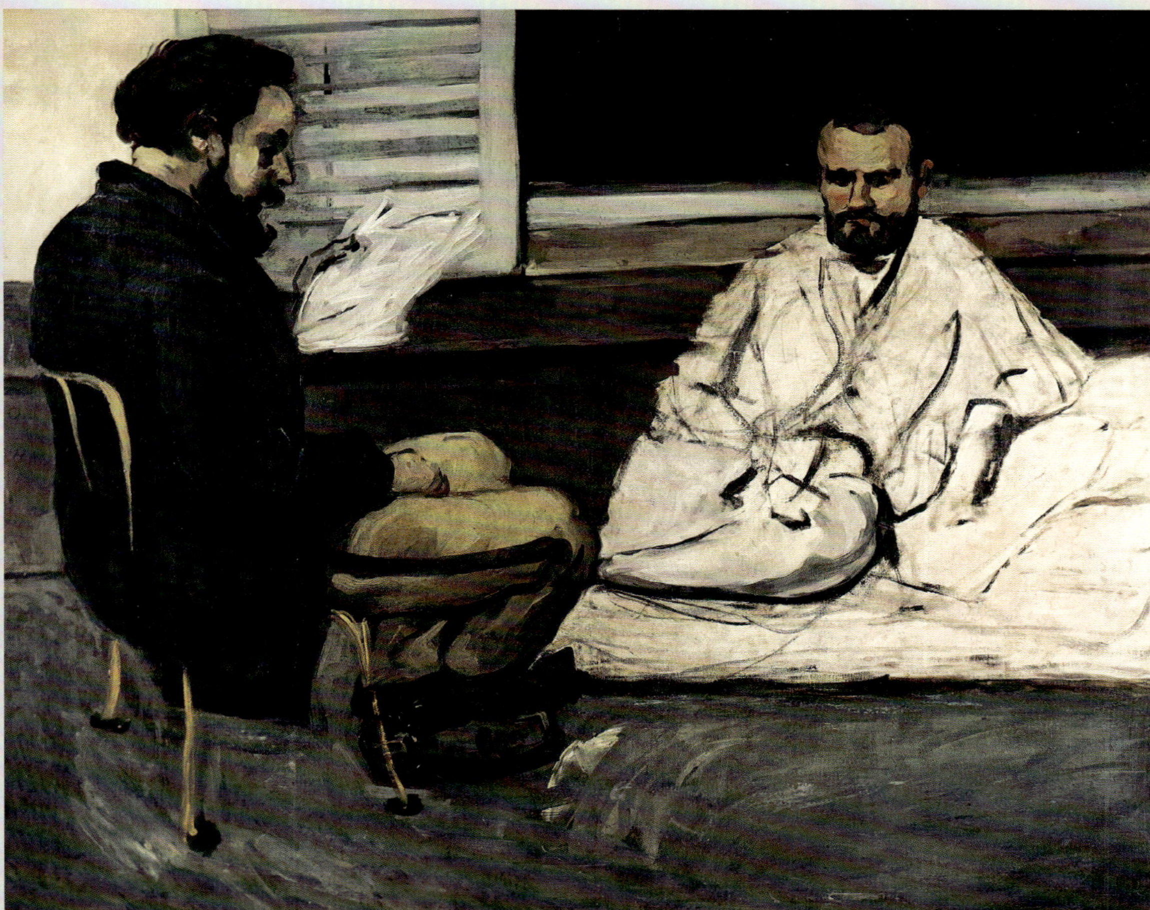

Paul Cézanne, *Paul Alexis Reading a Manuscript by Émile Zola*, 1869–70
Oil on canvas, 4 ft. 3 ¼ in. × 5 ft. 3 in. (1.3 × 1.6 m)
Museu de Arte de São Paulo, São Paulo

IMAGES IN THE SPOTLIGHT

Édouard Manet
Portrait of Émile Zola
1868
Oil on canvas,
4 ft. 9 ¾ in. × 3 ft. 9 in.
(1.47 × 1.14 m)
Musée d'Orsay, Paris

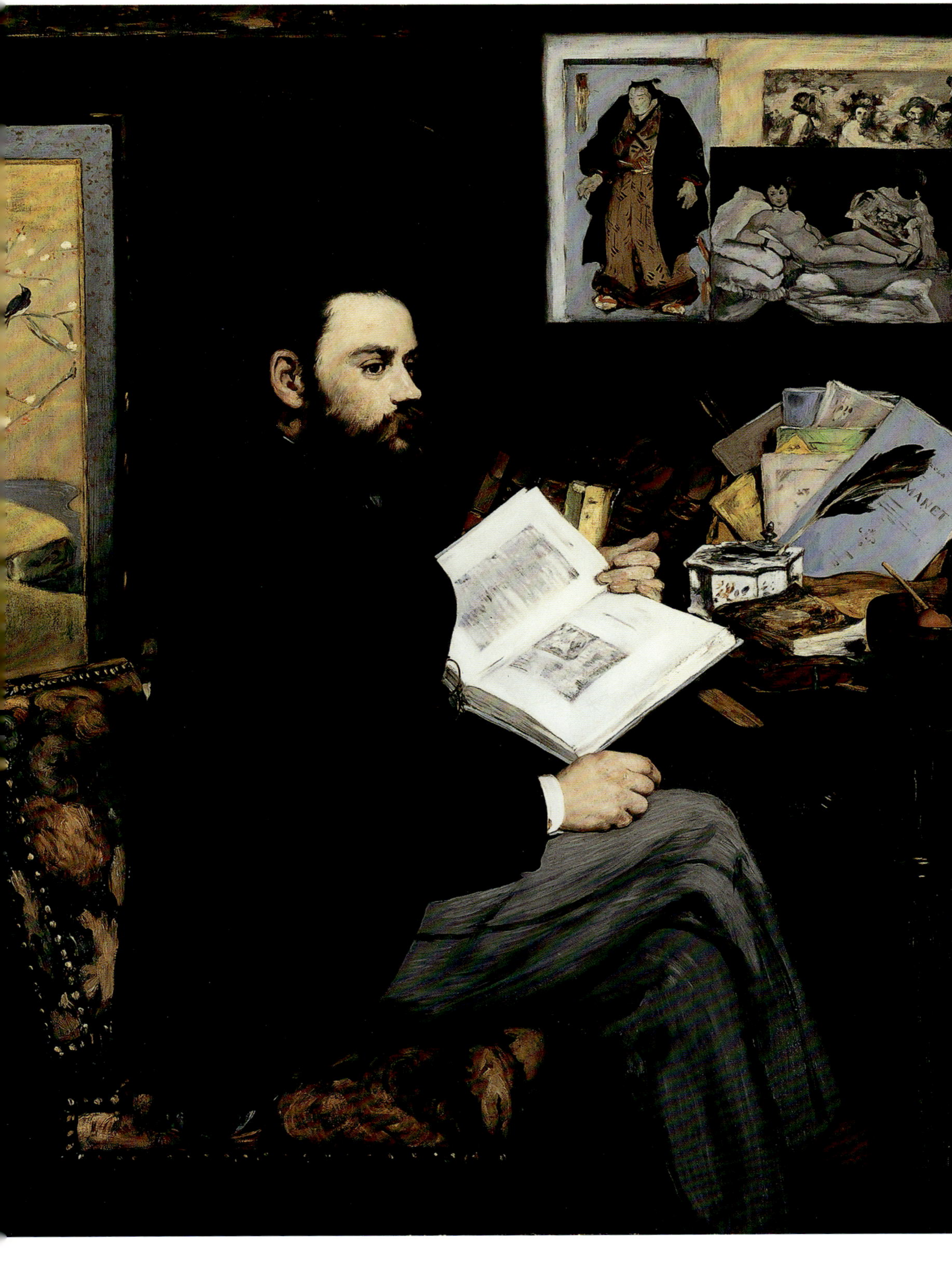
MANET

Portrait of Émile Zola
Édouard Manet, 1868

When ferocious criticism was unleashed on Manet's *Olympia* in the 1865 Salon, Zola stood up for his friend, defending the man he considered to be one of the masters of the new generation. He took pen in hand again two years later when Manet erected his own pavilion on the outskirts of the Universal Exposition. As a gesture of thanks, Manet painted the author's portrait, sealing the friendship between two men, who were both highly talented and hungry for recognition. Exhibited in the 1868 Salon in the year that it was painted, the portrait became a manifesto, a revenge on bourgeois convention by both men.

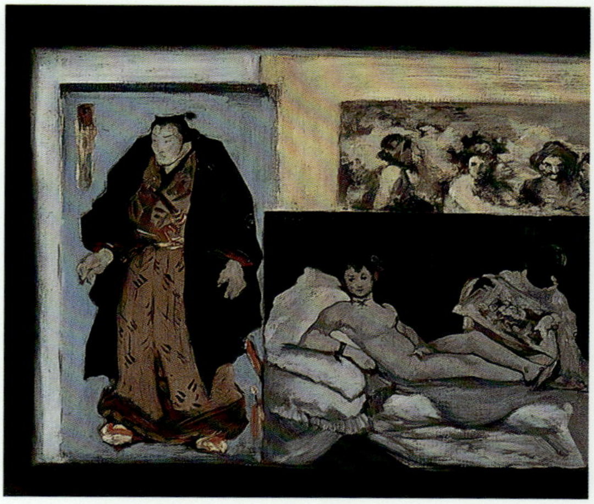

A reproduction of Manet's Olympia *appears prominently beside* The Triumph of Bacchus *by Velázquez. The assemblage testifies to Zola's support in the midst of the polemics directed against* Olympia*, as well as the two men's shared taste for Japanese art and Spanish realist painting.*

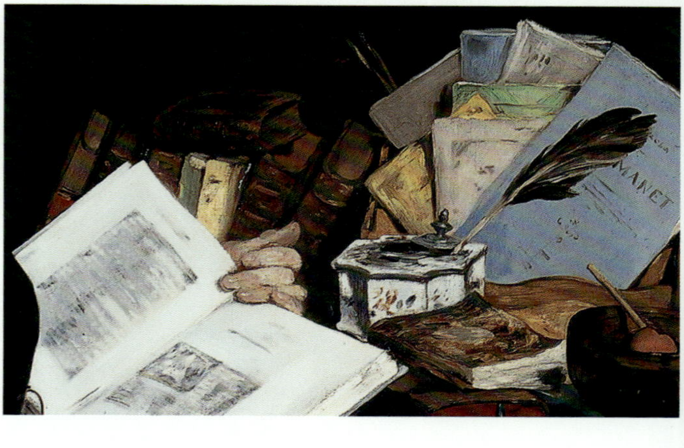

The cheerful clutter on the work table, with its heaps of books, the quill pen, and inkstand, bears witness to the writer's world. The pamphlet with a blue cover was published by Zola in defense of the painter in 1867. These surroundings were actually artfully recomposed, because the portrait sittings all took place in Manet's studio on Rue Guyot.

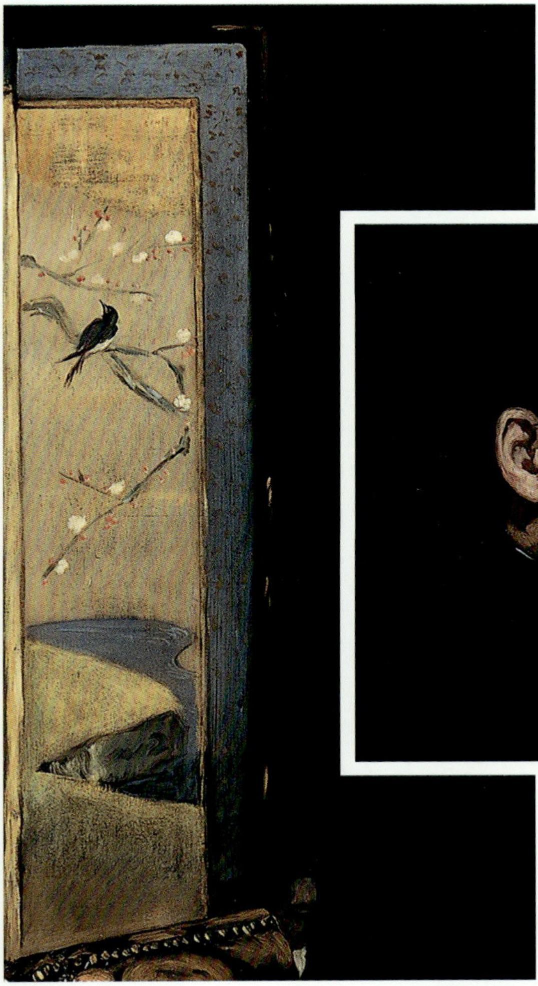

The Japanese screen in the background emphasizes their shared interest in Far Eastern art and distant horizons.

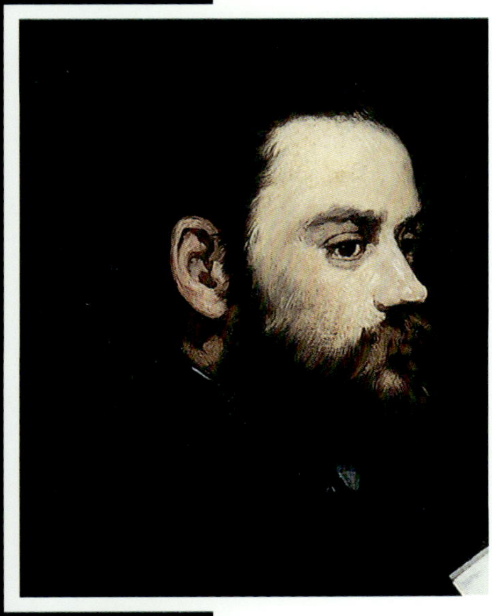

Zola's handsome face is seen in three-quarters view. It demonstrates Manet's style, which was considered too flat and harshly illuminated. It was an approach that Manet developed very deliberately after distancing himself from academicism.

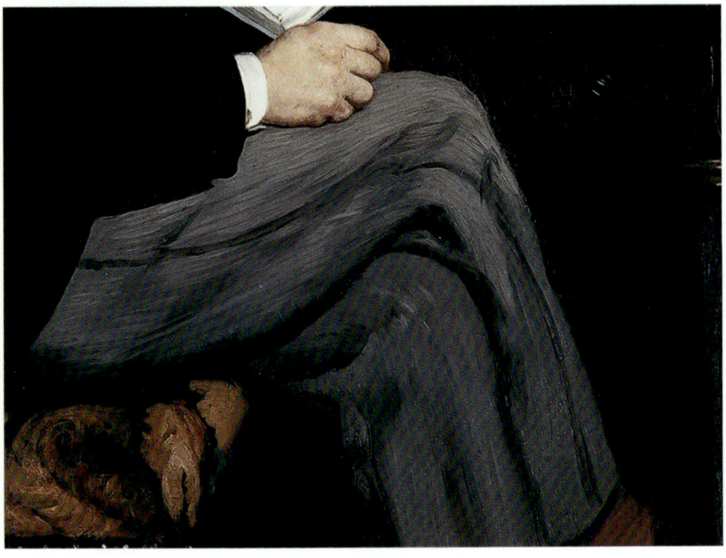

Like the chair's upholstery, the trousers are rapidly brushed in, demonstrating Manet's free hand in painting. His brushstrokes could be applied quickly when greater detail was superfluous.

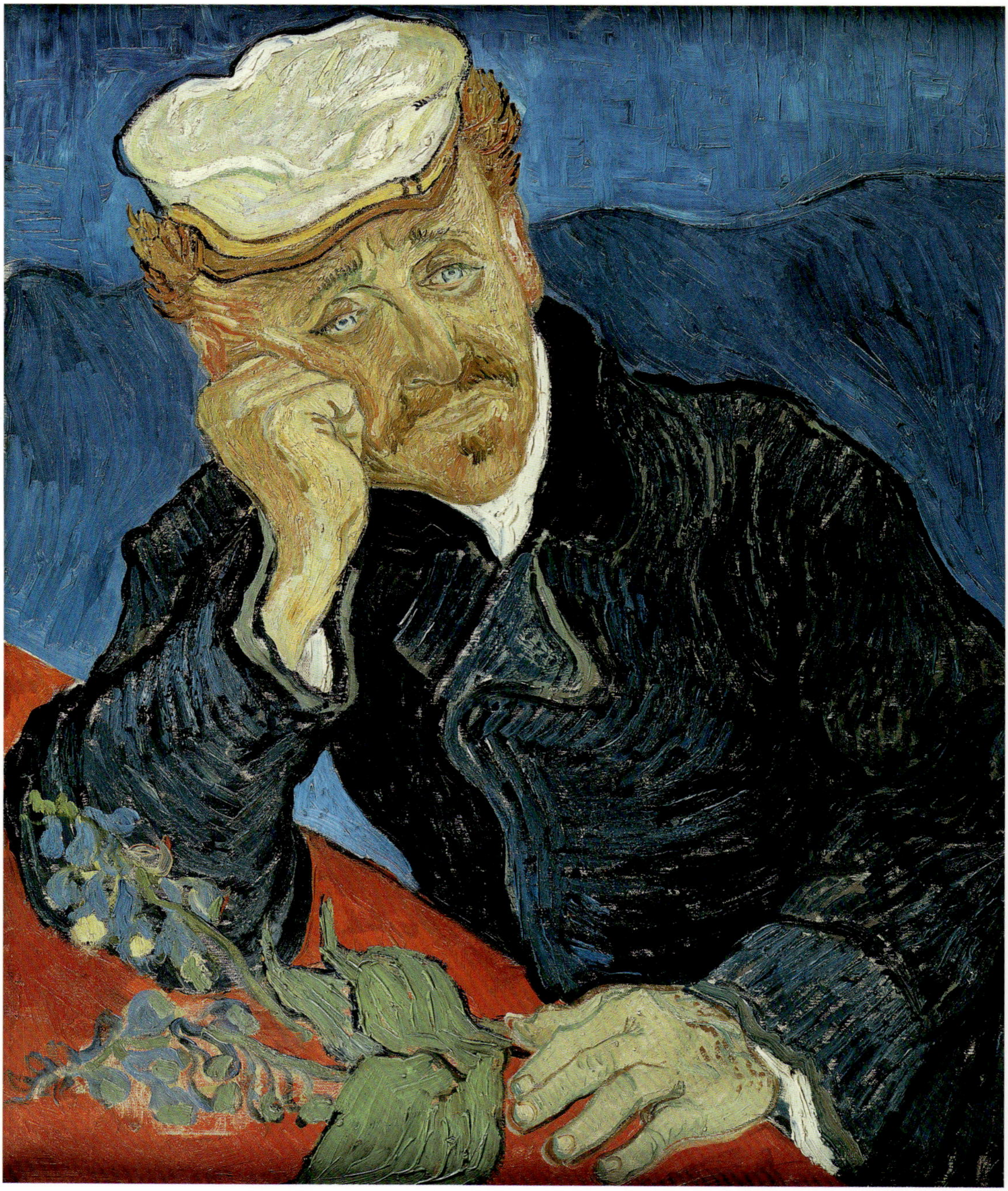

Vincent Van Gogh
Portrait of Doctor Gachet
1890
Oil on canvas, 26 ¾ × 22 ½ in. (68 × 57 cm)
Musée d'Orsay, Paris

A New Role for Dealers and Collectors

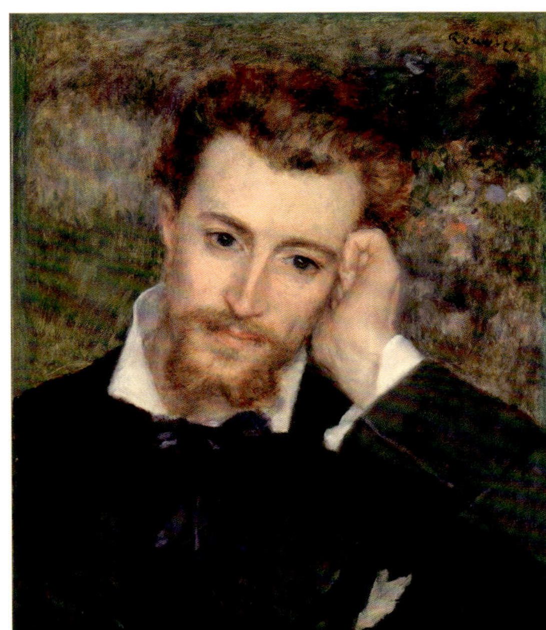

Auguste Renoir
Eugène Murer
1877
Oil on canvas, 18 ½ × 15 ½ in.
(47 × 39.4 cm)
The Metropolitan Museum of Art, New York

Defying academic rules and rejecting the Salon's dictates, the impressionists made their presence known outside the system they had defied. They overturned the givens of the art world as it had functioned up to this point. Partly to assert themselves as artists, and partly to merely survive, they organized exhibitions and auctions that put them in direct contact with collectors. The business of art dealers was based upon retail sales, and the most forward-looking among them recognized that their profession was changing. The role of the gallerist began to emerge: his function was to engage with living artists and foster the development of their work, advocate for their paintings among collectors, and seek to promote artists by arranging exhibitions, sales, and publications. Paul Durand-Ruel was a noteworthy example.

Patrons and Collectors

The impressionists, some of them penniless and hungry, managed to survive and continue to develop their art in good times and bad, thanks to the support provided by collectors and patrons, whose profiles varied widely. Some

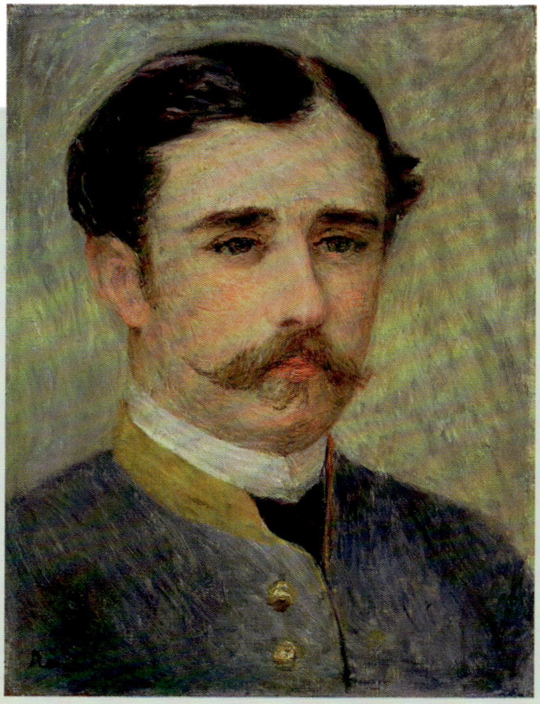

THE CHARPENTIERS AND THE ADVENTURE OF *LA VIE MODERNE*

An editor of the realist writers, including Zola, de Maupassant, and Flaubert, Georges Charpentier (1846–1901) purchased his first impressionist painting in 1875 at the sale organized at Drouot by Durand-Ruel. It was a work by Renoir, who was to become a close friend, and who in turn introduced him to Monet, Pissarro, and Sisley. Charpentier, whose financial support enabled the impressionist artists to navigate through some difficult times, went on to collect their works. With his wife's encouragement, he launched an artistic review, *La Vie moderne*, in 1879. He also organized one-man shows in its offices: Monet in 1880 and Sisley in 1881. His objective? "Our exhibitions will transport the artist's studio to the street corner, a place that is accessible to everyone, which collectors can visit whenever they wish." The venture lasted four years.

Auguste Renoir
Monsieur Charpentier
c. 1879
Oil on canvas, 12 ¾ × 9 ⅞ in. (32.5 × 25 cm)
The Barnes Foundation, Philadelphia

were friends, including the singer Jean-Baptiste Faure (1830-1914), an important art collector who gave financial support to Paul Durand-Ruel. Some were better-off members of the group, like Gustave Caillebotte (1848-1894) and Henri Rouart (1833-1912). Others were prominent businessmen, such as Gaudibert, a ship owner from Le Havre, who bought the first Monets and provided an allowance to the painter, who had been devastated by the death of his patron in 1870. An ordinary government bureaucrat, Victor Chocquet (1821-1891) developed a passion for impressionist art, which he had discovered at Drouot's sale in 1875, when it was still derided by the public. He became one of the group's most loyal supporters, even through their darkest years. A childhood friend of Guillaumin, the pastry chef Eugène Murer (1845-1906) was an unconditional admirer of the impressionists, purchasing their works and entertaining them at monthly dinners, until he sold his business in 1881 and retired to Auvers-sur-Oise. The homeopathic doctor Georges de Bellio (1828-1894), Romanian by birth,

"Nothing is funnier than seeing this man in his white apron, a chef's hat on his head, exiting his shop and darting over to the studio of one of the leading lights of impressionism. He never leaves without a canvas of one size or another."
Article published in *Le Gaulois*, January 1880, about Eugène Murer.

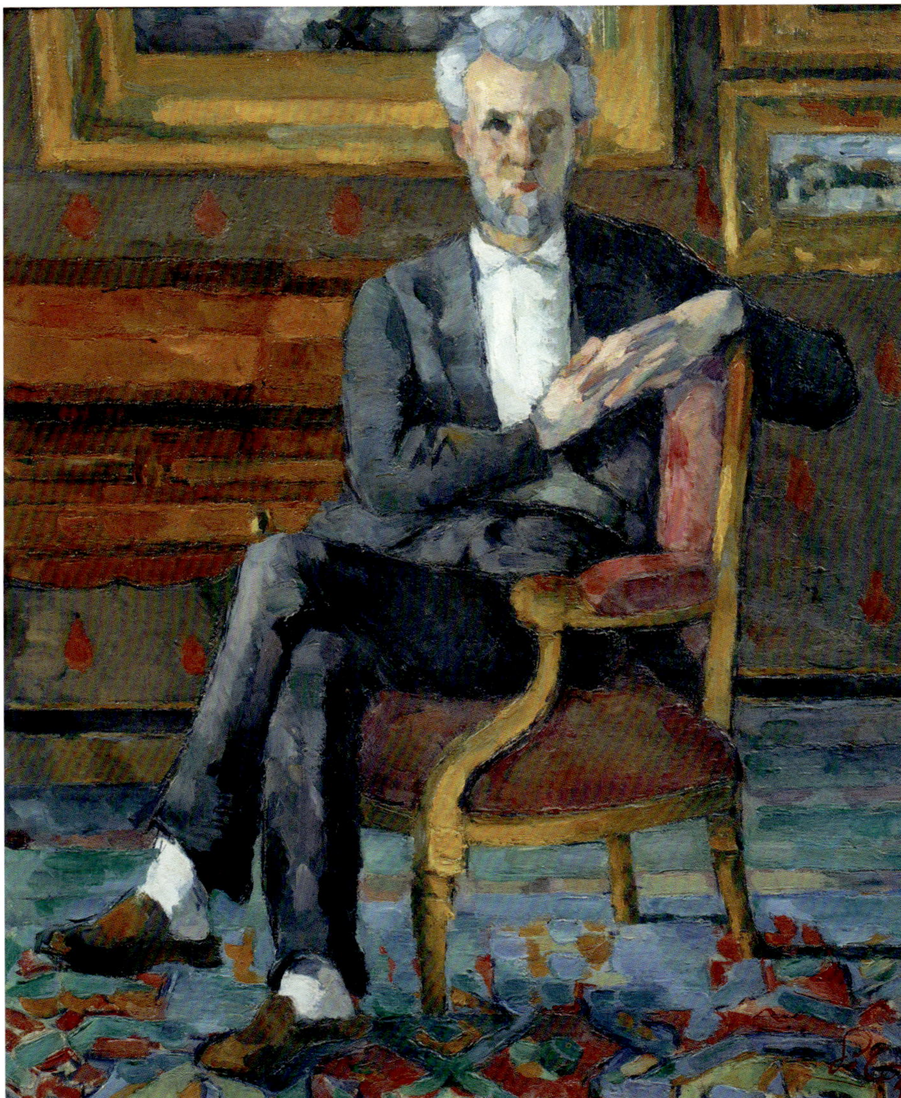

Paul Cézanne
Portrait of Victor Chocquet
1877
Oil on canvas, 18 ⅛ × 15 in. (46 × 38 cm)
Colombus Gallery of Fine Art,
Columbus, Ohio

"You would see him in the vanguard every time the impressionists had an opportunity to show their works.... I recall seeing him struggle to win over well-known critics, such as Albert Wolff, and antagonistic artists who came solely to ridicule."

Théodore Duret on Victor Chocquet, preface to the sale catalog for Chocquet's collection, 1899.

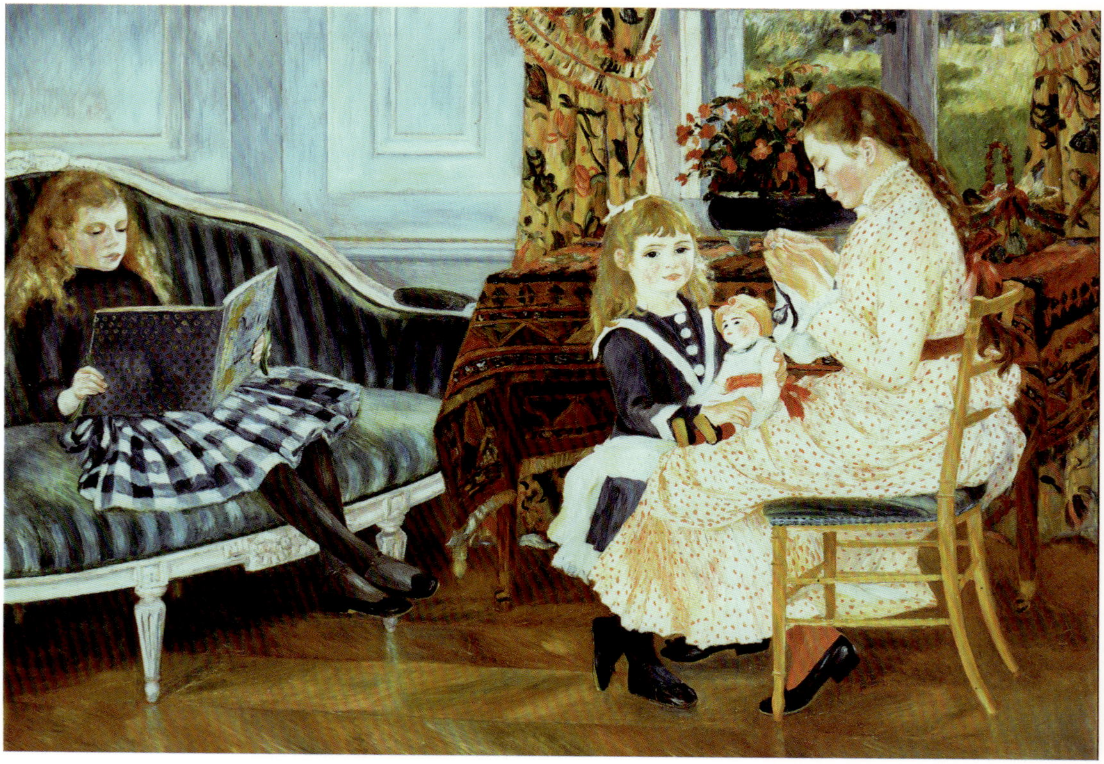

Auguste Renoir
Children's Afternoon at Wargemont
1884
Oil on canvas, 4 ft. 2 in. × 5 ft. 8 in.
(1.27 × 1.73 m)
Nationalgalerie, Staatliche Museen
zu Berlin, Berlin

was an art lover who purchased his first impressionist canvas in 1874. A devotee from the outset, he amassed such an extensive collection that he had to rent a space across from his own home to house the works. Throughout his life, he maintained close relationships with these painters who had become his friends. He helped them financially, recommended their work to his collector friends, and attended their dinners. His sudden death left the entire group saddened and diminished. Paul Gachet (1828-1909), another homeopathic physician, became involved with the artistic avant-garde in its very early years, frequenting the brasseries where Courbet gathered with his friends. He moved to Auvers-sur-Oise in 1872, where he set up an engraving workshop, and he collected, supported, advised, and cared for his artist friends, Pissarro, Cézanne, Guillaumin, and Van Gogh. Finally, the banker Paul Bérard met Renoir at the Charpentiers' salon. He invited the artist to stay, for several summers, at his imposing family estate of Wargemont, near Dieppe. Grateful for this ongoing patronage, Renoir painted a portrait of the family, received commissions for decorative panels, and above all seized the opportunity to paint from nature on the Normandy coast.

TERRIBLE PUBLICITY
In April 1878, Jean-Baptiste Faure sold part of his collection for a disastrously low amount. A few months later, Ernest Hoschedé, who had picked up some bargains at the first sale in 1874, declared bankruptcy and had to liquidate his collection. Again, the sale was a financial debacle and very bad publicity for the artists.

"Any time one of us has an urgent need for cash, he runs over to the Café Riche at lunchtime; he's sure to find Monsieur de Bellio, who'll buy any painting offered to him without even pausing to look at it."

Renoir to Vollard.

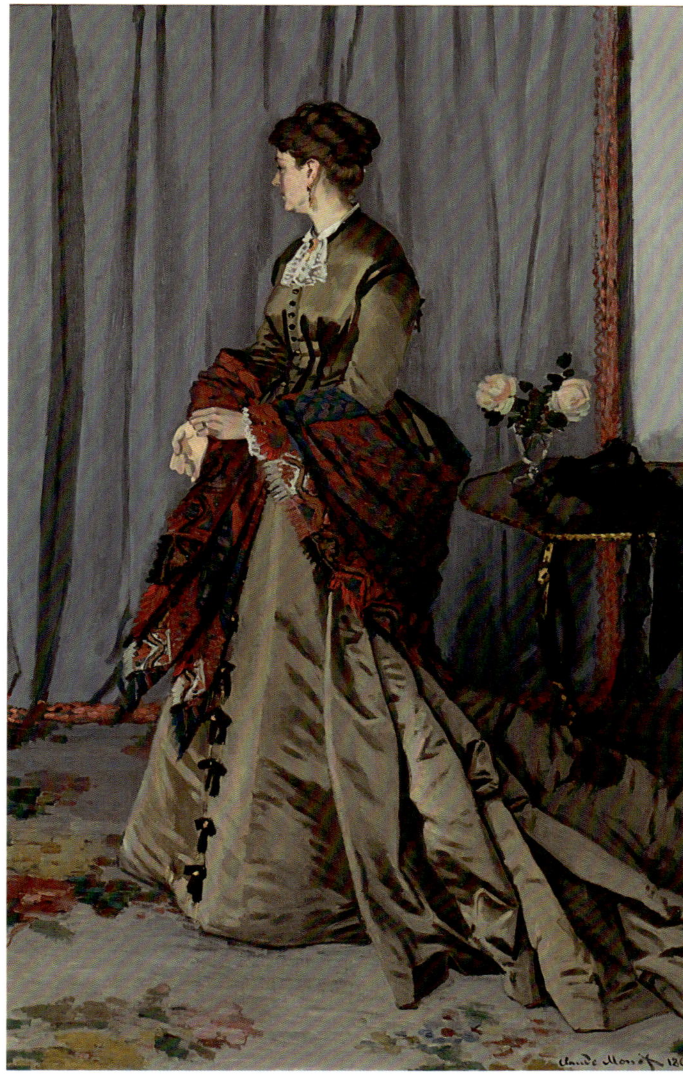

Claude Monet
Madame Louis Joachim Gaudibert
1868
Oil on canvas, 7 ft. 1 ½ in. × 4 ft. 6 ½ in. (2.17 × 1.39 m)
Musée d'Orsay, Paris

ERNEST HOSCHEDÉ: SPLENDOR AND DECADENCE

A wealthy dealer in textiles and the owner of a department store, Ernest Hoschedé (1837–1891) lived a life of luxury. With his wife, Alice, he received visitors to his estate in Montgeron, providing transport from Paris in a specially chartered train. Manet, Sisley, and Monet all stayed there. Hoschedé was an art lover who soon began to collect impressionist canvases, a providential development for those artists who were in need of funds. An accomplished businessman, he successfully resold various works (making two sales at Drouot in 1874) and purchased others. But his business activities unraveled so dramatically that he declared bankruptcy in 1877. The forced sale of his collection at Drouot was a disaster: the canvases went for less than the price he'd paid to acquire them. It was a doubly hard blow to the artists, who lost a collector and once again found themselves discredited in the marketplace. "The Hoschedé sale has killed me," Pissarro wrote to Murer. Meanwhile, Hoschedé's wife, Alice, moved with her six children to Claude Monet's family home. After the death of his first wife, she married him, formalizing a longstanding liaison.

"The story of his humble, honest life is inseparable from that of the impressionist group. You'd see paintings by Monet, Pissarro, Renoir, and later Van Gogh, Cézanne, and Gauguin in his storefront."

Octave Mirbeau, obituary for "Père" Tanguy, *L'Écho de Paris*, February 3, 1894.

The Art Sellers: Père Martin and Père Tanguy

Known for fiercely haggling over paintings that he later tried to place with collectors, "Père" Martin (1817-1891), as he was nicknamed, was among those who took a very early interest in the impressionists. An upholsterer, then an actor, who later became an antique dealer before becoming fascinated by art, he admired the Barbizon painters, Boudin, and Jongkind. An unsophisticated and simple shopkeeper if compared to Durand-Ruel, he was nevertheless enlightened in his tastes, and the impressionists could turn to him when they had no other recourse. They actually selected Martin to be the temporary manager of the Anonymous Cooperative Society of Artists (Painters, Sculptors, Engravers, etc.), which they established in 1874 to organize their first exhibition.

An art supplier in Montmartre, "Père" Tanguy (1825-1894), as he was affectionately called by the artists, operated a little shop on the Rue Clauzel in Montmartre. Having worked as a plasterer and butcher before becoming a paint-maker, he was beloved for his kindness and humility. An ardent anarchist, he saw these brightly colored paintings as harbingers of the social revolution for which he fervently hoped. Helping out the penniless impressionists, he was willing to accept pictures in exchange for his merchandise, and he would also take paintings on consignment to help their sales. Painters gathered in the back of his store to debate about art. Père Tanguy was among the first to take an interest in Van Gogh and Cézanne; Vollard first saw their work when it was displayed in his shop window. When Tanguy died, he had amassed a significant collection, whose quality spoke volumes about this modest man.

Vincent Van Gogh
Père Tanguy
1887–88
Oil on canvas, 25 ⅝ × 20 in. (65 × 51 cm)
Musée Rodin, Paris

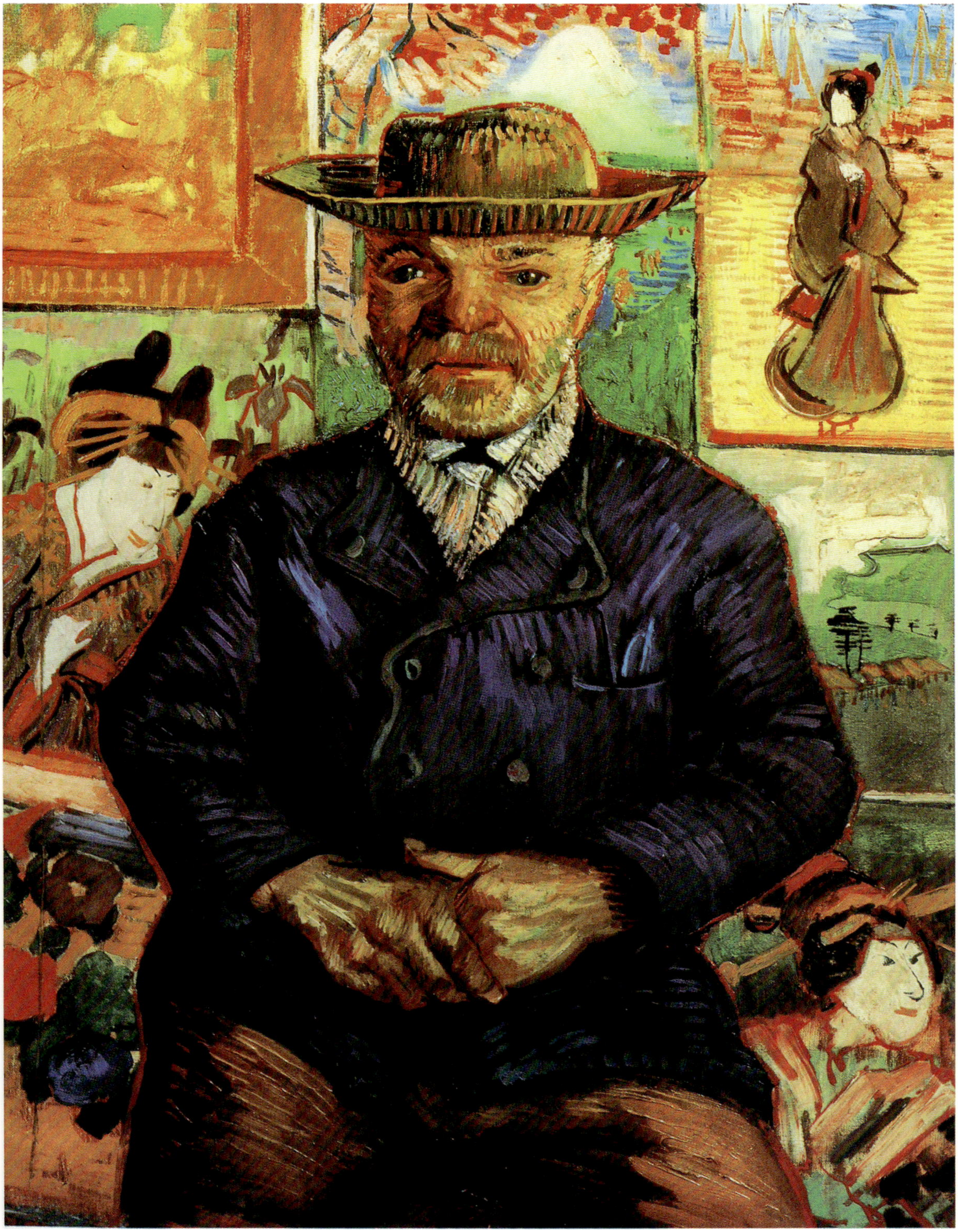

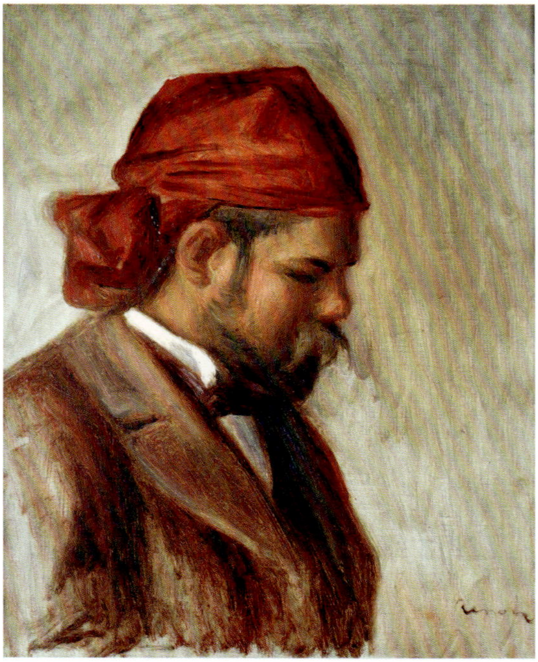

Auguste Renoir
Ambroise Vollard in a Red Scarf
c. 1899
Oil on canvas, 11 ⅜ × 8 ⅞ in. (30 × 25 cm)
Petit Palais, Musée des Beaux-Arts de la Ville de Paris, Paris

"He had the weary air of a Carthaginian general."

Renoir, on meeting Ambroise Vollard in autumn 1895 at his residence in the Château des Brouillards, on the summit of Montmartre.

Enlightened Gallerists

Durand-Ruel remains the gallerist most closely associated with the impressionist movement from its early days, but others took an interest in developments in later years and tried to attract some of the movement's participants.

In the early 1880s, when Durand-Ruel was experiencing serious financial problems, Georges Petit (1856-1920) approached some of the major figures of impressionism. He had opened opulent premises at the intersection of the Rue de Sèze and the Rue Godot-de-Mauroy in 1882. At a Universal Exposition, an event in which Monet, Sisley, Pissarro, and Berthe Morisot participated, he presented an array of French and international painters. Uneasy about Durand-Ruel's situation, and suffering from chronic financial problems, Monet, Sisley, and Pissarro succumbed to Petit's coaxing. In 1887, Monet and Sisley each had a one-man show there. In 1889, Georges Petit organized a joint Monet/Rodin exhibition that attracted considerable attention. In 1892, he presented two retrospectives, one on Renoir, and the other on Pissarro. In 1899, after Sisley's death, he took on responsibility for the sale of the contents of Pissarro's studio for the benefit of the artist's children.

Théo Van Gogh (1854-1891), Vincent's brother, moved to Paris in 1878, where he worked for the Galerie Boussod-Valadon (formerly the Maison Goupil). Keenly perceptive, he soon became interested in the new artistic trends. In 1884, he had the chance to purchase one of Pissarro's works on behalf of Boussod-Valadon, and one by Sisley the following

"The more advantageously the paintings are displayed and the greater the luxury of the gallery, which is really very beautiful, the more the crowd will be impressed… an exhibition of work by all of us presented in the same space—that's where I think we'd find success."
Monet, letter to Durand-Ruel, arguing for an agreement between the two dealers, shortly after Georges Petit inaugurated his new gallery space.

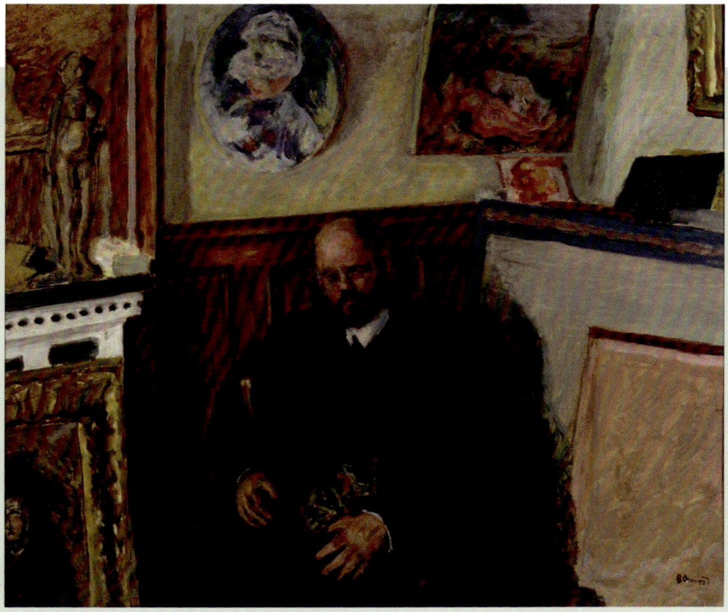

Pierre Bonnard
Ambroise Vollard and His Cat
c. 1924
Oil on canvas, 3 ft. 2 in. × 3 ft. 7 ¾ in.
(96.5 × 111 cm)
Petit Palais, Musée des Beaux-Arts
de la Ville de Paris, Paris

Vollard organized dinners in "the cellar," the windowless area used as a storage space, adjoining his gallery in Rue Laffitte. He entertained the artists, serving them specialties from La Réunion, the island where he had lived before coming to Paris to pursue his studies.

year; both were quickly sold at a gratifying profit. During 1887, he purchased about a dozen works by Monet for the gallery, having visited the artist in Giverny. He traveled to Moret to meet Sisley, made contact with Degas, and cultivated a friendship with Pissarro, who sent him canvases in hopes of selling them. Monet exhibited at Boussod-Valadon and signed a contract with the gallery in 1886. In late 1887, Théo Van Gogh organized a small exhibition that displayed the earliest works of neo-impressionism. Despite the hesitancy of his employers, who had more conservative tastes, Théo courageously continued to act as intermediary, trying to sell the canvases entrusted to him by Monet, Sisley, Pissarro, Degas, and Gauguin to collectors. Théo died young in 1891.

Ambroise Vollard (1868–1939) made his appearance in the art market shortly after the deaths of Théo Van Gogh and Père Tanguy. He developed close ties with the impressionists and became the dealer for Renoir, Degas, and Cézanne, for whom he organized the first one-man show in 1895. Vollard was a link with the next generation, showing work by Van Gogh, the Nabis, and later Matisse and Picasso. In 1893 he inaugurated his gallery on Rue Lafitte with an exhibition devoted to the work of Manet. It was effectively a modernist manifesto.

"We've just learned of the death of Théo Van Gogh, the kindly and intelligent connoisseur who did so much to inform the public about the work of the most independent artists."

Georges Aurier, *Mercure de France*, January 1891.

FOCUS

Durand-Ruel (1831–1922)

It was in London, during the Franco-Prussian War of 1870, that Daubigny introduced Paul Durand-Ruel to Monet and Pissarro. All of them had chosen to live in exile there. Immediately captivated by their modernity, Durand-Ruel exhibited their work in his gallery on New Bond Street. This was a watershed moment. Despite his own financial ups-and-downs, and the disastrous lack of proceeds from exhibitions and sales, Durand-Ruel never flagged in his support of the impressionists. This commitment was to be a lifelong struggle.

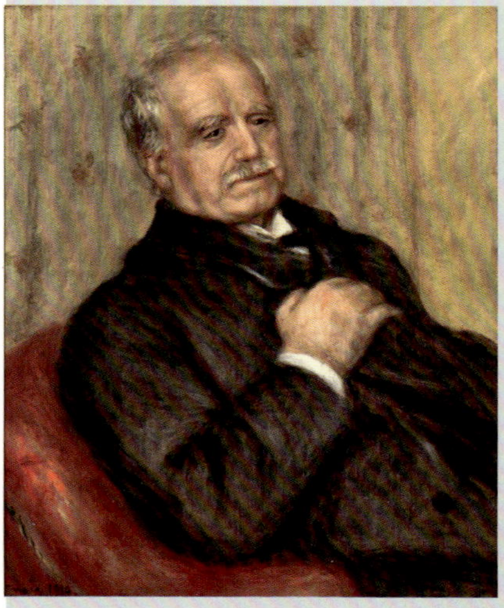

Auguste Renoir, *Portrait of Paul Durand-Ruel,* 1910
Oil on canvas, 25 ⅝ × 21 ¼ in. (65 × 54 cm)
Private collection

Unfailing Support

When he returned to France in 1872, Durand-Ruel approached the École des Batignolles group and purchased a substantial number of paintings by Manet and his young admirers. He became a staunch advocate of their art and one of their financial supporters. He bought their canvases, organized exhibitions, and helped them when in need. When the impressionists came under virulent attack, he loaned his Parisian gallery space for the second impressionist exhibition in 1876. In 1882, he once again rented out his gallery for the group's seventh exhibition. Paul Durand-Ruel experienced financial problems that sometimes compelled him to pull back from his business activities, but he persevered, even when some of the impressionists, uneasy about the financial difficulties their dealer experienced after the crash in 1882, began to show their work in Georges Petit's gallery. Competition with Petit, who organized the series of International Expositions of Painting, pushed Durand-Ruel to react. In 1883, Durand-Ruel organized one-man shows for Monet, Renoir, Sisley, and Pissarro, in rented space near the Madeleine.
He also opened an offensive on the international front. He was unconditional in his support for the impressionists, despite his business difficulties, the state of his finances, his disputes with the artists, and their periodic disloyalties. Renoir was the only one who remained loyal throughout.

KEY PARISIAN ADDRESSES

The son of an art dealer, Paul Durand-Ruel opened his own gallery in 1869 in the ninth arrondissement, at 16 Rue Laffitte and 11 Rue Le Pelletier. He was a supporter of Delacroix and the Barbizon school painters from the outset and, following his first meeting with Monet and Pissarro in 1870 in London, an unswerving supporter of the impressionists. His own apartment at 35 Rue de Rome was filled with eighteenth-century furniture, and its walls were hung with his own collection of impressionist paintings. Always eager to promote the art that he supported, Durand-Ruel gave free public access to his collection in 1898.

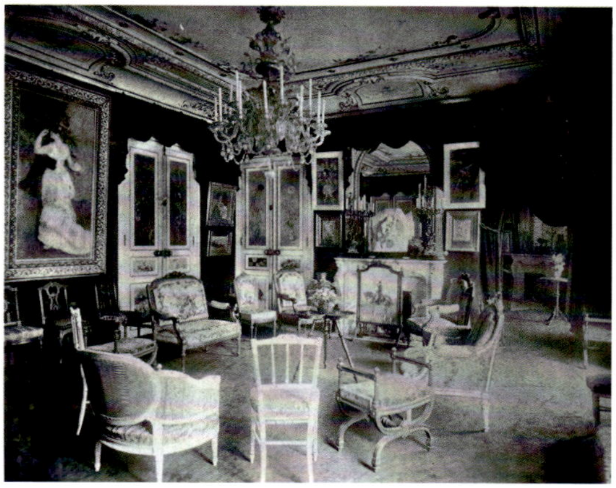

Paul Durand-Ruel’s drawing room at 35 Rue de Rome in Paris

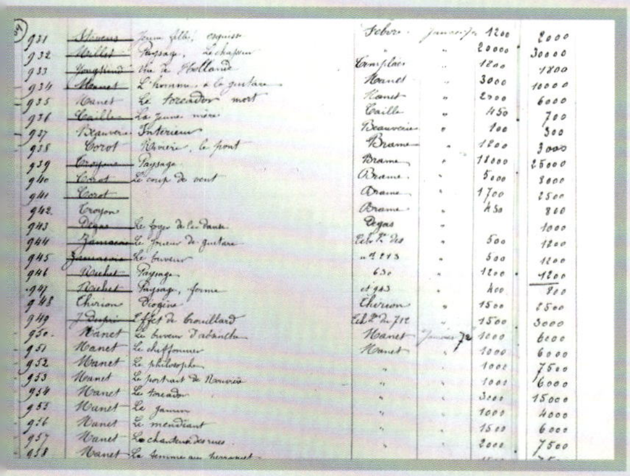

Durand-Ruel’s inventory listing, open to the page showing purchases from Manet in January 1872
Durand-Ruel Archives

LIMITED RESOURCES

With only limited capital, Paul Durand-Ruel always operated on the credit sources available to him from the time he began his business activities in 1865. He defaulted on payments in 1874 and 1884, but managed to negotiate moratoriums with his creditors both times, and later repaid them in full. It was not until 1894 that all his debts were cleared, after more than twenty years of commitment to the impressionists’ cause.

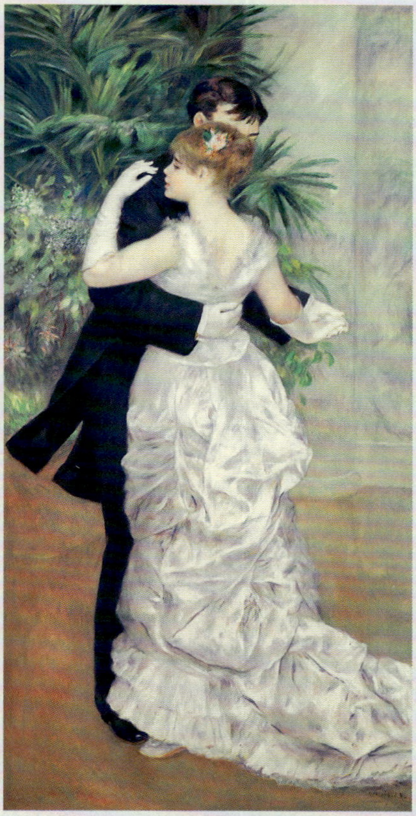

Auguste Renoir, *City Dance*, 1882–83
Oil on canvas, 5 ft. 10 ¾ in. × 2 ft. 11 ½ in. (180 × 90 cm)
Musée d’Orsay, Paris

Along with *Country Dance*, its companion piece, *City Dance* was consigned to Durand-Ruel in 1883. He purchased both paintings in 1886. This canvas was acquired by the State’s national collections through a settlement in 1978.

"Attacked and vilified by partisans of the Academy and its antiquated doctrines, by the most celebrated art critics, by the entire press corps, and by most of my colleagues, they [the impressionists] began to be the laughingstocks of the Salons and the public.... And I, guilty of having exhibited and daring to defend such works, was treated like an idiot and a man of bad faith. Little by little, the confidence I had once inspired evaporated, and I became suspect by my best clients."

Paul Durand-Ruel, quoted by Lionello Venturi, *Les Archives de l'impressionnisme*, 1939.

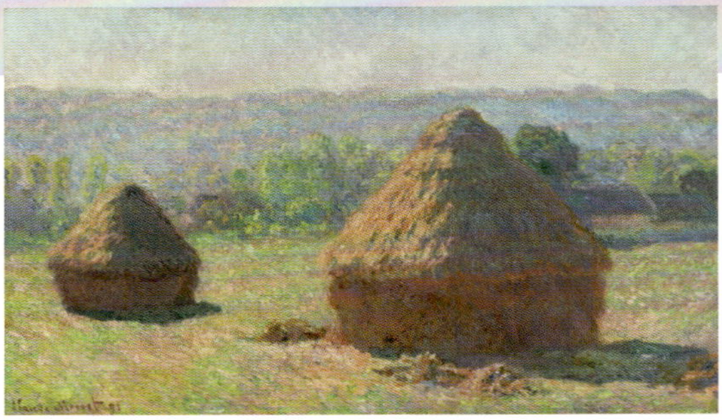

Claude Monet, *Haystacks, End of Summer*, 1891
Oil on canvas, 1 ft. 11 ½ in. × 3 ft. 3 ½ in. (60 × 100 cm)
Musée d'Orsay, Paris

Purchased early by Durand-Ruel, *Haystacks, End of Summer* remained with his family until 1952.

"You think I don't display your pictures enough.... I show nothing but them. I haven't occupied myself with anything else for several years. I've put all my heart, all my time, and all my family's fortune into them."
Paul Durand-Ruel, letter to Monet, January 22, 1886.

The Development of the International Market

In 1870, when they were all living in London in exile, Durand-Ruel began to exhibit Monet and Pissarro there. After returning to Paris, in 1874 he was forced to close his London branch due to financial pressure. In 1880, he again began to organize exhibitions in London, including a major show of sixty-five impressionist canvases at Dowdeswell's Galleries on New Bond Street in 1883. He mounted a show in Brussels in 1885 at the Hôtel du Grand Miroir where Degas, Monet, Pissarro, Renoir, and Sisley were represented. In 1891, he sent works to the eighth exhibition of the avant-garde group, Les XX, in Brussels, maintaining his ties with the Belgian artistic scene. He also tried to develop markets in Germany, Austria, Holland, Russia, and Sweden. Foreseeing that the international market was the key to success, he willingly loaned paintings to exhibitions abroad. In 1905, he organized the most comprehensive impressionist exhibition ever in London's Grafton Galleries. It included 315 works, of which 196 were from his own collection.

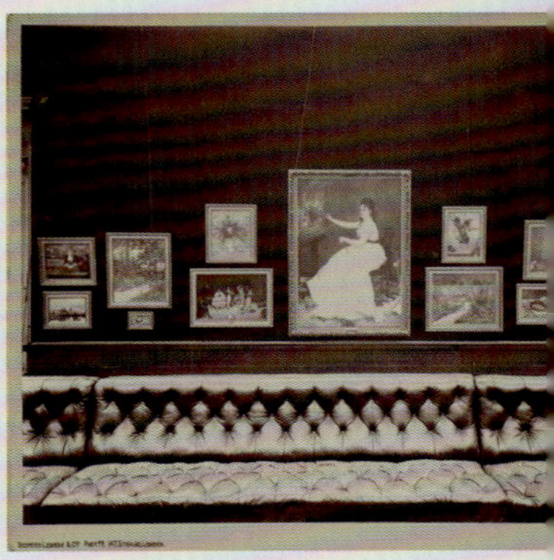

Bedford Lemere & Co.
View of the impressionist exhibition room in the Grafton Galleries in London
Musée d'Orsay, Paris

THE CONQUEST OF AMERICA

In 1886, Durand-Ruel accepted an invitation from the American Art Association in New York and exhibited a large selection of impressionist works. Despite skepticism from some of the painters, he presented almost three hundred canvases, including works by Monet, Manet, Pissarro, Renoir, Berthe Morisot, and Sisley. Critics received the show favorably, and the exhibition stimulated interest in this new art, which seemed in step with modernity. Sensing an opportunity, Durand-Ruel organized a second exhibition the following year, and in 1887 he opened a branch in New York for his three sons to manage. While the results were less than spectacular, the popularity of impressionism in the United States was attributable to Durand-Ruel's determined efforts to conquer this new market.

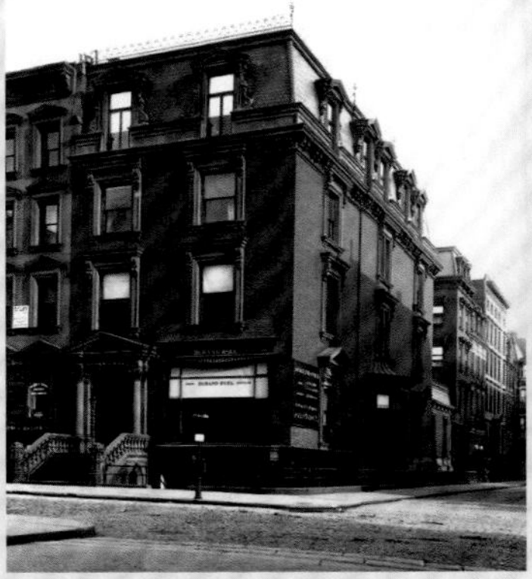

Third Durand-Ruel gallery in New York (1894–1904), 389 Fifth Avenue, exterior view

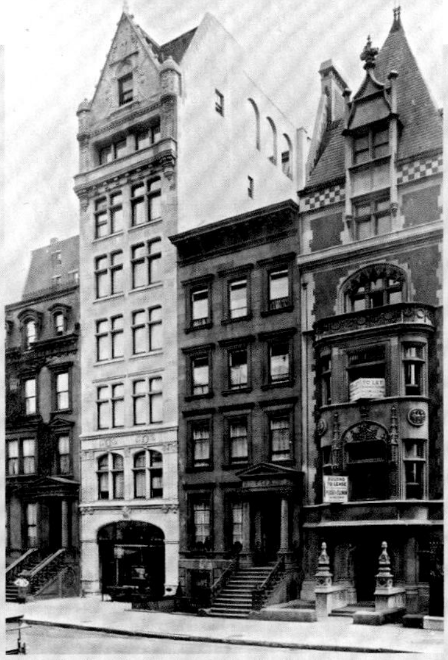

Fifth Durand-Ruel gallery in New York (1913–50), 12 East 57 Street, exterior view

"Don't suppose that the Americans are savages. On the contrary, they're less ignorant and less prosaic than French art lovers."
Paul Durand-Ruel, letter to Fantin-Latour, August 21, 1886.

THE WELL-CONNECTED MISS CASSATT

Mary Cassatt, whose brother Alexander was a Pennsylvania railroad magnate, had close ties with the American business classes. She played an important role in promoting the popularity of impressionism in the United States. Her friend, Henry Havemeyer, known as the "Sugar King," and his wife Louisine followed her advice and began to amass a peerless collection, now in New York's Metropolitan Museum of Art. Mrs. Palmer, the wife of a wealthy businessman, met Mary Cassatt in Paris in 1889, and also purchased one of the world's most important impressionist collections, now in the Art Institute of Chicago.

REVOLUTIONARY METHODS

As a dealer, Paul Durand-Ruel introduced entirely novel practices to the art world. His new principles included unconditional support of his artists, the exclusivity he tried to impose, the establishment of art journals when financial circumstances permitted, collaboration between the artistic and financial worlds to develop his business, the organization of one-man (rather than group) shows, and the development of an international network. When he received the Légion d'honneur in 1920, it was in acknowledgement of his contributions to foreign trade, not his activities in the fine arts.

"Now I'm about to confess my great crime, the one that surpasses all others. For a long time now I've been buying paintings, and I value most highly the works of very original and knowledgeable artists, many of whom are men of genius. I confess to imposing these works on collectors."

Paul Durand-Ruel, 1885.

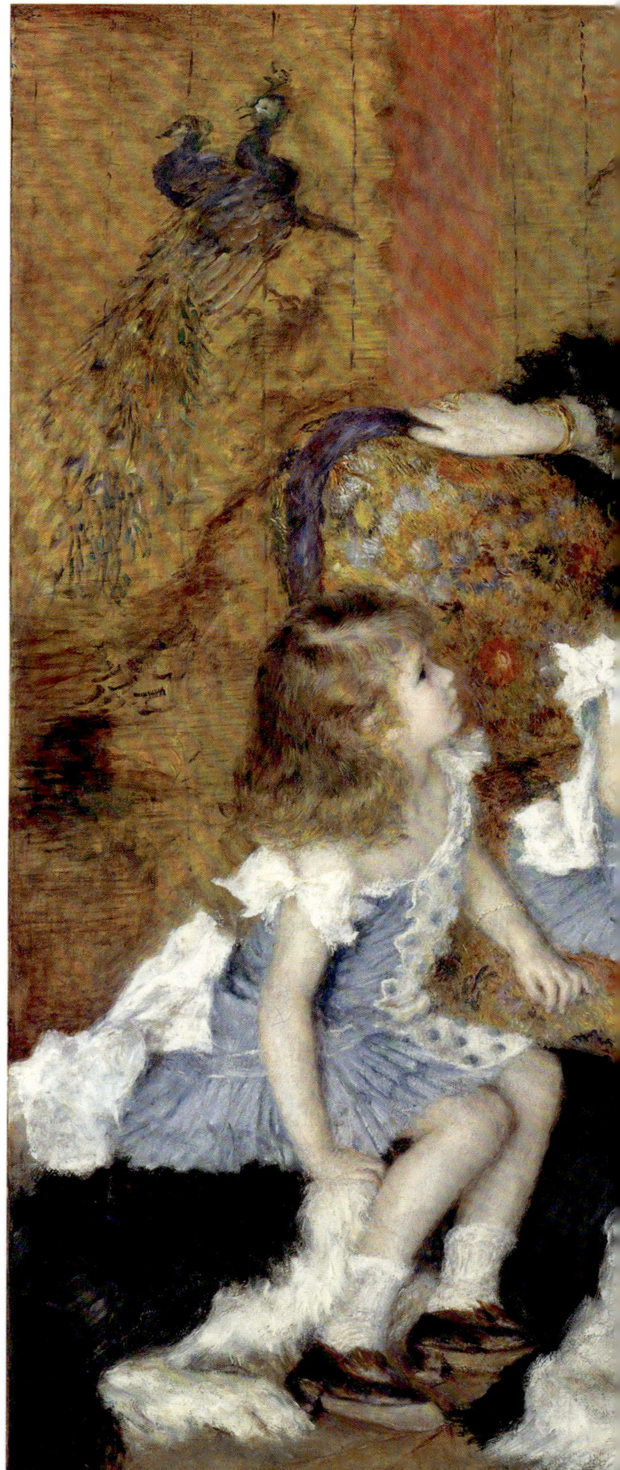

Auguste Renoir
Madame Charpentier and Her Children
1878
Oil on canvas, 5 ft. × 6 ft. 3 in. (1.54 × 1.90 m)
The Metropolitan Museum of Art, New York

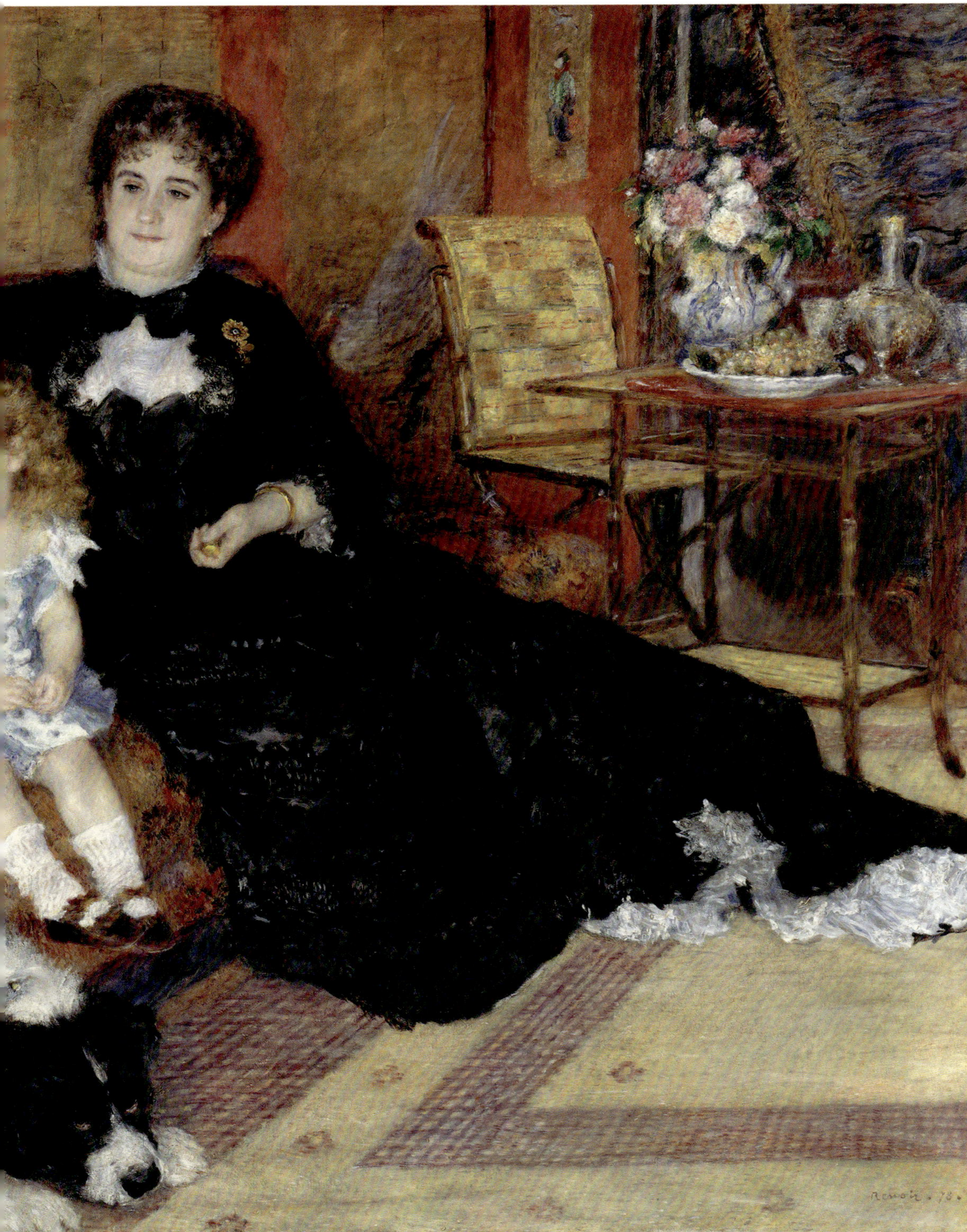

Madame Charpentier and Her Children

Auguste Renoir, 1878

Displayed in the 1879 Salon, this canvas by Renoir occupied a place of honor thanks to the social connections of the model and its patron, the publisher Georges Charpentier. The family's home welcomed political figures, duchesses, and actresses for noteworthy soirées. This portrait inaugurated Renoir's success and the beginning of his apogee.

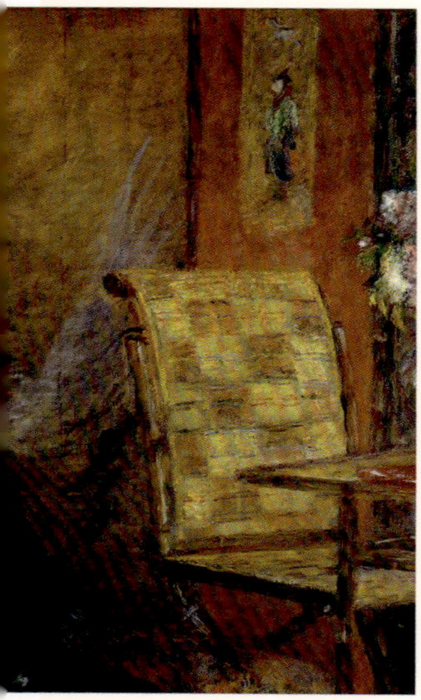

The still life on the table in the background is a pure piece of virtuosic painting that Renoir, a true lover of the good things in life, found irresistible.

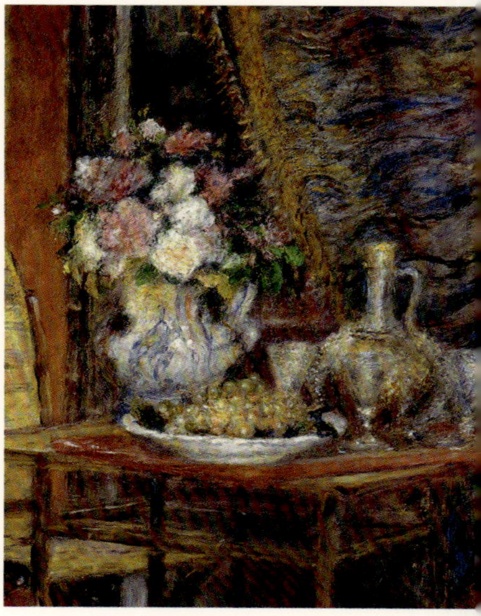

For his setting, Renoir chose the Charpentiers' Japanese drawing room, a stunning backdrop where gold tones predominate. It is an enveloping, intimate spot, a testament to the refined taste of these enlightened patrons.

Recalling Japanese prints, the composition is flat, ignoring the effects of perspective. The figures are staged on a diagonal that leaves the foreground partially empty; the border of the carpet is the only indication of spacial depth.

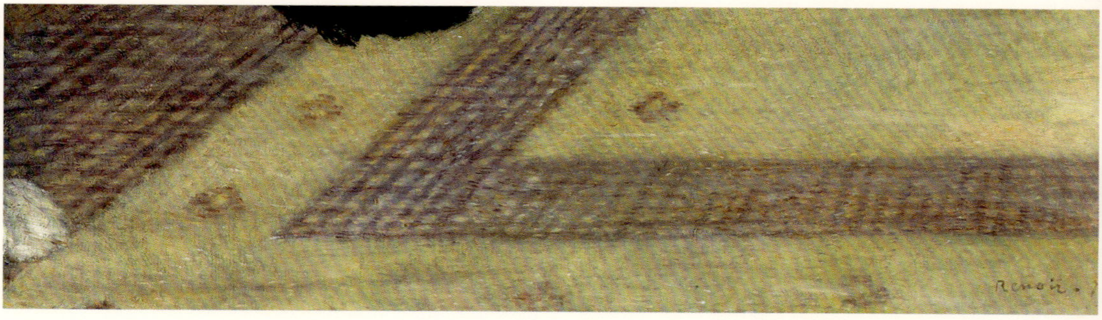

THE BOURGEOIS PORTRAIT

Renoir managed to inject an atmosphere of familial informality into this scene, which was reworked in his studio. He also fulfilled his obligation to depict the opulence and social distinction expected of this type of commission.

An imposing presence in her elegant Worth gown, Madame Charpentier may seem distant, but there is also a gentleness in her gaze that embraces the two children. They are attired in matching girls' outfits, as was customary at the time.

The rendering of the two children introduces a delightful spontaneity to the scene. Politely seated on the sofa, his hands clasped in his lap, three-year-old Paul casts an admiring glance at his sister Georgette. She is nonchalantly sitting on an enormous dog, whose black and white fur echoes their mother's elegant gown.

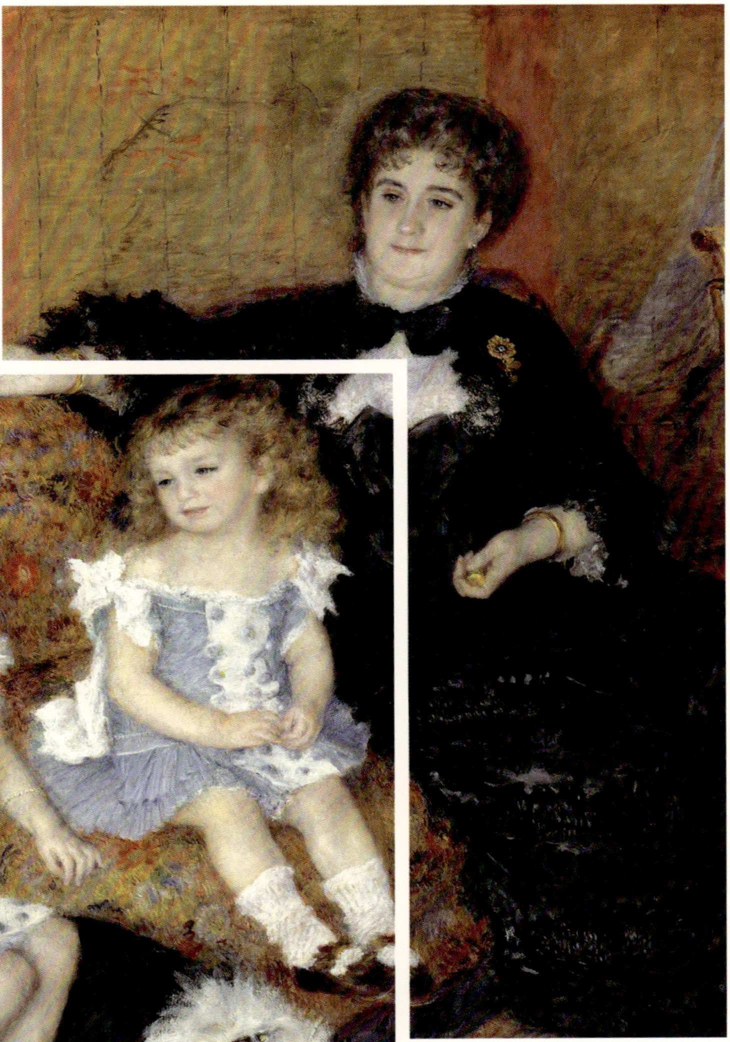

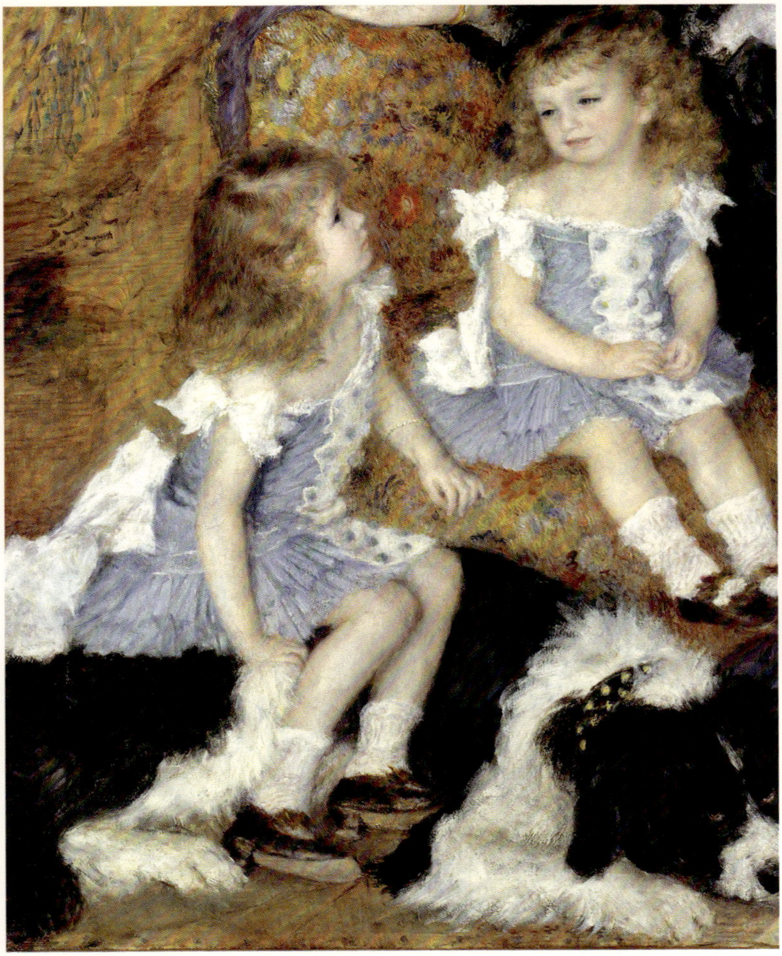

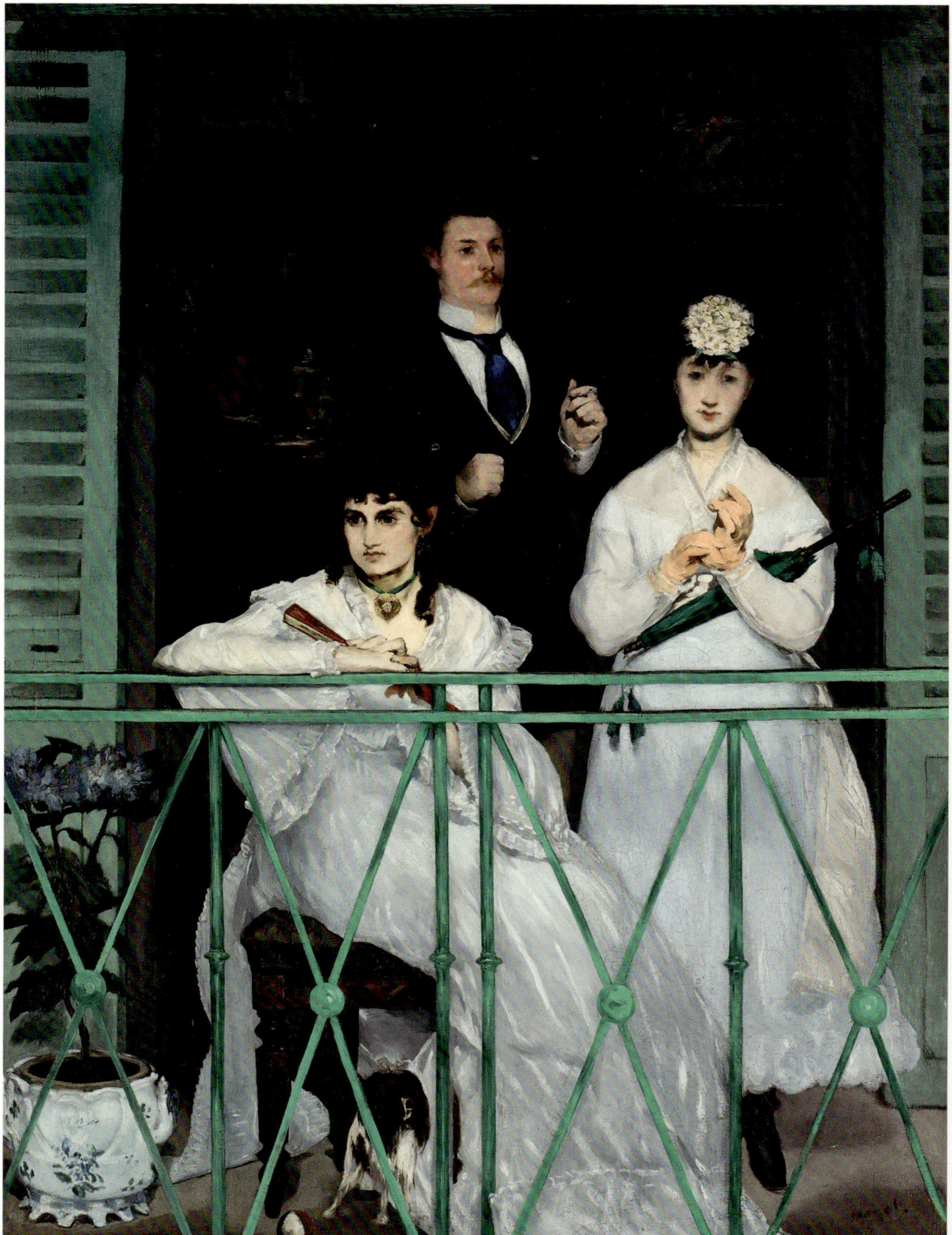

Édouard Manet
The Balcony
1868–69
Oil on canvas, 5 ft. 7 in. × 4 ft. 1 in. (1.70 × 1.25 m)
Musée d'Orsay, Paris

A Hard Life and Belated Recognition

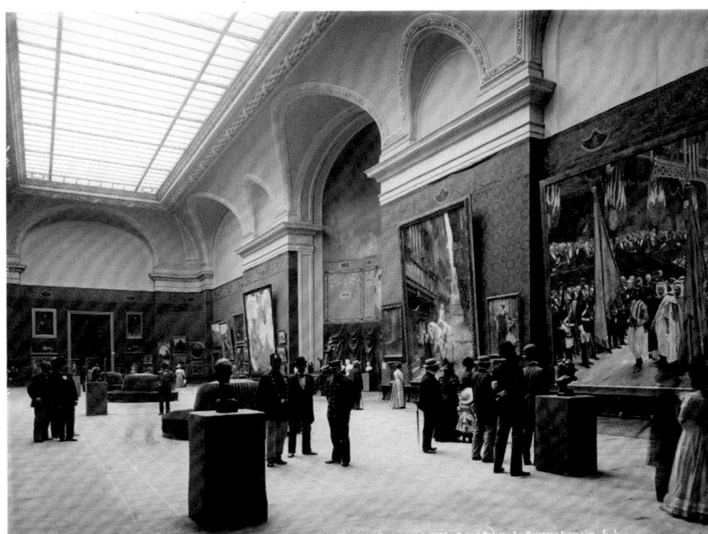

The French painting section in the Grand Palais during the 1900 Exposition Universelle

Young painters who defiantly chose to break with academic rules and principles faced long years of contempt, and some experienced acute poverty. The road before them was hard and painful. Not only was it difficult to exhibit in the face of such vicious critical disdain, but many of them suffered extreme financial deprivation.

Some, including Manet, Berthe Morisot, Caillebotte, Bazille, and Degas, were sheltered from financial worries, but others were condemned to struggle with poverty. The enthusiasm that surrounded the first impressionist exhibition soon diminished. Profits were nonexistent, and the artists had to contend with critics' attacks and widespread scorn, not to mention the incessant internecine quarrels and dissensions within the group. Renoir was penniless and was among the first to break away and try his luck at the Salon. He met with success there as early as 1879, when he presented *Madame*

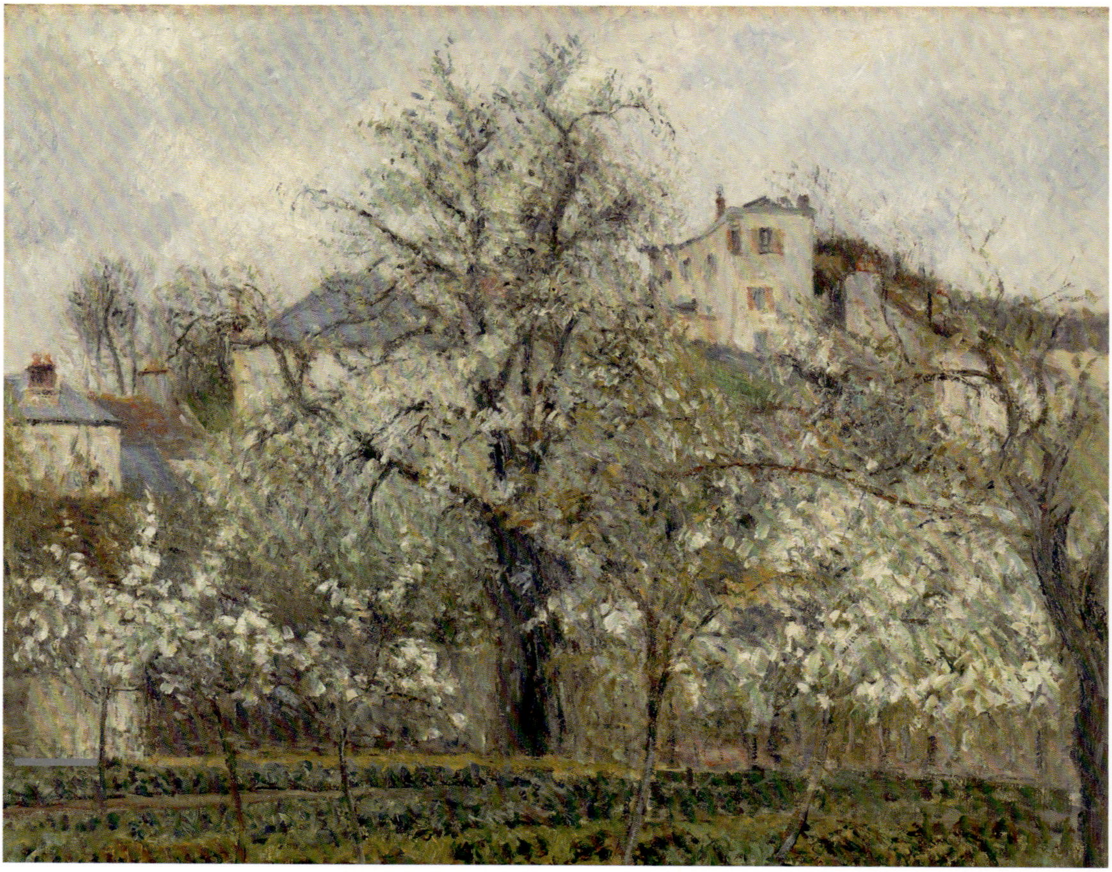

Camille Pissarro
Spring Plum Trees in Flower, also known as
Kitchen Garden, Trees in Flower: Spring, Pontoise
1877
Oil on canvas, 25 ¾ × 31 ⅞ in, (65.5 × 81 cm)
Musée d'Orsay, Paris

Charpentier and Her Children. Monet and Sisley, tired of living hand to mouth, followed Renoir's example. Financial need was an important issue that could not be ignored, even though Degas fulminated against the comrades he considered renegades. Renoir felt the need to justify his actions: "My submission to the Salon was above all a business decision," he wrote in 1881 to Paul Durand-Ruel. "In any case, it's like taking certain medicines: even if it doesn't help you, it won't harm you."

But finances were not the only concern. "If it took courage to enter upon a way of poverty, how much more was needed to continue for many years making unbelievable efforts without any encouragement?" as John Rewald wrote in his landmark work, *The History of Impressionism.* The violent criticism was at its worst in the early years, but it was slow to abate, and recognition in France came very late. And it was the height of injustice that the real

PISSARRO'S HARDSHIPS

"I don't see any way out.... It's going very badly. I take no pleasure in my studies because of this idea that I'll have to abandon art and look for something else to do, if it's possible to start a new apprenticeship. So sad."
Pissarro, letter to Murer, 1878.

Tell Gauguin that after thirty years of painting, I'm stuck in a ditch. The next generation should keep this in mind. It's a lottery, not a jackpot!"
Pissarro, letter to Murer, August 1884.

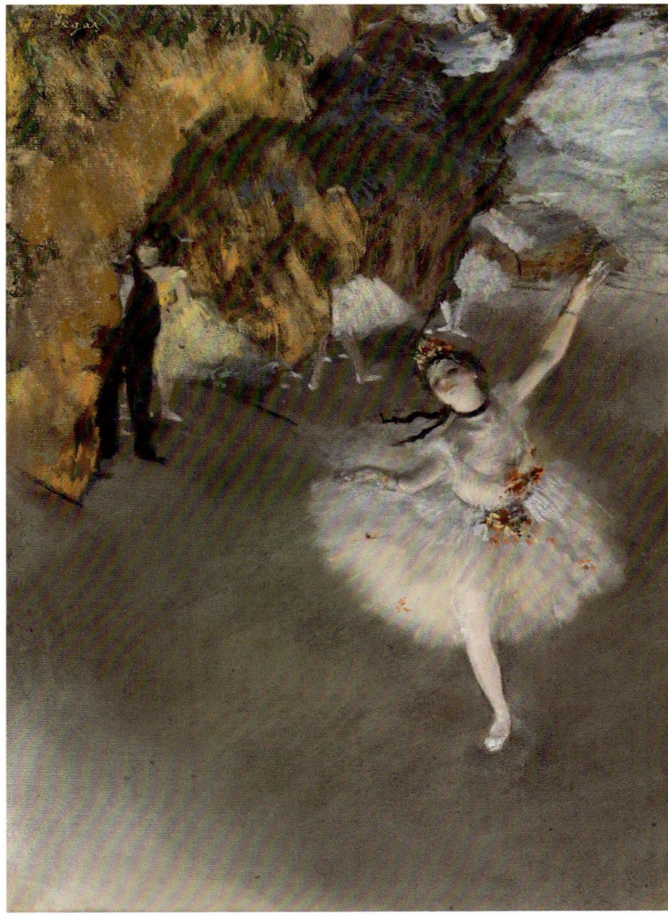

Edgar Degas
Ballet, also known as *The Star*
c. 1876
Pastel on paper, 23 × 12 ¾ in. (58.4 × 32.4 cm)
Musée d'Orsay, Paris, conserved at the Musée du Louvre

"The brotherhood of painters is in terrible trouble. The dealers have too many canvases.... Let's hope the buyers come back, but this is certainly not a good time."
Eugène Manet, letter to Berthe Morisot, September 1876.

"An aura of desolation seems to hang over the impressionist camp. The money isn't exactly pouring into their coffers and the work is just left drying where it hangs. We're living in very troubled times, and I don't know when our poor art of painting will regain some of its luster."
Cézanne, letter to Zola, August 24, 1877.

protagonists were not the first to benefit. As the columnist Houssaye so accurately observed in an article written in 1882: "Impressionism is a victim of scathing sarcasm when it goes under the name of Manet, Monet, Renoir, Caillebotte, or Degas, and receives all manner of reverence when called Bastien-Lepage, Duez, Gervex, Bompard, Danton, Goeneutte, Butin, Mangeant, Jean Béraud, or Dagnan-Bouveret" (all academic artists). The breath of fresh air brought by impressionism was just beginning to infiltrate works by academic artists, albeit in a very watered-down fashion. But it was these artists who were recognized, because their conventional, insipid style made the approach more acceptable. Houssaye saw things as they were, but other critics actually deceived themselves on the origins of the freshening breeze that was blowing through the Salon. Edmond de Goncourt, ignoring the recent link with impressionism, wrote in his *Journal* in 1882: "One thing struck me at the Salon—it was Jongkind's influence. Now all the landscapes of any merit seem inspired by this painter." Needless to say, this neglect was a bitter pill for the impressionists:

MORE COLOR!

In addition to the grinding poverty that some of the painters confronted, there was the additional indignity of being unable to purchase the supplies that were necessary to paint. Some found themselves limited in what they could produce. "Paint—I don't even have the money to buy paints, so I confine myself to drawing. It's less expensive," wrote Gauguin to Pissarro in the spring of 1885. "Please ask Durand-Ruel to take something, no matter what the price, so I can buy some colors."

"I wouldn't be unhappy to be able to read, while I am still above ground, the laudatory article that you'll write about me when I'm dead."

Manet, letter to Albert Wolff, May 1882. Monet would be awarded the coveted Légion d'Honneur just before he died.

financial difficulties remained pressing and severe for Monet, Pissarro, and Sisley. Despite the efforts of Durand-Ruel, who constantly tried new initiatives, the proceeds were negligible and money did not flow. Sisley died in 1899, one year after his wife, and never really saw the recognition that his work achieved posthumously. Other impressionists did experience this satisfaction, although the audience's resistance was easily reawakened and persisted for a long time. In 1890, fierce opposition had to be overcome for Manet's *Olympia*, purchased by the proceeds of a public subscription, to finally enter the Musée du Louvre. Similarly, in 1894, an epic battle had to be fought so that Caillebotte's bequest would be at least partially accepted by the State. Forty of the sixty canvases he so generously offered actually entered the museum and are today among the treasures of the Musée d'Orsay.

The official recognition of impressionism in France can be dated to the Universal Exposition of 1900. Its vast exhibition *Centenary Exhibition of French Art* honored both impressionists and academic artists on an equal footing. However, even decades after the first impressionist exhibition, the victory remained tenuous. It is hard to say whether Monet's gift of *Water Lilies* in 1918 and his project for displaying the canvases in the Orangerie would have come to fruition without the intervention of President Georges Clemenceau–that is still debatable.

SUBMISSIONS TO THE SALON

Recognition—but above all the need for material survival—motivated the impressionists' submissions to the Salon. Faced with the critical and financial catastrophe of the impressionist exhibitions, and seeing Renoir's success in the Salon that same year, Sisley wrote to Duret on March 14, 1879: "I'm tired of vegetating as I have for so long. The moment has come for me to make a decision. It is true that our exhibitions have served a purpose, and have in that way been very useful, but... it will be a long time before one can get by without the prestige associated with official exhibitions. I am therefore determined to send something to the Salon." His submission was rejected.

MONET'S CRIES FOR HELP

Monet's correspondence is studded with cries for help that demonstrate the extreme precariousness of his financial situation. His desperate letters were initially addressed to Bazille and to his first collector from Le Havre, Gaudibert, and later, after 1870, to Manet, Caillebotte, Zola, and the collectors de Bellio, Hoschedé, Faure, Chocquet, and Gachet.

"Could you, and would you, do me a great favor? If I am not paid the sum of 600 francs by tomorrow evening, Tuesday, our furniture and all our possessions will be sold and we will be on the street.... It is very painful to have to reveal this situation to my poor wife. I am making one last attempt in turning to you."
Monet, letter to Zola, winter 1876–77.

"Could you lend me 100 francs one more time and come see me in Paris as soon as you'd like so I can repay you with a painting?"
Monet, letter to Doctor Gachet, April 1878.

"I am totally disgusted and demoralized by the existence I've been leading for so long. If this is where I've gotten at this age [Monet was then thirty-nine], there's no hope left.... Every day brings fresh torments, every day new difficulties arise from which we'll never escape."
Monet, letter to de Bellio, March 10, 1879.

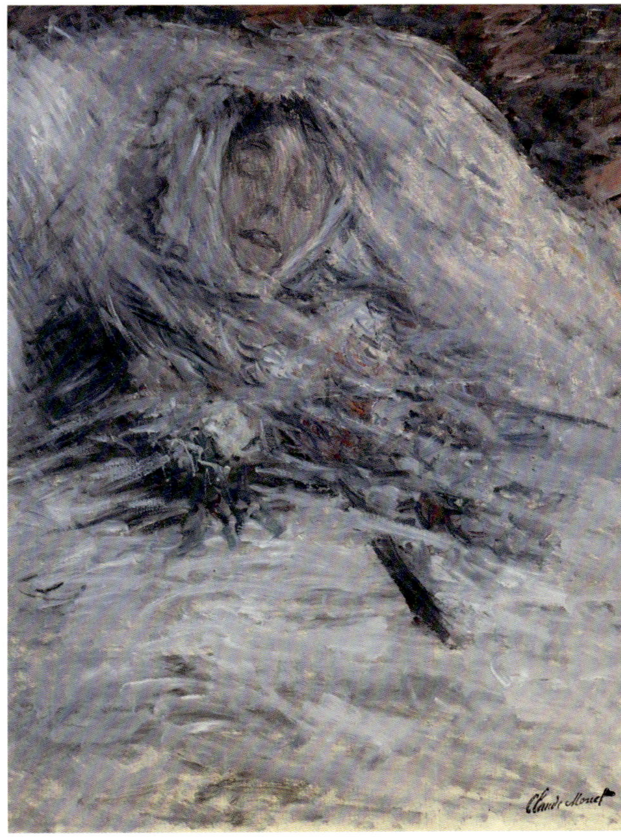

Claude Monet
Camille on Her Deathbed
1879
Oil on canvas, 35 ⅜ × 26 ¾ in. (90 × 68 cm)
Musée d'Orsay, Paris

"I'm here to ask you for another favor; it would be to go to the pawn shop and get the medallion whose receipt I include. It's the only memento my wife was able to keep, and I'd like to place it around her neck before she's gone forever."
Monet, letter to de Bellio, September 5, 1879, the day following the death of his first wife Camille.

Impressionism and the Arts

Members of the same artistic and intellectual community, painters, musicians, writers, and photographers debated together in cafés and studios. Their paths crossed at performances and exhibitions. Far from being a phenomenon confined to the fine arts, the explorations pursued by the impressionist painters were echoed in other artistic disciplines, including music, literature, and photography.

"To Edgar Degas, who paints life as I would like to be able to paint it."

Dedication by Guy de Maupassant in a copy of *Pierre and Jean* for his friend Degas.

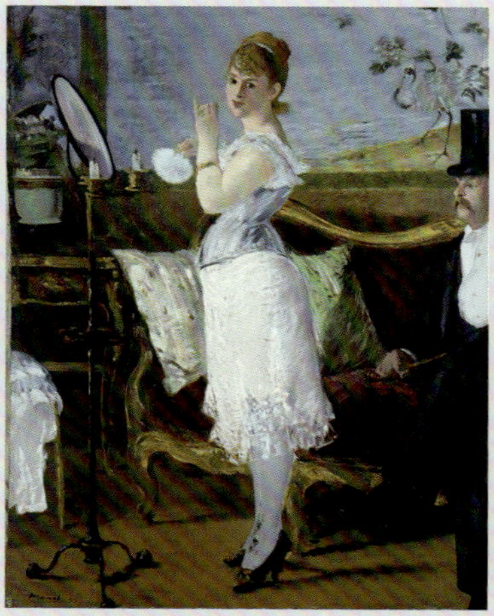

Édouard Manet, *Nana*, 1877
Oil on canvas, 5 ft. × 3 ft. 8 in. (1.54 × 1.15 m)
Hamburger Kunsthalle, Hamburg

Literature

The nineteenth century was an era of great change, during which literary styles (such as naturalism and symbolism) emerged, very reminiscent of the pictorial experimentation that was being carried out by the impressionists at the same time. A supporter of Manet and the impressionists before making an abrupt volte-face, Émile Zola also took the contemporary world as the subject of his work. The Goncourt brothers, as well as Balzac and his work *The Human Comedy*, demonstrated the same interest in describing the reality of their own time; they were attracted to subjects that had hitherto been considered inconsequential. Mallarmé was nicknamed "my little impressionist poet" by none other than Victor Hugo. Paul Valéry was close to Berthe Morisot and married her niece; he took inspiration from Degas for his intriguing novel *An Evening with Mr Teste* (1896). Guy de Maupassant's work was akin to the impressionist spirit; the writer frequented many of the same places, including La Grenouillère in Argenteuil, which he described in *Yvette* (1885). That same year, he also met Monet in Étretat. Marcel Proust's work came later, but it could be considered one of the closest literary equivalents. Abandoning conventional narration, the real subject of *In Search of Lost Time* is the description of the most tenuous, ephemeral impressions.

Music

Without being a style in itself, impressionism in music was reflected in a search for harmonic color and pure timbres. Ravel, Fauré, and especially Debussy, composed their music by breaking up and fragmenting chords, evoking the dappled stippling of colors by a painter's brushstrokes. Their choice of themes, such as Debussy's *The Sea*, was another echo of their kinship. Emmanuel Chabrier, a close friend of Manet, Monet, and Renoir, was among the pioneers of this new approach to composition. The musician collected impressionist works and appears in Degas's painting, *The Orchestra at the Opera*. Bazille was a music lover and amateur performer who organized musical soirées in his studio. He invited the singer Jean-Baptiste Faure and his friend the composer Edmond Maître to participate.

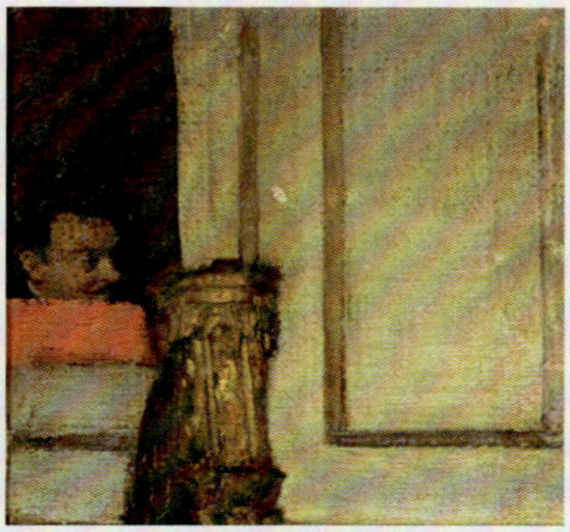

Edgar Degas, *The Orchestra at the Opéra* (detail), c. 1870
Oil on canvas, 22 ¼ × 18 ⅛ in. (56.5 × 46 cm)
Musée d'Orsay, Paris

Photography

Whether in the forest of Fontainebleau or along the Normandy coast, photographers were pioneers experimenting with a new tool that they wanted to elevate to the level of art. They planted their tripods in the same places where the impressionists set up their easels. Seizing the moment, capturing the ephemeral, and grasping the spirit of their own time were all shared preoccupations. As techniques for developing photographic effects improved after 1885, pictorialist photographers strove to convey atmospheres and impressions, just as painters did with their brushes. The Lumière brothers invented cinematography in 1895, and in 1903 they registered the first of many patents that were the origin of color photography. Using a process involving potato starch, autochromes had tiny specks colored red, green, and blue that recreated the impression of color on the retina. Perhaps it was the ultimate version of pointillism.

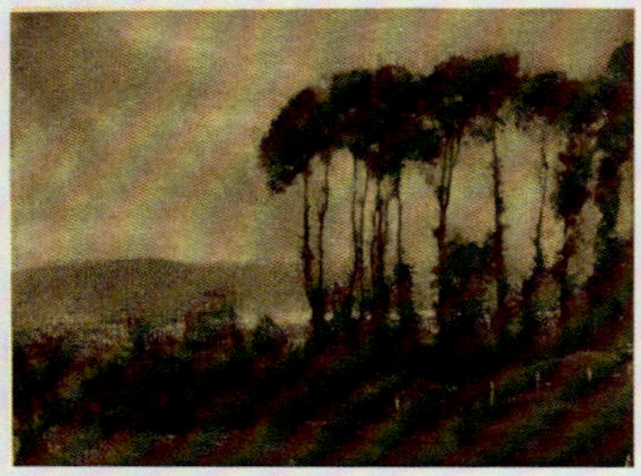

Robert Demachy, *Toucques Valley*, 1906
Heliogravure, 6 ⅛ × 8 in. (15.5 × 20.4 cm)
Musée d'Orsay, Paris

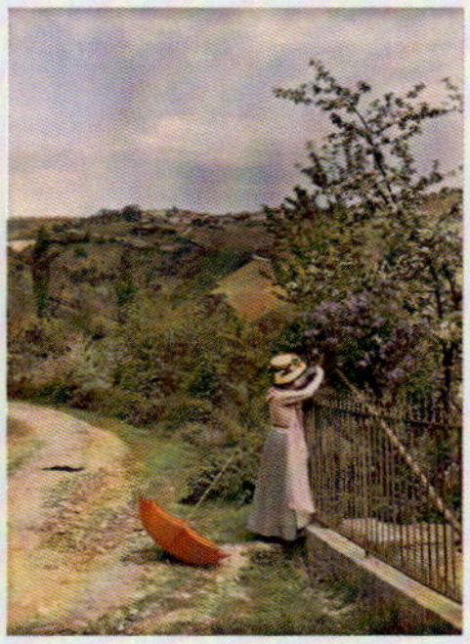

Lumière Brothers, *Young Woman and Lilacs*, 1906, autochrome plate, 5 ⅛ × 7 ⅛ in. (13 × 18 cm), Institut Lumière, Lyon

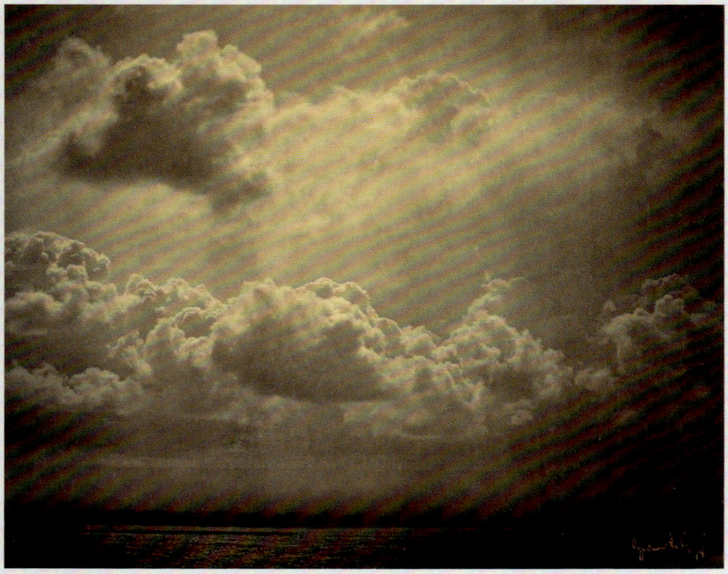

Gustave Le Gray, *Study of Clouds*, 1856–57
Albumin paper print, 12 ⅝ × 15 ⅜ in. (32 × 39 cm)
Musée d'Orsay, Paris

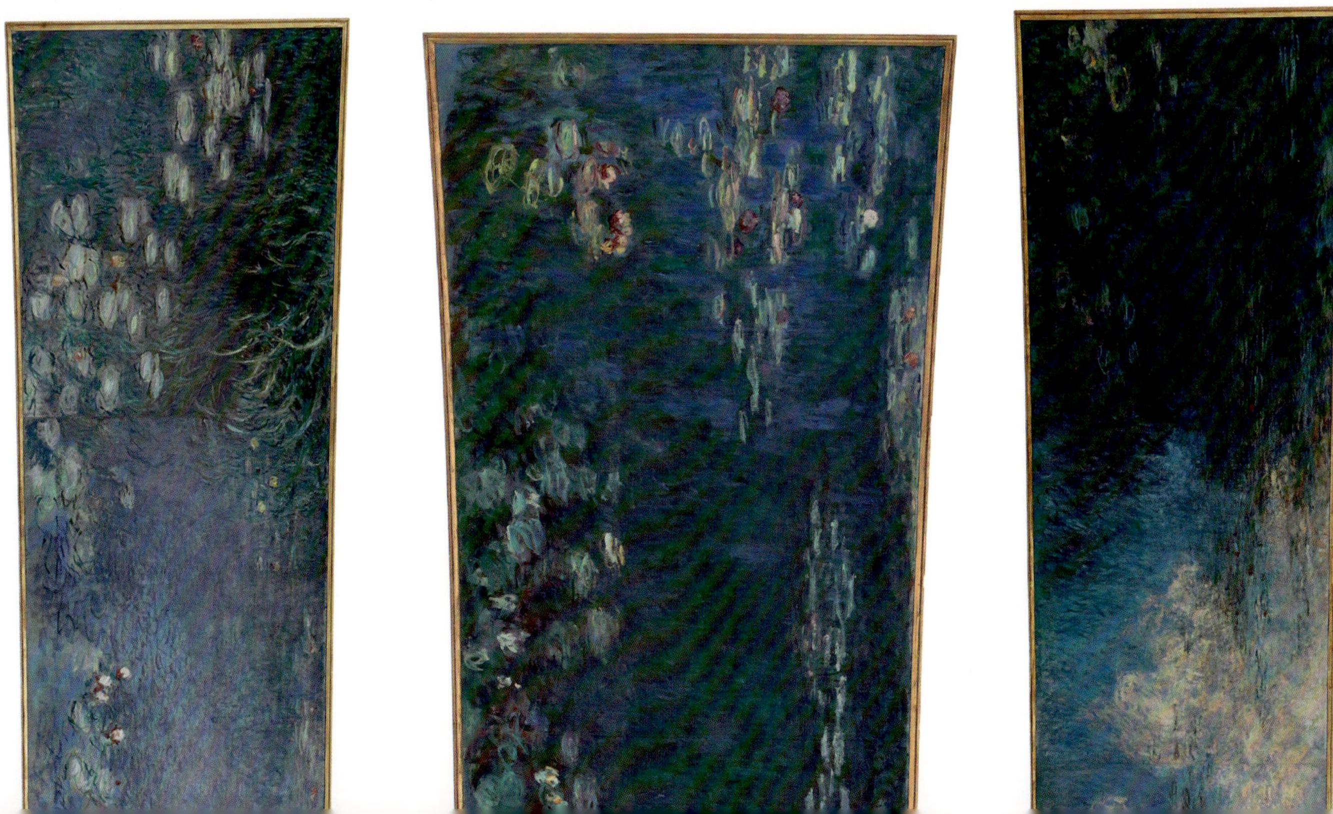

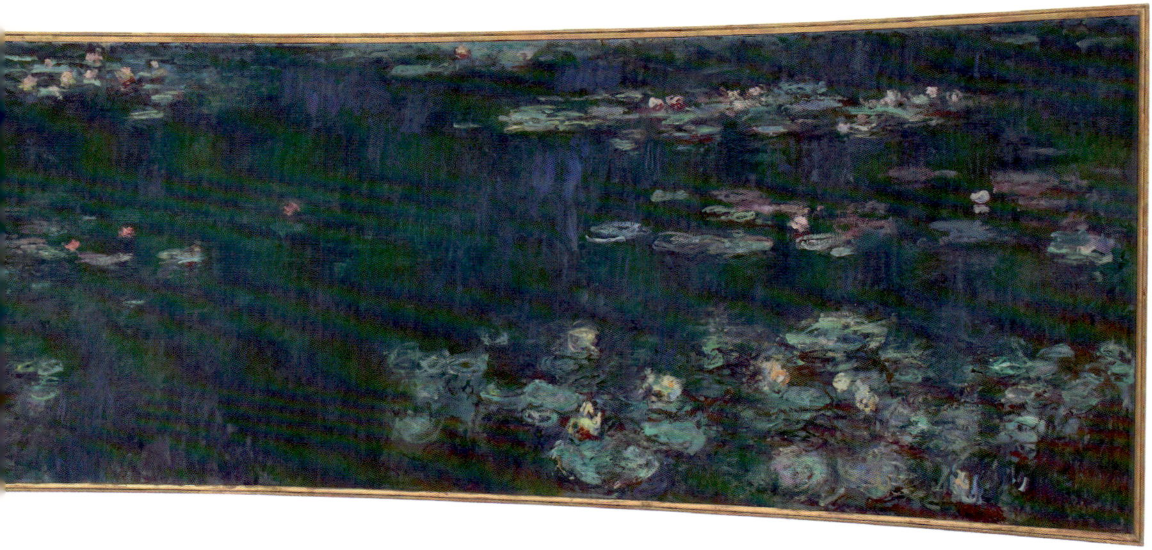

Claude Monet
The Water Lily Pond: Clouds
1915–16
Oil on canvas, triptych, each panel
6 ft. 6 ¾ in. × 13 ft. 11 ¼ in. (2.00 × 4.25 m)
Musée de l'Orangerie, Paris

Claude Monet
The Water Lily Pond: Green Reflections
1914–18
Oil on canvas, triptych, each panel
6 ft. 6 ¾ in. × 13 ft. 11 ¼ in. (2.00 × 4.25 m)
Musée de l'Orangerie, Paris

Claude Monet
The Water Lily Pond: Morning
1914–18
Oil on canvas, four panels of
6 ft. 6 ¾ in. × 6 ft. 11 ½ in. (2.00 × 2.13 m),
6 ft. 6 ¾ in. × 13 ft. 11 ¼ in. (2.00 × 4.25 m),
6 ft. 6 ¾ in. × 13 ft. 11 ¼ in. (2.00 × 4.25 m),
and 6 ft. 6 ¾ in. × 11 ½ in. (2.00 × 2.13 m)
Musée de l'Orangerie, Paris

Water Lilies

Claude Monet, 1914–18

Immediately following the armistice in 1918, Monet decided to donate several canvases from his *Water Lilies* series to the State. Following protracted negotiations, and thanks to the indefatigable support of his friend Georges Clemenceau, who had become President of the Council, the document confirming the donation of eight panels was signed in 1922. The paintings were hung in the Orangerie in 1927, just after the painter's death. They are displayed in two oval galleries designed by Monet himself–a truly immersive work of art.

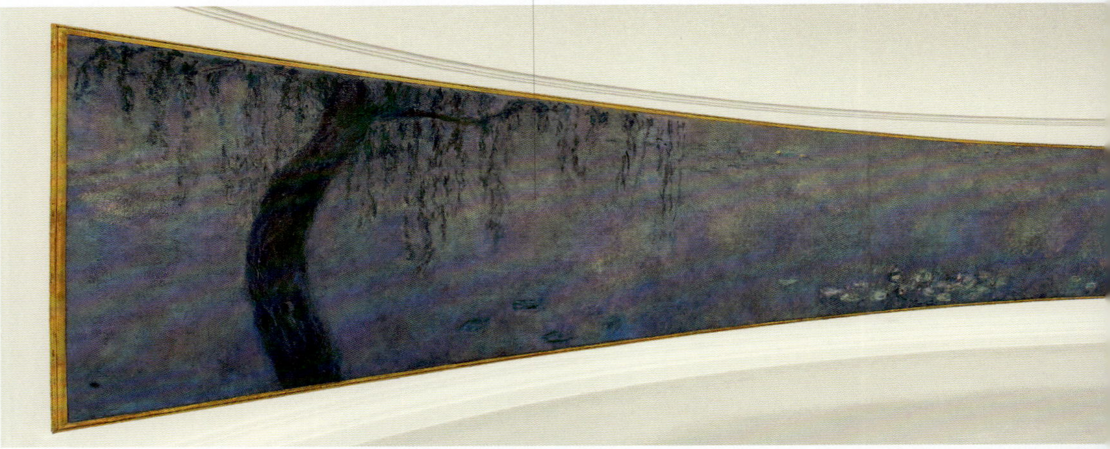

Claude Monet, *The Water Lily Pond: The Two Willows*, 1914–18
Oil on canvas, four panels of 6 ft. 6 ¾ in. × 13 ft. 11 ¼ in. (2.00 × 4.25 m)
Musée de l'Orangerie, Paris

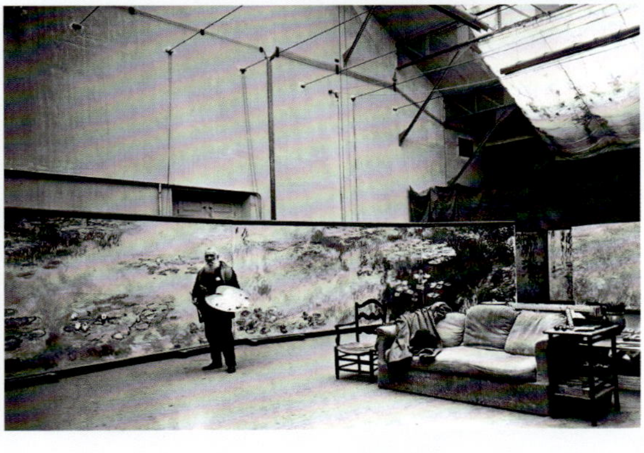

NATURE ON YOUR DOORSTEP

To facilitate his *Water Lilies* project, Monet built a vast studio, just steps away from the pond, where he could work all year round.

Henri Manuel, *Claude Monet in His Large Studio in Giverny*, c. 19
Durand-Ruel Archives

ENVIRONMENTAL ART

The panoramic format of the canvases and their staging in the galleries completely immerse the visitor in the paintings. Monet revolutionized the viewer's relationship with art, shattering the conventional visual barrier that puts distance between them. He created the first work of environmental art.

"You should know that I am consumed by this work. These landscapes of water and reflections have become an obsession. It's beyond what an old man's strength can do, but I still want to manage to convey what I feel."
Monet, letter to Geffroy, August 11, 1908.

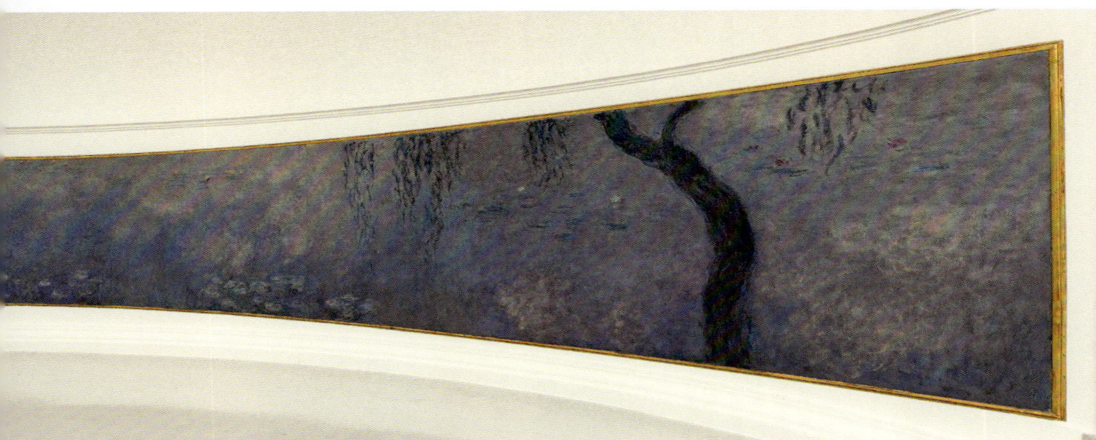

Captured on the water's surface, the passing clouds convey the pantheistic vision that Monet embraced at the end of his life. Here, the water and sky are one, merging on the painting's surface. The work is transformed into an abstract composition that anticipates the advent of abstract expressionism a quarter of a century later.

"The Orangerie is the Sistine Chapel of impressionism."

André Masson, 1952.

REDISCOVERY AND REDEMPTION

"An astonishing painting with neither drawing nor border," observed the critic Louis Gillet, following the inauguration of the galleries in the Orangerie. By 1927, impressionism was no longer in vogue. A myriad of new trends and "isms" followed one after the other in avant-garde circles, and *Water Lilies* did not really attract much attention. Not until the rise of abstract art in the 1950s did this major work once again astonish the viewer and inspire new artistic vocations.

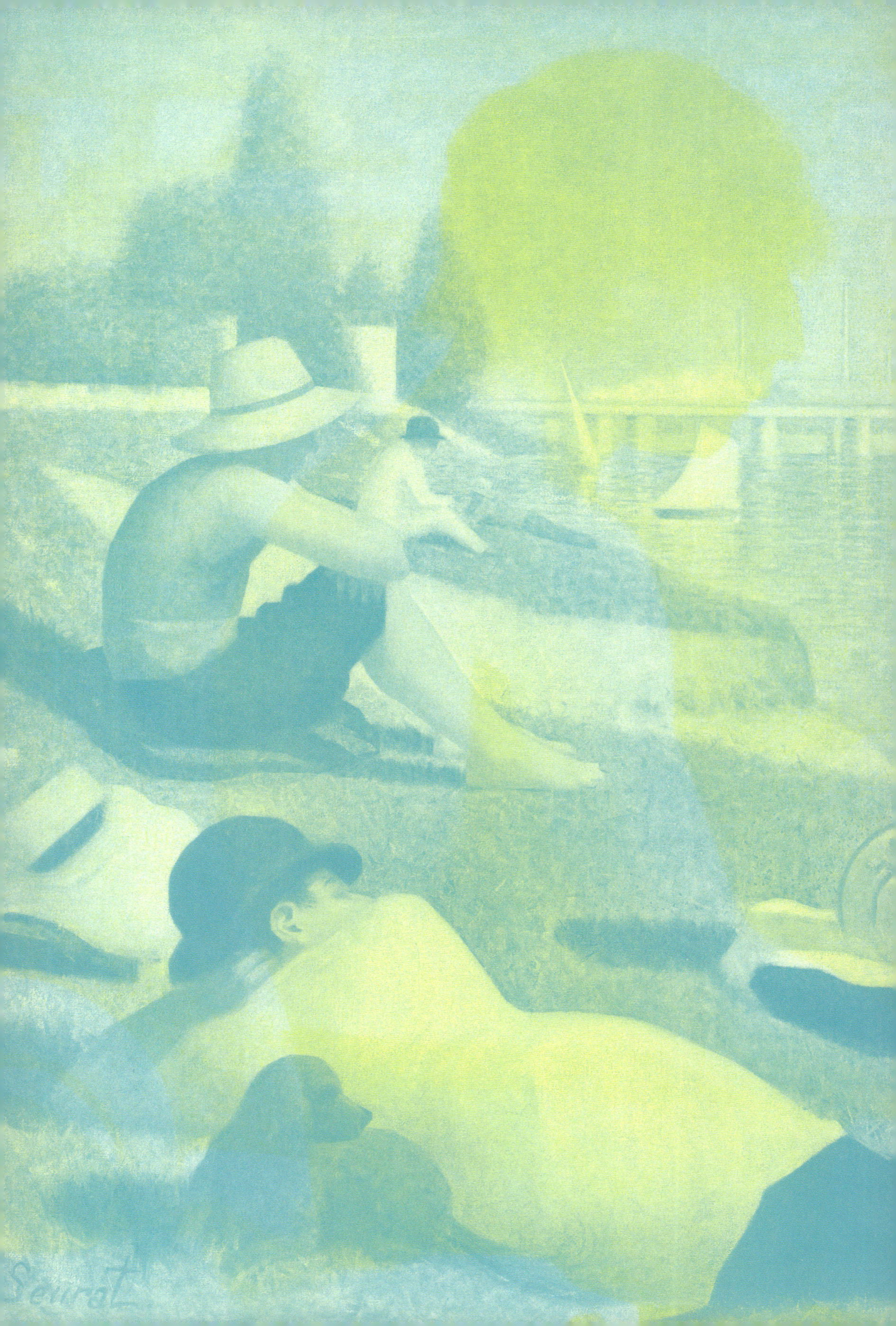
Seurat

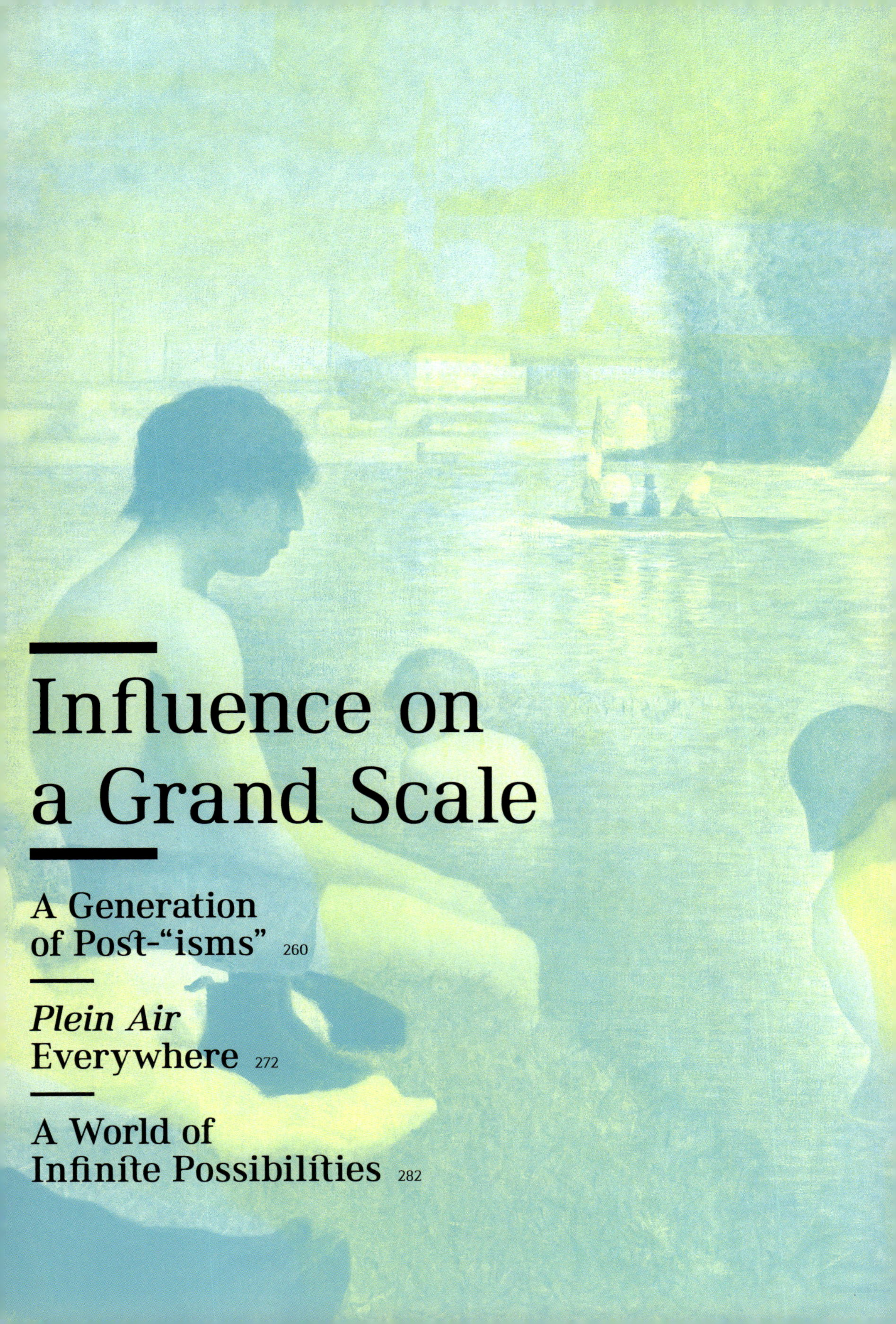

Influence on a Grand Scale

A Generation of Post-"isms" 260

Plein Air Everywhere 272

A World of Infinite Possibilities 282

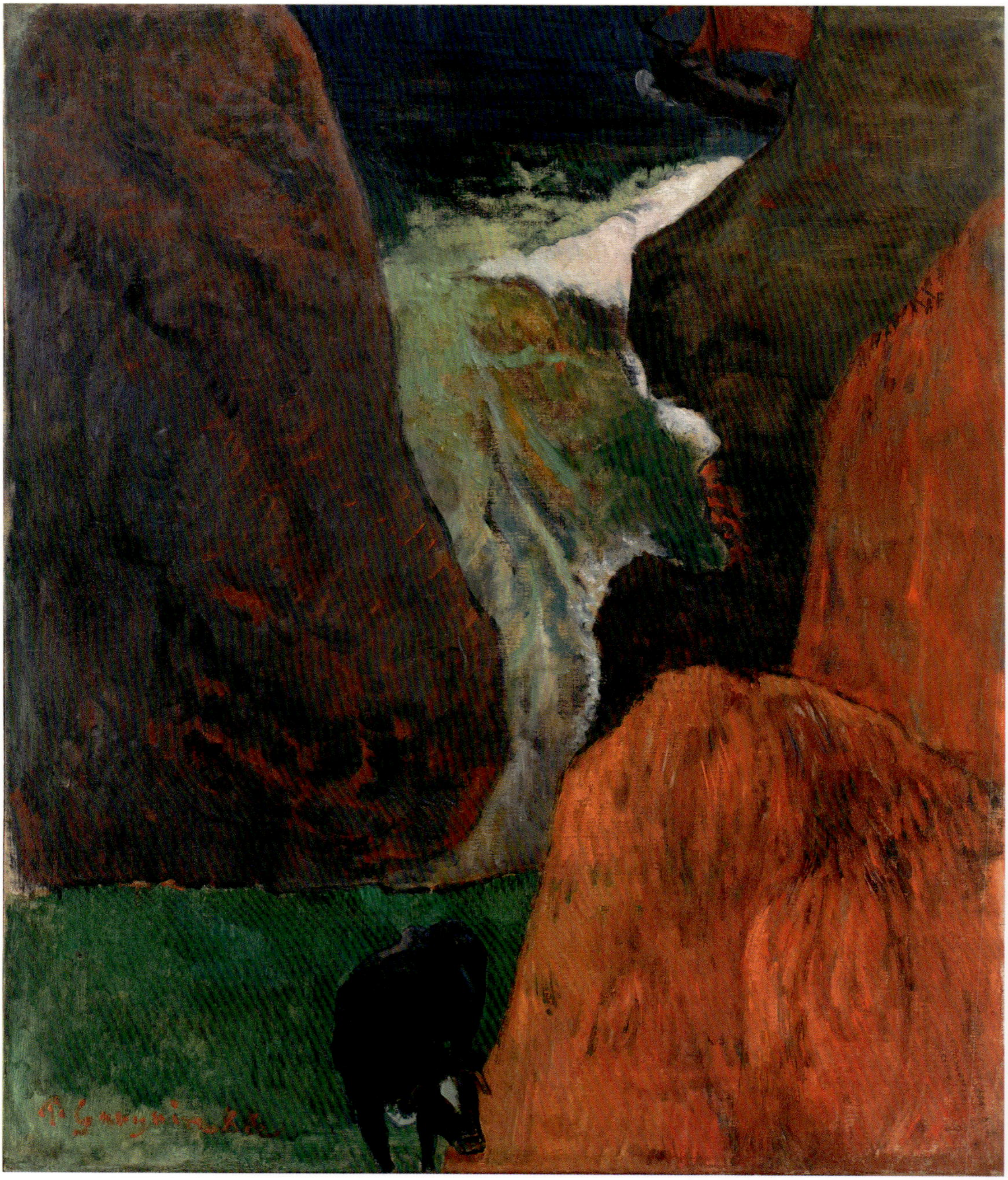

Paul Gauguin
Seascape with Cow on the Edge of the Cliff
1888
Oil on canvas, 25 ½ × 24 in. (72.5 × 61 cm)
Musée d'Orsay, Paris

A Generation of Post-"isms"

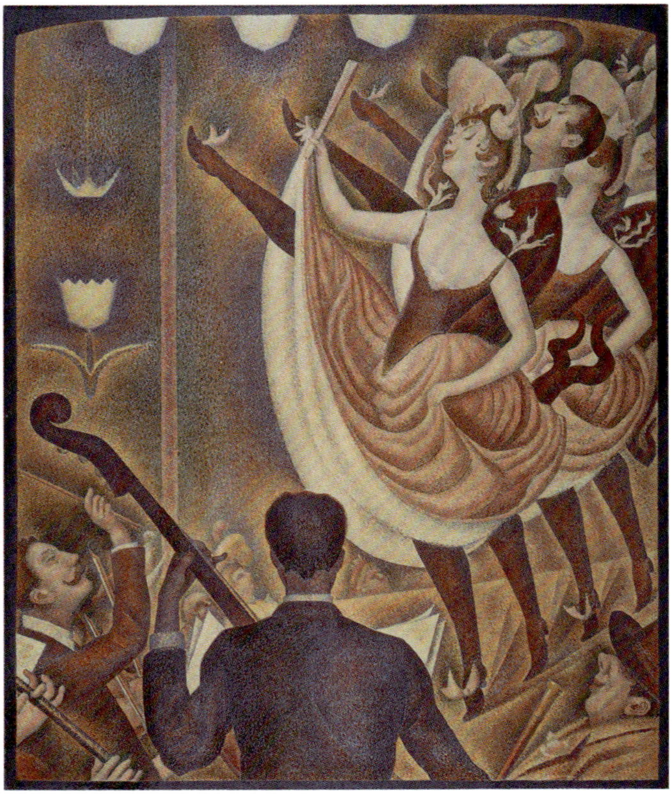

Georges Seurat
The Can-Can
1890
Oil on canvas, 5 ft. 6 ½ in. × 4 ft. 7 ½ in.
(1.69 × 1.41 m)
Kröller-Müller Museum, Otterlo

Revolutionary and innovative across many fields, impressionism paved the way for phenomenal artistic growth and development. Its legacy left a mark on all the avant-gardist styles, which succeeded one another at an ever-quickening pace. The trends of the future were already discernible as the impressionist group extended its reach. The eighth and last of their exhibitions in 1886 introduced newcomers Georges Seurat (1859-1891) and Paul Signac (1863-1935). Pissarro had been won over by their theories, and successfully negotiated to have the younger artists included. Initiated by Seurat, neo-impressionism pushed the fragmentation of the brushstroke and the use of pure color even further than the impressionists had. His studies led to pointillism, which applied almost to the letter Chevreul's scientific theories on the simultaneous contrast of colors. It was a concept that had originally inspired the impressionists. Pointillism is

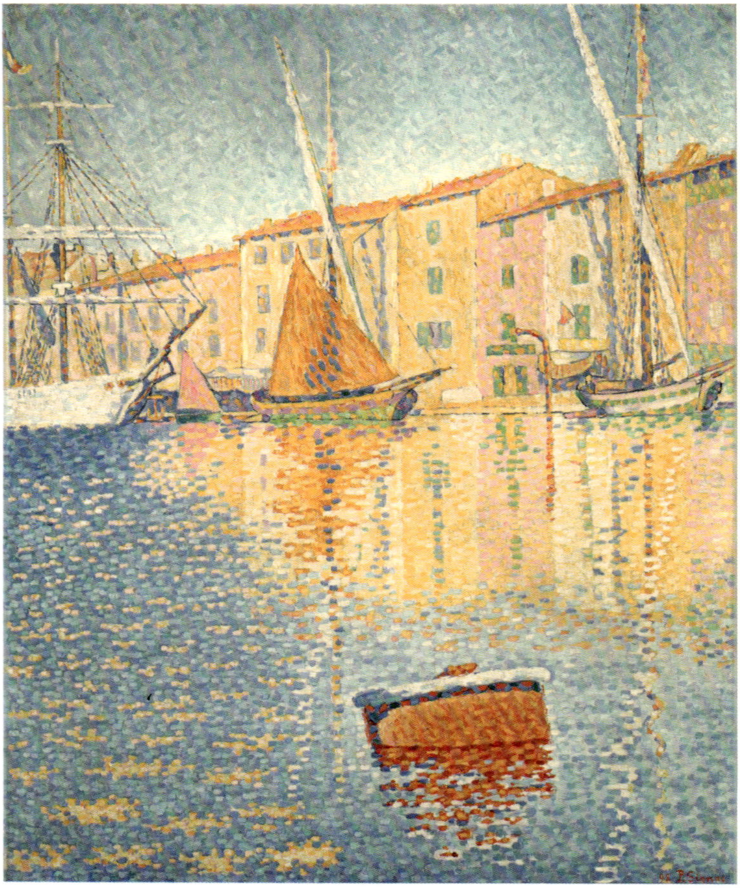

Paul Signac
The Red Buoy, Saint-Tropez
1895
Oil on canvas, 2 ft. × 3 ft. 1 ½ in. (61 × 95 cm)
Musée d'Orsay, Paris

"Neo-impressionism does not make dots—it divides. Division provides all the benefits of luminosity, coloration, and harmony by: (1) the optical blending of uniquely pure pigments; (2) the separation of various elements (local color, light color, and their interactions); (3) the balance of colors, etc."

Paul Signac, "From Eugène Delacroix to Neo-impressionism," *La Revue blanche*, 1899.

painstaking work: paint is applied using minuscule dots that the retina recomposes into the desired color effects. This new school painted views of Paris, outings to the countryside, and popular recreational activities—all subjects favored by the impressionists. Based on sketches drawn from nature, their canvases were executed in the studio using an almost scientifically rigorous technique that ultimately exhausted Georges Seurat, who died at a young age. It also took a toll on the school's other principal exponents Paul Signac, Henri Edmond Cross (1856–1910), Maximilien Luce (1858–1941), and Charles Angrand (1854–1926).

Gauguin began collaborating with the impressionists in 1879, participating in the fourth exhibition and continuing through the final show. Exceedingly independent, he demonstrated a unique style from the outset of his career. His synthetic approach utilized patches of color to define the flat pictorial space of the picture plane, embracing a vision transposed from reality. In search of authenticity, Gauguin took the radical step of leaving Paris to seek new horizons in Brittany. His quest later drove him to remote

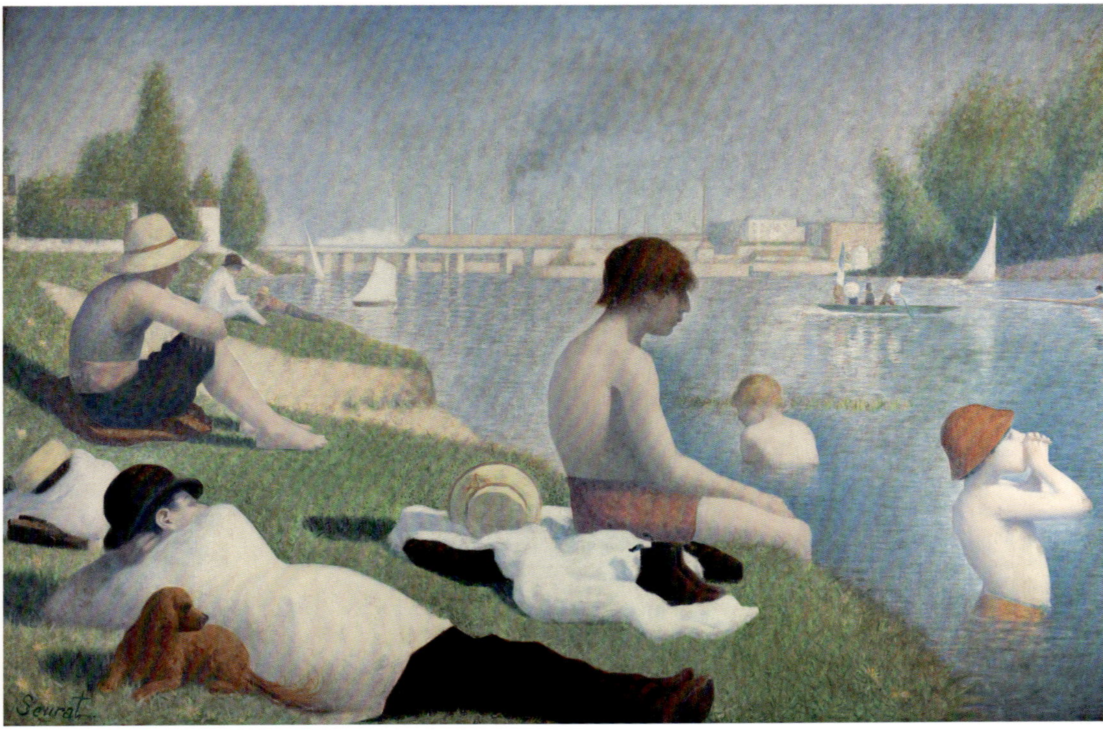

Rejected by the official Salon, Seurat exhibited at the Salon des Indépendants. He painted favorite impressionist themes, and inspired Pissarro, who was seeking new inspiration, to adopt this new technique.

Georges Seurat
Bathers at Asnières
1884
Oil on canvas, 6 ft. 7 ¼ in. × 9 ft. 10 in.
(2.01 × 3.00 m)
National Gallery, London

ARTIST THEORETICIANS

The impressionists were artists first and foremost, and they left it to others—advocates or antagonists—to name or decipher their work. Their successors, on the other hand, preferred to speak for themselves. Seurat elucidated his own theories and relayed them through Fénéon, his appointed spokesman. Gauguin willingly took up his pen to explain himself. Before anyone else could do it for them, the Nabis chose their own name and used the press to communicate and proclaim their vision. Over the course of the twentieth century, this practice culminated in the issuing of "manifestos" by avant-garde groups. These collective professions of faith were explicit and insistent, and they accompanied the birth of almost every new artistic movement.

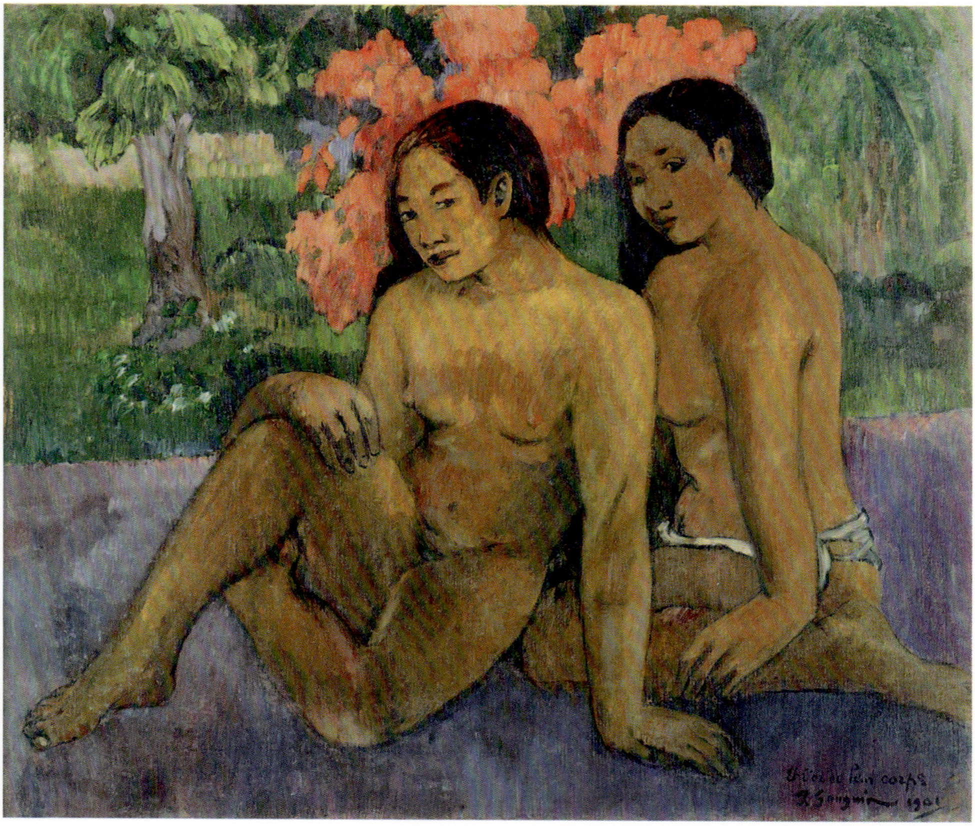

Paul Gauguin
And the Gold of Their Bodies
1901
Oil on canvas, 26 ⅜ × 31 ⅛ in. (67 × 79 cm)
Musée d'Orsay, Paris

"Don't copy nature too closely; art is an abstraction; take it from nature, dreaming as you behold it, and think about creation more than the result."

Paul Gauguin, letter to Emile Schuffenecker, August 1888.

destinations including Martinique, Tahiti, and the Marquesas Islands. In these distant places, "the savage" (as Gauguin called himself) finally found the genuine, primitive form of expression he sought.

Although subjected to virulent criticism over many long years, impressionism soon came to represent a liberating break and an exhilarating experience for young artists. They used the style as an inspiration for their own flight to freedom. When Vincent Van Gogh (1853-1890) arrived in Paris in 1886, he immediately adopted the impressionist manner, abandoning his earthy palette in the process. He did not participate in the group's exhibitions, but this Parisian interlude marked a decisive turning point in the

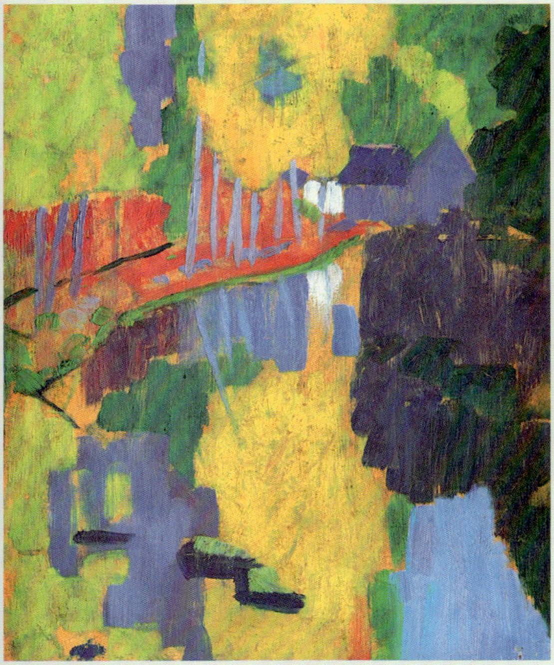

Paul Sérusier
The Talisman, also known as
The Aven River at the Bois d'Amour
1888
Oil on wood, 10 ⅝ × 8 ½ in. (27 × 21.5 cm)
Musée d'Orsay, Paris

This work, which became a talisman for the Nabis, was executed under the direction of Gauguin. Maurice Denis reports the lesson this way: "How do you see these trees?" "They're yellow." "So, use yellow. This shadow's rather blue, so use pure ultramarine to paint it. For the red leaves? Use vermilion."

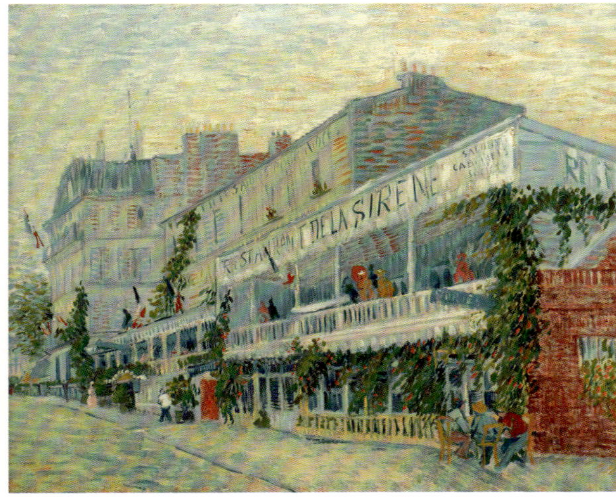

Vincent Van Gogh
The Restaurant de la Sirène at Asnières
1887
Oil on canvas, 21 ¼ × 25 ⅝ in. (54 × 65 cm)
Musée d'Orsay, Paris

Van Gogh's abrupt transition to bright colors and his embrace of more cheerful subjects, like this view of a restaurant on the banks of the Seine, demonstrate the immediate impact of impressionism on his work. Up until that point, he favored dark, somber tonalities.

artist's work. He soon found his own distinctive style: pure color, applied in patches and often outlined in black. His highly visible brushstrokes became increasingly agitated as the symptoms of his mental illness intensified.

The similarity is striking. Twenty years after the impressionists first gathered, the founding core group of a new school of painting met in the Académie Julian, one of the "free" schools. It was now 1888, and these comrades referred to themselves as the "Nabis." (The choice of this word, which means "prophet" in Hebrew, proclaimed their goal of seeking a new path that was both independent and visionary.) The Nabis frequented Pont-Aven, a small Breton village. Sérusier, who was then painting

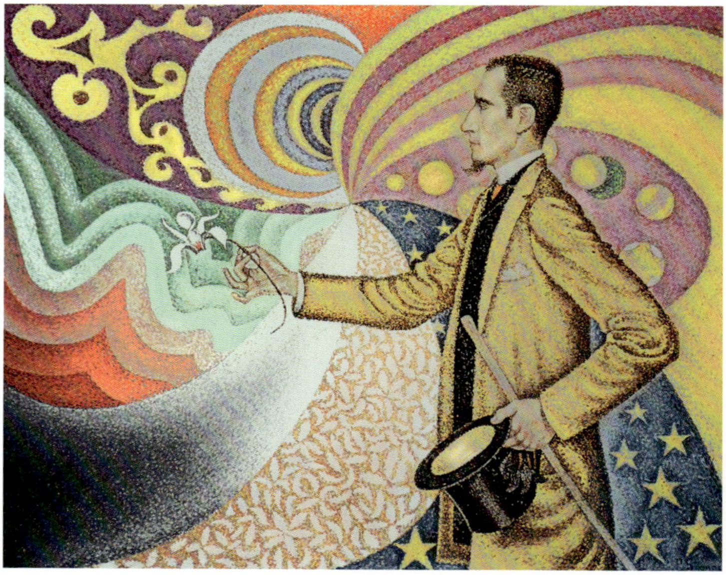

Paul Signac
Opus 217. Against the Enamel of a Background Rhythmic with Beats and Angles, Tones, and Tints, Portrait of M. Félix Fénéon in 1890
1890
Oil on canvas, 2 ft. 5 in. × 3 ft. ½ in. (73.5 × 92.5 cm)
Museum of Modern Art, New York

The Talisman (1888) under Gauguin's direction, received a masterly lesson there. Gauguin asserted the complete subjectivity of the artist above and beyond the subject matter. This lesson was another step along the path originally taken by the impressionists. Each Nabi appropriated aspects of the message in order to evolve individually. Maurice Denis chose to take a mystical direction; Ker-Xavier Roussel inclined toward primitivism. Pierre Bonnard and Jean Édouard Vuillard selected a distinctively intimist approach; their predilection for depictions of family life was a direct legacy of the impressionists, as was the fragmentation of their brushstrokes. The influence of Japanese art is very often perceptible in their compositions and framing of subjects.

Impressionist principles–rejection of convention, affirmation of the artist, arbitrary use of color, aversion to mimicry–were abrupt breaks with tradition. Their revolutionary ideas continued to inspire all the artists and movements of twentieth-century art. That small group of impressionist painters did more than create a new style or technique: they proclaimed to the next generation that the events of 1870 were irreversible. Artistic freedom must be full and complete. With this premise as a starting point, in art, everything became permissible.

FÉLIX FÉNÉON (1861–1944): DEFENDER OF NEO-IMPRESSIONISM

From the moment it was first introduced, neo-impressionism was scorned just as impressionism had been in its early years. But the new movement had an important advantage that made a profound difference: the full and complete support of a respected critic, Félix Fénéon. His writings gave substance to the theories adopted by Seurat and his friends. This close association between a critic and an artistic movement was unprecedented, but it was a formula that was to recur throughout the twentieth century: Apollinaire supported the cubists, Breton crowned himself the leading light of surrealism, and Pierre Restany became the spokesman for the New Realists.

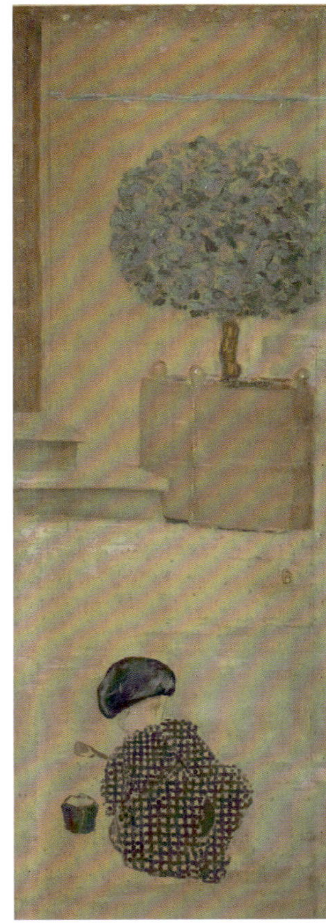

Pierre Bonnard
Child Making a Sand Castle (detail)
1894–95
5 ft. 5 ¾ in. × 1 ft. 7 ¾ in. (167 × 50 cm)
Musée d'Orsay, Paris

"Remember that a picture–before being a warhorse, a female nude, or a tale–is basically a flat surface covered with colors arranged in a particular order."

Maurice Denis, *Art et Critique*, 1890.

Édouard Vuillard
Public Gardens: Nannies, Conversation, The Red Parasol
1894
Oil on canvas, 6 ft. 11 ¾ in. × 5 ft. ¾ in.
(2.13 × 1.54 m)
Musée d'Orsay, Paris

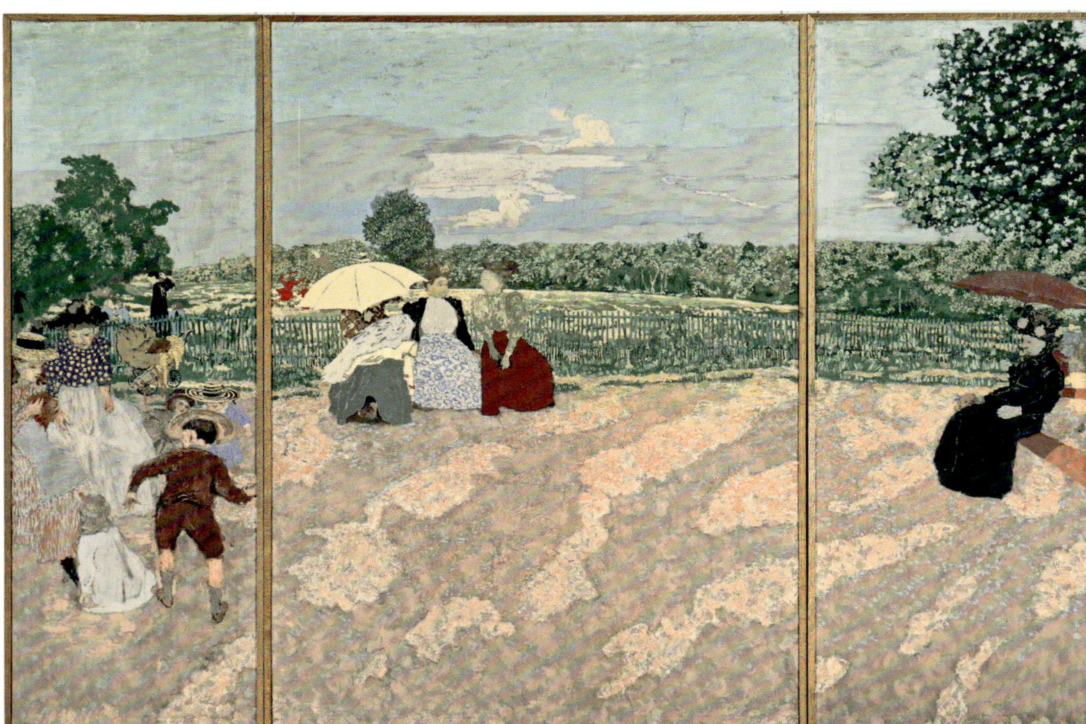

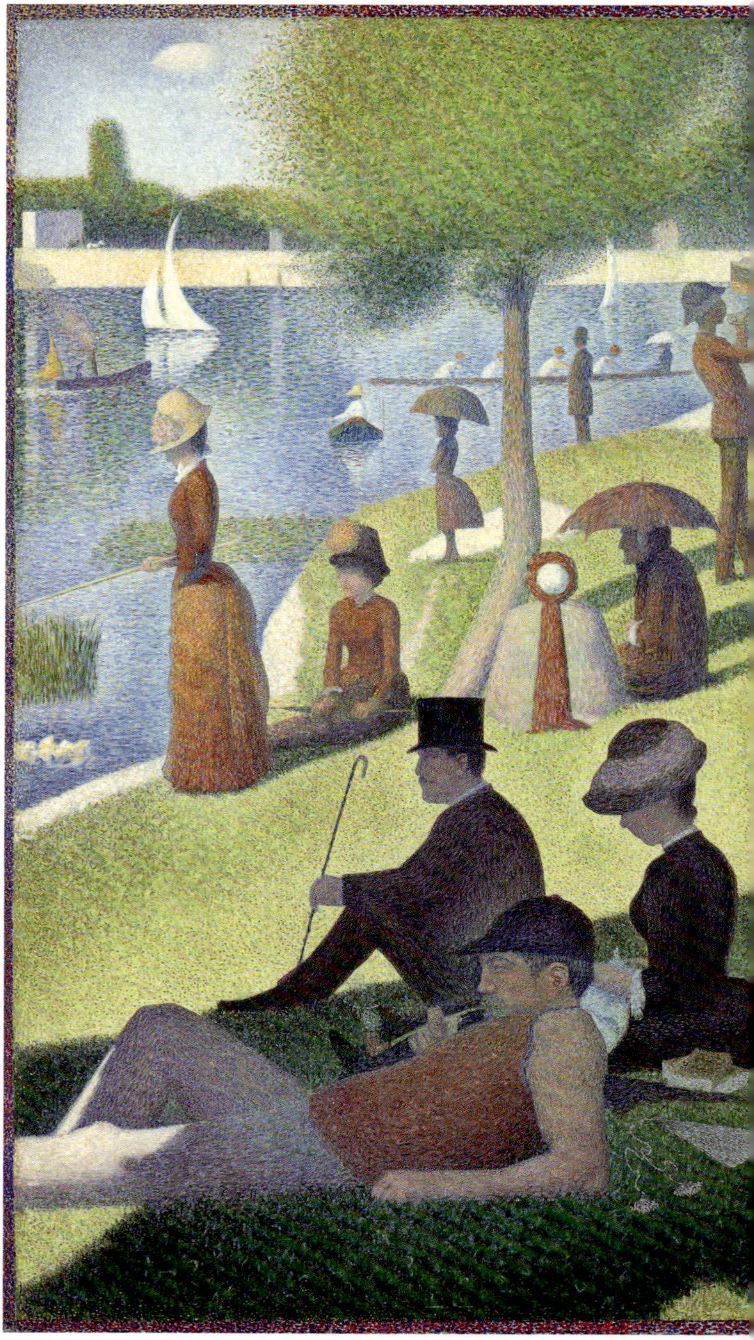

Georges Seurat
A Sunday on La Grande Jatte
1884–86
Oil on canvas,
6 ft. 9 ¾ in. × 10 ft. 1 ¼ in.
(2.08 × 3.08 m)
The Helen Birch Bartlett
Memorial Collection,
The Art Institute of Chicago,
Chicago

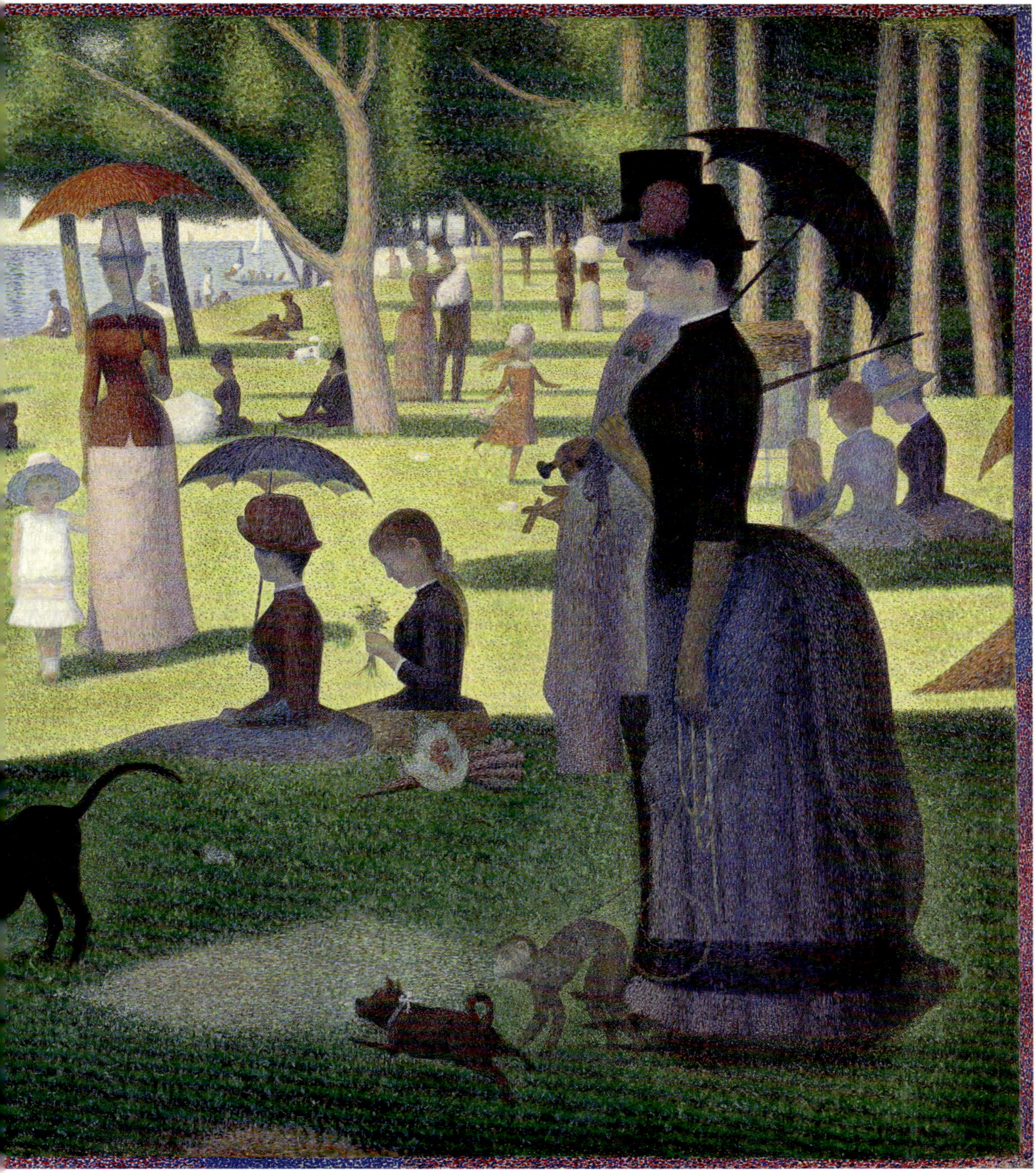

A Sunday on La Grande Jatte

Georges Seurat, 1884-86

Presented at the eighth and last impressionist exhibition, this large canvas reveals the experimental spirit of the young Seurat. He was the standard-bearer of the movement that was soon to overtake impressionism. His choice of subject–leisure activities by the river on a Sunday afternoon–was on a continuum with impressionism, but the approach to modeling indicates a new direction.

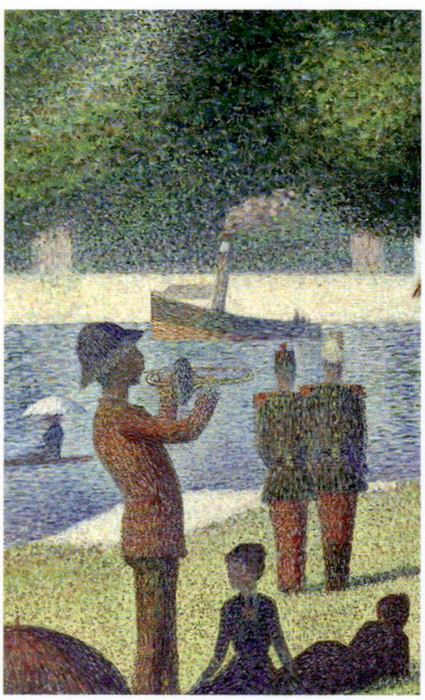

The use of divided brushstrokes follows to the letter Chevreul's scientific theories on the decomposition of colors. The application of tiny dots of pure color to the canvas eventually creates the desired tones. This extremely fastidious and demanding work was executed in the artist's studio.

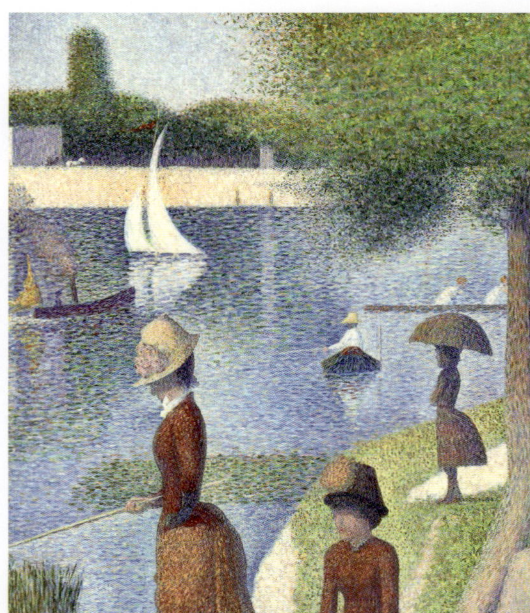

We see many of the impressionists' favorite subjects in this picture: the passing sailboats, the play of light and shadow, and the reflections on the water.

With his very different pictorial approach, Seurat used expanses of shadow and light to convey the experience of a lovely summer day.

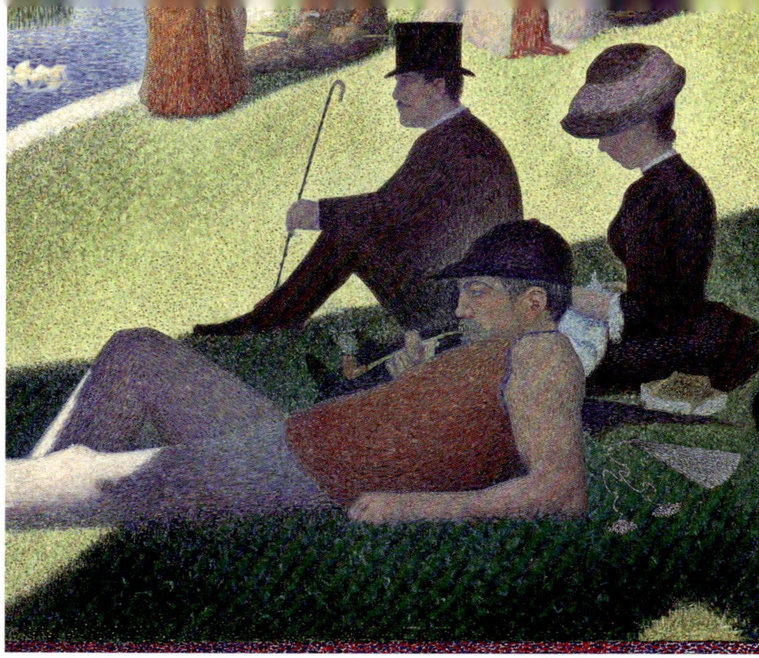

The Seine's riverbank, where social classes mingled for a relaxing Sunday afternoon, was a contemporary subject that the impressionists had embraced fifteen years earlier.

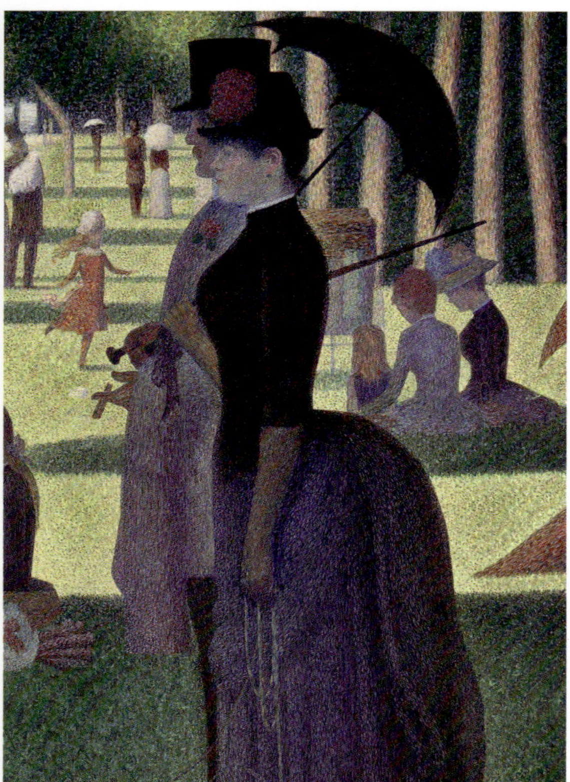

Seurat's meticulous technique has a hieratic effect that is at odds with the impressionist approach. In impressionist works, the outlines are deliberately vague, the brushstrokes rapid, and there is a sense of shifting light and circulating air. Seurat's painting has a static, rigid quality, leading the skeptical critic Octave Mirbeau to refer to it as "an Egyptian fantasy."

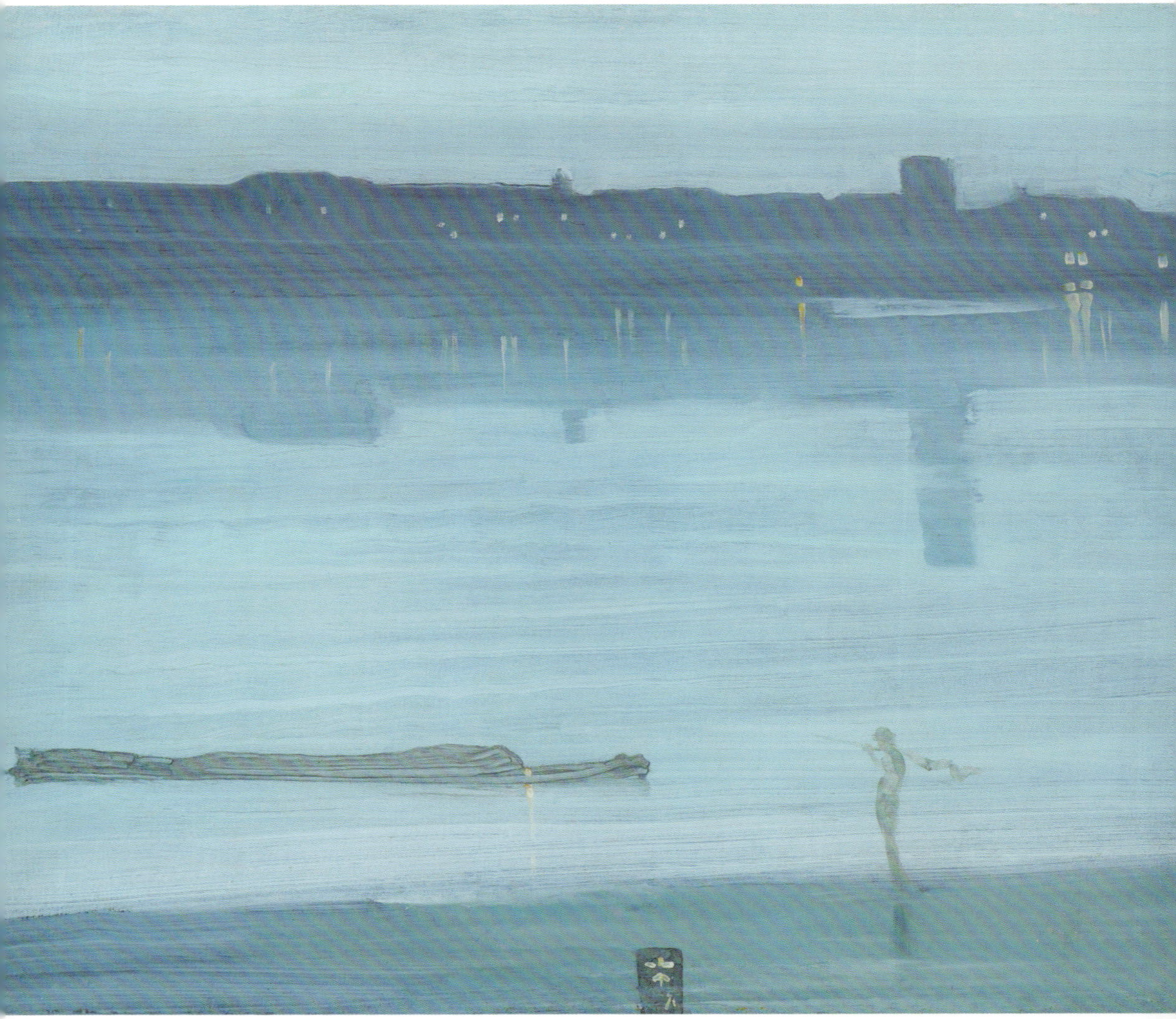

James Abbott McNeill Whistler
Nocturne: Blue and Silver–Chelsea
1871
Oil on wood, 19 ¾ × 23 ⅞ in. (50.2 × 60.8 cm)
Tate Collection, London

Plein Air Everywhere

Impressionism originated in France, around Paris, along the loops of the Seine and the coastline of Normandy. It was a style that soon spread beyond the confines of its native land. The movement's ideas circulated through the writings of its supporters and the initiatives of the gallerist Durand-Ruel, who was eager to display the works of the painters to an international audience. The artists traveled as well to England, Italy, and even Norway, which Monet visited in 1895. However, Paris remained the artistic capital, attracting young talents who thronged there to complete their training. The American artist Mary Cassatt moved to Paris to join the impressionist group. Many other foreign artists visited the city, absorbing the lessons of impressionism and later disseminating them back in their own countries.

Impressionism soon found followers all over Europe, particularly in Germany and Belgium, thanks to Durand-Ruel's activism. This trend was epitomized in the figure of the German painter Max Liebermann (1847–1935), who was won over by the impressionist style and began to collect works by artists of the group. He played the role of intermediary in Berlin for collectors and museum directors. In Brussels, from 1886 onward, the impressionist and neo-impressionist artists participated alongside Les XX and the Libre Esthétique. They exercised a direct influence that was particularly evident in the work of Théo Van Rysselberghe (1862–1926). Denmark, Sweden, and Norway

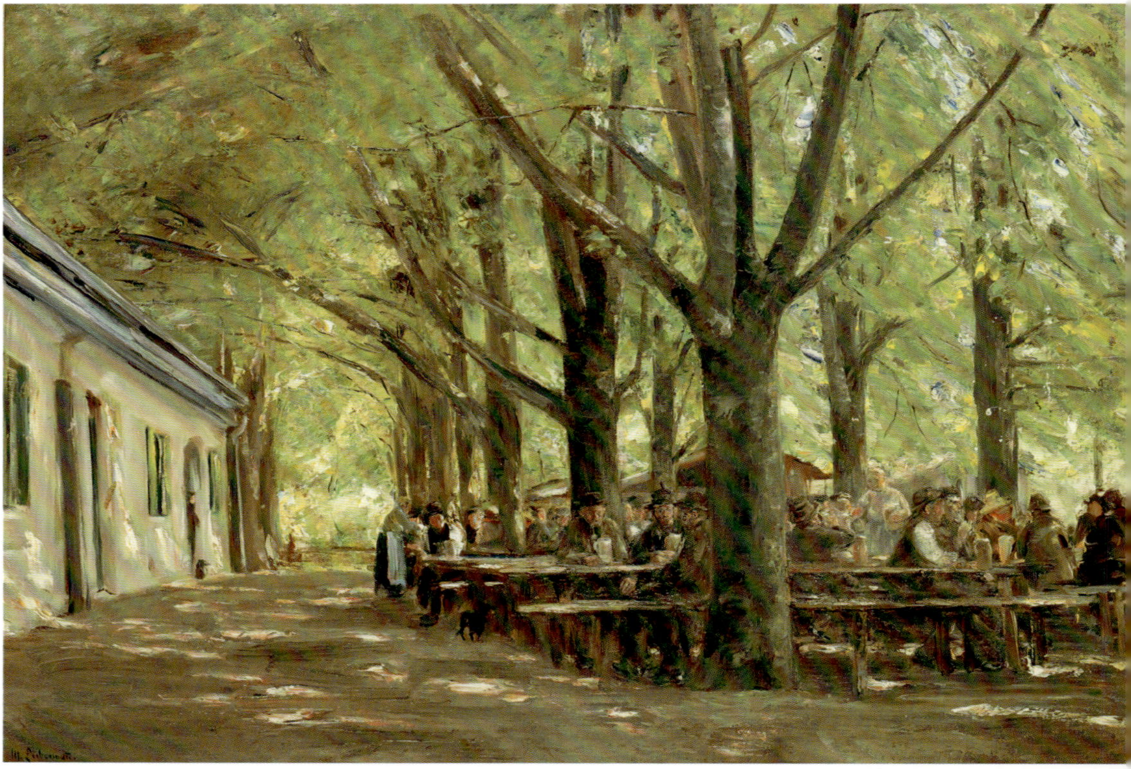

Max Liebermann
Country Pub in Brannenburg (Bavaria)
1893
Oil on canvas, 2 ft. 3 ½ in. × 3 ft. 3 ½ in.
(70 × 100 cm)
Musée d'Orsay, Paris

also embraced a freer, more colorful approach to landscape painting, which had finally been freed from the constraints of academic rules. The Norwegian painter Frits Thaulow (1847-1906) and the Swedish Carl Larsson (1853-1919) both studied the impressionists during their visits to Paris, and disseminated their ideas to their associates, each in his own way. Thaulow had been in Paris the year of the first impressionist exhibition and adopted *plein air* painting. He later participated in the International Exposition of Painting organized by Georges Petit, and retained his ties with the Parisian artistic scene throughout his life. Larsson had two extended stays in France, the first in Paris beginning in 1877, and the second from 1882 until 1889 in Grez-sur-Loing. He played an important role among the British and Scandinavian artists who had settled in the area around the forest of Fontainebleau, following the *plein air* painters. The British school of landscape painting had had a galvanizing effect on the early impressionists. However, impressionism had little direct influence on British art, aside from

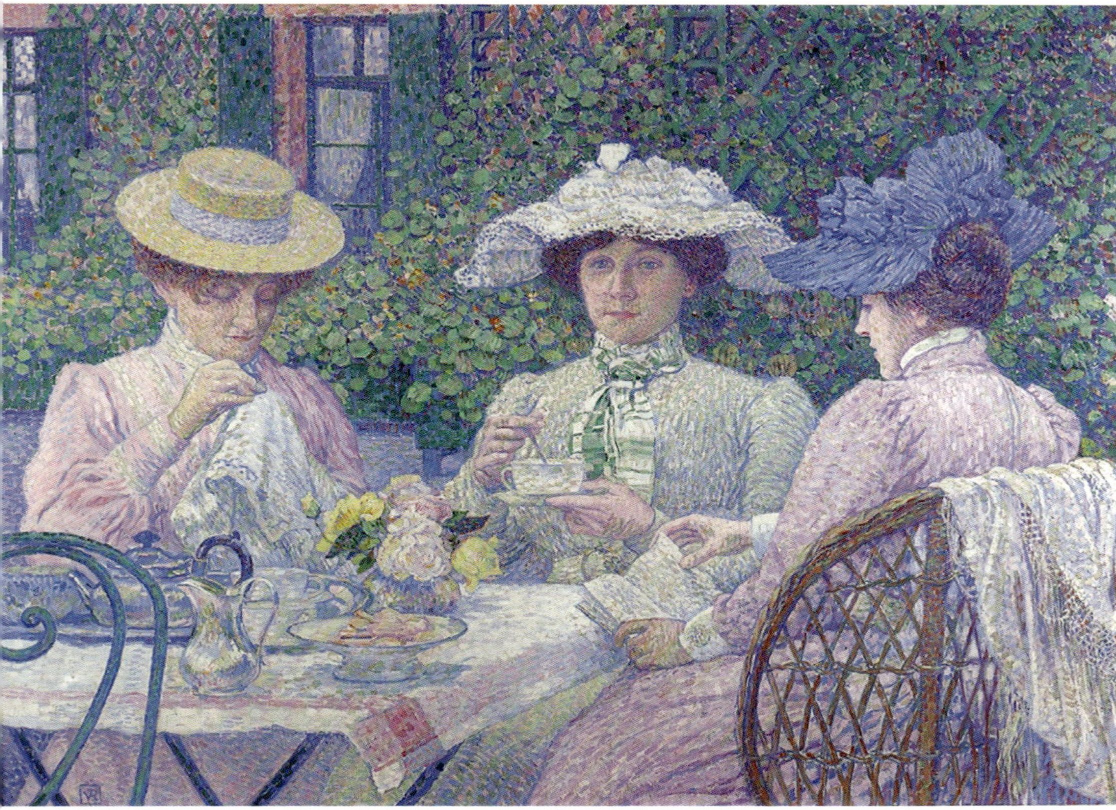

Théo Van Rysselberghe
Tea in the Garden
1903
Oil on canvas, 3 ft. 2 ½ in. × 4 ft. 3 ½ in.
(98 × 130 cm)
Musée d'Ixelles, Brussels

on Walter Sickert (1862-1942), who had extended stays in Dieppe between 1885 and 1922. It was in fact the American artist James Abbott Whistler (1834-1903) who established ties between London and Paris. Whistler arrived in Paris in 1855 to study painting and enrolled the following year in Gleyre's studio. He was soon assimilated into artistic circles, and the work he did in the 1860s foreshadowed impressionism to an astonishing degree. Whistler was close to Fantin-Latour, Manet, Degas, and the Goncourt brothers. Moving to London in 1859, he collected Japanese objets d'art for his house in Chelsea. Durand-Ruel exhibited Whistler's work in 1873, and the critics Duranty and Duret both applauded the paintings of this dandyish man-about-town; they viewed him as an exponent of impressionism.

In southern Europe, Spain was a decisive influence on Manet, who revered the great masters Velázquez and Goya, and traveled to Madrid in 1865 to study their work up close. Twenty years later, Joaquín Sorolla y Bastida (1863-1923) made the journey in reverse, arriving in Paris in 1885.

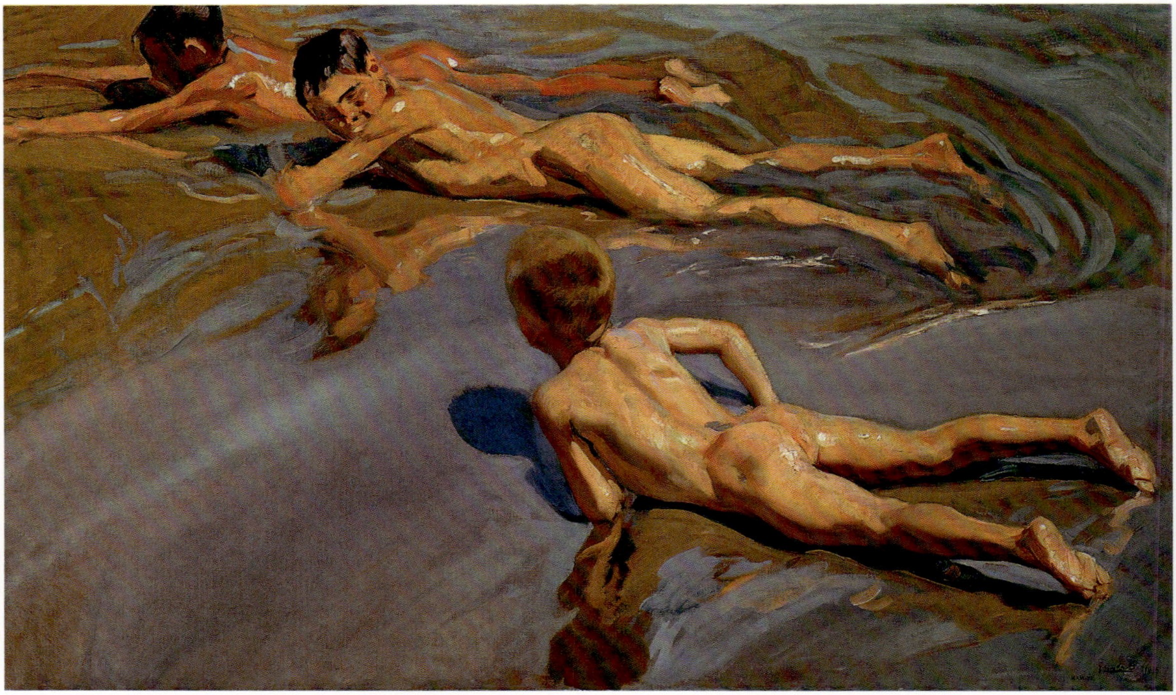

Joaquín Sorolla y Bastida
Children on the Beach
1909
Oil on canvas, 3 ft. 10 ½ in. × 6 ft. 1 in.
(1.18 × 1.85 m)
Museo Nacional del Prado, Madrid

The version of *plein air* painting that he developed through his study of impressionism earned him a medal at the 1900 Universal Exposition and another at an exhibition held in 1906 in the gallery run by Georges Petit, who was one of the strongest advocates of impressionism. In Italy, the liberation from conventional norms had begun in 1860 with a group of artists based in Florence, known as the Macchiaioli. Tired of the dominant schools of neoclassicism and romanticism, they introduced a new approach to painting. They were rejected, as the impressionists would be later, receiving their name from a hostile critic who saw nothing but "blotches" (*macchia* in Italian) in their work. This type of critical reaction was destined to have a long history.

Impressionism came to the United States in 1883 with Durand-Ruel's showing of works by Manet, Monet, Renoir, Pissarro, and Sisley at the International Exhibition in Boston. This show was a prelude to the large exhibition that the gallery owner organized in New York at the invitation

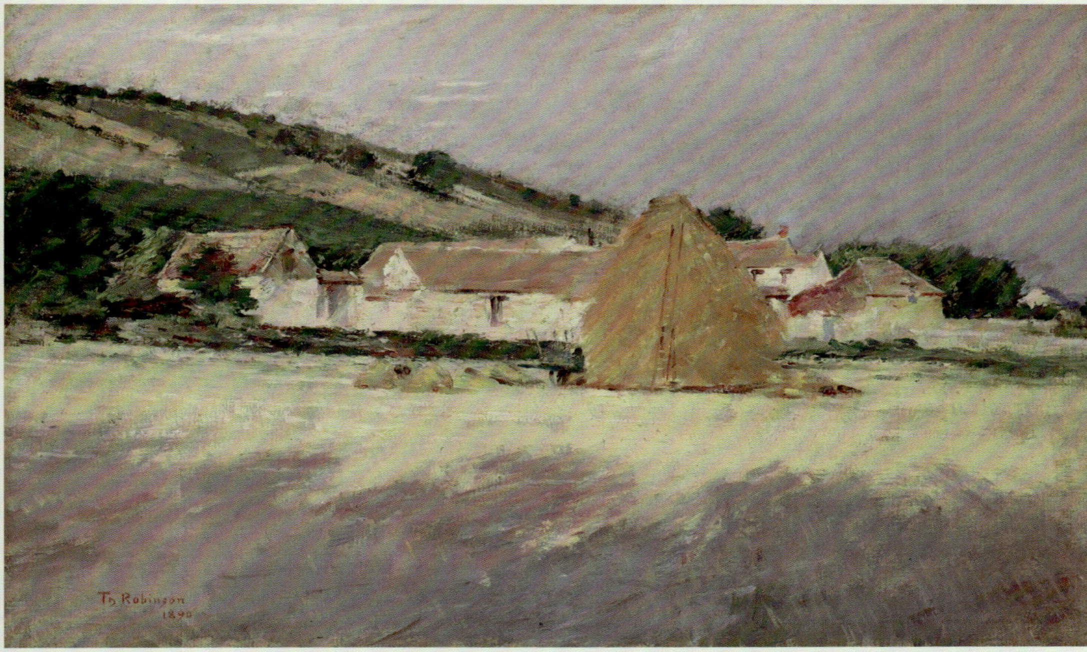

Monet quickly distanced himself from the colony's artists, who had settled close to his home in Giverny, but he developed an enduring friendship with Theodore Robinson. When Robinson returned to the United States in the early 1890s, he continued spreading his knowledge of impressionism through teaching, until his premature death in 1896.

Theodore Robinson
Scene in Giverny
1890
Oil on canvas, 16 × 25 ¾ in. (40.6 × 65.4 cm)
Detroit Institute of Arts, Detroit

of the American Art Association. A number of Americans, including William Merritt Chase (1849–1916), were already familiar with these artistic innovations, having spent time in Paris during their years of training. Childe Hassam (1859–1953) was already painting *en plein air* when he visited Europe in 1883. He lived in Paris for three years beginning in 1886. When he returned to America, he became in 1898 one of the founders of the artistic collaboration known as The Ten. Their objective was to establish a distinct artistic vocabulary, free of conventional restraints. Durand-Ruel came across these artists and exhibited their work in his New York gallery that same year. Meanwhile, in France, a colony of American painters was attracted by the revered figure of Monet. They gathered in Giverny from 1887 onward, becoming a focal point for the spread of impressionism. Among them was Theodore Robinson (1852–1896). He was a close friend of Monet's, and became a strong advocate of impressionism in France and the United States.

IMAGES IN THE SPOTLIGHT

James Abbott McNeill Whistler
Nocturne: Blue and Gold–
Old Battersea Bridge
c. 1872–75
Oil on canvas, 26 ⅞ × 20 ⅛ in.
(68.3 × 51.2 cm)
Tate Collection, London

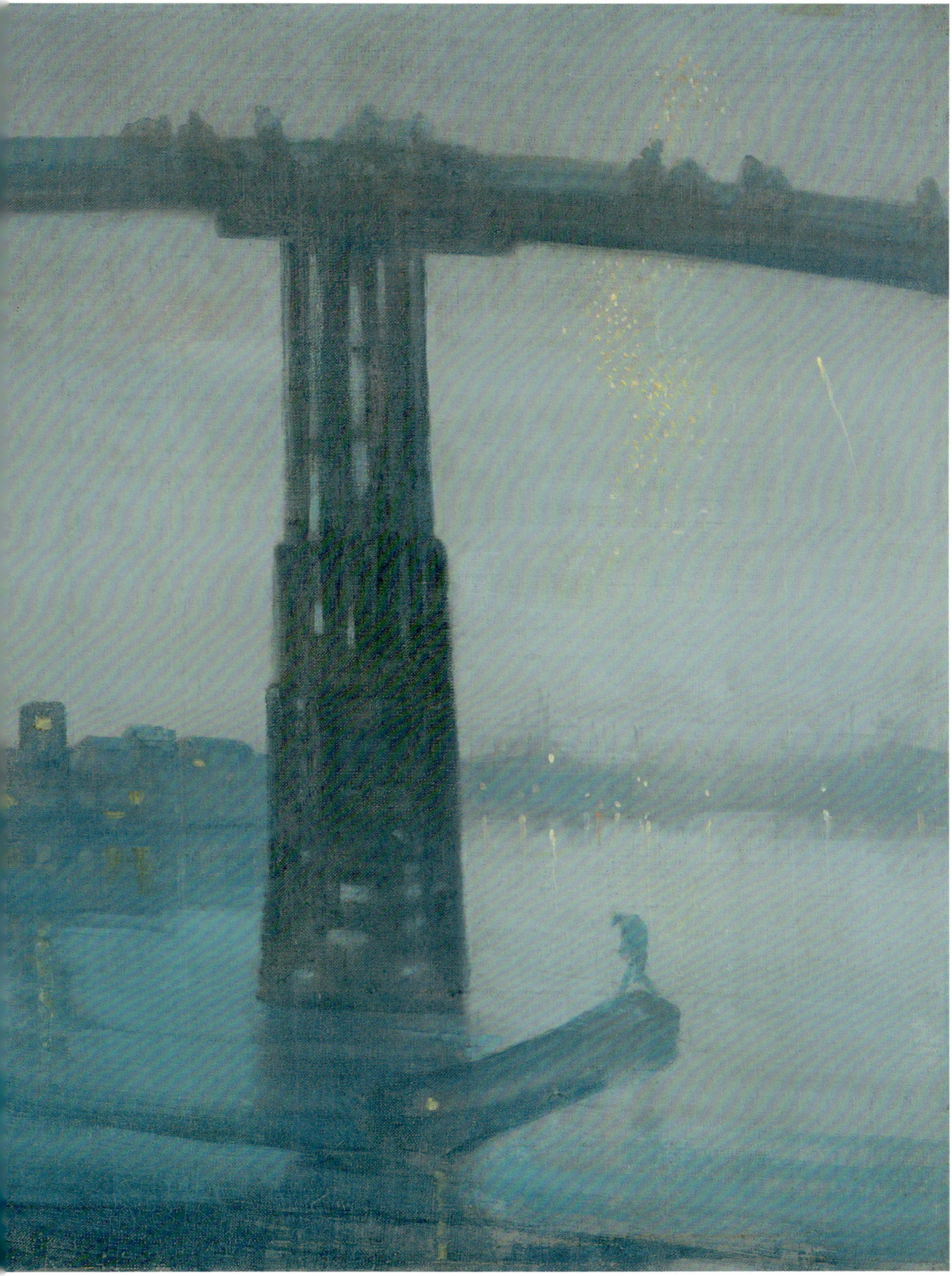

Nocturne: Blue and Gold–Old Battersea Bridge

James Abbott McNeill Whistler, c. 1872–75

A forerunner of the impressionists, the American artist Whistler was the movement's leading exponent in England. The influence of Japanese art, the subtlety of his palette with its refined pastel tonalities, and a certain mannered restraint characterized his very individualistic oeuvre.

Emphasized by the bridge's vertical support, the picture's elongated format recalls the panel of a Japanese screen.

A MUSICAL AIR

"Symphony," "nocturne," "variations"—the titles that Whistler gave to his paintings demonstrate his profound affinity with music, while his tone-on-tone palette defies painterly conventions.

WHISTLER AND PAINTING IN SERIES

This work was exhibited in 1876 under the title *Nocturne in Blue and Silver No. 5*, before being renamed in 1892. It was conceived from the outset as part of a series that Whistler was painting on the banks of the Thames in the 1870s. Whistler did not paint directly from nature, but he did give pride of place to his painterly impressions and sensibilities. Beginning in 1861, he was the first artist to work in series, well before Monet, who would later execute multiple compositions based on the same subject.

The reflection of lights on the river's calm waters seems to be the real subject of this work, just as it would become for the impressionists.

The dramatic intersection of the bridge's pier and roadway creates a barrier that boldly transects the picture's space. It is a direct reference to the Japanese prints that Whistler, an avid collector, so deeply admired.

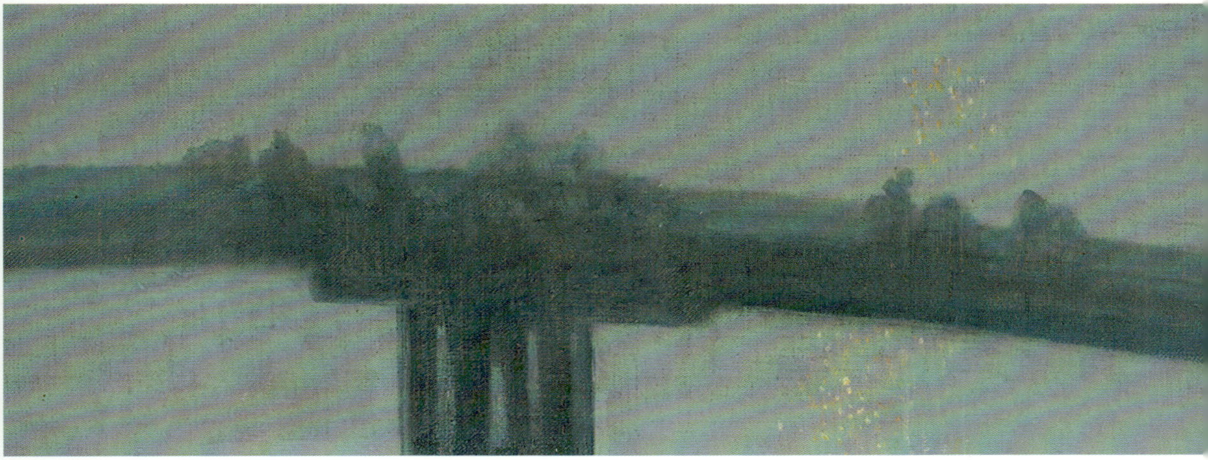

The boatman and the figures on the bridge are reduced to simplified notations. Any suggestion of anecdote or narrative is eliminated, leaving the canvas free to express pure impression.

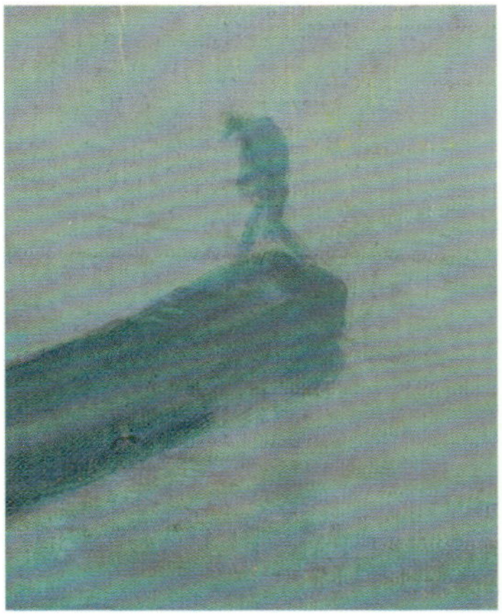

"These are impressions of my own; I make them my study."

Whistler, during the lawsuit he brought in 1878 against John Ruskin, who had harshly attacked the painter in one of his critical articles.

The foggy mists in the background and the glitter of fireworks in the sky demonstrate the painter's interest in capturing the ephemeral and impermanent.

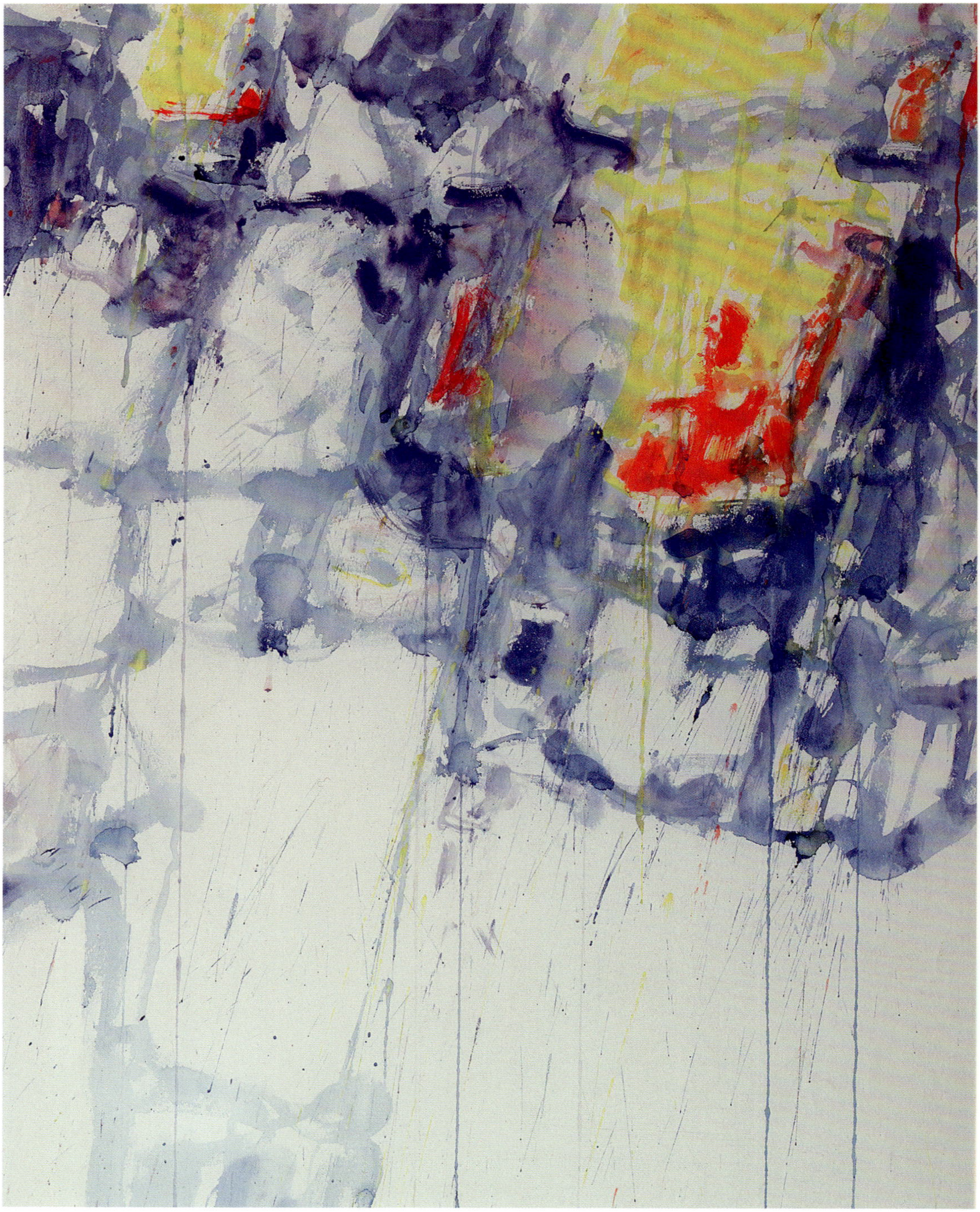

Sam Francis
Composition 1957
1957
Watercolor and gouache on paper,
30 ⅜ × 22 ¼ in. (77 × 56.5 cm)
Pallant House Gallery, Chichester

A World of Infinite Possibilities

Breaking the stranglehold, defying the rules, saying no to convention, inventing new ways of painting, and of being an artist: the impressionist revolution opened a world of infinite possibilities. Impressionism upended a system that was lackluster and moribund. It dealt the deathblow to tired academicism, and heralded the advent of a new era. All subsequent artistic movements would owe impressionism some form of debt.

In abandoning studio painting, the impressionists did more than breathe fresh air into the discipline. Painting from nature marked the beginning of physical involvement in the act of creation, breaking with the artist's traditionally safe position sitting in front of an easel. Taking the train to Argenteuil or the Normandy coast was more than a bid to capture the mood of the moment. It marked the beginning of the artist's physical involvement and the experience of being a stakeholder in the act of creation. It was

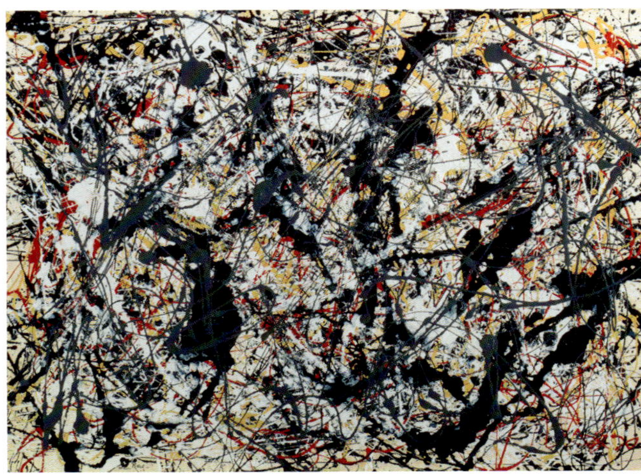

Jackson Pollock
Painting (Silver over Black, White, Yellow, and Red)
1948
Paint on paper mounted on canvas, 23 ⅝ × 31 ½ in. (60.1 × 80 cm)
Musée National d'Art Moderne/Centre de Création Industrielle, Centre Georges Pompidou, Paris

Painting a canvas laid on the floor with almost choreographed movements, Jackson Pollock invented the "all-over" style. Without borders or center, the painting escapes from the frame. This is a revolutionary concept, originally initiated by Monet with his *Water Lilies*.

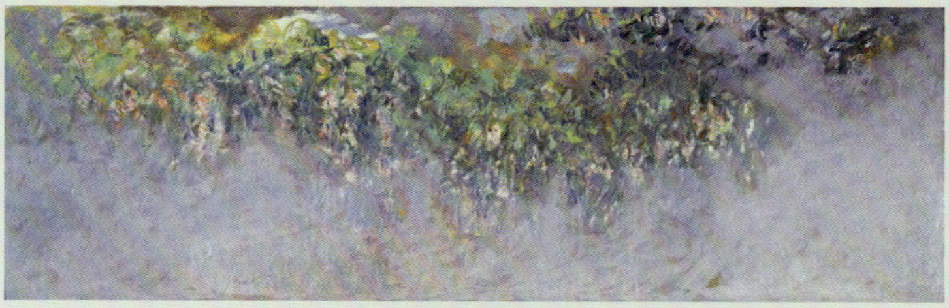

Claude Monet
Wisteria
1919–20
Oil on canvas, 3 ft. 3 ½ in. × 9 ft. 10 in. (1.0 × 3.0 m)
Musée Marmottan, Paris

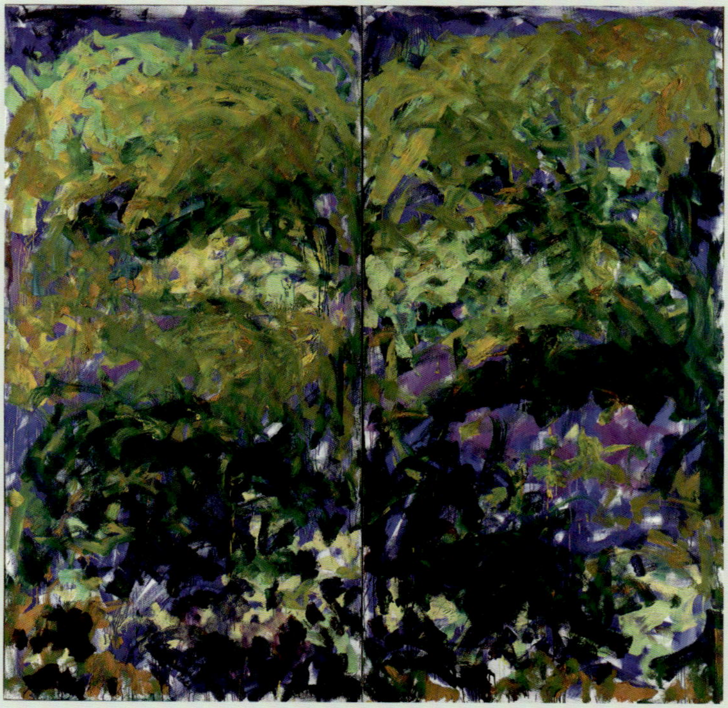

Joan Mitchell
The Grande Vallée IX (diptych)
1983–84
Oil on canvas, 8 ft. 6 ½ in. × 8 ft. 6 ½ in. (2.6 × 2.6 m)
Frac Normandie Collection, Rouen

Monet who unquestionably pushed this sense of merging with the subject to the maximum, practicing an instinctual art that heralded Jackson Pollock's lyrical abstraction decades later. Monet was the first and strongest advocate of rapid execution, gestural expression, and the physical aspect of painting. By the early 1950s his legacy had swept across both sides of the Atlantic. Long ignored, his *Water Lilies* in the Orangerie suddenly assumed an astonishing modernity, which continued in the work of the American abstract painter Sam Francis and the collaborating artists Joan Mitchell and Jean-Paul Riopelle, who actually moved to Vétheuil and then to Giverny, where the master himself had

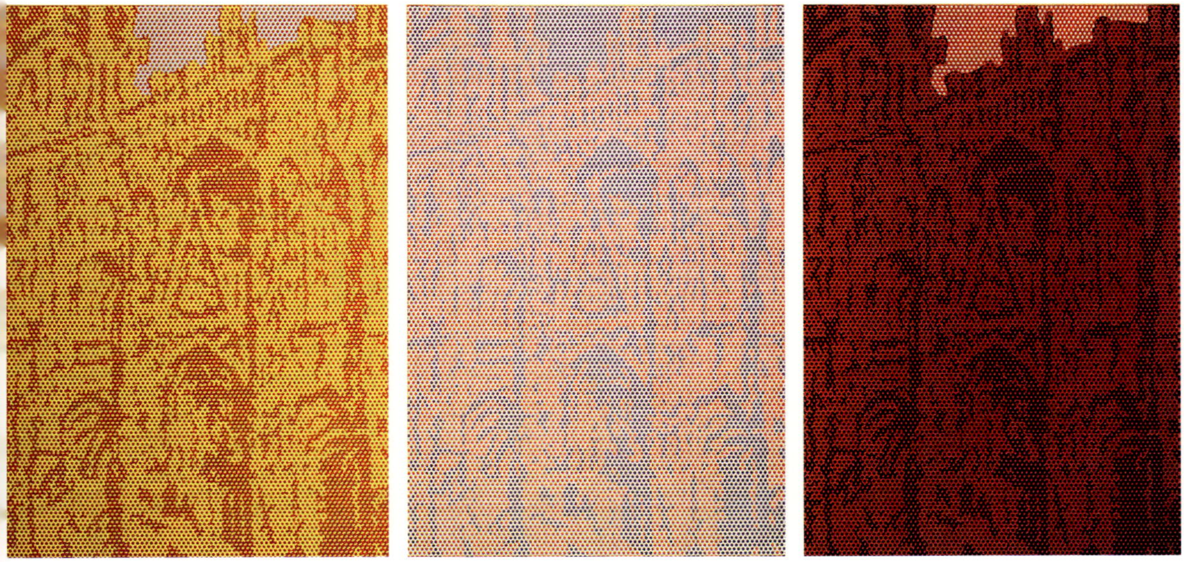

Roy Lichtenstein
Rouen Cathedral, Set 5
1969
Oil and magna on canvas,
5 ft. 3 ½ in. × 11 ft. 9 ¾ in.
(1.62 × 3.60 m)
Museum of Modern Art,
San Francisco

lived. American pop art pursued the exploration of painting in series, sweeping away the supremacy of abstract painting. The subject matter now consisted of Warhol's soup cans and celebrity photos. There are clear references to Monet in Roy Lichtenstein's *Rouen Cathedral* series. Monet actually designed the setting for his valedictory works, the *Water Lilies* in the Orangerie. In the evening of his long life, he created what was certainly the first environmental work of art, obliterating customary orientation points and immersing the viewer in a complete sensory experience. His work inspired the champions of environmental art, which emerged several decades later, from the 1960s onward.

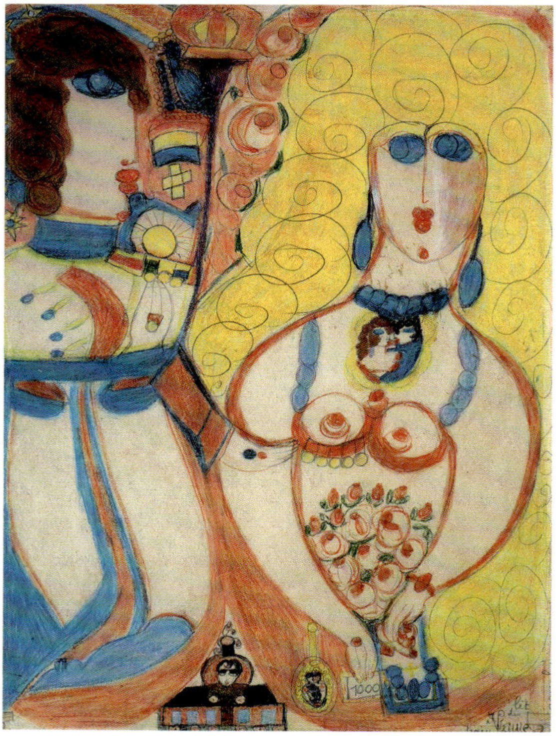

Aloïse
Lit du Train Veine a Couché
1940–50
Colored pencil on paper, recto and verso,
26 ¾ × 20 ⅛ in. (68 × 51 cm)
ABCD Collection, Bruno Decharme

CLEAR-EYED INNOCENCE

In proclaiming the "innocence of the eye," the impressionists challenged established protocols. They marked a complete break from tradition, and there was no looking back. Painting a picture did not necessarily require study, a preliminary drawing or sketch, the application of colors to create subtle modeling, or finishing with a fine glaze. The eye, the emotions, and pure sensation can and should be the only guides for the real artist. This is the true lesson of impressionism. Diplomas, medals, and "good work" have nothing to do with art. Creativity does not come from performing dogs; it requires inspiration, a "soul." Impressionism's horizon continued to broaden and the struggle went on. Jean Dubuffet (1901–1985) battled to earn recognition for *art brut*; for him, the artworks of autodidacts, psychiatric patients, and children were invaluable treasures.

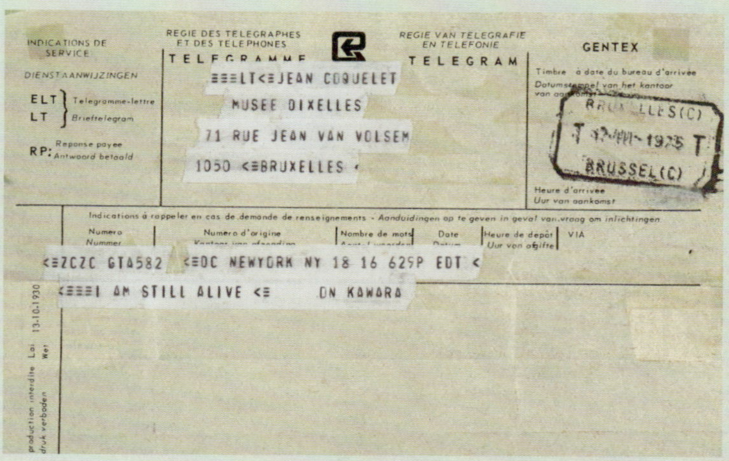
INDICATIONS DE SERVICE
DIENSTAANWIJZINGEN
ELT Telegramme-lettre
LT Brieftelegram
RP: Reponse payee / Antwoord betaald
REGIE DES TELEGRAPHES ET DES TELEPHONES
TELEGRAMME
REGIE VAN TELEGRAFIE EN TELEFONIE
TELEGRAM
GENTEX
≡≡≡LT<≡JEAN COQUELET
MUSEE DIXELLES
71 RUE JEAN VAN VOLSEM
1050 <≡BRUXELLES
<≡ZCZC GTA582 <≡DC NEWYORK NY 18 16 625P EDT <
<≡≡≡I AM STILL ALIVE <≡ ON KAWARA

Since 1969, the American artist On Kawara has been sending telegrams to acquaintances across the world at regular intervals. These missives invariably include the four words "I am still alive." The work's mocking existential message, its repetition in series, and even its method of dissemination—the entire ensemble of processes is pure artistic creation.

On Kawara
Telegram dated March 12, 1975, from the series *I Am Still Alive*
8 telegrams dated March 12, 13, 24, and 30, April 13 and 29, May 10, 1975. On one of the telegrams the date is illegible
Telegram sent from New York by On Kawara to Jean Coquelet at the Musée d'Ixelles, Brussels, bearing the text "I am still alive"
Dactylograph, 5 ¼ × 7 ¾ in. (13.3 × 19.7 cm)
Musée National d'Art Moderne/Centre de Création Industrielle, Centre Georges Pompidou, Paris

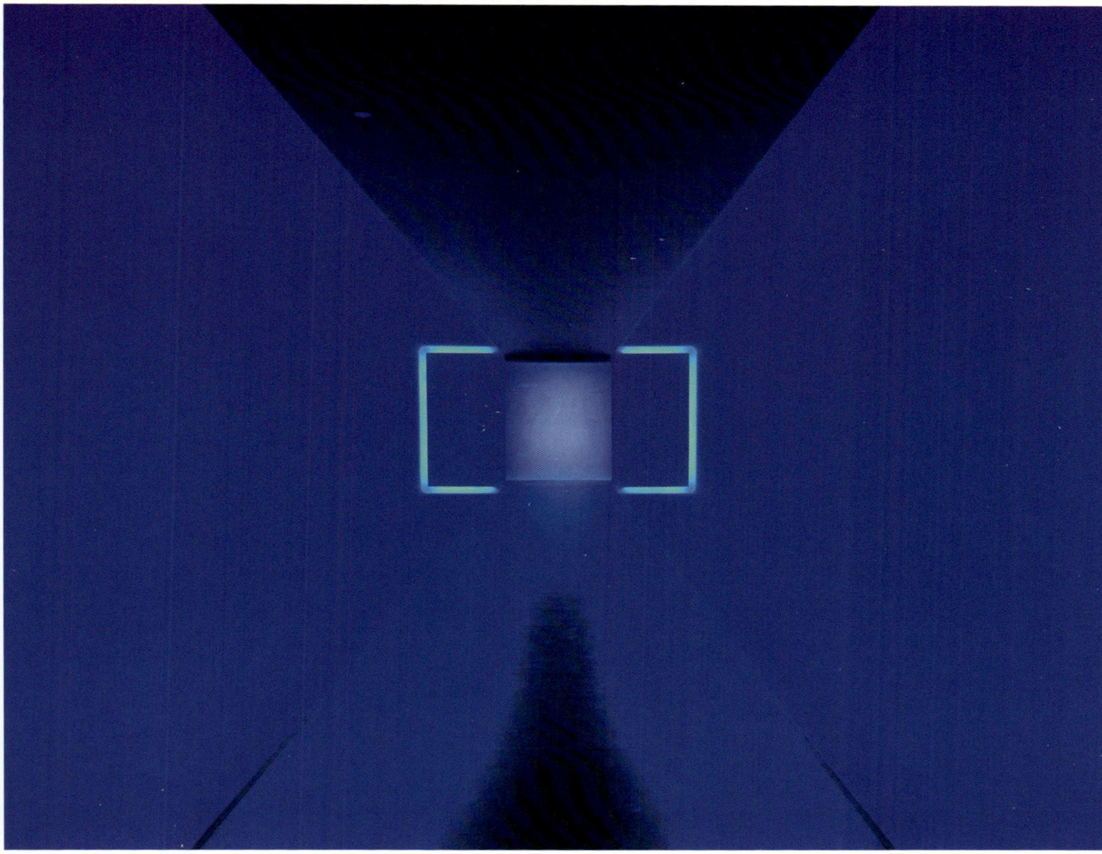

James Turrell
The Light Inside
1999
Various materials
Museum of Fine Arts, Houston

Inviting the viewer to dive into a sea of colored light, the American artist James Turrell creates "perceptual environments." They offer the opportunity to live a metaphysical and sensory experience, in which the spectators find themselves disconnected from all frames of reference and all reality.

THE ART OF DISSIDENCE

The impressionists lived outside convention. They were nevertheless determined to survive, and they created their own networking systems. They invented new ways of interacting, and debated freely in Parisian cafés, exploring new ways of exhibiting and selling their works. Taking entire responsibility for their destinies—from purchasing tubes of paint to disseminating their art—was a first. But it was not an end in itself. Conceptual art, collective studios, squats, utilization of new networks like the Internet, interactive works—artists can now proclaim themselves to be nonconformist and experimental, pioneers in every aspect of creation. The artist renews forms, seeks alternative paths, and cultivates independent ideas. The impressionists created this timeless spirit of modernity.

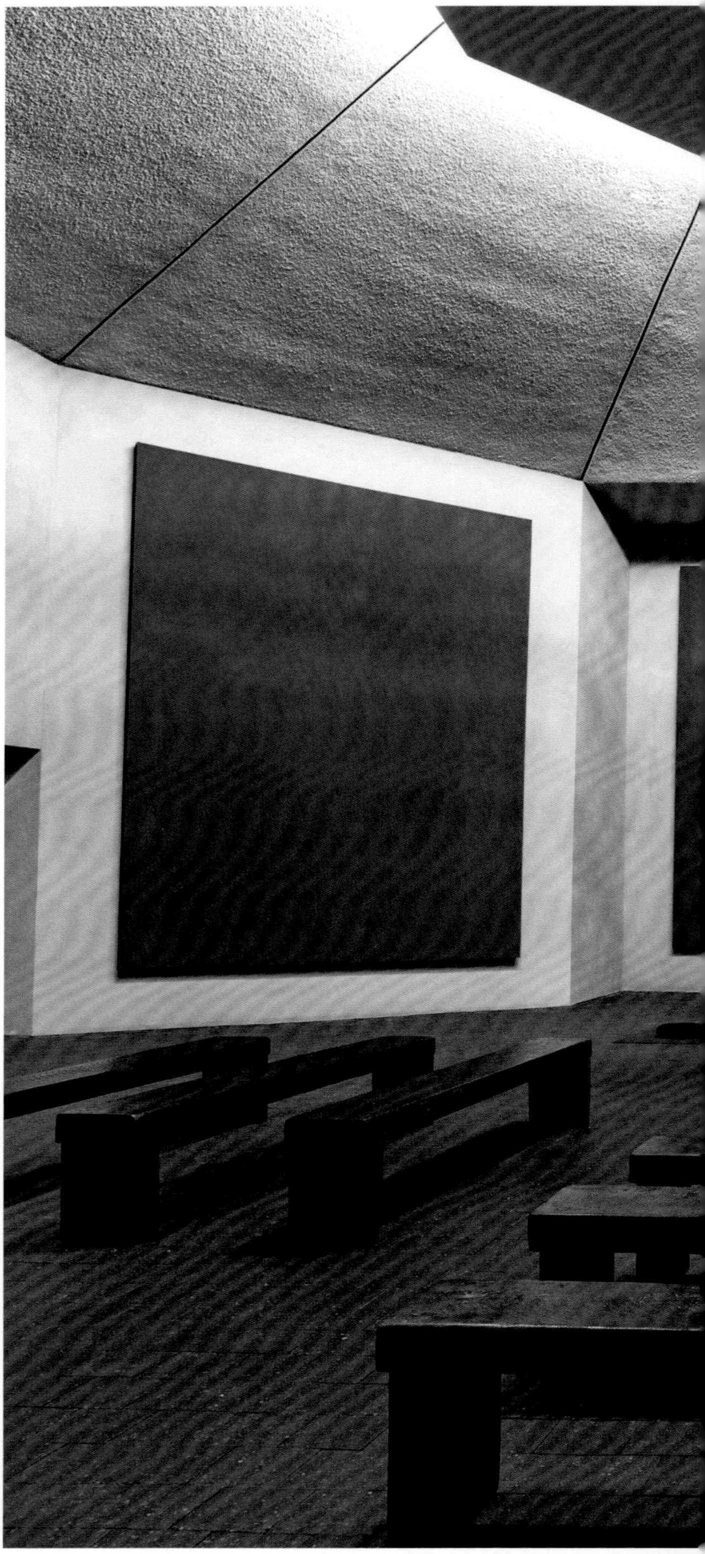

Mark Rothko
The Rothko Chapel
1964
Houston, Texas

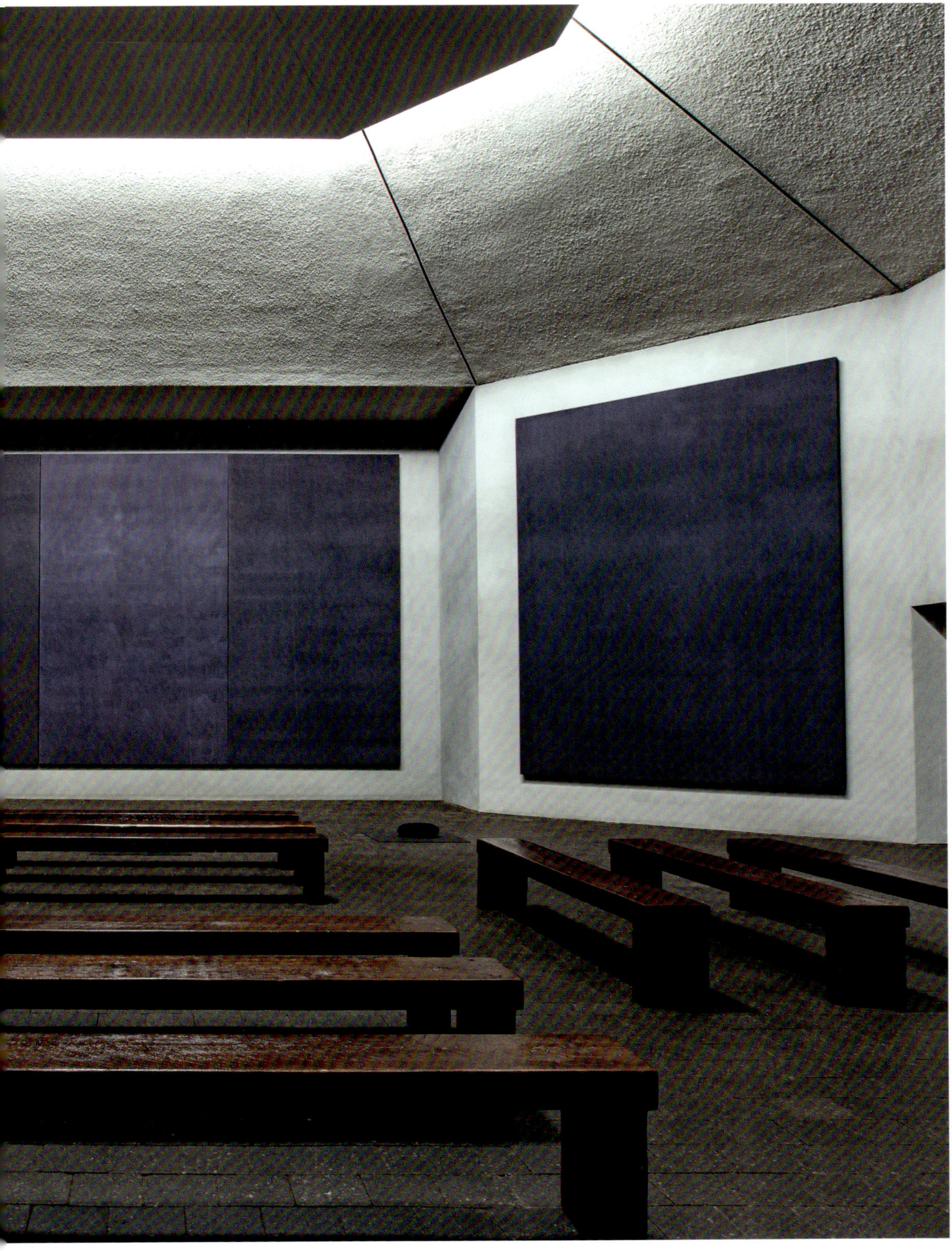

The Rothko Chapel

Mark Rothko, 1964

In 1964, the American abstract painter Mark Rothko (1903–1970) received a commission from the collectors John and Dominique de Menil to create the decor for a sacred space. The chapel was built expressly as a setting for Rothko's work, and he participated actively in drawing up the plans.

The choice of a Greek cross design echoes the rigor of the tenets of modernism and abstract art. The octagonal space completely envelops the viewer, inviting entrance into another dimension. The fourteen painted panels—three triptychs and five single panels—are arranged to surround the visitor. They compose a single unified work whose impact is enhanced by the extreme austerity of the architecture.

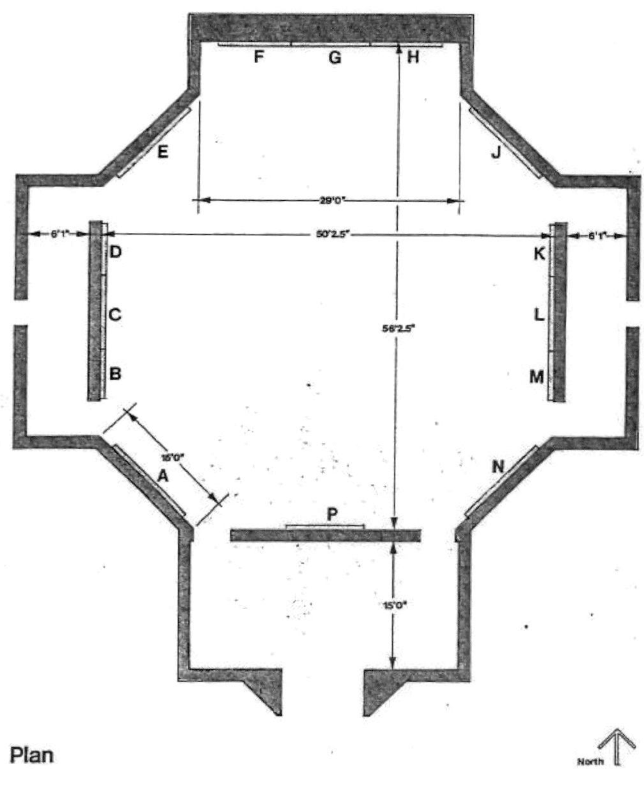

Rothko Chapel floor plan

A study in shades of black, the austere simplicity of the work invites contemplation. Depending on the time of day and the natural illumination that is admitted through the skylight, the restrained relief of the brushstrokes and the subtle variations of red, brown, and purple are revealed.

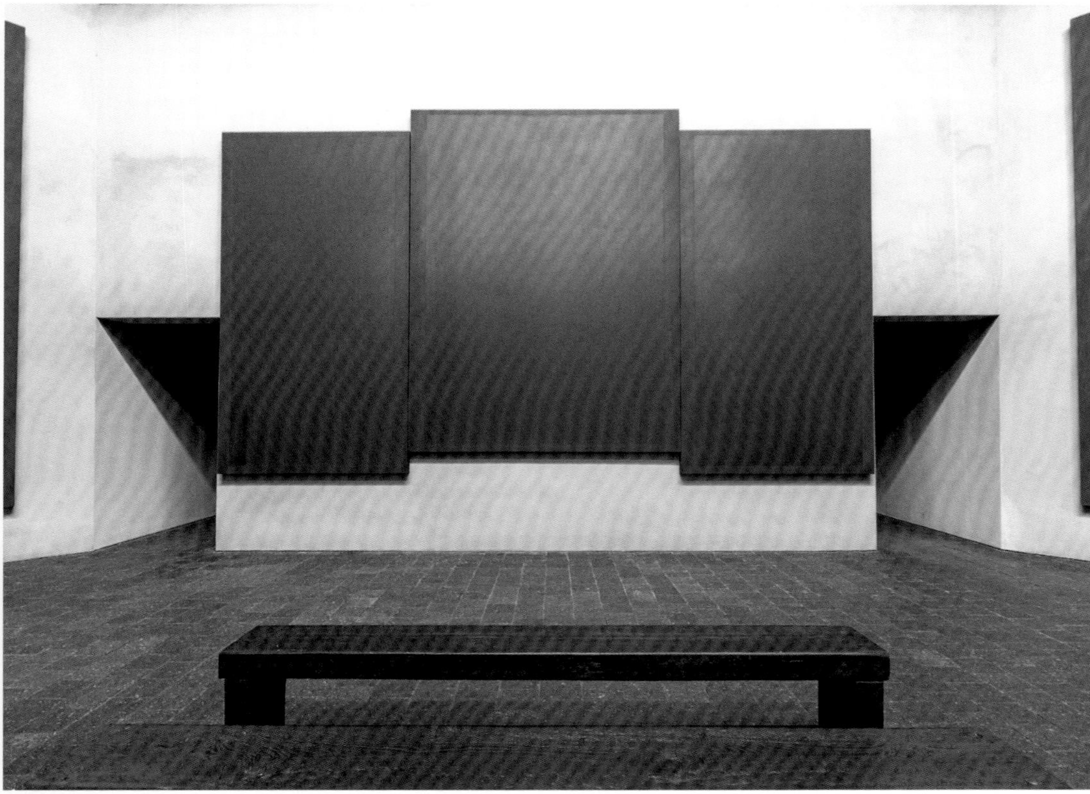

ART AS SPIRITUAL EXPERIENCE

A place of ecumenical contemplation, this chapel in Houston was inaugurated in 1971, one year after the artist's death. Rothko dedicated all his energy to the project, as Monet did for his *Water Lilies* in the Orangerie. He participated in the planning, actually creating a full-size maquette. For both artists, it was the culmination of a career, and perhaps a testament. Although they hang in a museum, Monet's *Water Lilies* are displayed as the artist wished, in two oval galleries separated from the outside world by an entrance room that sets them apart. Like Rothko much later, the intention was to create a totally immersive space for unmediated reflection in the presence of the painting. This is art that evokes a spiritual experience.

"Real creators, always working at the edge of their perceptions, may reach spiritual regions bordering on the sacred."

Dominique de Menil.

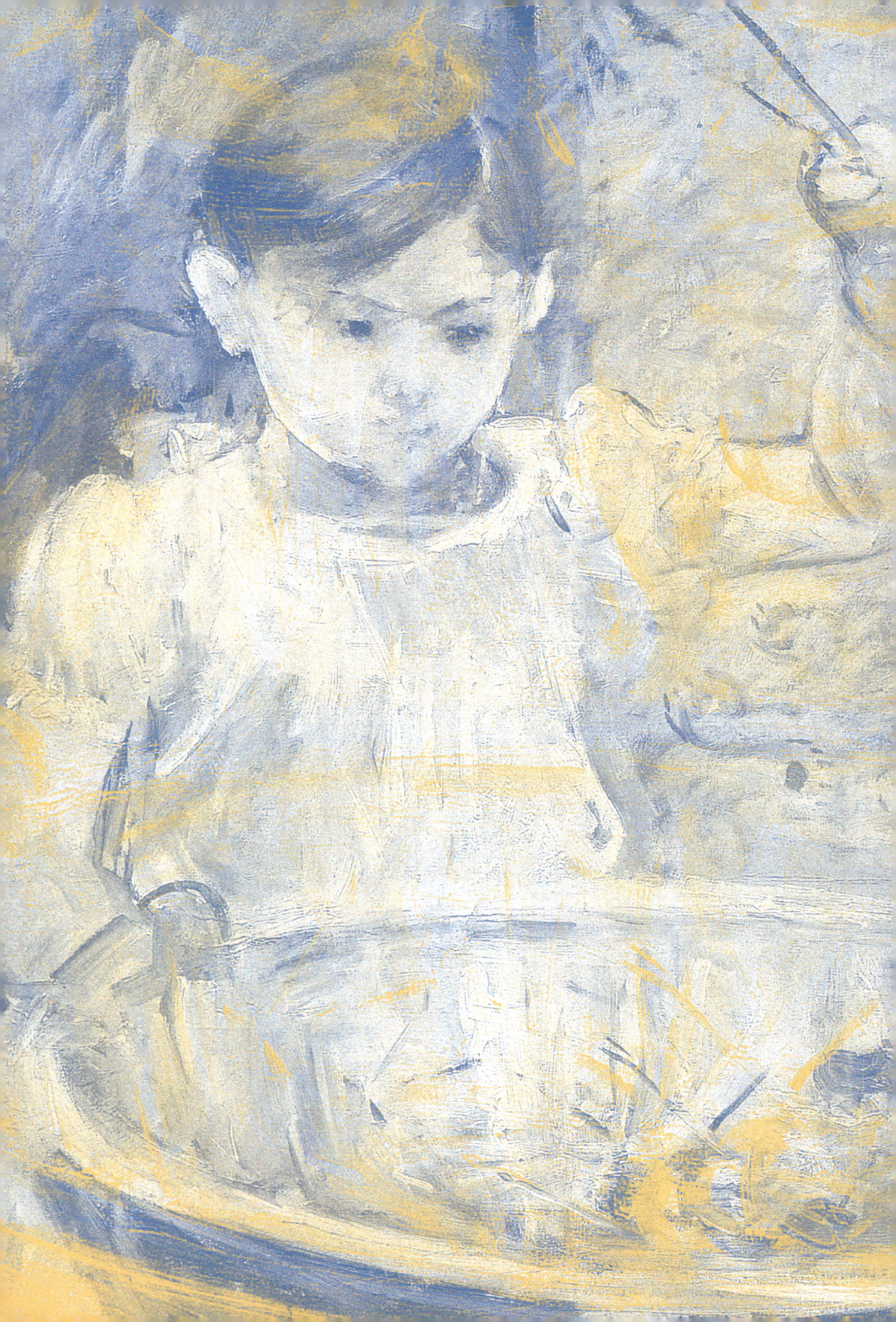

Biographies

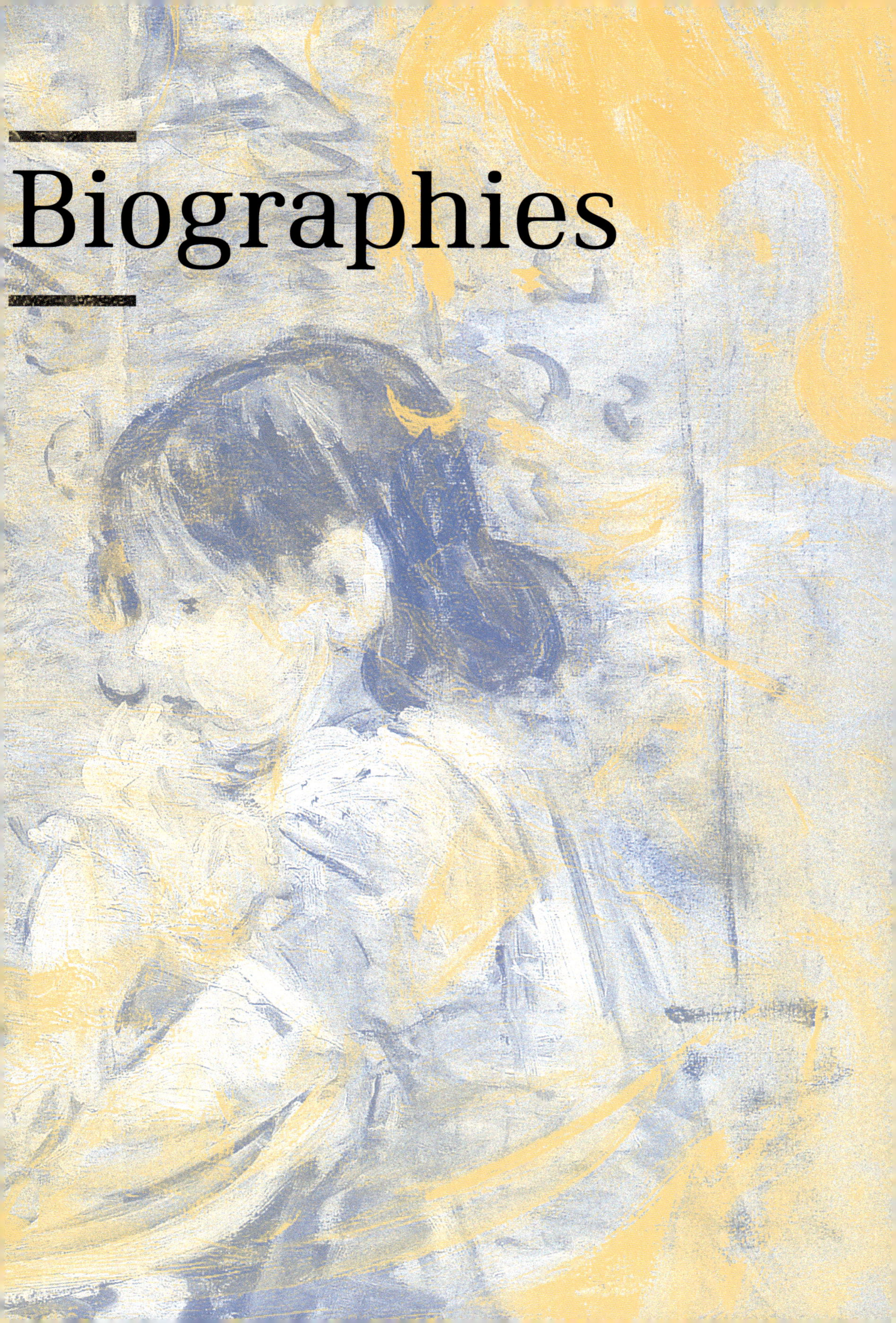

Claude Monet

The undisputed master of impressionism, Claude Monet was nevertheless perennially dissatisfied, forever in search of an artistic ideal and never really succumbing to the siren call of fame and recognition. Before achieving success, he had to undergo the trials and tribulations of a life marked by poverty, disappointment, and derision.

Monet was born in Paris but he grew up in Le Havre, where he was noted for his talents as a caricaturist. Struck by the young man's skill, the artist Eugène Boudin encouraged him to paint *en plein air*. "All of a sudden it was like a veil had been torn away. Now I understood, now I grasped what painting could be," wrote Monet, adding: "If I have become a painter, I owe it to Eugène Boudin." Convinced of his calling, he returned to Paris to study his trade at the Académie Suisse, a free studio where he met Pissarro. He performed his military service in Algeria, where the dazzling light left a lasting impression on him. He pursued his artistic career, alternating between visits to Normandy, the forest of Fontainebleau, and the Île-de-France and Paris. He experienced his first success in 1866 with *Woman in a Green Dress*. But this recognition was short-lived. Monet's audacious technique, which broke with academic convention, was understood only by a few enlightened viewers–although

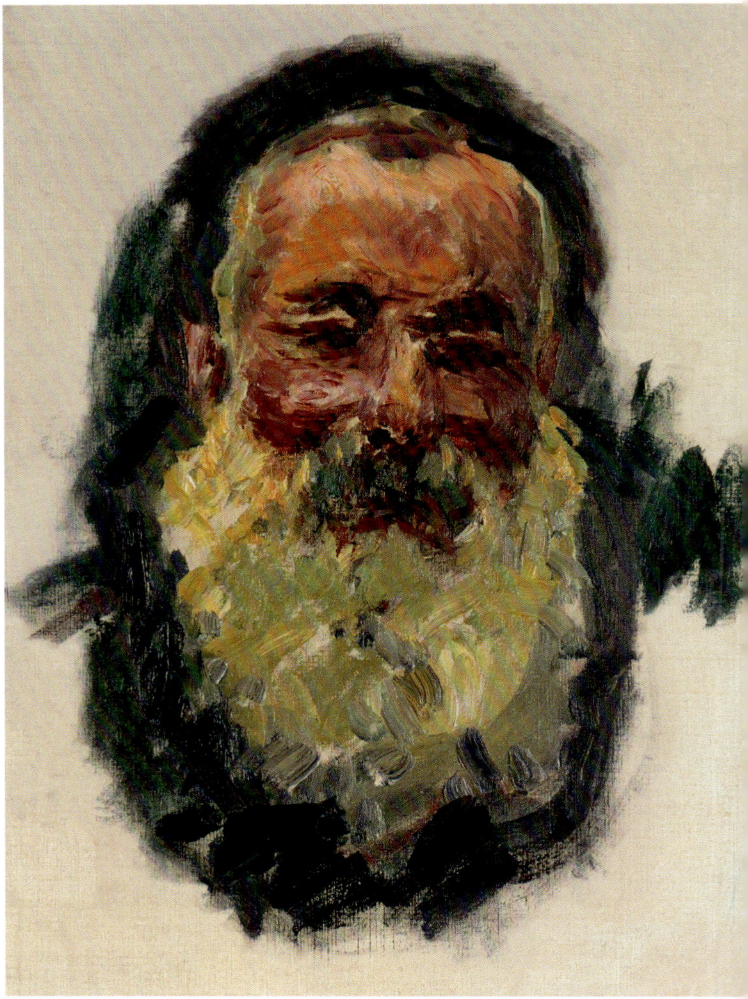

Claude Monet, *Self-Portrait*, 1917
Oil on canvas, 27 ½ × 21 ⅝ in. (70 × 55 cm)
Musée d'Orsay, Paris

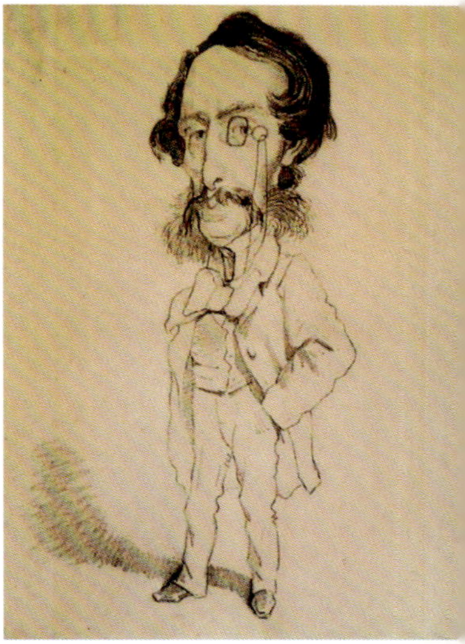

Claude Monet, *Mario Uchard*, c. 1858
Pencil, 12 ½ × 9 ¾ in. (32 x 24.5 cm)
Art Institute of Chicago, Chicago

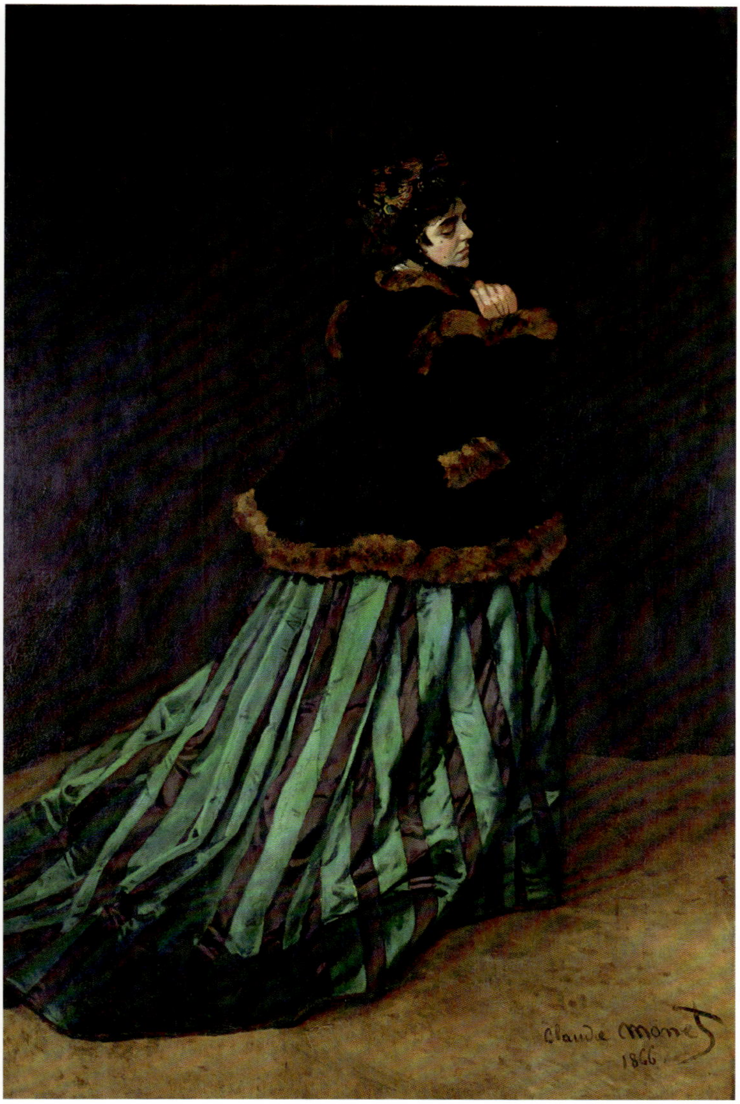

Claude Monet, *Camille*, also known as *Woman in a Green Dress*, 1866, oil on canvas, 7 ft. 7 in. × 4 ft. 11 ½ in. (2.31 × 1.51 m), Kunsthalle, Der Kunstverein in Bremen, Bremen

those who did were men of distinction such as Courbet, Zola, and Manet. They encouraged him to persevere, despite critical disdain and financial difficulties. His time in London, where he took refuge in 1870 when war broke out, provided encouragement; he discovered Turner's work and met Paul Durand-Ruel, who became his dealer. But he was weary of being rejected by the Salon, the only place where young artists could exhibit and make a name for themselves. In collaboration with other avant-garde painters including Renoir, Berthe Morisot, and Pissarro, he decided to establish an association of independent artists and present his works outside of official channels.

Key Dates

1840

Born in Paris on November 14

1859

Attends the Académie Suisse

1870

Lives in London

1874

Participates in the first impressionist exhibition

1879

Death of his wife Camille

1883

Discovers Giverny

1890

Undertakes major work to transform the garden in Giverny

1892

Marries Alice Hoschedé

1900

Begins the first series of Water Lilies

1908

Visits Venice

1918

Offers to donate Water Lilies to the State

1926

Dies in Giverny on December 5

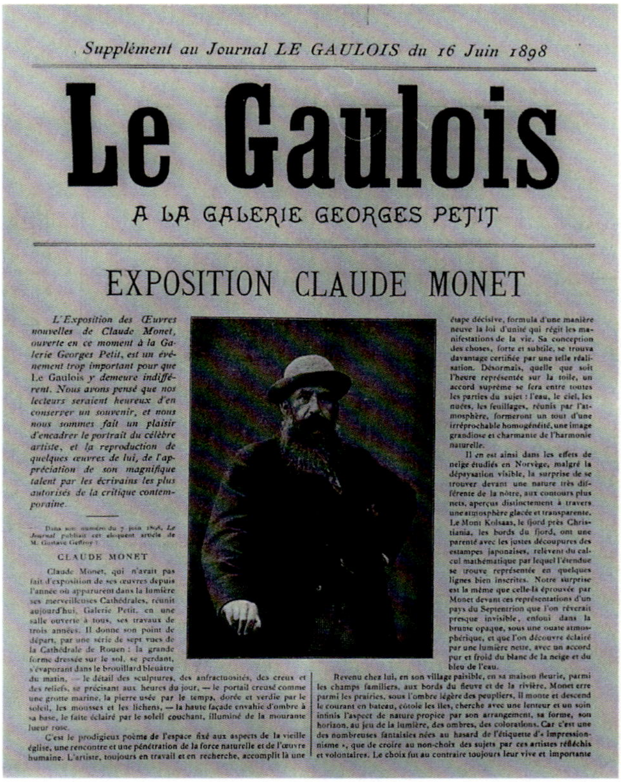

Supplément au Journal LE GAULOIS du 16 Juin 1898

Le Gaulois

A LA GALERIE GEORGES PETIT

EXPOSITION CLAUDE MONET

L'Exposition des Œuvres nouvelles de Claude Monet, ouverte en ce moment à la Galerie Georges Petit, est un événement trop important pour que Le Gaulois *y demeure indifférent. Nous avons pensé que nos lecteurs seraient heureux d'en conserver un souvenir, et nous nous sommes fait un plaisir d'encadrer le portrait du célèbre artiste, et la reproduction de quelques œuvres de lui, de l'appréciation de son magnifique talent par les écrivains les plus autorisés de la critique contemporaine.*

— Dans son numéro du 7 juin 1898, *Le Journal* publiait cet éloquent article de M. Gustave Geffroy :

CLAUDE MONET

Claude Monet, qui n'avait pas fait d'exposition de ses œuvres depuis l'année où apparurent dans la lumière ses merveilleuses Cathédrales, réunit aujourd'hui, Galerie Petit, en une salle ouverte à tous, ses travaux de trois années. Il donne son point de départ, par une série de sept vues de la Cathédrale de Rouen : la grande forme dressée sur le sol, se perdant, s'évaporant dans le brouillard bleuâtre du matin, — le détail des sculptures, des anfractuosités, des creux et des reliefs, se précisant aux heures du jour, — le portail creusé comme une grotte marine, la pierre usée par le temps, dorée et verdie par le soleil, les mousses et les lichens, — la haute façade envahie d'ombre à sa base, le faîte éclairé par le soleil couchant, illuminé de la mourante lueur rose.

C'est le prodigieux poème de l'espace fixé aux aspects de la vieille église, une rencontre et une pénétration de la force naturelle et de l'œuvre humaine. L'artiste, toujours en travail et en recherche, accomplit là une étape décisive, formula d'une manière neuve la loi d'unité qui régit les manifestations de la vie. Sa conception des choses, forte et subtile, se trouva davantage certifiée par une telle réalisation. Désormais, quelle que soit l'heure représentée sur la toile, un accord suprême se fera entre toutes les parties du sujet : l'eau, le ciel, les nuées, les feuillages, réunis par l'atmosphère, formeront un tout d'une irréprochable homogénéité, une image grandiose et charmante de l'harmonie naturelle.

Il en est ainsi dans les effets de neige étudiés en Norvège, malgré la dépaysation visible, la surprise de se trouver devant une nature très différente de la nôtre, aux contours plus nets, aperçus distinctement à travers une atmosphère glacée et transparente. Le Mont Kolsaas, le fjord près Christiania, les bords du fjord, ont une parenté avec les justes découpures des estampes japonaises, relèvent du calcul mathématique par lequel l'étendue se trouve représentée en quelques lignes bien inscrites. Notre surprise est la même que celle-là éprouvée par Monet devant ces représentations d'un pays du Septentrion que l'on rêverait presque invisible, enfoui dans la brume opaque, sous une ouate atmosphérique, et que l'on découvre éclairé par une lumière nette, avec un accord pur et froid du blanc de la neige et du bleu de l'eau.

Revenu chez lui, en son village paisible, en sa maison fleurie, parmi les champs familiers, aux bords du fleuve et de la rivière, Monet erre parmi les prairies, sous l'ombre légère des peupliers, il monte et descend le courant en bateau, côtoie les îles, cherche avec une lenteur et un soin infinis l'aspect de nature propice par son arrangement, sa forme, son horizon, au jeu de la lumière, des ombres, des colorations. Car c'est une des nombreuses fantaisies nées au hasard de l'étiquette d'« impressionnisme », que de croire au non-choix des sujets par ces artistes réfléchis et volontaires. Le choix fut au contraire toujours leur vive et importante

Le Gaulois, June 16, 1898
Supplement devoted to an exhibition of Monet's works

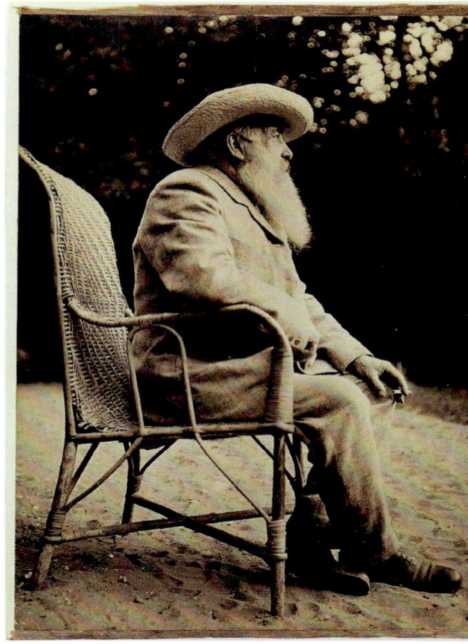

Sacha Guitry, *Claude Monet in the Garden at Giverny,* 1915
Palladiotype, 15 ⅛ × 11 ⅝ in. (38.4 × 29.5 cm)
Musée d'Orsay, Paris

In 1874, the first exhibition opened in the photographer Nadar's studio, in Paris, where he displayed the famous *Impression, Sunrise.* This pictorial thunderbolt was mocked by the press, which referred ironically to "impressionism," little supposing that this belittling term would be immortalized in the history of art.

Throughout the 1870s, Monet worked assiduously, painting the banks of the Seine, the Gare Saint-Lazare, and the busy Rue Montorgueil. However, he escaped financial hardship only with the support of his friends Manet, Caillebotte, Zola, and Ernest Hoschedé, who purchased pictures from him. The death of his wife Camille in 1879 marked the most difficult period of his life. But at last the critics became more receptive to his work: aged over forty, Monet was finally able to paint without fearing for his future. He came upon Giverny in 1883. It was a decisive moment in both his life and his work. He settled in the Normandy village, which became his base, and undertook a series of canvases on the same theme, painted at different times of day. The *Haystacks,* the *Poplars,* and

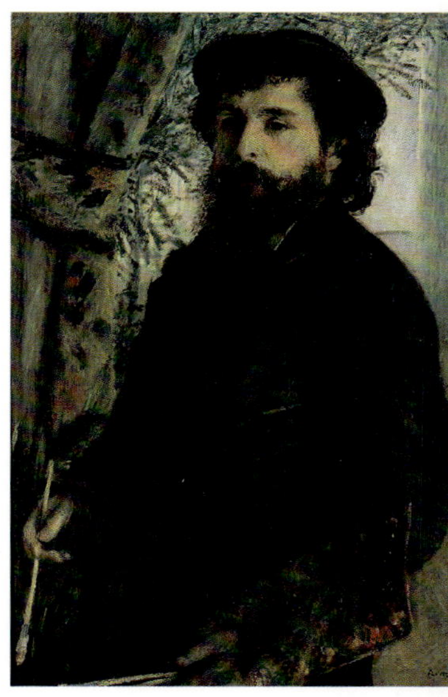

Auguste Renoir, *Portrait of Claude Monet,* 1875
Oil on canvas, 33 ½ × 23 ⅞ in. (85 × 60.5 cm)
Musée d'Orsay, Paris

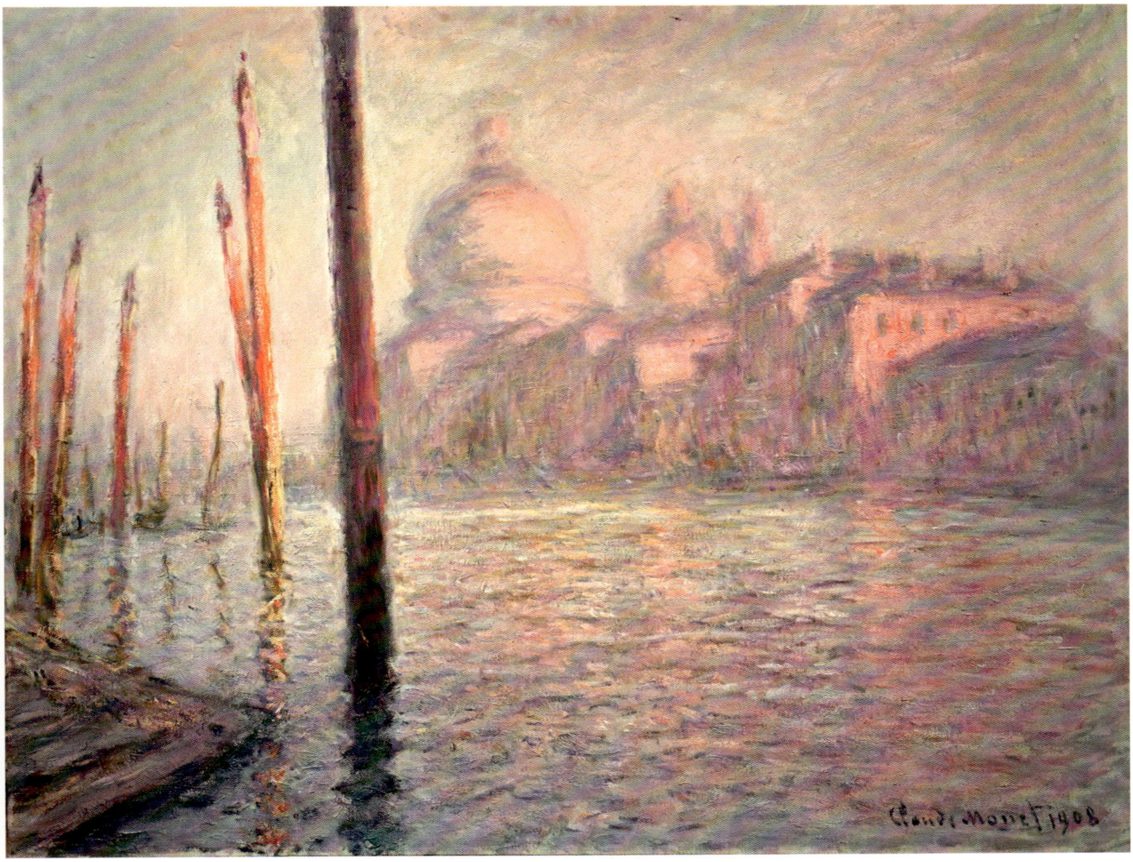

Claude Monet, *The Grand Canal, Venice*, 1908
Oil on canvas, 2 ft. 4 ¾ in. × 3 ft. ¼ in. (73 × 92 cm), private collection

the *Rouen Cathedral* series demonstrate his search for "instantaneousness," his desire to convey the ephemeral effects of light and its reflections. His newfound financial wellbeing allowed him to travel to a variety of destinations: to the Côte d'Azur with Renoir, to Norway, and to Venice with his second wife, Alice, the widow of Ernest Hoschedé. He was able to purchase the house in Giverny in 1890. Here he inaugurated his new creation: his garden with its famous pool covered with water lilies. They were to be the subject of his final works. He replaced fruit trees with roses, clematis, and wisteria. A Japanese-style bridge was built above the pool, and greenhouses were constructed in 1892. Monet envisioned vast decorative painted panels, and designed a huge, luminous studio in his garden, where his friend Clemenceau frequently came to visit. Monet addressed Clemenceau when he declared in 1918 that he wished "to offer a bouquet of flowers to France." The country had been devastated by four years of war. This monumental work was installed in the Orangerie in the Tuileries gardens. Galleries expressly designed for *Water Lilies* were inaugurated in 1927, a few months after the painter died.

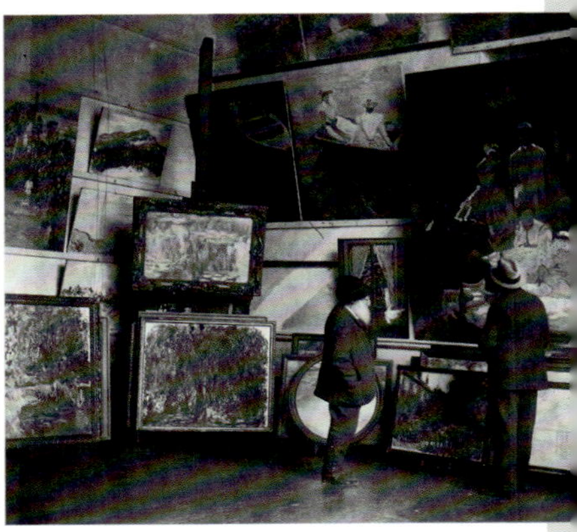

Claude Monet showing the central section of *The Luncheon on the Grass* to the Duke of Trévise in 1920
Jean-Dominique Rey Archives, Paris

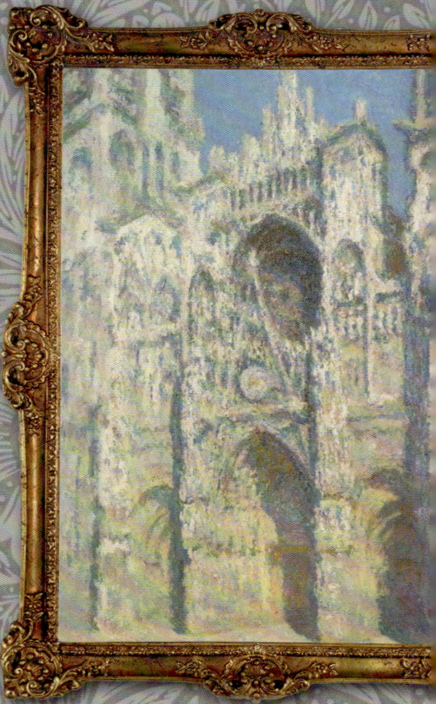
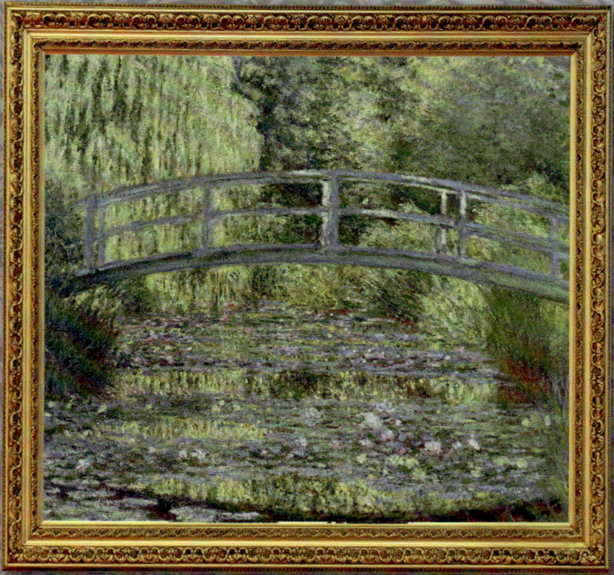
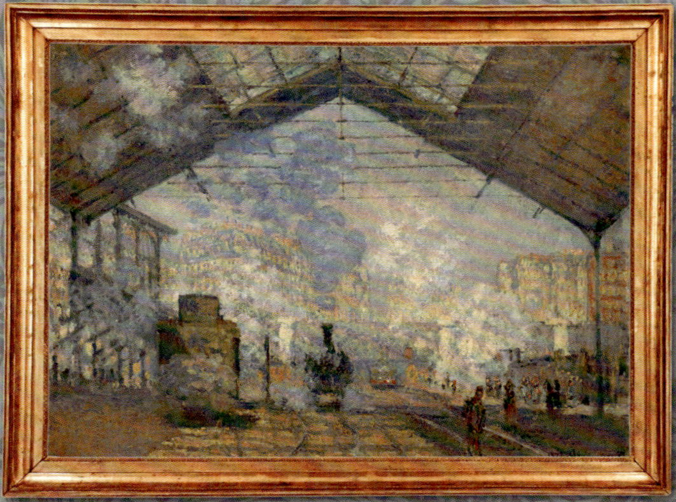
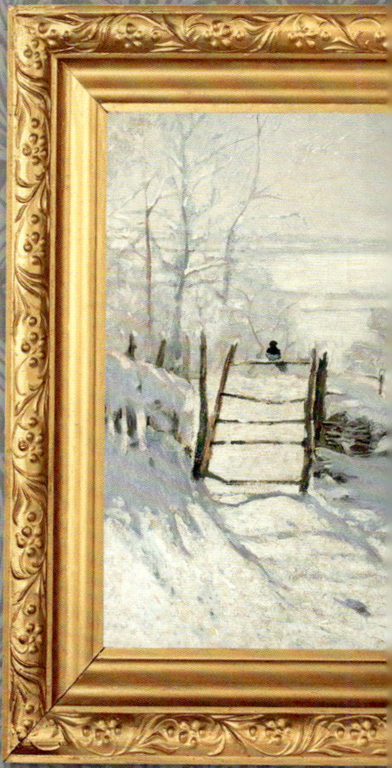

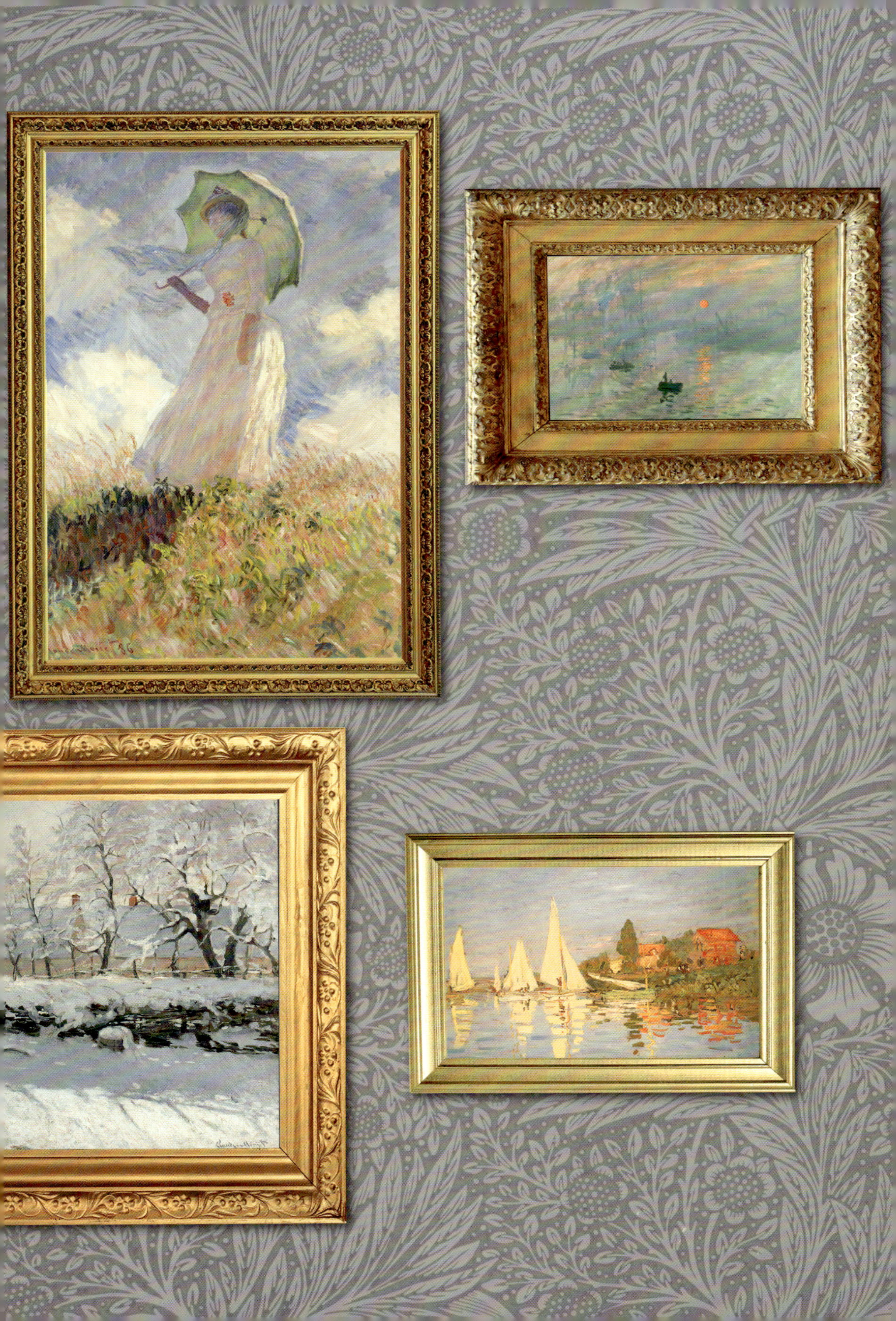

Camille Pissarro

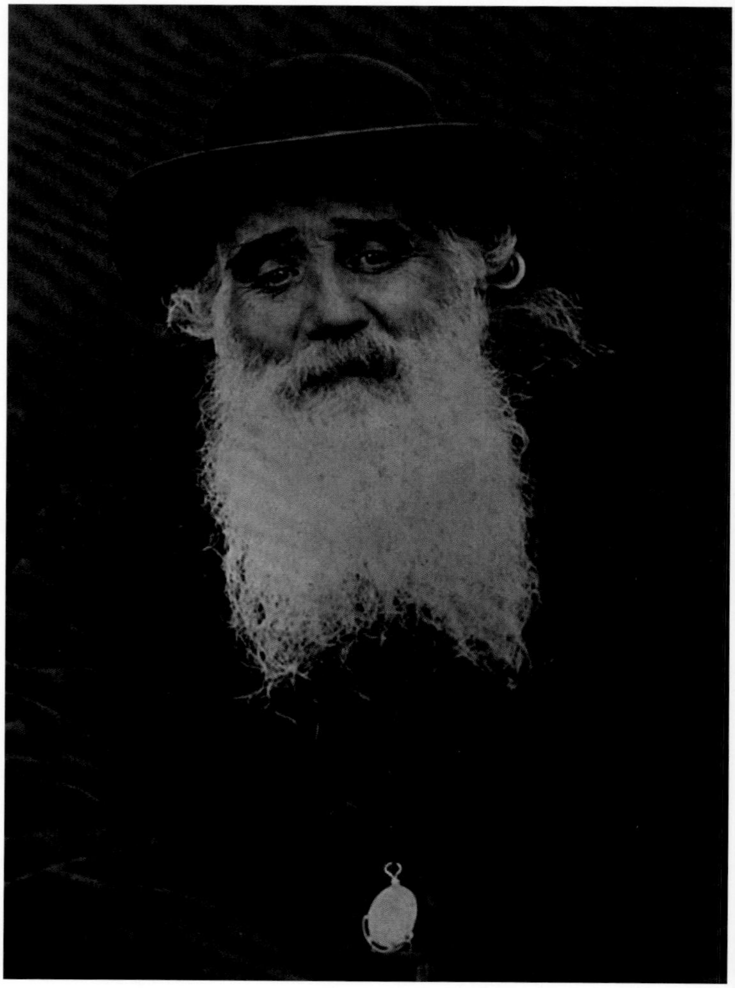

Photograph of Camille Pissarro
Durand-Ruel Archives, Paris

With his long beard, imposing figure, and natural charisma, Pissarro was compared to Moses by his impressionist friends. Blessed with a rare degree of energy and sensitivity, the oldest of the founders of impressionism nevertheless had to struggle with critics, rivalries, and numerous other challenges. Born in the Netherlands Antilles, as a young man he had to confront his father, who had planned for his son to enter the family business there. When he finally managed to free himself from these obligations, he was already twenty-five. He arrived in Paris before the 1855 Universal Exposition closed its doors. There he discovered the paintings of Ingres, Delacroix, Courbet, and Corot, who offered invaluable advice and urged him to paint *en plein air*. Initially a student at the École des Beaux-Arts, he soon joined the Académie Suisse (named for its founder, the painter Charles Suisse), a free studio where he met Monet, Cézanne, and the future impressionists. He exhibited fairly often at the Salon.

Primarily a landscape painter, he settled in Pontoise in 1866 with his companion Julie and his son Lucien, who became a painter like his father. Pissarro also spent a considerable amount of time in Paris, where he frequented the neighborhood around the Nouvelle Athènes, the Café Guerbois, and the haunts of Zola and Manet, who spearheaded the artistic

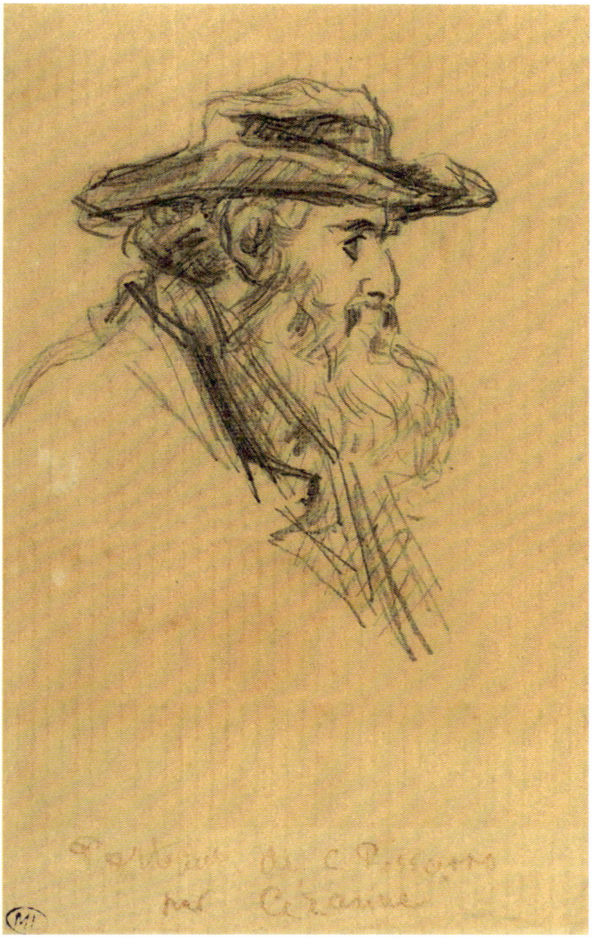

Paul Cézanne, *Portrait of Pissarro*, graphite, 5 ¼ × 4 in. (13.3 × 10.3 cm)
Musée d'Orsay, Paris, conserved at the Musée du Louvre

avant-garde. Fleeing the Franco-Prussian War, he encountered Monet in London in 1870, and became acquainted with Paul Durand-Ruel, who in turn introduced him to his friend the painter Daubigny. Returning to France, Pissarro devoted all his energy to creating an independent association of artists, who soon became known as "impressionists." He was the only member of this group to participate in all the exhibitions, despite the dissensions that raged over many years. He was naturally generous and willingly shared his advice, initially with Cézanne, whom he met in 1872. Five years later, he advised Gauguin, too, and invited him to exhibit with his impressionist friends. "He was such a professor that he could have taught stones to draw correctly," Mary Cassatt said of him. Van Gogh thought that, with Pissarro's participation, "discussions took on a broader scope."

Key Dates

1830

Born in the Antilles on July 10

1855

Moves to Paris

1870

Lives in London

1872

Moves to Pontoise

1874

Participates in the first impressionist exhibition

1884

Moves to Eragny; meets Signac and Seurat

1885

Adopts the pointillist method

1892

Exhibits successfully at Durand-Ruel's gallery

1903

Dies in Paris on November 13

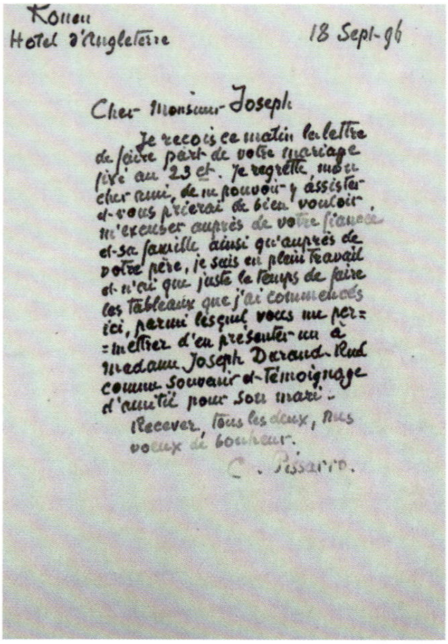

Rouen
Hotel d'Angleterre 18 Sept-96

Cher Monsieur Joseph

Je reçois ce matin la lettre de faire part de votre mariage fixé au 23 ct. Je regrette, mon cher ami, de ne pouvoir y assister et vous prierai de bien vouloir m'excuser auprès de votre fiancée et sa famille ainsi qu'auprès de votre père, je suis en plein travail et n'ai que juste le temps de faire les tableaux que j'ai commencés ici, parmi lesquels vous me permettrez d'en présenter un à madame Joseph Durand-Ruel comme souvenir et témoignage d'amitié pour son mari.

Recevez, tous les deux, mes voeux de bonheur.

C. Pissarro.

Camille Pissarro, letter to Joseph Durand-Ruel, September 18, 1896

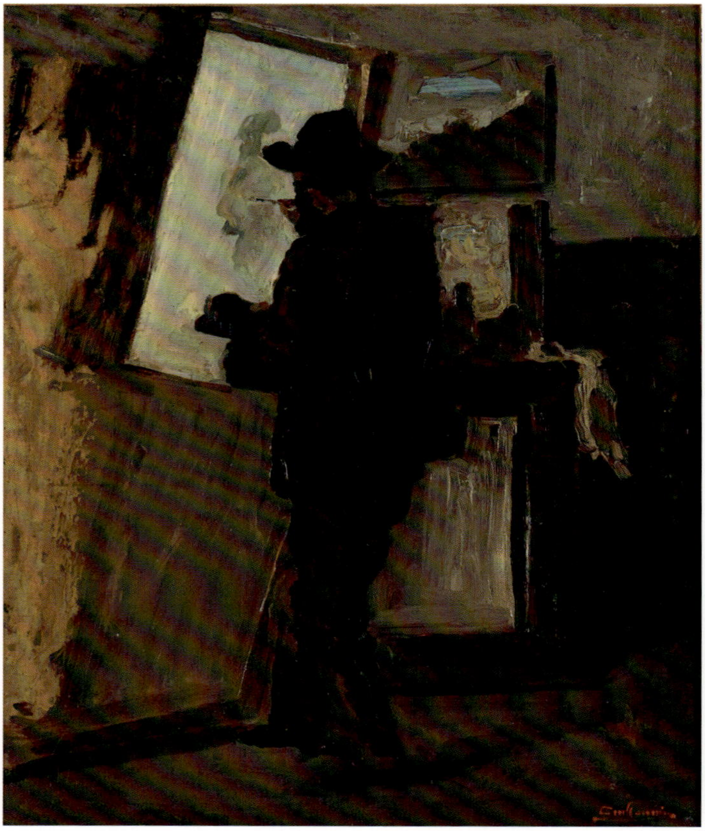

Armand Guillaumin, *Portrait of Pissarro*, c. 1868
Oil on canvas, 17 ⅞ × 14 ⅞ in. (45.5 × 37.8 cm)
Musée Municipal de l'Evêché, Limoges

He was also intensely conscious of the era's social problems, and felt a closeness to the lower and working classes. His approach to landscape was not that of a city dweller on an idle country jaunt, or of a bourgeois gentleman on a boating excursion, but of a painter attentive to the realities of the world of laborers and peasants. An admirer of Millet, he acknowledged the artist's moral and artistic influence. He was politically engaged in the socialist and anarchist movements, and his defense of these ideas resulted in a brief exile to Belgium following the assassination of French president Sadi Carnot in 1894. His political views no doubt contributed to his attraction to the pointillists, who were outspoken anarchists. He adopted their technique of divided brushstrokes after

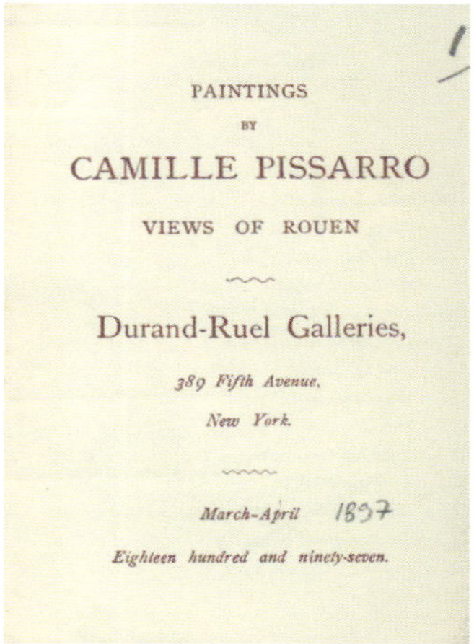

1

PAINTINGS
BY
CAMILLE PISSARRO
VIEWS OF ROUEN

Durand-Ruel Galleries,
389 Fifth Avenue,
New York.

March–April 1897
Eighteen hundred and ninety-seven.

New York exhibition catalog, 1897

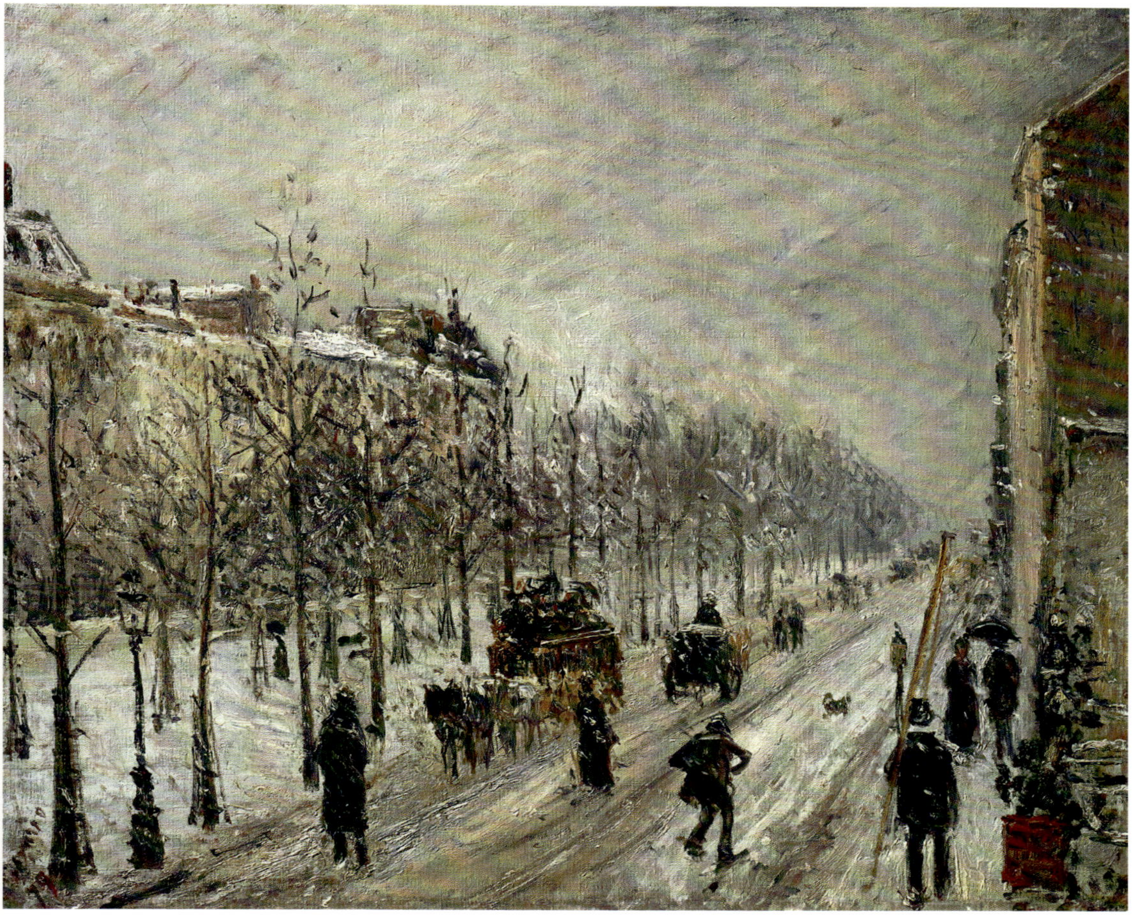

Camille Pissarro, *The Outer Boulevards, Snow Effect*, 1879
Oil on canvas, 21 ¼ × 25 ⅝ in. (54 × 65 cm)
Musée Marmottan Monet, Paris

meeting Signac and Seurat in 1884. However, these paintings did not sell well. The divisionist technique was too restrictive for Pissarro, and his eyesight was failing. He reverted to the impressionist style in the 1890s, whereas his son Lucien remained one of the foremost exponents of pointillism.

A new era finally began for Pissarro, who achieved success following an important exhibition organized by the dealer Paul Durand-Ruel in 1892. Following the example of his friend Monet, who was godfather to his son, Pissarro created several series based on the same subject, most often a city scene. They varied not in terms of the time of day they were painted, but rather from the point of view. He painted numerous pictures in Rouen, Dieppe, and Paris, often seen from his window. His bird's-eye views of the quays, the Grands Boulevards, and the Tuileries gardens were always well composed. In art as in friendship, Pissarro consistently demonstrated unwavering loyalty.

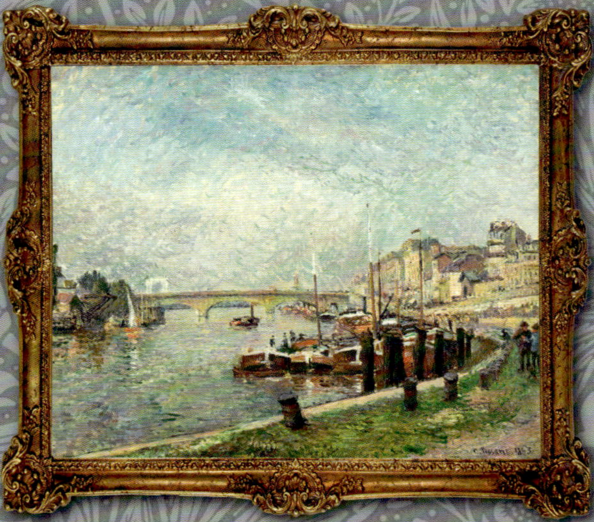

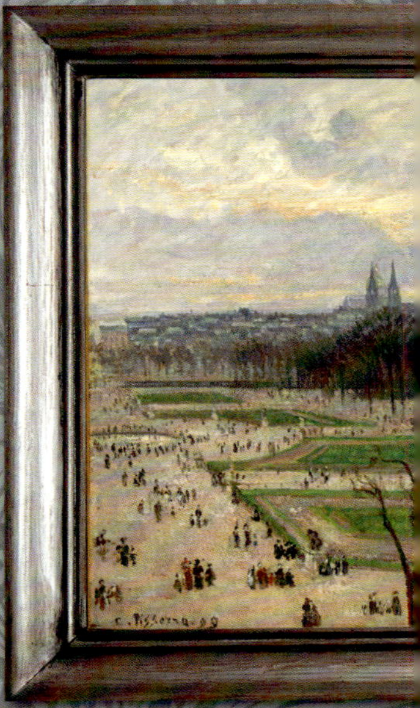

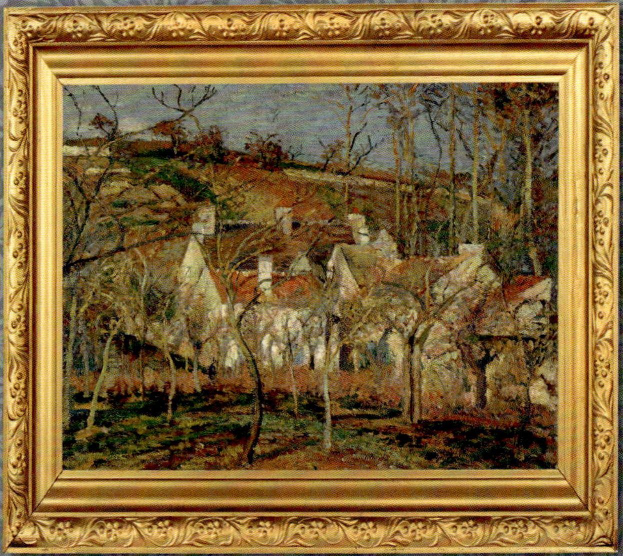

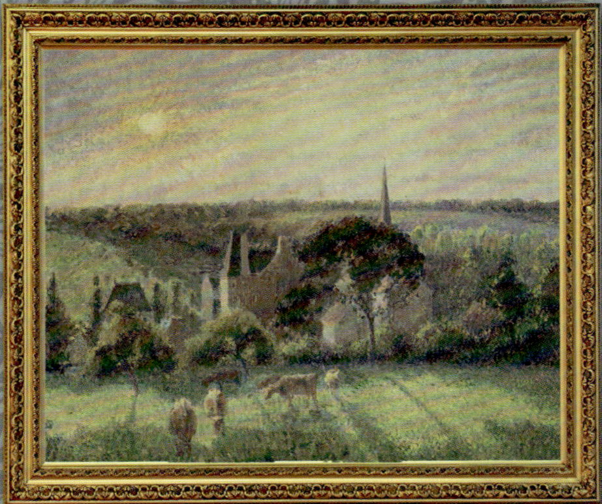

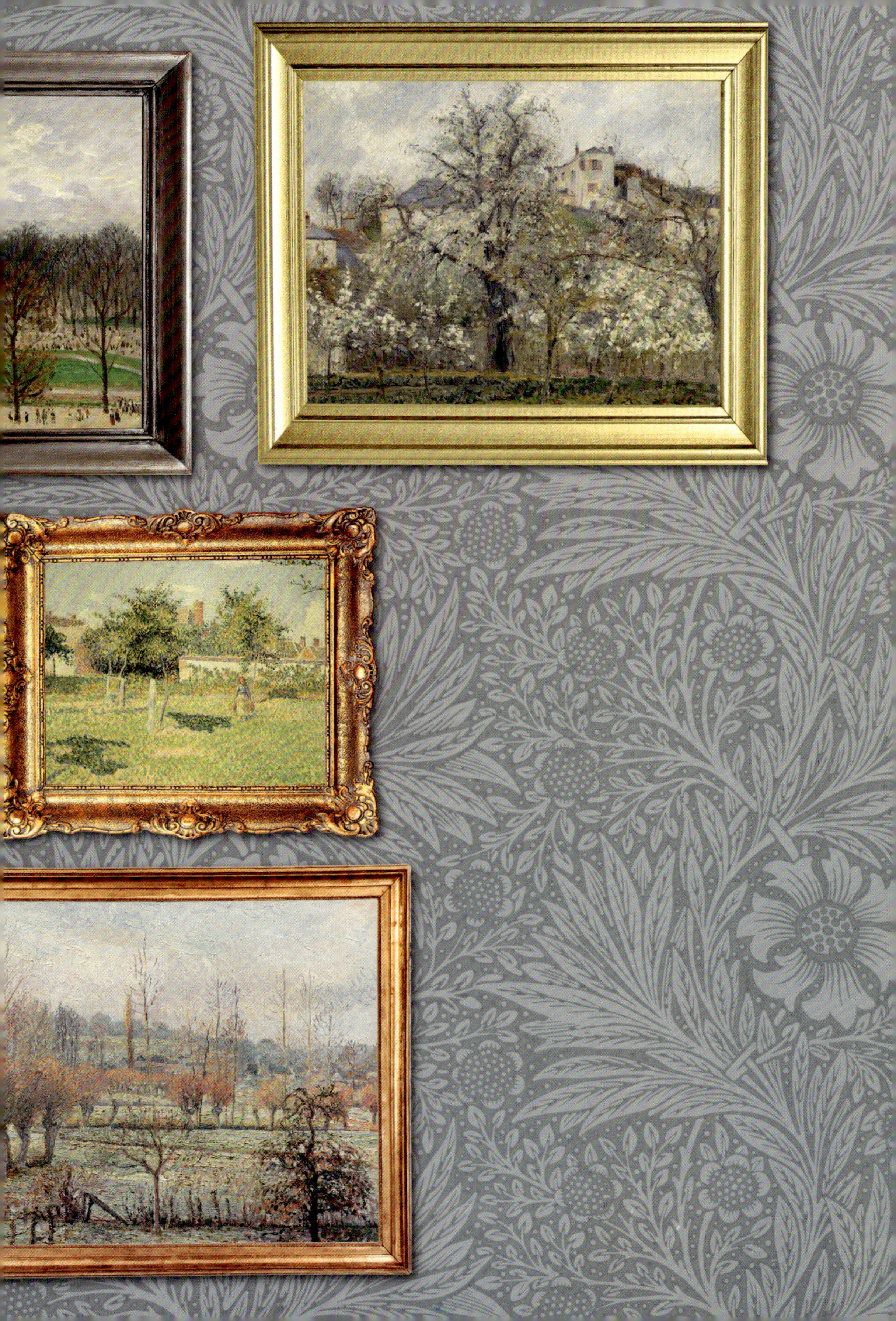

Pierre Auguste Renoir

The painter of *Dance at Le Moulin de la Galette* would certainly have made an excellent musician: his teacher, the French composer Charles Gounod, found his pupil to be gifted and intelligent. But young Renoir was equally brilliant at drawing, and his parents, a couple from Limoges who had limited means, decided he should pursue that path. So, aged thirteen, Renoir took an apprenticeship in a porcelain-decorating workshop. Having saved the money he had earned painting awnings and fans in his spare time, Renoir entered the École des Beaux-Arts in 1862 and took lessons from the painter Charles Gleyre. At Gleyre's studio he met Monet, Sisley, and Bazille, who quickly became companions, and joined him in traveling to the forest of Fontainebleau to paint from nature, *en plein air*. Working side by side, the young artists encouraged each other along the path to impressionism.

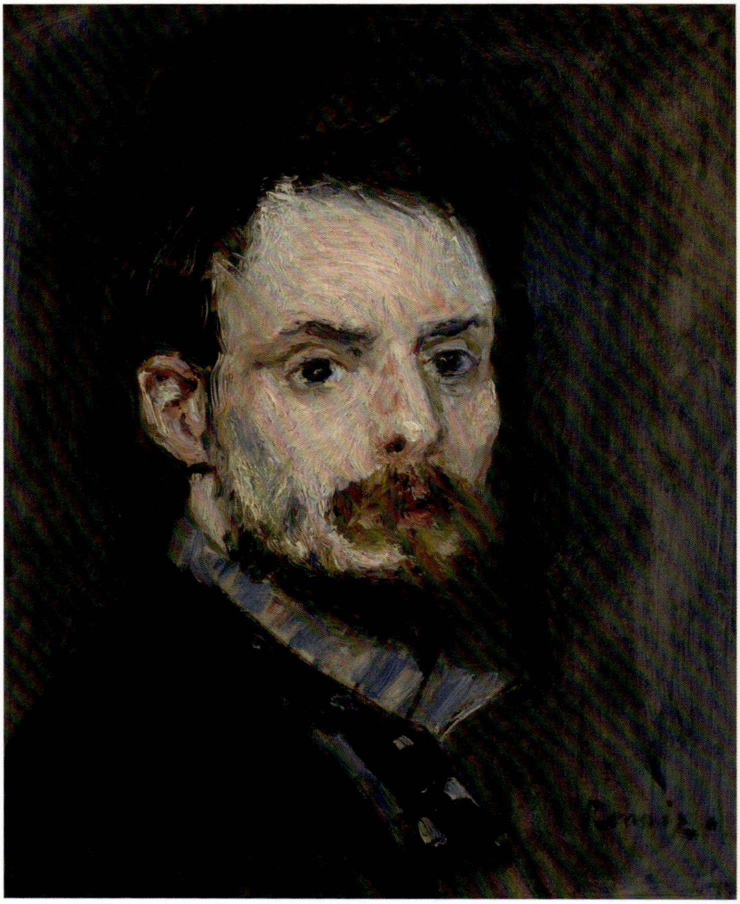

Auguste Renoir, *Self-Portrait*, c. 1875, oil on canvas, 15 ⅜ × 12 ½ in. (39.1 × 31.6 cm)
Sterling and Francine Art Institute, Williamstown, MA

Particularly close to Monet, Renoir gradually freed himself from the influence of Courbet and began to use a brighter palette. Together, the two young men painted the same subjects, including La Grenouillère, a café and dance hall on the banks of the Seine at Croissy, near Paris. In contrast to his friends, Renoir was more interested in the human figure than in landscape. In 1874, he chose to submit *La Loge (The Theater Box)*, *Dancer* and *The Parisian Girl* to present at the first impressionist exhibition.

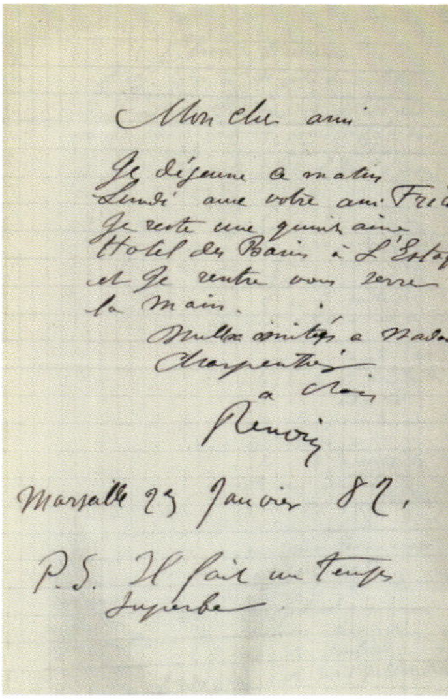

Mon cher ami

Je déjeune ce matin
Lundi avec votre ami Fri[illegible]
Je reste une quinzaine
Hotel des Bains à L'Estaque
et je rentre vous serrer
la main.

Mille amitiés à Madame
Charpentier
à vous
Renoir

Marseille 23 Janvier 82.

P.S. Il fait un temps
superbe

Renoir, letter to Georges Charpentier
January 23, 1882

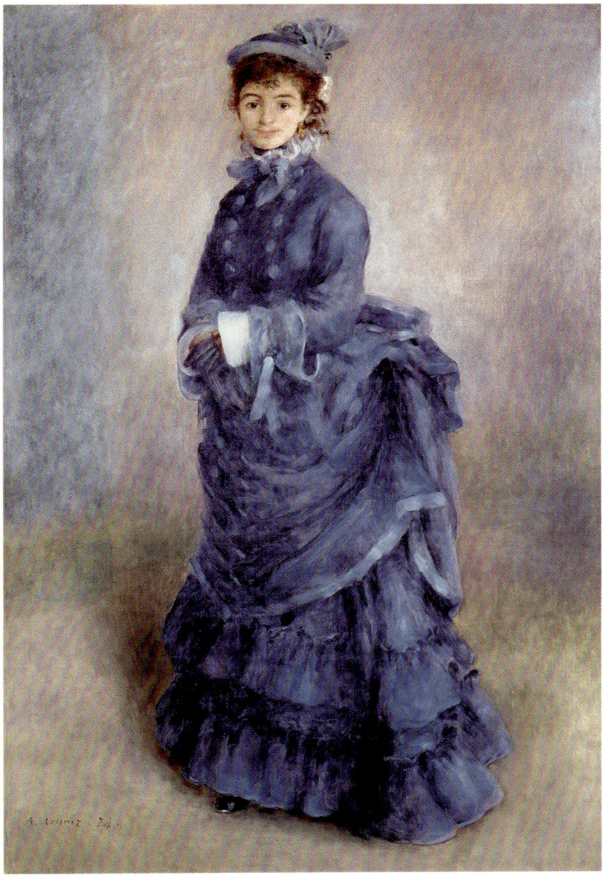

Auguste Renoir, *The Parisian Girl*, 1874
Oil on canvas, 5 ft. 4 ¼ in. × 3 ft. 6 ¾ in. (1.63 × 1.08 m), National Museum Cardiff, Wales

Living in Montmartre on Rue Cortot, Renoir selected a novel topic for *Dance at Le Moulin de la Galette*. He executed numerous studies and arranged for his friends to pose there, but he completed the canvas in his studio. With a greater affinity for form than his colleagues, and despite continuing criticism, he began to arouse the interest of several collectors, including the publisher Georges Charpentier, who introduced him to well-off clients who commissioned portraits. Renoir was amiable, poised, and accommodating, a man who was equally at ease in bourgeois drawing rooms and popular gathering places. He maintained a simple way of life. "The secret is to have few needs," he said. However, concerned that his membership in an avant-garde movement might harm his still fragile success, he decided not to take part in some of the impressionist exhibitions beginning in 1880. Furthermore, he felt that he had reached a stylistic impasse. "[A] sort of break occurred in my

Key Dates

1841

Born in Limoges on February 25

1854

Apprenticed to a porcelain-painting workshop

1862

Admitted to the École des Beaux-Arts

1874

Participates in the first impressionist exhibition

1879

Accepted into the Salon

1881

Travels to Algeria and Italy

1903

Moves to Cagnes-sur-Mer

1919

Dies in Cagnes-sur-Mer on December 3

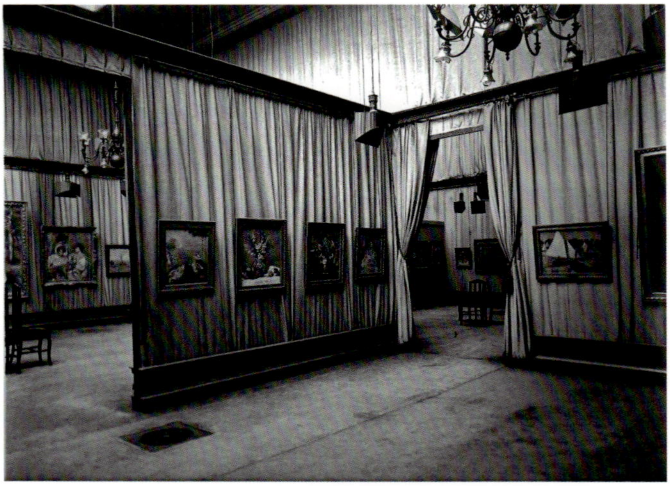

Renoir exhibition at Durand-Ruel's gallery on Rue Laffitte, Paris, 1920

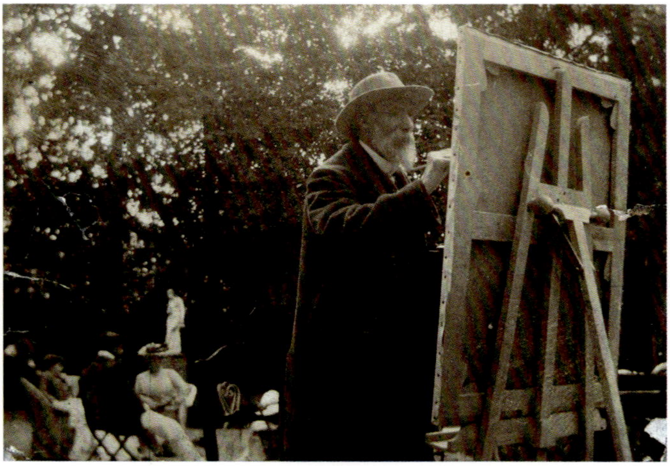

Renoir working at his easel, 1901

work. I had got to the end of impressionism and had reached the conclusion that I could neither paint nor draw." In 1881, he weathered a crisis that drove him to travel to Algeria and then Italy. There his studies of the Renaissance masters strengthened his determination to revert to the primacy of drawing over color. He also stopped in L'Estaque to visit his friend Cézanne. They had always been close, despite their differences in style and personality. Heartened, he took part in the seventh impressionist exhibition in 1882 and presented some of his loveliest compositions, including *Luncheon of the Boating Party* and the companion panels *City Dance* and *Country Dance*.

This prosperous period was further brightened when he met his future wife Aline. But a new period of despondency

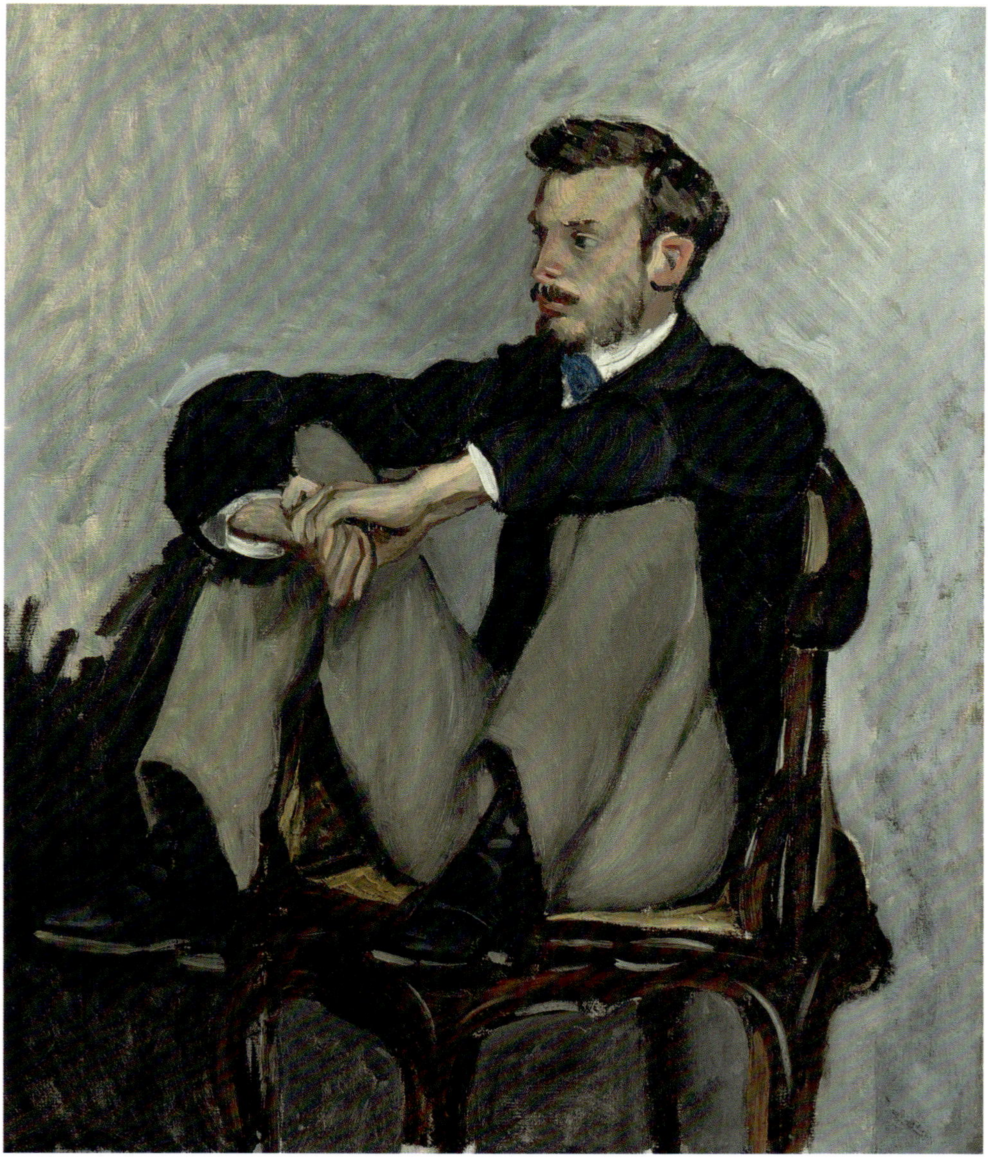

Frédéric Bazille, *Pierre-Auguste Renoir,* c. 1868–69
Oil on canvas, 24 ⅛ × 19 ⅝ in. (61.2 × 50 cm), Musée d'Orsay, Paris

followed, aggravated by health problems. Obliged to spend long periods in the south of France, he decided to move to Cagnes-sur-Mer on the Côte d'Azur in 1903, even though he felt that the light there was too harsh. He painted members of his family, including his sons Pierre, Jean (the future film director) and Claude, as well as lush nude bathers. He was finally enjoying success and recognition—he was awarded the Légion d'Honneur in 1901—but his strength was failing. He was gradually paralyzed by arthritis and could only move about in a wheelchair. At the end of his life, he was no longer able to hold brushes in his hand, and had to have them tied to his fingers so he could still work. Right up until his final breath in 1919, he never gave up painting.

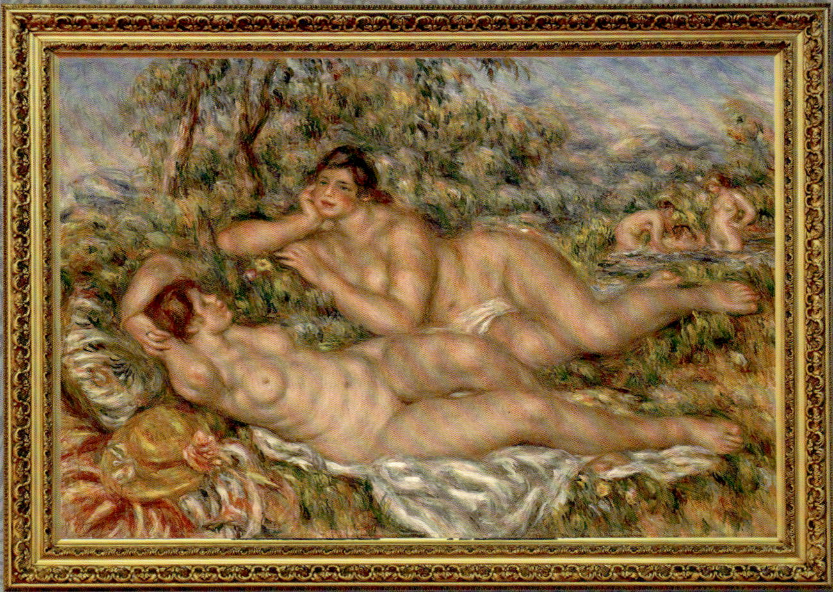

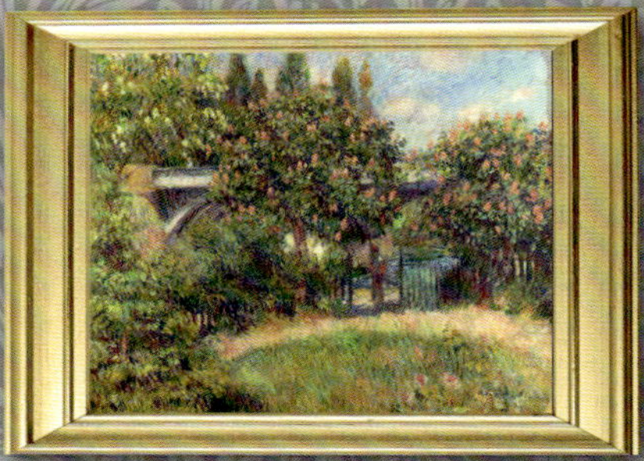

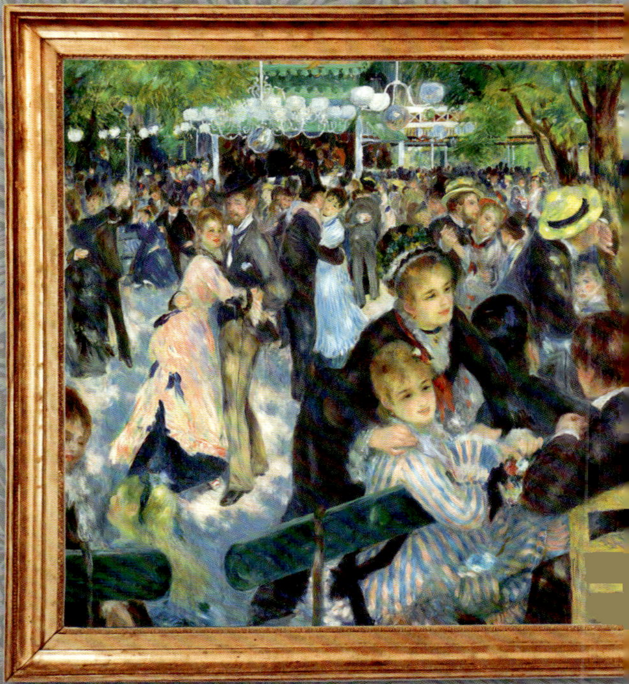

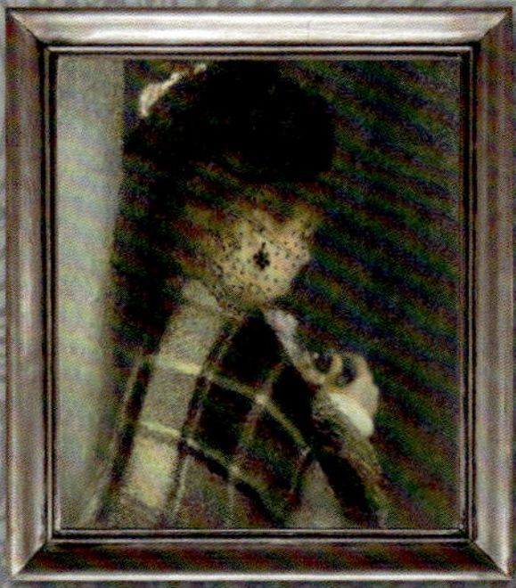

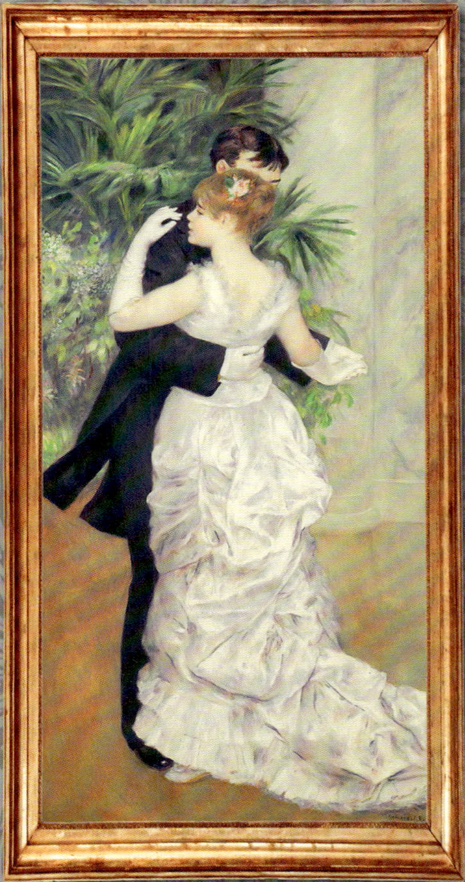

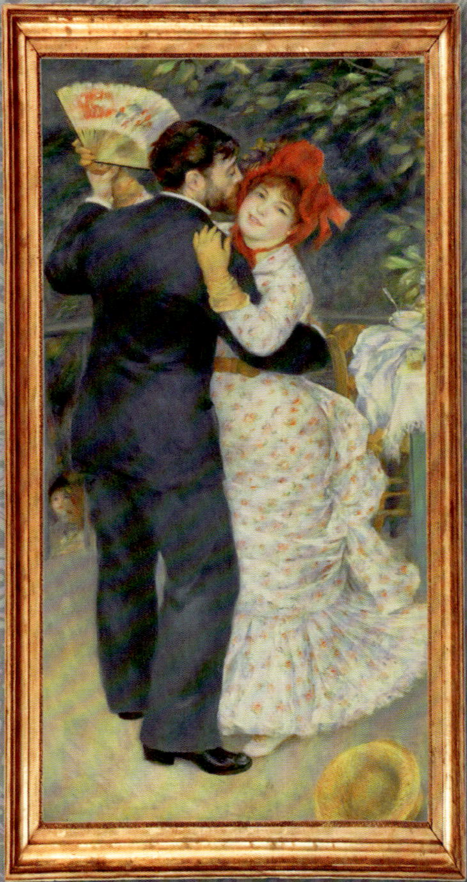

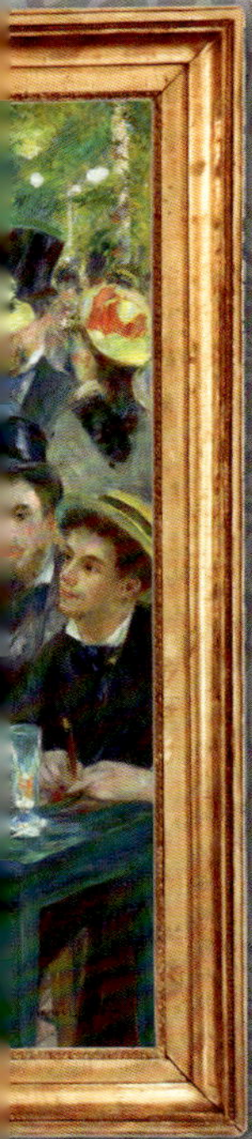

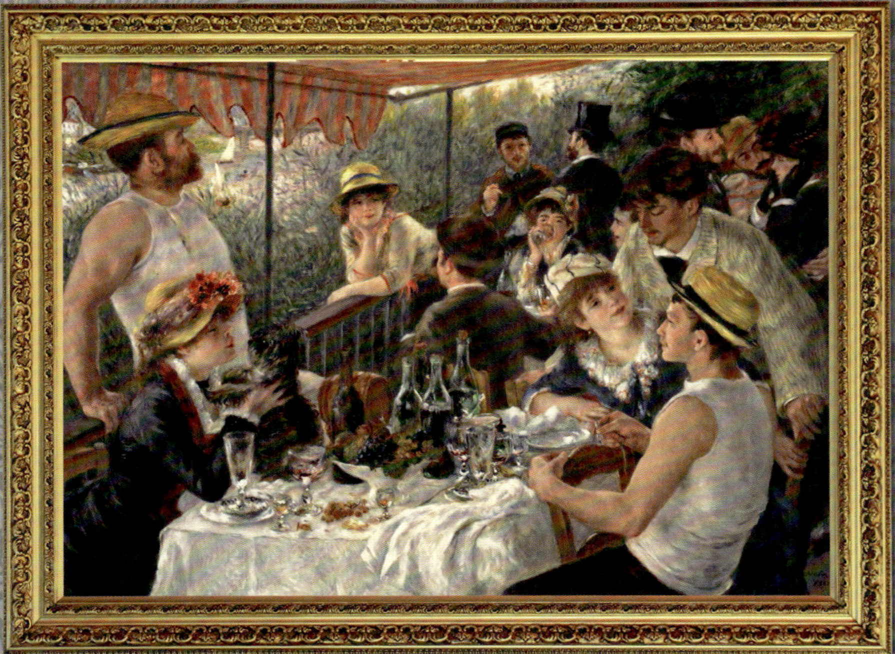

Edgar Degas

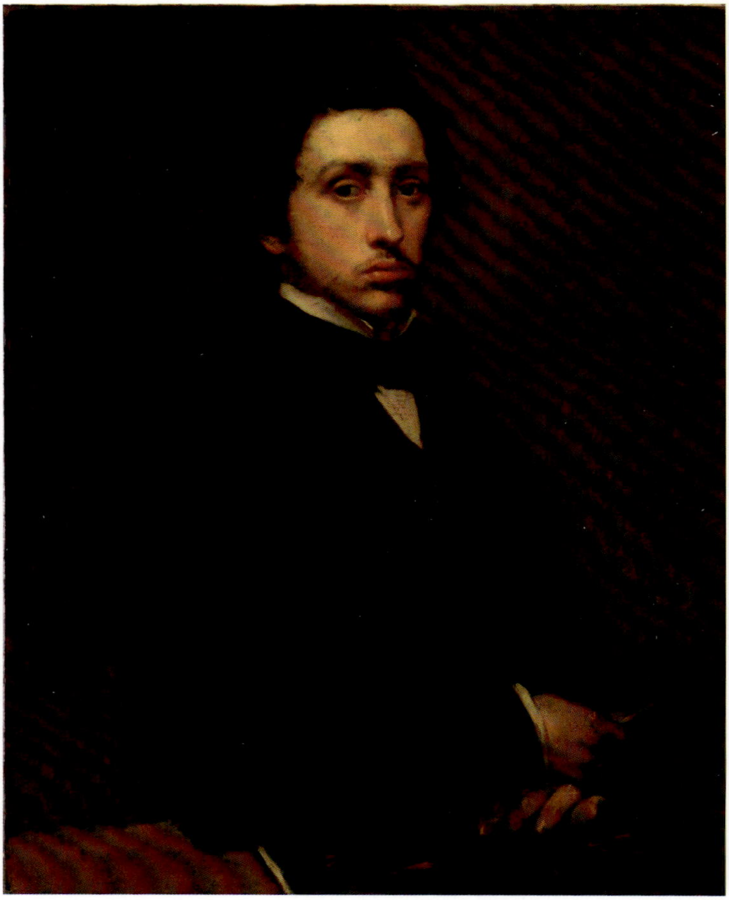

Edgar Degas, *Portrait of the Artist*, also known as *Degas with Charcoal Holder*, 1855
Oil on paper mounted on canvas, 32 ⅛ × 25 ⅝ in. (81.5 × 65 cm), Musée d'Orsay, Paris

Gruff yet sensitive, arrogant and discerning, intransigent and restless, Edgar Degas was a man of paradoxes. The painter was from a prosperous bourgeois background, born to a wealthy banking family. He was a recognized artist and well-informed collector. He maintained loyal friendships and kept himself fiercely independent from official circles and fashionable fads.

He followed a traditional course of study at the Lycée Louis-le-Grand in Paris, and was admitted to the École des Beaux-Arts in 1855. He studied under Louis Lamothe, a student of Ingres, whom he admired. He conscientiously frequented the Louvre and made careful copies of the old masters. Between 1856 and 1860, he made several visits to Italy, the home of his ancestors. Naples, Rome, Florence, and Venice offered him the opportunity to complete his training and perfect his knowledge of painting and drawing. His portraits were masterpieces of realism and psychology, and were favorably received by critics. His work was frequently admitted to the Salon but, rather than engaging in academic artistic circles, he preferred frequenting the Café Guerbois and the Nouvelle Athènes, where he encountered Manet, Zola, and the adherents of the "new painting." Together with Manet, he joined the infantry when war broke out in 1870.

Two years later, he sailed to New Orleans, where his mother's family lived. There

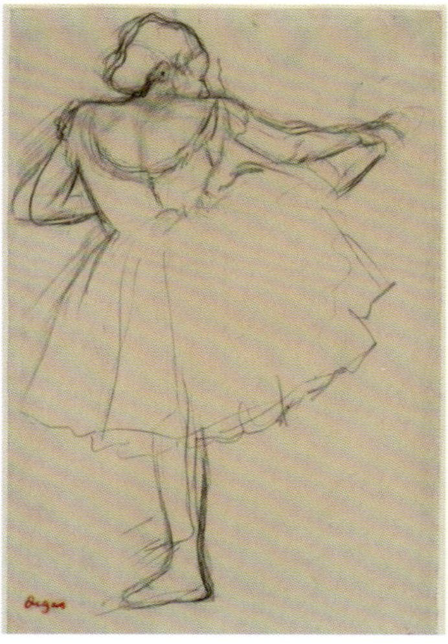

Edgar Degas, *Dancer at the Barre*
Black pencil, 11 ⅞ × 7 ⅞ in. (30 × 20 cm)
Musée d'Orsay, Paris, conserved
at the Musée du Louvre

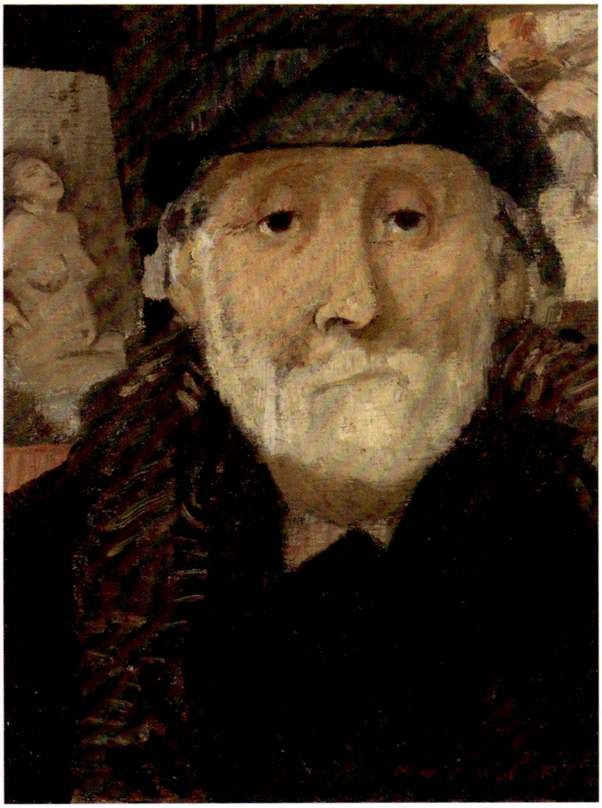

Maurice Denis, *Portrait of the Painter Degas*, 1906
Oil on canvas, 13 × 9 ½ in. (33 × 24 cm)
Musée d'Art Moderne, Troyes

Key Dates

1834
Born in Paris on July 19

1855
Admitted to the École des Beaux-Arts

1856
Travels in Italy

1870
Volunteers for the National Guard

1872
Travels to the United States

1878
Family bankruptcy

1889
Travels to Spain and Morocco with Italian artist Giovanni Boldini

1896
Exhibits his photographs

1917
Dies in Paris on September 27

he painted his extraordinary *A Cotton Office in New Orleans*, an astonishingly modernist work. In Paris, he turned his attention to racecourses, the stock exchange, the circus, theaters, and the opera. All of these subjects offered him the opportunity to depict his contemporaries with no concessions to convention. Although he was admitted to the Salon, he wholeheartedly engaged with the future impressionists and exhibited alongside them, despite their differences in style and point of view. "You need natural life, but I need an artificial one," he said. He preferred working in the studio to *plein air* painting, and figures to landscapes. He also refused to sacrifice drawing to color. For Degas, painting was a carefully considered and constructed art. He used off-center compositions, novel perspectives, and a photographer's eye to express a sense of life and movement, and to capture the fleeting moment. He was also among the first to recognize photography as an artistic medium.

Although he had previously been sheltered from financial concerns, Degas found his situation threatened by his family's bankruptcy in 1878. However, he never made any concessions in his art, refusing all official honors. He was admired by his contemporaries and appreciated by collectors, but he was a poor manager. He freely spent whatever

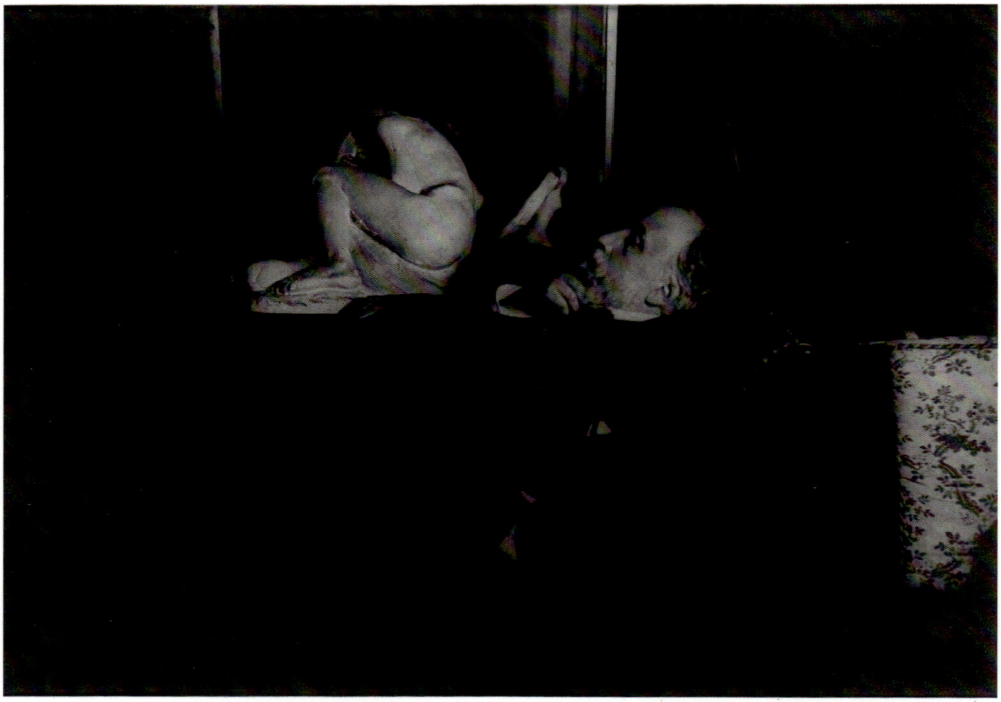

Edgar Degas, *Self-Portrait Beside a Statue by Bartholomé*, 1895
Silver print, Musée d'Orsay, Paris

money he earned buying pictures, and his periods of prosperity were short-lived. These tribulations did not improve his temperament. He became increasingly irascible, and some of his impressionist friends found him impossible to deal with. He was sometimes bitter, regretting the solitude that he had allowed to engulf him. Some judged him to be a misogynist, but he maintained a deep friendship with Mary Cassatt, Berthe Morisot, and her daughter Julie. "Monsieur Degas is always the same, a bit mad, but charming in spirit," wrote Berthe Morisot.

Driven by his creative energy, Edgar Degas was always experimenting with something new. He practiced every technique, including pastel and engraving, tirelessly exploring the subject that fascinated him–human reality. Dancers and women absorbed in ironing or bathing seem to come to life under his brush or pencil, as well as in his bold pastels. When his sight began to fail, he focused increasingly on his sculptural work, until he was forced to retire at the age of almost eighty. In 1917, Mary Cassatt and Monet walked in the cortège that accompanied his body for burial in the cemetery on Montmartre.

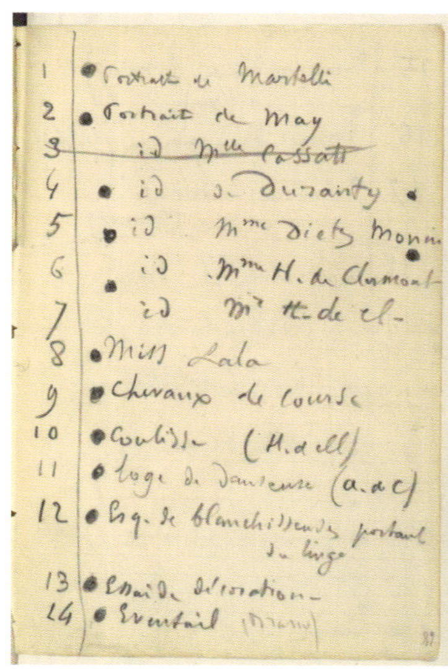
1 Portrait de Martelli
2 Portrait de May
3 id Mlle Cassatt
4 id de Duranty
5 id Mme Dietz Monnin
6 id Mme H. de Clermont
7 id Mr H. de Cl-
8 Miss Lala
9 Chevaux de course
10 Coulisse
11 Loge de danseuse
12 Esq. de blanchisseuses portant du linge
13 Etude de décoration
14 Eventail

Degas's inventory of works
Black pencil
Bibliothèque Nationale de France, Paris

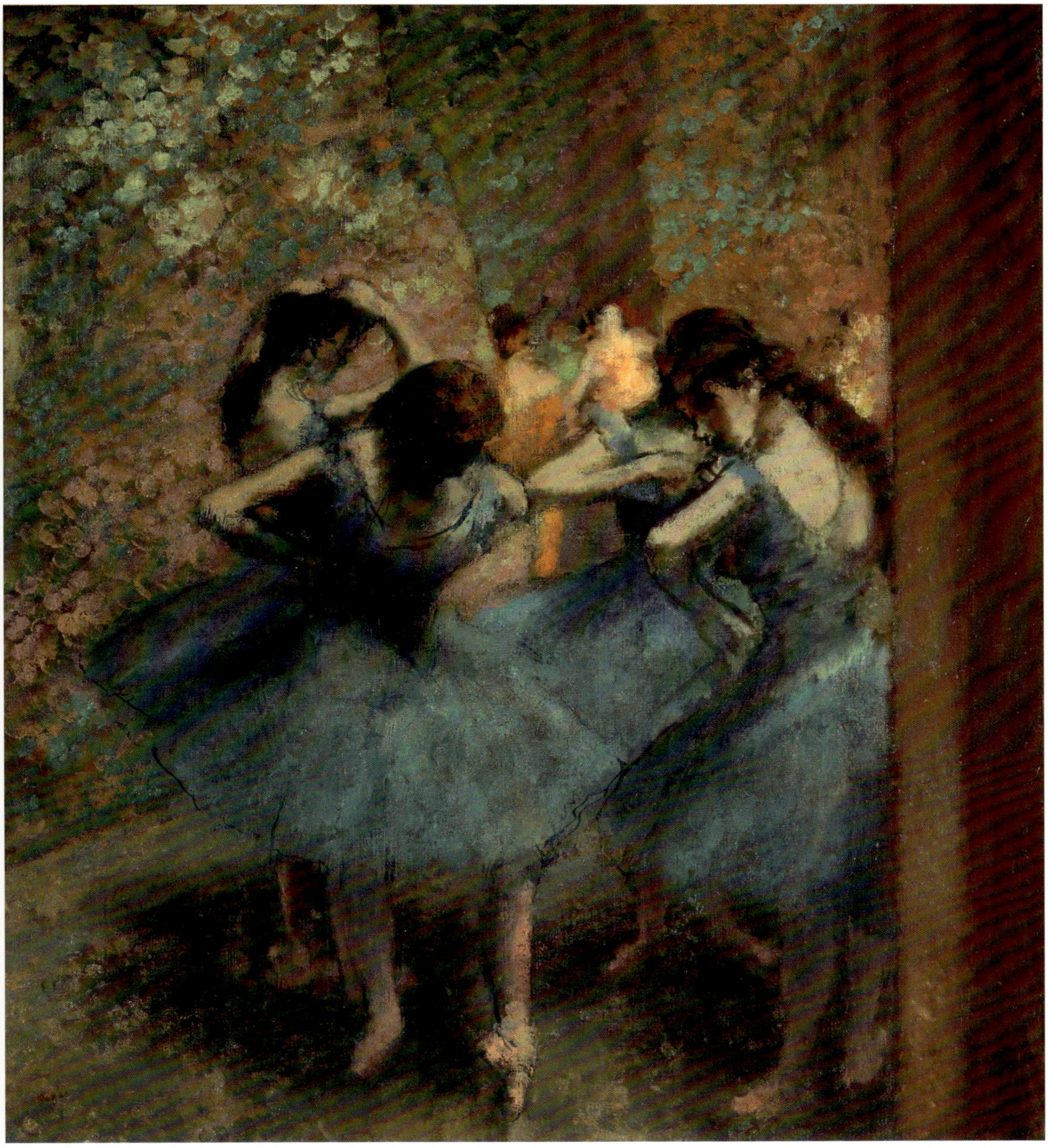

Edgar Degas, *Blue Dancers*, c. 1890
Oil on canvas, 15 ⅜ × 35 ¼ in. (39 × 89.5 cm)
Musée d'Orsay, Paris

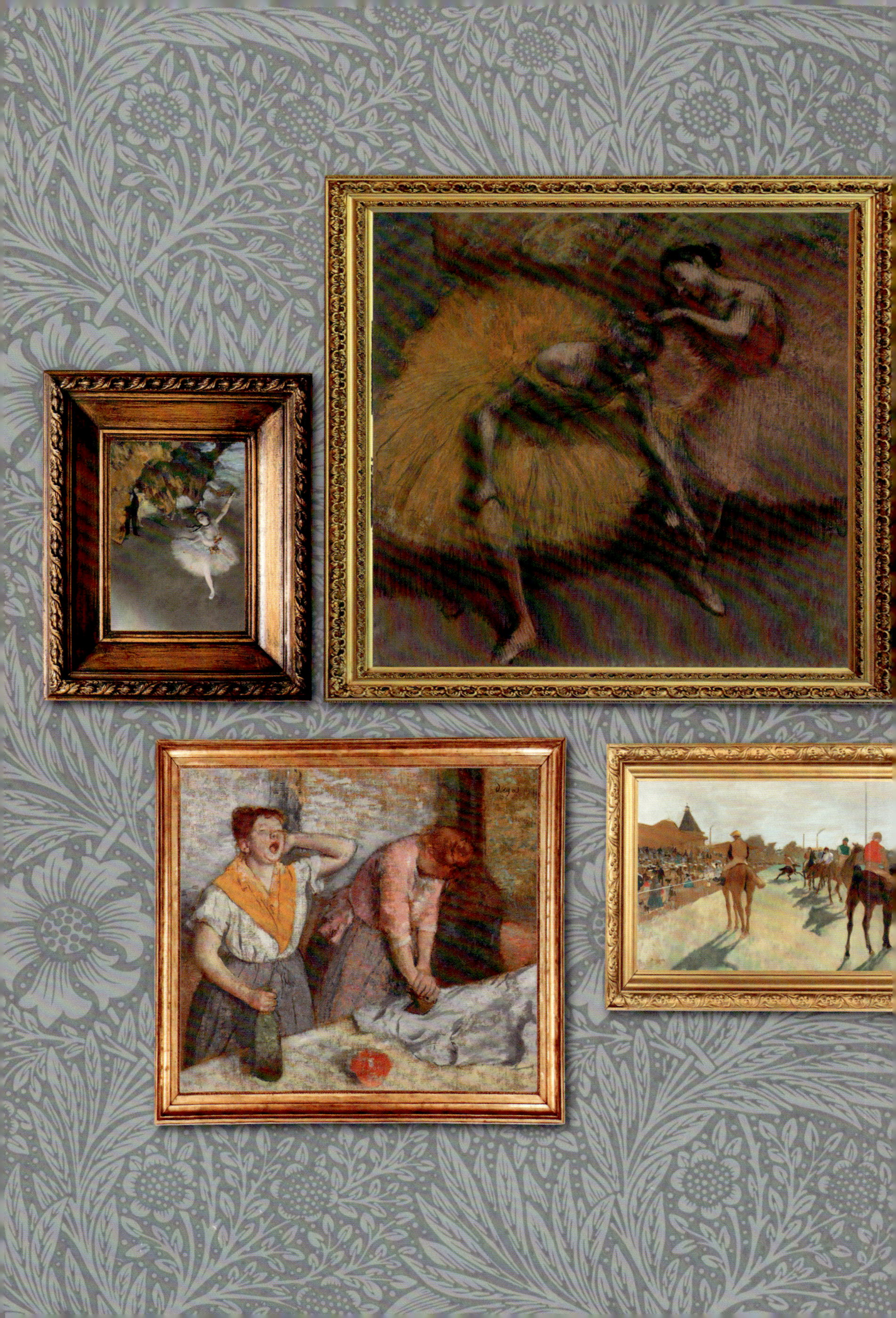

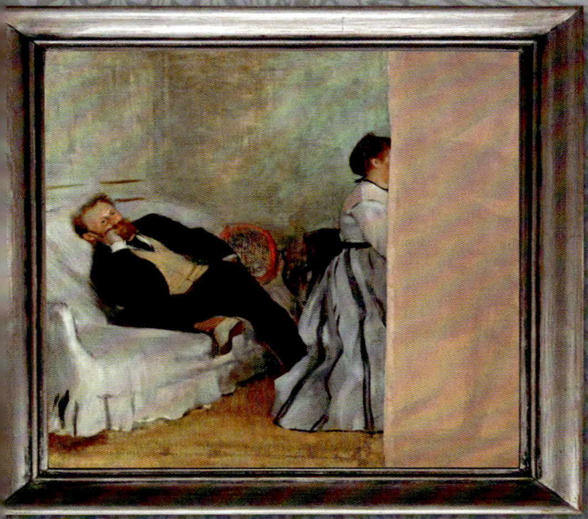
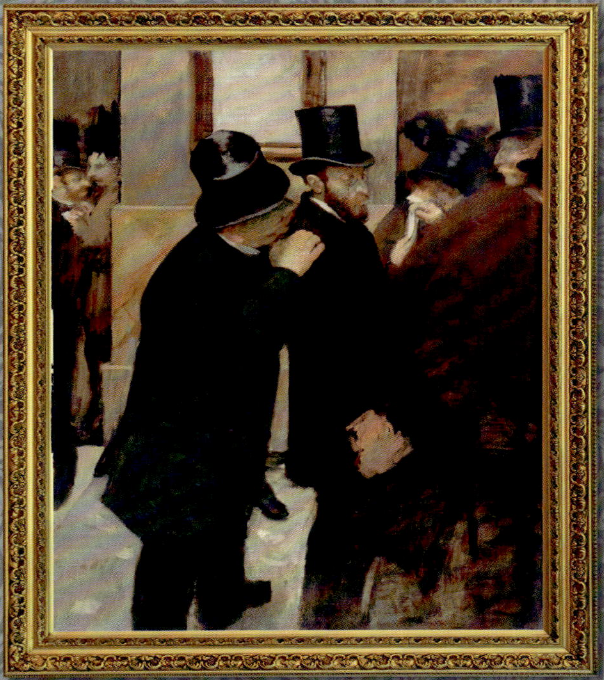
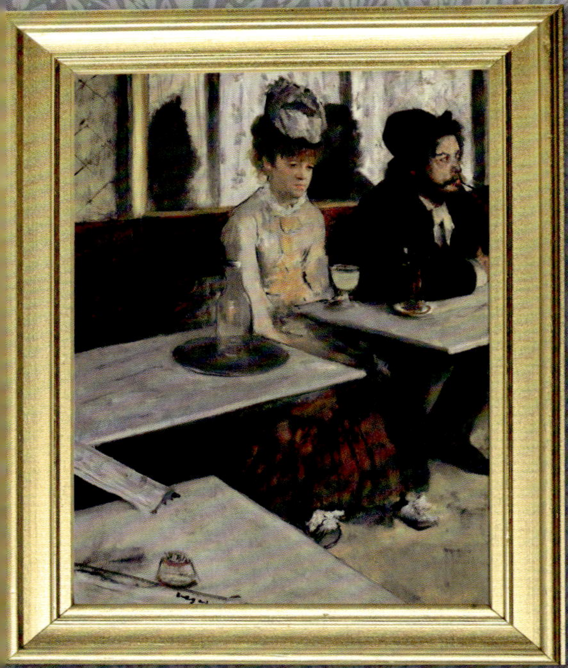
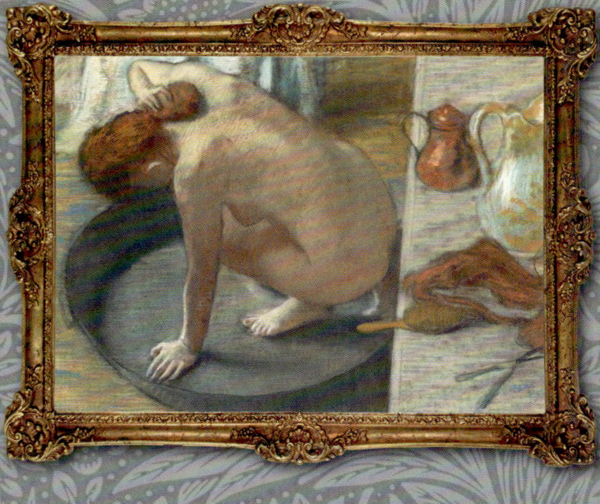

Frédéric Bazille

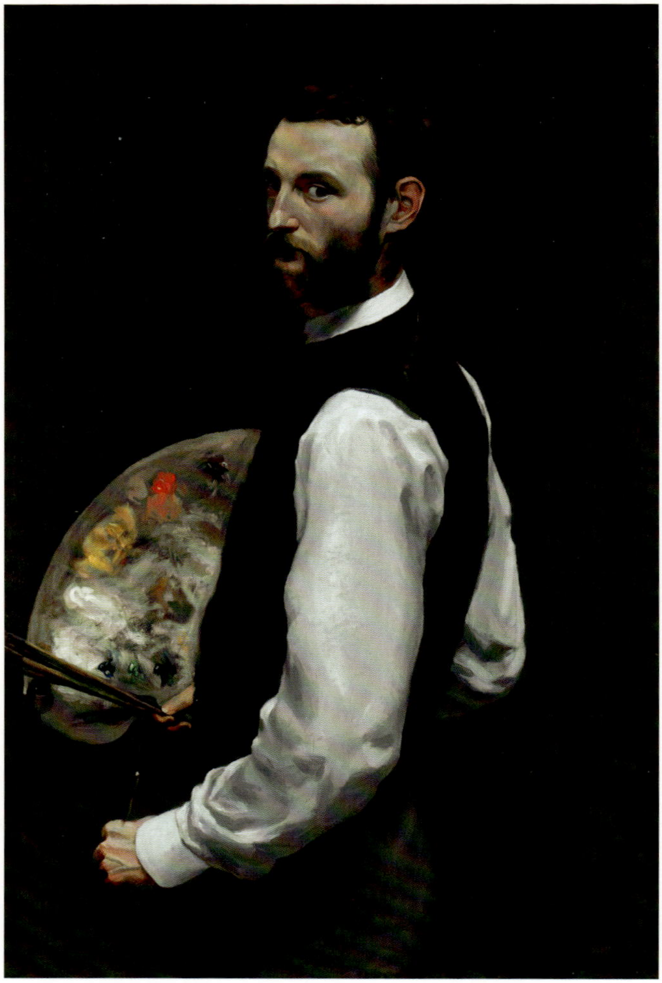

Frédéric Bazille, *Self-Portrait with Palette*, c. 1865
Oil on canvas, 3 ft. 7 in. × 2 ft. 4 in. (108.9 × 71.1 cm), The Art Institute of Chicago, Chicago

Frédéric Bazille was tragically killed in 1870 in the Franco-Prussian War, and so did not have the time to demonstrate the full extent of his talent. However, his destiny was tied to that of the impressionists. He shared in their beginnings, their hopes, and their setbacks. Born in Montpellier to a prosperous family of winemakers, Bazille initially began to study medicine, before dedicating himself full time to his passion for painting and drawing. Studying in Paris, he was admitted to painter Charles Gleyre's studio in 1862, where he met Sisley, Renoir, and Monet. They became the closest of friends. They worked together *en plein air*, painting from nature. To their surprise, some of these canvases were accepted by the Salon: "Apart from Manet, whom no one dares to refuse, I am the least ill-treated. Monet was entirely rejected.… I was supported by Cabanel [an academic painter] to my astonishment."

His tall figure can be seen in portraits painted by Renoir, who showed him engrossed in front of his easel, as if observed surreptitiously. Fantin-Letour showed him standing in the elegant attire of a dandy. Bazille painted himself in his picture, *Bazille's Studio*, where we see him at the side of Édouard Manet, whom he regarded as a master. His studio was a welcoming retreat for Monet and Renoir when they were penniless. Everyone gathered there to engage in heated and passionate

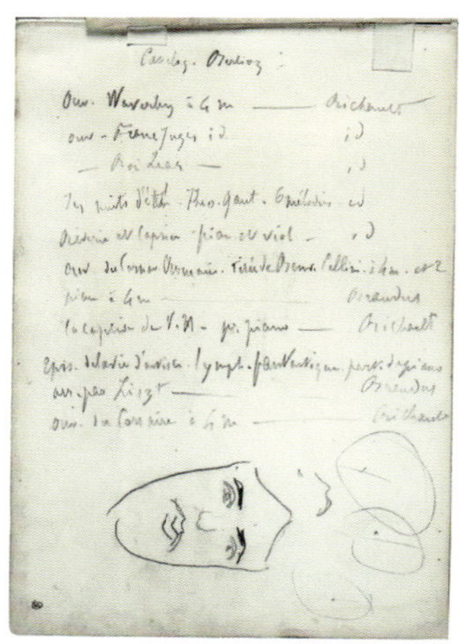

Frédéric Bazille, *Berlioz*, c. 1867–70
Graphite on paper,
9 ¾ × 13 ⅞ in. (24.8 × 35.3 cm)
Musée Fabre, Montpellier

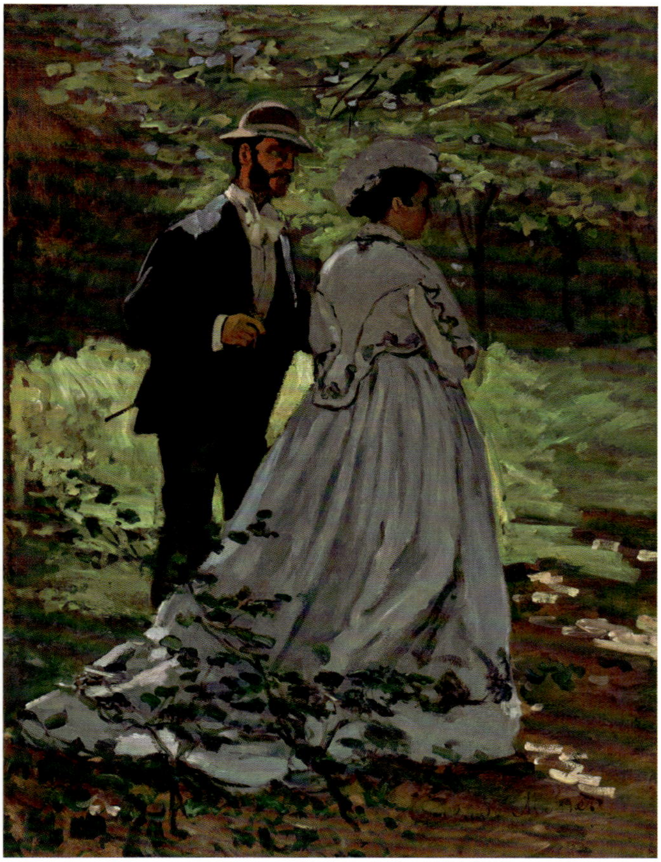

Claude Monet, *Bazille and Camille (Study for* The Luncheon on the Grass*)*, 1865
Oil on canvas, 3 ft. ½ in. × 2 ft. 3 ¼ (93 × 68.9 cm), Musée d'Orsay, Paris

Key Dates

1841

Born in Montpellier on December 6

1862

Enters Charles Gleyre's atelier in Paris

1866

Accepted by the Salon

1870

Dies at the front in the Franco-Prussian War on November 28

discussions on art. We see canvases by his friends Renoir and Monet hanging next to his own work on the walls of his studio. Bazille did not entirely disregard landscape, but he favored depictions of the human figure and the contemporary world. In his paintings of his family, each individual is captured in a natural pose, a departure from traditional practice. Tackling the male nude, the academic genre *par excellence*, he chose to represent young men in swimsuits, creating a scene of contemporary life. His technique is more conventional and less daring than Monet's, but his handling of light, often showing sharp contrasts, demonstrates the young painter's promising originality. The impressionists deeply mourned the premature passing of their warm and generous comrade, who fell at the front during the Franco-Prussian War before his twenty-ninth birthday.

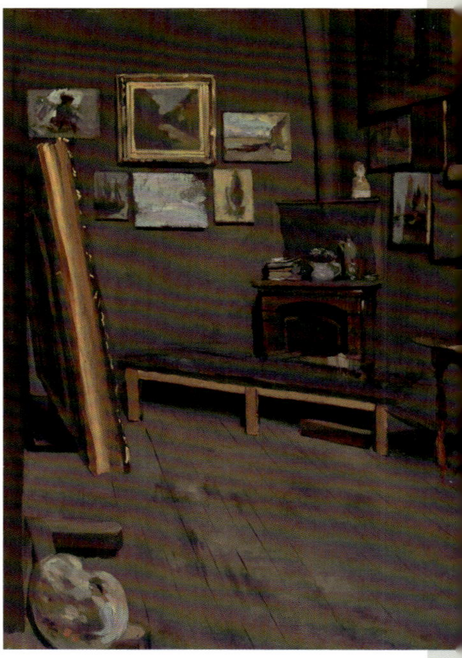

Frédéric Bazille, *The Artist's Studio, Rue Visconti,* May 1867
Oil on canvas, 25 ¼ × 19 ¼ in. (64 × 49 cm)
Virginia Museum of Fine Arts, Richmond

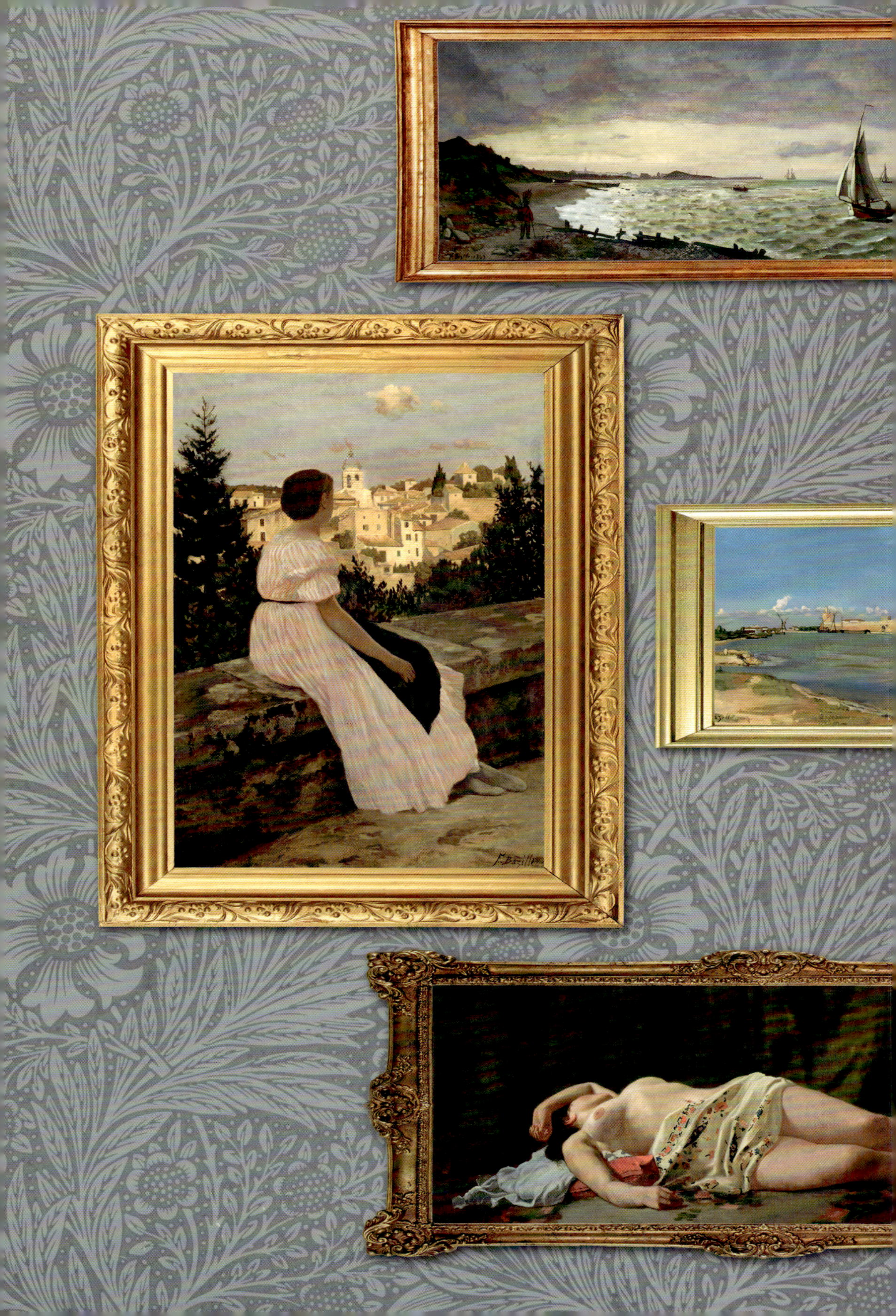

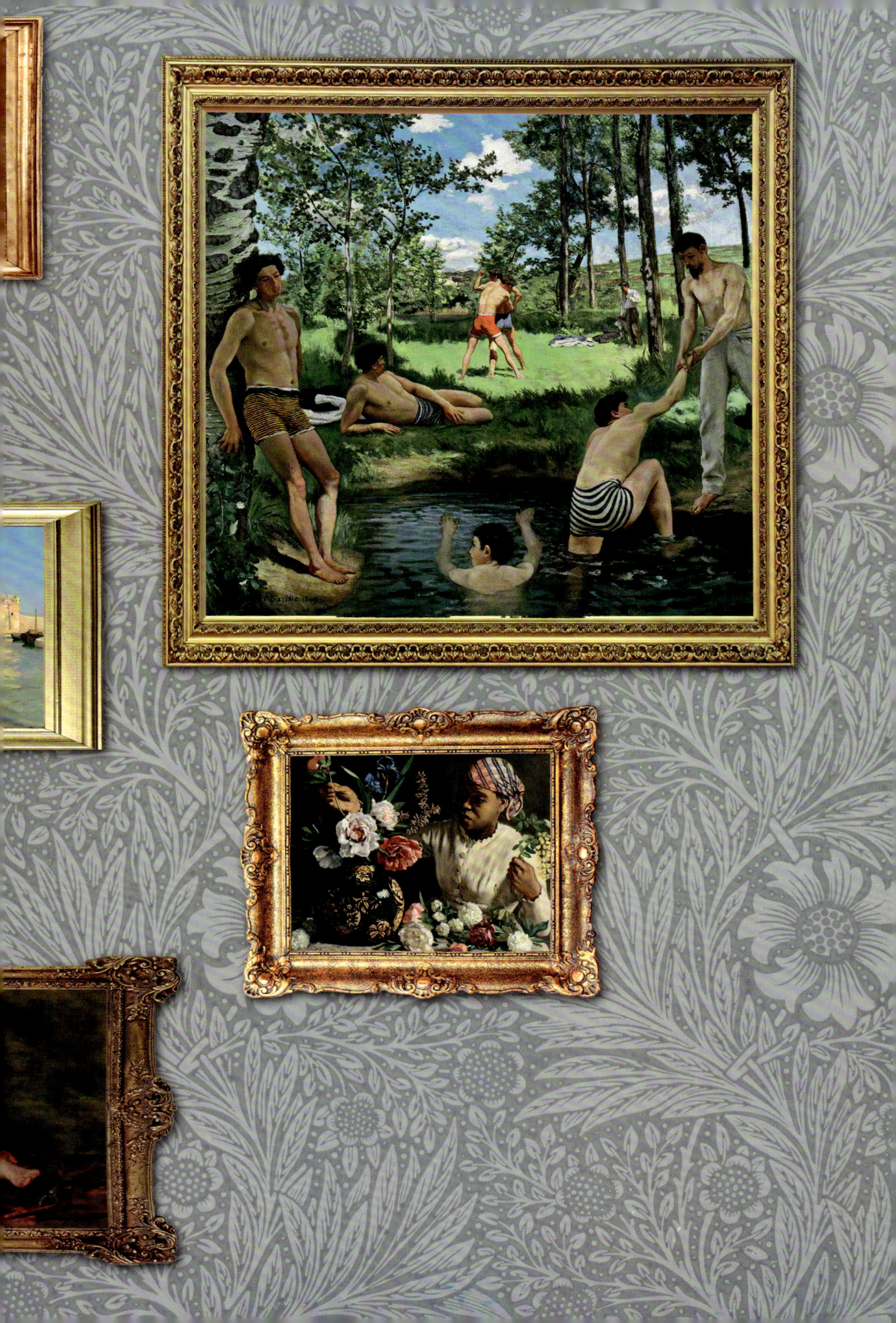

Gustave Caillebotte

Gustave Caillebotte, *Self-Portrait*, c. 1889
Oil on canvas, 21 ⅝ × 18 ⅛ in. (55 × 46 cm)
Private collection

"We've just lost a sincere and devoted friend … one we can deeply mourn; he was good and generous, and what's more, a talented painter." This is how Pissarro honored Caillebotte's memory when he died in 1894 at the age of forty-five. Gustave Caillebotte was indeed devoted and generous, and he was also discreet and sensitive. He was among the most fervent advocates of impressionism. Like Degas, he came from the bourgeoisie, pursuing rigorous academic studies before starting a career as a painter. He received a law degree in 1870, and was mobilized during the Franco-Prussian War. He later traveled around Scandinavia and Italy, before joining the painter Léon Bonnat's atelier in 1872. Admitted to the École des Beaux-Arts in 1873, he quickly mastered traditional techniques and soon turned away from academicism, which he found unsatisfactory. He approached Degas through the intermediary of his friend Henri Rouart, and became acquainted with the impressionists during their first exhibition in Nadar's studio in 1874. Caillebotte's magnificent painting *The Floor Planers* was rejected by the Salon the following year. Initially dejected by this setback, he accepted an invitation to participate in the second impressionist exhibition, becoming its efficient organizer and the principal source of its financial

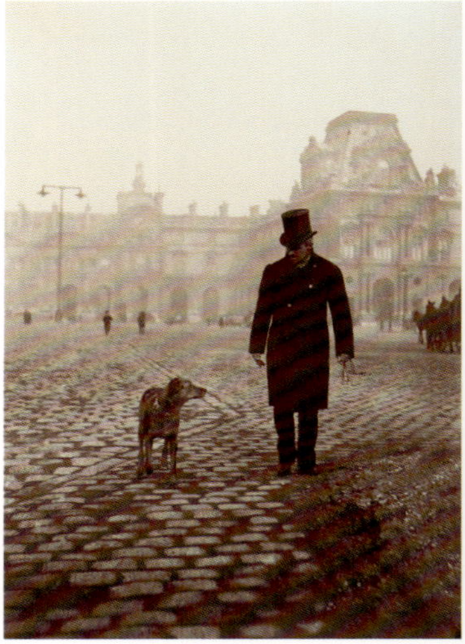

Gustave Caillebotte and His Dog on the Place du Carrousel (detail), February 1892
Flexible gelatin silver bromide negative, 6 ⅛ × 4 ⅛ in. (15.5 × 10.5 cm); silver print, 5 ⅞ × 4 ⅛ in. (15 × 10.5 cm), private collection

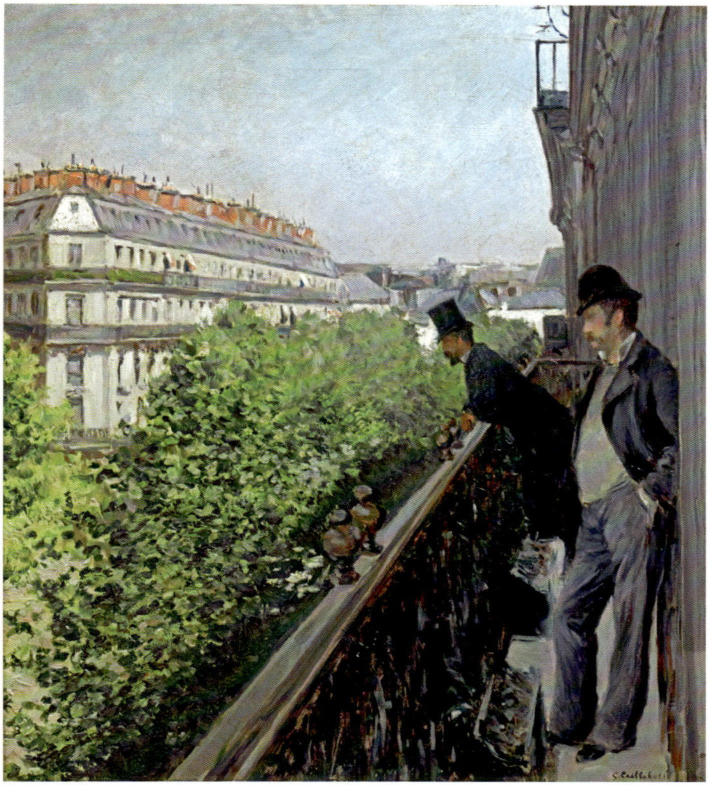

Gustave Caillebotte, *A Balcony, Boulevard Haussmann*, c. 1880
Oil on canvas, 23 ⅝ × 24 ⅜ in. (60 × 62 cm)
Private collection

Key Dates

1848

Born in Paris on August 19

1870

Receives law degree

1873

Enters the École des Beaux-Arts

1876

Participates in the second impressionist exhibition

1881

Purchases a property in Petit-Genevilliers with his brother Martial

1884

Purchases The Balcony by Manet

1888

Participates in the Les XX exhibition in Brussels

1894

Dies in Gennevilliers on February 21

1896

His bequest is partially accepted by the State (67 of 96 paintings)

support. His own pictorial style and his preference for painting figures linked him most closely with Degas or Manet, but he devoted all his energy to defending the impressionists. He offered much-needed financial help to Monet, in particular. He purchased many paintings, and thus amassed the finest and first impressionist collection long before these works achieved recognition and success. From the outset, he planned to bequeath his holdings to the State. He maintained an unwavering friendship with Renoir, who visited frequently and who named him godfather of his eldest son. He was equally close to Monet, and signed as a witness at his marriage. But he was unquestionably closest of all to his brother Martial, five years his junior. Martial was a musician and amateur photographer, and they shared a passion for sailing. They competed in regattas together and invested

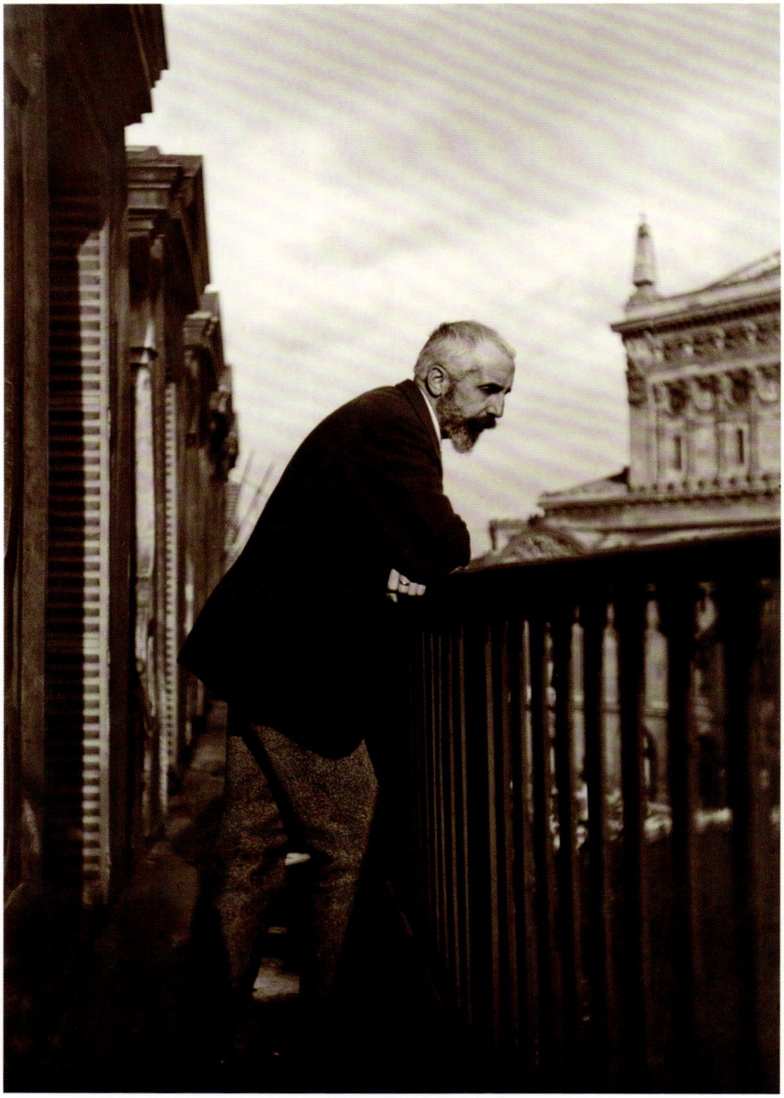

Martial Caillebotte, *Me on the Balcony*, December 1891, flexible gelatin silver bromide negative, 6 ⅛ × 4 ½ in. (15.5 × 11.5 cm); silver print, 6 ⅛ × 4 ⅛ in. (15.5 × 10.5 cm), private collection

in the first sailing clubs. Gustave even drew up plans for sailboat designs. He was generous with useful advice for the young Signac, who was also an accomplished sailor. Forming an inseparable duo, the Caillebotte brothers lived together until Martial married in 1887. Moving to his property in Petit-Genevilliers, Gustave Caillebotte gave free rein to his passion for gardening and horticulture. He had explored every artistic genre–landscape, still life, interiors, nudes, portraits, regattas, and the streets of Paris–but now

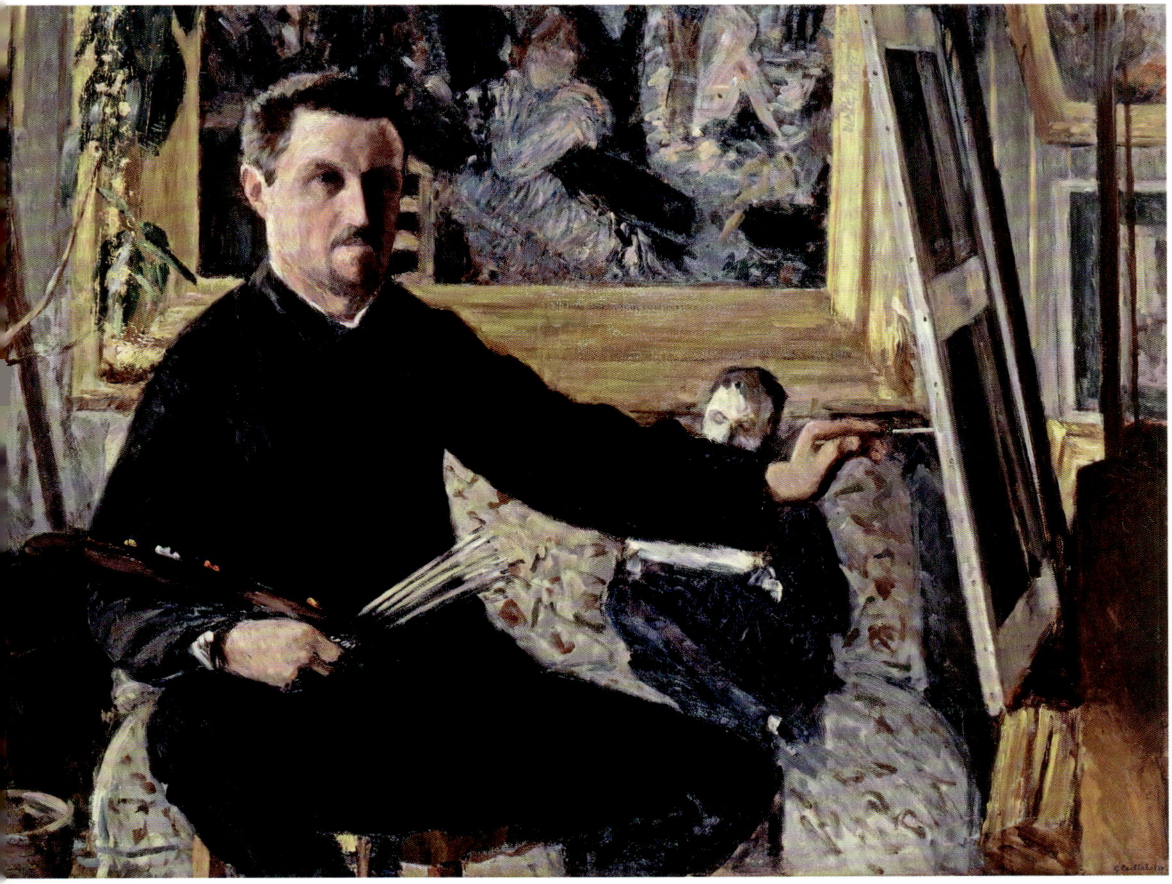

Gustave Caillebotte, *Self-Portrait at an Easel*, c. 1879–80
Oil on canvas, 2 ft. 11 ½ in. × 3 ft. 9 ¼ in. (90 × 115 cm), private collection

his flowers and garden became almost exclusive subjects for him, well before Monet began his transformation of Giverny. His premature death prevented him from completing the landscape design he had begun: he had envisioned banks of flowers overflowing the space and giving the impression of a luxuriant greenhouse. "He was only beginning his career when we lost him," mourned Monet. His brother Martial struggled to persuade the State to accept even a portion of the collection he had bequeathed. It included works by Degas, Manet, Cézanne, Monet, Renoir, and many others. There was just one name missing from the list: Caillebotte.

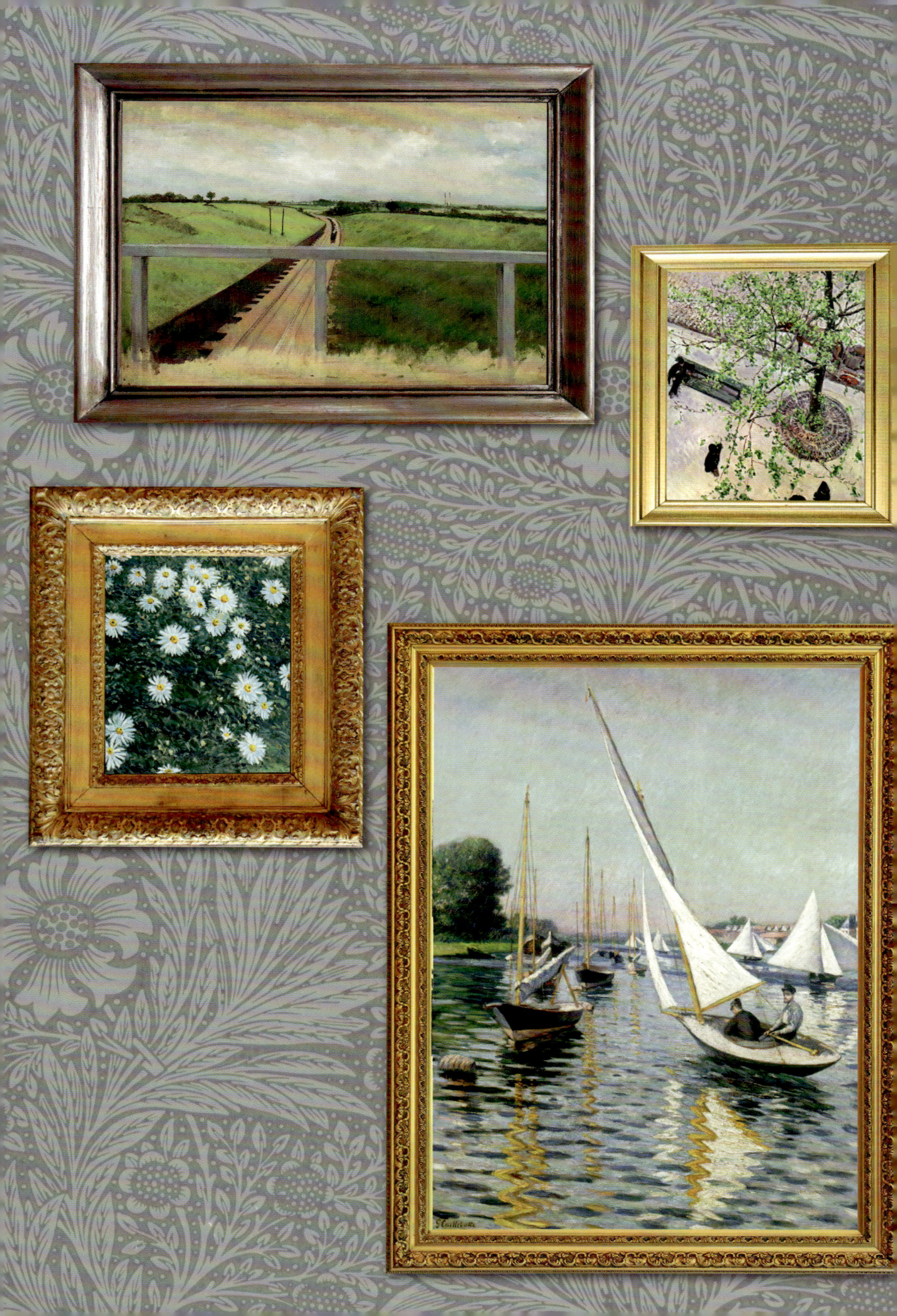

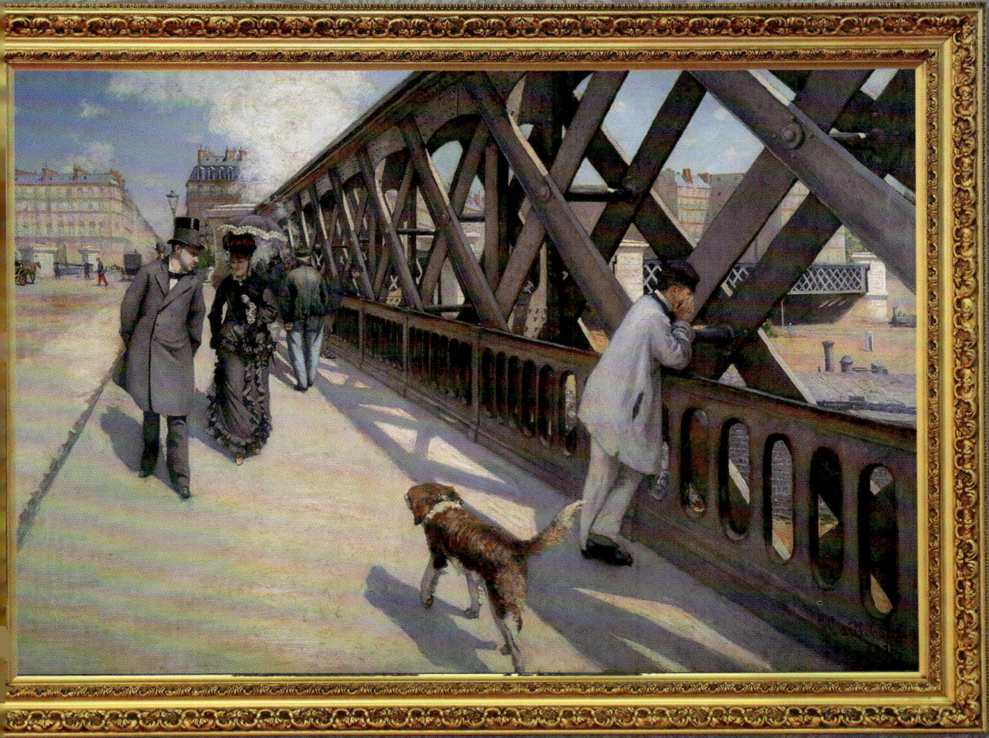

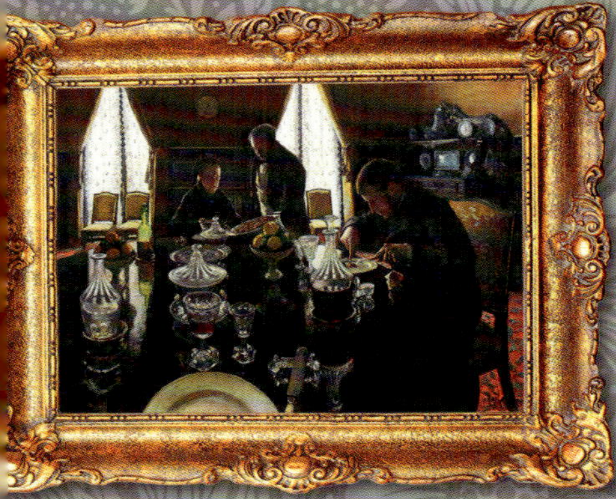

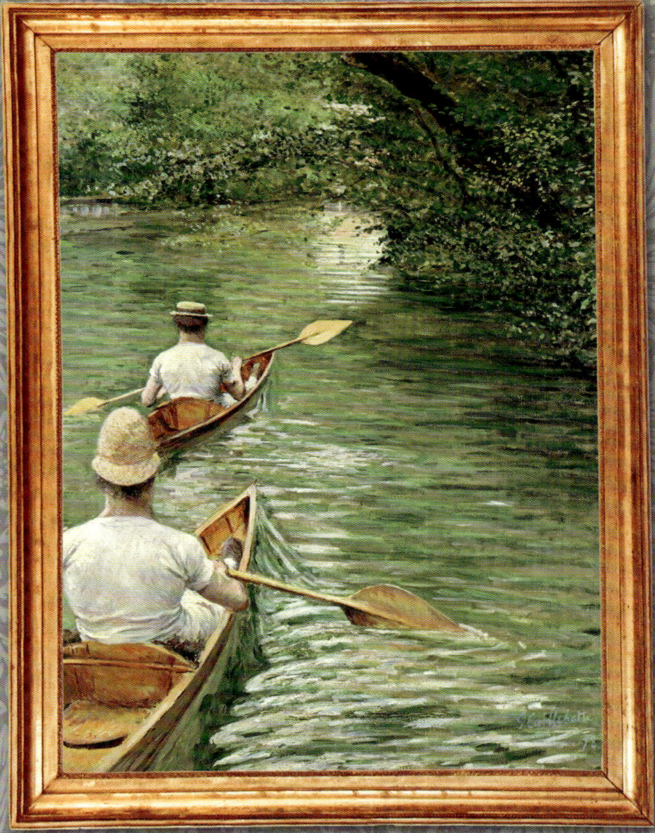

Alfred Sisley

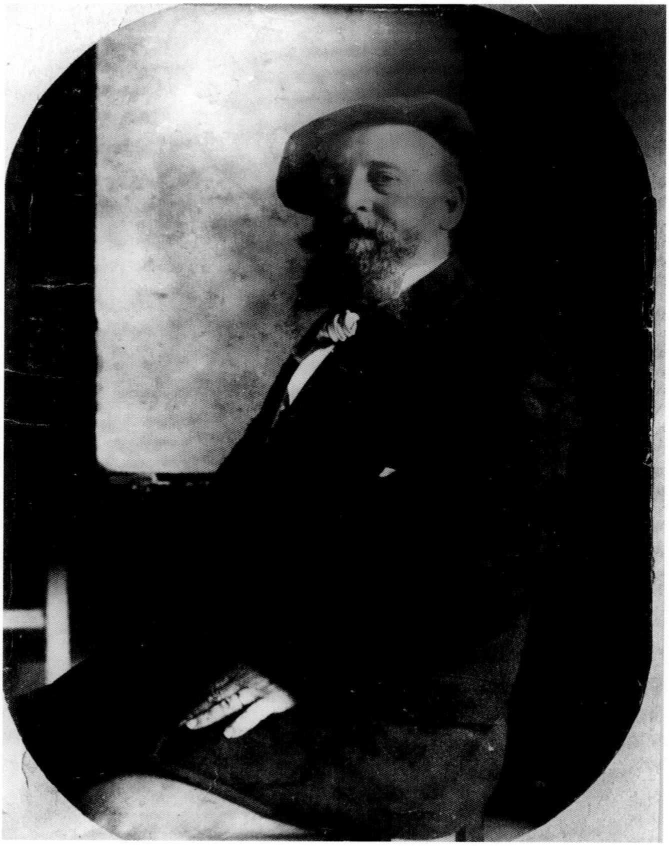

Alfred Sisley posing in front of a blank canvas
Private collection

"Sisley lived the life of a selfless, reflective landscape painter, with a deep love of nature, who distanced himself from social life," wrote the journalist and art critic Gustave Geffroy. Living in retirement in Moret-sur-Loing, the painter was never really recognized during his lifetime, only gaining recognition after his death in 1899.

Born in Paris to British parents, Alfred Sisley grew up in a prosperous family of wealthy professionals. In 1857, his father sent him to London to pursue business studies, a topic of no interest to Alfred. Even at a young age, he preferred to marvel at the canvases of Constable and Turner. Returning to Paris, he enrolled in Charles Gleyre's studio, although Gleyre was very critical of landscape painting. "He didn't give much help to his students, but he did have the merit of leaving them alone," Renoir acknowledged. It also allowed Sisley to meet Monet, Bazille, and Renoir; they banded together to form the "Gang of Four." The group went to paint from nature in the forest of Fontainebleau, the Île-de-France, and Normandy. Sisley's compositions were solidly constructed, almost classical in form. The Salon accepted some, and rejected others. Buoyed by these early successes, though, and comfortably off because of his family's money, Sisley frequently came to the aid of his less fortunate friends. However, the Franco-Prussian War left his father bankrupt, and Sisley's studio was destroyed by looting soldiers. Already the father of two children, the artist suddenly found himself in severe straits. Not allowing himself to become discouraged, however, he participated actively in the first impressionist exhibition in 1874, as well as in those that followed. His landscapes were well-balanced realist compositions executed with a subtle, refined palette. However, this stylistic discipline did not bring the success he hoped for, and the efforts of his dealer Paul Durand-Ruel remained fruitless. Shy and solitary, Sisley increasingly turned inward. In 1880, he withdrew

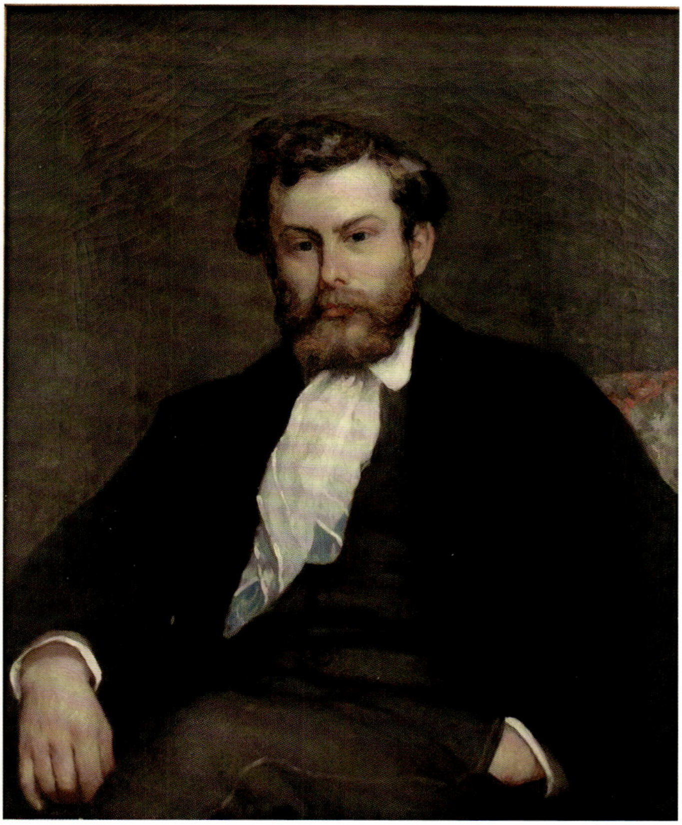

Auguste Renoir, *Portrait of the Painter Alfred Sisley*, 1864
Oil on canvas, 32 ¼ × 26 in. (82 × 66 cm)
E. G. Bührle Collection, Zurich

to Moret-sur-Loing with his family, distancing himself further from Parisian artistic circles. At Monet's suggestion, he embarked on a significant series of paintings on the same theme, including the church in Moret, which he captured at various times of day across the seasons. It was also to Monet, who was a regular visitor, that Sisley commended his children before his death. Somewhat embittered, Sisley succumbed to inexorable bouts of depression, the effects of which are noticeable in his paintings. Some have criticized his consistency, and his fidelity to the impressionist style, implying that he was not capable of reinventing himself. Shortly after his death in 1899, however, collectors began to take an interest in his paintings, and their prices began to climb.

Key Dates

1839

Born in Paris on October 30

1857

Begins studies in London

1860

Enrolls in Charles Gleyre's studio

1870

His studio in Bougival is destroyed by Prussian troops

1874

Participates in the first impressionist exhibition

1875

Moves to Marly-le-Roi

1880

Settles close to Moret-sur-Loing

1897

Marries his mistress, Eugénie Lescouezec, in Cardiff

1899

Dies in Moret on January 29

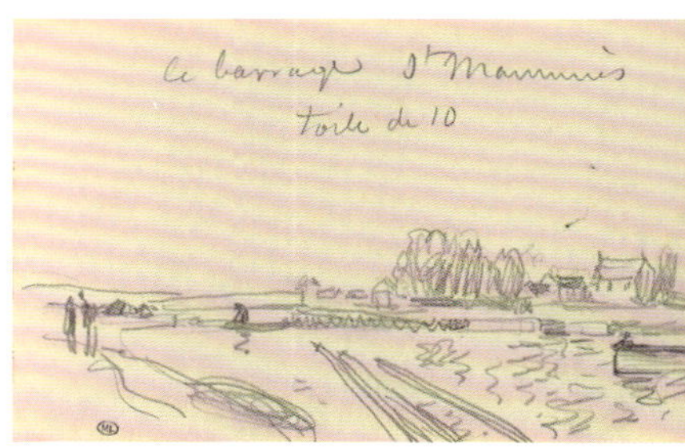

Alfred Sisley, *The Dam at Saint-Mammès*
Graphite, 4 ¾ × 7 ⅝ in. (12 × 19.5 cm)
Musée d'Orsay, Paris

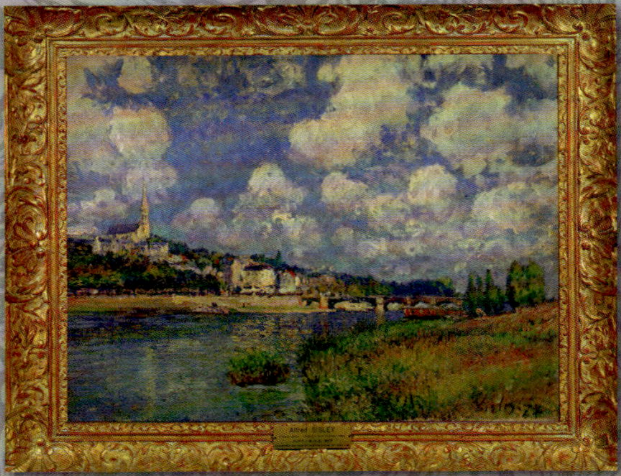

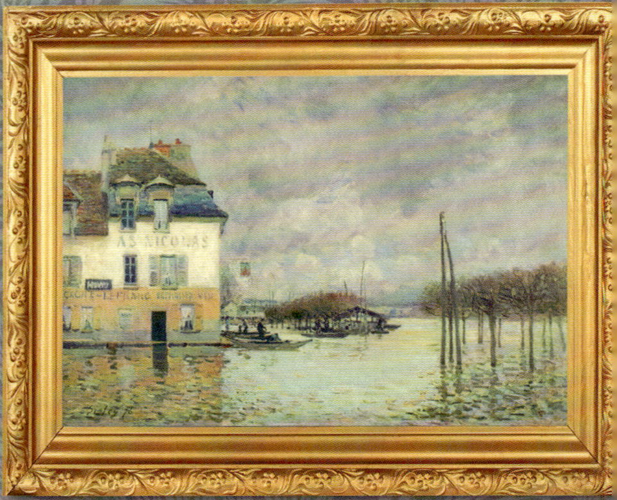

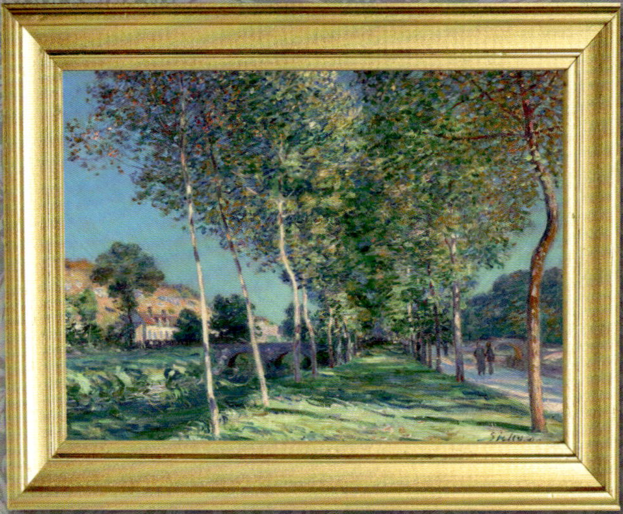

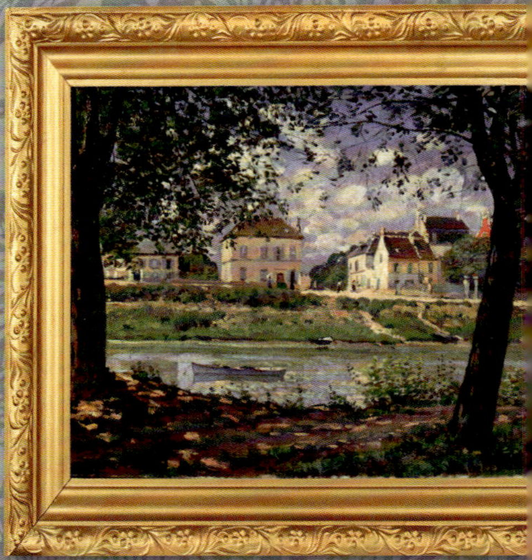

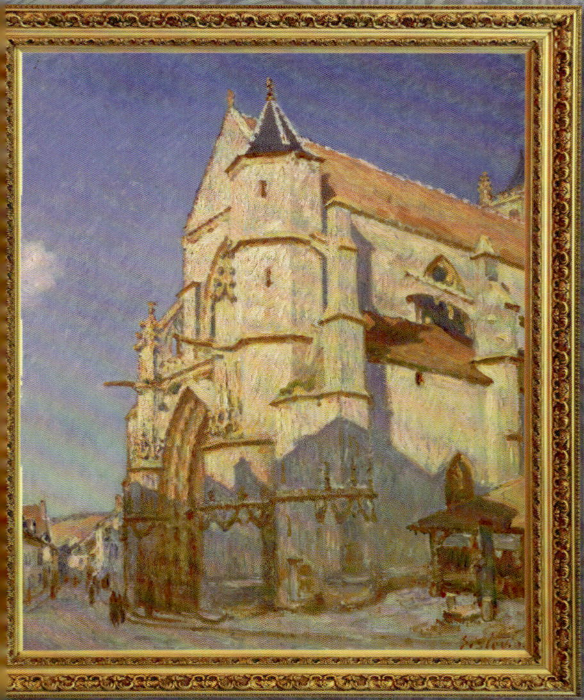

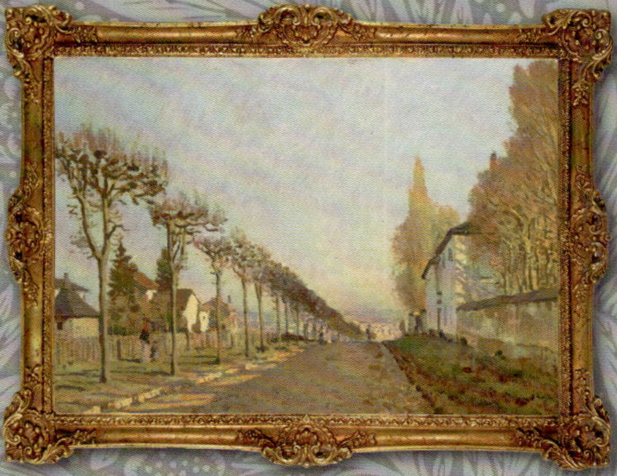

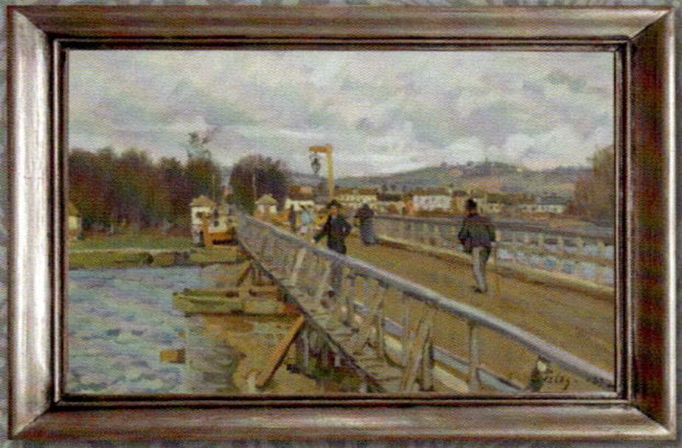

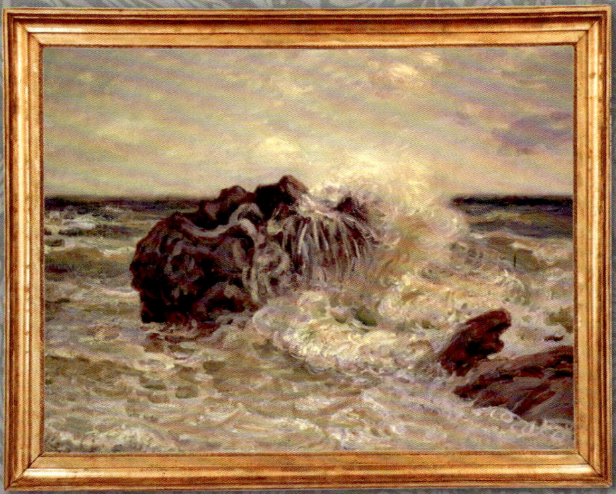

Berthe Morisot

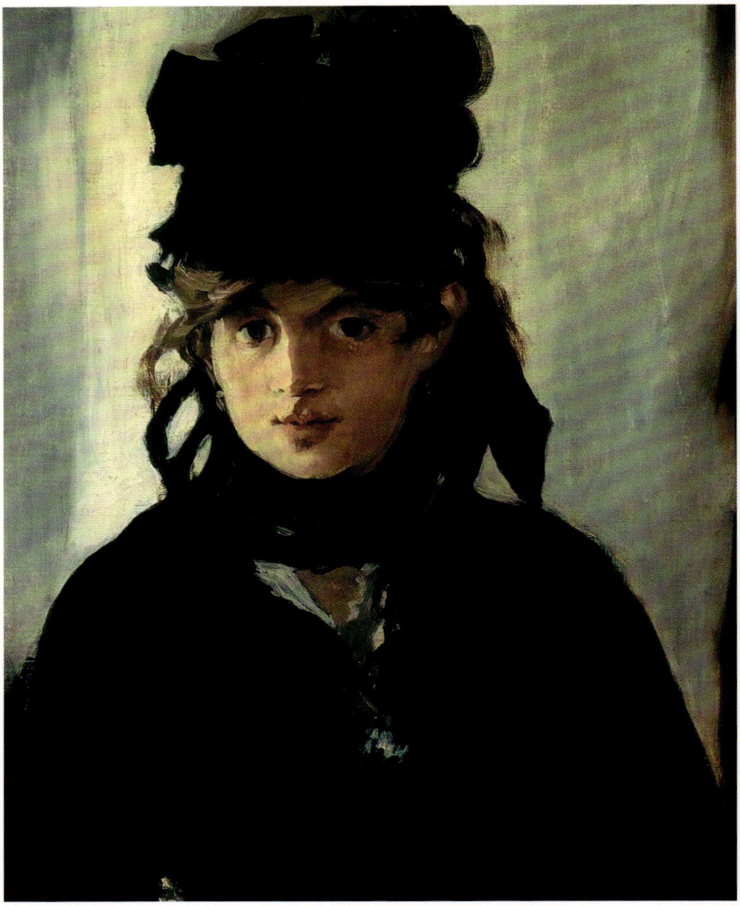

Édouard Manet, *Berthe Morisot with a Bouquet of Violets*, 1872
Oil on canvas, 21 ⅝ × 15 in. (55 × 38 cm)
Musée d'Orsay, Paris

Stéphane Mallarmé called her "the lovely painter," "the angel of the incomplete," and "the sorceress." Berthe Morisot's charms were not lost on her contemporaries. Admired for her personality and beauty, as well as for her artistic talent, she played a leading role in the history of late nineteenth-century painting.

The daughter of a prominent government official, Berthe Morisot grew up in a bourgeois family that frequently hosted distinguished figures including Rossini, Jules Ferry, and Alfred Stevens. Her parents were sufficiently open-minded to allow their daughters to copy old master paintings in the Louvre, renowned for being a gathering place for artists, where everybody knew each other, if not through friendship, then through point of view, name, history, or habit. She and her sister Edma became acquainted with Fantin-Latour, and she also met Corot, who gave her a few painting lessons. The École des Beaux-Arts, which refused to accept female students, was not an option for her; however, she was accepted by the Salon in 1864, and the following year her father built her a studio in the family's garden. Tall and slender, extremely distinguished in her bearing and intelligence, Berthe Morisot was a dark Baudelairean beauty, who was enigmatic, very courteous, and fiercely independent. She turned down offers of

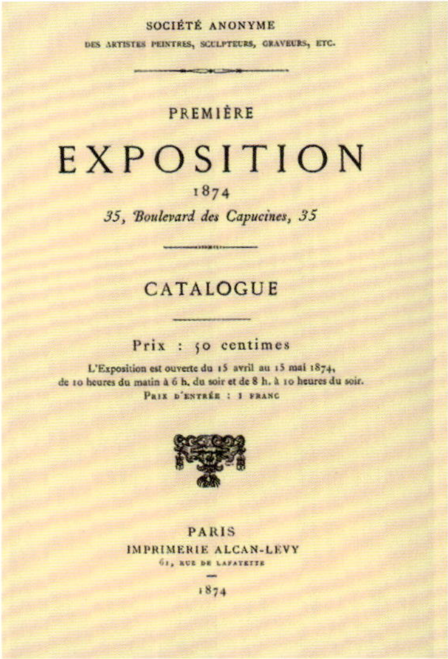

SOCIÉTÉ ANONYME
DES ARTISTES PEINTRES, SCULPTEURS, GRAVEURS, ETC.

PREMIÈRE
EXPOSITION
1874
35, Boulevard des Capucines, 35

CATALOGUE

Prix : 50 centimes
L'Exposition est ouverte du 15 avril au 15 mai 1874,
de 10 heures du matin à 6 h. du soir et de 8 h. à 10 heures du soir.
PRIX D'ENTRÉE : 1 FRANC

PARIS
IMPRIMERIE ALCAN-LEVY
61, RUE DE LAFAYETTE
1874

Cover of the catalog for the first impressionist exhibition in 1874

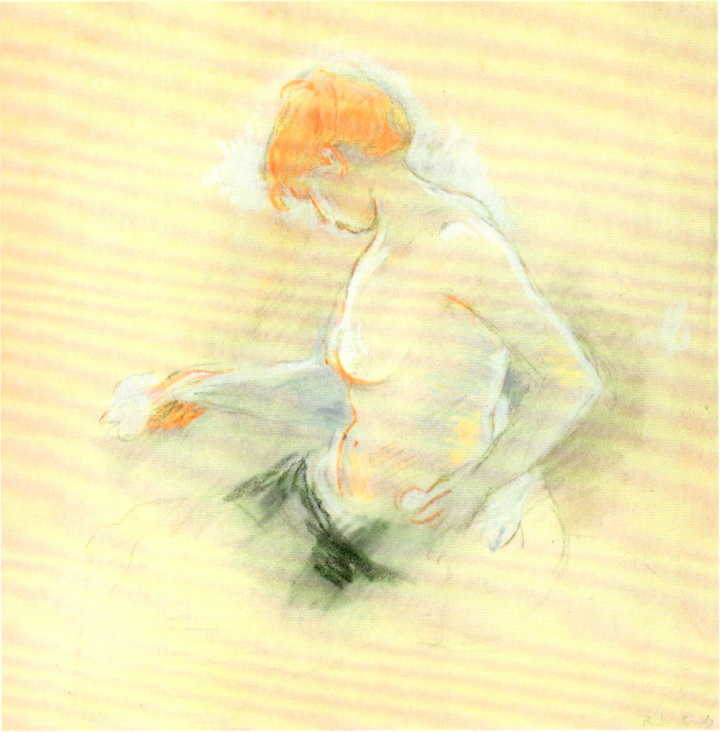

Berthe Morisot, *Young Woman Drying Herself*, 1886–87
Pastel, 16 ½ × 16 ⅛ in. (42 × 41 cm)
Private collection

marriage from Puvis de Chavannes and Jules Ferry politely but decisively.

In 1868, she began to pose for Édouard Manet, who made her one of his favorite models. She can be seen in *The Balcony*, with a distant, dreamy air and a distinctive presence. This young woman, an intimist painter and an artist of the avant-garde, also promoted her own works, and participated in the first impressionist exhibition in 1874. She married Eugène Manet, the painter's brother, the same year, and gave birth four years later to their daughter Julie. Having recently given birth, she was not able to take part in the 1879 exhibition, the only break in her unwavering loyalty to the movement. She and her husband financed the seventh showing of this avant-garde exhibition in 1882. After Édouard Manet's death in 1883, the couple organized a retrospective of his work at the École des Beaux-Arts. They frequently got together with "our friend Renoir," Monet, Degas–when she was present,

Key Dates

1841

Born in Bourges on January 14

1858

Copies old masters at the Louvre

1860

Takes lessons from Corot

1864

First submission of a painting to the Salon

1868

Meets Édouard Manet

1874

Participates in the first impressionist exhibition; marries Eugène Manet, Édouard's brother

1878

Birth of daughter Julie

1882

Finances the seventh impressionist exhibition with her husband

1892

Death of Eugène Manet

1895

Dies in Paris on March 2

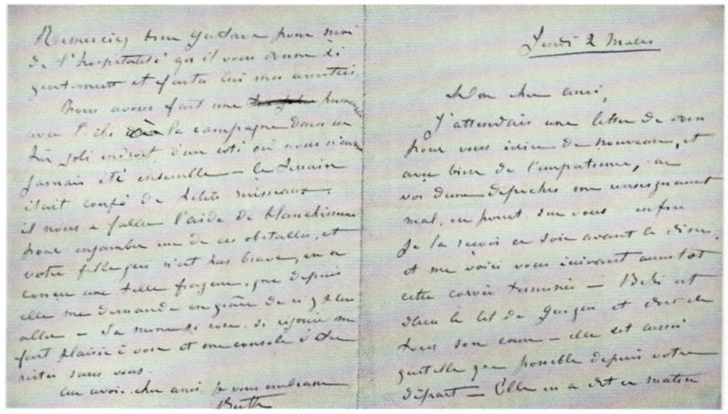

Berthe Morisot, letter
Private collection

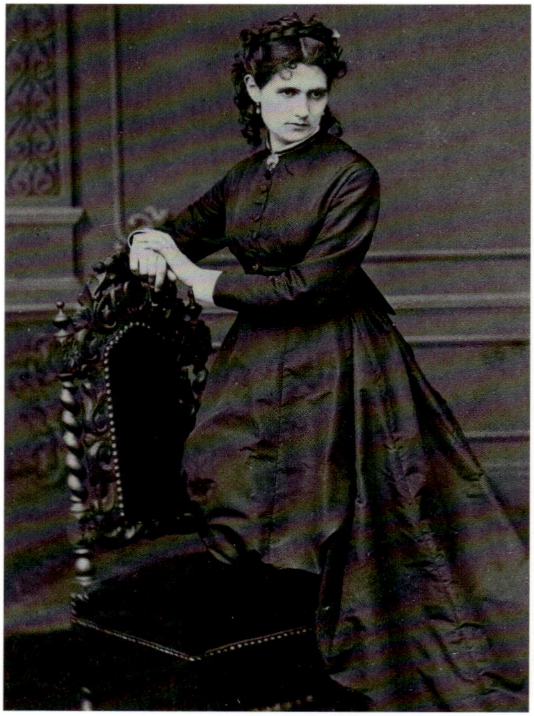

Contemporary photograph of Berthe Morisot
Private collection

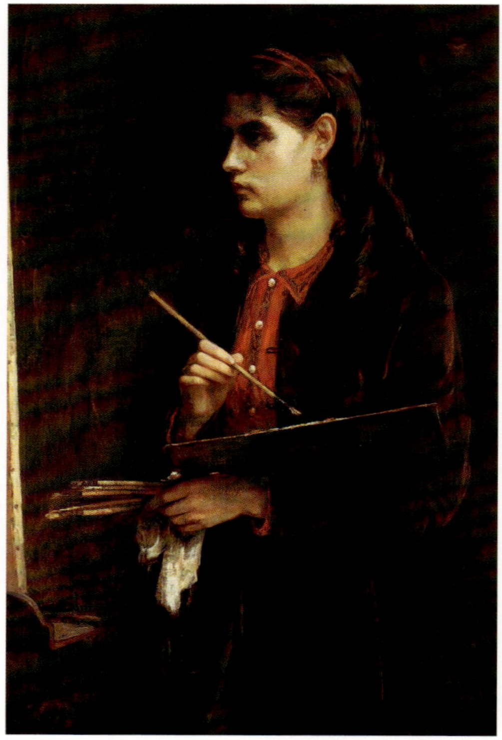

Edma Morisot, *Portrait of Berthe Morisot Painting*, 1865
Oil on canvas, 39 ⅜ × 28 in. (100 × 71 cm)
Private collection, Paris

it was said that even Degas became gracious–Caillebotte, and Mallarmé. “It wasn’t just a coterie of intellectuals that you’d meet at Berthe Morisot’s home. It was simply a very congenial crowd. Berthe Morisot admired a particular type of person. She was only attracted to people of the highest caliber,” recalled Jean Renoir. He spoke of her salon as a “center of authentic Parisian civilization.” Stéphane Mallarmé was certainly one of the most frequent visitors and, after Eugène died, he became tutor to the young Julie Manet. Following Berthe Morisot’s death, Degas, Renoir, Monet, and Mallarmé assumed responsibility for organizing a posthumous exhibition at Durand-Ruel’s gallery. The poet wrote the preface of the catalog for the artist. As Paul Valéry observed, “Her singular achievement was to live her painting and paint her life.”

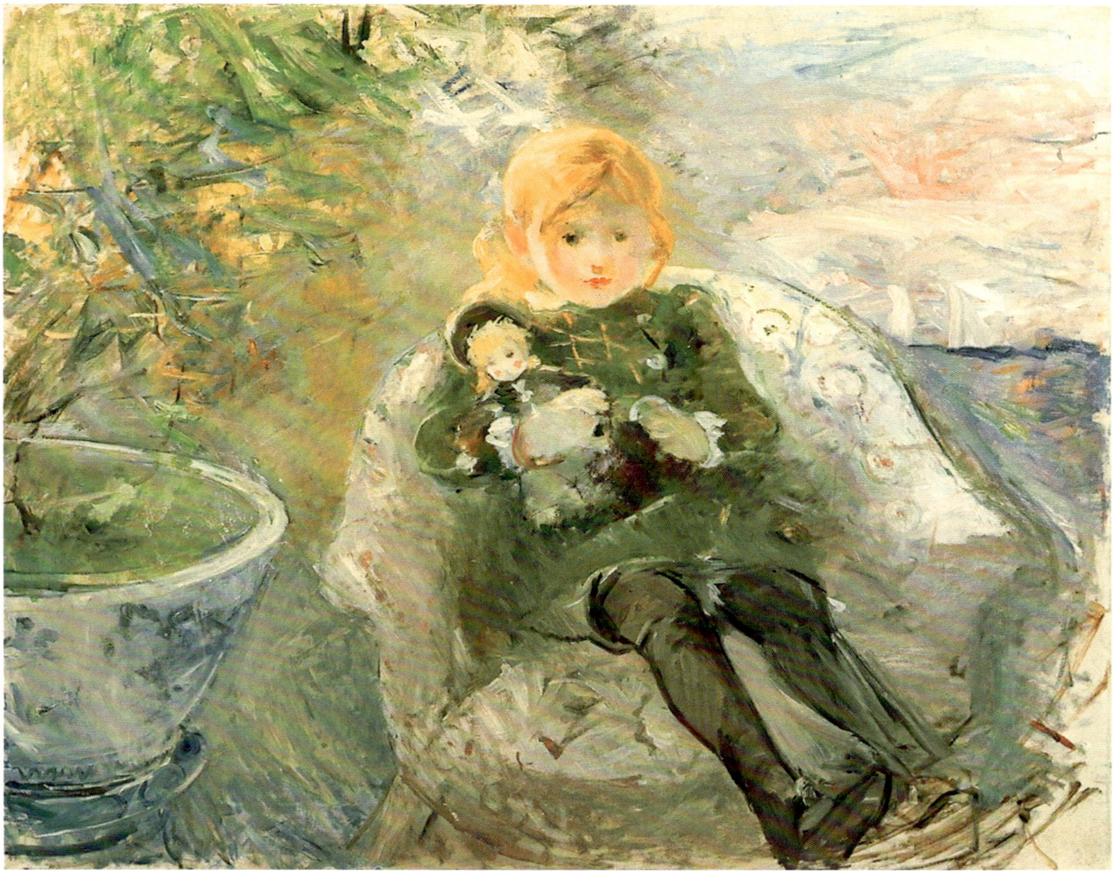

Berthe Morisot, *Julie with a Doll*, 1884
Oil on canvas, 32 ¼ × 39 ⅜ in. (82 × 100 cm)
Private collection

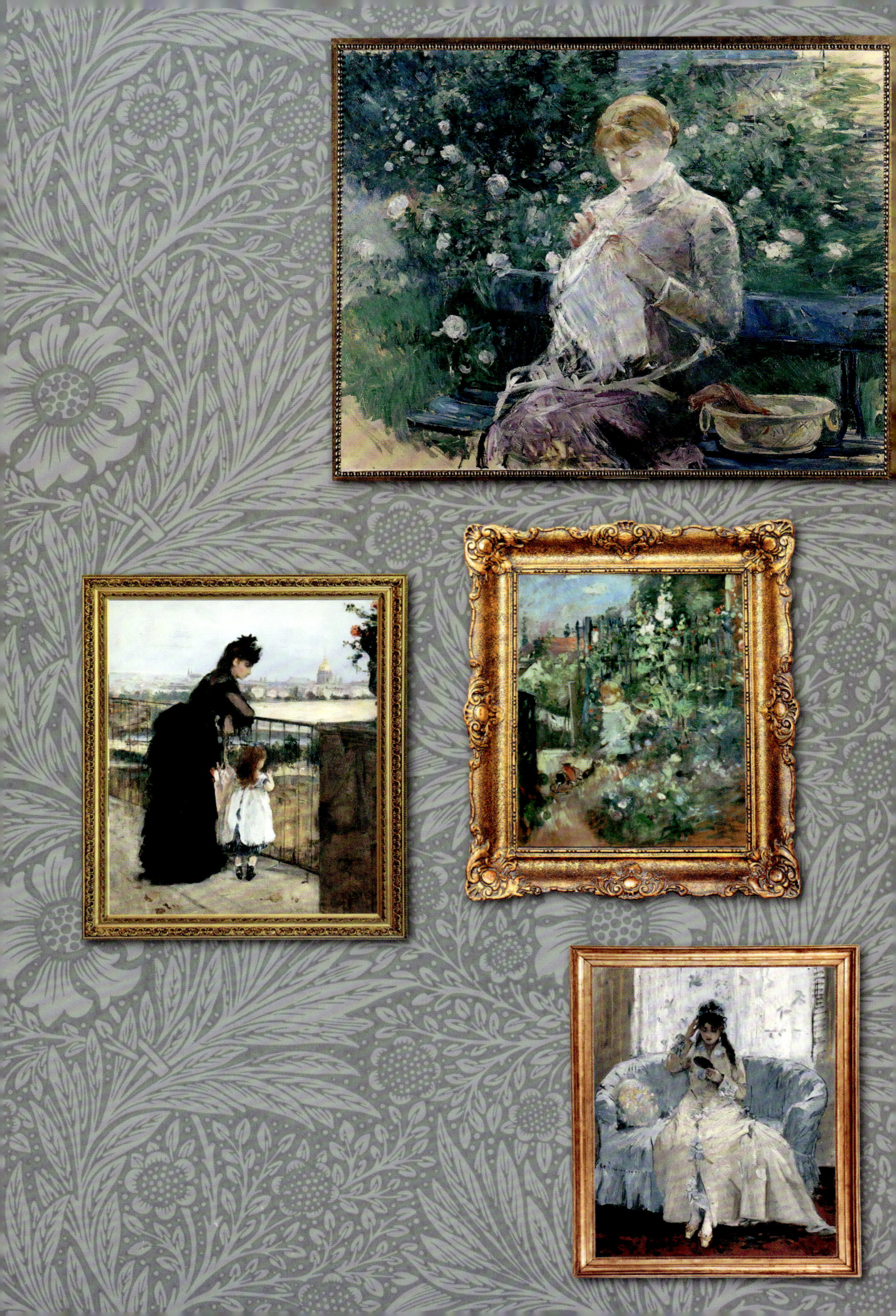

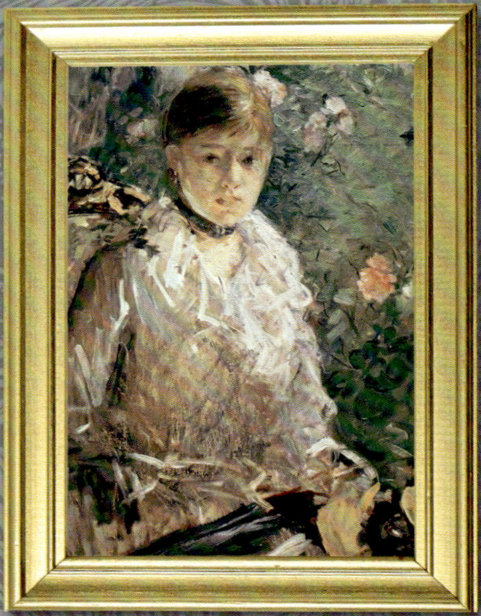
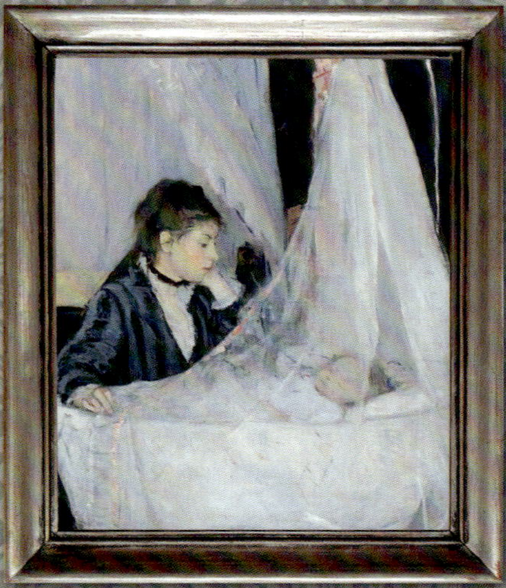
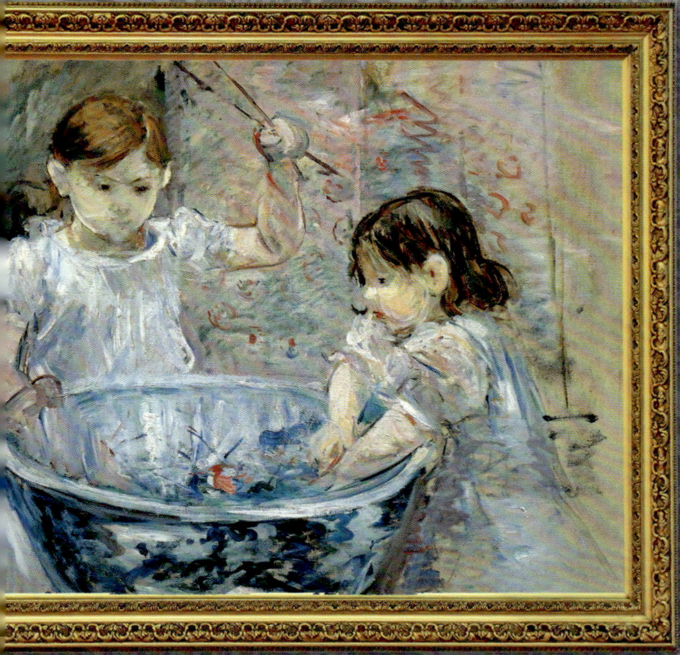
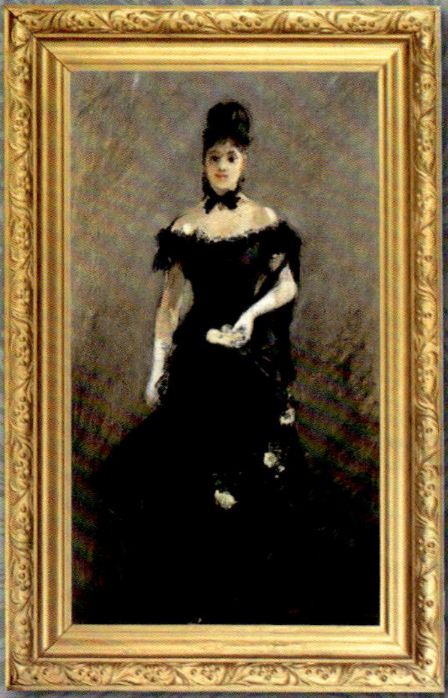
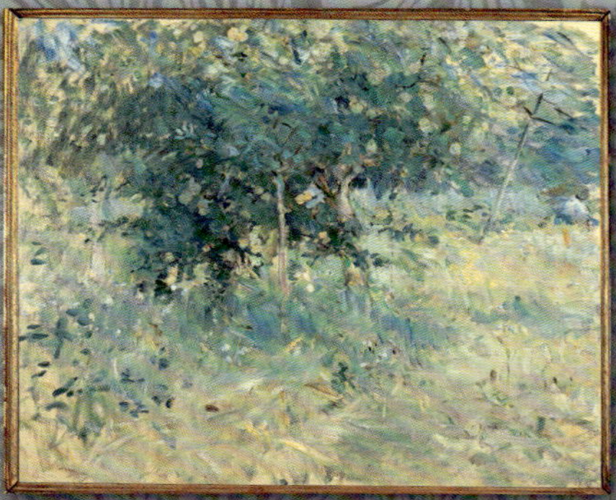

Mary Cassatt

The only American artist to join the impressionists, Mary Cassatt spent almost her entire life in France, where her family had distant ancestors. Born in Pennsylvania in 1844, she enrolled in the Pennsylvania Academy of the Fine Arts in Philadelphia in 1860, aged barely sixteen. But she was disappointed by academic teaching and decided to move to Paris with her mother and a friend. She became a student of Thomas Couture and Jean-Léon Gérôme, visited Barbizon, the landscape painters' retreat, and discovered the works of Courbet and Manet. She left for the United States when the Franco-Prussian War broke out in 1870, but returned to Europe the following year and started on a long tour through Italy, Spain, and the Netherlands. This journey was for both pleasure and study, and she was particularly struck by the paintings of Correggio and Rubens.

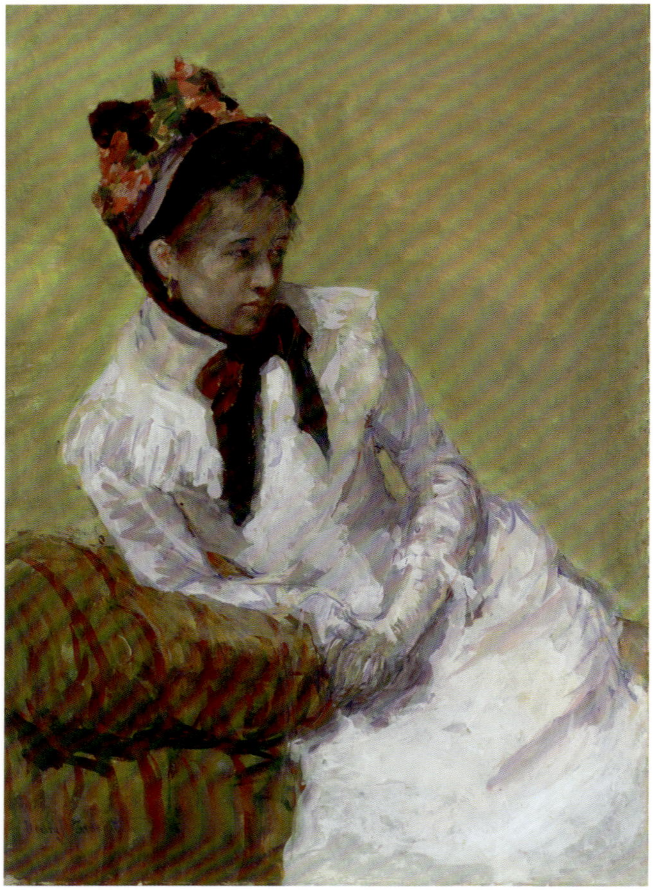

Mary Cassatt, *Portrait of the Artist*, c. 1878
Oil on canvas, 23 ⅝ × 16 ⅛ in. (60 × 41.1 cm), The Metropolitan Museum of Art, New York

Returning to Paris, the young woman began to submit paintings to the Salon on a regular basis. However, after meeting Degas around 1875, she was persuaded to join the impressionists. Degas became a kind of mentor for her and she was close to him, sometimes posing as his model.

She exhibited with the group for the first time in 1879, demonstrating her ability as a portraitist more than as a landscape painter. She admired the work of Pissarro, Manet, and Renoir, and developed a close friendship with Berthe Morisot. Both

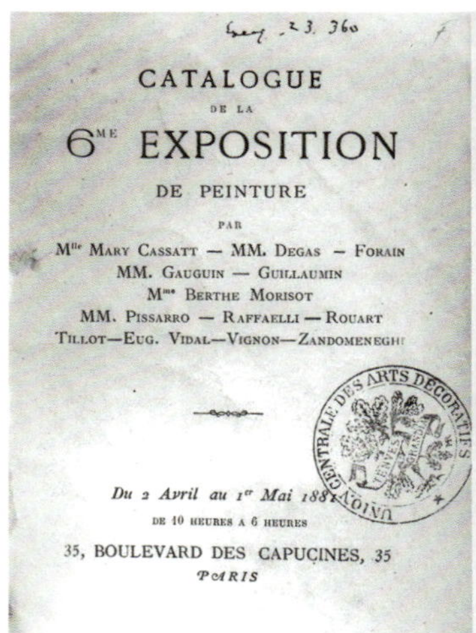

CATALOGUE
DE LA
6ME EXPOSITION
DE PEINTURE
PAR
Mlle Mary Cassatt — MM. Degas — Forain
MM. Gauguin — Guillaumin
Mme Berthe Morisot
MM. Pissarro — Raffaelli — Rouart
Tillot—Eug. Vidal—Vignon—Zandomeneghi

Du 2 Avril au 1er Mai 1881
de 10 heures à 6 heures
35, BOULEVARD DES CAPUCINES, 35
PARIS

Title page of the catalog for the sixth impressionist exhibition in 1881

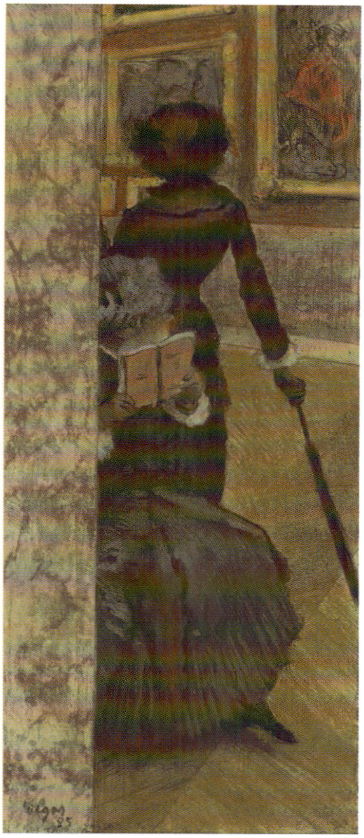

Edgar Degas, *Mary Cassatt at the Louvre: The Paintings Gallery*, 1885
Etching, aquatint, and drypoint, highlighted with pastel on tan wove paper, 12 × 5 in. (30.5 × 12.7 cm) without the margins
The Art Institute of Chicago, Chicago

Key Dates

1844

Born in Pittsburgh, Pennsylvania on May 22

1865

Moves to Paris to study painting

1879

Participates in the fourth impressionist exhibition

1890

Discovers Japanese art

1894

Purchases the Château de Beaufresne

1926

Dies in Paris on June 14

artists tended to paint intimist subjects—portraits of women, often mothers, and children. She was joined in Paris by her parents and sister, who died in 1882.

The discovery of Japanese art and prints by Utamaro and Hiroshige inspired her to experiment with a new technique, engraving, and she mastered the art of intaglio. She undertook an additional role, complementing her other numerous skills, becoming an intermediary between French art dealers and American collectors. She encouraged Paul Durand-Ruel to organize exhibitions in the United States, and advised her friend Louisine Havemeyer, one of the first and most significant American collectors.

Toward the end of her life, her parents and brother died. Living in the Château de Beaufresne in Mesnil-Théribus in the Oise region of northern France, she gradually lost her sight and her health deteriorated. She stopped painting in 1914 and died twelve years later. Save for a few brief visits to America, she had spent her entire life in her adopted country.

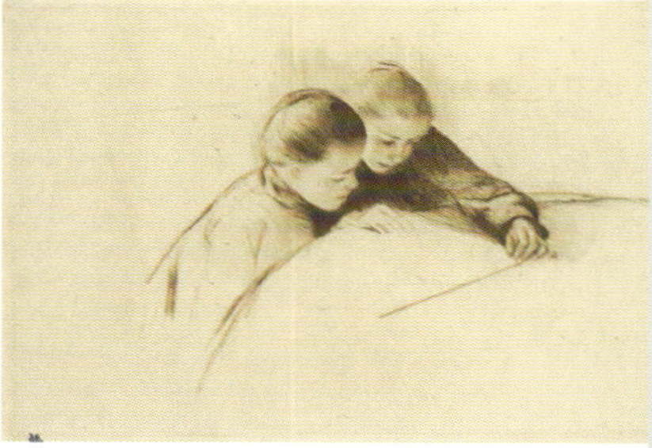

Mary Cassatt, *Reading*, 1889
Drypoint, 6 ¼ × 9 ⅛ in. (15.8 × 23.3 cm)
Bibliothèque Nationale de France, Paris

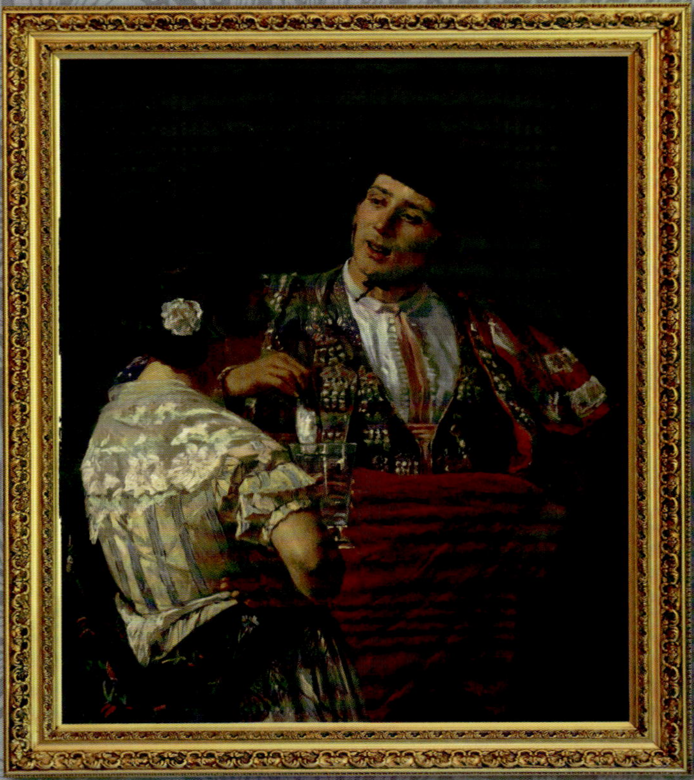

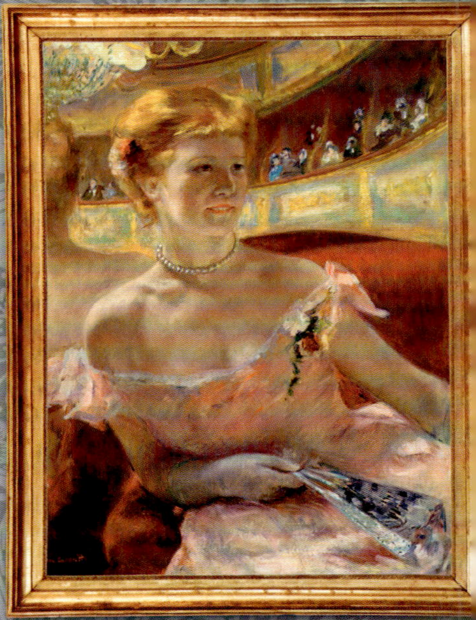

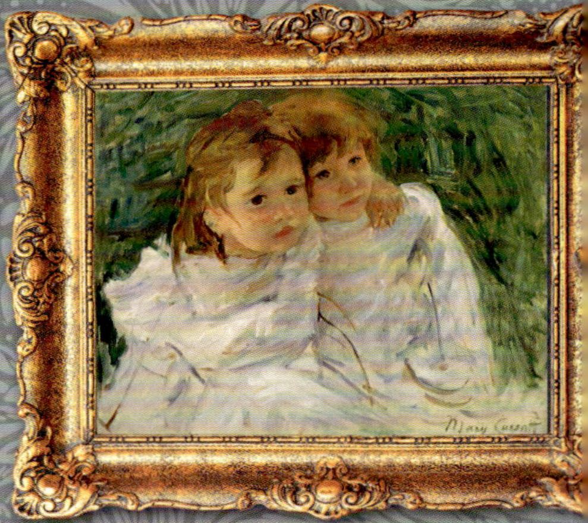
Mary Cassatt

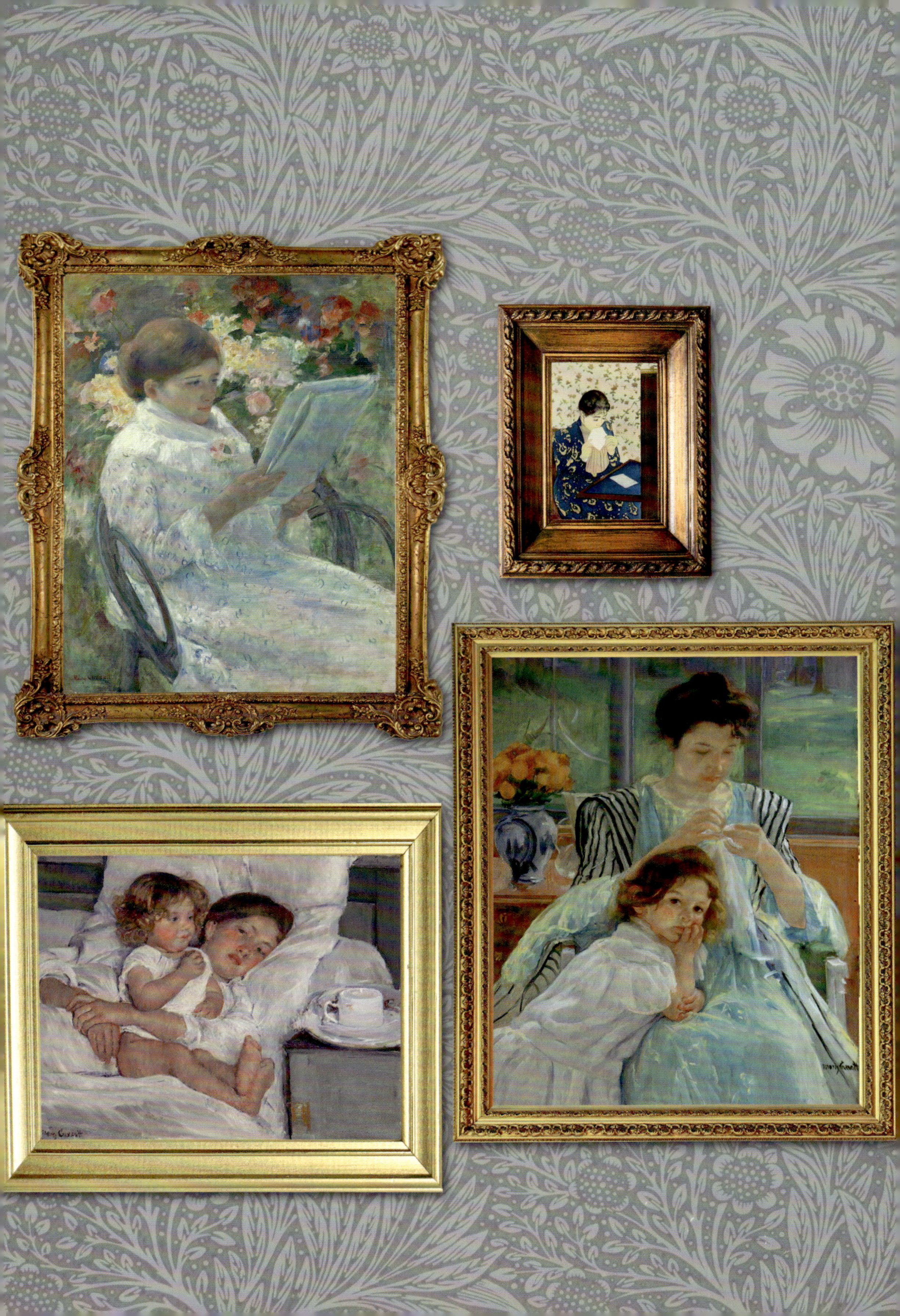

Paul Cézanne

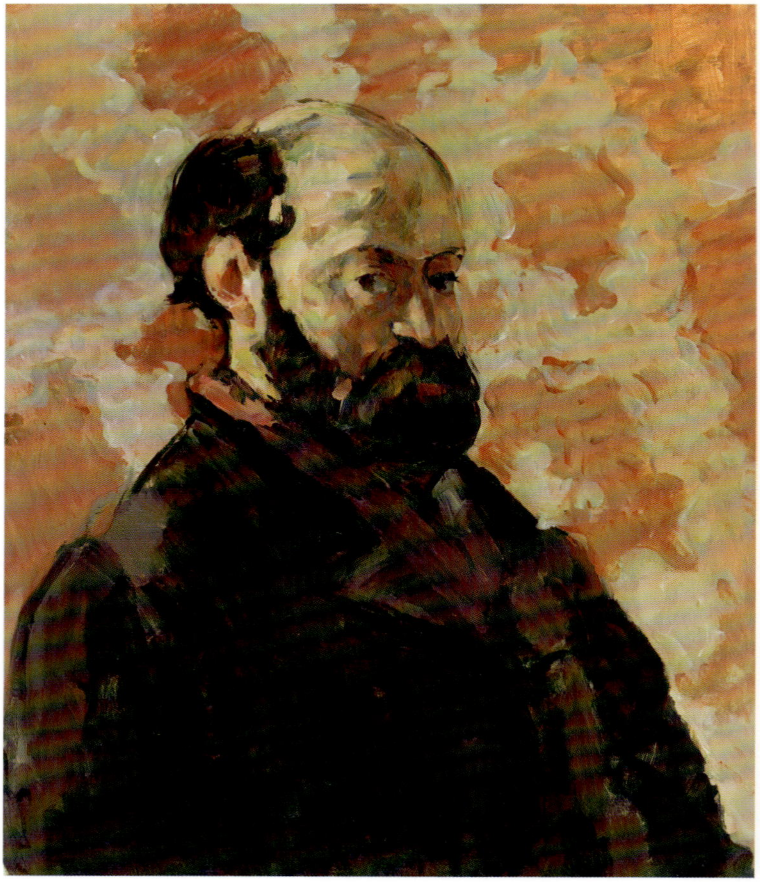

Paul Cézanne, *Portrait of the Artist with Pink Background*, c. 1875
Oil on canvas, 26 × 21 ⅝ in. (66 × 55 cm), Musée d'Orsay, Paris

"This poetic, fantastical, bacchic, erotic, antique, physical, geometrical friend of ours"—such was the verbal portrait of Cézanne proffered by his friend Baptistin Baille, another native of Aix-en-Provence. They were both students at the Collège Bourbon, which Émile Zola also attended in the 1850s. Enrolled in the municipal school of design, Cézanne was forced by his father, a banker, to study law, but he rapidly abandoned these studies to join Zola in Paris in 1861. Initially he was enthusiastic—"It's fantastic, stunning, amazing"—but the artist who would later paint the famous Sainte-Victoire mountain was soon disenchanted. "I thought that by leaving Aix I should leave behind the boredom that pursues me. Actually, I have done nothing but change my abode and the boredom has followed me." Before he finally settled back in Provence, Cézanne traveled constantly between Paris and his native city.

His first stay in Paris did give him the opportunity to make several significant contacts. At Charles Suisse's academy he met Pissarro. "He was a father to me, a man to confide in, almost like the good Lord himself," Cézanne admitted. The older artist encouraged him to experiment with *plein air* painting. He also met Bazille, Monet, and Renoir. Cézanne had an intriguing personality. He was solitary, gruff, and even somewhat crude; he was certainly a character. Hypersensitive, highly cultivated, well

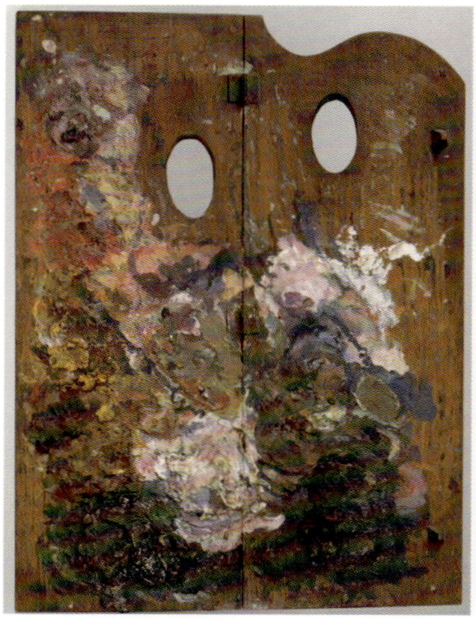

Paul Cézanne's folding palette
Musée d'Orsay, Paris

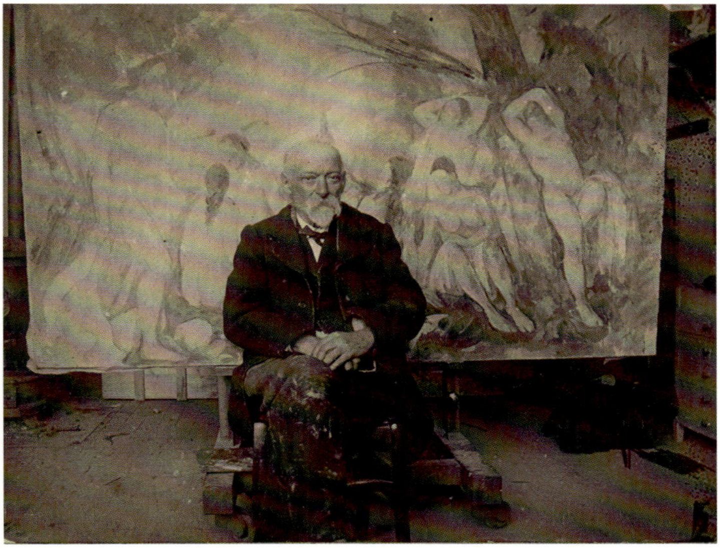

Émile Bernard, *Paul Cézanne Seated in His Studio at Les Lauves, in front of* The Large Bathers, 1905
Silver print, 3 ¼ × 4 ¼ in. (8.2 × 10.7 cm)
Musée d'Orsay, Paris

schooled in classical literature, he avoided society life. Feeling a need to protect himself from the outside world, he made something of a game of his rustic simplicity. As he punningly said to Manet, whom he admired: "I won't shake hands [*mains* in French], Monsieur Manet, as I've not washed for a week." Willfully provocative, Cézanne enjoyed outraging the bourgeois mentality, even if the bourgeois in question was Manet himself. Cézanne was often seen sporting a blue coat, a white jacket covered with paint marks from brushes and other instruments, and an old crushed hat. The painter from Aix cultivated his marginality, and it didn't go unnoticed; his conduct was met with general incomprehension. He brushed off an initial rejection by the Salon, which never admitted any of his canvases to its hallowed halls. However, that setback did not stop him from working with relentless tenacity and ambition. Creating something beautiful was not enough to satisfy him. He wanted to make something "'admirable."

Key Dates

1839

Born in Aix-en-Provence on January 19

1861

First visit to Paris; meets Camille Pissarro

1869

Meets Hortense Fiquet, who becomes his mistress

1872

Birth of their son Paul

1873

Meets Doctor Gachet in Auvers-sur-Oise

1874

Participates in the first impressionist exhibition

1878

Paints in L'Estaque

1880

Meets Huysmans, who supports the impressionists

1881

Meets Paul Gauguin at Pissarro's home in Pontoise

1886

Publication of Zola's novel His Masterpiece*: quarrels with the author. Marries Hortense Fiquet shortly before his father's death*

1906

Dies in Aix-en-Provence on October 23

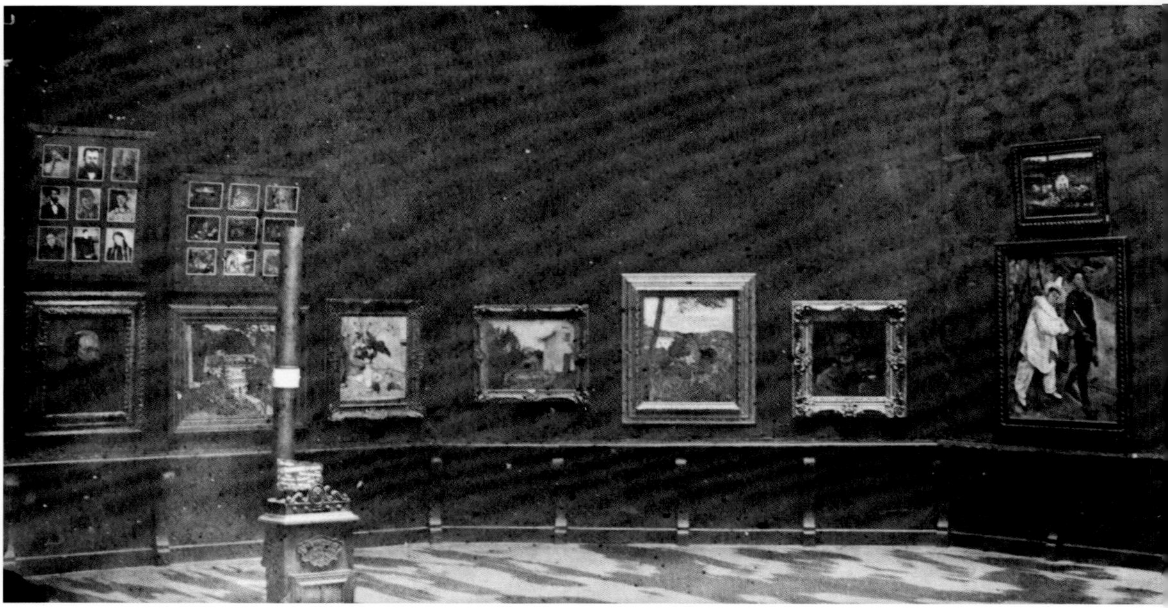

The Cézanne room at the Salon d'Automne in 1904
Musée d'Orsay, Paris

He painted with Pissarro in Pontoise and Auvers-sur-Oise, where he met Doctor Gachet, who treated Vincent Van Gogh. He also participated in the first three impressionist exhibitions. He made the acquaintance of the young Gauguin, worked with his friends Renoir and Monet, and was championed by Huysmans and Zola. "I wanted to make impressionism something strong and enduring, like the art in museums," he said.

He was a troubled, dissatisfied man, who was haunted by doubts despite his determination, and struggled to contain violent impulses.

In 1886, Zola published his novel *His Masterpiece*, the story of a failed artist. Believing he recognized himself in the protagonist, Cézanne severed relations with him, even though they had been friends since childhood and he had been a witness at the writer's marriage. Shortly before his father's death that same year, he married his mistress Hortense, the mother of his son Paul. His inheritance allowed him to dedicate himself exclusively to painting, freed him from financial concerns, and allowed him to "work in silence." "I could never bear to have someone watch me work; I don't want to paint in front of anyone," he admitted late in life. Sequestered in Aix, he painted landscapes, still lifes, and portraits that only a few enlightened artists and collectors appreciated. He socialized very rarely, but he cultivated lasting friendships with other artists including Monet, who introduced him to Clemenceau, Rodin, and Mary Cassatt when they visited his home in 1894. He also befriended Renoir, who became his neighbor in the south of France. Toward the end of his life, he received an increasing number of visits from art dealers, including Ambroise Vollard and Gaston Bernheim-Jeune. Younger artists came to call: Maurice Denis, who painted his *Homage to Cézanne*, and Émile Bernard and Ker-Xavier Roussel, with whom

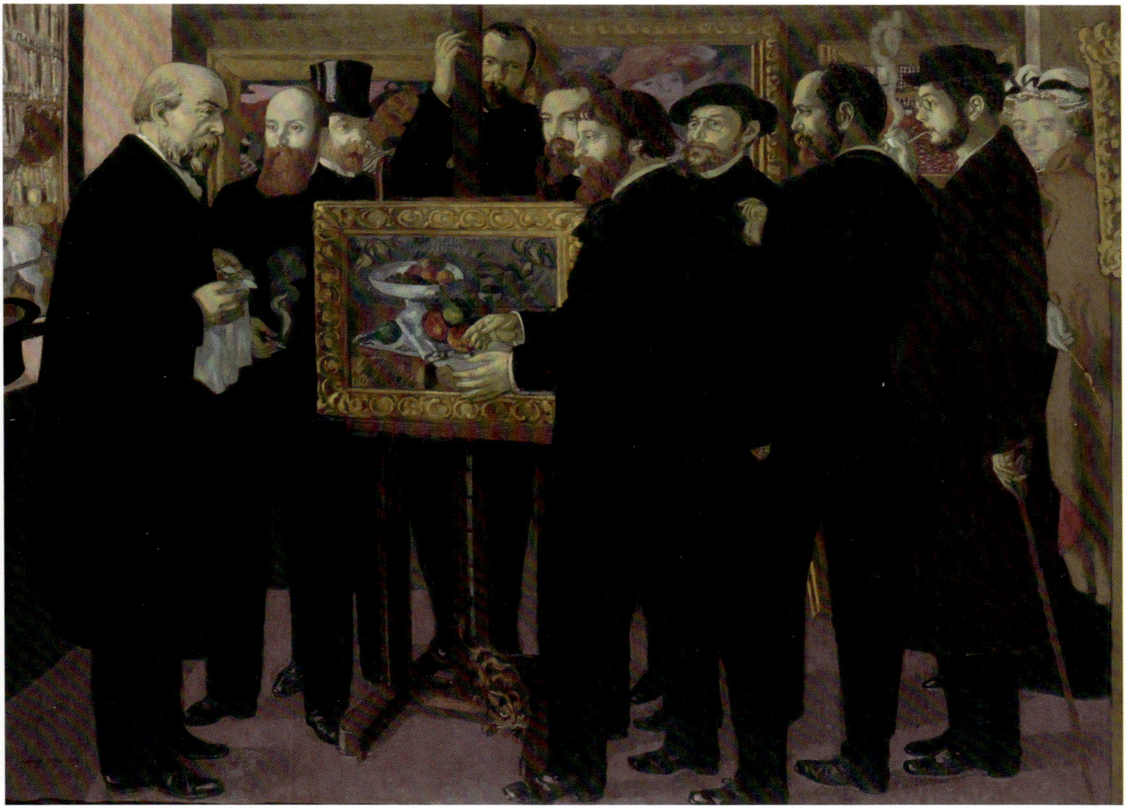

Maurice Denis, *Homage to Cézanne*, 1900
Oil on canvas, 5 ft. 11 in. × 7 ft. 10 ½ in. (1.8 × 2.4 m)
Musée d'Orsay, Paris

he shared some advice. "There are two things in the painter: the eye and the mind. Each of them should aid the other. You have to work on their mutual development. The eye for its vision of nature, and the mind for its ability to organize sensations as a means of expression." A year after his death in 1906, everyone had the chance to reflect on the magnitude of his achievement at the retrospective held at the Salon d'Automne in Paris.

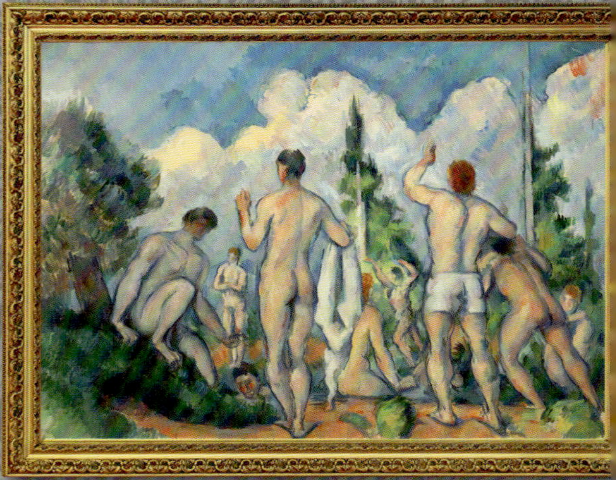
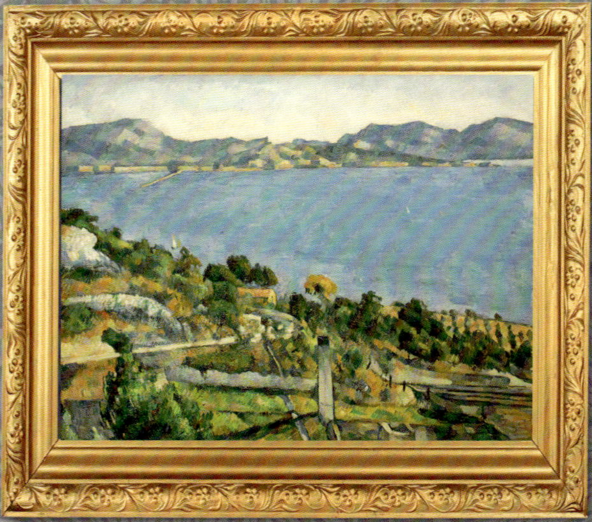
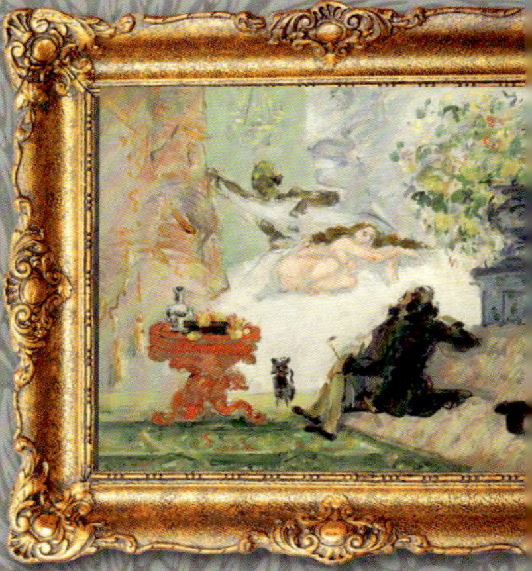
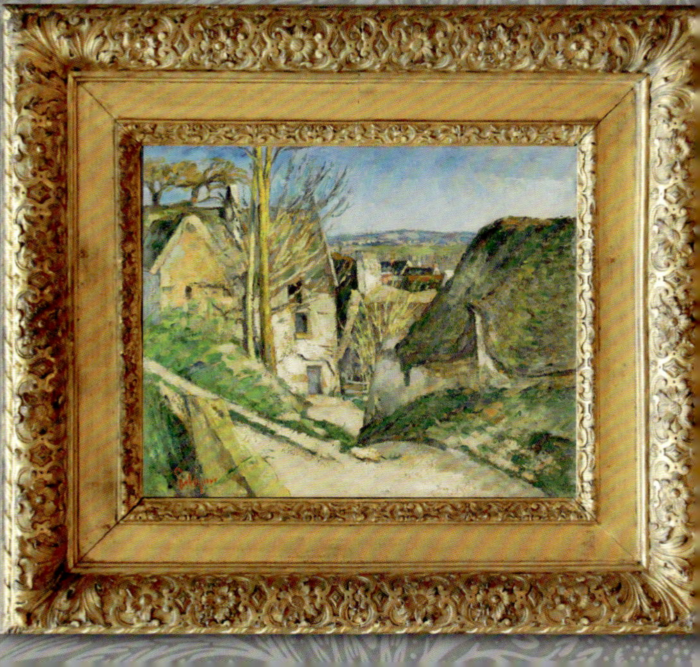

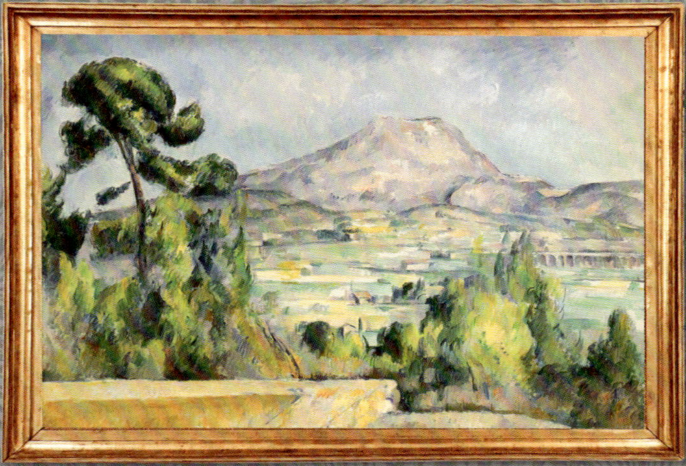

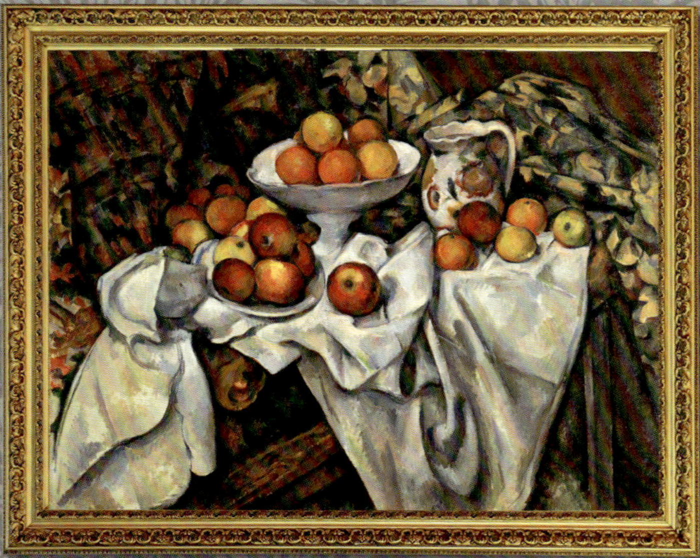

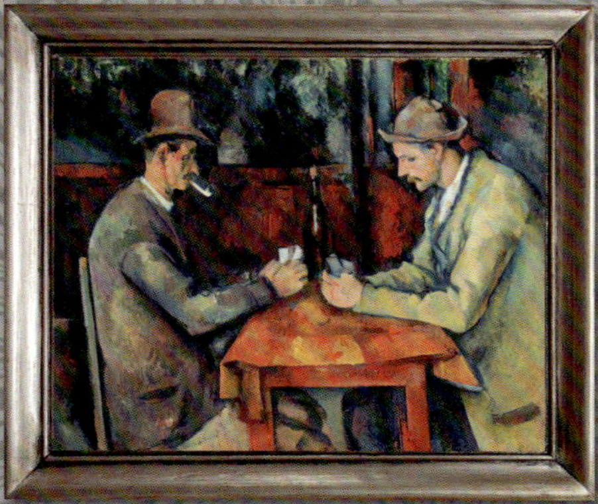

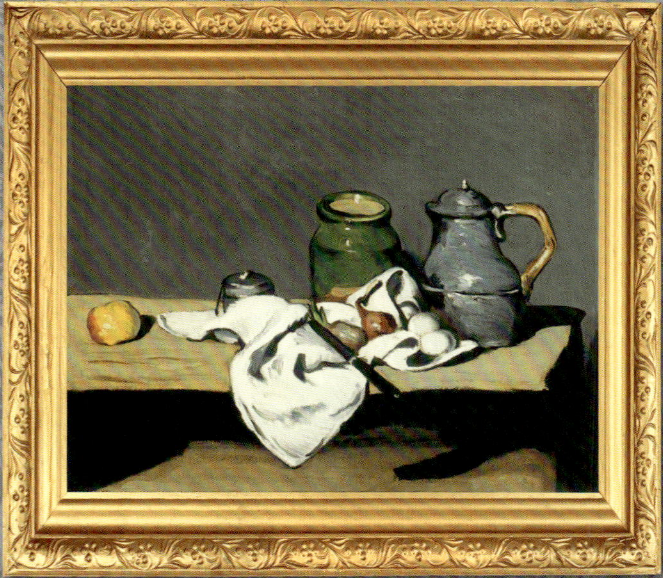

Armand Guillaumin

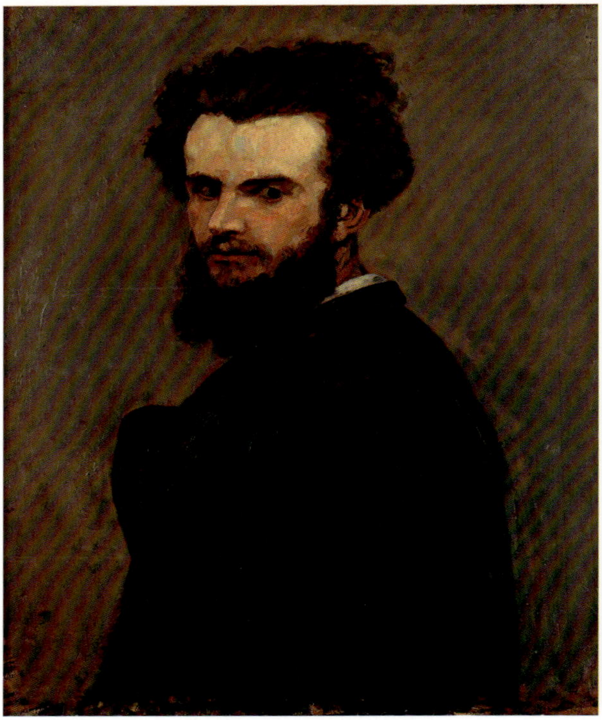

Armand Guillaumin, *Portrait of the Artist*, c. 1875
Oil on canvas, 28 ¾ × 23 ⅝ in. (73 × 60 cm)
Musée d'Orsay, Paris

Guillaumin was perhaps the most modest of the impressionists. He has not received the same recognition as Pissarro, Sisley, or even Caillebotte, yet was the last surviving member of the group.

He was born in Paris in 1841 but spent his childhood in Moulins-sur-Allier with his working-class family. When he was seventeen, he moved to Paris to work in a shop belonging to one of his uncles, spending his free time painting and drawing. He entered the Académie Suisse three years later and became friends with Pissarro and Cézanne, who said of him: "Guillaumin is an artist with a great future, and he's also a fine fellow who's good company." They went together to paint from nature around Paris and along the banks of the Oise and the Seine. With no outside financial support, he continued to work for a living, renting an old studio on the Île de la Cité that Daumier had once occupied.

Self taught, he participated in the first impressionist exhibition, and demonstrated his loyalty to the group by taking part in most of their later shows. He developed close ties with Van Gogh and Gauguin, who were always impatient to see his new canvases. His dense application of paint and intense palette earned him the nickname of "the mad" or "ferocious" colorist. "At first glance, his paintings appear to be a slushy mess of clashing tones and crude forms, a mass of vermilion and Prussian-blue slashes. But stand back and take a fresh look. Everything falls into place: the perspective is clear, the violent tonalities moderate, the warring colors reconcile, and the viewer is

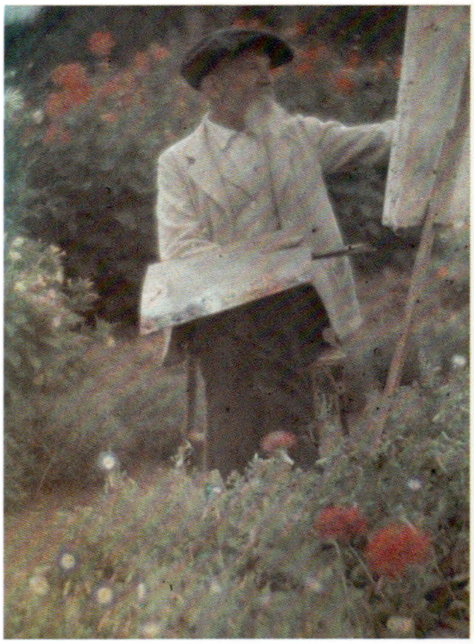

Paul Burty Haviland, *Armand Guillaumin Painting at Crozant*, 1917
Autochrome, 7 × 4 ⅞ in. (17.8 × 12.5 cm)
Musée d'Orsay, Paris

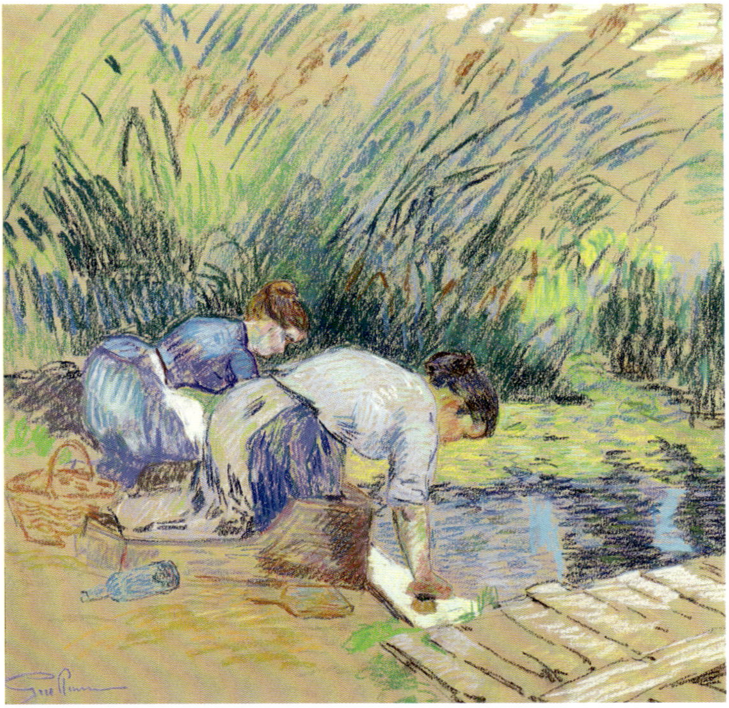

Armand Guillaumin, *Two Laundresses*
Pastel on paper, 18 ⅞ × 18 ⅞ in. (48 × 48 cm), private collection

astounded by the unexpected delicacy of certain portions of these canvases," wrote Huysmans in 1883.

Guillaumin was able to dedicate himself to painting full time in 1891–not owing to commercial success, but because he won the hefty sum of 100,000 francs in a lottery. This newfound independence allowed him to travel through France; he took a liking to the Auvergne and the Creuse region, where he eventually settled down. Although faithful to the impressionist style, he gradually distanced himself from other members of the group and tried to reinvent himself. The lively, colorful intensity of his palette impressed Signac and foreshadowed fauvist painting. The last survivor of the 1840s generation, he died in 1927.

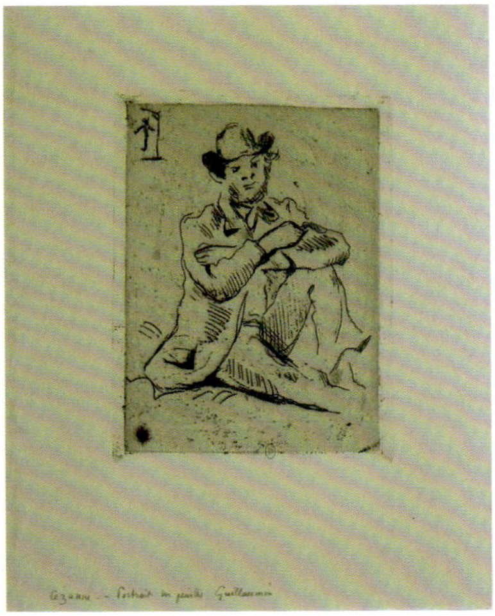

Paul Cézanne, *Portrait of Armand Guillaumin*, 1873
Etching, 10 ¼ × 8 ¼ in. (26.1 × 21 cm)
Bibliothèque de l'INHA, Paris

Key Dates

1841

Born in Paris on February 16

1851

Employed in his uncle's shop

1861

Enrolls in the Académie Suisse

1863

Participates in the Salon des Refusés

1874

Participates in the first impressionist exhibition

1887

Marries his cousin Marie-Joséphine

1891

Wins 100,000 francs in a lottery

1927

Dies in Orly on December 6

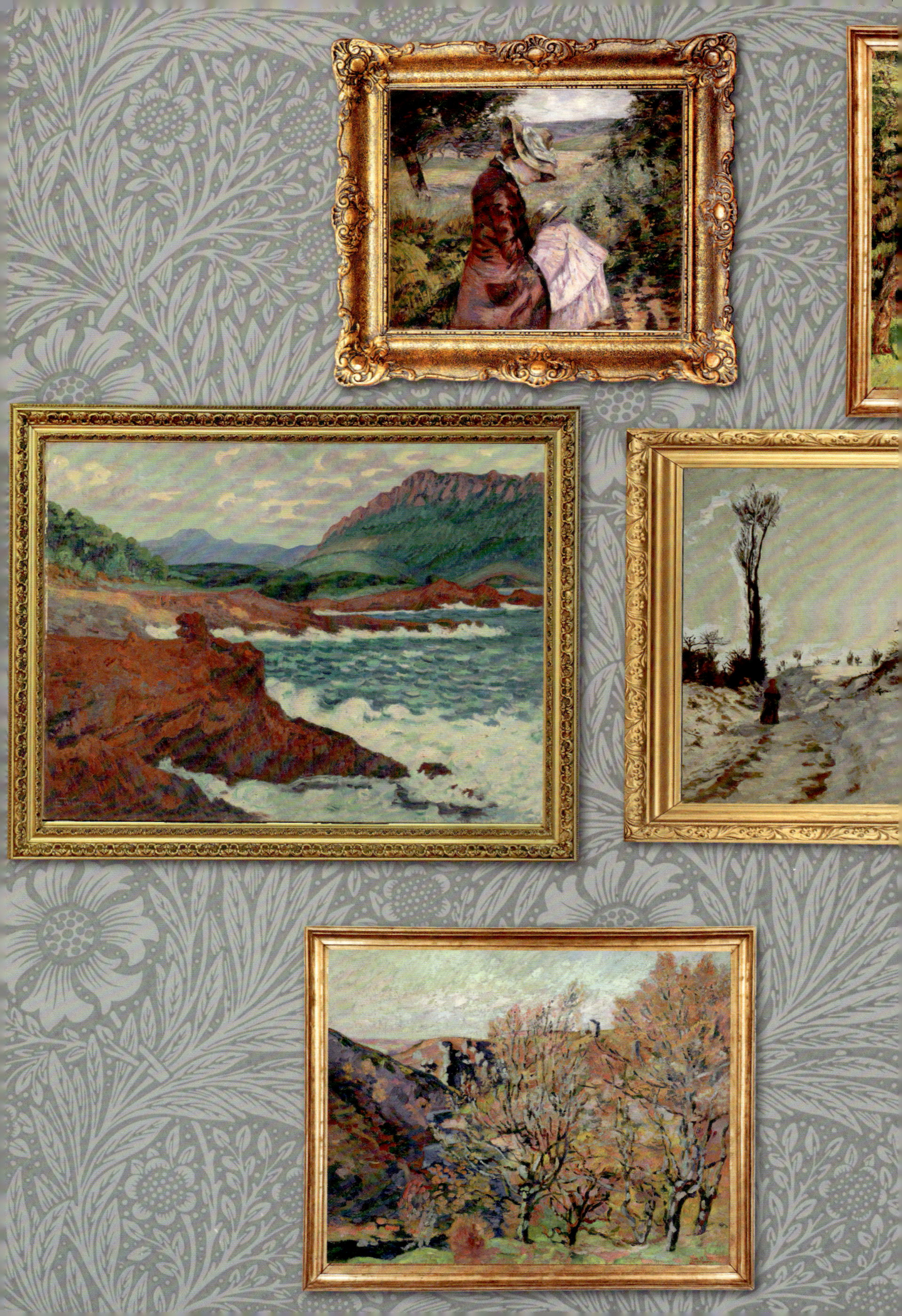

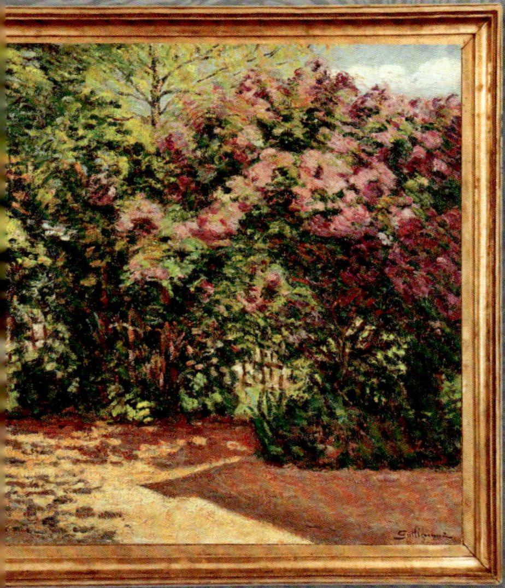
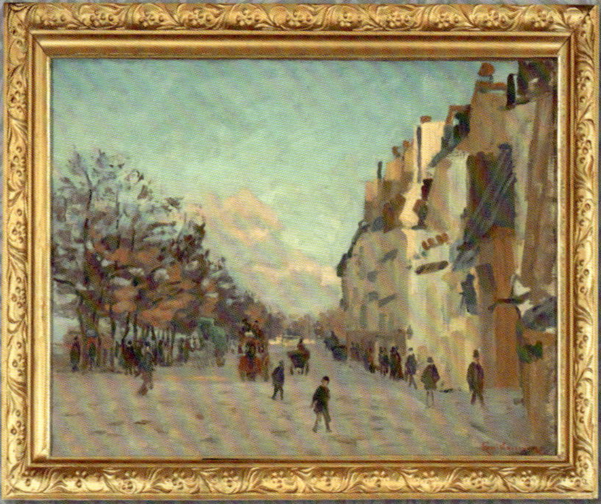
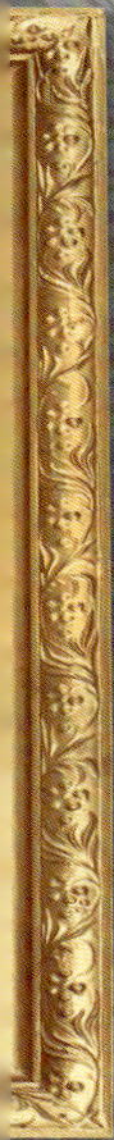
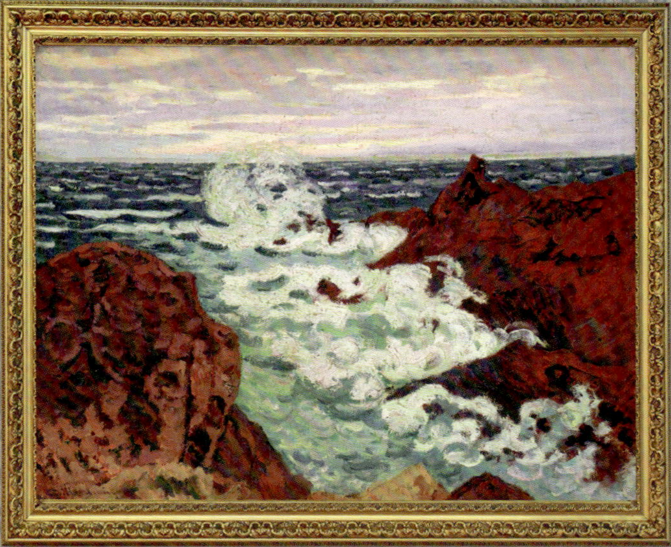
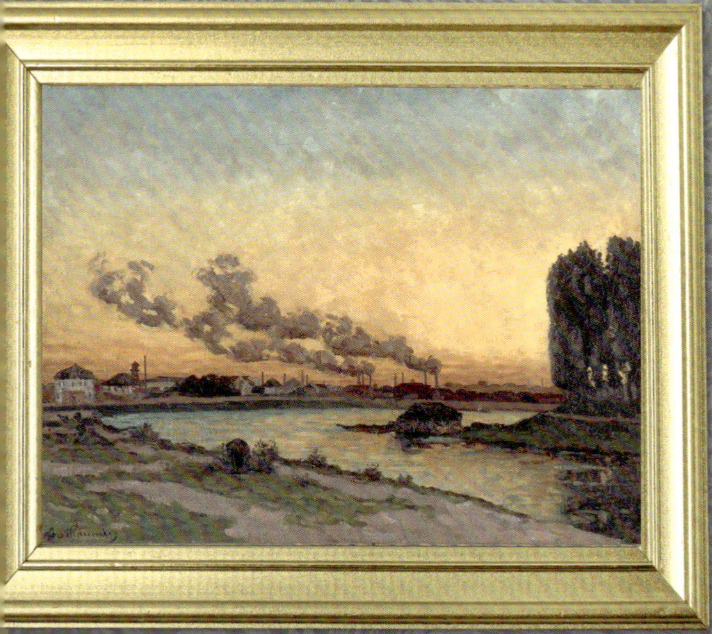

Georges Seurat

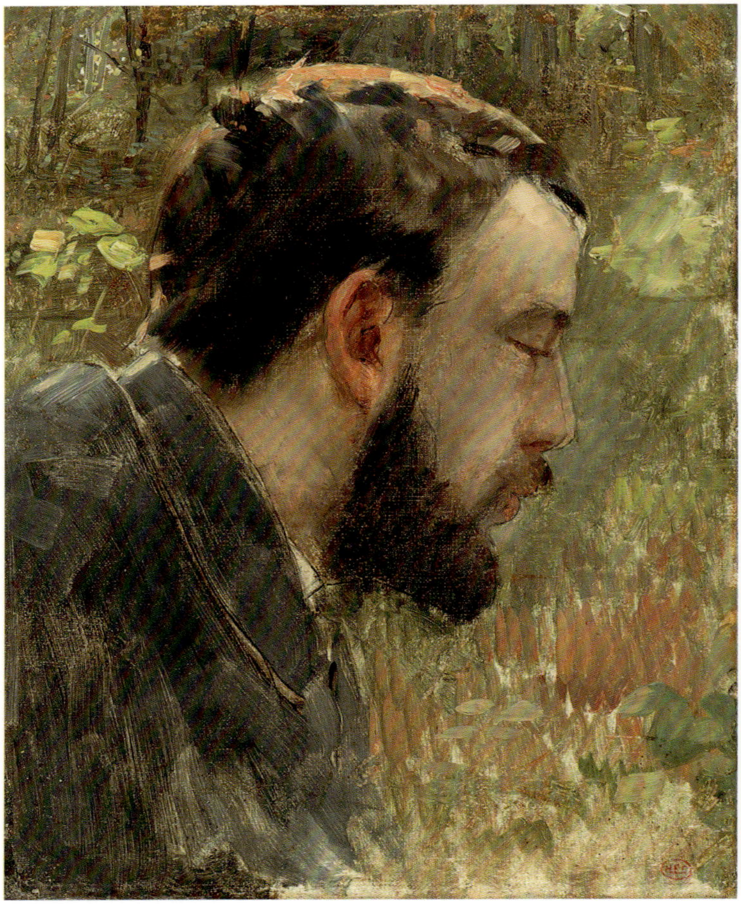

Henri-Edmond Cross, *Portrait of Seurat*
Oil on canvas, 16 ⅛ × 13 in. (41 × 33 cm)
Private collection

Georges Seurat was one of those blazing figures who streaks across the history of art like a shooting star, intensely brilliant and ephemeral. His work represented a turning point that definitively affected aesthetic and pictorial development.

Seurat was born in Paris and grew up in a rather austere bourgeois household. The young Seurat met Edmond Aman-Jean, who was to remain among his closest friends, at the municipal design school where they were both studying. Admitted to the École des Beaux-Arts in 1878, he joined the studio of the painter Henri Lehmann and copied Ingres, whom he greatly admired. But he was fascinated above all by the color theories developed by Chevreul, Charles Blanc, and Ogden Nicholas Rood. Before leaving for Brest to perform his military service the following year, he visited the fourth impressionist exhibition with Aman-Jean. It was a genuine revelation for the two young artists. When he returned to Paris, he shared Aman-Jean's studio, studied the work of Delacroix, and pursued theoretical research. Intellectual speculation and profound, almost scientific consideration of the laws of optics and color were of fundamental importance to Seurat. He was also a very close observer of nature. His first large picture, *Bathers at Asnières*, took him an entire year to complete and

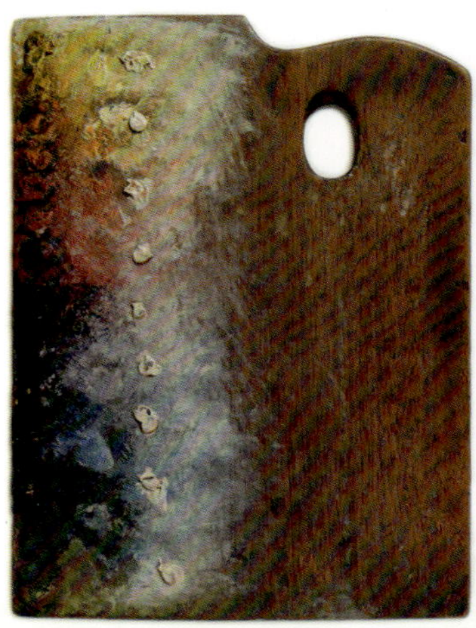

Seurat's palette
Musée d'Orsay, Paris

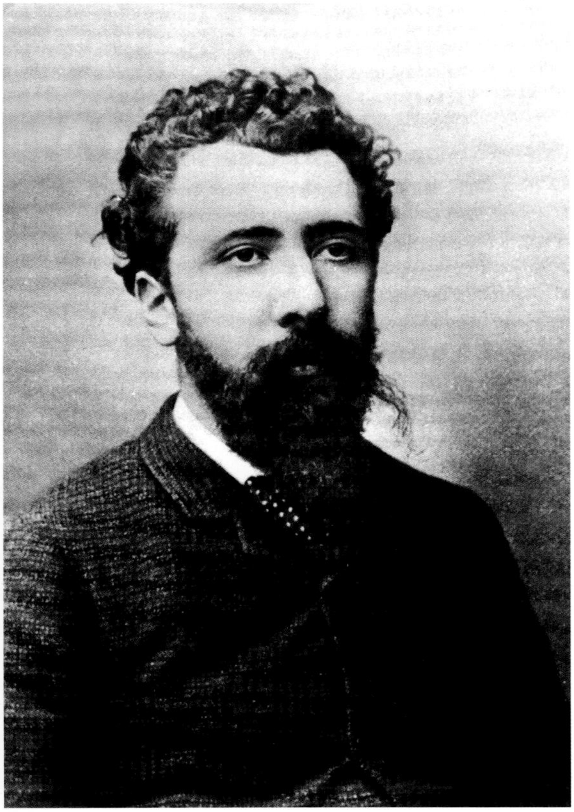

Georges Seurat in 1888

required dozens of drawings and painted sketches. The work was rejected by the 1884 Salon. Seurat became a member of the Society of Independent Artists, and through it met Signac, who also adopted this new aesthetic initiative. Every year thereafter, Seurat dedicated himself to completing the vast and ambitious compositions that marked his brief career. Misunderstood by most of his contemporaries, Seurat aroused some interest among some of his colleagues, such as Guillaumin and Pissarro. However, the painter of *A Sunday on La Grande Jatte* had no wish to attract imitators. Not only did he fear for the originality of his style, but also he did not want it reduced to a mere method of applying paint for less informed artists. Despite the opposition of some members of the group, Seurat, with Pissarro's support, participated in the last impressionist exhibition in 1886. It was on this occasion that the art critic Félix Fénéon first used the term

Key Dates

1859

Born in Paris on December 2

1878

Admitted to the École des Beaux-Arts

1879

Visits the fourth impressionist exhibition

1883

One of his drawings is displayed in the Salon

1884

Joins the Society of Independent Artists and becomes close to Paul Signac

1885

Introduced to Pissarro by Signac and Guillaumin

1886

Participates in the last impressionist exhibition; Félix Fénéon names the movement "neo-impressionism." Durand-Ruel exhibits A Sunday on La Grande Jatte *in New York*

1887

Participates in the Salon des XX in Brussels; meets Van Gogh

1889

Beginning of his liaison with Madeleine Knoblock

1891

Dies in Paris on March 29

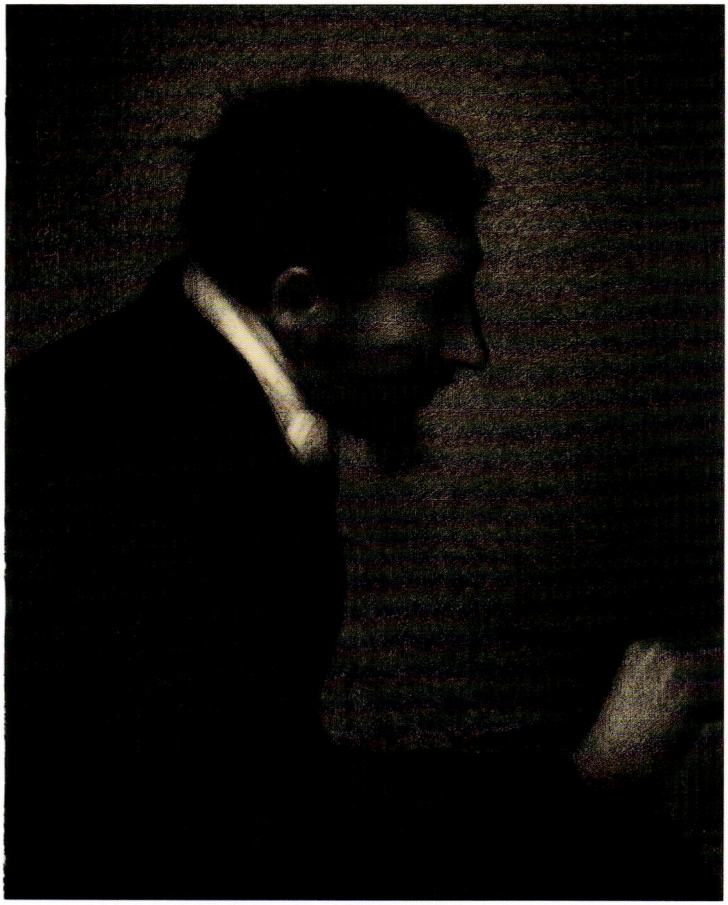

Georges Seurat, *Aman-Jean*, 1882–83
Conté pencil, 24 ½ × 18 ¾ in. (62.2 × 47.5 cm)
The Metropolitan Museum of Art, New York

"neo-impressionism" to describe Seurat's art, and he became a zealous champion of the style.

Seurat frequently showed his work in Brussels at the Salon des XX, which exhibited work by avant-garde artists. He became the leading light of pointillism, and established ties with other painters, including Van Gogh, whom he met in 1887. Consumed by the conception and execution of his huge compositions for most of the year, he spent his summers in Normandy in Somme Bay or the Nord-Pas-de-Calais region. He'd return with views of Port-en-Bessin, Crotoy, Gravelines, and Honfleur that featured subtly shimmering chromatic effects. In 1889, Madeleine Knoblock, a young model, became his mistress and gave birth to their son a year later. She apparently posed for the only portrait known to have been painted by Seurat, *Young Woman Powdering Herself.* Seurat almost certainly produced this work to silence detractors who criticized him for his supposed inability to do

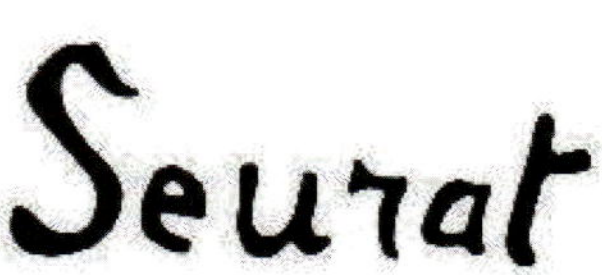

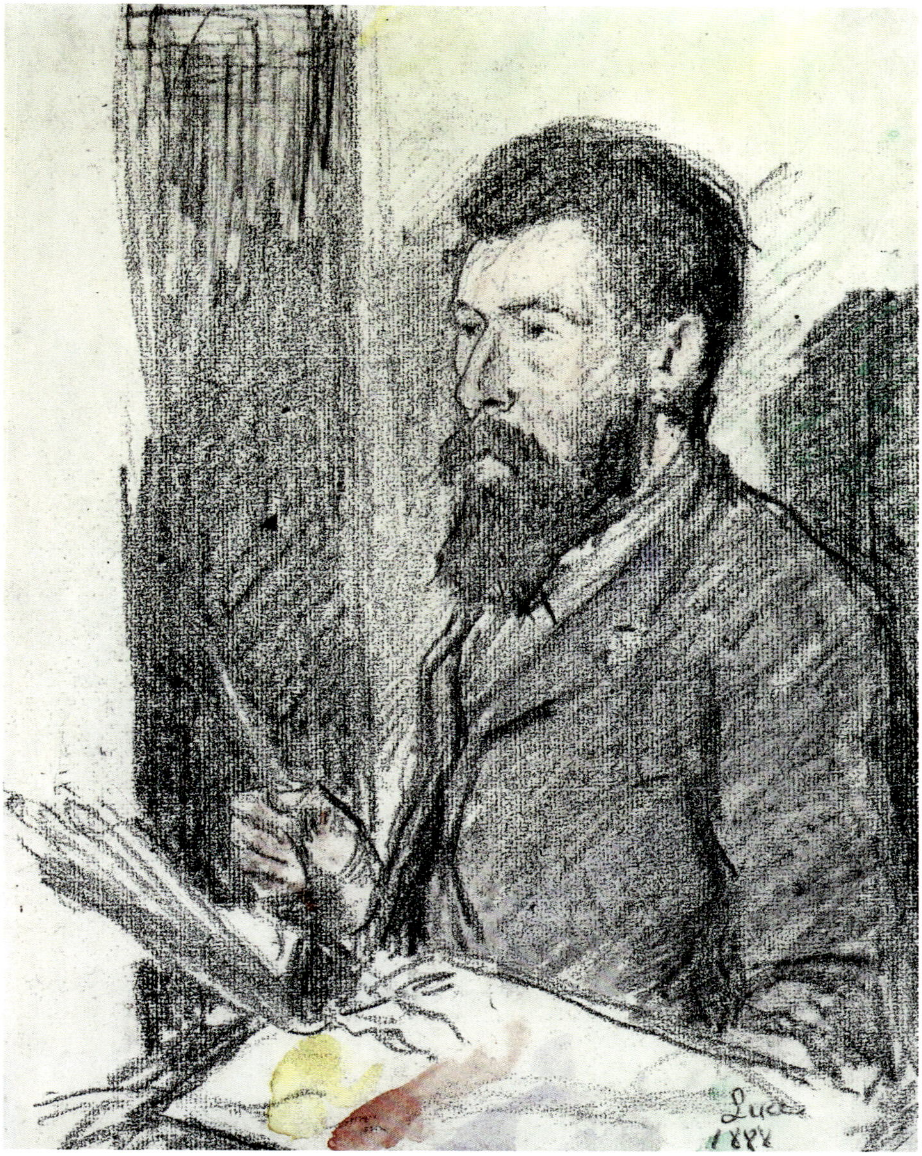

Maximilien Luce, *Portrait of Seurat*, 1888
Charcoal and watercolor on paper, 11 ⅝ × 9 in. (29.5 × 23 cm)
Private collection

this kind of painting. Illness struck suddenly when he was just thirty-one; he died a few days later, before he could complete *The Circus*, the third panel of a series dedicated to public amusements, along with *Circus Sideshow* and *The Can-Can.* He left behind six large paintings and several landscapes that had significant influence and resonance for later artists. According to Apollinaire, "His research was impressive and above all had the merit of paving the way for numerous new seekers."

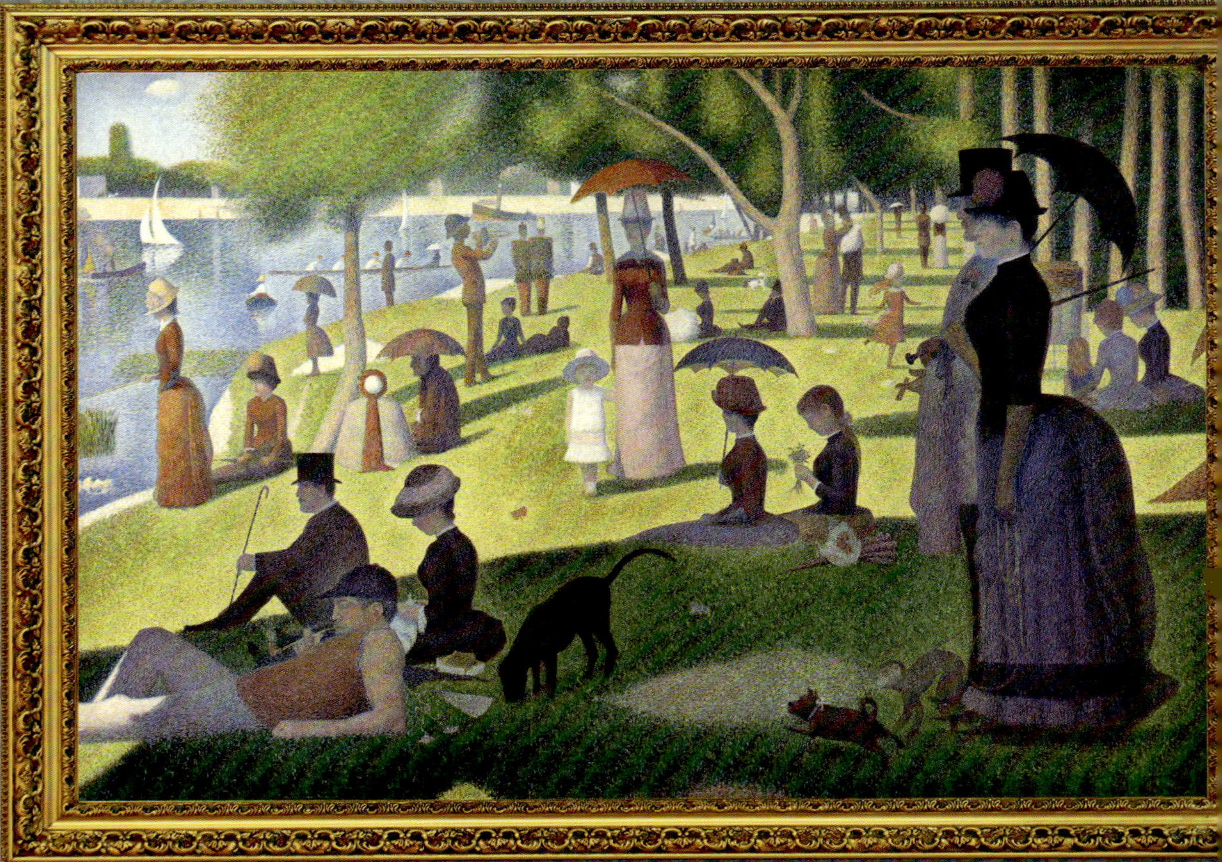

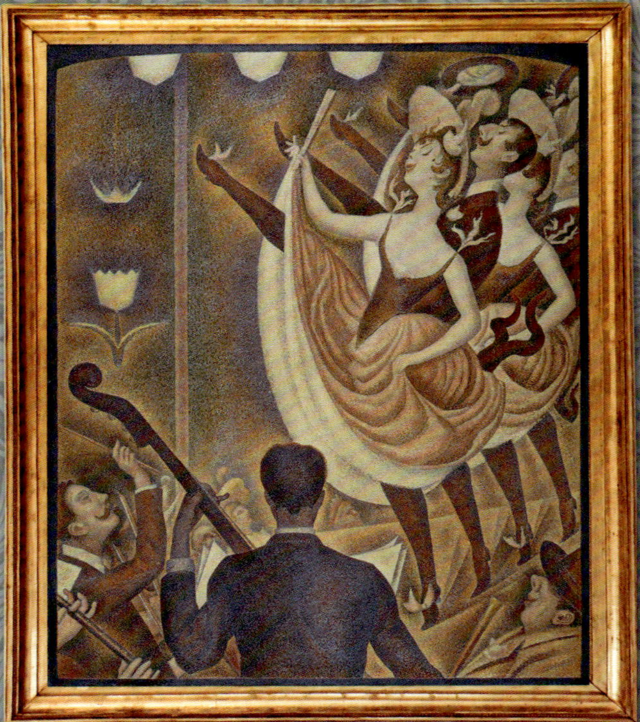

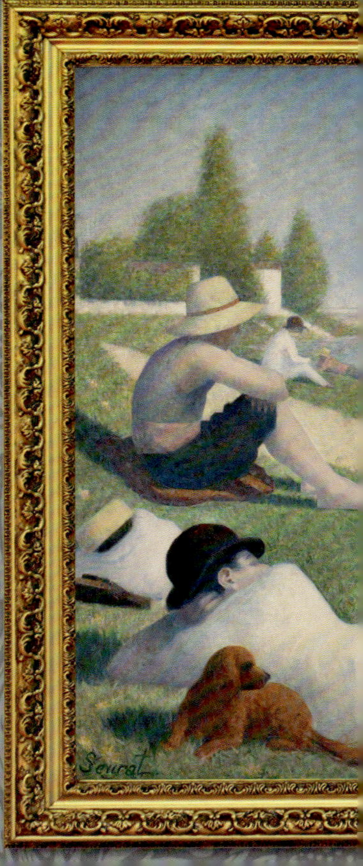
Seurat

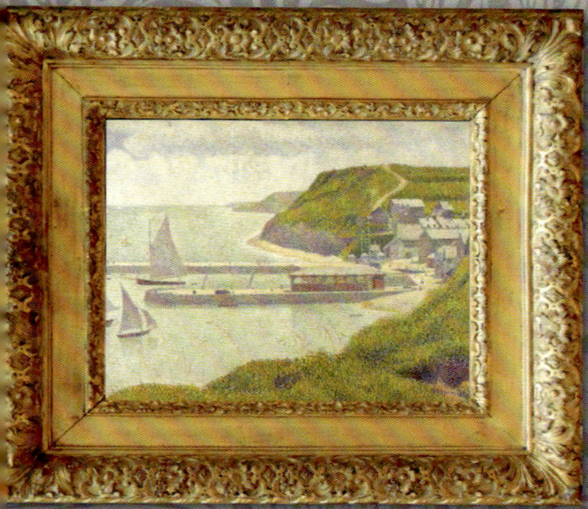
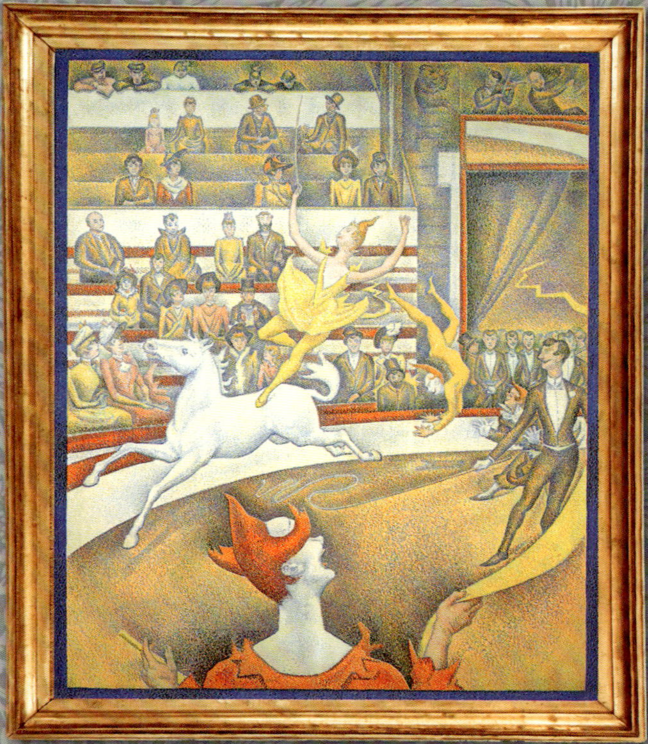
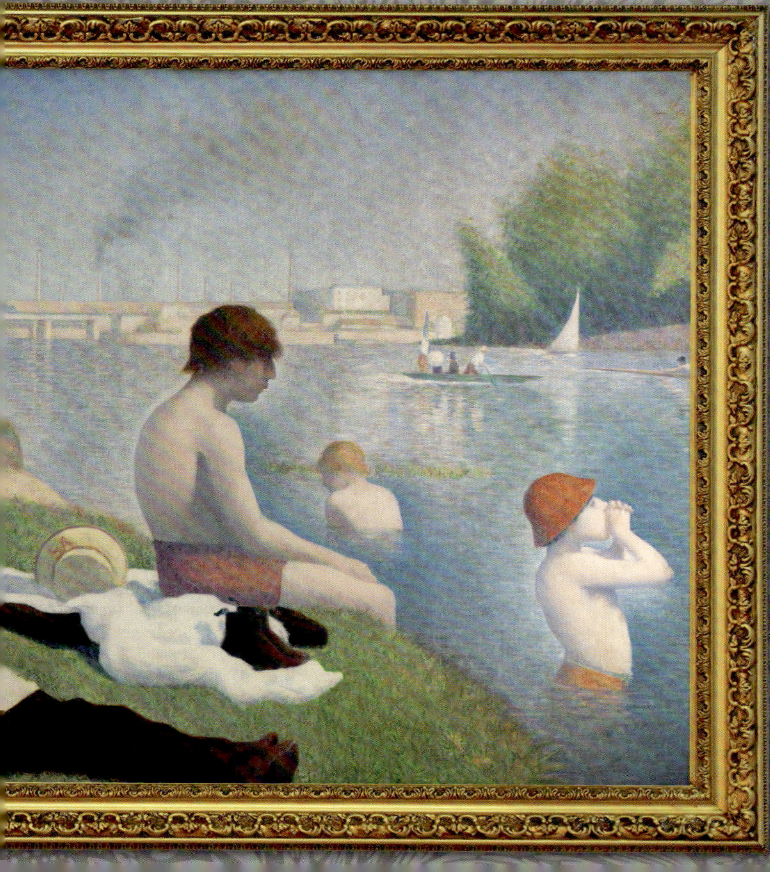

Captions to the Virtual Galleries

The paintings by each artist have been reproduced at a size proportional to the other works in their virtual gallery.

Claude Monet

Pages 298-99

The Water Lily Pond: Harmony in Green, 1899, oil on canvas, 2 ft. 11 in. × 3 ft 1 in. (89 × 93 cm), Musée d'Orsay, Paris

Rouen Cathedral, the Portal and Tour Saint-Romain (Bright Sun), also known as *Harmony in Blue and Gold,* 1893-94, oil on canvas, 3 ft. 6 ¼ in. × 2 ft. 5 in. (107 × 73.5 cm), Musée d'Orsay, Paris

Study of a Figure Outdoors: Woman with a Parasol, Facing Left, 1886, oil on canvas, 4 ft. 3 ½ in. × 2 ft. 10 ½ in. (131 × 88 cm), Musée d'Orsay, Paris

Impression, Sunrise, 1872, oil on canvas, 18 ⅞ × 24 ⅞ in. (48 × 63 cm), Musée Marmottan, Paris

The Gare Saint-Lazare, 1877, oil on canvas, 2 ft. 5 ¾ in. × 3 ft. 5 in. (75 × 104 cm), Musée d'Orsay, Paris

The Magpie, 1868-69, oil on canvas, 2 ft. 11 in. × 4 ft. 3 ¼ in. (89 × 130 cm), Musée d'Orsay, Paris

Regattas at Argenteuil, 1872, oil on canvas, 18 ⅞ × 29 ½ in. (48 × 75 cm), Musée d'Orsay, Paris

Camille Pissaro

Pages 304-5

Quai de Paris and Pont Corneille in Rouen, Sunshine, 1883, oil on canvas, 21 ⅜ × 25 ⅜ in. (54.3 × 64.4 cm), Philadelphia Museum of Art, Philadelphia

The Garden of the Tuileries on a Winter Afternoon, 1899, oil on canvas, 2 ft. 5 in. × 3 ft. ¼ in. (74 × 92 cm), The Metropolitan Museum of Art, New York

Spring Plum Trees in Flower, also known as *Kitchen Garden, Trees in Flower: Spring, Pontoise,* 1877, oil on canvas, 25 ¾ × 31 ⅞ in. (65.5 × 81 cm), Paris, Musée d'Orsay, Paris

Red Roofs, Corner of a Village, Winter, 1877, oil on canvas, 21 ¼ × 25 ⅝ in. (54 × 65 cm), Musée d'Orsay, Paris

Woman in an Orchard, also known as *Spring Sunshine in the Meadow at Éragny,* 1887, oil on canvas, 17 ⅞ × 25 ⅝ in. (45.4 × 65 cm), Musée d'Orsay, Paris

Landscape in Éragny: Church and Farm in Éragny, 1895, oil on canvas, 23 ⅝ × 28 ⅞ in. (60 × 73.4 cm), Musée d'Orsay, Paris

White Frost, Morning, also known as *Effect of Snow, Éragny,* 1894, oil on canvas, 2 ft. 4 ¾ in. × 3 ft. ¼ in. (73 × 92 cm), Musée d'Orsay, Paris

Auguste Renoir

Pages 310-11

The Bathers, 1918-19, oil on canvas, 3 ft. 7 ¼ in. × 5 ft. 3 in. (110 × 160 cm), Musée d'Orsay, Paris

City Dance, 1882-83, oil on canvas, 5 ft. 10 ¾ in. × 2 ft. 11 ½ in. (180 × 90 cm), Musée d'Orsay, Paris

Country Dance, 1882-83, oil on canvas, 5 ft. 10 ¾ in. × 2 ft. 11 ½ in. (180 × 90 cm), Musée d'Orsay, Paris

Railroad Bridge at Chatou, also known as *The Pink Chestnut Trees,* 1881, oil on canvas, 21 ¼ × 25 ¾ in. (54 × 65.5 cm), Musée d'Orsay, Paris

Dance at Le Moulin de la Galette, 1876, oil on canvas, 4 ft. 3 ½ in. × 5 ft. 9 in. (131 × 175 cm), Musée d'Orsay, Paris

The Luncheon of the Boating Party, 1881, oil on canvas, 4 ft. 3 in. × 5 ft 7 ¾ in. (129 × 172 cm), Phillips Collection, Washington, D.C.

Young Woman with a Veil, c. 1870, oil on canvas, 24 1/8 × 20 in. (61.3 × 50.8 cm), Musée d'Orsay, Paris

Edgar Degas

Pages 316-17

Ballet, also known as *The Star*, c. 1876, pastel on paper, 23 × 12 ¾ in. (58.4 × 32.4 cm), Musée d'Orsay, Paris, conserved at the Musée du Louvre

Two Dancers, Yellow and Pink, 1898, pastel, 3 ft. 5 ¾ in. × 3 ft. 6 ½ in. (106 × 108 cm), Museo de Bellas Artes, Buenos Aires

Portrait of Monsieur and Madame Édouard Manet, c. 1868, oil on canvas, 25 ⅝ × 28 in. (65 × 71 cm), Kitakyushu Municipal Museum of Art, Kitakyushu

Portraits at the Stock Exchange, 1878-79, oil on canvas, 3 ft. 3 ¾ in. × 2 ft. 8 ¼ in. (100 × 82 cm), Musée d'Orsay, Paris

Women Ironing, c. 1884-86, oil on canvas, 29 ⅞ × 32 in. (76 × 81.5 cm), Musée d'Orsay, Paris

The Parade, also known as *Racehorses in Front of the Tribunes*, c. 1866-68, oil on paper mounted on canvas, 18 1/8 × 24 in. (46 × 61 cm), Musée d'Orsay, Paris

In a Café, also known as *L'Absinthe* or *The Absinthe Drinker*, 1875-76, oil on canvas, 3 ft. 1 ¼ in. × 2 ft. 3 in. (92 × 68.5 cm), Musée d'Orsay, Paris

The Tub, 1886, pastel on board, 23 ⅝ × 32 ⅝ in. (60 × 83 cm), Musée d'Orsay, Paris

Frédéric Bazille

Pages 320-21

The Beach at Sainte-Adresse, 1865, oil on canvas, 1 ft. 11 in. × 4 ft. 7 in. (58.4 × 140 cm), High Museum of Art, Atlanta

Summer Scene, 1869, oil on canvas, 5 ft. 1 ½ in. × 5 ft. 2 ¼ in. (156 × 158 cm), Fogg Art Museum, Harvard University Art Museums, Cambridge

The Pink Dress, late summer 1864, oil on canvas, 4 ft. 9 ¾ in. × 3 ft. 7 ¼ in. (147 × 110 cm), Musée d'Orsay, Paris

The Ramparts at Aigues-Mortes, Setting Sun, 1867, oil on canvas, 1 ft 11 in. × 3 ft. 3 ¼ in. (60 × 100 cm), National Gallery of Art, Washington, DC

African Woman with Peonies, spring 1870, oil on canvas, 23 ⅞ × 29 ⅝ in. (60.5 × 75.4 cm), Musée Fabre, Montpellier

Nude Study, also known as *Reclining Nude*, 1864, oil on canvas, 2 ft. 3 ¾ in. × 6 ft. 3 in. (70.5 × 190.5 cm), Musée Fabre, Montpellier

Gustave Caillebotte

Pages 326-27

Landscape with Railroad Tracks, 1872-73, oil on canvas, 2 ft. 8 in. × 3 ft. 9 ¾ in. (81 × 116 cm), private collection

The Boulevard Seen from Above, c. 1880, oil on canvas, 25 ⅝ × 21 ¼ in. (65 × 54 cm), private collection

The Pont de l'Europe, 1876, oil on canvas, 4 ft. 1 in. × 5 ft. 11 in. (124.7 × 180.6 cm), Musée du Petit Palais, Geneva

Marguerites, 1892, oil on canvas, 25 ⅝ × 21 ¼ in. (65 × 54 cm), private collection

Regatta at Argenteuil, 1893, oil on canvas, 5 ft. 1 ¾ in. × 3 ft. 10 in. (157 × 117 cm), private collection

The Luncheon, 1876, oil on canvas, 20 ½ × 29 ½ in. (52 × 75 cm), private collection

The Canoe Paddlers, 1878, oil on canvas, 5 ft. 1 ¼ in. × 3 ft. 6 ¾ in. (155.5 × 108.5 cm), Musée des Beaux-Arts, Rennes

Alfred Sisley

Pages 330-31

View of Saint-Cloud near Paris, 1877, oil on canvas, 21 ⅝ × 25 ⅝ in. (55 × 65 cm), Musée du Louvre, Paris

The Church at Moret, Evening, 1894, oil on canvas, 3 ft. 3 ¾ in. × 2 ft. 8 ½ in. (101 × 82 cm), Petit Palais, Musée des Beaux-Arts de la Ville de Paris, Paris

The Flood at Port-Marly, 1876, oil on canvas, 23 ⅝ × 31 ⅞ in. (60 × 81 cm), Musée d'Orsay, Paris

Footbridge at Argenteuil (Val d'Oise), 1872, oil on canvas, 15 ⅜ × 23 ⅝ in. (39 × 60 cm), Musée d'Orsay, Paris

The Chemin de la Machine, Louveciennes, 1873, oil on canvas, 21 ½ × 28 ¾ in. (54.5 × 73 cm), Musée d'Orsay, Paris

The Lane of Poplars at Moret-sur-Loing, 1890, oil on canvas, 25 ⅝ × 31 ⅞ in. (65 × 81 cm), Musée d'Orsay, Paris

View of Villeneuve-la-Garenne, 1872, oil on canvas, 31 1/8 × 31 ½ in. (79 × 80 cm), Hermitage Museum, Saint Petersburg

The Wave, Lady's Cove, Langland Bay, 1897, oil on canvas, 25 ⅝ × 32 in. (65 × 81.5 cm), private collection

Berthe Morisot

Pages 336-37

Pasie Sewing in the Garden in Bougival, 1881, oil on board, 2 ft. 8 ¼ in. × 3 ft. 3 ¾ in. (81.7 × 101 cm), Musée des Beaux-Arts, Pau

Young Girl by a Window, 1878, oil on canvas, 29 ⅞ × 24 in. (76 × 61 cm), Musée Fabre, Montpellier

The Cradle, 1872, oil on canvas, 22 × 18 1/8 in. (56 × 46 cm), Musée d'Orsay, Paris

Lady and Child on the Terrace, also known as *Woman and Child on the Balcony*, 1872, oil on canvas, 23 ⅝ × 19 ⅝ in. (60 × 50 cm), private collection, Switzerland

Child with Hollyhocks, 1881, oil on canvas, 19 ⅞ × 16 ⅝ in. (50.6 × 42.2 cm), private collection

Children with a Bowl, 1886, oil on canvas, 2 ft. 4 ¾ in. × 3 ft. ¼ in. (73 × 92 cm), Musée Marmottan-Monet, Paris

Woman in Black, also known as *Before the Theater*, 1875, oil on canvas, 22 ½ × 12 1/8 in. (57 × 31 cm), private collection

Young Woman at the Mirror, 1876, oil on canvas, 21 ¼ × 17 ¾ in. (54 × 45 cm), private collection

Garden at Bougival, also known as *The Garden of Doctor Robin*, 1884, oil on canvas, 18 ⅞ × 21 ⅝ in. (48 × 55 cm), private collection

Mary Cassatt

Pages 340-41

Offering the Panal *to the Bullfighter*, 1873, oil on canvas, 3 ft. 3 ½ in. × 2 ft. 9 ½ in. (100.6 × 85.1 cm), Sterling and Francine Clark Art Institute, Williamstown

Woman with a Pearl Necklace in a Loge, 1879, oil on canvas, 32 × 23 ½ in. (81.3 × 59.7 cm), Philadelphia Museum of Art, Philadelphia

Woman Reading in the Garden, 1878-79, oil on canvas, 35 ⅜ × 25 ⅝ in. (89.9 × 65.2 cm), The Art Institute of Chicago, Chicago

The Letter, 1890-91, colored etching, 13 ⅝ × 8 ⅞ in. (34.6 × 22.7 cm), Bibliothèque Nationale de France, Paris

The Sisters, c. 1885, oil on canvas, 18 ¼ × 21 ⅞ in. (46.3 × 55.5 cm), Art Gallery and Museum, Glasgow

Breakfast in Bed, 1897, oil on canvas, 23 × 29 in. (58.4 × 73.7 cm), Huntington Library and Art Gallery, San Marino

Young Mother Sewing, 1900, oil on canvas, 3 ft. ½ in. × 2 ft. 5 in. (92.4 × 73.7 cm), The Metropolitan Museum of Art, New York

Armand Guillaumin

Pages 350–51

Madame Guillaumin Reading, c. 1887, oil on canvas, 18 ¼ × 21 ⅝ in. (46.5 × 55 cm), private collection

Lilacs (The Artist's Garden at Saint-Val near Malesherbes), n.d., oil on canvas, 25 ¼ × 31 ½ in. (64 × 80 cm), Musée Bonnat-Helleu, Bayonne

Quai de la Gare, Effect of Snow, 1873, oil on canvas, 19 ⅞ × 24 in. (50.5 × 61.2 cm), Musée d'Orsay, Paris

View of Agay, 1895, oil on canvas, 2 ft. 4 ¾ in. × 3 ft. ¼ in. (73 × 92 cm), Musée d'Orsay, Paris

Rutted Path, Effect of Snow, 1869, oil on canvas, 26 × 21 ⅝ in. (66 × 55 cm), Musée d'Orsay, Paris

Storm in Agay, 1895, oil on canvas, 25 ¾ × 31 ⅞ in. (65.5 × 81 cm), Musée des Beaux-Arts, Rouen

The Valley of the Sedelle, Crozant, c. 1898, oil on canvas, 23 ⅝ × 29 ⅛ in. (60 × 74 cm), Musée Marmottan-Monet, Paris

Sunset at Ivry, 1878, oil on canvas, 25 ⅝ × 31 ⅞ in. (65 × 81 cm), Musée d'Orsay, Paris

Paul Cézanne

Pages 346–47

Bathers, c. 1890–92, oil on canvas, 23 ⅝ × 32 ¼ in. (60 × 82 cm), Musée d'Orsay, Paris

Mont Sainte-Victoire, c. 1890, oil on canvas, 2 ft. 1 ½ in. × 3 ft. ¼ in. (65 × 92 cm), Musée d'Orsay, Paris

The Bay of Marseille Seen from L'Estaque, also known as *L'Estaque*, c. 1878–79, oil on canvas, 22 ⅞ × 28 ⅜ in. (58 × 72 cm), Musée d'Orsay, Paris

A Modern Olympia, 1873, oil on canvas, 18 1/8 × 21 ⅝ in. (46 × 55 cm), Musée d'Orsay, Paris

Apples and Oranges, c. 1899, oil on canvas, 2 ft. 5 ¼ in. × 3 ft. ½ in. (74 × 93 cm), Musée d'Orsay, Paris

The Hanged Man's House, Auvers-sur-Oise, 1873, oil on canvas, 21 ⅝ × 26 in. (55 × 66 cm). Musée d'Orsay, Paris

The Card Players, c. 1890, oil on canvas, 18 ½ × 22 ½ in. (47 × 57 cm), Musée d'Orsay

Still Life with Kettle, c. 1867–69, oil on canvas, 25 ⅜ × 31 ⅞ in. (64.5 × 81 cm), Musée d'Orsay, Paris

Georges Seurat

Pages 356–57

A Sunday on La Grande Jatte, 1884–86, oil on canvas, 6 ft 9 ¾ in. × 10 ft. 1 ¼ in. (207.5 × 308.1 cm), The Helen Birch Bartlett Memorial Collection, The Art Institute of Chicago, Chicago

Harbor at Port-en-Bassin at High Tide, 1888, oil on canvas, 26 ⅜ × 32 ¼ in. (67 × 82 cm), Musée d'Orsay, Paris

Circus, 1891, oil on canvas, 6 ft 1 in. × 5 ft. (185.5 × 152.5 cm), Musée d'Orsay, Paris

The Can-Can, 1890, oil on canvas, 5 ft 6 ½ in. × 4 ft 7 ½ in. (169.1 × 141 cm), Kröller-Müller Museum, Otterlo

Bathers at Asnières, 1884, oil on canvas, 6 ft. 7 ¼ in. × 9 ft. 10 in. (201 × 300 cm), National Gallery, London

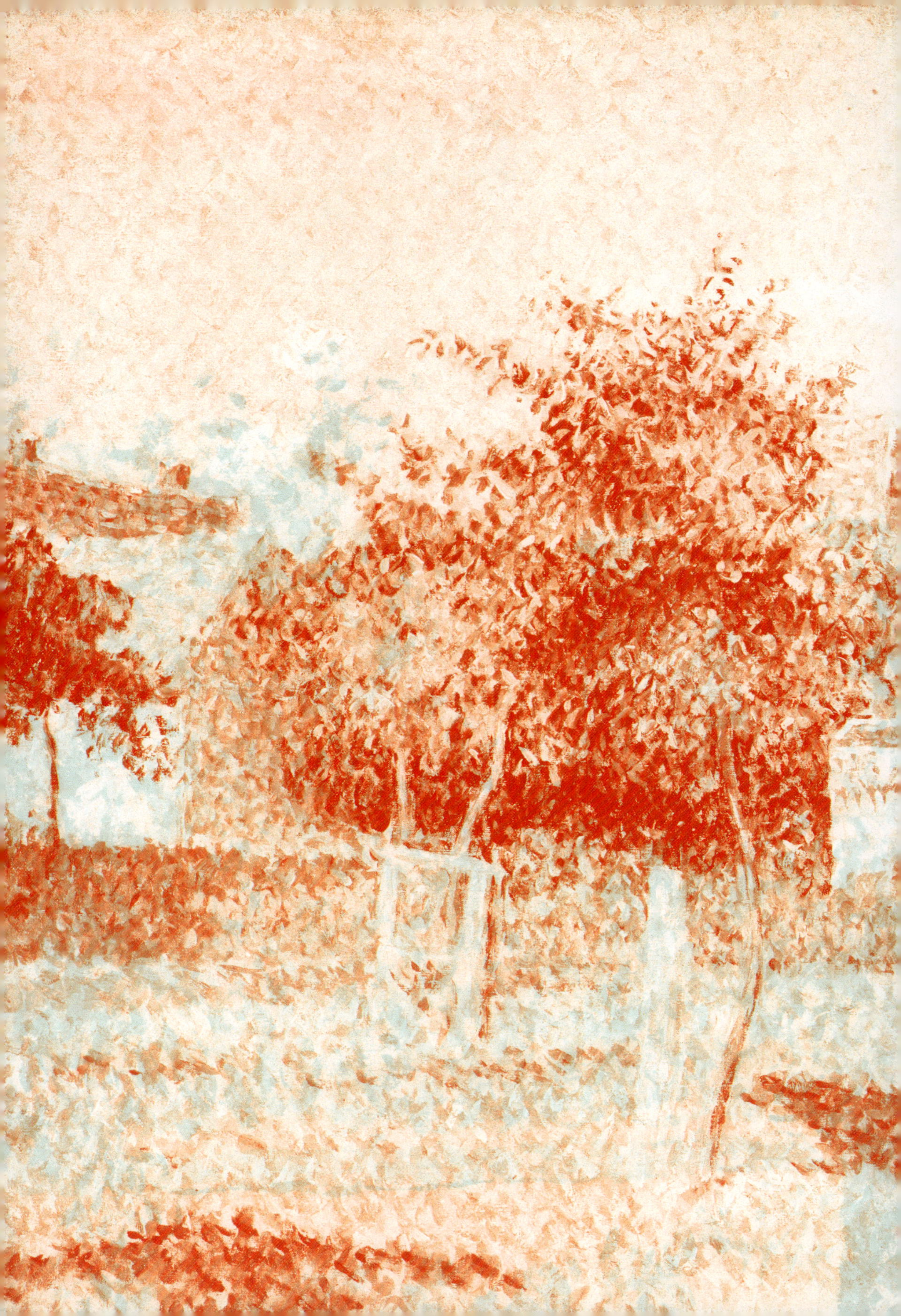

Appendixes

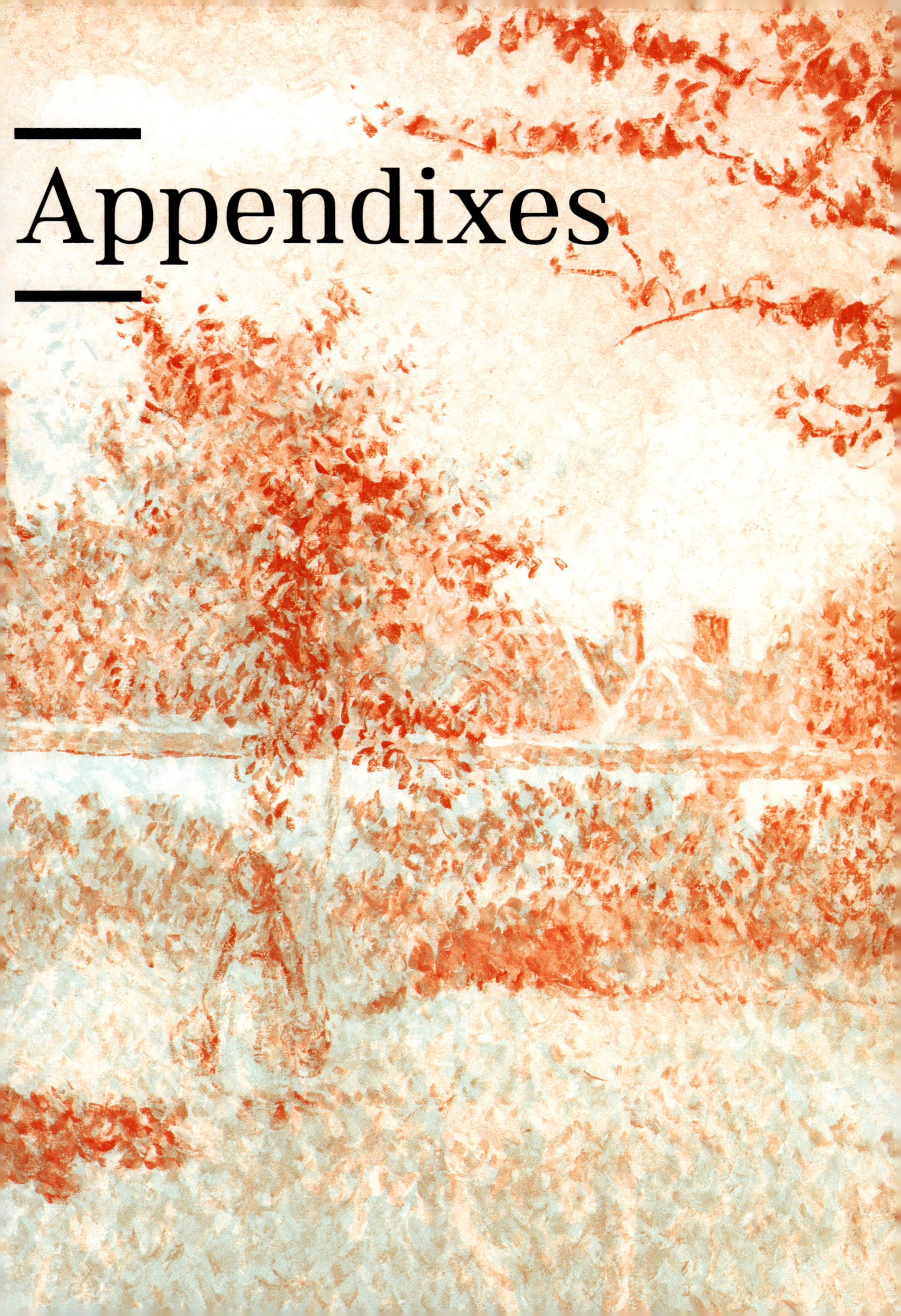

Index of Proper Names

Page numbers in bold refer to illustrations

Alexis, Paul **223**
Alphand, Jean-Charles-Adolphe 21
Aman-Jean, Edmond (Amand Edmond Jean) 352
Angrand, Charles 262
Astruc, Zacharie 38, **85**, 188

Baltard, Victor 21
Balzac, Honoré de 15, 252
Banville, Théodore de 39
Bastien-Lepage, Jules 249
Baudelaire, Charles 9, **10**, 24, 25, 34, 35, 39, 63, 86, 87, 93
Bazille, Frédéric **10**, 23, 38, 39, 79, **80–83**, **85**, 102, 107–8, 110, 112, **113**, **116–19**, **142**, 186, 201, **205**, 247, 251, 253, 306, 309, **318–21**, 328, 342, 359
Bellio, Georges de 230, 233, 251
Bérard, Paul 128, 232
Bernard, Émile 343, 344
Bernheim-Jeune, Gaston 344
Bonaparte, Louis-Napoleon 8
Bonington, Richard Parkes **98**
Bonnard, Pierre **237**, 266, **267**
Bouard, Ernest-Auguste **54**
Boudin, Eugène-Louis 107, 110, **111**, 129, 135, 188, 234, 294
Bouguereau, William **73**, 74
Bracquemond, Félix 25, 188, 191, 192

Cabanel, Alexandre 74, **93**, 318
Caillebotte, Gustave **11**, 15, **18**, **19**, **23**, 25, **28–31**, 58, **67**, **68–71**, **109**, **132**, **136**, **140**, **143**, **146**, 171, **173**, 190, 191, **192**, 193, 199, 200, 201, **204**, 222, 230, 247, 249–50, 251, 296, **322–27**, 334, 348, 359
Caillebotte, Martial **67**, 324
Camp, Maxime Du 74
Carolus-Durand (Duran, Charles Auguste Émile) 25, **79**
Cassatt, Mary 25, **26**, **78**, **139**, **191**, 192, 193, 208, **209**, 222, 241, 273, 301, 314, **338–41**, 344, 360
Castagnary, Jules-Antoine 39, 190, 202, 219
Cézanne, Paul 9, 10, 13, 23, 31, 38, **47**, **50**, 68, 70, 75, 79, 102, 122, 125, 185, **186**, 188, **189**, 190, 191, **200**, 201, **223**, **231**, 232, 233, 234, 237, 249, **300–5**, 308, 325, **342–47**, 348, 349
Chabrier, Emmanuel 253
Cham (Amédée de Noé) **214**
Champfleury (Jules François Félix Fleury-Husson) 34, 39
Charpentier, Georges 54, 222, **230**, 232, 244, 306
Chase, William Merritt 277
Chevreul, Michel-Eugène 9, 51, 154, 261, 270, 352
Chocquet, Victor 230, **231**, 251
Claretie, Jules 92, 216
Clay, Jean 111, 216
Clemenceau, Georges 250, 256, 297, 344
Constable, John **98**, 328
Corbaz, Aloïse **286**
Corot, Jean-Baptiste-Camille **96**, 102, 110, 113, 144, 186, 187, 197, 300, 332, 333
Courbet, Gustave **8**, 10, 13, 39, **46**, 49, **53**, **66**, 74, **76**, 96, **99**, 108, 110, 185, 186, 219, 232, 300, 306, 338
Couture, Thomas **74**, 84, 338
Cross, Henri-Edmond 262, 352

Daguerre, Louis 63
Danton, Georges Jacques 249
Daubigny, Charles-François 9, 10, 97, 98, **100–3**, 109, 186, 197, 238, 301
Daumier, Honoré Victorin **63**, **92**, 348
Debussy, Claude 14, 253
Degas, Edgar 23, 25, 26, 30, **32**, 33, **36**, 38, **39**, **49**, **62**, **64**, **65**, 70, **78**, 102, **141**, **145**, **157**, 170, **171**, 174, **184**, 185, 188, 190, 191, **192**, 193, 197, 199–200, 201, 202, **203**, **204**, 208, **209**, 217, **219**, **220**, 221, 222, 237, 240, 247, 248, **249**, 252, **253**, 259, 275, **312–17**, 322, 323, 325, 328, 333, 334, 338, 339
Delacroix, Eugène 9, 74, **76**, 78, 98, 239, 262, 300, 352
Demachy, Robert **253**
Denis, Maurice 265, 266, 267, 313, **344**, 345
Desboutin, Marcellin 39, 190
Diaz de la Peña, Narcisse 97, 186
Dubuffet, Jean 286
Dumas, Alexandre 8
Durand-Ruel, Paul 98, 102, 167, 176, 190, 193, 221, 229–30, 234, 236, **238**, **239**, 240, 241, 248, 250, 273, 275–77, 295, 300, 301, 302, 303, 308, 328, 334, 339, 353
Duranty, Louis Edmond 11, 38, 39, 170, 190, 197, **219**, 275
Duret, Théodore 12, 24, 25, 38, 161, 187, 199, 212, **218**, 219, 231, 250, 275

Fantin-Latour, Henri 9, 34, 38, 75, **85**, 241, 275, 332
Fauré, Gabriel 82, 253
Faure, Jean-Baptiste 230, 232, 251, 253
Fénéon, Félix 51, 222, 263, **266**, 353
Ferry, Jules 24, 233, 332
Flaubert, Gustave 230
Fournaise, Alphonse 54, 60, 61
Fournaise, Alphonsine 54, 59, 61
Francis, Samuel Lewis, known as Sam **282**, 284

Fromentin, Eugène **98**

Gachet, Paul 39, 189, **228**, 232, 251, 343, 344
Garnier, Charles 11, 33
Gaudibert, Louis-Joachim 230, **233**, 251
Gauguin, Paul **13**, 14, 122, 125, 126, 191, 192, **193**, 222, 234, 237, 248, 250, **260**, 262, 263, **264**, 265, 266, 301, 343, 344, 348
Gautier, Théophile 86, 92
Géricault, Théodore 76, 98
Gérôme, Jean-Léon **72**, 74, 187, 338
Gervex, Henri **75**, 249
Gleyre, Charles 79, 83, 107, 110, 275, 306, 318, 319, 328, 329
Goncourt, Edmond de 24, 25, 54, 249, 252, 275
Goncourt, Jules de 24, 25, 54, 252, 275
Gonzalès, Eva **208**, **209**
Grey, Henri **53**
Gounod, Charles 306
Guichard, Joseph 188, 209
Guillaumin, Armand 23, **44**, 75, 79, 125, **159**, 161, **163**, 188, 191, 192, 193, 201, 230, 232, 302, **348–51**, 353, 361
Guys, Constantin 38

Hassam, Frederick Childe 277
Haussmann, Georges Eugène 8, 19, **20**, 22, 30, 45, 48, 130
Havemeyer, Henry 171, 241
Havemeyer, Louisine 241, 339
Hiroshige, Utagawa 25, **27**, 339
Hittorff, Jacques Ignace 21
Hokusai, Katsushika 25, **26**
Hoschedé, Alice 126, 175, 233, 295
Hoschedé, Ernest 166, 232, 233, 251, 296, 297
Hoschedé, Suzanne **178–81**
Huysmans, Joris-Karl 199, 219, 220, 343, 344, 349

Ingres, Jean-Auguste-Dominique **9**, 10, 39, 75, 76, 78, 300, 312, 352
Isabey, Jean-Baptiste 111

Jongkind, Johan Barthold 75, 107, **110**, 197, 234, 249

Laforgue, Jules 158, 220, 222
Larsson, Carl Olaf 274
Le Gray, Gustave **66**, **253**
Leroy, Louis 22, 189, 196, 215, 217
Lichtenstein, Roy Fox **285**
Liebermann, Max 273, **274**
Luce, Maximilien 262, 355
Lumière, Auguste **15**, **253**
Lumière, Louis **15**, **253**

Maître, Edmond **80–83**, **85**, 253
Mallarmé, Étienne, known as Stéphane 11, 199, **220**, **221**, 252, 332, 334
Manet, Édouard **9**, **10**, 11, 13, 14, 23, **25**, **34**, **38**, 39, **48**, 75, 76, **77**, 78, 79, **80–83**, 84, 85, **86**, **87**, **88–91**, 92, 93, 108, **109**, 114, **115**, 122, 171, 185, 186, 188, 197, 201, **208**, 209, **218**, **219**, 220, **221**, 223, **224–27**, 233, 237–238, 239, 241, **246**, 247, 249, 250, 251, **252**, 253, 275, 276, 295, 296, 300, 312, 318, 323, 325, 332, 333, 338, 343, 359
Manet, Eugène 124, 133, 193, 209, **210–13**, 249, 333, 334
Manet, Julie 124, **133**, **142**, **173**, 174, 208, **209**, **210–13**, 220, 221, 314, 333, 334, **335**
Marey, Étienne-Jules 12, 64
Martin, Pierre-Firmin, known as Père 234
Marx, Karl 46
Masson, André 257
Mauclair, Camille 153, 157
Maupassant, Guy de 128, 174, 220, 230, 252
Meissonier, Ernest 64, 74
Menil, Dominique de 290, 291
Menil, John de 291
Mérimée, Prosper 78
Meurent, Victorine 90
Millet, Jean-François 8, **9**, 10, 74, 96, **97**, 111, 190, 302
Mirbeau, Octave 167, 220, 222, 234, 271
Mitchell, Joan **284**
Monet, Claude 10, **11**, 13, **15**, **22**, 23, **25**, **26**, **27**, 30, 38, 39, **45**, **55**, 79, **80–83**, **85**, 92, 97, 98, 102, **106**, 107, 108, 109, 110, 111, **112**, **113**, 114, **115**, **122**, **126**, **127**, 128, **129**, **130**, **131**, 132, **134**, **135**, **137**, **143**, **144**, **145**, **146**, **147**, **152**, **154**, 155, **156**, **158**, 160, **161**, **164–67**, 170, 171, **172**, **174–76**, 177, **178–81**, 185, 188, 190, **191**, 192, 193, **194–97**, **198**, 199, 200, **201**, **206**, 218, 220, 222, 230, **233**, 234, 236–37, 238, 239, **240**, 241, 248–50, **251**, 252, 253, **254–57**, 273, 276, 277, 280, 283, **284**, 285, 291, **294–99**, 300, 301, 303, 306, 314, 318, 319, 323, 325, 328, 329, 333, 334, 342, 344, 358
Monet, Jean **114**, 131, 143, 181
Moore, George 167, 203
Moreau, Gustave 33, 98
Morisot, Berthe 23, 30, 78, 102, 119, **124**, **133**, **138**, **140**, **142**, **153**, **169**, 170, 171, **173**, 174, **188**, 190, **191**, 192, 193, 201, **204**, 208, **209**, **210–13**, 220, 221, 222, 236, 241, 247, 249, 252, 295, 314, **332–37**, 338, 360
Morisot, Edma **188**, 332, 334
Muybridge, Eadweard 12, 64
Murer, Eugène **229**

Nadar (Gaspar-Félix Tournachon) 8, 38, **63**, **67**, 187, 188, 190, 296, 322
Napoleon III 8, 19, 20, 23, 33, 34, 45, 48, 53, 75, 77
Nieuwerkerke, Émilien, Count of 74, 78, 102
Nittis, Giuseppe De 188

On Kawara **286**

Petit, Georges 218, 222, 236, 238, 274, 276
Pissarro, Camille **21**, 23, 30, **37**, 38, 39, 49, 51, 75, 78, 79, 98, 102, **107**, 108, 122, **123**, **125**, **126**, 128, **133**, **144**, 159, **160**, **162**, **177**, 185, 186, **187**, 188, **189**, 190, 191, 192, **193**, 199, 201, 202, **207**, 217, 218, 222, 230, 232, 233, 234, 237, 238, 239, 240, 241, **248**, 250, 261, 263, 276, 294, 295, **300–5**, 338, 342, 343, 344, 348, 353, 358
Pissarro, Lucien 21, 193, 300, 303
Pollock, Jackson **283**, 284
Proudhon, Pierre-Joseph 39, **46**, 139
Proust, Antonin 38, 86, 87, 93
Proust, Marcel 43, 252
Puvis de Chavannes, Pierre 119, 332

Raffaëlli, Jean-François 192, 203
Ravel, Maurice 253
Redon, Odilon 103, 193
Renoir, Auguste **20**, **23**, 30, **35**, 38, **40–43**, **50**, 54, **56–59**, **60**, **61**, 78, 79, **80–83**, **85**, 102, 107, **108**, 110, 112, **113**, **114**, **120**, 121, 122, **128**, **131**, **132**, **147**, **148–51**, **155**, 156, **158**, **163**, **168**, **170**, 185, 188, 190, 191, 192, 193, 197, 199, 200, 201, **202**, **205**, 215, **217**, 218, 220, 221, 222, **229**, **230**, **232**, 233, 234, **236**, 237, **238**, **239**, 240, 241, **242–45**, 247–49, 250, 253, 276, 295, 296, 297, **306–11**, 318, 319, 323, 325, 328, 329, 333, 334, 338, 342, 344, 358
Restany, Pierre 266
Rewald, John 39, 75, 156, 159, 163, 197, 248
Riopelle, Jean-Paul 284
Rivière, Georges 141, 215
Robinson, Theodore **277**
Rodin, Auguste 9, 11, **12**, 15, 222, 236, 344
Rothko, Mark **288–91**
Rouart, Henri 188, 190, 191, 192, 193, 230, 322
Rousseau, Théodore **94**, 97, 113, 197
Roussel, François Xavier, known as Ker-Xavier 266, 344
Rubens, Peter Paul 76, 78, 156, 338
Ruskin, John 281
Rysselberghe, Théo Van 273, **275**

Saint-Victor, Paul de 92, 96
Scholderer, Otto **85**
Schuffenecker, Claude-Émile, known as Émile 193, 264
Sérusier, Paul 13, **265**
Seurat, Georges 14, 51, 193, **261**, 262, **263**, 266, **268–71**, 301, 303, **352–57**, 361
Sickert, Walter Richard 275
Signac, Paul 14, 51, 193, 261, **262**, **266**, 301, 303, 324, 349, 353
Sisley, Alfred 23, 30, 38, **47**, 79, 102, 107, 108, 110, 112, **113**, 122, **124**, **125**, **145**, **146**, **147**, 160, **162**, **172**, **177**, **185**, 188, **190**, 191, 192, 193, 199–200, 201, **207**, 218, 222, 230, 233, 236–37, 238, 240, 241, 248, 250, 276, 306, 318, **328–31**, 348, 360
Sorolla, Joaquín 275, **276**
Suisse, Charles 79, 300, 342

Talbot, William Henry Fox 63, **66**
Tanguy, Julien-François, known as Père 234, **235**, 237
Thaulow, Johan Frederik, known as Frits 274
Tintoretto (Jacopo Robusti) 78
Titian (Tiziano Vecellio) 76, 77, 78, 156
Troyon, Constant **95**, 97, 111
Turner, Joseph Mallord William 98, 295, 328
Turrell, James **287**

Utamaro, Kitagawa 25, 339

Valéry, Paul 220, 252, 334
Van Gogh, Théodorus, known as Théo 236–37
Van Gogh, Vincent 13, 14, 122, 222, **228**, 232, 234, **235**, 237, 264, **265**, 301, 344, 348, 353, 354
Velázquez, Diego 78, 226, 275
Veronese, Paolo Caliari 76
Viollet-le-Duc, Eugène Emmanuel 78, 79
Vollard, Ambroise 61, 233, 234, **236**, **237**, 344
Vuillard, Jean Édouard 266, **267**

Warhol, Andy 285
Whistler, James Abbott McNeill 9, 25, 75, 222, **272**, 275, **278–81**
Wolff, Albert 190, 217, 218, 231, 250

Zola, Émile 13, 15, 20, 25, 37, 38, 45, 47, **80–83**, **85**, 102, 188, 197, 220, **223**, **224–27**, 230, 249, 251, 252, 295, 296, 300, 312, 342, 343, 344

Selected Bibliography

Bomford, David, et al. *Art in the Making: Impressionism.* An exhibition catalog. New Haven and London: National Gallery, 1990.

Callen, Anthea. *The Art of Impressionism: Painting Technique & the Making of Modernity.* New Haven: Yale University Press, 2000.

De Montebello, Philippe. *Monet's Years at Giverny: Beyond Impressionism.* New York: Metropolitan Museum of Art, 2012.

Guegan, Stephane, and Alice Thomine-Berrada. *Birth of Impressionism: Masterpieces from the Musée d'Orsay.* New York: Prestel, 2010.

Herbert, Robert L. *Impressionism: Art, Leisure, and Parisian Society.* New Haven: Yale University Press, 1988.

House, John. *Impressionism: Paint and Politics.* New Haven: Yale University Press, 2004.

Kelder, Diane. *The Great Book of French Impressionism.* New York: Abbeville Press, 1997.

Moffett, Charles S., et al. *The New Painting: Impressionism 1874-1886.* San Francisco: Fine Arts Museums of San Francisco, 1986.

Nochlin, Linda, ed. *Impressionism and Post-Impressionism, 1874-1904: Sources and Documents.* Englewood Cliffs, N.J.: Prentice-Hall, 1966.

Patry, Sylvie. *Inventing Impressionism: Paul Durand-Ruel and the Modern Art Market.* An exhibition catalog. London: National Gallery Company, 2015.

Rewald, John. *The History of Impressionism.* New York: Museum of Modern Art, 1946. Revised edition, 1961.

Seitz, William C. *Claude Monet.* New York: Abrams, 1983.

Tinterow, Gary, and Henri Loyrette. *Origins of Impressionism.* An exhibition catalog. New York: Metropolitan Museum of Art, 1994.

Photographic Credits and Copyrights

t: top; c: center; b: bottom; l: left; r: right

© 2012, The Philadelphia Museum of Art / Art Resource / Scala, Florence: pp. 191b, 340t; © 2016, Museum of Fine Arts, Boston: pp. 25t, 27t, 136, 176tr; © Adagp Images: p. 285; © AISA/Leemage: p. 223; © AKG-Images: pp. 36b, 48t, 109t, 115t, 129b, 131c, 147c, 158t, 192l, 329t; © AKG-Images / CDA / Guillot: p. 135t, b; © AKG-Images / Erich Lessing: p. 295; © AKG-Images / Interfoto / Groth-Schmachtenberger: p. 353; © AKG-Images / The National Gallery of Art, Washington, DC: p. 114t; All rights reserved: pp. 19, 67tl, 157l, 169, 171l, 296tl, 316tr, 322b, 324, 326bl, 332b, t, 333, 334t, cr, cl; © Archives Alinari, Florence, Dist. RMN-Grand Palais / Fratelli Alinari: pp. 27b, 206c; © Archives Charmet / Bridgeman Images: pp. 51, 53t, 54b, 76b; © Archives Durand-Ruel / © Durand-Ruel & Cie: pp. 238, 239bl, t, 241tr, 256b, 300, 302b, tl, 308t; © Archives Durand-Ruel / © Photo Sidman / © Durand-Ruel & Cie: p. 241tl © Archives Flammarion: pp. 113bl, 206t; © Artcurial, Paris: p. 158b; © Art, Dist. RMN-Grand Palais / Image Philadelphia Museum of Art: p. 20l; Art Gallery and Museum, Kelvingrove, Glasgow, Scotland / © Culture and Sport Glasgow (Museums) / Bridgeman Images: p. 340b; © Ashmolean Museum, University of Oxford, UK / Bridgeman Images: p. 120; © Atelier 53, Paris: p. 335; © Bibliothèque des Arts Decoratifs, Paris, France / Archives Charmet / Bridgeman Images: p. 338b; © Bibliothèque Littéraire Jacques Doucet: p. 220; © BnF: pp. 92, 215, 339b; © BnF/The Fogg Art Museum, Harvard University: p. 38; © BnF, Dist. RMN-Grand Palais / Image BnF: pp. 26tl, 26tr, 63, 67b, 314b, 341tr; © BPK, Berlin, Dist. RMN-GP: p.252; © BPK, Berlin, Dist. RMN-GP / Elke Walford: p. 47t; © BPK, Berlin, Dist. RMN-GP / Jörg P. Anders: p. 232; © C. Lancien, C. Loisel / Réunion des Musées Métropolitains Rouen Normandy: p. 177tr; © Centre Pompidou, MNAM-CCI, Dist. RMN-Grand Palais / Georges Meguerditchian: p. 286b; © Centre Pompidou, MNAM-CCI, Dist. RMN-Grand Palais / Philippe Migeat: p. 283; © Christie's Images / Bridgeman Images: pp. 352t, 355; © Colección Carmen Thyssen-Bornemisza en Depósito en el Museo Thyssen-Bornemisza/ Scala, Florence: p. 133t; © Collection Sirot-Angel/Leemage: pp. 308b, 328; © Courtesy of the Comité Caillebotte: pp. 67r, 322t, 323, 325, 326br, tr, tl; © Courtesy of the National Gallery of Art, Washington. NGA Images: pp. 319t, 320cr; © D.C., USA / Bridgeman Images: pp. 23t, 87b, 139; © D.C., USA / Acquired 1923 / Bridgeman Images: pp. 56-59; © Detroit Institute of Arts, USA / Gift of Mrs. Christian H. Hecker / Bridgeman Images: p. 277; © Dreyfus: pp. 337b, cr; © Electa/Leemage: p. 348t; © Estate of Joan Mitchell / Jacqueline Hyde: p. 284b; © FineArtImages/Leemage: p. 330br; © Fitzwilliam Museum, University of Cambridge, UK / Bridgeman Images: pp. 147b, 160, 168; © Fogg Art Museum, Harvard Art Museums, USA / Gift of Mr. and Mrs. F. Meynier de Salinelles / Bridgeman Images: p. 321t; © Galerie Hopkins-Custot: pp. 142b, 209t, 210-13,

336b; © Gusman/Leemage: p. 48b; © Harvard University Art Museums, USA / Gift of Mr. And Mrs. F. Meynier de Salinelles / The Bridgeman Art Library: pp. 116-19, 205t; © Huntington Library and Art Gallery, San Marino, CA, USA / © The Huntington Library, Art Collections & Botanical Gardens / Bridgeman Images: p. 341bl; © INHA, Dist. RMN-Grand Palais / Image INHA: p. 349b; © Institut Lumière/Famille Lumière: p. 253cr; © Kharbine Tapabor: pp. 214, 216; © Laporte/Leemage: p. 55b; © Leemage: pp. 173b, 327t; © Léon et Lévy / Roger-Viollet: p. 247; © 2016, London, Courtauld Institute Galleries, 2016: pp. 41-43; © Look and Learn / Bridgeman Images: p. 54t ; © Look and Learn / Illustrated Papers Collection / Bridgeman Images: p. 52; © Luisa/Ricciarini/Leemage: p. 219; © Lylho/Leemage: p. 140t; © MBA, MBA, Rennes. RMN-Grand Palais / Adélaïde Beaudoin: p. 193t; © Metropolitan Museum of Art, New York, USA / Bridgeman Images: p. 146br; Musée Fabre Montpellier Méditerranée Métropole / © Frédéric Jaulmes: pp. 98c, 319b, 320b, 321b; © Municipal Museum of Art, Kitakyushu, Japan / Bridgeman Images: p. 317tl; © MuMa Le Havre / David Fogel: pp. 177bl, br; © MuMa Le Havre / Charles Maslard: p. 159; © MuMa Le Havre / Florian Kleinefenn: p. 110; © Musée Baron Gérard - Bayeux: p. 143b; © Musée Bonnat, Bayonne, France / Bridgeman Images: p. 351tl; © Musée des Beaux-Arts de Rennes - Photographic credit Louis Deschamps: pp. 109b, 327br; © Musée d'Orsay, Dist. RMN / Alexis Brandt: p. 253cl; © Musée d'Orsay, Dist. RMN / Patrice Schmidt: pp. 25b, 62, 66tl, 80-83, 107, 129t, 149-51, 161b, 175tl, tc, 192r, 207bl, 217, 233, 240b, 246, 249, 253t, 260, 265r, 298tr, 309, 310bl, t, cl, 316tl, 317tr, 320cl, 342t, 344, 348b, 357tr; © Musée des Beaux-Arts, Rouen, France / Bridgeman Images: p. 351c; © Musée d'Orsay, Paris, France / Bridgeman Images: pp. 143t, 145bl, 294t; © Musée Marmottan-Monet, Paris, France / Bridgeman Image: pp. 11br, 12tl, 162t, 173t, 175b, 284t, 303, 337c, 350b; © Museo Nacional del Prado, Dist. RMN-GP / Image from the Prado: p. 276; © Museum of Fine Arts, Boston: p. 198; © Museum of Fine Arts, Houston, Texas, USA / Museum Commission, Funded by Isabel B. and Wallace S. Wilson / Bridgeman Images: p. 287; © Museum of Modern Art, New York, USA / Bridgeman Images: p. 266; © National Museum, Stockholm, Sweden / Bridgeman Images: pp. 113br, 205bl; © National Gallery, London, UK / The Bridgeman Art Library: pp. 140b, 203; © National Museum Wales / Bridgeman Images: p. 307; Pallant House Gallery, Chichester, UK / Kearley Bequest through The Art Fund (1989) / Bridgeman Images: p. 282; © Niarchos Collection, Athens: p. 235; © Philadelphia Museum of Art, Philadelphia: pp. 176br, 304tl; © Photo Josse/Leemage: pp. 185, 189t, b, 231, 236, 330t, 346cr; Private Collection / Bridgeman Images: pp. 73, 145t, 153 331b, 349t, 350t; © Private collection / © Christie's Images / Bridgeman Images: pp. 133b, 146bl, 336cr; © Pushkin Museum, Moscow, Russia / Bridgeman Images: p. 22; © Kröller-Müller Museum, Otterlo, Netherlands / Artothek / Bridgeman Images: pp. 261, 356b; © RMN-Grand Palais / All rights reserved: pp. 94, 98t, 194-97, 297b, 299tr, 342b; © RMN-Grand Palais / Daniel Arnaudet: pp. 154, 172t; © RMN-Grand Palais / Michèle Bellot: p. 145c; © RMN-Grand Palais / Gérard Blot: pp. 21, 152, 313; © RMN-Grand Palais / Gérard Blot / Hervé Lewandowski: p. 8b; © RMN-Grand Palais / Lutz Braun: p. 87t; © RMN-Grand Palais / Agence Bulloz: pp. 53b, 113tr, 177tl, 218, 237, 331t, 347t; © RMN-Grand Palais/ Thierry Ollivier: pp. 49t, 204c; © RMN-Grand Palais / Jean Schormans: p. 201; © RMN-Grand Palais / Benoît Touchard: pp. 100-3, 124, 336t; © RMN-Grand Palais / Michel Urtado: pp. 132t, 205br; © RMN-Grand Palais (Musée du Louvre): p. 98b; © RMN-Grand Palais (Musée du Louvre) / Philippe Fuzeau: p.76t; © RMN-Grand Palais (Musée de l'Orangerie) / Franck Raux: p. 163b; © RMN-Grand Palais (Musée de l'Orangerie) / Michel Urtado: pp. 146tr, 254-55, 256t, 257t; © RMN-Grand Palais (Musée d'Orsay) / All rights reserved: pp. 75, 106; © RMN-Grand Palais (Musée d'Orsay) / Martine Beck-Coppola: p. 23b; © RMN-Grand Palais (Musée d'Orsay) / Michèle Bellot: pp. 306b, 312b; © RMN-Grand Palais (Musée d'Orsay) / Jean-Gilles Berizzi: pp. 45, 138, 187, 296b, 304c; © RMN-Grand Palais (Musée d'Orsay) / Gérard Blot: pp. 50r, 228, 331cl; © RMN-Grand Palais (Musée d'Orsay) / Adrien Didierjean: pp. 50l, 329b; © RMN-Grand Palais (Musée d'Orsay) / Christian Jean: p. 162b; © RMN-Grand Palais (Musée d'Orsay) / Hervé Lewandowski: pp. 8t, 9br, bl, 10bl, 11bl, 13r, 14tl, 20r, 32, 35, 36t, 39, 46, 47b, 49b, 55t, 61, 65b, 66tr, b, 68-72, 74, 77, 79, 85, 88-91, 93, 95, 97, 99, 111-12, 114b, 115b, 122, 123t, b, 124b, 126b, 130, 131b, 134, 137, 141, 142t, 144t, 145br, 146tl, 147t, 156, 161t, 163t, 165-67, 171r, 172b, 175tr, 179-81, 184, 186, 188, 190, 191c, 193b, 200, 204b, 207tl, tr, br, 209bl, 221, 225-27, 239br, 248, 251, 253b, 262, 264, 265l, 267t, 274, 298tl, bl, 299tl, br, 304b, 305c, tr, 310r, 311tl, tr, 312t, 314t, 315, 316bl, br, 317br, bl, 330c, bl, 331cr, 337tr, 345, 346b, t, 347c, br, bl, 350cr, cl, 351tr, 357tl; © RMN-Grand Palais (Musée d'Orsay) / René-Gabriel Ojéda: pp. 44, 96, 351b, 343; © RMN-Grand Palais (Musée d'Orsay) / Thierry Ollivier: p. 26br; © RMN-Grand Palais (Musée d'Orsay) / Tony Querrec: pp. 301, 318b, 302tr, 352b; © RMN-Grand Palais (Musée d'Orsay) / Philippe Schmidt: p. 299bl; © RMN-Grand Palais (Musée d'Orsay) / Jean Schormans: p. 267b; © RMN-Grand Palais (Musée d'Orsay) / Michel Urtado: p. 305b; © Rothko Chapel, Houston, Texas. Photo by Runaway Productions: pp. 288-89, 291; © Rothko Chapel, Houston, Texas. S.I Morris Associates, Courtesy of Rothko Chapel: p. 290; © Samuel Courtauld Trust, The Courtauld Gallery, London, UK / Bridgeman Images: p. 144b; © Schweizerisches Institut für Kunstwissenschaft, Zürich, Lutz Hartmann: p. 125b; © Sotheby's / AKG-Images: pp. 15br, 127; © Sterling and Francine Clark Art Institute, Williamstown, Massachusetts, USA / Bridgeman Images: pp. 60, 306t, 340l; © Studio Sébert Photographes: p.132b, 327bl; © Tallandier/ Bridgeman Images: pp. 11t, 33; © Tate, London, Dist. RMN-Grand Palais / Tate Photography: pp. 272, 279-81; © The Art Institute of Chicago: pp. 28-31, 113tl, 268-71, 294b, 318t, 356t; © The Art Institute of Chicago / Gift of Arthur M. Wood, Sr. in Memory of Pauline Palmer Wood / Bridgeman Images: pp. 176tl, 240t; © The Art Institute of Chicago / Gift of Mrs. Albert J. Beveridge in Memory of Her Aunt, Delia Spencer Field / Bridgeman Images: pp. 209br, 341tl; © The Art Institute of Chicago / Mr. and Mrs. Martin A. Ryerson Collection / Bridgeman Images: p. 131t; © The Art Institute of Chicago / Stickney Fund / Bridgeman Images: pp. 191t, 204t; © The Barber Institute of Fine Arts, University of Birmingham / Bridgeman Images: p. 174; © The Barnes Foundation, Philadelphia, Pennsylvania, USA / Bridgeman Images: p. 230; © The Bridgeman Art Library / Metropolitan Museum of Art, New York, United States, Lauros / Giraudon: p. 26bl; © The Cleveland Museum of Art: p. 18; © The High Museum of Art, Atlanta: p. 320t; © The J. Paul Getty Museum, Los Angeles: p. 64; © The Metropolitan Museum of Art, Dist. RMN-/ Image of the MMA: pp. 65t, 86, 128, 157r, 176bl, 229, 242-45, 304tr, 338t, 341br, 346cl, 354t; © The National Gallery, London, Dist. RMN/ National Gallery Photographic Department: pp. 34, 37, 78, 108, 170, 202, 205bc, 208, 209bc, 263, 357b, 339t; © The Phillips Collection, Washington, D.C., USA / Acquired 1923 / Bridgeman Images: p. 311b; © The Solomon R. Guggenheim Foundation / Art Resource, NY, Dist. RMN-Grand Palais / The Solomon R. Guggenheim Foundation / Art Resource, NY: p. 125t; © Toledo Museum of Art: p. 155; © Wildenstein Institute: pp. 176c, 296tr.

Front cover: Claude Monet, *San Giorgio Maggiore by Twilight* (detail), 1908, © AKG-images
Back cover, from top left: Edgar Degas, *Blue Dancers*, c. 1890, © RMN-Grand Palais (Musée d'Orsay) / Hervé Lewandowski; Gustave Caillebotte, *The Boulevard Seen from Above*, c. 1880, © Courtesy Comité Caillebotte; Paul Signac, *The Red Buoy, Saint-Tropez*, 1895, © RMN-Grand Palais (Musée d'Orsay) / Hervé Lewandowski; Auguste Renoir, *The Skiff*, 1875, © The National Gallery, London, Dist. RMN / National Gallery Photographic Department